The Complete Payment Book

C O N T E M P O R A R Y
BOOKS, INC.
CHICAGO

Published by Contemporary Books, Inc.
180 North Michigan Avenue, Chicago, Illinois 60601
Manufactured in the United States of America
International Standard Book Number: 0-8092-5710-6

Published simultaneously in Canada by
Beaverbooks, Ltd.
150 Lesmill Road
Don Mills, Ontario M3B 2T5
Canada

This edition published by arrangement
with Delphi Information Sciences Corporation

SCOPE

Interest Rates

8¾% to 26% - every ¼%

Terms

1 year to 10 yrs - every year

15, 20, 25, 30, 35 and 40 years

All monthly payments have been rounded upward to the next highest cent so they will completely pay off (amortize) the loan within its given term.

8.750% MONTHLY AMORTIZING PAYMENTS

AMOUNT OF LOAN	NUMBER OF YEARS IN TERM							
	1	2	3	4	5	6	7	8
$ 50	4.37	2.28	1.59	1.24	1.04	.90	.80	.73
100	8.74	4.56	3.17	2.48	2.07	1.80	1.60	1.46
200	17.47	9.12	6.34	4.96	4.13	3.59	3.20	2.91
300	26.21	13.68	9.51	7.43	6 20	5.38	4.79	4.36
400	34.94	18.23	12.68	9.91	8.26	7.17	6.39	5.81
500	43.67	22.79	15 85	12.39	10.32	8.96	7.99	7.27
600	52.41	27.35	19.02	14.86	12.39	10.75	9.58	8.72
700	61.14	31.90	22.18	17.34	14.45	12.54	11.18	10.17
800	69.87	36.46	25.35	19.82	16.51	14.33	12.77	11.62
900	78.61	41.02	28.52	22.29	18.58	16.12	14.37	13.07
1000	87.34	45.58	31.69	24.77	20.64	17.91	15.97	14.53
2000	174.68	91.15	63.37	49.54	41.28	35.81	31.93	29.05
3000	262.01	136.72	95.06	74.30	61.92	53.71	47.89	43.57
4000	349.35	182.29	126.74	99.07	82.55	71.61	63.85	58.09
5000	436.68	227.86	158.42	123.84	103.19	89.51	79.82	72.61
6000	524.02	273.43	190.11	148.60	123.83	107.42	95.78	87.13
7000	611.35	319.00	221.79	173.37	144.47	125.32	111.74	101.65
8000	698.69	364.57	253.47	198.14	165.10	143.22	127.70	116.17
9000	786.03	410.14	285.16	222.90	185.74	161.12	143.67	130.69
10000	873.36	455.71	316.84	247.67	206.38	179.02	159.63	145.21
11000	960.70	501.28	348.52	272.44	227.01	196.92	175.59	159.73
12000	1048.03	546.85	380.21	297.20	247.65	214.83	191.55	174.26
13000	1135.37	592.42	411.89	321.97	268.29	232.73	207.52	188.78
14000	1222.70	637.99	443.57	346.74	288.93	250.63	223.48	203.30
15000	1310.04	683.56	475.26	371.50	309.56	268.53	239.44	217.82
16000	1397.37	729.13	506.94	396.27	330.20	286.43	255.40	232.34
17000	1484.71	774.70	538.62	421.04	350.84	304.33	271.37	246.86
18000	1572.05	820.27	570.31	445.80	371.48	322.24	287.33	261.38
19000	1659.38	865.84	601.99	470.57	392.11	340.14	303.29	275.90
20000	1746.72	911.41	633.68	495.34	412.75	358.04	319.25	290.42
21000	1834.05	956.98	665.36	520.10	433.39	375.94	335.22	304.94
22000	1921.39	1002.55	697.04	544.87	454.02	393.84	351.18	319.46
23000	2008.72	1048.12	728.73	569.63	474.66	411.74	367.14	333.98
24000	2096.06	1093.69	760.41	594.40	495.30	429.65	383.10	348.51
25000	2183.39	1139.26	792.09	619.17	515.94	447.55	399.07	363.03
26000	2270.73	1184.83	823.78	643.93	536.57	465.45	415.03	377.55
27000	2358.07	1230.40	855.46	668.70	557.21	483.35	430.99	392.07
28000	2445.40	1275.97	887.14	693.47	577.85	501.25	446.95	406.59
29000	2532.74	1321.54	918.83	718.23	598.48	519.15	462.92	421.11
30000	2620.07	1367.11	950.51	743.00	619.12	537.06	478.88	435.63
31000	2707.41	1412.68	982.19	767.77	639.76	554.96	494.84	450.15
32000	2794.74	1458.25	1013.88	792.53	660.40	572.86	510.80	464.67
33000	2882.08	1503.82	1045.56	817.30	681.03	590.76	526.77	479.19
34000	2969.41	1549.39	1077.24	842.07	701.67	608.66	542.73	493.71
35000	3056.75	1594.96	1108.93	866.83	722.31	626.56	558.69	508.23
40000	3493.43	1822.81	1267.35	990.67	825.49	716.07	638.50	580.84
45000	3930.11	2050.66	1425.76	1114.50	928.68	805.58	718.32	653.44
50000	4366.78	2278.51	1584.18	1238.33	1031.87	895.09	798.13	726.05
55000	4803.46	2506.36	1742.60	1362.16	1135.05	984.60	877.94	798.65
60000	5240.14	2734.21	1901.02	1486.00	1238.24	1074.11	957.75	871.26
65000	5676.82	2962.06	2059.43	1609.83	1341.43	1163.62	1037.57	943.86
70000	6113.50	3189.91	2217.85	1733.66	1444.61	1253.12	1117.38	1016.46
75000	6550.17	3417.76	2376.27	1857.49	1547.80	1342.63	1197.19	1089.07
80000	6986.85	3645.61	2534.69	1981.33	1650.98	1432.14	1277.00	1161.67
85000	7423.53	3873.47	2693.10	2105.16	1754.17	1521.65	1356.82	1234.28
90000	7860.21	4101.32	2851.52	2228.99	1857.36	1611.16	1436.63	1306.88
95000	8296.89	4329.17	3009.94	2352.82	1960.54	1700.67	1516.44	1379.48
100000	8733.56	4557.02	3168.36	2476.66	2063.73	1790.18	1596.25	1452.09
105000	9170.24	4784.87	3326.77	2600.49	2166.91	1879.68	1676.07	1524.69
110000	9606.92	5012.72	3485.19	2724.32	2270.10	1969.19	1755.88	1597.30
115000	10043.60	5240.57	3643.61	2848.15	2373.29	2058.70	1835.69	1669.90
120000	10480.28	5468.42	3802.03	2971.99	2476.47	2148.21	1915.50	1742.51
125000	10916.95	5696.27	3960.44	3095.82	2579.66	2237.72	1995.32	1815.11
130000	11353.63	5924.12	4118.86	3219.65	2682.85	2327.23	2075.13	1887.71
135000	11790.31	6151.97	4277.28	3343.48	2786.03	2416.74	2154.94	1960.32
140000	12226.99	6379.82	4435.70	3467.32	2889.22	2506.24	2234.75	2032.92
145000	12663.67	6607.67	4594.11	3591.15	2992.40	2595.75	2314.57	2105.53
150000	13100.34	6835.52	4752.53	3714.98	3095.59	2685.26	2394.38	2178.13
155000	13537.02	7063.37	4910.95	3838.81	3198.78	2774.77	2474.19	2250.74
160000	13973.70	7291.22	5069.37	3962.65	3301.96	2864.28	2554.00	2323.34

MONTHLY AMORTIZING PAYMENTS   8.750%

AMOUNT OF LOAN	NUMBER OF YEARS IN TERM							
	9	10	15	20	25	30	35	40
$ 50	.68	.63	.50	.45	.42	.40	.39	.38
100	1.35	1.26	1.00	.89	.83	.79	.77	.76
200	2.69	2.51	2.00	1.77	1.65	1.58	1.54	1.51
300	4.03	3.76	3.00	2.66	2.47	2.37	2.30	2.26
400	5.37	5.02	4.00	3.54	3.29	3.15	3.07	3.01
500	6.71	6.27	5.00	4.42	4.12	3.94	3.83	3.77
600	8.05	7.52	6.00	5.31	4.94	4.73	4.60	4.52
700	9.39	8.78	7.00	6.19	5.76	5.51	5.36	5.27
800	10.73	10.03	8.00	7.07	6.58	6.30	6.13	6.02
900	12.07	11.28	9.00	7.96	7.40	7.09	6.89	6.77
1000	13.42	12.54	10.00	8.84	8.23	7.87	7.66	7.53
2000	26.83	25.07	19.99	17.68	16.45	15.74	15.31	15.05
3000	40.24	37.60	29.99	26.52	24.67	23.61	22.97	22.57
4000	53.65	50.14	39.98	35.35	32.89	31.47	30.62	30.09
5000	67.06	62.67	49.98	44.19	41.11	39.34	38.27	37.61
6000	80.47	75.20	59.97	53.03	49.33	47.21	45.93	45.14
7000	93.88	87.73	69.97	61.86	57.56	55.07	53.58	52.66
8000	107.29	100.27	79.96	70.70	65.78	62.94	61.23	60.18
9000	120.70	112.80	89.96	79.54	74.00	70.81	68.89	67.70
10000	134.11	125.33	99.95	88.38	82.22	78.68	76.54	75.22
11000	147.52	137.86	109.94	97.21	90.44	86.54	84.19	82.74
12000	160.93	150.40	119.94	106.05	98.66	94.41	91.85	90.27
13000	174.34	162.93	129.93	114.89	106.88	102.28	99.50	97.79
14000	187.76	175.46	139.93	123.72	115.11	110.14	107.16	105.31
15000	201.17	188.00	149.92	132.56	123.33	118.01	114.81	112.83
16000	214.58	200.53	159.92	141.40	131.55	125.88	122.46	120.35
17000	227.99	213.06	169.91	150.24	139.77	133.74	130.12	127.87
18000	241.40	225.59	179.91	159.07	147.99	141.61	137.77	135.40
19000	254.81	238.13	189.90	167.91	156.21	149.48	145.42	142.92
20000	268.22	250.66	199.89	176.75	164.43	157.35	153.08	150.44
21000	281.63	263.19	209.89	185.58	172.66	165.21	160.73	157.96
22000	295.04	275.72	219.88	194.42	180.88	173.08	168.38	165.48
23000	308.45	288.26	229.88	203.26	189.10	180.95	176.04	173.00
24000	321.86	300.79	239.87	212.10	197.32	188.82	183.69	180.53
25000	335.27	313.32	249.87	220.93	205.54	196.68	191.35	188.05
26000	348.68	325.85	259.86	229.77	213.76	204.55	199.00	195.57
27000	362.10	338.39	269.86	238.61	221.98	212.41	206.65	203.09
28000	375.51	350.92	279.85	247.44	230.21	220.28	214.31	210.61
29000	388.92	363.45	289.85	256.28	238.43	228.15	221.96	218.13
30000	402.33	375.99	299.84	265.12	246.65	236.02	229.61	225.66
31000	415.74	388.52	309.83	273.96	254.87	243.88	237.27	233.18
32000	429.15	401.05	319.83	282.79	263.09	251.75	244.92	240.70
33000	442.56	413.58	329.82	291.63	271.31	259.62	252.57	248.22
34000	455.97	426.12	339.82	300.47	279.53	267.48	260.23	255.74
35000	469.38	438.65	349.81	309.30	287.76	275.35	267.88	263.26
40000	536.44	501.31	399.78	353.49	328.86	314.69	306.15	300.87
45000	603.49	563.98	449.76	397.67	369.97	354.02	344.42	338.48
50000	670.54	626.64	499.73	441.86	411.08	393.36	382.69	376.09
55000	737.60	689.30	549.70	486.05	452.18	432.69	420.95	413.70
60000	804.65	751.97	599.67	530.23	493.29	472.03	459.22	451.31
65000	871.70	814.63	649.65	574.42	534.40	511.36	497.49	488.92
70000	938.76	877.29	699.62	618.60	575.51	550.70	535.76	526.52
75000	1005.81	939.96	749.59	662.79	616.61	590.03	574.03	564.13
80000	1072.87	1002.62	799.56	706.97	657.72	629.37	612.30	601.74
85000	1139.92	1065.28	849.54	751.16	698.83	668.70	650.56	639.35
90000	1206.97	1127.95	899.51	795.34	739.93	708.04	688.83	676.96
95000	1274.03	1190.61	949.48	839.53	781.04	747.37	727.10	714.57
100000	1341.08	1253.27	999.45	883.72	822.15	786.71	765.37	752.18
105000	1408.14	1315.94	1049.43	927.90	863.26	826.04	803.64	789.78
110000	1475.19	1378.60	1099.40	972.09	904.36	865.38	841.90	827.39
115000	1542.24	1441.26	1149.37	1016.27	945.47	904.71	880.17	865.00
120000	1609.30	1503.93	1199.34	1060.46	986.58	944.05	918.44	902.61
125000	1676.35	1566.59	1249.32	1104.64	1027.68	983.38	956.71	940.22
130000	1743.40	1629.25	1299.29	1148.83	1068.79	1022.72	994.98	977.83
135000	1810.46	1691.92	1349.26	1193.01	1109.90	1062.05	1033.25	1015.44
140000	1877.51	1754.58	1399.23	1237.20	1151.01	1101.39	1071.51	1053.04
145000	1944.57	1817.24	1449.21	1281.39	1192.11	1140.72	1109.78	1090.65
150000	2011.62	1879.91	1499.18	1325.57	1233.22	1180.06	1148.05	1128.26
155000	2078.67	1942.57	1549.15	1369.76	1274.33	1219.39	1186.32	1165.87
160000	2145.73	2005.23	1599.12	1413.94	1315.43	1258.73	1224.59	1203.48

9.000%   MONTHLY AMORTIZING PAYMENTS

AMOUNT OF LOAN	NUMBER OF YEARS IN TERM							
	1	2	3	4	5	6	7	8
$ 50	4.38	2.29	1.59	1.25	1.04	.91	.81	.74
100	8.75	4.57	3.18	2.49	2.08	1.81	1.61	1.47
200	17.50	9.14	6.36	4.98	4.16	3.61	3.22	2.94
300	26.24	13.71	9.54	7.47	6.23	5.41	4.83	4.40
400	34.99	18.28	12.72	9.96	8.31	7.22	6.44	5.87
500	43.73	22.85	15.90	12.45	10.38	9.02	8.05	7.33
600	52.48	27.42	19.08	14.94	12.46	10.82	9.66	8.80
700	61.22	31.98	22.26	17.42	14.54	12.62	11.27	10.26
800	69.97	36.55	25.44	19.91	16.61	14.43	12.88	11.73
900	78.71	41.12	28.62	22.40	18.69	16.23	14.49	13.19
1000	87.46	45.69	31.80	24.89	20.76	18.03	16.09	14.66
2000	174.91	91.37	63.60	49.78	41.52	36.06	32.18	29.31
3000	262.36	137.06	95.40	74.66	62.28	54.08	48.27	43.96
4000	349.81	182.74	127.20	99.55	83.04	72.11	64.36	58.61
5000	437.26	228.43	159.00	124.43	103.80	90.13	80.45	73.26
6000	524.71	274.11	190.80	149.32	124.56	108.16	96.54	87.91
7000	612.17	319.80	222.60	174.20	145.31	126.18	112.63	102.56
8000	699.62	365.48	254.40	199.09	166.07	144.21	128.72	117.21
9000	787.07	411.17	286.20	223.97	186.83	162.23	144.81	131.86
10000	874.52	456.85	318.00	248.86	207.59	180.26	160.90	146.51
11000	961.97	502.54	349.80	273.74	228.35	198.29	176.98	161.16
12000	1049.42	548.22	381.60	298.63	249.11	216.31	193.07	175.81
13000	1136.87	593.91	413.40	323.51	269.86	234.34	209.16	190.46
14000	1224.33	639.59	445.20	348.40	290.62	252.36	225.25	205.11
15000	1311.78	685.28	477.00	373.28	311.38	270.39	241.34	219.76
16000	1399.23	730.96	508.80	398.17	332.14	288.41	257.43	234.41
17000	1486.68	776.65	540.60	423.05	352.90	306.44	273.52	249.06
18000	1574.13	822.33	572.40	447.94	373.66	324.46	289.61	263.71
19000	1661.58	868.02	604.20	472.82	394.41	342.49	305.70	278.38
20000	1749.03	913.70	636.00	497.71	415.17	360.52	321.79	293.01
21000	1836.49	959.38	667.80	522.59	435.93	378.54	337.88	307.66
22000	1923.94	1005.07	699.60	547.48	456.69	396.57	353.96	322.31
23000	2011.39	1050.75	731.40	572.36	477.45	414.59	370.05	336.96
24000	2098.84	1096.44	763.20	597.25	498.21	432.62	386.14	351.61
25000	2186.29	1142.12	795.00	622.13	518.96	450.64	402.23	366.26
26000	2273.74	1187.81	826.80	647.02	539.72	468.67	418.32	380.91
27000	2361.19	1233.49	858.60	671.90	560.48	486.69	434.41	395.56
28000	2448.65	1279.18	890.40	696.79	581.24	504.72	450.50	410.21
29000	2536.10	1324.86	922.20	721.67	602.00	522.75	466.59	424.86
30000	2623.55	1370.55	954.00	746.56	622.76	540.77	482.68	439.51
31000	2711.00	1416.23	985.80	771.44	643.51	558.80	498.77	454.16
32000	2798.45	1461.92	1017.60	796.33	664.27	576.82	514.86	468.81
33000	2885.90	1507.60	1049.40	821.21	685.03	594.85	530.94	483.46
34000	2973.36	1553.29	1081.20	846.10	705.79	612.87	547.03	498.11
35000	3060.81	1598.97	1113.00	870.98	726.55	630.90	563.12	512.76
40000	3498.06	1827.39	1271.99	995.41	830.34	721.03	643.57	586.01
45000	3935.32	2055.82	1430.99	1119.83	934.13	811.15	724.01	659.26
50000	4372.58	2284.24	1589.99	1244.26	1037.92	901.28	804.46	732.52
55000	4809.84	2512.67	1748.99	1368.68	1141.71	991.41	884.90	805.77
60000	5247.09	2741.09	1907.99	1493.11	1245.51	1081.54	965.35	879.02
65000	5684.35	2969.51	2066.99	1617.53	1349.30	1171.66	1045.80	952.27
70000	6121.61	3197.94	2225.99	1741.96	1453.09	1261.79	1126.24	1025.52
75000	6558.87	3426.36	2384.98	1866.38	1556.88	1351.92	1206.69	1098.77
80000	6996.12	3654.78	2543.98	1990.81	1660.67	1442.05	1287.13	1172.02
85000	7433.38	3883.21	2702.98	2115.23	1764.47	1532.18	1367.58	1245.27
90000	7870.64	4111.63	2861.98	2239.66	1868.26	1622.30	1448.02	1318.52
95000	8307.90	4340.06	3020.98	2364.08	1972.05	1712.43	1528.47	1391.77
100000	8745.15	4568.48	3179.98	2488.51	2075.84	1802.56	1608.91	1465.03
105000	9182.41	4796.90	3338.98	2612.93	2179.63	1892.69	1689.36	1538.28
110000	9619.67	5025.33	3497.98	2737.36	2283.42	1982.81	1769.80	1611.53
115000	10056.92	5253.75	3656.97	2861.78	2387.22	2072.94	1850.25	1684.78
120000	10494.18	5482.17	3815.97	2986.21	2491.01	2163.07	1930.69	1758.03
125000	10931.44	5710.60	3974.97	3110.64	2594.80	2253.20	2011.14	1831.28
130000	11368.70	5939.02	4133.97	3235.06	2698.59	2343.32	2091.59	1904.53
135000	11805.95	6167.45	4292.97	3359.49	2802.38	2433.45	2172.03	1977.78
140000	12243.21	6395.87	4451.97	3483.91	2906.17	2523.58	2252.48	2051.03
145000	12680.47	6624.29	4610.97	3608.34	3009.97	2613.71	2332.92	2124.28
150000	13117.73	6852.72	4769.96	3732.76	3113.76	2703.84	2413.37	2197.54
155000	13554.98	7081.14	4928.96	3857.19	3217.55	2793.96	2493.81	2270.79
160000	13992.24	7309.56	5087.96	3981.61	3321.34	2884.09	2574.26	2344.04

6

MONTHLY AMORTIZING PAYMENTS 9.000%

AMOUNT OF LOAN	NUMBER OF YEARS IN TERM							
	9	10	15	20	25	30	35	40
$ 50	.68	.64	.51	.45	.42	.41	.40	.39
100	1.36	1.27	1.02	.90	.84	.81	.79	.78
200	2.71	2.54	2.03	1.80	1.68	1.61	1.57	1.55
300	4.07	3.81	3.05	2.70	2.52	2.42	2.36	2.32
400	5.42	5.07	4.06	3.60	3.36	3.22	3.14	3.09
500	6.78	6.34	5.08	4.50	4.20	4.03	3.92	3.86
600	8.13	7.61	6.09	5.40	5.04	4.83	4.71	4.63
700	9.49	8.87	7.10	6.30	5.88	5.64	5.49	5.40
800	10.84	10.14	8.12	7.20	6.72	6.44	6.28	6.18
900	12.19	11.41	9.13	8.1u	7.56	7.25	7.06	6.95
1000	13.55	12.67	10.15	9.00	8.40	8.05	7.84	7.72
2000	27.09	25.34	20.29	18.00	16.79	16.10	15.68	15.43
3000	40.63	38.01	30.43	27.00	25.18	24.14	23.52	23.15
4000	54.18	50.68	40.58	35.99	33.57	32.19	31.36	30.86
5000	67.72	63.34	50.72	44.99	41.96	40.24	39.20	38.57
6000	81.26	76.01	60.86	53.99	50.36	48.28	47.04	46.29
7000	94.81	88.68	71.00	62.99	58.75	56.33	54.88	54.00
8000	108.35	101.35	81.15	71.98	67.14	64.37	62.72	61.71
9000	121.89	114.01	91.29	80.98	75.53	72.42	70.56	69.43
10000	135.43	126.68	101.43	89.98	83.92	80.47	78.40	77.14
11000	148.98	139.35	111.57	98.97	92.32	88.51	86.24	84.85
12000	162.52	152.02	121.72	107.97	100.71	96.56	94.08	92.57
13000	176.06	164.68	131.86	116.97	109.10	104.61	101.92	100.28
14000	189.61	177.35	142.00	125.97	117.49	112.65	109.76	108.00
15000	203.15	190.02	152.14	134.96	125.88	120.70	117.60	115.71
16000	216.69	202.69	162.29	143.96	134.28	128.74	125.44	123.42
17000	230.23	215.35	172.43	152.96	142.67	136.79	133.28	131.14
18000	243.78	228.02	182.57	161.96	151.06	144.84	141.12	138.85
19000	257.32	240.69	192.72	170.95	159.45	152.88	148.96	146.56
20000	270.86	253.36	202.86	179.95	167.84	160.93	156.80	154.28
21000	284.41	266.02	213.00	188.95	176.24	168.98	164.64	161.99
22000	297.95	278.69	223.14	197.94	184.63	177.02	172.48	169.70
23000	311.49	291.36	233.29	206.94	193.02	185.07	180.32	177.42
24000	325.03	304.03	243.43	215.94	201.41	193.11	188.16	185.13
25000	338.58	316.69	253.57	224.94	209.80	201.16	196.00	192.85
26000	352.12	329.36	263.71	233.93	218.20	209.21	203.84	200.56
27000	365.66	342.03	273.86	242.93	226.59	217.25	211.68	208.27
28000	379.21	354.70	284.00	251.93	234.98	225.30	219.52	215.99
29000	392.75	367.36	294.14	260.93	243.37	233.35	227.36	223.70
30000	406.29	380.03	304.28	269.92	251.76	241.39	235.20	231.41
31000	419.84	392.70	314.43	278.92	260.16	249.44	243.04	239.13
32000	433.38	405.37	324.57	287.92	268.55	257.48	250.88	246.84
33000	446.92	418.04	334.71	296.91	276.94	265.53	258.72	254.55
34000	460.46	430.70	344.86	305.91	285.33	273.58	266.56	262.27
35000	474.01	443.37	355.00	314.91	293.72	281.62	274.40	269.98
40000	541.72	506.71	405.71	359.90	335.68	321.85	313.60	308.55
45000	609.44	570.05	456.42	404.88	377.64	362.09	352.80	347.12
50000	677.15	633.38	507.14	449.87	419.60	402.32	392.00	385.69
55000	744.86	696.72	557.85	494.85	461.56	442.55	431.20	424.25
60000	812.58	760.06	608.56	539.84	503.52	482.78	470.40	462.82
65000	880.29	823.40	659.28	584.83	545.48	523.01	509.60	501.39
70000	948.01	886.74	709.99	629.81	587.44	563.24	548.80	539.96
75000	1015.72	950.07	760.70	674.80	629.40	603.47	588.00	578.53
80000	1083.44	1013.41	811.42	719.79	671.36	643.70	627.20	617.09
85000	1151.15	1076.75	862.13	764.77	713.32	683.93	666.40	655.66
90000	1218.87	1140.09	912.84	809.76	755.28	724.17	705.60	694.23
95000	1286.58	1203.42	963.56	854.74	797.24	764.40	744.80	732.80
100000	1354.30	1266.76	1014.27	899.73	839.20	804.63	784.00	771.37
105000	1422.01	1330.10	1064.98	944.72	881.16	844.86	823.20	809.93
110000	1489.72	1393.44	1115.70	989.70	923.12	885.09	862.40	848.50
115000	1557.44	1456.78	1166.41	1034.69	965.08	925.32	901.60	887.07
120000	1625.15	1520.11	1217.12	1079.68	1007.04	965.55	940.80	925.64
125000	1692.87	1583.45	1267.84	1124.66	1049.00	1005.78	980.00	964.21
130000	1760.58	1646.79	1318.55	1169.65	1090.96	1046.01	1019.20	1002.77
135000	1828.30	1710.13	1369.26	1214.64	1132.92	1086.25	1058.40	1041.34
140000	1896.01	1773.47	1419.98	1259.62	1174.88	1126.48	1097.60	1079.91
145000	1963.73	1836.80	1470.69	1304.61	1216.84	1166.71	1136.79	1118.48
150000	2031.44	1900.14	1521.40	1349.59	1258.80	1206.94	1175.99	1157.05
155000	2099.16	1963.48	1572.12	1394.58	1300.76	1247.17	1215.19	1195.62
160000	2166.87	2026.82	1622.83	1439.57	1342.72	1287.40	1254.39	1234.18

AMOUNT OF LOAN	NUMBER OF YEARS IN TERM							
	1	2	3	4	5	6	7	8
$ 50	4.38	2.29	1.60	1.26	1.05	.91	.82	.74
100	8.76	4.58	3.20	2.51	2.09	1.82	1.63	1.48
200	17.52	9.16	6.39	5.01	4.18	3.63	3.25	2.96
300	26.28	13.74	9.58	7.51	6.27	5.45	4.87	4.44
400	35.03	18.32	12.77	10.01	8.36	7.26	6.49	5.92
500	43.79	22.90	15.96	12.51	10.44	9.08	8.11	7.40
600	52.55	27.48	19.15	15.01	12.53	10.89	9.73	8.87
700	61.30	32.06	22.35	17.51	14.62	12.71	11.36	10.35
800	70.06	36.64	25.54	20.01	16.71	14.52	12.98	11.83
900	78.82	41.22	28.73	22.51	18.80	16.34	14.60	13.31
1000	87.57	45.80	31.92	25.01	20.88	18.15	16.22	14.79
2000	175.14	91.60	63.84	50.01	41.76	36.30	32.44	29.57
3000	262.71	137.40	95.75	75.02	62.64	54.45	48.65	44.35
4000	350.27	183.20	127.67	100.02	83.52	72.60	64.87	59.13
5000	437.84	229.00	159.59	125.02	104.40	90.75	81.09	73.91
6000	525.41	274.80	191.50	150.03	125.28	108.90	97.30	88.69
7000	612.98	320.60	223.42	175.03	146.16	127.05	113.52	103.47
8000	700.54	366.40	255.33	200.04	167.04	145.20	129.73	118.25
9000	788.11	412.20	287.25	225.04	187.92	163.35	145.95	133.03
10000	875.68	458.00	319.17	250.04	208.80	181.50	162.17	147.81
11000	963.25	503.80	351.08	275.05	229.68	199.65	178.38	162.59
12000	1050.81	549.60	383.00	300.05	250.56	217.80	194.60	177.37
13000	1138.38	595.40	414.92	325.06	271.44	235.95	210.82	192.15
14000	1225.95	641.20	446.83	350.06	292.32	254.10	227.03	206.93
15000	1313.52	687.00	478.75	375.06	313.20	272.25	243.25	221.71
16000	1401.08	732.80	510.66	400.07	334.08	290.40	259.46	236.49
17000	1488.65	778.60	542.58	425.07	354.96	308.55	275.68	251.27
18000	1576.22	824.40	574.50	450.08	375.84	326.70	291.90	266.05
19000	1663.79	870.20	606.41	475.08	396.72	344.85	308.11	280.83
20000	1751.35	916.00	638.33	500.08	417.60	363.00	324.33	295.61
21000	1838.92	961.80	670.25	525.09	438.48	381.15	340.55	310.39
22000	1926.49	1007.59	702.16	550.09	459.36	399.30	356.76	325.17
23000	2014.06	1053.39	734.08	575.10	480.24	417.45	372.98	339.95
24000	2101.62	1099.19	765.99	600.10	501.12	435.60	389.19	354.73
25000	2189.19	1144.99	797.91	625.10	522.00	453.75	405.41	369.51
26000	2276.76	1190.79	829.83	650.11	542.88	471.90	421.63	384.29
27000	2364.33	1236.59	861.74	675.11	563.76	490.05	437.84	399.07
28000	2451.89	1282.39	893.66	700.11	584.64	508.20	454.06	413.85
29000	2539.46	1328.19	925.58	725.12	605.52	526.35	470.28	428.63
30000	2627.03	1373.99	957.49	750.12	626.40	544.50	486.49	443.41
31000	2714.60	1419.79	989.41	775.13	647.28	562.65	502.71	458.19
32000	2802.16	1465.59	1021.32	800.13	668.16	580.80	518.92	472.97
33000	2889.73	1511.39	1053.24	825.13	689.04	598.95	535.14	487.75
34000	2977.30	1557.19	1085.16	850.14	709.92	617.10	551.36	502.53
35000	3064.87	1602.99	1117.07	875.14	730.80	635.25	567.57	517.31
40000	3502.70	1831.99	1276.65	1000.16	835.20	726.00	648.65	591.21
45000	3940.54	2060.98	1436.23	1125.18	939.60	816.75	729.74	665.11
50000	4378.38	2289.98	1595.82	1250.20	1044.00	907.50	810.82	739.02
55000	4816.21	2518.98	1755.40	1375.22	1148.40	998.25	891.90	812.92
60000	5254.05	2747.98	1914.98	1500.24	1252.80	1089.00	972.98	886.82
65000	5691.89	2976.97	2074.56	1625.26	1357.20	1179.75	1054.06	960.72
70000	6129.73	3205.97	2234.14	1750.28	1461.60	1270.50	1135.14	1034.62
75000	6567.56	3434.97	2393.72	1875.30	1566.00	1361.24	1216.22	1108.52
80000	7005.40	3663.97	2553.30	2000.32	1670.40	1451.99	1297.30	1182.42
85000	7443.24	3892.97	2712.88	2125.34	1774.80	1542.74	1378.39	1256.32
90000	7881.08	4121.96	2872.46	2250.36	1879.20	1633.49	1459.47	1330.22
95000	8318.91	4350.96	3032.05	2375.39	1983.60	1724.24	1540.55	1404.13
100000	8756.75	4579.96	3191.63	2500.40	2087.99	1814.99	1621.63	1478.03
105000	9194.59	4808.96	3351.21	2625.42	2192.39	1905.74	1702.71	1551.93
110000	9632.42	5037.95	3510.79	2750.44	2296.79	1996.49	1783.79	1625.83
115000	10070.26	5266.95	3670.37	2875.46	2401.19	2087.24	1864.87	1699.73
120000	10508.10	5495.95	3829.95	3000.48	2505.59	2177.99	1945.95	1773.63
125000	10945.94	5724.95	3989.53	3125.50	2609.99	2268.74	2027.04	1847.53
130000	11383.77	5953.94	4149.11	3250.51	2714.39	2359.49	2108.12	1921.43
135000	11821.61	6182.94	4308.69	3375.53	2818.79	2450.24	2189.20	1995.33
140000	12259.45	6411.94	4468.27	3500.55	2923.19	2540.99	2270.28	2069.24
145000	12697.29	6640.94	4627.86	3625.57	3027.59	2631.74	2351.36	2143.14
150000	13135.12	6869.93	4787.44	3750.59	3131.99	2722.48	2432.44	2217.04
155000	13572.96	7098.93	4947.02	3875.61	3236.39	2813.23	2513.52	2290.94
160000	14010.80	7327.93	5106.60	4000.63	3340.79	2903.98	2594.60	2364.84

AMOUNT OF LOAN	NUMBER OF YEARS IN TERM							
	9	10	15	20	25	30	35	40
$ 50	.69	.65	.52	.46	.43	.42	.41	.40
100	1.37	1.29	1.03	.92	.86	.83	.81	.80
200	2.74	2.57	2.06	1.84	1.72	1.65	1.61	1.59
300	4.11	3.85	3.09	2.75	2.57	2.47	2.41	2.38
400	5.48	5.13	4.12	3.67	3.43	3.30	3.22	3.17
500	6.84	6.41	5.15	4.58	4.29	4.12	4.02	3.96
600	8.21	7.69	6.18	5.50	5.14	4.94	4.82	4.75
700	9.58	8.97	7.21	6.42	6.00	5.76	5.62	5.54
800	10.95	10.25	8.24	7.33	6.86	6.59	6.43	6.33
900	12.31	11.53	9.27	8.25	7.71	7.41	7.23	7.12
1000	13.68	12.81	10.30	9.16	8.57	8.23	8.03	7.91
2000	27.36	25.61	20.59	18.32	17.13	16.46	16.06	15.82
3000	41.03	38.41	30.88	27.48	25.70	24.69	24.09	23.72
4000	54.71	51.22	41.17	36.64	34.26	32.91	32.11	31.63
5000	68.38	64.02	51.46	45.80	42.82	41.14	40.14	39.54
6000	82.06	76.82	61.76	54.96	51.39	49.37	48.17	47.44
7000	95.74	89.63	72.05	64.12	59.95	57.59	56.20	55.35
8000	109.41	102.43	82.34	73.27	68.52	65.82	64.22	63.26
9000	123.09	115.23	92.63	82.43	77.08	74.05	72.25	71.16
10000	136.76	128.04	102.92	91.59	85.64	82.27	80.28	79.07
11000	150.44	140.84	113.22	100.75	94.21	90.50	88.31	86.98
12000	164.11	153.64	123.51	109.91	102.77	98.73	96.33	94.88
13000	177.79	166.45	133.80	119.07	111.33	106.95	104.36	102.79
14000	191.47	179.25	144.09	128.23	119.90	115.18	112.39	110.70
15000	205.14	192.05	154.38	137.39	128.46	123.41	120.42	118.60
16000	218.82	204.86	164.68	146.54	137.03	131.63	128.44	126.51
17000	232.49	217.66	174.97	155.70	145.59	139.86	136.47	134.42
18000	246.17	230.46	185.26	164.86	154.15	148.09	144.50	142.32
19000	259.84	243.27	195.55	174.02	162.72	156.31	152.53	150.23
20000	273.52	256.07	205.84	183.18	171.28	164.54	160.55	158.14
21000	287.20	268.87	216.14	192.34	179.85	172.77	168.58	166.04
22000	300.87	281.68	226.43	201.50	188.41	180.99	176.61	173.95
23000	314.55	294.48	236.72	210.65	196.97	189.22	184.64	181.86
24000	328.22	307.28	247.01	219.81	205.54	197.45	192.66	189.76
25000	341.90	320.09	257.30	228.97	214.10	205.67	200.69	197.67
26000	355.58	332.89	267.59	238.13	222.66	213.90	208.72	205.58
27000	369.25	345.69	277.89	247.29	231.23	222.13	216.75	213.48
28000	382.93	358.50	288.18	256.45	239.79	230.35	224.77	221.39
29000	396.60	371.30	298.47	265.61	248.36	238.58	232.80	229.30
30000	410.28	384.10	308.76	274.77	256.92	246.81	240.83	237.20
31000	423.95	396.91	319.05	283.92	265.48	255.03	248.86	245.11
32000	437.63	409.71	329.35	293.08	274.05	263.26	256.88	253.02
33000	451.31	422.51	339.64	302.24	282.61	271.49	264.91	260.92
34000	464.98	435.32	349.93	311.40	291.17	279.71	272.94	268.83
35000	478.66	448.12	360.22	320.56	299.74	287.94	280.97	276.74
40000	547.04	512.14	411.68	366.35	342.56	329.08	321.10	316.27
45000	615.41	576.15	463.14	412.15	385.38	370.21	361.24	355.80
50000	683.79	640.17	514.60	457.94	428.20	411.34	401.38	395.34
55000	752.17	704.18	566.06	503.73	471.02	452.48	441.51	434.87
60000	820.55	768.20	617.52	549.53	513.83	493.61	481.65	474.40
65000	888.93	832.22	668.98	595.32	556.65	534.74	521.79	513.93
70000	957.31	896.23	720.44	641.11	599.47	575.88	561.93	553.47
75000	1025.69	960.25	771.90	686.91	642.29	617.01	602.06	593.00
80000	1094.07	1024.27	823.36	732.70	685.11	658.15	642.20	632.53
85000	1162.45	1088.28	874.82	778.49	727.93	699.28	682.34	672.07
90000	1230.82	1152.30	926.28	824.29	770.75	740.41	722.47	711.60
95000	1299.20	1216.32	977.74	870.08	813.57	781.55	762.61	751.13
100000	1367.58	1280.33	1029.20	915.87	856.39	822.68	802.75	790.67
105000	1435.96	1344.35	1080.66	961.67	899.21	863.81	842.89	830.20
110000	1504.34	1408.36	1132.12	1007.46	942.03	904.95	883.02	869.73
115000	1572.72	1472.38	1183.58	1053.25	984.84	946.08	923.16	909.26
120000	1641.10	1536.40	1235.04	1099.05	1027.66	987.22	963.30	948.80
125000	1709.48	1600.41	1286.50	1144.84	1070.48	1028.35	1003.44	988.33
130000	1777.86	1664.43	1337.95	1190.63	1113.30	1069.48	1043.57	1027.86
135000	1846.23	1728.45	1389.41	1236.43	1156.12	1110.62	1083.71	1067.40
140000	1914.61	1792.46	1440.87	1282.22	1198.94	1151.75	1123.85	1106.93
145000	1982.99	1856.48	1492.33	1328.01	1241.76	1192.88	1163.98	1146.46
150000	2051.37	1920.50	1543.79	1373.81	1284.58	1234.02	1204.12	1186.00
155000	2119.75	1984.51	1595.25	1419.60	1327.40	1275.15	1244.26	1225.53
160000	2188.13	2048.53	1646.71	1465.39	1370.22	1316.29	1284.40	1265.06

AMOUNT OF LOAN	NUMBER OF YEARS IN TERM							
	1	2	3	4	5	6	7	8
$ 50	4.39	2.30	1.61	1.26	1.06	.92	.82	.75
100	8.77	4.60	3.21	2.52	2.11	1.83	1.64	1.50
200	17.54	9.19	6.41	5.03	4.21	3.66	3.27	2.99
300	26.31	13.78	9.61	7.54	6.31	5.49	4.91	4.48
400	35.08	18.37	12.82	10.05	8.41	7.31	6.54	5.97
500	43.85	22.96	16.02	12.57	10.51	9.14	8.18	7.46
600	52.62	27.55	19.22	15.08	12.61	10.97	9.81	8.95
700	61.38	32.15	22.43	17.59	14.71	12.80	11.45	10.44
800	70.15	36.74	25.63	20.10	16.81	14.62	13.08	11.93
900	78.92	41.33	28.83	22.62	18.91	16.45	14.71	13.42
1000	87.69	45.92	32.04	25.13	21.01	18.28	16.35	14.92
2000	175.37	91.83	64.07	50.25	42.01	36.55	32.69	29.83
3000	263.06	137.75	96.10	75.37	63.01	54.83	49.04	44.74
4000	350.74	183.66	128.14	100.50	84.01	73.10	65.38	59.65
5000	438.42	229.58	160.17	125.62	105.01	91.38	81.72	74.56
6000	526.11	275.49	192.20	150.74	126.02	109.65	98.07	89.47
7000	613.79	321.41	224.24	175.87	147.02	127.93	114.41	104.38
8000	701.47	367.32	256.27	200.99	168.02	146.20	130.76	119.29
9000	789.16	413.24	288.30	226.11	189.02	164.48	147.10	134.20
10000	876.84	459.15	320.33	251.24	210.02	182.75	163.44	149.11
11000	964.52	505.06	352.37	276.36	231.03	201.03	179.79	164.02
12000	1052.21	550.98	384.40	301.48	252.03	219.30	196.13	178.94
13000	1139.89	596.89	416.43	326.61	273.03	237.58	212.48	193.85
14000	1227.57	642.81	448.47	351.73	294.03	255.85	228.82	208.76
15000	1315.26	688.72	480.50	376.85	315.03	274.13	245.16	223.67
16000	1402.94	734.64	512.53	401.98	336.03	292.40	261.51	238.58
17000	1490.62	780.55	544.57	427.10	357.04	310.67	277.85	253.49
18000	1578.31	826.47	576.60	452.22	378.04	328.95	294.20	268.40
19000	1665.99	872.38	608.63	477.34	399.04	347.22	310.54	283.31
20000	1753.68	918.29	640.66	502.47	420.04	365.50	326.88	298.22
21000	1841.36	964.21	672.70	527.59	441.04	383.77	343.23	313.13
22000	1929.04	1010.12	704.73	552.71	462.05	402.05	359.57	328.04
23000	2016.73	1056.04	736.76	577.84	483.05	420.32	375.92	342.96
24000	2104.41	1101.95	768.80	602.96	504.05	438.60	392.26	357.87
25000	2192.09	1147.87	800.83	628.08	525.05	456.87	408.60	372.78
26000	2279.78	1193.78	832.86	653.21	546.05	475.15	424.95	387.69
27000	2367.46	1239.70	864.89	678.33	567.06	493.42	441.29	402.60
28000	2455.14	1285.61	896.93	703.45	588.06	511.70	457.64	417.51
29000	2542.83	1331.53	928.96	728.58	609.06	529.97	473.98	432.42
30000	2630.51	1377.44	960.99	753.70	630.06	548.25	490.32	447.33
31000	2718.19	1423.35	993.03	778.82	651.06	566.52	506.67	462.24
32000	2805.88	1469.27	1025.06	803.95	672.07	584.80	523.01	477.15
33000	2893.56	1515.18	1057.09	829.07	693.07	603.07	539.36	492.06
34000	2981.24	1561.10	1089.13	854.19	714.07	621.34	555.70	506.98
35000	3068.93	1607.01	1121.16	879.31	735.07	639.62	572.04	521.89
40000	3507.35	1836.58	1281.32	1004.93	840.08	730.99	653.76	596.44
45000	3945.76	2066.16	1441.49	1130.55	945.09	822.37	735.48	670.99
50000	4384.18	2295.73	1601.65	1256.16	1050.10	913.74	817.20	745.55
55000	4822.60	2525.30	1761.82	1381.78	1155.11	1005.11	898.92	820.10
60000	5261.01	2754.87	1921.98	1507.39	1260.12	1096.49	980.64	894.66
65000	5699.43	2984.45	2082.15	1633.01	1365.13	1187.86	1062.36	969.21
70000	6137.85	3214.02	2242.31	1758.62	1470.14	1279.23	1144.08	1043.77
75000	6576.27	3443.59	2402.48	1884.24	1575.14	1370.61	1225.80	1118.32
80000	7014.69	3673.16	2562.64	2009.86	1680.15	1461.98	1307.52	1192.88
85000	7453.10	3902.74	2722.81	2135.47	1785.16	1553.35	1389.24	1267.43
90000	7891.52	4132.31	2882.97	2261.09	1890.17	1644.73	1470.96	1341.98
95000	8329.94	4361.88	3043.14	2386.70	1995.18	1736.10	1552.68	1416.54
100000	8768.36	4591.45	3203.30	2512.32	2100.19	1827.48	1634.40	1491.09
105000	9206.77	4821.03	3363.46	2637.93	2205.20	1918.85	1716.12	1565.65
110000	9645.19	5050.60	3523.63	2763.55	2310.21	2010.22	1797.84	1640.20
115000	10083.61	5280.17	3683.79	2889.17	2415.22	2101.59	1879.56	1714.76
120000	10522.03	5509.74	3843.96	3014.78	2520.23	2192.97	1961.28	1789.31
125000	10960.44	5739.32	4004.12	3140.40	2625.24	2284.34	2043.00	1863.87
130000	11398.86	5968.89	4164.29	3266.01	2730.25	2375.71	2124.72	1938.42
135000	11837.28	6198.46	4324.45	3391.63	2835.26	2467.09	2206.44	2012.97
140000	12275.70	6428.03	4484.62	3517.24	2940.27	2558.46	2288.16	2087.53
145000	12714.11	6657.61	4644.78	3642.86	3045.27	2649.84	2369.88	2162.08
150000	13152.53	6887.18	4804.95	3768.48	3150.28	2741.21	2451.60	2236.64
155000	13590.95	7116.75	4965.11	3894.09	3255.29	2832.58	2533.32	2311.19
160000	14029.37	7346.32	5125.28	4019.71	3360.30	2923.96	2615.04	2385.75

AMOUNT OF LOAN	NUMBER OF YEARS IN TERM							
	9	10	15	20	25	30	35	40
$ 50	.70	.65	.53	.47	.44	.43	.42	.41
100	1.39	1.30	1.05	.94	.88	.85	.83	.82
200	2.77	2.59	2.09	1.87	1.75	1.69	1.65	1.63
300	4.15	3.89	3.14	2.80	2.63	2.53	2.47	2.44
400	5.53	5.18	4.18	3.73	3.50	3.37	3.29	3.25
500	6.91	6.47	5.23	4.67	4.37	4.21	4.11	4.06
600	8.29	7.77	6.27	5.60	5.25	5.05	4.93	4.87
700	9.67	9.06	7.31	6.53	6.12	5.89	5.76	5.68
800	11.05	10.36	8.36	7.46	6.99	6.73	6.58	6.49
900	12.43	11.65	9.40	8.39	7.87	7.57	7.40	7.30
1000	13.81	12.94	10.45	9.33	8.74	8.41	8.22	8.11
2000	27.62	25.88	20.89	18.65	17.48	16.82	16.44	16.21
3000	41.43	38.82	31.33	27.97	26.22	25.23	24.65	24.31
4000	55.24	51.76	41.77	37.29	34.95	33.64	32.87	32.41
5000	69.05	64.70	52.22	46.61	43.69	42.05	41.09	40.51
6000	82.86	77.64	62.66	55.93	52.43	50.46	49.30	48.61
7000	96.67	90.58	73.10	65.25	61.16	58.86	57.52	56.71
8000	110.48	103.52	83.54	74.58	69.90	67.27	65.73	64.81
9000	124.29	116.46	93.99	83.90	78.64	75.68	73.95	72.91
10000	138.10	129.40	104.43	93.22	87.37	84.09	82.17	81.01
11000	151.91	142.34	114.87	102.54	96.11	92.50	90.38	89.11
12000	165.72	155.28	125.31	111.86	104.85	100.91	98.60	97.21
13000	179.53	168.22	135.75	121.18	113.59	109.32	106.81	105.31
14000	193.34	181.16	146.20	130.50	122.32	117.72	115.03	113.41
15000	207.15	194.10	156.64	139.82	131.06	126.13	123.25	121.51
16000	220.95	207.04	167.08	149.15	139.80	134.54	131.46	129.61
17000	234.76	219.98	177.52	158.47	148.53	142.95	139.68	137.72
18000	248.57	232.92	187.97	167.79	157.27	151.36	147.90	145.82
19000	262.38	245.86	198.41	177.11	166.01	159.77	156.11	153.92
20000	276.19	258.80	208.85	186.43	174.74	168.18	164.33	162.02
21000	290.00	271.74	219.29	195.75	183.48	176.58	172.54	170.12
22000	303.81	284.68	229.73	205.07	192.22	184.99	180.76	178.22
23000	317.62	297.62	240.18	214.40	200.96	193.40	188.98	186.32
24000	331.43	310.56	250.62	223.72	209.69	201.81	197.19	194.42
25000	345.24	323.50	261.06	233.04	218.43	210.22	205.41	202.52
26000	359.05	336.44	271.50	242.36	227.17	218.63	213.62	210.62
27000	372.86	349.38	281.95	251.68	235.90	227.04	221.84	218.72
28000	386.67	362.32	292.39	261.00	244.64	235.44	230.06	226.82
29000	400.48	375.26	302.83	270.32	253.38	243.85	238.27	234.92
30000	414.29	388.20	313.27	279.64	262.11	252.26	246.49	243.02
31000	428.10	401.14	323.71	288.97	270.85	260.67	254.70	251.12
32000	441.90	414.08	334.16	298.29	279.59	269.08	262.92	259.22
33000	455.71	427.02	344.60	307.61	288.32	277.49	271.14	267.33
34000	469.52	439.96	355.04	316.93	297.06	285.90	279.35	275.43
35000	483.33	452.90	365.48	326.25	305.80	294.30	287.57	283.53
40000	552.38	517.60	417.69	372.86	349.48	336.35	328.65	324.03
45000	621.43	582.29	469.91	419.46	393.17	378.39	369.73	364.53
50000	690.47	646.99	522.12	466.07	436.85	420.43	410.81	405.04
55000	759.52	711.69	574.33	512.68	480.54	462.47	451.89	445.54
60000	828.57	776.39	626.54	559.28	524.22	504.52	492.97	486.04
65000	897.61	841.09	678.75	605.89	567.91	546.56	534.05	526.55
70000	966.66	905.79	730.96	652.50	611.59	588.60	575.13	567.05
75000	1035.71	970.49	783.17	699.10	655.28	630.65	616.21	607.55
80000	1104.75	1035.19	835.38	745.71	698.96	672.69	657.29	648.05
85000	1173.80	1099.88	887.60	792.32	742.65	714.73	698.37	688.56
90000	1242.85	1164.58	939.81	838.92	786.33	756.77	739.46	729.06
95000	1311.89	1229.28	992.02	885.53	830.02	798.82	780.54	769.56
100000	1380.94	1293.98	1044.23	932.14	873.70	840.86	821.62	810.07
105000	1449.99	1358.68	1096.44	978.74	917.39	882.90	862.70	850.57
110000	1519.03	1423.38	1148.65	1025.35	961.07	924.94	903.78	891.07
115000	1588.08	1488.08	1200.86	1071.96	1004.76	966.99	944.86	931.58
120000	1657.13	1552.78	1253.07	1118.56	1048.44	1009.03	985.94	972.08
125000	1726.18	1617.47	1305.29	1165.17	1092.13	1051.07	1027.02	1012.58
130000	1795.22	1682.17	1357.50	1211.78	1135.81	1093.12	1068.10	1053.09
135000	1864.27	1746.87	1409.71	1258.38	1179.50	1135.16	1109.18	1093.59
140000	1933.32	1811.57	1461.92	1304.99	1223.18	1177.20	1150.26	1134.09
145000	2002.36	1876.27	1514.13	1351.60	1266.87	1219.24	1191.34	1174.59
150000	2071.41	1940.97	1566.34	1398.20	1310.55	1261.29	1232.42	1215.10
155000	2140.46	2005.67	1618.55	1444.81	1354.24	1303.33	1273.50	1255.60
160000	2209.50	2070.37	1670.76	1491.41	1397.92	1345.37	1314.58	1296.10

MONTHLY AMORTIZING PAYMENTS

AMOUNT OF LOAN	NUMBER OF YEARS IN TERM							
	1	2	3	4	5	6	7	8
$ 50	4.39	2.31	1.61	1.27	1.06	.92	.83	.76
100	8.78	4.61	3.22	2.53	2.12	1.85	1.65	1.51
200	17.56	9.21	6.43	5.05	4.23	3.69	3.30	3.01
300	26.34	13.81	9.65	7.58	6.34	5.53	4.95	4.52
400	35.12	18.42	12.86	10.10	8.45	7.37	6.59	6.02
500	43.90	23.02	16.08	12.63	10.57	9.21	8.24	7.53
600	52.68	27.62	19.29	15.15	12.68	11.05	9.89	9.03
700	61.46	32.23	22.51	17.67	14.79	12.89	11.54	10.53
800	70.24	36.83	25.72	20.20	16.90	14.73	13.18	12.04
900	79.02	41.43	28.94	22.72	19.02	16.57	14.83	13.54
1000	87.80	46.03	32.15	25.25	21.13	18.41	16.48	15.05
2000	175.60	92.06	64.30	50.49	42.25	36.81	32.95	30.09
3000	263.40	138.09	96.45	75.73	63.38	55.21	49.42	45.13
4000	351.20	184.12	128.60	100.98	84.50	73.61	65.89	60.17
5000	439.00	230.15	160.75	126.22	105.63	92.01	82.37	75.22
6000	526.80	276.18	192.90	151.46	126.75	110.41	98.84	90.26
7000	614.60	322.21	225.05	176.70	147.87	128.81	115.31	105.30
8000	702.40	368.24	257.20	201.95	169.00	147.21	131.78	120.34
9000	790.20	414.27	289.35	227.19	190.12	165.61	148.26	135.38
10000	878.00	460.30	321.50	252.43	211.25	184.01	164.73	150.43
11000	965.80	506.33	353.65	277.67	232.37	202.41	181.20	165.47
12000	1053.60	552.36	385.80	302.92	253.50	220.81	197.67	180.51
13000	1141.40	598.39	417.95	328.16	274.62	239.21	214.14	195.55
14000	1229.20	644.42	450.10	353.40	295.74	257.61	230.62	210.60
15000	1317.00	690.45	482.25	378.65	316.87	276.01	247.09	225.64
16000	1404.80	736.48	514.40	403.89	337.99	294.41	263.56	240.68
17000	1492.60	782.51	546.55	429.13	359.12	312.81	280.03	255.72
18000	1580.40	828.54	578.70	454.37	380.24	331.21	296.51	270.76
19000	1668.20	874.57	610.85	479.62	401.37	349.61	312.98	285.81
20000	1756.00	920.60	643.00	504.86	422.49	368.01	329.45	300.85
21000	1843.80	966.63	675.15	530.10	443.61	386.41	345.92	315.89
22000	1931.60	1012.66	707.30	555.34	464.74	404.81	362.40	330.93
23000	2019.40	1058.69	739.45	580.59	485.86	423.21	378.87	345.98
24000	2107.20	1104.72	771.60	605.83	506.99	441.61	395.34	361.02
25000	2195.00	1150.75	803.75	631.07	528.11	460.01	411.81	376.06
26000	2282.80	1196.78	835.90	656.31	549.24	478.41	428.28	391.10
27000	2370.60	1242.80	868.05	681.56	570.36	496.81	444.76	406.14
28000	2458.40	1288.83	900.20	706.80	591.48	515.21	461.23	421.19
29000	2546.20	1334.86	932.35	732.04	612.61	533.61	477.70	436.23
30000	2633.99	1380.89	964.50	757.29	633.73	552.01	494.17	451.27
31000	2721.79	1426.92	996.65	782.53	654.86	570.41	510.65	466.31
32000	2809.59	1472.95	1028.80	807.77	675.98	588.81	527.12	481.36
33000	2897.39	1518.98	1060.95	833.01	697.11	607.21	543.59	496.40
34000	2985.19	1565.01	1093.10	858.26	718.23	625.61	560.06	511.44
35000	3072.99	1611.04	1125.25	883.50	739.35	644.01	576.54	526.48
40000	3511.99	1841.19	1286.00	1009.71	844.97	736.01	658.90	601.69
45000	3950.99	2071.34	1446.75	1135.93	950.60	828.01	741.26	676.90
50000	4389.99	2301.49	1607.50	1262.14	1056.22	920.01	823.62	752.12
55000	4828.99	2531.63	1768.25	1388.35	1161.84	1012.01	905.98	827.33
60000	5267.98	2761.78	1929.00	1514.57	1267.46	1104.01	988.34	902.54
65000	5706.98	2991.93	2089.75	1640.78	1373.08	1196.01	1070.70	977.75
70000	6145.98	3222.08	2250.50	1766.99	1478.70	1288.01	1153.07	1052.96
75000	6584.98	3452.23	2411.25	1893.21	1584.32	1380.01	1235.43	1128.17
80000	7023.98	3682.37	2572.00	2019.42	1689.94	1472.01	1317.79	1203.38
85000	7462.98	3912.52	2732.75	2145.63	1795.57	1564.01	1400.15	1278.59
90000	7901.97	4142.67	2893.50	2271.85	1901.19	1656.01	1482.51	1353.80
95000	8340.97	4372.82	3054.25	2398.06	2006.81	1748.01	1564.87	1429.01
100000	8779.97	4602.97	3215.00	2524.27	2112.43	1840.01	1647.23	1504.23
105000	9218.97	4833.12	3375.75	2650.49	2218.05	1932.01	1729.60	1579.44
110000	9657.97	5063.26	3536.50	2776.70	2323.67	2024.01	1811.96	1654.65
115000	10096.97	5293.41	3697.25	2902.91	2429.29	2116.01	1894.32	1729.86
120000	10535.96	5523.56	3858.00	3029.13	2534.91	2208.01	1976.68	1805.07
125000	10974.96	5753.71	4018.75	3155.34	2640.54	2300.01	2059.04	1880.28
130000	11413.96	5983.86	4179.50	3281.55	2746.16	2392.01	2141.40	1955.49
135000	11852.96	6214.00	4340.25	3407.77	2851.78	2484.01	2223.76	2030.70
140000	12291.96	6444.15	4501.00	3533.98	2957.40	2576.01	2306.13	2105.91
145000	12730.96	6674.30	4661.75	3660.20	3063.02	2668.01	2388.49	2181.12
150000	13169.95	6904.45	4822.50	3786.41	3168.64	2760.01	2470.85	2256.34
155000	13608.95	7134.60	4983.25	3912.62	3274.26	2852.01	2553.21	2331.55
160000	14047.95	7364.74	5144.00	4038.84	3379.88	2944.01	2635.57	2406.76

AMOUNT OF LOAN	NUMBER OF YEARS IN TERM							
	9	10	15	20	25	30	35	40
$ 50	.70	.66	.53	.48	.45	.43	.43	.42
100	1.40	1.31	1.06	.95	.90	.86	.85	.83
200	2.79	2.62	2.12	1.90	1.79	1.72	1.69	1.66
300	4.19	3.93	3.18	2.85	2.68	2.58	2.53	2.49
400	5.58	5.24	4.24	3.80	3.57	3.44	3.37	3.32
500	6.98	6.54	5.30	4.75	4.46	4.30	4.21	4.15
600	8.37	7.85	6.36	5.70	5.35	5.16	5.05	4.98
700	9.77	9.16	7.42	6.64	6.24	6.02	5.89	5.81
800	11.16	10.47	8.48	7.59	7.13	6.88	6.73	6.64
900	12.55	11.77	9.54	8.54	8.03	7.74	7.57	7.47
1000	13.95	13.08	10.60	9.49	8.92	8.60	8.41	8.30
2000	27.89	26.16	21.19	18.98	17.83	17.19	16.82	16.60
3000	41.84	39.24	31.79	28.46	26.74	25.78	25.22	24.89
4000	55.78	52.31	42.38	37.95	35.65	34.37	33.63	33.19
5000	69.72	65.39	52.97	47.43	44.56	42.96	42.03	41.48
6000	83.67	78.47	63.57	56.92	53.47	51.55	50.44	49.78
7000	97.61	91.54	74.16	66.40	62.38	60.15	58.85	58.07
8000	111.55	104.62	84.75	75.89	71.30	68.74	67.25	66.37
9000	125.50	117.70	95.35	85.37	80.21	77.33	75.66	74.67
10000	139.44	130.78	105.94	94.86	89.12	85.92	84.06	82.96
11000	153.39	143.85	116.53	104.34	98.03	94.51	92.47	91.26
12000	167.33	156.93	127.13	113.83	106.94	103.10	100.88	99.55
13000	181.27	170.01	137.72	123.31	115.85	111.70	109.28	107.85
14000	195.22	183.08	148.32	132.80	124.76	120.29	117.69	116.14
15000	209.16	196.16	158.91	142.28	133.68	128.88	126.09	124.44
16000	223.10	209.24	169.50	151.77	142.59	137.47	134.50	132.73
17000	237.05	222.31	180.10	161.25	151.50	146.06	142.91	141.03
18000	250.99	235.39	190.69	170.74	160.41	154.65	151.31	149.33
19000	264.93	248.47	201.28	180.22	169.32	163.24	159.72	157.62
20000	278.88	261.55	211.88	189.71	178.23	171.84	168.12	165.92
21000	292.82	274.62	222.47	199.19	187.14	180.43	176.53	174.21
22000	306.77	287.70	233.06	208.68	196.06	189.02	184.93	182.51
23000	320.71	300.78	243.66	218.16	204.97	197.61	193.34	190.80
24000	334.65	313.85	254.25	227.65	213.88	206.20	201.75	199.10
25000	348.60	326.93	264.85	237.13	222.79	214.79	210.15	207.39
26000	362.54	340.01	275.44	246.62	231.70	223.39	218.56	215.69
27000	376.48	353.08	286.03	256.10	240.61	231.98	226.96	223.99
28000	390.43	366.16	296.63	265.59	249.52	240.57	235.37	232.28
29000	404.37	379.24	307.22	275.07	258.43	249.16	243.78	240.58
30000	418.31	392.32	317.81	284.56	267.35	257.75	252.18	248.87
31000	432.26	405.39	328.41	294.05	276.26	266.34	260.59	257.17
32000	446.20	418.47	339.00	303.53	285.17	274.93	268.99	265.46
33000	460.15	431.55	349.59	313.02	294.08	283.53	277.40	273.76
34000	474.09	444.62	360.19	322.50	302.99	292.12	285.81	282.05
35000	488.03	457.70	370.78	331.99	311.90	300.71	294.21	290.35
40000	557.75	523.09	423.75	379.41	356.46	343.67	336.24	331.83
45000	627.47	588.47	476.72	426.84	401.02	386.62	378.27	373.31
50000	697.19	653.86	529.69	474.26	445.57	429.58	420.30	414.78
55000	766.91	719.24	582.65	521.69	490.13	472.54	462.33	456.26
60000	836.62	784.63	635.62	569.12	534.69	515.50	504.36	497.74
65000	906.34	850.01	688.59	616.54	579.24	558.46	546.39	539.22
70000	976.06	915.40	741.56	663.97	623.80	601.41	588.42	580.70
75000	1045.78	980.78	794.53	711.39	668.36	644.37	630.45	622.17
80000	1115.50	1046.17	847.50	758.82	712.91	687.33	672.48	663.65
85000	1185.22	1111.55	900.46	806.24	757.47	730.29	714.51	705.13
90000	1254.93	1176.94	953.43	853.67	802.03	773.24	756.54	746.61
95000	1324.65	1242.32	1006.40	901.10	846.59	816.20	798.56	788.09
100000	1394.37	1307.71	1059.37	948.52	891.14	859.16	840.59	829.56
105000	1464.09	1373.09	1112.34	995.95	935.70	902.12	882.62	871.04
110000	1533.81	1438.48	1165.30	1043.37	980.26	945.07	924.65	912.52
115000	1603.53	1503.86	1218.27	1090.80	1024.81	988.03	966.68	954.00
120000	1673.24	1569.25	1271.24	1138.23	1069.37	1030.99	1008.71	995.48
125000	1742.96	1634.63	1324.21	1185.65	1113.93	1073.95	1050.74	1036.95
130000	1812.68	1700.02	1377.18	1233.08	1158.48	1116.91	1092.77	1078.43
135000	1882.40	1765.40	1430.14	1280.50	1203.04	1159.86	1134.80	1119.91
140000	1952.12	1830.79	1483.11	1327.93	1247.60	1202.82	1176.83	1161.39
145000	2021.84	1896.17	1536.08	1375.35	1292.15	1245.78	1218.86	1202.86
150000	2091.55	1961.56	1589.05	1422.78	1336.71	1288.74	1260.89	1244.34
155000	2161.27	2026.94	1642.02	1470.21	1381.27	1331.69	1302.92	1285.82
160000	2230.99	2092.33	1694.99	1517.63	1425.82	1374.65	1344.95	1327.30

AMOUNT OF LOAN	NUMBER OF YEARS IN TERM							
	1	**2**	**3**	**4**	**5**	**6**	**7**	**8**
$ 50	4.40	2.31	1.62	1.27	1.07	.93	.84	.76
100	8.80	4.62	3.23	2.54	2.13	1.86	1.67	1.52
200	17.59	9.23	6.46	5.08	4.25	3.71	3.33	3.04
300	26.38	13.85	9.69	7.61	6.38	5.56	4.99	4.56
400	35.17	18.46	12.91	10.15	8.50	7.42	6.65	6.07
500	43.96	23.08	16.14	12.69	10.63	9.27	8.31	7.59
600	52.75	27.69	19.37	15.22	12.75	11.12	9.97	9.11
700	61.55	32.31	22.59	17.76	14.88	12.97	11.63	10.63
800	70.34	36.92	25.82	20.30	17.00	14.83	13.29	12.14
900	79.13	41.54	29.05	22.83	19.13	16.68	14.95	13.66
1000	87.92	46.15	32.27	25.37	21.25	18.53	16.61	15.18
2000	175.84	92.29	64.54	50.73	42.50	37.06	33.21	30.35
3000	263.75	138.44	96.81	76.09	63.75	55.58	49.81	45.53
4000	351.67	184.58	129.07	101.46	84.99	74.11	66.41	60.70
5000	439.58	230.73	161.34	126.82	106.24	92.63	83.01	75.88
6000	527.50	276.87	193.61	152.18	127.49	111.16	99.61	91.05
7000	615.42	323.02	225.88	177.54	148.73	129.69	116.21	106.22
8000	703.33	369.16	258.14	202.91	169.98	148.21	132.81	121.40
9000	791.25	415.31	290.41	228.27	191.23	166.74	149.42	136.57
10000	879.16	461.45	322.68	253.63	212.48	185.26	166.02	151.75
11000	967.08	507.60	354.94	278.99	233.72	203.79	182.62	166.92
12000	1055.00	553.74	387.21	304.36	254.97	222.32	199.22	182.09
13000	1142.91	599.89	419.48	329.72	276.22	240.84	215.82	197.27
14000	1230.83	646.03	451.75	355.08	297.46	259.37	232.42	212.44
15000	1318.74	692.18	484.01	380.44	318.71	277.89	249.02	227.62
16000	1406.66	738.32	516.28	405.81	339.96	296.42	265.62	242.79
17000	1494.58	784.47	548.55	431.17	361.20	314.94	282.23	257.97
18000	1582.49	830.61	580.81	456.53	382.45	333.47	298.83	273.14
19000	1670.41	876.76	613.08	481.89	403.70	352.00	315.43	288.31
20000	1758.32	922.90	645.35	507.26	424.95	370.52	332.03	303.49
21000	1846.24	969.05	677.62	532.62	446.19	389.05	348.63	318.66
22000	1934.15	1015.19	709.88	557.98	467.44	407.57	365.23	333.84
23000	2022.07	1061.34	742.15	583.34	488.69	426.10	381.83	349.01
24000	2109.99	1107.48	774.42	608.71	509.93	444.63	398.43	364.18
25000	2197.90	1153.63	806.68	634.07	531.18	463.15	415.03	379.36
26000	2285.82	1199.77	838.95	659.43	552.43	481.68	431.64	394.53
27000	2373.73	1245.92	871.22	684.79	573.68	500.20	448.24	409.71
28000	2461.65	1292.06	903.49	710.16	594.92	518.73	464.84	424.88
29000	2549.57	1338.21	935.75	735.52	616.17	537.25	481.44	440.06
30000	2637.48	1384.35	968.02	760.88	637.42	555.78	498.04	455.23
31000	2725.40	1430.50	1000.29	786.25	658.66	574.31	514.64	470.40
32000	2813.31	1476.64	1032.55	811.61	679.91	592.83	531.24	485.58
33000	2901.23	1522.79	1064.82	836.97	701.16	611.36	547.84	500.75
34000	2989.15	1568.93	1097.09	862.33	722.40	629.88	564.45	515.93
35000	3077.06	1615.08	1129.36	887.70	743.65	648.41	581.05	531.10
40000	3516.64	1845.80	1290.69	1014.51	849.89	741.04	664.05	606.97
45000	3956.22	2076.53	1452.03	1141.32	956.12	833.67	747.06	682.84
50000	4395.80	2307.25	1613.36	1268.13	1062.36	926.30	830.06	758.71
55000	4835.38	2537.98	1774.70	1394.95	1168.59	1018.93	913.07	834.58
60000	5274.96	2768.70	1936.04	1521.76	1274.83	1111.56	996.08	910.45
65000	5714.54	2999.42	2097.37	1648.57	1381.06	1204.18	1079.08	986.33
70000	6154.12	3230.15	2258.71	1775.39	1487.30	1296.81	1162.09	1062.20
75000	6593.70	3460.87	2420.04	1902.20	1593.53	1389.44	1245.09	1138.07
80000	7033.28	3691.60	2581.38	2029.01	1699.77	1482.07	1328.10	1213.94
85000	7472.86	3922.32	2742.72	2155.82	1806.00	1574.70	1411.11	1289.81
90000	7912.43	4153.05	2904.05	2282.64	1912.24	1667.33	1494.11	1365.68
95000	8352.01	4383.77	3065.39	2409.45	2018.47	1759.96	1577.12	1441.55
100000	8791.59	4614.50	3226.72	2536.26	2124.71	1852.59	1660.12	1517.42
105000	9231.17	4845.22	3388.06	2663.08	2230.94	1945.22	1743.13	1593.29
110000	9670.75	5075.95	3549.40	2789.89	2337.18	2037.85	1826.14	1669.16
115000	10110.33	5306.67	3710.73	2916.70	2443.42	2130.48	1909.14	1745.03
120000	10549.91	5537.40	3872.07	3043.52	2549.65	2223.11	1992.15	1820.90
125000	10989.49	5768.12	4033.40	3170.33	2655.89	2315.73	2075.15	1896.78
130000	11429.07	5998.85	4194.74	3297.14	2762.12	2408.36	2158.16	1972.65
135000	11868.65	6229.57	4356.08	3423.95	2868.36	2500.99	2241.16	2048.52
140000	12308.23	6460.29	4517.41	3550.77	2974.59	2593.62	2324.17	2124.39
145000	12747.81	6691.02	4678.75	3677.58	3080.83	2686.25	2407.18	2200.26
150000	13187.39	6921.74	4840.08	3804.39	3187.06	2778.88	2490.18	2276.13
155000	13626.97	7152.47	5001.42	3931.21	3293.30	2871.51	2573.19	2352.00
160000	14066.55	7383.19	5162.75	4058.02	3399.53	2964.14	2656.19	2427.87

AMOUNT OF LOAN	NUMBER OF YEARS IN TERM							
	9	10	15	20	25	30	35	40
$ 50	.71	.67	.54	.49	.46	.44	.43	.43
100	1.41	1.33	1.08	.97	.91	.88	.86	.85
200	2.82	2.65	2.15	1.94	1.82	1.76	1.72	1.70
300	4.23	3.97	3.23	2.90	2.73	2.64	2.58	2.55
400	5.64	5.29	4.30	3.87	3.64	3.52	3.44	3.40
500	7.04	6.61	5.38	4.83	4.55	4.39	4.30	4.25
600	8.45	7.93	6.45	5.80	5.46	5.27	5.16	5.10
700	9.86	9.26	7.53	6.76	6.37	6.15	6.02	5.95
800	11.27	10.58	8.60	7.73	7.27	7.03	6.88	6.80
900	12.68	11.90	9.68	8.69	8.18	7.90	7.74	7.65
1000	14.08	13.22	10.75	9.66	9.09	8.78	8.60	8.50
2000	28.16	26.44	21.50	19.31	18.18	17.56	17.20	16.99
3000	42.24	39.65	32.24	28.96	27.27	26.33	25.80	25.48
4000	56.32	52.87	42.99	38.61	36.35	35.11	34.39	33.97
5000	70.40	66.08	53.74	48.26	45.44	43.88	42.99	42.46
6000	84.48	79.30	64.48	57.91	54.53	52.66	51.59	50.95
7000	98.56	92.51	75.23	67.56	63.61	61.44	60.18	59.45
8000	112.63	105.73	85.97	77.21	72.70	70.21	68.78	67.94
9000	126.71	118.94	96.72	86.86	81.79	78.99	77.38	76.43
10000	140.79	132.16	107.47	96.51	90.88	87.76	85.97	84.92
11000	154.87	145.37	118.21	106.16	99.96	96.54	94.57	93.41
12000	168.95	158.59	128.96	115.81	109.05	105.31	103.17	101.90
13000	183.03	171.80	139.70	125.46	118.14	114.09	111.76	110.39
14000	197.11	185.02	150.45	135.11	127.22	122.87	120.36	118.89
15000	211.19	198.23	161.20	144.76	136.31	131.64	128.96	127.38
16000	225.26	211.45	171.94	154.41	145.40	140.42	137.55	135.87
17000	239.34	224.66	182.69	164.06	154.48	149.19	146.15	144.36
18000	253.42	237.88	193.43	173.71	163.57	157.97	154.75	152.85
19000	267.50	251.09	204.18	183.36	172.66	166.74	163.34	161.34
20000	281.58	264.31	214.93	193.01	181.75	175.52	171.94	169.83
21000	295.66	277.52	225.67	202.66	190.83	184.30	180.54	178.33
22000	309.74	290.74	236.42	212.31	199.92	193.07	189.13	186.82
23000	323.81	303.95	247.16	221.96	209.01	201.85	197.73	195.31
24000	337.89	317.17	257.91	231.61	218.09	210.62	206.33	203.80
25000	351.97	330.38	268.66	241.26	227.18	219.40	214.92	212.29
26000	366.05	343.60	279.40	250.91	236.27	228.17	223.52	220.78
27000	380.13	356.81	290.15	260.56	245.35	236.95	232.12	229.27
28000	394.21	370.03	300.89	270.21	254.44	245.73	240.71	237.77
29000	408.29	383.24	311.64	279.86	263.53	254.50	249.31	246.26
30000	422.37	396.46	322.39	289.51	272.62	263.28	257.91	254.75
31000	436.44	409.67	333.13	299.16	281.70	272.05	266.50	263.24
32000	450.52	422.89	343.88	308.81	290.79	280.83	275.10	271.73
33000	464.60	436.10	354.62	318.46	299.88	289.60	283.70	280.22
34000	478.68	449.32	365.37	328.11	308.96	298.38	292.29	288.71
35000	492.76	462.53	376.12	337.76	318.05	307.16	300.89	297.21
40000	563.15	528.61	429.85	386.01	363.49	351.03	343.87	339.66
45000	633.55	594.68	483.58	434.26	408.92	394.91	386.86	382.12
50000	703.94	660.76	537.31	482.52	454.36	438.79	429.84	424.58
55000	774.33	726.83	591.04	530.77	499.79	482.67	472.82	467.04
60000	844.73	792.91	644.77	579.02	545.23	526.55	515.81	509.49
65000	915.12	858.98	698.50	627.27	590.66	570.43	558.79	551.95
70000	985.51	925.06	752.23	675.52	636.10	614.31	601.78	594.41
75000	1055.91	991.14	805.96	723.77	681.53	658.18	644.76	636.86
80000	1126.30	1057.21	859.69	772.02	726.97	702.06	687.74	679.32
85000	1196.69	1123.29	913.42	820.27	772.40	745.94	730.73	721.78
90000	1267.09	1189.36	967.15	868.52	817.84	789.82	773.71	764.24
95000	1337.48	1255.44	1020.88	916.78	863.27	833.70	816.69	806.69
100000	1407.87	1321.51	1074.61	965.03	908.71	877.58	859.68	849.15
105000	1478.27	1387.59	1128.34	1013.28	954.14	921.46	902.66	891.61
110000	1548.66	1453.66	1182.07	1061.53	999.58	965.33	945.64	934.07
115000	1619.05	1519.74	1235.80	1109.78	1045.01	1009.21	988.63	976.52
120000	1689.45	1585.81	1289.53	1158.03	1090.45	1053.09	1031.61	1018.98
125000	1759.84	1651.89	1343.26	1206.28	1135.88	1096.97	1074.60	1061.44
130000	1830.23	1717.96	1396.99	1254.53	1181.32	1140.85	1117.58	1103.89
135000	1900.63	1784.04	1450.72	1302.78	1226.75	1184.73	1160.56	1146.35
140000	1971.02	1850.12	1504.45	1351.04	1272.19	1228.61	1203.55	1188.81
145000	2041.41	1916.19	1558.18	1399.29	1317.62	1272.48	1246.53	1231.27
150000	2111.81	1982.27	1611.91	1447.54	1363.06	1316.36	1289.51	1273.72
155000	2182.20	2048.34	1665.64	1495.79	1408.49	1360.24	1332.50	1316.18
160000	2252.59	2114.42	1719.37	1544.04	1453.93	1404.12	1375.48	1358.64

10.250% MONTHLY AMORTIZING PAYMENTS

AMOUNT OF LOAN	NUMBER OF YEARS IN TERM							
	1	2	3	4	5	6	7	8
$ 50	4.41	2.32	1.62	1.28	1.07	.94	.84	.77
100	8.81	4.63	3.24	2.55	2.14	1.87	1.68	1.54
200	17.61	9.26	6.48	5.10	4.28	3.74	3.35	3.07
300	26.41	13.88	9.72	7.65	6.42	5.60	5.02	4.60
400	35.22	18.51	12.96	10.20	8.55	7.47	6.70	6.13
500	44.02	23.14	16.20	12.75	10.69	9.33	8.37	7.66
600	52.82	27.76	19.44	15.29	12.83	11.20	10.04	9.19
700	61.63	32.39	22.67	17.84	14.96	13.06	11.72	10.72
800	70.43	37.01	25.91	20.39	17.10	14.93	13.39	12.25
900	79.23	41.64	29.15	22.94	19.24	16.79	15.06	13.78
1000	88.04	46.27	32.39	25.49	21.38	18.66	16.74	15.31
2000	176.07	92.53	64.77	50.97	42.75	37.31	33.47	30.62
3000	264.10	138.79	97.16	76.45	64.12	55.96	50.20	45.93
4000	352.13	185.05	129.54	101.94	85.49	74.61	66.93	61.23
5000	440.17	231.31	161.93	127.42	106.86	93.27	83.66	76.54
6000	528.20	277.57	194.31	152.90	128.23	111.92	100.39	91.85
7000	616.23	323.83	226.70	178.38	149.60	130.57	117.12	107.15
8000	704.26	370.09	259.08	203.87	170.97	149.22	133.85	122.46
9000	792.29	416.35	291.47	229.35	192.34	167.87	150.58	137.77
10000	880.33	462.61	323.85	254.83	213.71	186.53	167.31	153.07
11000	968.36	508.87	356.24	280.32	235.08	205.18	184.04	168.38
12000	1056.39	555.13	388.62	305.80	256.45	223.83	200.77	183.69
13000	1144.42	601.39	421.01	331.28	277.82	242.48	217.50	198.99
14000	1232.46	647.65	453.39	356.76	299.19	261.14	234.23	214.30
15000	1320.49	693.91	485.78	382.25	320.56	279.79	250.96	229.61
16000	1408.52	740.17	518.16	407.73	341.93	298.44	267.70	244.91
17000	1496.55	786.43	550.54	433.21	363.30	317.09	284.43	260.22
18000	1584.58	832.69	582.93	458.70	384.67	335.74	301.16	275.53
19000	1672.62	878.95	615.31	484.18	406.04	354.40	317.89	290.83
20000	1760.65	925.21	647.70	509.66	427.41	373.05	334.62	306.14
21000	1848.68	971.47	680.08	535.14	448.78	391.70	351.35	321.45
22000	1936.71	1017.73	712.47	560.63	470.15	410.35	368.08	336.75
23000	2024.75	1063.99	744.85	586.11	491.52	429.00	384.81	352.06
24000	2112.78	1110.25	777.24	611.59	512.89	447.66	401.54	367.37
25000	2200.81	1156.51	809.62	637.08	534.26	466.31	418.27	382.67
26000	2288.84	1202.78	842.01	662.56	555.63	484.96	435.00	397.98
27000	2376.87	1249.04	874.39	688.04	577.00	503.61	451.73	413.29
28000	2464.91	1295.30	906.78	713.52	598.37	522.27	468.46	428.59
29000	2552.94	1341.56	939.16	739.01	619.74	540.92	485.19	443.90
30000	2640.97	1387.82	971.55	764.49	641.11	559.57	501.92	459.21
31000	2729.00	1434.08	1003.93	789.97	662.48	578.22	518.65	474.51
32000	2817.04	1480.34	1036.32	815.46	683.85	596.87	535.39	489.82
33000	2905.07	1526.60	1068.70	840.94	705.22	615.53	552.12	505.13
34000	2993.10	1572.86	1101.08	866.42	726.59	634.18	568.85	520.44
35000	3081.13	1619.12	1133.47	891.90	747.96	652.83	585.58	535.74
40000	3521.29	1850.42	1295.39	1019.32	854.82	746.09	669.23	612.28
45000	3961.45	2081.72	1457.32	1146.73	961.67	839.35	752.88	688.81
50000	4401.62	2313.02	1619.24	1274.15	1068.52	932.61	836.54	765.34
55000	4841.78	2544.33	1781.16	1401.56	1175.37	1025.87	920.19	841.88
60000	5281.94	2775.63	1943.09	1528.97	1282.22	1119.13	1003.84	918.41
65000	5722.10	3006.93	2105.01	1656.39	1389.07	1212.40	1087.50	994.95
70000	6162.26	3238.23	2266.93	1783.80	1495.92	1305.66	1171.15	1071.48
75000	6602.42	3469.53	2428.86	1911.22	1602.77	1398.92	1254.80	1148.01
80000	7042.58	3700.84	2590.78	2038.63	1709.63	1492.18	1338.46	1224.55
85000	7482.74	3932.14	2752.70	2166.04	1816.48	1585.44	1422.11	1301.08
90000	7922.90	4163.44	2914.63	2293.46	1923.33	1678.70	1505.76	1377.61
95000	8363.06	4394.74	3076.55	2420.87	2030.18	1771.96	1589.42	1454.15
100000	8803.23	4626.04	3238.47	2548.29	2137.03	1865.22	1673.07	1530.68
105000	9243.39	4857.35	3400.40	2675.70	2243.88	1958.48	1756.72	1607.22
110000	9683.55	5088.65	3562.32	2803.11	2350.73	2051.74	1840.38	1683.75
115000	10123.71	5319.95	3724.24	2930.53	2457.59	2145.00	1924.03	1760.28
120000	10563.87	5551.25	3886.17	3057.94	2564.44	2238.26	2007.68	1836.82
125000	11004.03	5782.55	4048.09	3185.36	2671.29	2331.52	2091.34	1913.35
130000	11444.19	6013.86	4210.01	3312.77	2778.14	2424.79	2174.99	1989.89
135000	11884.35	6245.16	4371.94	3440.18	2884.99	2518.05	2258.64	2066.42
140000	12324.51	6476.46	4533.86	3567.60	2991.84	2611.31	2342.30	2142.95
145000	12764.67	6707.76	4695.78	3695.01	3098.69	2704.57	2425.95	2219.49
150000	13204.84	6939.06	4857.71	3822.43	3205.54	2797.83	2509.60	2296.02
155000	13645.00	7170.37	5019.63	3949.84	3312.40	2891.09	2593.25	2372.55
160000	14085.16	7401.67	5181.56	4077.26	3419.25	2984.35	2676.91	2449.09

MONTHLY AMORTIZING PAYMENTS 10.250%

AMOUNT OF LOAN	NUMBER OF YEARS IN TERM							
	9	10	15	20	25	30	35	40
$ 50	.72	.67	.55	.50	.47	.45	.44	.44
100	1.43	1.34	1.09	.99	.93	.90	.88	.87
200	2.85	2.68	2.18	1.97	1.86	1.80	1.76	1.74
300	4.27	4.01	3.27	2.95	2.78	2.69	2.64	2.61
400	5.69	5.35	4.36	3.93	3.71	3.59	3.52	3.48
500	7.11	6.68	5.45	4.91	4.64	4.49	4.40	4.35
600	8.53	8.02	6.54	5.89	5.56	5.38	5.28	5.22
700	9.96	9.35	7.63	6.88	6.49	6.28	6.16	6.09
800	11.38	10.69	8.72	7.86	7.42	7.17	7.04	6.96
900	12.80	12.02	9.81	8.84	8.34	8.07	7.91	7.82
1000	14.22	13.36	10.90	9.82	9.27	8.97	8.79	8.69
2000	28.43	26.71	21.80	19.64	18.53	17.93	17.57	17.38
3000	42.65	40.07	32.70	29.45	27.80	26.89	26.37	26.07
4000	56.86	53.42	43.60	39.27	37.06	35.85	35.16	34.76
5000	71.08	66.77	54.50	49.09	46.32	44.81	43.95	43.45
6000	85.29	80.13	65.40	58.90	55.59	53.77	52.74	52.13
7000	99.51	93.48	76.30	68.72	64.85	62.73	61.52	60.82
8000	113.72	106.84	87.20	78.54	74.12	71.69	70.31	69.51
9000	127.93	120.19	98.10	88.35	83.38	80.65	79.10	78.20
10000	142.15	133.54	109.00	98.17	92.64	89.62	87.89	86.89
11000	156.36	146.90	119.90	107.99	101.91	98.58	96.68	95.58
12000	170.58	160.25	130.80	117.80	111.17	107.54	105.47	104.28
13000	184.79	173.61	141.70	127.62	120.43	116.50	114.26	112.95
14000	199.01	186.96	152.60	137.44	129.70	125.46	123.04	121.64
15000	213.22	200.31	163.50	147.25	138.96	134.42	131.83	130.33
16000	227.44	213.67	174.40	157.07	148.23	143.38	140.62	139.02
17000	241.65	227.02	185.30	166.88	157.49	152.34	149.41	147.70
18000	255.86	240.38	196.20	176.70	166.75	161.30	158.20	156.39
19000	270.08	253.73	207.10	186.52	176.02	170.26	166.99	165.08
20000	284.29	267.08	218.00	196.33	185.28	179.23	175.78	173.77
21000	298.51	280.44	228.89	206.15	194.55	188.19	184.56	182.46
22000	312.72	293.79	239.79	215.97	203.81	197.15	193.35	191.15
23000	326.94	307.14	250.69	225.78	213.07	206.11	202.14	199.83
24000	341.15	320.50	261.59	235.60	222.34	215.07	210.93	208.52
25000	355.37	333.85	272.49	245.42	231.60	224.03	219.72	217.21
26000	369.58	347.21	283.39	255.23	240.86	232.99	228.51	225.90
27000	383.79	360.56	294.29	265.05	250.13	241.95	237.30	234.59
28000	398.01	373.91	305.19	274.87	259.39	250.91	246.08	243.27
29000	412.22	387.27	316.09	284.68	268.66	259.87	254.87	251.96
30000	426.44	400.62	326.99	294.50	277.92	268.84	263.66	260.65
31000	440.65	413.98	337.89	304.31	287.18	277.80	272.45	269.34
32000	454.87	427.33	348.79	314.13	296.45	286.76	281.24	278.03
33000	469.08	440.68	359.69	323.95	305.71	295.72	290.03	286.72
34000	483.30	454.04	370.59	333.76	314.98	304.68	298.82	295.40
35000	497.51	467.39	381.49	343.58	324.24	313.64	307.60	304.09
40000	568.58	534.16	435.99	392.66	370.56	358.45	351.55	347.53
45000	639.65	600.93	490.48	441.74	416.88	403.25	395.49	390.97
50000	710.73	667.70	544.98	490.83	463.20	448.06	439.43	434.41
55000	781.80	734.47	599.48	539.91	509.52	492.86	483.38	477.86
60000	852.87	801.24	653.98	588.99	555.83	537.67	527.32	521.30
65000	923.94	868.01	708.47	638.07	602.15	582.47	571.26	564.74
70000	995.01	934.78	762.97	687.16	648.47	627.28	615.20	608.18
75000	1066.09	1001.55	817.47	736.24	694.79	672.08	659.15	651.62
80000	1137.16	1068.32	871.97	785.32	741.11	716.89	703.09	695.06
85000	1208.23	1135.09	926.46	834.40	787.43	761.69	747.03	738.50
90000	1279.30	1201.86	980.96	883.48	833.75	806.50	790.98	781.94
95000	1350.37	1268.63	1035.46	932.57	880.07	851.30	834.92	825.38
100000	1421.45	1335.40	1089.96	981.65	926.39	896.11	878.86	868.82
105000	1492.52	1402.16	1144.45	1030.73	972.71	940.91	922.80	912.26
110000	1563.59	1468.93	1198.95	1079.81	1019.03	985.72	966.75	955.71
115000	1634.66	1535.70	1253.45	1128.89	1065.35	1030.52	1010.69	999.15
120000	1705.74	1602.47	1307.95	1177.98	1111.66	1075.33	1054.63	1042.59
125000	1776.81	1669.24	1362.44	1227.06	1157.98	1120.13	1098.57	1086.03
130000	1847.88	1736.01	1416.94	1276.14	1204.30	1164.94	1142.52	1129.47
135000	1918.95	1802.78	1471.44	1325.22	1250.62	1209.74	1186.46	1172.91
140000	1990.02	1869.55	1525.94	1374.31	1296.94	1254.55	1230.40	1216.35
145000	2061.10	1936.32	1580.43	1423.39	1343.26	1299.35	1274.35	1259.79
150000	2132.17	2003.09	1634.93	1472.47	1389.58	1344.16	1318.29	1303.23
155000	2203.24	2069.86	1689.43	1521.55	1435.90	1388.96	1362.23	1346.67
160000	2274.31	2136.63	1743.93	1570.63	1482.22	1433.77	1406.17	1390.11

17

MONTHLY AMORTIZING PAYMENTS

AMOUNT OF LOAN	NUMBER OF YEARS IN TERM							
	1	2	3	4	5	6	7	8
$ 50	4.41	2.32	1.63	1.29	1.08	.94	.85	.78
100	8.82	4.64	3.26	2.57	2.15	1.88	1.69	1.55
200	17.63	9.28	6.51	5.13	4.30	3.76	3.38	3.09
300	26.45	13.92	9.76	7.69	6.45	5.64	5.06	4.64
400	35.26	18.56	13.01	10.25	8.60	7.52	6.75	6.18
500	44.08	23.19	16.26	12.81	10.75	9.39	8.44	7.73
600	52.89	27.83	19.51	15.37	12.90	11.27	10.12	9.27
700	61.71	32.47	22.76	17.93	15.05	13.15	11.81	10.81
800	70.52	37.11	26.01	20.49	17.20	15.03	13.49	12.36
900	79.34	41.74	29.26	23.05	19.35	16.91	15.18	13.90
1000	88.15	46.38	32.51	25.61	21.50	18.78	16.87	15.45
2000	176.30	92.76	65.01	51.21	42.99	37.56	33.73	30.89
3000	264.45	139.13	97.51	76.82	64.49	56.34	50.59	46.33
4000	352.60	185.51	130.01	102.42	85.98	75.12	67.45	61.77
5000	440.75	231.89	162.52	128.02	107.47	93.90	84.31	77.21
6000	528.90	278.26	195.02	153.63	128.97	112.68	101.17	92.65
7000	617.05	324.64	227.52	179.23	150.46	131.46	118.03	108.09
8000	705.19	371.01	260.02	204.83	171.96	150.24	134.89	123.53
9000	793.34	417.39	292.53	230.44	193.45	169.02	151.75	138.97
10000	881.49	463.77	325.03	256.04	214.94	187.79	168.61	154.41
11000	969.64	510.14	357.53	281.64	236.44	206.57	185.47	169.85
12000	1057.79	556.52	390.03	307.25	257.93	225.35	202.33	185.29
13000	1145.94	602.89	422.54	332.85	279.43	244.13	219.19	200.73
14000	1234.09	649.27	455.04	358.45	300.92	262.91	236.05	216.17
15000	1322.23	695.65	487.54	384.06	322.41	281.69	252.92	231.61
16000	1410.38	742.02	520.04	409.66	343.91	300.47	269.78	247.05
17000	1498.53	788.40	552.55	435.26	365.40	319.25	286.64	262.49
18000	1586.68	834.77	585.05	460.87	386.90	338.03	303.50	277.93
19000	1674.83	881.15	617.55	486.47	408.39	356.81	320.36	293.37
20000	1762.98	927.53	650.05	512.07	429.88	375.58	337.22	308.81
21000	1851.13	973.90	682.56	537.68	451.38	394.36	354.08	324.25
22000	1939.27	1020.28	715.06	563.28	472.87	413.14	370.94	339.69
23000	2027.42	1066.65	747.56	588.88	494.36	431.92	387.80	355.13
24000	2115.57	1113.03	780.06	614.49	515.86	450.70	404.66	370.57
25000	2203.72	1159.41	812.57	640.09	537.35	469.48	421.52	386.01
26000	2291.87	1205.78	845.07	665.69	558.85	488.26	438.38	401.45
27000	2380.02	1252.16	877.57	691.30	580.34	507.04	455.24	416.89
28000	2468.17	1298.53	910.07	716.90	601.83	525.82	472.10	432.33
29000	2556.31	1344.91	942.58	742.50	623.33	544.60	488.96	447.77
30000	2644.46	1391.29	975.08	768.11	644.82	563.37	505.83	463.21
31000	2732.61	1437.66	1007.58	793.71	666.32	582.15	522.69	478.65
32000	2820.76	1484.04	1040.08	819.31	687.81	600.93	539.55	494.09
33000	2908.91	1530.41	1072.59	844.92	709.30	619.71	556.41	509.53
34000	2997.06	1576.79	1105.09	870.52	730.80	638.49	573.27	524.97
35000	3085.21	1623.17	1137.59	896.12	752.29	657.27	590.13	540.41
40000	3525.95	1855.05	1300.10	1024.14	859.76	751.16	674.43	617.61
45000	3966.69	2086.93	1462.61	1152.16	967.23	845.06	758.74	694.81
50000	4407.44	2318.81	1625.13	1280.17	1074.70	938.95	843.04	772.01
55000	4848.18	2550.69	1787.64	1408.19	1182.17	1032.85	927.34	849.21
60000	5288.92	2782.57	1950.15	1536.21	1289.64	1126.74	1011.65	926.41
65000	5729.66	3014.45	2112.66	1664.22	1397.11	1220.64	1095.95	1003.61
70000	6170.41	3246.33	2275.18	1792.24	1504.58	1314.53	1180.25	1080.81
75000	6611.15	3478.21	2437.69	1920.26	1612.05	1408.43	1264.56	1158.01
80000	7051.89	3710.09	2600.20	2048.28	1719.52	1502.32	1348.86	1235.21
85000	7492.64	3941.97	2762.71	2176.29	1826.99	1596.22	1433.16	1312.41
90000	7933.38	4173.85	2925.22	2304.31	1934.46	1690.11	1517.47	1389.61
95000	8374.12	4405.73	3087.74	2432.33	2041.93	1784.01	1601.77	1466.81
100000	8814.87	4637.61	3250.25	2560.34	2149.40	1877.90	1686.07	1544.01
105000	9255.61	4869.49	3412.76	2688.36	2256.86	1971.80	1770.38	1621.21
110000	9696.35	5101.37	3575.27	2816.38	2364.33	2065.69	1854.68	1698.41
115000	10137.09	5333.25	3737.79	2944.39	2471.80	2159.59	1938.98	1775.61
120000	10577.84	5565.13	3900.30	3072.41	2579.27	2253.48	2023.29	1852.81
125000	11018.58	5797.01	4062.81	3200.43	2686.74	2347.38	2107.59	1930.01
130000	11459.32	6028.89	4225.32	3328.44	2794.21	2441.27	2191.89	2007.21
135000	11900.07	6260.77	4387.83	3456.46	2901.68	2535.17	2276.20	2084.41
140000	12340.81	6492.65	4550.35	3584.48	3009.15	2629.06	2360.50	2161.61
145000	12781.55	6724.53	4712.86	3712.50	3116.62	2722.96	2444.80	2238.81
150000	13222.30	6956.41	4875.37	3840.51	3224.09	2816.85	2529.11	2316.01
155000	13663.04	7188.29	5037.88	3968.53	3331.56	2910.75	2613.41	2393.21
160000	14103.78	7420.17	5200.40	4096.55	3439.03	3004.64	2697.71	2470.41

AMOUNT OF LOAN	NUMBER OF YEARS IN TERM							
	9	10	15	20	25	30	35	40
$ 50	.72	.68	.56	.50	.48	.46	.45	.45
100	1.44	1.35	1.11	1.00	.95	.92	.90	.89
200	2.88	2.70	2.22	2.00	1.89	1.83	1.80	1.78
300	4.31	4.05	3.32	3.00	2.84	2.75	2.70	2.67
400	5.75	5.40	4.43	4.00	3.78	3.66	3.60	3.56
500	7.18	6.75	5.53	5.00	4.73	4.58	4.50	4.45
600	8.62	8.10	6.64	6.00	5.67	5.49	5.39	5.34
700	10.05	9.45	7.74	6.99	6.61	6.41	6.29	6.22
800	11.49	10.80	8.85	7.99	7.56	7.32	7.19	7.11
900	12.92	12.15	9.95	8.99	8.50	8.24	8.09	8.00
1000	14.36	13.50	11.06	9.99	9.45	9.15	8.99	8.89
2000	28.71	26.99	22.11	19.97	18.89	18.30	17.97	17.78
3000	43.06	40.49	33.17	29.96	28.33	27.45	26.95	26.66
4000	57.41	53.98	44.22	39.94	37.77	36.59	35.93	35.55
5000	71.76	67.47	55.27	49.92	47.21	45.74	44.91	44.43
6000	86.11	80.97	66.33	59.91	56.66	54.89	53.89	53.32
7000	100.46	94.46	77.38	69.89	66.10	64.04	62.87	62.20
8000	114.81	107.95	88.44	79.88	75.54	73.18	71.86	71.09
9000	129.16	121.45	99.49	89.86	84.98	82.33	80.84	79.98
10000	143.51	134.94	110.54	99.84	94.42	91.48	89.82	88.86
11000	157.86	148.43	121.60	109.83	103.86	100.63	98.80	97.75
12000	172.22	161.93	132.65	119.81	113.31	109.77	107.78	106.63
13000	186.57	175.42	143.71	129.79	122.75	118.92	116.76	115.52
14000	200.92	188.91	154.76	139.78	132.19	128.07	125.74	124.40
15000	215.27	202.41	165.81	149.76	141.63	137.22	134.73	133.29
16000	229.62	215.90	176.87	159.75	151.07	146.36	143.71	142.18
17000	243.97	229.39	187.92	169.73	160.52	155.51	152.69	151.06
18000	258.32	242.89	198.98	179.71	169.96	164.66	161.67	159.95
19000	272.67	256.38	210.03	189.70	179.40	173.81	170.65	168.83
20000	287.02	269.87	221.08	199.68	188.84	182.95	179.63	177.72
21000	301.37	283.37	232.14	209.66	198.28	192.10	188.61	186.60
22000	315.72	296.86	243.19	219.65	207.72	201.25	197.59	195.49
23000	330.07	310.36	254.25	229.63	217.17	210.40	206.58	204.38
24000	344.43	323.85	265.30	239.62	226.61	219.54	215.56	213.26
25000	358.78	337.34	276.35	249.60	236.05	228.69	224.54	222.15
26000	373.13	350.84	287.41	259.58	245.49	237.84	233.52	231.03
27000	387.48	364.33	298.46	269.57	254.93	246.98	242.50	239.92
28000	401.83	377.82	309.52	279.55	264.38	256.13	251.48	248.80
29000	416.18	391.32	320.57	289.54	273.82	265.28	260.46	257.69
30000	430.53	404.81	331.62	299.52	283.26	274.43	269.45	266.58
31000	444.88	418.30	342.68	309.50	292.70	283.57	278.43	275.46
32000	459.23	431.80	353.73	319.49	302.14	292.72	287.41	284.35
33000	473.58	445.29	364.79	329.47	311.58	301.87	296.39	293.23
34000	487.93	458.78	375.84	339.45	321.03	311.02	305.37	302.12
35000	502.29	472.28	386.89	349.44	330.47	320.16	314.35	311.00
40000	574.04	539.74	442.16	399.36	377.68	365.90	359.26	355.43
45000	645.79	607.21	497.43	449.28	424.89	411.64	404.17	399.86
50000	717.55	674.68	552.70	499.19	472.10	457.37	449.07	444.29
55000	789.30	742.15	607.97	549.11	519.30	503.11	493.98	488.72
60000	861.06	809.61	663.24	599.03	566.51	548.85	538.89	533.15
65000	932.81	877.08	718.51	648.95	613.72	594.59	583.79	577.58
70000	1004.57	944.55	773.78	698.87	660.93	640.32	628.70	622.00
75000	1076.32	1012.02	829.05	748.79	708.14	686.06	673.61	666.43
80000	1148.07	1079.48	884.32	798.71	755.35	731.80	718.51	710.86
85000	1219.83	1146.95	939.59	848.63	802.56	777.53	763.42	755.29
90000	1291.58	1214.42	994.86	898.55	849.77	823.27	808.33	799.72
95000	1363.34	1281.89	1050.13	948.47	896.98	869.01	853.23	844.15
100000	1435.09	1349.35	1105.40	998.38	944.19	914.74	898.14	888.58
105000	1506.85	1416.82	1160.67	1048.30	991.40	960.48	943.05	933.00
110000	1578.60	1484.29	1215.94	1098.22	1038.60	1006.22	987.95	977.43
115000	1650.35	1551.76	1271.21	1148.14	1085.81	1051.96	1032.86	1021.86
120000	1722.11	1619.22	1326.48	1198.06	1133.02	1097.69	1077.77	1066.29
125000	1793.86	1686.69	1381.75	1247.98	1180.23	1143.43	1122.67	1110.72
130000	1865.62	1754.16	1437.02	1297.90	1227.44	1189.17	1167.58	1155.15
135000	1937.37	1821.63	1492.29	1347.82	1274.65	1234.90	1212.49	1199.57
140000	2009.13	1889.09	1547.56	1397.74	1321.86	1280.64	1257.39	1244.00
145000	2080.88	1956.56	1602.83	1447.66	1369.07	1326.38	1302.30	1288.43
150000	2152.63	2024.03	1658.10	1497.57	1416.28	1372.11	1347.21	1332.86
155000	2224.39	2091.50	1713.37	1547.49	1463.49	1417.85	1392.11	1377.29
160000	2296.14	2158.96	1768.64	1597.41	1510.70	1463.59	1437.02	1421.72

10.750% MONTHLY AMORTIZING PAYMENTS

AMOUNT OF LOAN	NUMBER OF YEARS IN TERM							
	1	2	3	4	5	6	7	8
$ 50	4.42	2.33	1.64	1.29	1.09	.95	.85	.78
100	8.83	4.65	3.27	2.58	2.17	1.90	1.70	1.56
200	17.66	9.30	6.53	5.15	4.33	3.79	3.40	3.12
300	26.48	13.95	9.79	7.72	6.49	5.68	5.10	4.68
400	35.31	18.60	13.05	10.29	8.65	7.57	6.80	6.23
500	44.14	23.25	16.32	12.87	10.81	9.46	8.50	7.79
600	52.96	27.90	19.58	15.44	12.98	11.35	10.20	9.35
700	61.79	32.55	22.84	18.01	15.14	13.24	11.90	10.91
800	70.62	37.20	26.10	20.58	17.30	15.13	13.60	12.46
900	79.44	41.85	29.36	23.16	19.46	17.02	15.30	14.02
1000	88.27	46.50	32.63	25.73	21.62	18.91	17.00	15.58
2000	176.54	92.99	65.25	51.45	43.24	37.82	33.99	31.15
3000	264.80	139.48	97.87	77.18	64.86	56.72	50.98	46.73
4000	353.07	185.97	130.49	102.90	86.48	75.63	67.97	62.30
5000	441.33	232.46	163.11	128.63	108.09	94.54	84.96	77.87
6000	529.60	278.96	195.73	154.35	129.71	113.44	101.95	93.45
7000	617.86	325.45	228.35	180.07	151.33	132.35	118.94	109.02
8000	706.13	371.94	260.97	205.80	172.95	151.26	135.94	124.60
9000	794.39	418.43	293.59	231.52	194.57	170.16	152.93	140.17
10000	882.66	464.92	326.21	257.25	216.18	189.07	169.92	155.74
11000	970.92	511.42	358.83	282.97	237.80	207.97	186.91	171.32
12000	1059.19	557.91	391.45	308.70	259.42	226.88	203.90	186.89
13000	1147.45	604.40	424.07	334.42	281.04	245.79	220.89	202.47
14000	1235.72	650.89	456.69	360.14	302.66	264.69	237.88	218.04
15000	1323.98	697.38	489.31	385.87	324.27	283.60	254.87	233.61
16000	1412.25	743.87	521.93	411.59	345.89	302.51	271.87	249.19
17000	1500.51	790.37	554.55	437.32	367.51	321.41	288.86	264.76
18000	1588.78	836.86	587.17	463.04	389.13	340.32	305.85	280.34
19000	1677.04	883.35	619.79	488.77	410.75	359.22	322.84	295.91
20000	1765.31	929.84	652.41	514.49	432.36	378.13	339.83	311.48
21000	1853.57	976.33	685.03	540.21	453.98	397.04	356.82	327.06
22000	1941.84	1022.83	717.65	565.94	475.60	415.94	373.81	342.63
23000	2030.10	1069.32	750.28	591.66	497.22	434.85	390.80	358.20
24000	2118.37	1115.81	782.90	617.39	518.84	453.76	407.80	373.78
25000	2206.63	1162.30	815.52	643.11	540.45	472.66	424.79	389.35
26000	2294.90	1208.79	848.14	668.84	562.07	491.57	441.78	404.93
27000	2383.16	1255.29	880.76	694.56	583.69	510.47	458.77	420.50
28000	2471.43	1301.78	913.38	720.28	605.31	529.38	475.76	436.07
29000	2559.69	1348.27	946.00	746.01	626.93	548.29	492.75	451.65
30000	2647.96	1394.76	978.62	771.73	648.54	567.19	509.74	467.22
31000	2736.22	1441.25	1011.24	797.46	670.16	586.10	526.73	482.80
32000	2824.49	1487.74	1043.86	823.18	691.78	605.01	543.73	498.37
33000	2912.75	1534.24	1076.48	848.91	713.40	623.91	560.72	513.94
34000	3001.02	1580.73	1109.10	874.63	735.02	642.82	577.71	529.52
35000	3089.28	1627.22	1141.72	900.35	756.63	661.72	594.70	545.09
40000	3530.61	1859.68	1304.82	1028.98	864.72	756.26	679.66	622.96
45000	3971.93	2092.14	1467.93	1157.60	972.81	850.79	764.61	700.83
50000	4413.26	2324.60	1631.03	1286.22	1080.90	945.32	849.57	778.70
55000	4854.58	2557.06	1794.13	1414.84	1188.99	1039.85	934.52	856.57
60000	5295.91	2789.52	1957.23	1543.46	1297.08	1134.38	1019.48	934.44
65000	5737.24	3021.98	2120.33	1672.08	1405.17	1228.91	1104.44	1012.31
70000	6178.56	3254.43	2283.44	1800.70	1513.26	1323.44	1189.39	1090.18
75000	6619.89	3486.89	2446.54	1929.33	1621.35	1417.98	1274.35	1168.05
80000	7061.21	3719.35	2609.64	2057.95	1729.44	1512.51	1359.31	1245.92
85000	7502.54	3951.81	2772.74	2186.57	1837.53	1607.04	1444.26	1323.79
90000	7943.86	4184.27	2935.85	2315.19	1945.62	1701.57	1529.22	1401.66
95000	8385.19	4416.73	3098.95	2443.81	2053.71	1796.10	1614.18	1479.53
100000	8826.51	4649.19	3262.05	2572.43	2161.80	1890.63	1699.13	1557.40
105000	9267.84	4881.65	3425.15	2701.05	2269.89	1985.16	1784.09	1635.26
110000	9709.16	5114.11	3588.25	2829.68	2377.98	2079.70	1869.04	1713.13
115000	10150.49	5346.57	3751.36	2958.30	2486.07	2174.23	1954.00	1791.00
120000	10591.82	5579.03	3914.46	3086.92	2594.16	2268.76	2038.96	1868.87
125000	11033.14	5811.49	4077.56	3215.54	2702.25	2363.29	2123.91	1946.74
130000	11474.47	6043.95	4240.66	3344.16	2810.34	2457.82	2208.87	2024.61
135000	11915.79	6276.41	4403.77	3472.78	2918.43	2552.35	2293.83	2102.48
140000	12357.12	6508.86	4566.87	3601.40	3026.52	2646.88	2378.78	2180.35
145000	12798.44	6741.32	4729.97	3730.03	3134.61	2741.42	2463.74	2258.22
150000	13239.77	6973.78	4893.07	3858.65	3242.70	2835.95	2548.70	2336.09
155000	13681.09	7206.24	5056.18	3987.27	3350.79	2930.48	2633.65	2413.96
160000	14122.42	7438.70	5219.28	4115.89	3458.88	3025.01	2718.61	2491.83

AMOUNT OF LOAN	NUMBER OF YEARS IN TERM							
	9	10	15	20	25	30	35	40
$ 50	.73	.69	.57	.51	.49	.47	.46	.46
100	1.45	1.37	1.13	1.02	.97	.94	.92	.91
200	2.90	2.73	2.25	2.04	1.93	1.87	1.84	1.82
300	4.35	4.10	3.37	3.05	2.89	2.81	2.76	2.73
400	5.80	5.46	4.49	4.07	3.85	3.74	3.68	3.64
500	7.25	6.82	5.61	5.08	4.82	4.67	4.59	4.55
600	8.70	8.19	6.73	6.10	5.78	5.61	5.51	5.46
700	10.15	9.55	7.85	7.11	6.74	6.54	6.43	6.36
800	11.60	10.91	8.97	8.13	7.70	7.47	7.35	7.27
900	13.04	12.28	10.09	9.14	8.66	8.41	8.26	8.18
1000	14.49	13.64	11.21	10.16	9.63	9.34	9.18	9.09
2000	28.98	27.27	22.42	20.31	19.25	18.67	18.36	18.17
3000	43.47	40.91	33.63	30.46	28.87	28.01	27.53	27.26
4000	57.96	54.54	44.84	40.61	38.49	37.34	36.71	36.34
5000	72.45	68.17	56.05	50.77	48.11	46.68	45.88	45.42
6000	86.93	81.81	67.26	60.92	57.73	56.01	55.06	54.51
7000	101.42	95.44	78.47	71.07	67.35	65.35	64.23	63.59
8000	115.91	109.08	89.68	81.22	76.97	74.68	73.41	72.68
9000	130.40	122.71	100.89	91.38	86.59	84.02	82.58	81.76
10000	144.89	136.34	112.10	101.53	96.21	93.35	91.76	90.84
11000	159.37	149.98	123.31	111.68	105.84	102.69	100.93	99.93
12000	173.86	163.61	134.52	121.83	115.46	112.02	110.11	109.01
13000	188.35	177.25	145.73	131.98	125.08	121.36	119.28	118.10
14000	202.84	190.88	156.94	142.14	134.70	130.69	128.46	127.18
15000	217.33	204.51	168.15	152.29	144.32	140.03	137.63	136.26
16000	231.81	218.15	179.36	162.44	153.94	149.36	146.81	145.35
17000	246.30	231.78	190.57	172.59	163.56	158.70	155.98	154.43
18000	260.79	245.41	201.78	182.75	173.18	168.03	165.16	163.52
19000	275.28	259.05	212.99	192.90	182.80	177.37	174.33	172.60
20000	289.77	272.68	224.19	203.05	192.42	186.70	183.51	181.68
21000	304.25	286.32	235.40	213.20	202.04	196.04	192.68	190.77
22000	318.74	299.95	246.61	223.36	211.67	205.37	201.86	199.85
23000	333.23	313.58	257.82	233.51	221.29	214.71	211.03	208.94
24000	347.72	327.22	269.03	243.66	230.91	224.04	220.21	218.02
25000	362.21	340.85	280.24	253.81	240.53	233.38	229.38	227.10
26000	376.69	354.49	291.45	263.96	250.15	242.71	238.56	236.19
27000	391.18	368.12	302.66	274.12	259.77	252.04	247.73	245.27
28000	405.67	381.75	313.87	284.27	269.39	261.38	256.91	254.36
29000	420.16	395.39	325.08	294.42	279.01	270.71	266.08	263.44
30000	434.65	409.02	336.29	304.57	288.63	280.05	275.26	272.52
31000	449.13	422.65	347.50	314.73	298.25	289.38	284.43	281.61
32000	463.62	436.29	358.71	324.88	307.87	298.72	293.61	290.69
33000	478.11	449.92	369.92	335.03	317.50	308.05	302.78	299.78
34000	492.60	463.56	381.13	345.18	327.12	317.39	311.96	308.86
35000	507.09	477.19	392.34	355.34	336.74	326.72	321.13	317.94
40000	579.53	545.36	448.38	406.10	384.84	373.40	367.01	363.36
45000	651.97	613.53	504.43	456.86	432.95	420.07	412.88	408.78
50000	724.41	681.70	560.48	507.62	481.05	466.75	458.76	454.20
55000	796.85	749.87	616.53	558.38	529.16	513.42	504.63	499.62
60000	869.29	818.04	672.57	609.14	577.26	560.09	550.51	545.04
65000	941.73	886.21	728.62	659.90	625.37	606.77	596.38	590.46
70000	1014.17	954.38	784.67	710.67	673.47	653.44	642.26	635.88
75000	1086.61	1022.55	840.72	761.43	721.57	700.12	688.13	681.30
80000	1159.05	1090.71	896.76	812.19	769.68	746.79	734.01	726.72
85000	1231.49	1158.88	952.81	862.95	817.78	793.46	779.88	772.14
90000	1303.93	1227.05	1008.86	913.71	865.89	840.14	825.76	817.56
95000	1376.37	1295.22	1064.91	964.47	913.99	886.81	871.63	862.98
100000	1448.81	1363.39	1120.95	1015.23	962.10	933.49	917.51	908.40
105000	1521.25	1431.56	1177.00	1066.00	1010.20	980.16	963.38	953.82
110000	1593.69	1499.73	1233.05	1116.76	1058.31	1026.83	1009.26	999.24
115000	1666.13	1567.90	1289.10	1167.52	1106.41	1073.51	1055.13	1044.66
120000	1738.57	1636.07	1345.14	1218.28	1154.52	1120.18	1101.01	1090.08
125000	1811.01	1704.24	1401.19	1269.04	1202.62	1166.86	1146.88	1135.50
130000	1883.45	1772.41	1457.24	1319.80	1250.73	1213.53	1192.76	1180.92
135000	1955.89	1840.58	1513.28	1370.58	1298.83	1260.20	1238.63	1226.34
140000	2028.33	1908.75	1569.33	1421.33	1346.93	1306.88	1284.51	1271.76
145000	2100.77	1976.92	1625.38	1472.09	1395.04	1353.55	1330.38	1317.18
150000	2173.21	2045.09	1681.43	1522.85	1443.14	1400.23	1376.26	1362.60
155000	2245.65	2113.25	1737.47	1573.61	1491.25	1446.90	1422.13	1408.02
160000	2316.09	2181.42	1793.52	1624.37	1539.35	1493.58	1468.01	1453.44

11.000% MONTHLY AMORTIZING PAYMENTS

AMOUNT OF LOAN	NUMBER OF YEARS IN TERM							
	1	2	3	4	5	6	7	8
$ 50	4.42	2.34	1.64	1.30	1.09	.96	.86	.79
100	8.84	4.67	3.28	2.59	2.18	1.91	1.72	1.58
200	17.68	9.33	6.55	5.17	4.35	3.81	3.43	3.15
300	26.52	13.99	9.83	7.76	6.53	5.72	5.14	4.72
400	35.36	18.65	13.10	10.34	8.70	7.62	6.85	6.29
500	44.20	23.31	16.37	12.93	10.88	9.52	8.57	7.86
600	53.03	27.97	19.65	15.51	13.05	11.43	10.28	9.43
700	61.87	32.63	22.92	18.10	15.22	13.33	11.99	11.00
800	70.71	37.29	26.20	20.68	17.40	15.23	13.70	12.57
900	79.55	41.95	29.47	23.27	19.57	17.14	15.42	14.14
1000	88.39	46.61	32.74	25.85	21.75	19.04	17.13	15.71
2000	176.77	93.22	65.48	51.70	43.49	38.07	34.25	31.42
3000	265.15	139.83	98.22	77.54	65.23	57.11	51.37	47.13
4000	353.53	186.44	130.96	103.39	86.97	76.14	68.49	62.84
5000	441.91	233.04	163.70	129.23	108.72	95.18	85.62	78.55
6000	530.29	279.65	196.44	155.08	130.46	114.21	102.74	94.26
7000	618.68	326.26	229.18	180.92	152.20	133.24	119.86	109.96
8000	707.06	372.87	261.91	206.77	173.94	152.28	136.98	125.67
9000	795.44	419.48	294.65	232.61	195.69	171.31	154.11	141.38
10000	883.82	466.08	327.39	258.46	217.43	190.35	171.23	157.09
11000	972.20	512.69	360.13	284.31	239.17	209.38	188.35	172.80
12000	1060.58	559.30	392.87	310.15	260.91	228.41	205.47	188.51
13000	1148.97	605.91	425.61	336.00	282.66	247.45	222.60	204.21
14000	1237.35	652.51	458.35	361.84	304.40	266.48	239.72	219.92
15000	1325.73	699.12	491.09	387.69	326.14	285.52	256.84	235.63
16000	1414.11	745.73	523.82	413.53	347.88	304.55	273.96	251.34
17000	1502.49	792.34	556.56	439.38	369.63	323.58	291.09	267.05
18000	1590.87	838.95	589.30	465.22	391.37	342.62	308.21	282.76
19000	1679.26	885.55	622.04	491.07	413.11	361.65	325.33	298.47
20000	1767.64	932.16	654.78	516.92	434.85	380.69	342.45	314.17
21000	1856.02	978.77	687.52	542.76	456.60	399.72	359.58	329.88
22000	1944.40	1025.38	720.26	568.61	478.34	418.75	376.70	345.59
23000	2032.78	1071.99	753.00	594.45	500.08	437.79	393.82	361.30
24000	2121.16	1118.59	785.73	620.30	521.82	456.82	410.94	377.01
25000	2209.55	1165.20	818.47	646.14	543.57	475.86	428.07	392.72
26000	2297.93	1211.81	851.21	671.99	565.31	494.89	445.19	408.42
27000	2386.31	1258.42	883.95	697.83	587.05	513.93	462.31	424.13
28000	2474.69	1305.02	916.69	723.68	608.79	532.96	479.43	439.84
29000	2563.07	1351.63	949.43	749.53	630.54	551.99	496.56	455.55
30000	2651.45	1398.24	982.17	775.37	652.28	571.03	513.68	471.26
31000	2739.84	1444.85	1014.91	801.22	674.02	590.06	530.80	486.97
32000	2828.22	1491.46	1047.64	827.06	695.76	609.10	547.92	502.67
33000	2916.60	1538.06	1080.38	852.91	717.50	628.13	565.05	518.38
34000	3004.98	1584.67	1113.12	878.75	739.25	647.16	582.17	534.09
35000	3093.36	1631.28	1145.86	904.60	760.99	666.20	599.29	549.80
40000	3535.27	1864.32	1309.55	1033.83	869.70	761.37	684.90	628.34
45000	3977.18	2097.36	1473.25	1163.05	978.41	856.54	770.51	706.88
50000	4419.09	2330.40	1636.94	1292.28	1087.13	951.71	856.13	785.43
55000	4861.00	2563.44	1800.63	1421.51	1195.84	1046.88	941.74	863.97
60000	5302.90	2796.48	1964.33	1550.74	1304.55	1142.05	1027.35	942.51
65000	5744.81	3029.51	2128.02	1679.96	1413.26	1237.22	1112.96	1021.05
70000	6186.72	3262.55	2291.72	1809.19	1521.97	1332.39	1198.58	1099.59
75000	6628.63	3495.59	2455.41	1938.42	1630.69	1427.56	1284.19	1178.14
80000	7070.54	3728.63	2619.10	2067.65	1739.40	1522.73	1369.80	1256.68
85000	7512.45	3961.67	2782.80	2196.87	1848.11	1617.90	1455.41	1335.22
90000	7954.35	4194.71	2946.49	2326.10	1956.82	1713.07	1541.02	1413.76
95000	8396.26	4427.75	3110.18	2455.33	2065.54	1808.24	1626.64	1492.31
100000	8838.17	4660.79	3273.88	2584.56	2174.25	1903.41	1712.25	1570.85
105000	9280.08	4893.83	3437.57	2713.78	2282.96	1998.58	1797.86	1649.39
110000	9721.99	5126.87	3601.26	2843.01	2391.67	2093.75	1883.47	1727.93
115000	10163.90	5359.91	3764.96	2972.24	2500.38	2188.92	1969.09	1806.47
120000	10605.80	5592.95	3928.65	3101.47	2609.10	2284.09	2054.70	1885.02
125000	11047.71	5825.98	4092.34	3230.70	2717.81	2379.26	2140.31	1963.56
130000	11489.62	6059.02	4256.04	3359.92	2826.52	2474.44	2225.92	2042.10
135000	11931.53	6292.06	4419.73	3489.15	2935.23	2569.61	2311.53	2120.64
140000	12373.44	6525.10	4583.43	3618.38	3043.94	2664.78	2397.15	2199.18
145000	12815.35	6758.14	4747.12	3747.61	3152.66	2759.95	2482.76	2277.73
150000	13257.25	6991.18	4910.81	3876.83	3261.37	2855.12	2568.37	2356.27
155000	13699.16	7224.22	5074.51	4006.06	3370.08	2950.29	2653.98	2434.81
160000	14141.07	7457.26	5238.20	4135.29	3478.79	3045.46	2739.59	2513.35

22

AMOUNT OF LOAN	NUMBER OF YEARS IN TERM							
	9	10	15	20	25	30	35	40
$ 50	.74	.69	.57	.52	.50	.48	.47	.47
100	1.47	1.38	1.14	1.04	.99	.96	.94	.93
200	2.93	2.76	2.28	2.07	1.97	1.91	1.88	1.86
300	4.39	4.14	3.41	3.10	2.95	2.86	2.82	2.79
400	5.86	5.51	4.55	4.13	3.93	3.81	3.75	3.72
500	7.32	6.89	5.69	5.17	4.91	4.77	4.69	4.65
600	8.78	8.27	6.82	6.20	5.89	5.72	5.63	5.57
700	10.24	9.65	7.96	7.23	6.87	6.67	6.56	6.50
800	11.71	11.02	9.10	8.26	7.85	7.62	7.50	7.43
900	13.17	12.40	10.23	9.29	8.83	8.58	8.44	8.36
1000	14.63	13.78	11.37	10.33	9.81	9.53	9.37	9.29
2000	29.26	27.56	22.74	20.65	19.61	19.05	18.74	18.57
3000	43.88	41.33	34.10	30.97	29.41	28.57	28.11	27.85
4000	58.51	55.11	45.47	41.29	39.21	38.10	37.48	37.14
5000	73.13	68.88	56.83	51.61	49.01	47.62	46.85	46.42
6000	87.76	82.66	68.20	61.94	58.81	57.14	56.22	55.70
7000	102.39	96.43	79.57	72.26	68.61	66.67	65.59	64.99
8000	117.01	110.21	90.93	82.58	78.41	76.19	74.96	74.27
9000	131.64	123.98	102.30	92.90	88.22	85.71	84.33	83.55
10000	146.26	137.76	113.66	103.22	98.02	95.24	93.70	92.83
11000	160.89	151.53	125.03	113.55	107.82	104.76	103.07	102.12
12000	175.52	165.31	136.40	123.87	117.62	114.28	112.44	111.40
13000	190.14	179.08	147.76	134.19	127.42	123.81	121.81	120.68
14000	204.77	192.86	159.13	144.51	137.22	133.33	131.18	129.97
15000	219.39	206.63	170.49	154.83	147.02	142.85	140.55	139.25
16000	234.02	220.41	181.86	165.16	156.82	152.38	149.92	148.53
17000	248.64	234.18	193.23	175.48	166.62	161.90	159.29	157.82
18000	263.27	247.96	204.59	185.80	176.43	171.42	168.66	167.10
19000	277.90	261.73	215.96	196.12	186.23	180.95	178.03	176.38
20000	292.52	275.51	227.32	206.44	196.03	190.47	187.40	185.66
21000	307.15	289.28	238.69	216.76	205.83	199.99	196.77	194.95
22000	321.77	303.06	250.06	227.09	215.63	209.52	206.14	204.23
23000	336.40	316.83	261.42	237.41	225.43	219.04	215.51	213.51
24000	351.03	330.61	272.79	247.73	235.23	228.56	224.87	222.80
25000	365.65	344.38	284.15	258.05	245.03	238.09	234.24	232.08
26000	380.28	358.16	295.52	268.37	254.83	247.61	243.61	241.36
27000	394.90	371.93	306.89	278.70	264.64	257.13	252.98	250.64
28000	409.53	385.71	318.25	289.02	274.44	266.66	262.35	259.93
29000	424.15	399.48	329.62	299.34	284.24	276.18	271.72	269.21
30000	438.78	413.26	340.98	309.66	294.04	285.70	281.09	278.49
31000	453.41	427.03	352.35	319.98	303.84	295.23	290.46	287.78
32000	468.03	440.81	363.72	330.31	313.64	304.75	299.83	297.06
33000	482.66	454.58	375.08	340.63	323.44	314.27	309.20	306.34
34000	497.28	468.36	386.45	350.95	333.24	323.79	318.57	315.63
35000	511.91	482.13	397.81	361.27	343.04	333.32	327.94	324.91
40000	585.04	551.01	454.64	412.88	392.05	380.93	374.79	371.32
45000	658.17	619.88	511.47	464.49	441.06	428.55	421.64	417.74
50000	731.30	688.76	568.30	516.10	490.06	476.17	468.48	464.15
55000	804.43	757.63	625.13	567.71	539.07	523.78	515.33	510.57
60000	877.56	826.51	681.96	619.32	588.07	571.40	562.18	556.98
65000	950.69	895.38	738.79	670.93	637.08	619.02	609.03	603.40
70000	1023.82	964.26	795.62	722.54	686.08	666.63	655.88	649.81
75000	1096.94	1033.13	852.45	774.15	735.09	714.25	702.72	696.23
80000	1170.07	1102.01	909.28	825.76	784.10	761.86	749.57	742.64
85000	1243.20	1170.88	966.11	877.37	833.10	809.48	796.42	789.06
90000	1316.33	1239.76	1022.94	928.97	882.11	857.10	843.27	835.47
95000	1389.46	1308.63	1079.77	980.58	931.11	904.71	890.11	881.88
100000	1462.59	1377.51	1136.60	1032.19	980.12	952.33	936.96	928.30
105000	1535.72	1446.38	1193.43	1083.80	1029.12	999.94	983.81	974.71
110000	1608.85	1515.26	1250.26	1135.41	1078.13	1047.56	1030.66	1021.13
115000	1681.98	1584.13	1307.09	1187.02	1127.14	1095.18	1077.51	1067.54
120000	1755.11	1653.01	1363.92	1238.63	1176.14	1142.79	1124.35	1113.96
125000	1828.24	1721.88	1420.75	1290.24	1225.15	1190.41	1171.20	1160.37
130000	1901.37	1790.76	1477.58	1341.85	1274.15	1238.03	1218.05	1206.79
135000	1974.50	1859.63	1534.41	1393.46	1323.16	1285.64	1264.90	1253.20
140000	2047.63	1928.51	1591.24	1445.07	1372.16	1333.26	1311.75	1299.62
145000	2120.75	1997.38	1648.07	1496.68	1421.17	1380.87	1358.59	1346.03
150000	2193.88	2066.26	1704.90	1548.29	1470.17	1428.49	1405.44	1392.45
155000	2267.01	2135.13	1761.73	1599.90	1519.18	1476.11	1452.29	1438.86
160000	2340.14	2204.01	1818.56	1651.51	1568.19	1523.72	1499.14	1485.28

AMOUNT OF LOAN	NUMBER OF YEARS IN TERM							
	1	2	3	4	5	6	7	8
$ 50	4.43	2.34	1.65	1.30	1.10	.96	.87	.80
100	8.85	4.68	3.29	2.60	2.19	1.92	1.73	1.59
200	17.70	9.35	6.58	5.20	4.38	3.84	3.46	3.17
300	26.55	14.02	9.86	7.80	6.57	5.75	5.18	4.76
400	35.40	18.69	13.15	10.39	8.75	7.67	6.91	6.34
500	44.25	23.37	16.43	12.99	10.94	9.59	8.63	7.93
600	53.10	28.04	19.72	15.59	13.13	11.50	10.36	9.51
700	61.95	32.71	23.01	18.18	15.31	13.42	12.08	11.10
800	70.80	37.38	26.29	20.78	17.50	15.33	13.81	12.68
900	79.65	42.06	29.58	23.38	19.69	17.25	15.53	14.26
1000	88.50	46.73	32.86	25.97	21.87	19.17	17.26	15.85
2000	177.00	93.45	65.72	51.94	43.74	38.33	34.51	31.69
3000	265.50	140.18	98.58	77.91	65.61	57.49	51.77	47.54
4000	354.00	186.90	131.43	103.87	87.47	76.65	69.02	63.38
5000	442.50	233.62	164.29	129.84	109.34	95.82	86.28	79.22
6000	530.99	280.35	197.15	155.81	131.21	114.98	103.53	95.07
7000	619.49	327.07	230.01	181.77	153.08	134.14	120.78	110.91
8000	707.99	373.80	262.86	207.74	174.94	153.30	138.04	126.75
9000	796.49	420.52	295.72	233.71	196.81	172.47	155.29	142.60
10000	884.99	467.24	328.58	259.68	218.68	191.63	172.55	158.44
11000	973.49	513.97	361.43	285.64	240.55	210.79	189.80	174.28
12000	1061.98	560.69	394.29	311.61	262.41	229.95	207.06	190.13
13000	1150.48	607.42	427.15	337.58	284.28	249.12	224.31	205.97
14000	1238.98	654.14	460.01	363.54	306.15	268.28	241.56	221.82
15000	1327.48	700.86	492.86	389.51	328.01	287.44	258.82	237.66
16000	1415.98	747.59	525.72	415.48	349.88	306.60	276.07	253.50
17000	1504.48	794.31	558.58	441.45	371.75	325.77	293.33	269.35
18000	1592.97	841.04	591.44	467.41	393.62	344.93	310.58	285.19
19000	1681.47	887.76	624.29	493.38	415.48	364.09	327.83	301.03
20000	1769.97	934.48	657.15	519.35	437.35	383.25	345.09	316.88
21000	1858.47	981.21	690.01	545.31	459.22	402.41	362.34	332.72
22000	1946.97	1027.93	722.86	571.28	481.09	421.58	379.60	348.56
23000	2035.47	1074.66	755.72	597.25	502.95	440.74	396.85	364.41
24000	2123.96	1121.38	788.58	623.22	524.82	459.90	414.11	380.25
25000	2212.46	1168.10	821.44	649.18	546.69	479.06	431.36	396.09
26000	2300.96	1214.83	854.29	675.15	568.56	498.23	448.61	411.94
27000	2389.46	1261.55	887.15	701.12	590.42	517.39	465.87	427.78
28000	2477.96	1308.28	920.01	727.08	612.29	536.55	483.12	443.63
29000	2566.46	1355.00	952.86	753.05	634.16	555.71	500.38	459.47
30000	2654.95	1401.72	985.72	779.02	656.02	574.88	517.63	475.31
31000	2743.45	1448.45	1018.58	804.99	677.89	594.04	534.88	491.16
32000	2831.95	1495.17	1051.44	830.95	699.76	613.20	552.14	507.00
33000	2920.45	1541.90	1084.29	856.92	721.63	632.36	569.39	522.84
34000	3008.95	1588.62	1117.15	882.89	743.49	651.53	586.65	538.69
35000	3097.45	1635.34	1150.01	908.85	765.36	670.69	603.90	554.53
40000	3539.94	1868.96	1314.29	1038.69	874.70	766.50	690.17	633.75
45000	3982.43	2102.58	1478.58	1168.52	984.03	862.31	776.44	712.97
50000	4424.92	2336.20	1642.87	1298.36	1093.37	958.12	862.71	792.18
55000	4867.41	2569.82	1807.15	1428.20	1202.71	1053.94	948.98	871.40
60000	5309.90	2803.44	1971.44	1558.03	1312.04	1149.75	1035.26	950.62
65000	5752.40	3037.06	2135.73	1687.87	1421.38	1245.56	1121.53	1029.84
70000	6194.89	3270.68	2300.01	1817.70	1530.72	1341.37	1207.80	1109.06
75000	6637.38	3504.30	2464.30	1947.54	1640.05	1437.18	1294.07	1188.27
80000	7079.87	3737.92	2628.58	2077.37	1749.39	1532.99	1380.34	1267.49
85000	7522.36	3971.54	2792.87	2207.21	1858.73	1628.81	1466.61	1346.71
90000	7964.85	4205.16	2957.16	2337.04	1968.06	1724.62	1552.88	1425.93
95000	8407.34	4438.78	3121.44	2466.88	2077.40	1820.43	1639.15	1505.15
100000	8849.84	4672.40	3285.73	2596.71	2186.74	1916.24	1725.42	1584.36
105000	9292.33	4906.02	3450.01	2726.55	2296.07	2012.05	1811.69	1663.58
110000	9734.82	5139.64	3614.30	2856.39	2405.41	2107.87	1897.96	1742.80
115000	10177.31	5373.26	3778.59	2986.22	2514.75	2203.68	1984.23	1822.02
120000	10619.80	5606.88	3942.87	3116.06	2624.08	2299.49	2070.51	1901.24
125000	11062.29	5840.50	4107.16	3245.89	2733.42	2395.30	2156.78	1980.45
130000	11504.79	6074.12	4271.45	3375.73	2842.76	2491.11	2243.05	2059.67
135000	11947.28	6307.74	4435.73	3505.56	2952.09	2586.93	2329.32	2138.89
140000	12389.77	6541.36	4600.02	3635.40	3061.43	2682.74	2415.59	2218.11
145000	12832.26	6774.98	4764.30	3765.23	3170.76	2778.55	2501.86	2297.32
150000	13274.75	7008.60	4928.59	3895.07	3280.10	2874.36	2588.13	2376.54
155000	13717.24	7242.22	5092.88	4024.91	3389.44	2970.17	2674.40	2455.76
160000	14159.74	7475.84	5257.16	4154.74	3498.77	3065.98	2760.67	2534.98

MONTHLY AMORTIZING PAYMENTS   11.250%

AMOUNT OF LOAN	NUMBER OF YEARS IN TERM							
	9	10	15	20	25	30	35	40
$ 50	.74	.70	.58	.53	.50	.49	.48	.48
100	1.48	1.40	1.16	1.05	1.00	.98	.96	.95
200	2.96	2.79	2.31	2.10	2.00	1.95	1.92	1.90
300	4.43	4.18	3.46	3.15	3.00	2.92	2.87	2.85
400	5.91	5.57	4.61	4.20	4.00	3.89	3.83	3.80
500	7.39	6.96	5.77	5.25	5.00	4.86	4.79	4.75
600	8.86	8.36	6.92	6.30	5.99	5.83	5.74	5.69
700	10.34	9.75	8.07	7.35	6.99	6.80	6.70	6.64
800	11.82	11.14	9.22	8.40	7.99	7.78	7.66	7.59
900	13.29	12.53	10.38	9.45	8.99	8.75	8.61	8.54
1000	14.77	13.92	11.53	10.50	9.99	9.72	9.57	9.49
2000	29.53	27.84	23.05	20.99	19.97	19.43	19.13	18.97
3000	44.30	41.76	34.58	31.48	29.95	29.14	28.70	28.45
4000	59.06	55.67	46.10	41.98	39.93	38.86	38.26	37.94
5000	73.83	69.59	57.62	52.47	49.92	48.57	47.83	47.42
6000	88.59	83.51	69.15	62.96	59.90	58.28	57.39	56.90
7000	103.36	97.42	80.67	73.45	69.88	67.99	66.96	66.38
8000	118.12	111.34	92.19	83.95	79.86	77.71	76.52	75.87
9000	132.88	125.26	103.72	94.44	89.85	87.42	86.09	85.35
10000	147.65	139.17	115.24	104.93	99.83	97.13	95.65	94.83
11000	162.41	153.09	126.76	115.42	109.81	106.84	105.22	104.31
12000	177.18	167.01	138.29	125.92	119.79	116.56	114.78	113.80
13000	191.94	180.92	149.81	136.41	129.78	126.27	124.35	123.28
14000	206.71	194.84	161.33	146.90	139.76	135.98	133.91	132.76
15000	221.47	208.76	172.86	157.39	149.74	145.69	143.48	142.24
16000	236.24	222.68	184.38	167.89	159.72	155.41	153.04	151.73
17000	251.00	236.59	195.90	178.38	169.71	165.12	162.61	161.21
18000	265.76	250.51	207.43	188.87	179.69	174.83	172.17	170.69
19000	280.53	264.43	218.95	199.36	189.67	184.54	181.74	180.17
20000	295.29	278.34	230.47	209.86	199.65	194.26	191.30	189.66
21000	310.06	292.26	242.00	220.35	209.64	203.97	200.87	199.14
22000	324.82	306.18	253.52	230.84	219.62	213.68	210.43	208.62
23000	339.59	320.09	265.04	241.33	229.60	223.40	220.00	218.10
24000	354.35	334.01	276.57	251.83	239.58	233.11	229.56	227.59
25000	369.12	347.93	288.09	262.32	249.56	242.82	239.13	237.07
26000	383.88	361.84	299.61	272.81	259.55	252.53	248.69	246.55
27000	398.64	375.76	311.14	283.30	269.53	262.25	258.26	256.03
28000	413.41	389.68	322.66	293.80	279.51	271.96	267.82	265.52
29000	428.17	403.59	334.18	304.29	289.49	281.67	277.39	275.00
30000	442.94	417.51	345.71	314.78	299.48	291.39	286.95	284.48
31000	457.70	431.43	357.23	325.27	309.46	301.10	296.52	293.96
32000	472.47	445.35	368.76	335.77	319.44	310.81	306.08	303.45
33000	487.23	459.26	380.28	346.26	329.42	320.52	315.65	312.93
34000	502.00	473.18	391.80	356.75	339.41	330.23	325.21	322.41
35000	516.76	487.10	403.33	367.24	349.39	339.95	334.78	331.90
40000	590.58	556.68	460.94	419.71	399.30	388.51	382.60	379.31
45000	664.40	626.27	518.56	472.17	449.21	437.07	430.43	426.72
50000	738.23	695.85	576.18	524.63	499.12	485.64	478.25	474.13
55000	812.05	765.43	633.79	577.10	549.04	534.20	526.08	521.55
60000	885.87	835.02	691.41	629.56	598.95	582.76	573.90	568.96
65000	959.69	904.60	749.03	682.02	648.86	631.32	621.73	616.37
70000	1033.51	974.19	806.65	734.48	698.77	679.89	669.55	663.79
75000	1107.34	1043.77	864.26	786.95	748.68	728.45	717.38	711.20
80000	1181.16	1113.36	921.88	839.41	798.60	777.01	765.20	758.61
85000	1254.98	1182.94	979.50	891.87	848.51	825.58	813.02	806.02
90000	1328.80	1252.53	1037.12	944.34	898.42	874.14	860.85	853.44
95000	1402.62	1322.11	1094.73	996.80	948.33	922.70	908.67	900.85
100000	1476.45	1391.69	1152.35	1049.26	998.24	971.27	956.50	948.26
105000	1550.27	1461.28	1209.97	1101.72	1048.16	1019.83	1004.32	995.68
110000	1624.09	1530.86	1267.58	1154.19	1098.07	1068.39	1052.15	1043.09
115000	1697.91	1600.45	1325.20	1206.65	1147.98	1116.96	1099.97	1090.50
120000	1771.73	1670.03	1382.82	1259.11	1197.89	1165.52	1147.80	1137.91
125000	1845.56	1739.62	1440.44	1311.58	1247.80	1214.08	1195.62	1185.33
130000	1919.38	1809.20	1498.05	1364.04	1297.72	1262.64	1243.45	1232.74
135000	1993.20	1878.79	1555.67	1416.50	1347.63	1311.21	1291.27	1280.15
140000	2067.02	1948.37	1613.29	1468.96	1397.54	1359.77	1339.10	1327.57
145000	2140.84	2017.95	1670.90	1521.43	1447.45	1408.33	1386.92	1374.98
150000	2214.67	2087.54	1728.52	1573.89	1497.36	1456.90	1434.75	1422.39
155000	2288.49	2157.12	1786.14	1626.35	1547.28	1505.46	1482.57	1469.80
160000	2362.31	2226.71	1843.76	1678.81	1597.19	1554.02	1530.40	1517.22

MONTHLY AMORTIZING PAYMENTS

AMOUNT OF LOAN	NUMBER OF YEARS IN TERM							
	1	2	3	4	5	6	7	8
$ 50	4.44	2.35	1.65	1.31	1.10	.97	.87	.80
100	8.87	4.69	3.30	2.61	2.20	1.93	1.74	1.60
200	17.73	9.37	6.60	5.22	4.40	3.86	3.48	3.20
300	26.59	14.06	9.90	7.83	6.60	5.79	5.22	4.80
400	35.45	18.74	13.20	10.44	8.80	7.72	6.96	6.40
500	44.31	23.43	16.49	13.05	11.00	9.65	8.70	7.99
600	53.17	28.11	19.79	15.66	13.20	11.58	10.44	9.59
700	62.04	32.79	23.09	18.27	15.40	13.51	12.18	11.19
800	70.90	37.48	26.39	20.88	17.60	15.44	13.91	12.79
900	79.76	42.16	29.68	23.49	19.80	17.37	15.65	14.39
1000	88.62	46.85	32.98	26.09	22.00	19.30	17.39	15.98
2000	177.24	93.69	65.96	52.18	43.99	38.59	34.78	31.96
3000	265.85	140.53	98.93	78.27	65.98	57.88	52.16	47.94
4000	354.47	187.37	131.91	104.36	87.98	77.17	69.55	63.92
5000	443.08	234.21	164.89	130.45	109.97	96.46	86.94	79.90
6000	531.70	281.05	197.86	156.54	131.96	115.75	104.32	95.88
7000	620.31	327.89	230.84	182.63	153.95	135.04	121.71	111.86
8000	708.93	374.73	263.81	208.72	175.95	154.33	139.10	127.84
9000	797.54	421.57	296.79	234.81	197.94	173.63	156.48	143.82
10000	886.16	468.41	329.77	260.90	219.93	192.92	173.87	159.80
11000	974.77	515.25	362.74	286.98	241.92	212.21	191.26	175.78
12000	1063.39	562.09	395.72	313.07	263.92	231.50	208.64	191.76
13000	1152.00	608.93	428.69	339.16	285.91	250.79	226.03	207.74
14000	1240.62	655.77	461.67	365.25	307.90	270.08	243.42	223.72
15000	1329.23	702.61	494.65	391.34	329.89	289.37	260.80	239.70
16000	1417.85	749.45	527.62	417.43	351.89	308.66	278.19	255.67
17000	1506.46	796.29	560.60	443.52	373.88	327.95	295.57	271.65
18000	1595.08	843.13	593.57	469.61	395.87	347.25	312.96	287.63
19000	1683.69	889.97	626.55	495.70	417.86	366.54	330.35	303.61
20000	1772.31	936.81	659.53	521.79	439.86	385.83	347.73	319.59
21000	1860.92	983.65	692.50	547.87	461.85	405.12	365.12	335.57
22000	1949.54	1030.49	725.48	573.96	483.84	424.41	382.51	351.55
23000	2038.15	1077.33	758.45	600.05	505.83	443.70	399.89	367.53
24000	2126.77	1124.17	791.43	626.14	527.83	462.99	417.28	383.51
25000	2215.38	1171.01	824.41	652.23	549.82	482.28	434.67	399.49
26000	2304.00	1217.85	857.38	678.32	571.81	501.58	452.05	415.47
27000	2392.61	1264.69	890.36	704.41	593.81	520.87	469.44	431.45
28000	2481.23	1311.53	923.33	730.50	615.80	540.16	486.83	447.43
29000	2569.84	1358.37	956.31	756.59	637.79	559.45	504.21	463.41
30000	2658.46	1405.21	989.29	782.68	659.78	578.74	521.60	479.39
31000	2747.07	1452.05	1022.26	808.76	681.78	598.03	538.99	495.37
32000	2835.69	1498.90	1055.24	834.85	703.77	617.32	556.37	511.34
33000	2924.30	1545.74	1088.21	860.94	725.76	636.61	573.76	527.32
34000	3012.92	1592.58	1121.19	887.03	747.75	655.90	591.14	543.30
35000	3101.53	1639.42	1154.17	913.12	769.75	675.20	608.53	559.28
40000	3544.61	1873.62	1319.05	1043.57	879.71	771.65	695.46	639.18
45000	3987.68	2107.82	1483.93	1174.01	989.67	868.11	782.40	719.08
50000	4430.76	2342.02	1648.81	1304.46	1099.64	964.56	869.33	798.97
55000	4873.83	2576.22	1813.69	1434.90	1209.60	1061.02	956.26	878.87
60000	5316.91	2810.42	1978.57	1565.35	1319.56	1157.47	1043.19	958.77
65000	5759.98	3044.63	2143.45	1695.79	1429.52	1253.93	1130.12	1038.66
70000	6203.06	3278.83	2308.33	1826.24	1539.49	1350.39	1217.06	1118.56
75000	6646.13	3513.03	2473.21	1956.68	1649.45	1446.84	1303.99	1198.46
80000	7089.21	3747.23	2638.09	2087.13	1759.41	1543.30	1390.92	1278.35
85000	7532.28	3981.43	2802.97	2217.57	1869.38	1639.75	1477.85	1358.25
90000	7975.36	4215.63	2967.85	2348.02	1979.34	1736.21	1564.79	1438.15
95000	8418.44	4449.83	3132.73	2478.46	2089.30	1832.66	1651.72	1518.05
100000	8861.51	4684.04	3297.61	2608.91	2199.27	1929.12	1738.65	1597.94
105000	9304.59	4918.24	3462.49	2739.35	2309.23	2025.58	1825.58	1677.84
110000	9747.66	5152.44	3627.37	2869.80	2419.19	2122.03	1912.52	1757.74
115000	10190.74	5386.64	3792.25	3000.24	2529.15	2218.49	1999.45	1837.63
120000	10633.81	5620.84	3957.13	3130.69	2639.12	2314.94	2086.38	1917.53
125000	11076.89	5855.04	4122.01	3261.13	2749.08	2411.40	2173.31	1997.43
130000	11519.96	6089.25	4286.89	3391.58	2859.04	2507.86	2260.24	2077.32
135000	11963.04	6323.45	4451.77	3522.02	2969.01	2604.31	2347.18	2157.22
140000	12406.11	6557.65	4616.65	3652.47	3078.97	2700.77	2434.11	2237.12
145000	12849.19	6791.85	4781.53	3782.91	3188.93	2797.22	2521.04	2317.01
150000	13292.26	7026.05	4946.41	3913.36	3298.90	2893.68	2607.97	2396.91
155000	13735.34	7260.25	5111.29	4043.80	3408.86	2990.13	2694.91	2476.81
160000	14178.41	7494.46	5276.17	4174.25	3518.82	3086.59	2781.84	2556.70

AMOUNT OF LOAN	NUMBER OF YEARS IN TERM							
	9	10	15	20	25	30	35	40
$ 50	.75	.71	.59	.54	.51	.50	.49	.49
100	1.50	1.41	1.17	1.07	1.02	1.00	.98	.97
200	2.99	2.82	2.34	2.14	2.04	1.99	1.96	1.94
300	4.48	4.22	3.51	3.20	3.05	2.98	2.93	2.91
400	5.97	5.63	4.68	4.27	4.07	3.97	3.91	3.88
500	7.46	7.03	5.85	5.34	5.09	4.96	4.89	4.85
600	8.95	8.44	7.01	6.40	6.10	5.95	5.86	5.81
700	10.44	9.85	8.18	7.47	7.12	6.94	6.84	6.78
800	11.93	11.25	9.35	8.54	8.14	7.93	7.81	7.75
900	13.42	12.66	10.52	9.60	9.15	8.92	8.79	8.72
1000	14.91	14.06	11.69	10.67	10.17	9.91	9.77	9.69
2000	29.81	28.12	23.37	21.33	20.33	19.81	19.53	19.37
3000	44.72	42.18	35.05	32.00	30.50	29.71	29.29	29.05
4000	59.62	56.24	46.73	42.66	40.66	39.62	39.05	38.74
5000	74.52	70.30	58.41	53.33	50.83	49.52	48.81	48.42
6000	89.43	84.36	70.10	63.99	60.99	59.42	58.57	58.10
7000	104.33	98.42	81.78	74.66	71.16	69.33	68.33	67.78
8000	119.23	112.48	93.46	85.32	81.32	79.23	78.09	77.47
9000	134.14	126.54	105.14	95.98	91.49	89.13	87.85	87.15
10000	149.04	140.60	116.82	106.65	101.65	99.03	97.62	96.83
11000	163.95	154.66	128.51	117.31	111.82	108.94	107.38	106.52
12000	178.85	168.72	140.19	127.98	121.98	118.84	117.14	116.20
13000	193.75	182.78	151.87	138.64	132.15	128.74	126.90	125.88
14000	208.66	196.84	163.55	149.31	142.31	138.65	136.66	135.56
15000	223.56	210.90	175.23	159.97	152.48	148.55	146.42	145.25
16000	238.46	224.96	186.92	170.63	162.64	158.45	156.18	154.93
17000	253.37	239.02	198.60	181.30	172.80	168.35	165.94	164.61
18000	268.27	253.08	210.28	191.96	182.97	178.26	175.70	174.30
19000	283.17	267.14	221.96	202.63	193.13	188.16	185.47	183.98
20000	298.08	281.20	233.64	213.29	203.30	198.06	195.23	193.66
21000	312.98	295.26	245.32	223.96	213.46	207.97	204.99	203.34
22000	327.89	309.31	257.01	234.62	223.63	217.87	214.75	213.03
23000	342.79	323.37	268.69	245.28	233.79	227.77	224.51	222.71
24000	357.69	337.43	280.37	255.95	243.96	237.67	234.27	232.39
25000	372.60	351.49	292.05	266.61	254.12	247.58	244.03	242.08
26000	387.50	365.55	303.73	277.28	264.29	257.48	253.79	251.76
27000	402.40	379.61	315.42	287.94	274.45	267.38	263.55	261.44
28000	417.31	393.67	327.10	298.61	284.62	277.29	273.32	271.12
29000	432.21	407.73	338.78	309.27	294.78	287.19	283.08	280.81
30000	447.11	421.79	350.46	319.93	304.95	297.09	292.84	290.49
31000	462.02	435.85	362.14	330.60	315.11	307.00	302.60	300.17
32000	476.92	449.91	373.83	341.26	325.28	316.90	312.36	309.86
33000	491.83	463.97	385.51	351.93	335.44	326.80	322.12	319.54
34000	506.73	478.03	397.19	362.59	345.60	336.70	331.88	329.22
35000	521.63	492.09	408.87	373.26	355.77	346.61	341.64	338.90
40000	596.15	562.39	467.28	426.58	406.59	396.12	390.45	387.32
45000	670.67	632.68	525.69	479.90	457.42	445.64	439.25	435.73
50000	745.19	702.98	584.10	533.22	508.24	495.15	488.06	484.15
55000	819.71	773.28	642.51	586.54	559.06	544.67	536.86	532.56
60000	894.22	843.58	700.92	639.86	609.89	594.18	585.67	580.97
65000	968.74	913.88	759.33	693.18	660.71	643.69	634.47	629.39
70000	1043.26	984.17	817.74	746.51	711.53	693.21	683.28	677.80
75000	1117.78	1054.47	876.15	799.83	762.36	742.72	732.09	726.22
80000	1192.30	1124.77	934.56	853.15	813.18	792.24	780.89	774.63
85000	1266.82	1195.07	992.97	906.47	864.00	841.75	829.70	823.04
90000	1341.33	1265.36	1051.38	959.79	914.83	891.27	878.50	871.46
95000	1415.85	1335.66	1109.79	1013.11	965.65	940.78	927.31	919.87
100000	1490.37	1405.96	1168.19	1066.43	1016.47	990.30	976.11	968.29
105000	1564.89	1476.26	1226.60	1119.76	1067.30	1039.81	1024.92	1016.70
110000	1639.41	1546.55	1285.01	1173.08	1118.12	1089.33	1073.72	1065.12
115000	1713.93	1616.85	1343.42	1226.40	1168.94	1138.84	1122.53	1113.53
120000	1788.44	1687.15	1401.83	1279.72	1219.77	1188.35	1171.33	1161.94
125000	1862.96	1757.45	1460.24	1333.04	1270.59	1237.87	1220.14	1210.36
130000	1937.48	1827.75	1518.65	1386.36	1321.41	1287.38	1268.94	1258.77
135000	2012.00	1898.04	1577.06	1439.69	1372.24	1336.90	1317.75	1307.19
140000	2086.52	1968.34	1635.47	1493.01	1423.06	1386.41	1366.56	1355.60
145000	2161.04	2038.64	1693.88	1546.33	1473.88	1435.93	1415.36	1404.01
150000	2235.55	2108.94	1752.29	1599.65	1524.71	1485.44	1464.17	1452.43
155000	2310.07	2179.23	1810.70	1652.97	1575.53	1534.96	1512.97	1500.84
160000	2384.59	2249.53	1869.11	1706.29	1626.36	1584.47	1561.78	1549.26

MONTHLY AMORTIZING PAYMENTS

AMOUNT OF LOAN	NUMBER OF YEARS IN TERM							
	1	2	3	4	5	6	7	8
$ 50	4.44	2.35	1.66	1.32	1.11	.98	.88	.81
100	8.88	4.70	3.31	2.63	2.22	1.95	1.76	1.62
200	17.75	9.40	6.62	5.25	4.43	3.89	3.51	3.23
300	26.62	14.09	9.93	7.87	6.64	5.83	5.26	4.84
400	35.50	18.79	13.24	10.49	8.85	7.77	7.01	6.45
500	44.37	23.48	16.55	13.11	11.06	9.72	8.76	8.06
600	53.24	28.18	19.86	15.73	13.28	11.66	10.52	9.67
700	62.12	32.87	23.17	18.35	15.49	13.60	12.27	11.29
800	70.99	37.57	26.48	20.97	17.70	15.54	14.02	12.90
900	79.86	42.27	29.79	23.60	19.91	17.48	15.77	14.51
1000	88.74	46.96	33.10	26.22	22.12	19.43	17.52	16.12
2000	177.47	93.92	66.20	52.43	44.24	38.85	35.04	32.24
3000	266.20	140.88	99.29	78.64	66.36	58.27	52.56	48.35
4000	354.93	187.83	132.39	104.85	88.48	77.69	70.08	64.47
5000	443.66	234.79	165.48	131.06	110.60	97.11	87.60	80.58
6000	532.40	281.75	198.58	157.27	132.71	116.53	105.12	96.70
7000	621.13	328.70	231.67	183.48	154.83	135.95	122.64	112.82
8000	709.86	375.66	264.77	209.70	176.95	155.37	140.16	128.93
9000	798.59	422.62	297.86	235.91	199.07	174.79	157.68	145.05
10000	887.32	469.57	330.96	262.12	221.19	194.21	175.20	161.16
11000	976.06	516.53	364.05	288.33	243.31	213.63	192.72	177.28
12000	1064.79	563.49	397.15	314.54	265.42	233.05	210.24	193.39
13000	1153.52	610.44	430.24	340.75	287.54	252.47	227.76	209.51
14000	1242.25	657.40	463.34	366.96	309.66	271.89	245.28	225.63
15000	1330.98	704.36	496.43	393.17	331.78	291.31	262.79	241.74
16000	1419.72	751.31	529.53	419.39	353.90	310.73	280.31	257.86
17000	1508.45	798.27	562.62	445.60	376.02	330.15	297.83	273.97
18000	1597.18	845.23	595.72	471.81	398.13	349.57	315.35	290.09
19000	1685.91	892.18	628.81	498.02	420.25	368.99	332.87	306.21
20000	1774.64	939.14	661.91	524.23	442.37	388.41	350.39	322.32
21000	1863.37	986.10	695.00	550.44	464.49	407.83	367.91	338.44
22000	1952.11	1033.05	728.10	576.65	486.61	427.25	385.43	354.55
23000	2040.84	1080.01	761.19	602.86	508.73	446.67	402.95	370.67
24000	2129.57	1126.97	794.29	629.08	530.84	466.10	420.47	386.78
25000	2218.30	1173.93	827.38	655.29	552.96	485.52	437.99	402.90
26000	2307.03	1220.88	860.48	681.50	575.08	504.94	455.51	419.02
27000	2395.77	1267.84	893.57	707.71	597.20	524.36	473.03	435.13
28000	2484.50	1314.80	926.67	733.92	619.32	543.78	490.55	451.25
29000	2573.23	1361.75	959.76	760.13	641.44	563.20	508.07	467.36
30000	2661.96	1408.71	992.86	786.34	663.55	582.62	525.58	483.48
31000	2750.69	1455.67	1025.95	812.55	685.67	602.04	543.10	499.59
32000	2839.43	1502.62	1059.05	838.77	707.79	621.46	560.62	515.71
33000	2928.16	1549.58	1092.14	864.98	729.91	640.88	578.14	531.83
34000	3016.89	1596.54	1125.24	891.19	752.03	660.30	595.66	547.94
35000	3105.62	1643.49	1158.33	917.40	774.15	679.72	613.18	564.06
40000	3549.28	1878.28	1323.81	1048.46	884.74	776.82	700.78	644.64
45000	3992.94	2113.06	1489.28	1179.51	995.33	873.92	788.37	725.22
50000	4436.60	2347.85	1654.76	1310.57	1105.92	971.03	875.97	805.79
55000	4880.26	2582.63	1820.23	1441.62	1216.51	1068.13	963.57	886.37
60000	5323.92	2817.41	1985.71	1572.68	1327.10	1165.23	1051.16	966.95
65000	5767.58	3052.20	2151.18	1703.74	1437.70	1262.33	1138.76	1047.53
70000	6211.24	3286.98	2316.66	1834.79	1548.29	1359.44	1226.36	1128.11
75000	6654.90	3521.77	2482.13	1965.85	1658.88	1456.54	1313.95	1208.69
80000	7098.56	3756.55	2647.61	2096.91	1769.47	1553.64	1401.55	1289.27
85000	7542.21	3991.33	2813.08	2227.96	1880.06	1650.74	1489.15	1369.85
90000	7985.87	4226.12	2978.56	2359.02	1990.65	1747.84	1576.74	1450.43
95000	8429.53	4460.90	3144.03	2490.07	2101.25	1844.95	1664.34	1531.01
100000	8873.19	4695.69	3309.51	2621.13	2211.84	1942.05	1751.94	1611.58
105000	9316.85	4930.47	3474.98	2752.19	2322.43	2039.15	1839.53	1692.16
110000	9760.51	5165.25	3640.46	2883.24	2433.02	2136.25	1927.13	1772.74
115000	10204.17	5400.04	3805.93	3014.30	2543.61	2233.35	2014.73	1853.32
120000	10647.83	5634.82	3971.41	3145.36	2654.20	2330.46	2102.32	1933.90
125000	11091.49	5869.61	4136.88	3276.41	2764.80	2427.56	2189.92	2014.48
130000	11535.15	6104.39	4302.36	3407.47	2875.39	2524.66	2277.52	2095.06
135000	11978.81	6339.17	4467.83	3538.52	2985.98	2621.76	2365.11	2175.64
140000	12422.47	6573.96	4633.31	3669.58	3096.57	2718.87	2452.71	2256.22
145000	12866.13	6808.74	4798.78	3800.64	3207.16	2815.97	2540.31	2336.80
150000	13309.79	7043.53	4964.26	3931.69	3317.75	2913.07	2627.90	2417.37
155000	13753.45	7278.31	5129.73	4062.75	3428.34	3010.17	2715.50	2497.95
160000	14197.11	7513.09	5295.21	4193.81	3538.94	3107.27	2803.10	2578.53

AMOUNT OF LOAN	NUMBER OF YEARS IN TERM							
	9	10	15	20	25	30	35	40
$ 50	.76	.72	.60	.55	.52	.51	.50	.50
100	1.51	1.43	1.19	1.09	1.04	1.01	1.00	.99
200	3.01	2.85	2.37	2.17	2.07	2.02	2.00	1.98
300	4.52	4.27	3.56	3.26	3.11	3.03	2.99	2.97
400	6.02	5.69	4.74	4.34	4.14	4.04	3.99	3.96
500	7.53	7.11	5.93	5.42	5.18	5.05	4.98	4.95
600	9.03	8.53	7.11	6.51	6.21	6.06	5.98	5.94
700	10.54	9.95	8.29	7.59	7.25	7.07	6.98	6.92
800	12.04	11.37	9.48	8.67	8.28	8.08	7.97	7.91
900	13.54	12.79	10.66	9.76	9.32	9.09	8.97	8.90
1000	15.05	14.21	11.85	10.84	10.35	10.10	9.96	9.89
2000	30.09	28.41	23.69	21.68	20.70	20.19	19.92	19.77
3000	45.14	42.61	35.53	32.52	31.05	30.29	29.88	29.66
4000	60.18	56.82	47.37	43.35	41.40	40.38	39.84	39.54
5000	75.22	71.02	59.21	54.19	51.74	50.48	49.79	49.42
6000	90.27	85.22	71.05	65.03	62.09	60.57	59.75	59.31
7000	105.31	99.43	82.89	75.86	72.44	70.66	69.71	69.19
8000	120.35	113.63	94.74	86.70	82.79	80.76	79.67	79.07
9000	135.40	127.83	106.58	97.54	93.14	90.85	89.63	88.96
10000	150.44	142.03	118.42	108.38	103.48	100.95	99.58	98.84
11000	165.48	156.24	130.26	119.21	113.83	111.04	109.54	108.73
12000	180.53	170.44	142.10	130.05	124.18	121.13	119.50	118.61
13000	195.57	184.64	153.94	140.89	134.53	131.23	129.46	128.49
14000	210.62	198.85	165.78	151.72	144.88	141.32	139.42	138.38
15000	225.66	213.05	177.62	162.56	155.22	151.42	149.37	148.26
16000	240.70	227.25	189.47	173.40	165.57	161.51	159.33	158.14
17000	255.75	241.46	201.31	184.24	175.92	171.60	169.29	168.03
18000	270.79	255.66	213.15	195.07	186.27	181.70	179.25	177.91
19000	285.83	269.86	224.99	205.91	196.62	191.79	189.21	187.79
20000	300.88	284.06	236.83	216.75	206.96	201.89	199.16	197.68
21000	315.92	298.27	248.67	227.58	217.31	211.98	209.12	207.56
22000	330.96	312.47	260.51	238.42	227.66	222.08	219.08	217.45
23000	346.01	326.67	272.36	249.26	238.01	232.17	229.04	227.33
24000	361.05	340.88	284.20	260.09	248.36	242.26	239.00	237.21
25000	376.10	355.08	296.04	270.93	258.70	252.36	248.95	247.10
26000	391.14	369.28	307.88	281.77	269.05	262.45	258.91	256.98
27000	406.18	383.48	319.72	292.61	279.40	272.55	268.87	266.86
28000	421.23	397.69	331.56	303.44	289.75	282.64	278.83	276.75
29000	436.27	411.89	343.40	314.28	300.10	292.73	288.79	286.63
30000	451.31	426.09	355.24	325.12	310.44	302.83	298.74	296.51
31000	466.36	440.30	367.09	335.95	320.79	312.92	308.70	306.40
32000	481.40	454.50	378.93	346.79	331.14	323.02	318.66	316.28
33000	496.44	468.70	390.77	357.63	341.49	333.11	328.62	326.17
34000	511.49	482.91	402.61	368.46	351.84	343.20	338.57	336.05
35000	526.53	497.11	414.45	379.30	362.18	353.30	348.53	345.93
40000	601.75	568.12	473.66	433.49	413.92	403.77	398.32	395.35
45000	676.97	639.14	532.86	487.67	465.66	454.24	448.11	444.77
50000	752.19	710.15	592.07	541.86	517.40	504.71	497.90	494.19
55000	827.40	781.17	651.28	596.04	569.14	555.18	547.69	543.61
60000	902.62	852.18	710.48	650.23	620.88	605.65	597.48	593.02
65000	977.84	923.20	769.69	704.41	672.62	656.12	647.27	642.44
70000	1053.06	994.21	828.90	758.60	724.36	706.59	697.06	691.86
75000	1128.28	1065.23	888.10	812.79	776.10	757.06	746.85	741.28
80000	1203.49	1136.24	947.31	866.97	827.84	807.53	796.64	790.70
85000	1278.71	1207.26	1006.52	921.16	879.58	858.00	846.43	840.11
90000	1353.93	1278.27	1065.72	975.34	931.32	908.47	896.22	889.53
95000	1429.15	1349.28	1124.93	1029.53	983.06	958.94	946.01	938.95
100000	1504.37	1420.30	1184.14	1083.71	1034.80	1009.41	995.80	988.37
105000	1579.58	1491.31	1243.34	1137.90	1086.54	1059.89	1045.59	1037.79
110000	1654.80	1562.33	1302.55	1192.08	1138.28	1110.36	1095.38	1087.21
115000	1730.02	1633.34	1361.76	1246.27	1190.02	1160.83	1145.17	1136.62
120000	1805.24	1704.36	1420.96	1300.45	1241.76	1211.30	1194.96	1186.04
125000	1880.46	1775.37	1480.17	1354.64	1293.50	1261.77	1244.75	1235.46
130000	1955.67	1846.39	1539.38	1408.82	1345.24	1312.24	1294.54	1284.88
135000	2030.89	1917.40	1598.58	1463.01	1396.98	1362.71	1344.33	1334.30
140000	2106.11	1988.42	1657.79	1517.19	1448.72	1413.18	1394.12	1383.71
145000	2181.33	2059.43	1717.00	1571.38	1500.46	1463.65	1443.91	1433.13
150000	2256.55	2130.45	1776.20	1625.57	1552.20	1514.12	1493.70	1482.55
155000	2331.76	2201.46	1835.41	1679.75	1603.94	1564.59	1543.49	1531.97
160000	2406.98	2272.48	1894.62	1733.94	1655.68	1615.06	1593.28	1581.39

MONTHLY AMORTIZING PAYMENTS

AMOUNT OF LOAN	NUMBER OF YEARS IN TERM							
	1	2	3	4	5	6	7	8
$ 50	4.45	2.36	1.67	1.32	1.12	.98	.89	.82
100	8.89	4.71	3.33	2.64	2.23	1.96	1.77	1.63
200	17.77	9.42	6.65	5.27	4.45	3.92	3.54	3.26
300	26.66	14.13	9.97	7.91	6.68	5.87	5.30	4.88
400	35.54	18.83	13.29	10.54	8.90	7.83	7.07	6.51
500	44.43	23.54	16.61	13.17	11.13	9.78	8.83	8.13
600	53.31	28.25	19.93	15.81	13.35	11.74	10.60	9.76
700	62.20	32.96	23.26	18.44	15.58	13.69	12.36	11.38
800	71.08	37.66	26.58	21.07	17.80	15.65	14.13	13.01
900	79.97	42.37	29.90	23.71	20.03	17.60	15.89	14.63
1000	88.85	47.08	33.22	26.34	22.25	19.56	17.66	16.26
2000	177.70	94.15	66.43	52.67	44.49	39.11	35.31	32.51
3000	266.55	141.23	99.65	79.01	66.74	58.66	52.96	48.76
4000	355.40	188.30	132.86	105.34	88.98	78.21	70.62	65.02
5000	444.25	235.37	166.08	131.67	111.23	97.76	88.27	81.27
6000	533.10	282.45	199.29	158.01	133.47	117.31	105.92	97.52
7000	621.95	329.52	232.51	184.34	155.72	136.86	123.57	113.77
8000	710.80	376.59	265.72	210.68	177.96	156.41	141.23	130.03
9000	799.64	423.67	298.93	237.01	200.21	175.96	158.88	146.28
10000	888.49	470.74	332.15	263.34	222.45	195.51	176.53	162.53
11000	977.34	517.81	365.36	289.68	244.69	215.06	194.19	178.79
12000	1066.19	564.89	398.58	316.01	266.94	234.61	211.84	195.04
13000	1155.05	611.96	431.79	342.34	289.18	254.16	229.49	211.29
14000	1243.89	659.03	465.01	368.68	311.43	273.71	247.14	227.54
15000	1332.74	706.11	498.22	395.01	333.67	293.26	264.80	243.80
16000	1421.59	753.18	531.43	421.35	355.92	312.81	282.45	260.05
17000	1510.43	800.25	564.65	447.68	378.16	332.36	300.10	276.30
18000	1599.28	847.33	597.86	474.01	400.41	351.91	317.75	292.56
19000	1688.13	894.40	631.08	500.35	422.65	371.46	335.41	308.81
20000	1776.98	941.47	664.29	526.68	444.89	391.01	353.06	325.06
21000	1865.83	988.55	697.51	553.02	467.14	410.56	370.71	341.31
22000	1954.68	1035.62	730.72	579.35	489.38	430.11	388.37	357.57
23000	2043.53	1082.69	763.93	605.68	511.63	449.66	406.02	373.82
24000	2132.38	1129.77	797.15	632.02	533.87	469.21	423.67	390.07
25000	2221.22	1176.84	830.36	658.35	556.12	488.76	441.32	406.33
26000	2310.07	1223.92	863.58	684.68	578.36	508.31	458.98	422.58
27000	2398.92	1270.99	896.79	711.02	600.61	527.86	476.63	438.83
28000	2487.77	1318.06	930.01	737.35	622.85	547.41	494.28	455.08
29000	2576.62	1365.14	963.22	763.69	645.09	566.96	511.93	471.34
30000	2665.47	1412.21	996.43	790.02	667.34	586.51	529.59	487.59
31000	2754.32	1459.28	1029.65	816.35	689.58	606.06	547.24	503.84
32000	2843.17	1506.36	1062.86	842.69	711.83	625.61	564.89	520.10
33000	2932.02	1553.43	1096.08	869.02	734.07	645.16	582.55	536.35
34000	3020.86	1600.50	1129.29	895.36	756.32	664.71	600.20	552.60
35000	3109.71	1647.58	1162.51	921.69	778.56	684.26	617.85	568.85
40000	3553.96	1882.94	1328.58	1053.36	889.78	782.01	706.11	650.12
45000	3998.20	2118.31	1494.65	1185.03	1001.01	879.76	794.38	731.38
50000	4442.44	2353.68	1660.72	1316.70	1112.23	977.51	882.64	812.65
55000	4886.69	2589.05	1826.79	1448.37	1223.45	1075.27	970.91	893.91
60000	5330.93	2824.41	1992.86	1580.04	1334.67	1173.02	1059.17	975.18
65000	5775.18	3059.78	2158.94	1711.70	1445.89	1270.77	1147.43	1056.44
70000	6219.42	3295.15	2325.01	1843.37	1557.12	1368.52	1235.70	1137.70
75000	6663.66	3530.52	2491.08	1975.04	1668.34	1466.27	1323.96	1218.97
80000	7107.91	3765.88	2657.15	2106.71	1779.56	1564.02	1412.22	1300.23
85000	7552.15	4001.25	2823.22	2238.38	1890.78	1661.77	1500.49	1381.50
90000	7996.40	4236.62	2989.29	2370.05	2002.01	1759.52	1588.75	1462.76
95000	8440.64	4471.98	3155.36	2501.72	2113.23	1857.27	1677.01	1544.02
100000	8884.88	4707.35	3321.44	2633.39	2224.45	1955.02	1765.28	1625.29
105000	9329.13	4942.72	3487.51	2765.06	2335.67	2052.78	1853.54	1706.55
110000	9773.37	5178.09	3653.58	2896.73	2446.89	2150.53	1941.81	1787.82
115000	10217.62	5413.45	3819.65	3028.40	2558.12	2248.28	2030.07	1869.08
120000	10661.86	5648.82	3985.72	3160.07	2669.34	2346.03	2118.33	1950.35
125000	11106.10	5884.19	4151.79	3291.73	2780.56	2443.78	2206.60	2031.61
130000	11550.35	6119.56	4317.87	3423.40	2891.78	2541.53	2294.86	2112.87
135000	11994.59	6354.92	4483.94	3555.07	3003.01	2639.28	2383.12	2194.14
140000	12438.84	6590.29	4650.01	3686.74	3114.23	2737.03	2471.39	2275.40
145000	12883.08	6825.66	4816.08	3818.41	3225.45	2834.78	2559.65	2356.67
150000	13327.32	7061.03	4982.15	3950.08	3336.67	2932.53	2647.91	2437.93
155000	13771.57	7296.39	5148.22	4081.75	3447.89	3030.28	2736.18	2519.20
160000	14215.81	7531.76	5314.29	4213.42	3559.12	3128.04	2824.44	2600.46

AMOUNT OF LOAN	NUMBER OF YEARS IN TERM							
	9	10	15	20	25	30	35	40
$ 50	.76	.72	.61	.56	.53	.52	.51	.51
100	1.52	1.44	1.21	1.11	1.06	1.03	1.02	1.01
200	3.04	2.87	2.41	2.21	2.11	2.06	2.04	2.02
300	4.56	4.31	3.61	3.31	3.16	3.09	3.05	3.03
400	6.08	5.74	4.81	4.41	4.22	4.12	4.07	4.04
500	7.60	7.18	6.01	5.51	5.27	5.15	5.08	5.05
600	9.12	8.61	7.21	6.61	6.32	6.18	6.10	6.06
700	10.63	10.05	8.41	7.71	7.38	7.21	7.11	7.06
800	12.15	11.48	9.61	8.81	8.43	8.23	8.13	8.07
900	13.67	12.92	10.81	9.91	9.48	9.26	9.14	9.08
1000	15.19	14.35	12.01	11.02	10.54	10.29	10.16	10.09
2000	30.37	28.70	24.01	22.03	21.07	20.58	20.32	20.17
3000	45.56	43.05	36.01	33.04	31.60	30.86	30.47	30.26
4000	60.74	57.39	48.01	44.05	42.13	41.15	40.63	40.34
5000	75.93	71.74	60.01	55.06	52.67	51.44	50.78	50.43
6000	91.11	86.09	72.02	66.07	63.20	61.72	60.94	60.51
7000	106.29	100.43	84.02	77.08	73.73	72.01	71.09	70.60
8000	121.48	114.78	96.02	88.09	84.26	82.29	81.25	80.68
9000	136.66	129.13	108.02	99.10	94.80	92.58	91.40	90.77
10000	151.85	143.48	120.02	110.11	105.33	102.87	101.56	100.85
11000	167.03	157.82	132.02	121.12	115.86	113.15	111.72	110.94
12000	182.22	172.17	144.03	132.14	126.39	123.44	121.87	121.02
13000	197.40	186.52	156.03	143.15	136.92	133.72	132.03	131.11
14000	212.58	200.86	168.03	154.16	147.46	144.01	142.18	141.19
15000	227.77	215.21	180.03	165.17	157.99	154.30	152.34	151.28
16000	242.95	229.56	192.03	176.18	168.52	164.58	162.49	161.36
17000	258.14	243.91	204.03	187.19	179.05	174.87	172.65	171.45
18000	273.32	258.25	216.04	198.20	189.59	185.16	182.80	181.53
19000	288.51	272.60	228.04	209.21	200.12	195.44	192.96	191.62
20000	303.69	286.95	240.04	220.22	210.65	205.73	203.11	201.70
21000	318.87	301.29	252.04	231.23	221.18	216.01	213.27	211.79
22000	334.06	315.64	264.04	242.24	231.71	226.30	223.43	221.87
23000	349.24	329.99	276.04	253.25	242.25	236.59	233.58	231.96
24000	364.43	344.34	288.05	264.27	252.78	246.87	243.74	242.04
25000	379.61	358.68	300.05	275.28	263.31	257.16	253.89	252.13
26000	394.80	373.03	312.05	286.29	273.84	267.44	264.05	262.21
27000	409.98	387.38	324.05	297.30	284.38	277.73	274.20	272.30
28000	425.16	401.72	336.05	308.31	294.91	288.02	284.36	282.38
29000	440.35	416.07	348.05	319.32	305.44	298.30	294.51	292.47
30000	455.53	430.42	360.06	330.33	315.97	308.59	304.67	302.55
31000	470.72	444.76	372.06	341.34	326.50	318.87	314.83	312.64
32000	485.90	459.11	384.06	352.35	337.04	329.16	324.98	322.72
33000	501.08	473.46	396.06	363.36	347.57	339.45	335.14	332.81
34000	516.27	487.81	408.06	374.37	358.10	349.73	345.29	342.89
35000	531.45	502.15	420.06	385.39	368.63	360.02	355.45	352.98
40000	607.37	573.89	480.07	440.44	421.29	411.45	406.22	403.40
45000	683.30	645.62	540.08	495.49	473.96	462.88	457.00	453.83
50000	759.22	717.36	600.09	550.55	526.62	514.31	507.78	504.25
55000	835.14	789.10	660.10	605.60	579.28	565.74	558.56	554.68
60000	911.06	860.83	720.11	660.66	631.94	617.17	609.33	605.10
65000	986.98	932.57	780.11	715.71	684.60	668.60	660.11	655.53
70000	1062.90	1004.30	840.12	770.77	737.26	720.03	710.89	705.95
75000	1138.82	1076.04	900.13	825.82	789.92	771.46	761.67	756.38
80000	1214.74	1147.77	960.14	880.87	842.58	822.90	812.44	806.80
85000	1290.66	1219.51	1020.15	935.93	895.25	874.33	863.22	857.23
90000	1366.59	1291.24	1080.16	990.98	947.91	925.76	914.00	907.65
95000	1442.51	1362.98	1140.16	1046.04	1000.57	977.19	964.78	958.08
100000	1518.43	1434.71	1200.17	1101.09	1053.23	1028.62	1015.55	1008.50
105000	1594.35	1506.45	1260.18	1156.15	1105.89	1080.05	1066.33	1058.93
110000	1670.27	1578.19	1320.19	1211.20	1158.55	1131.48	1117.11	1109.35
115000	1746.19	1649.92	1380.20	1266.25	1211.21	1182.91	1167.89	1159.78
120000	1822.11	1721.66	1440.21	1321.31	1263.87	1234.34	1218.66	1210.20
125000	1898.03	1793.39	1500.22	1376.36	1316.54	1285.77	1269.44	1260.63
130000	1973.96	1865.13	1560.22	1431.42	1369.20	1337.20	1320.22	1311.05
135000	2049.88	1936.86	1620.23	1486.47	1421.86	1388.63	1371.00	1361.48
140000	2125.80	2008.60	1680.24	1541.53	1474.52	1440.06	1421.77	1411.90
145000	2201.72	2080.33	1740.25	1596.58	1527.18	1491.49	1472.55	1462.33
150000	2277.64	2152.07	1800.26	1651.63	1579.84	1542.92	1523.33	1512.75
155000	2353.56	2223.80	1860.27	1706.69	1632.50	1594.35	1574.11	1563.18
160000	2429.48	2295.54	1920.27	1761.74	1685.16	1645.79	1624.88	1613.60

12.250%   MONTHLY AMORTIZING PAYMENTS

AMOUNT OF LOAN	NUMBER OF YEARS IN TERM							
	1	2	3	4	5	6	7	8
$ 50	4.45	2.36	1.67	1.33	1.12	.99	.89	.82
100	8.90	4.72	3.34	2.65	2.24	1.97	1.78	1.64
200	17.80	9.44	6.67	5.30	4.48	3.94	3.56	3.28
300	26.69	14.16	10.01	7.94	6.72	5.91	5.34	4.92
400	35.59	18.88	13.34	10.59	8.95	7.88	7.12	6.56
500	44.49	23.60	16.67	13.23	11.19	9.85	8.90	8.20
600	53.38	28.32	20.01	15.88	13.43	11.81	10.68	9.84
700	62.28	33.04	23.34	18.52	15.66	13.78	12.46	11.48
800	71.18	37.76	26.67	21.17	17.90	15.75	14.23	13.12
900	80.07	42.48	30.01	23.82	20.14	17.72	16.01	14.76
1000	88.97	47.20	33.34	26.46	22.38	19.69	17.79	16.40
2000	177.94	94.39	66.67	52.92	44.75	39.37	35.58	32.79
3000	266.90	141.58	100.01	79.38	67.12	59.05	53.37	49.18
4000	355.87	188.77	133.34	105.83	89.49	78.73	71.15	65.57
5000	444.83	235.96	166.67	132.29	111.86	98.41	88.94	81.96
6000	533.80	283.15	200.01	158.75	134.23	118.09	106.73	98.35
7000	622.77	330.34	233.34	185.20	156.60	137.77	124.51	114.74
8000	711.73	377.53	266.68	211.66	178.97	157.45	142.30	131.13
9000	800.70	424.72	300.01	238.12	201.34	177.13	160.09	147.52
10000	889.66	471.91	333.34	264.57	223.71	196.81	177.87	163.91
11000	978.63	519.10	366.68	291.03	246.09	216.49	195.66	180.30
12000	1067.59	566.29	400.01	317.49	268.46	236.17	213.45	196.69
13000	1156.56	613.48	433.34	343.94	290.83	255.85	231.23	213.08
14000	1245.53	660.67	466.68	370.40	313.20	275.53	249.02	229.47
15000	1334.49	707.86	500.01	396.86	335.57	295.21	266.81	245.86
16000	1423.46	755.05	533.35	423.31	357.94	314.89	284.59	262.25
17000	1512.42	802.24	566.68	449.77	380.31	334.57	302.38	278.64
18000	1601.39	849.43	600.01	476.23	402.68	354.25	320.17	295.03
19000	1690.35	896.62	633.35	502.68	425.05	373.93	337.95	311.42
20000	1779.32	943.81	666.68	529.14	447.42	393.61	355.74	327.82
21000	1868.29	991.00	700.02	555.60	469.80	413.29	373.53	344.21
22000	1957.25	1038.19	733.35	582.05	492.17	432.97	391.31	360.60
23000	2046.22	1085.38	766.68	608.51	514.54	452.66	409.10	376.99
24000	2135.18	1132.57	800.02	634.97	536.91	472.34	426.89	393.38
25000	2224.15	1179.76	833.35	661.42	559.28	492.02	444.67	409.77
26000	2313.12	1226.95	866.68	687.88	581.65	511.70	462.46	426.16
27000	2402.08	1274.14	900.02	714.34	604.02	531.38	480.25	442.55
28000	2491.05	1321.33	933.35	740.79	626.39	551.06	498.03	458.94
29000	2580.01	1368.52	966.69	767.25	648.76	570.74	515.82	475.33
30000	2668.98	1415.71	1000.02	793.71	671.13	590.42	533.61	491.72
31000	2757.94	1462.90	1033.35	820.16	693.51	610.10	551.39	508.11
32000	2846.91	1510.09	1066.69	846.62	715.88	629.78	569.18	524.50
33000	2935.88	1557.29	1100.02	873.08	738.25	649.46	586.97	540.89
34000	3024.84	1604.48	1133.36	899.53	760.62	669.14	604.75	557.28
35000	3113.81	1651.67	1166.69	925.99	782.99	688.82	622.54	573.67
40000	3558.64	1887.62	1333.36	1058.28	894.84	787.22	711.47	655.63
45000	4003.47	2123.57	1500.03	1190.56	1006.70	885.62	800.41	737.58
50000	4448.29	2359.52	1666.70	1322.84	1118.55	984.03	889.34	819.53
55000	4893.12	2595.47	1833.37	1455.13	1230.41	1082.43	978.27	901.48
60000	5337.95	2831.42	2000.04	1587.41	1342.26	1180.83	1067.21	983.44
65000	5782.78	3067.37	2166.70	1719.69	1454.12	1279.23	1156.14	1065.39
70000	6227.61	3303.33	2333.37	1851.98	1565.97	1377.64	1245.07	1147.34
75000	6672.44	3539.28	2500.04	1984.26	1677.83	1476.04	1334.01	1229.29
80000	7117.27	3775.23	2666.71	2116.55	1789.68	1574.44	1422.94	1311.25
85000	7562.10	4011.18	2833.38	2248.83	1901.54	1672.84	1511.88	1393.20
90000	8006.93	4247.13	3000.05	2381.11	2013.39	1771.24	1600.81	1475.15
95000	8451.75	4483.08	3166.72	2513.40	2125.25	1869.65	1689.74	1557.10
100000	8896.58	4719.04	3333.39	2645.68	2237.10	1968.05	1778.68	1639.06
105000	9341.41	4954.99	3500.06	2777.96	2348.96	2066.45	1867.61	1721.01
110000	9786.24	5190.94	3666.73	2910.25	2460.81	2164.85	1956.54	1802.96
115000	10231.07	5426.89	3833.40	3042.53	2572.67	2263.26	2045.48	1884.91
120000	10675.90	5662.84	4000.07	3174.82	2684.52	2361.66	2134.41	1966.87
125000	11120.73	5898.79	4166.74	3307.10	2796.38	2460.06	2223.34	2048.82
130000	11565.56	6134.74	4333.40	3439.38	2908.23	2558.46	2312.28	2130.77
135000	12010.39	6370.70	4500.07	3571.67	3020.09	2656.86	2401.21	2212.72
140000	12455.21	6606.65	4666.74	3703.95	3131.94	2755.27	2490.14	2294.68
145000	12900.04	6842.60	4833.41	3836.23	3243.80	2853.67	2579.08	2376.63
150000	13344.87	7078.55	5000.08	3968.52	3355.65	2952.07	2668.01	2458.58
155000	13789.70	7314.50	5166.75	4100.80	3467.51	3050.47	2756.94	2540.53
160000	14234.53	7550.45	5333.42	4233.09	3579.36	3148.88	2845.88	2622.49

32

AMOUNT OF LOAN	NUMBER OF YEARS IN TERM							
	9	10	15	20	25	30	35	40
$ 50	.77	.73	.61	.56	.54	.53	.52	.52
100	1.54	1.45	1.22	1.12	1.08	1.05	1.04	1.03
200	3.07	2.90	2.44	2.24	2.15	2.10	2.08	2.06
300	4.60	4.35	3.65	3.36	3.22	3.15	3.11	3.09
400	6.14	5.80	4.87	4.48	4.29	4.20	4.15	4.12
500	7.67	7.25	6.09	5.60	5.36	5.24	5.18	5.15
600	9.20	8.70	7.30	6.72	6.44	6.29	6.22	6.18
700	10.73	10.15	8.52	7.83	7.51	7.34	7.25	7.21
800	12.27	11.60	9.74	8.95	8.58	8.39	8.29	8.23
900	13.80	13.05	10.95	10.07	9.65	9.44	9.32	9.26
1000	15.33	14.50	12.17	11.19	10.72	10.48	10.36	10.29
2000	30.66	28.99	24.33	22.38	21.44	20.96	20.71	20.58
3000	45.98	43.48	36.49	33.56	32.16	31.44	31.07	30.87
4000	61.31	57.97	48.66	44.75	42.87	41.92	41.42	41.15
5000	76.63	72.46	60.82	55.93	53.59	52.40	51.77	51.44
6000	91.96	86.96	72.98	67.12	64.31	62.88	62.13	61.73
7000	107.28	101.45	85.15	78.30	75.03	73.36	72.48	72.01
8000	122.61	115.94	97.31	89.49	85.74	83.84	82.83	82.30
9000	137.93	130.43	109.47	100.68	96.46	94.32	93.19	92.59
10000	153.26	144.92	121.63	111.86	107.18	104.79	103.54	102.87
11000	168.59	159.42	133.80	123.05	117.90	115.27	113.90	113.16
12000	183.91	173.91	145.96	134.23	128.61	125.75	124.25	123.45
13000	199.24	188.40	158.12	145.42	139.33	136.23	134.60	133.73
14000	214.56	202.89	170.29	156.60	150.05	146.71	144.96	144.02
15000	229.89	217.38	182.45	167.79	160.77	157.19	155.31	154.31
16000	245.21	231.88	194.61	178.98	171.48	167.67	165.66	164.59
17000	260.54	246.37	206.78	190.16	182.20	178.15	176.02	174.88
18000	275.86	260.86	218.94	201.35	192.92	188.63	186.37	185.17
19000	291.19	275.35	231.10	212.53	203.64	199.11	196.73	195.46
20000	306.52	289.84	243.26	223.72	214.35	209.58	207.08	205.74
21000	321.84	304.34	255.43	234.90	225.07	220.06	217.43	216.03
22000	337.17	318.83	267.59	246.09	235.79	230.54	227.79	226.32
23000	352.49	333.32	279.75	257.27	246.51	241.02	238.14	236.60
24000	367.82	347.81	291.92	268.46	257.22	251.50	248.49	246.89
25000	383.14	362.30	304.08	279.65	267.94	261.98	258.85	257.18
26000	398.47	376.80	316.24	290.83	278.66	272.46	269.20	267.46
27000	413.79	391.29	328.41	302.02	289.38	282.94	279.56	277.75
28000	429.12	405.78	340.57	313.20	300.09	293.42	289.91	288.04
29000	444.45	420.27	352.73	324.39	310.81	303.89	300.26	298.32
30000	459.77	434.76	364.89	335.57	321.53	314.37	310.62	308.61
31000	475.10	449.26	377.06	346.76	332.25	324.85	320.97	318.90
32000	490.42	463.75	389.22	357.95	342.96	335.33	331.32	329.18
33000	505.75	478.24	401.38	369.13	353.68	345.81	341.68	339.47
34000	521.07	492.73	413.55	380.32	364.40	356.29	352.03	349.76
35000	536.40	507.22	425.71	391.50	375.12	366.77	362.38	360.05
40000	613.03	579.68	486.52	447.43	428.70	419.16	414.15	411.48
45000	689.65	652.14	547.34	503.36	482.29	471.56	465.92	462.91
50000	766.28	724.60	608.15	559.29	535.88	523.95	517.69	514.35
55000	842.91	797.06	668.97	615.22	589.46	576.35	569.46	565.78
60000	919.54	869.52	729.78	671.14	643.05	628.74	621.23	617.22
65000	996.17	941.98	790.60	727.07	696.64	681.14	673.00	668.65
70000	1072.79	1014.44	851.41	783.00	750.23	733.53	724.76	720.09
75000	1149.42	1086.90	912.23	838.93	803.81	785.93	776.53	771.52
80000	1226.05	1159.36	973.04	894.86	857.40	838.32	828.30	822.95
85000	1302.68	1231.82	1033.86	950.78	910.99	890.72	880.07	874.39
90000	1379.30	1304.28	1094.67	1006.71	964.57	943.11	931.84	925.82
95000	1455.93	1376.74	1155.49	1062.64	1018.16	995.51	983.61	977.26
100000	1532.56	1449.20	1216.30	1118.57	1071.75	1047.90	1035.38	1028.69
105000	1609.19	1521.66	1277.12	1174.50	1125.34	1100.30	1087.14	1080.13
110000	1685.82	1594.12	1337.93	1230.43	1178.92	1152.69	1138.91	1131.56
115000	1762.44	1666.58	1398.75	1286.35	1232.51	1205.09	1190.68	1182.99
120000	1839.07	1739.04	1459.56	1342.28	1286.10	1257.48	1242.45	1234.43
125000	1915.70	1811.50	1520.38	1398.21	1339.68	1309.88	1294.22	1285.86
130000	1992.33	1883.96	1581.19	1454.14	1393.27	1362.27	1345.99	1337.30
135000	2068.95	1956.42	1642.01	1510.07	1446.86	1414.67	1397.76	1388.73
140000	2145.58	2028.88	1702.82	1566.00	1500.45	1467.06	1449.52	1440.17
145000	2222.21	2101.34	1763.64	1621.92	1554.03	1519.45	1501.29	1491.60
150000	2298.84	2173.80	1824.45	1677.85	1607.62	1571.85	1553.06	1543.03
155000	2375.47	2246.26	1885.27	1733.78	1661.21	1624.24	1604.83	1594.47
160000	2452.09	2318.72	1946.08	1789.71	1714.80	1676.64	1656.60	1645.90

AMOUNT OF LOAN	NUMBER OF YEARS IN TERM							
	1	2	3	4	5	6	7	8
$ 50	4.46	2.37	1.68	1.33	1.13	1.00	.90	.83
100	8.91	4.74	3.35	2.66	2.25	1.99	1.80	1.66
200	17.82	9.47	6.70	5.32	4.50	3.97	3.59	3.31
300	26.73	14.20	10.04	7.98	6.75	5.95	5.38	4.96
400	35.64	18.93	13.39	10.64	9.00	7.93	7.17	6.62
500	44.55	23.66	16.73	13.29	11.25	9.91	8.97	8.27
600	53.45	28.39	20.08	15.95	13.50	11.89	10.76	9.92
700	62.36	33.12	23.42	18.61	15.75	13.87	12.55	11.58
800	71.27	37.85	26.77	21.27	18.00	15.85	14.34	13.23
900	80.18	42.58	30.11	23.93	20.25	17.84	16.13	14.88
1000	89.09	47.31	33.46	26.58	22.50	19.82	17.93	16.53
2000	178.17	94.62	66.91	53.16	45.00	39.63	35.85	33.06
3000	267.25	141.93	100.37	79.74	67.50	59.44	53.77	49.59
4000	356.34	189.23	133.82	106.32	90.00	79.25	71.69	66.12
5000	445.42	236.54	167.27	132.90	112.49	99.06	89.61	82.65
6000	534.50	283.85	200.73	159.48	134.99	118.87	107.53	99.18
7000	623.59	331.16	234.18	186.06	157.49	138.68	125.45	115.71
8000	712.67	378.46	267.63	212.64	179.99	158.49	143.37	132.24
9000	801.75	425.77	301.09	239.22	202.49	178.31	161.30	148.76
10000	890.83	473.08	334.54	265.80	224.98	198.12	179.22	165.29
11000	979.92	520.39	367.99	292.38	247.48	217.93	197.14	181.82
12000	1069.00	567.69	401.45	318.96	269.98	237.74	215.06	198.35
13000	1158.08	615.00	434.90	345.54	292.48	257.55	232.98	214.88
14000	1247.17	662.31	468.36	372.12	314.98	277.36	250.90	231.41
15000	1336.25	709.61	501.81	398.70	337.47	297.17	268.82	247.94
16000	1425.33	756.92	535.26	425.28	359.97	316.98	286.74	264.47
17000	1514.41	804.23	568.72	451.86	382.47	336.80	304.67	280.99
18000	1603.50	851.54	602.17	478.44	404.97	356.61	322.59	297.52
19000	1692.58	898.84	635.62	505.02	427.47	376.42	340.51	314.05
20000	1781.66	946.15	669.08	531.60	449.96	396.23	358.43	330.58
21000	1870.75	993.46	702.53	558.18	472.46	416.04	376.35	347.11
22000	1959.83	1040.77	735.98	584.76	494.96	435.85	394.27	363.64
23000	2048.91	1088.07	769.44	611.34	517.46	455.66	412.19	380.17
24000	2137.99	1135.38	802.89	637.92	539.96	475.47	430.11	396.70
25000	2227.08	1182.69	836.35	664.50	562.45	495.28	448.04	413.23
26000	2316.16	1230.00	869.80	691.08	584.95	515.10	465.96	429.75
27000	2405.24	1277.30	903.25	717.66	607.45	534.91	483.88	446.28
28000	2494.33	1324.61	936.71	744.24	629.95	554.72	501.80	462.81
29000	2583.41	1371.92	970.16	770.82	652.45	574.53	519.72	479.34
30000	2672.49	1419.22	1003.61	797.40	674.94	594.34	537.64	495.87
31000	2761.57	1466.53	1037.07	823.98	697.44	614.15	555.56	512.40
32000	2850.66	1513.84	1070.52	850.56	719.94	633.96	573.48	528.93
33000	2939.74	1561.15	1103.97	877.14	742.44	653.77	591.41	545.46
34000	3028.82	1608.45	1137.43	903.72	764.93	673.59	609.33	561.98
35000	3117.91	1655.76	1170.88	930.30	787.43	693.40	627.25	578.51
40000	3563.32	1892.30	1338.15	1063.20	899.92	792.45	716.85	661.16
45000	4008.73	2128.83	1505.42	1196.10	1012.41	891.51	806.46	743.80
50000	4454.15	2365.37	1672.69	1329.00	1124.90	990.56	896.07	826.45
55000	4899.56	2601.91	1839.95	1461.90	1237.39	1089.62	985.67	909.09
60000	5344.98	2838.44	2007.22	1594.80	1349.88	1188.68	1075.28	991.73
65000	5790.39	3074.98	2174.49	1727.70	1462.37	1287.73	1164.89	1074.38
70000	6235.81	3311.52	2341.76	1860.60	1574.86	1386.79	1254.49	1157.02
75000	6681.22	3548.05	2509.03	1993.50	1687.35	1485.84	1344.10	1239.67
80000	7126.63	3784.59	2676.30	2126.40	1799.84	1584.90	1433.70	1322.31
85000	7572.05	4021.13	2843.56	2259.30	1912.33	1683.96	1523.31	1404.95
90000	8017.46	4257.66	3010.83	2392.20	2024.82	1783.01	1612.92	1487.60
95000	8462.88	4494.20	3178.10	2525.10	2137.31	1882.07	1702.52	1570.24
100000	8908.29	4730.74	3345.37	2658.00	2249.80	1981.12	1792.13	1652.89
105000	9353.71	4967.27	3512.64	2790.90	2362.29	2080.18	1881.74	1735.53
110000	9799.12	5203.81	3679.90	2923.80	2474.78	2179.23	1971.34	1818.17
115000	10244.53	5440.35	3847.17	3056.70	2587.27	2278.29	2060.95	1900.82
120000	10689.95	5676.88	4014.44	3189.60	2699.76	2377.35	2150.55	1983.46
125000	11135.36	5913.42	4181.71	3322.50	2812.25	2476.40	2240.16	2066.11
130000	11580.78	6149.96	4348.98	3455.40	2924.74	2575.46	2329.77	2148.75
135000	12026.19	6386.49	4516.24	3588.30	3037.23	2674.51	2419.37	2231.39
140000	12471.61	6623.03	4683.51	3721.20	3149.72	2773.57	2508.98	2314.04
145000	12917.02	6859.56	4850.78	3854.10	3262.21	2872.63	2598.58	2396.68
150000	13362.43	7096.10	5018.05	3987.00	3374.70	2971.68	2688.19	2479.33
155000	13807.85	7332.64	5185.32	4119.90	3487.19	3070.74	2777.80	2561.97
160000	14253.26	7569.17	5352.59	4252.80	3599.68	3169.79	2867.40	2644.61

AMOUNT OF LOAN	NUMBER OF YEARS IN TERM							
	9	10	15	20	25	30	35	40
$ 50	.78	.74	.62	.57	.55	.54	.53	.53
100	1.55	1.47	1.24	1.14	1.10	1.07	1.06	1.05
200	3.10	2.93	2.47	2.28	2.19	2.14	2.12	2.10
300	4.65	4.40	3.70	3.41	3.28	3.21	3.17	3.15
400	6.19	5.86	4.94	4.55	4.37	4.27	4.23	4.20
500	7.74	7.32	6.17	5.69	5.46	5.34	5.28	5.25
600	9.29	8.79	7.40	6.82	6.55	6.41	6.34	6.30
700	10.83	10.25	8.63	7.96	7.64	7.48	7.39	7.35
800	12.38	11.72	9.87	9.09	8.73	8.54	8.45	8.40
900	13.93	13.18	11.10	10.23	9.82	9.61	9.50	9.45
1000	15.47	14.64	12.33	11.37	10.91	10.68	10.56	10.49
2000	30.94	29.28	24.66	22.73	21.81	21.35	21.11	20.98
3000	46.41	43.92	36.98	34.09	32.72	32.02	31.66	31.47
4000	61.88	58.56	49.31	45.45	43.62	42.70	42.22	41.96
5000	77.34	73.19	61.63	56.81	54.52	53.37	52.77	52.45
6000	92.81	87.83	73.96	68.17	65.43	64.04	63.32	62.94
7000	108.28	102.47	86.28	79.53	76.33	74.71	73.87	73.43
8000	123.75	117.11	98.61	90.90	87.23	85.39	84.43	83.92
9000	139.21	131.74	110.93	102.26	98.14	96.06	94.98	94.41
10000	154.68	146.38	123.26	113.62	109.04	106.73	105.53	104.90
11000	170.15	161.02	135.58	124.98	119.94	117.40	116.08	115.39
12000	185.62	175.66	147.91	136.34	130.85	128.08	126.64	125.88
13000	201.08	190.29	160.23	147.70	141.75	138.75	137.19	136.36
14000	216.55	204.93	172.56	159.06	152.65	149.42	147.74	146.85
15000	232.02	219.57	184.88	170.43	163.56	160.09	158.29	157.34
16000	247.49	234.21	197.21	181.79	174.46	170.77	168.85	167.83
17000	262.95	248.84	209.53	193.15	185.37	181.44	179.40	178.32
18000	278.42	263.48	221.86	204.51	196.27	192.11	189.95	188.81
19000	293.89	278.12	234.18	215.87	207.17	202.78	200.50	199.30
20000	309.36	292.76	246.51	227.23	218.08	213.46	211.06	209.79
21000	324.82	307.39	258.83	238.59	228.98	224.13	221.61	220.28
22000	340.29	322.03	271.16	249.96	239.88	234.80	232.16	230.77
23000	355.76	336.67	283.49	261.32	250.79	245.47	242.71	241.26
24000	371.23	351.31	295.81	272.68	261.69	256.15	253.27	251.75
25000	386.69	365.95	308.14	284.04	272.59	266.82	263.82	262.23
26000	402.16	380.58	320.46	295.40	283.50	277.49	274.37	272.72
27000	417.63	395.22	332.79	306.76	294.40	288.16	284.92	283.21
28000	433.10	409.86	345.11	318.12	305.30	298.84	295.48	293.70
29000	448.56	424.50	357.44	329.49	316.21	309.51	306.03	304.19
30000	464.03	439.13	369.76	340.85	327.11	320.18	316.58	314.68
31000	479.50	453.77	382.09	352.21	338.01	330.85	327.13	325.17
32000	494.97	468.41	394.41	363.57	348.92	341.53	337.69	335.66
33000	510.43	483.05	406.74	374.93	359.82	352.20	348.24	346.15
34000	525.90	497.68	419.06	386.29	370.73	362.87	358.79	356.64
35000	541.37	512.32	431.39	397.65	381.63	373.55	369.34	367.13
40000	618.71	585.51	493.01	454.46	436.15	426.91	422.11	419.57
45000	696.04	658.70	554.64	511.27	490.66	480.27	474.87	472.02
50000	773.38	731.89	616.27	568.08	545.18	533.63	527.63	524.46
55000	850.72	805.07	677.89	624.88	599.70	587.00	580.39	576.91
60000	928.06	878.26	739.52	681.69	654.22	640.36	633.16	629.36
65000	1005.40	951.45	801.14	738.50	708.74	693.72	685.92	681.80
70000	1082.73	1024.64	862.77	795.30	763.25	747.09	738.68	734.25
75000	1160.07	1097.83	924.40	852.11	817.77	800.45	791.45	786.69
80000	1237.41	1171.01	986.02	908.92	872.29	853.81	844.21	839.14
85000	1314.75	1244.20	1047.65	965.72	926.81	907.17	896.97	891.59
90000	1392.08	1317.39	1109.27	1022.53	981.32	960.54	949.73	944.03
95000	1469.42	1390.58	1170.90	1079.34	1035.84	1013.90	1002.50	996.48
100000	1546.76	1463.77	1232.53	1136.15	1090.36	1067.26	1055.26	1048.92
105000	1624.10	1536.95	1294.15	1192.95	1144.88	1120.63	1108.02	1101.37
110000	1701.44	1610.14	1355.78	1249.76	1199.39	1173.99	1160.78	1153.82
115000	1778.77	1683.33	1417.41	1306.57	1253.91	1227.35	1213.55	1206.26
120000	1856.11	1756.52	1479.03	1363.37	1308.43	1280.71	1266.31	1258.71
125000	1933.45	1829.71	1540.66	1420.18	1362.95	1334.08	1319.07	1311.15
130000	2010.79	1902.90	1602.28	1476.99	1417.47	1387.44	1371.84	1363.60
135000	2088.12	1976.08	1663.91	1533.79	1471.98	1440.80	1424.60	1416.05
140000	2165.46	2049.27	1725.54	1590.60	1526.50	1494.17	1477.36	1468.49
145000	2242.80	2122.46	1787.16	1647.41	1581.02	1547.53	1530.12	1520.94
150000	2320.14	2195.65	1848.79	1704.22	1635.54	1600.89	1582.89	1573.38
155000	2397.48	2268.84	1910.41	1761.02	1690.05	1654.25	1635.65	1625.83
160000	2474.81	2342.02	1972.04	1817.83	1744.57	1707.62	1688.41	1678.28

MONTHLY AMORTIZING PAYMENTS

AMOUNT OF LOAN	NUMBER OF YEARS IN TERM							
	1	2	3	4	5	6	7	8
$ 50	4.47	2.38	1.68	1.34	1.14	1.00	.91	.84
100	8.93	4.75	3.36	2.68	2.27	2.00	1.81	1.67
200	17.85	9.49	6.72	5.35	4.53	3.99	3.62	3.34
300	26.77	14.23	10.08	8.02	6.79	5.99	5.42	5.01
400	35.69	18.97	13.43	10.69	9.06	7.98	7.23	6.67
500	44.61	23.72	16.79	13.36	11.32	9.98	9.03	8.34
600	53.53	28.46	20.15	16.03	13.58	11.97	10.84	10.01
700	62.45	33.20	23.51	18.70	15.84	13.96	12.64	11.67
800	71.37	37.94	26.86	21.37	18.11	15.96	14.45	13.34
900	80.29	42.69	30.22	24.04	20.37	17.95	16.26	15.01
1000	89.21	47.43	33.58	26.71	22.63	19.95	18.06	16.67
2000	178.41	94.85	67.15	53.41	45.26	39.89	36.12	33.34
3000	267.61	142.28	100.73	80.12	67.88	59.83	54.17	50.01
4000	356.81	189.70	134.30	106.82	90.51	79.77	72.23	66.68
5000	446.01	237.13	167.87	133.52	113.13	99.72	90.29	83.34
6000	535.21	284.55	201.45	160.23	135.76	119.66	108.34	100.01
7000	624.41	331.98	235.02	186.93	158.38	139.60	126.40	116.68
8000	713.61	379.40	268.59	213.63	181.01	159.54	144.46	133.35
9000	802.81	426.83	302.17	240.34	203.63	179.49	162.51	150.01
10000	892.01	474.25	335.74	267.04	226.26	199.43	180.57	166.68
11000	981.21	521.67	369.32	293.74	248.88	219.37	198.62	183.35
12000	1070.61	569.10	402.89	320.45	271.51	239.31	216.68	200.02
13000	1159.61	616.52	436.46	347.15	294.13	259.26	234.74	216.69
14000	1248.81	663.95	470.04	373.86	316.76	279.20	252.79	233.35
15000	1338.01	711.37	503.61	400.56	339.38	299.14	270.85	250.02
16000	1427.21	758.80	537.18	427.26	362.01	319.08	288.91	266.69
17000	1516.41	806.22	570.76	453.97	384.64	339.03	306.96	283.36
18000	1605.61	853.65	604.33	480.67	407.26	358.97	325.02	300.02
19000	1694.81	901.07	637.90	507.37	429.89	378.91	343.08	316.69
20000	1784.01	948.49	671.48	534.08	452.51	398.85	361.13	333.36
21000	1873.21	995.92	705.05	560.78	475.14	418.80	379.19	350.03
22000	1962.41	1043.34	738.63	587.48	497.76	438.74	397.24	366.69
23000	2051.61	1090.77	772.20	614.19	520.39	458.68	415.30	383.36
24000	2140.81	1138.19	805.77	640.89	543.01	478.62	433.36	400.03
25000	2230.01	1185.62	839.35	667.59	565.64	498.56	451.41	416.70
26000	2319.21	1233.04	872.92	694.30	588.26	518.51	469.47	433.37
27000	2408.41	1280.47	906.49	721.00	610.89	538.45	487.53	450.03
28000	2497.61	1327.89	940.07	747.71	633.51	558.39	505.58	466.70
29000	2586.81	1375.31	973.64	774.41	656.14	578.33	523.64	483.37
30000	2676.01	1422.74	1007.21	801.11	678.76	598.28	541.69	500.04
31000	2765.21	1470.16	1040.79	827.82	701.39	618.22	559.75	516.70
32000	2854.41	1517.59	1074.36	854.52	724.01	638.16	577.81	533.37
33000	2943.61	1565.01	1107.94	881.22	746.64	658.10	595.86	550.04
34000	3032.81	1612.44	1141.51	907.93	769.27	678.05	613.92	566.71
35000	3122.01	1659.86	1175.08	934.63	791.89	697.99	631.98	583.38
40000	3568.01	1896.98	1342.95	1068.15	905.02	797.70	722.26	666.71
45000	4014.01	2134.11	1510.82	1201.67	1018.14	897.41	812.54	750.05
50000	4460.01	2371.23	1678.69	1335.18	1131.27	997.13	902.82	833.39
55000	4906.01	2608.35	1846.56	1468.70	1244.40	1096.84	993.10	916.73
60000	5352.01	2845.48	2014.42	1602.22	1357.52	1196.55	1083.38	1000.07
65000	5798.01	3082.60	2182.29	1735.74	1470.65	1296.26	1173.67	1083.41
70000	6244.01	3319.72	2350.16	1869.26	1583.78	1395.97	1263.95	1166.75
75000	6690.01	3556.84	2518.03	2002.77	1696.90	1495.69	1354.23	1250.08
80000	7136.01	3793.96	2685.90	2136.29	1810.03	1595.40	1444.51	1333.42
85000	7582.01	4031.09	2853.77	2269.81	1923.16	1695.11	1534.79	1416.76
90000	8028.01	4268.21	3021.63	2403.33	2036.28	1794.82	1625.07	1500.10
95000	8474.01	4505.33	3189.50	2536.85	2149.41	1894.53	1715.36	1583.44
100000	8920.01	4742.45	3357.37	2670.36	2262.54	1994.25	1805.64	1666.78
105000	9366.01	4979.58	3525.24	2803.88	2375.66	2093.96	1895.92	1750.12
110000	9812.01	5216.70	3693.11	2937.40	2488.79	2193.67	1986.20	1833.45
115000	10258.01	5453.82	3860.98	3070.92	2601.91	2293.38	2076.48	1916.79
120000	10704.01	5690.94	4028.84	3204.43	2715.04	2393.09	2166.76	2000.13
125000	11150.01	5928.07	4196.71	3337.95	2828.17	2492.81	2257.05	2083.47
130000	11596.01	6165.19	4364.58	3471.47	2941.29	2592.52	2347.33	2166.81
135000	12042.01	6402.31	4532.45	3604.99	3054.42	2692.23	2437.61	2250.15
140000	12488.01	6639.43	4700.32	3738.51	3167.55	2791.94	2527.89	2333.49
145000	12934.01	6876.55	4868.19	3872.02	3280.67	2891.65	2618.17	2416.82
150000	13380.01	7113.68	5036.05	4005.54	3393.80	2991.37	2708.45	2500.16
155000	13826.01	7350.80	5203.92	4139.06	3506.93	3091.08	2798.74	2583.50
160000	14272.01	7587.92	5371.79	4272.58	3620.05	3190.79	2889.02	2666.84

MONTHLY AMORTIZING PAYMENTS 12.750%

AMOUNT OF LOAN	NUMBER OF YEARS IN TERM							
	9	10	15	20	25	30	35	40
$ 50	.79	.74	.63	.58	.56	.55	.54	.54
100	1.57	1.48	1.25	1.16	1.11	1.09	1.08	1.07
200	3.13	2.96	2.50	2.31	2.22	2.18	2.16	2.14
300	4.69	4.44	3.75	3.47	3.33	3.27	3.23	3.21
400	6.25	5.92	5.00	4.62	4.44	4.35	4.31	4.28
500	7.81	7.40	6.25	5.77	5.55	5.44	5.38	5.35
600	9.37	8.88	7.50	6.93	6.66	6.53	6.46	6.42
700	10.93	10.35	8.75	8.08	7.77	7.61	7.53	7.49
800	12.49	11.83	10.00	9.24	8.88	8.70	8.61	8.56
900	14.05	13.31	11.24	10.39	9.99	9.79	9.68	9.63
1000	15.62	14.79	12.49	11.54	11.10	10.87	10.76	10.70
2000	31.23	29.57	24.98	23.08	22.19	21.74	21.51	21.39
3000	46.84	44.36	37.47	34.62	33.28	32.61	32.26	32.08
4000	62.45	59.14	49.96	46.16	44.37	43.47	43.01	42.77
5000	78.06	73.92	62.45	57.70	55.46	54.34	53.76	53.46
6000	93.67	88.71	74.94	69.23	66.55	65.21	64.52	64.16
7000	109.28	103.49	87.42	80.77	77.64	76.07	75.27	74.85
8000	124.89	118.28	99.91	92.31	88.73	86.94	86.02	85.54
9000	140.50	133.06	112.40	103.85	99.82	97.81	96.77	96.23
10000	156.11	147.84	124.89	115.39	110.91	108.67	107.52	106.92
11000	171.72	162.63	137.38	126.92	122.00	119.54	118.28	117.62
12000	187.33	177.41	149.87	138.46	133.09	130.41	129.03	128.31
13000	202.94	192.20	162.35	150.00	144.18	141.28	139.78	139.00
14000	218.55	206.98	174.84	161.54	155.27	152.14	150.53	149.69
15000	234.16	221.76	187.33	173.08	166.36	163.01	161.28	160.39
16000	249.77	236.55	199.82	184.61	177.45	173.88	172.04	171.08
17000	265.38	251.33	212.31	196.15	188.54	184.74	182.79	181.77
18000	280.99	266.12	224.80	207.69	199.63	195.61	193.54	192.46
19000	296.60	280.90	237.28	219.23	210.72	206.48	204.29	203.15
20000	312.21	295.68	249.77	230.77	221.82	217.34	215.04	213.84
21000	327.82	310.47	262.26	242.31	232.91	228.21	225.80	224.54
22000	343.43	325.25	274.75	253.84	244.00	239.08	236.55	235.23
23000	359.04	340.04	287.24	265.38	255.09	249.94	247.30	245.92
24000	374.65	354.82	299.73	276.92	266.18	260.81	258.05	256.61
25000	390.26	369.60	312.21	288.46	277.27	271.68	268.80	267.30
26000	405.87	384.39	324.70	300.00	288.36	282.55	279.56	278.00
27000	421.48	399.17	337.19	311.53	299.45	293.41	290.31	288.69
28000	437.09	413.96	349.68	323.07	310.54	304.28	301.06	299.38
29000	452.70	428.74	362.17	334.61	321.63	315.15	311.81	310.07
30000	468.31	443.52	374.66	346.15	332.72	326.01	322.56	320.76
31000	483.92	458.31	387.14	357.69	343.81	336.88	333.32	331.46
32000	499.53	473.09	399.63	369.22	354.90	347.75	344.07	342.15
33000	515.14	487.88	412.12	380.76	365.99	358.61	354.82	352.84
34000	530.75	502.66	424.61	392.30	377.08	369.48	365.57	363.53
35000	546.36	517.44	437.10	403.84	388.17	380.35	376.32	374.22
40000	624.41	591.36	499.54	461.53	443.63	434.68	430.08	427.68
45000	702.47	665.28	561.98	519.22	499.08	489.02	483.84	481.14
50000	780.52	739.20	624.42	576.91	554.53	543.35	537.60	534.60
55000	858.57	813.12	686.87	634.60	609.98	597.69	591.36	588.06
60000	936.62	887.04	749.31	692.29	665.44	652.02	645.12	641.52
65000	1014.67	960.96	811.75	749.98	720.89	706.36	698.88	694.98
70000	1092.72	1034.88	874.19	807.67	776.34	760.69	752.64	748.44
75000	1170.77	1108.80	936.63	865.36	831.79	815.02	806.40	801.90
80000	1248.82	1182.72	999.07	923.05	887.25	869.36	860.16	855.36
85000	1326.87	1256.64	1061.52	980.74	942.70	923.69	913.92	908.82
90000	1404.93	1330.56	1123.96	1038.44	998.15	978.03	967.68	962.28
95000	1482.98	1404.48	1186.40	1096.13	1053.60	1032.36	1021.44	1015.74
100000	1561.03	1478.40	1248.84	1153.82	1109.06	1086.70	1075.20	1069.20
105000	1639.08	1552.32	1311.28	1211.51	1164.51	1141.03	1128.96	1122.66
110000	1717.13	1626.24	1373.73	1269.20	1219.96	1195.37	1182.72	1176.12
115000	1795.18	1700.16	1436.17	1326.89	1275.42	1249.70	1236.48	1229.58
120000	1873.23	1774.08	1498.61	1384.58	1330.87	1304.04	1290.24	1283.04
125000	1951.28	1848.00	1561.05	1442.27	1386.32	1358.37	1344.00	1336.50
130000	2029.34	1921.92	1623.49	1499.96	1441.77	1412.71	1397.76	1389.96
135000	2107.39	1995.84	1685.93	1557.65	1497.23	1467.04	1451.52	1443.42
140000	2185.44	2069.76	1748.38	1615.34	1552.68	1521.38	1505.28	1496.88
145000	2263.49	2143.68	1810.82	1673.03	1608.13	1575.71	1559.04	1550.34
150000	2341.54	2217.60	1873.26	1730.72	1663.58	1630.04	1612.80	1603.80
155000	2419.59	2291.52	1935.70	1788.41	1719.04	1684.38	1666.56	1657.26
160000	2497.64	2365.44	1998.14	1846.10	1774.49	1738.71	1720.32	1710.72

37

MONTHLY AMORTIZING PAYMENTS

AMOUNT OF LOAN	NUMBER OF YEARS IN TERM							
	1	2	3	4	5	6	7	8
$ 50	4.47	2.38	1.69	1.35	1.14	1.01	.91	.85
100	8.94	4.76	3.37	2.69	2.28	2.01	1.82	1.69
200	17.87	9.51	6.74	5.37	4.56	4.02	3.64	3.37
300	26.80	14.27	10.11	8.05	6.83	6.03	5.46	5.05
400	35.73	19.02	13.48	10.74	9.11	8.03	7.28	6.73
500	44.66	23.78	16.85	13.42	11.38	10.04	9.10	8.41
600	53.60	28.53	20.22	16.10	13.66	12.05	10.92	10.09
700	62.53	33.28	23.59	18.78	15.93	14.06	12.74	11.77
800	71.46	38.04	26.96	21.47	18.21	16.06	14.56	13.45
900	80.39	42.79	30.33	24.15	20.48	18.07	16.38	15.13
1000	89.32	47.55	33.70	26.83	22.76	20.08	18.20	16.81
2000	178.64	95.09	67.39	53.66	45.51	40.15	36.39	33.62
3000	267.96	142.63	101.09	80.49	68.26	60.23	54.58	50.43
4000	357.27	190.17	134.78	107.31	91.02	80.30	72.77	67.23
5000	446.59	237.71	168.47	134.14	113.77	100.38	90.96	84.04
6000	535.91	285.26	202.17	160.97	136.52	120.45	109.16	100.85
7000	625.23	332.80	235.86	187.80	159.28	140.52	127.35	117.66
8000	714.54	380.34	269.56	214.62	182.03	160.60	145.54	134.46
9000	803.86	427.88	303.25	241.45	204.78	180.67	163.73	151.27
10000	893.18	475.42	336.94	268.28	227.54	200.75	181.92	168.08
11000	982.50	522.97	370.64	295.11	250.29	220.82	200.12	184.88
12000	1071.81	570.51	404.33	321.93	273.04	240.89	218.31	201.69
13000	1161.13	618.05	438.03	348.76	295.79	260.97	236.50	218.50
14000	1250.45	665.59	471.72	375.59	318.55	281.04	254.69	235.31
15000	1339.76	713.13	505.41	402.42	341.30	301.12	272.88	252.11
16000	1429.08	760.67	539.11	429.24	364.05	321.19	291.08	268.92
17000	1518.40	808.22	572.80	456.07	386.81	341.26	309.27	285.73
18000	1607.72	855.76	606.50	482.90	409.56	361.34	327.46	302.54
19000	1697.03	903.30	640.19	509.73	432.31	381.41	345.65	319.34
20000	1786.35	950.84	673.88	536.55	455.07	401.49	363.84	336.15
21000	1875.67	998.38	707.58	563.38	477.82	421.56	382.04	352.96
22000	1964.99	1045.93	741.27	590.21	500.57	441.64	400.23	369.76
23000	2054.30	1093.47	774.97	617.04	523.33	461.71	418.42	386.57
24000	2143.62	1141.01	808.66	643.86	546.08	481.78	436.61	403.38
25000	2232.94	1188.55	842.35	670.69	568.83	501.86	454.80	420.19
26000	2322.25	1236.09	876.05	697.52	591.58	521.93	473.00	436.99
27000	2411.57	1283.63	909.74	724.35	614.34	542.01	491.19	453.80
28000	2500.89	1331.18	943.44	751.17	637.09	562.08	509.38	470.61
29000	2590.21	1378.72	977.13	778.00	659.84	582.15	527.57	487.42
30000	2679.52	1426.26	1010.82	804.83	682.60	602.23	545.76	504.22
31000	2768.84	1473.80	1044.52	831.66	705.35	622.30	563.96	521.03
32000	2858.16	1521.34	1078.21	858.48	728.10	642.38	582.15	537.84
33000	2947.48	1568.89	1111.91	885.31	750.86	662.45	600.34	554.64
34000	3036.79	1616.43	1145.60	912.14	773.61	682.52	618.53	571.45
35000	3126.11	1663.97	1179.29	938.97	796.36	702.60	636.72	588.26
40000	3572.70	1901.68	1347.76	1073.10	910.13	802.97	727.68	672.30
45000	4019.28	2139.39	1516.23	1207.24	1023.89	903.34	818.64	756.33
50000	4465.87	2377.10	1684.70	1341.38	1137.66	1003.71	909.60	840.37
55000	4912.46	2614.81	1853.17	1475.52	1251.42	1104.08	1000.56	924.40
60000	5359.04	2852.51	2021.64	1609.65	1365.19	1204.45	1091.52	1008.44
65000	5805.63	3090.22	2190.11	1743.79	1478.95	1304.82	1182.48	1092.48
70000	6252.21	3327.93	2358.58	1877.93	1592.72	1405.19	1273.44	1176.51
75000	6698.80	3565.64	2527.05	2012.07	1706.49	1505.56	1364.40	1260.55
80000	7145.39	3803.35	2695.52	2146.20	1820.25	1605.93	1455.36	1344.59
85000	7591.97	4041.06	2863.99	2280.34	1934.02	1706.30	1546.32	1428.62
90000	8038.56	4278.77	3032.46	2414.48	2047.78	1806.67	1637.28	1512.66
95000	8485.15	4516.48	3200.93	2548.62	2161.55	1907.04	1728.24	1596.69
100000	8931.73	4754.19	3369.40	2682.75	2275.31	2007.42	1819.20	1680.73
105000	9378.32	4991.90	3537.87	2816.89	2389.08	2107.79	1910.16	1764.77
110000	9824.91	5229.61	3706.34	2951.03	2502.84	2208.16	2001.13	1848.80
115000	10271.49	5467.31	3874.81	3085.17	2616.61	2308.53	2092.08	1932.84
120000	10718.08	5705.02	4043.28	3219.30	2730.37	2408.90	2183.04	2016.88
125000	11164.66	5942.73	4211.75	3353.44	2844.14	2509.27	2274.00	2100.91
130000	11611.25	6180.44	4380.22	3487.58	2957.90	2609.64	2364.96	2184.95
135000	12057.84	6418.15	4548.69	3621.72	3071.67	2710.01	2455.92	2268.98
140000	12504.42	6655.86	4717.16	3755.85	3185.44	2810.38	2546.88	2353.02
145000	12951.01	6893.57	4885.63	3889.99	3299.20	2910.75	2637.84	2437.06
150000	13397.60	7131.28	5054.10	4024.13	3412.97	3011.12	2728.80	2521.09
155000	13844.18	7368.99	5222.57	4158.27	3526.73	3111.49	2819.76	2605.13
160000	14290.77	7606.70	5391.04	4292.40	3640.50	3211.86	2910.72	2689.17

MONTHLY AMORTIZING PAYMENTS   13.000%

AMOUNT OF LOAN	\multicolumn{8}{c}{NUMBER OF YEARS IN TERM}
	9	10	15	20	25	30	35	40
$ 50	.79	.75	.64	.59	.57	.56	.55	.55
100	1.58	1.50	1.27	1.18	1.13	1.11	1.10	1.09
200	3.16	2.99	2.54	2.35	2.26	2.22	2.20	2.18
300	4.73	4.48	3.80	3.52	3.39	3.32	3.29	3.27
400	6.31	5.98	5.07	4.69	4.52	4.43	4.39	4.36
500	7.88	7.47	6.33	5.86	5.64	5.54	5.48	5.45
600	9.46	8.96	7.60	7.03	6.77	6.64	6.58	6.54
700	11.03	10.46	8.86	8.21	7.90	7.75	7.67	7.63
800	12.61	11.95	10.13	9.38	9.03	8.85	8.77	8.72
900	14.18	13.44	11.39	10.55	10.16	9.96	9.86	9.81
1000	15.76	14.94	12.66	11.72	11.28	11.07	10.96	10.90
2000	31.51	29.87	25.31	23.44	22.56	22.13	21.91	21.80
3000	47.27	44.80	37.96	35.15	33.84	33.19	32.86	32.69
4000	63.02	59.73	50.61	46.87	45.12	44.25	43.81	43.59
5000	78.77	74.66	63.27	58.58	56.40	55.31	54.76	54.48
6000	94.53	89.59	75.92	70.30	67.68	66.38	65.72	65.38
7000	110.28	104.52	88.57	82.02	78.95	77.44	76.67	76.27
8000	126.03	119.45	101.22	93.73	90.23	88.50	87.62	87.17
9000	141.79	134.38	113.88	105.45	101.51	99.56	98.57	98.06
10000	157.54	149.32	126.53	117.16	112.79	110.62	109.52	108.96
11000	173.29	164.25	139.18	128.88	124.07	121.69	120.48	119.85
12000	189.05	179.18	151.83	140.59	135.35	132.75	131.43	130.75
13000	204.80	194.11	164.49	152.31	146.62	143.81	142.38	141.64
14000	220.56	209.04	177.14	164.03	157.90	154.87	153.33	152.54
15000	236.31	223.97	189.79	175.74	169.18	165.93	164.28	163.43
16000	252.06	238.90	202.44	187.46	180.46	177.00	175.24	174.33
17000	267.82	253.83	215.10	199.17	191.74	188.06	186.19	185.22
18000	283.57	268.76	227.75	210.89	203.02	199.12	197.14	196.12
19000	299.32	283.70	240.40	222.60	214.29	210.18	208.09	207.01
20000	315.08	298.63	253.05	234.32	225.57	221.24	219.04	217.91
21000	330.83	313.56	265.71	246.04	236.85	232.31	230.00	228.80
22000	346.58	328.49	278.36	257.75	248.13	243.37	240.95	239.70
23000	362.34	343.42	291.01	269.47	259.41	254.43	251.90	250.59
24000	378.09	358.35	303.66	281.18	270.69	265.49	262.85	261.49
25000	393.84	373.28	316.32	292.90	281.96	276.55	273.80	272.38
26000	409.60	388.21	328.97	304.61	293.24	287.62	284.76	283.28
27000	425.35	403.14	341.62	316.33	304.52	298.68	295.71	294.17
28000	441.11	418.08	354.27	328.05	315.80	309.74	306.66	305.07
29000	456.86	433.01	366.93	339.76	327.08	320.80	317.61	315.96
30000	472.61	447.94	379.58	351.48	338.36	331.86	328.56	326.86
31000	488.37	462.87	392.23	363.19	349.63	342.93	339.51	337.75
32000	504.12	477.80	404.88	374.91	360.91	353.99	350.47	348.65
33000	519.87	492.73	417.53	386.62	372.19	365.05	361.42	359.54
34000	535.63	507.66	430.19	398.34	383.47	376.11	372.37	370.44
35000	551.38	522.59	442.84	410.06	394.75	387.17	383.32	381.33
40000	630.15	597.25	506.10	468.64	451.14	442.48	438.08	435.81
45000	708.92	671.90	569.36	527.21	507.53	497.79	492.84	490.29
50000	787.68	746.56	632.63	585.79	563.92	553.10	547.60	544.76
55000	866.45	821.21	695.89	644.37	620.31	608.41	602.36	599.24
60000	945.22	895.87	759.15	702.95	676.71	663.72	657.12	653.71
65000	1023.99	970.52	822.41	761.53	733.10	719.03	711.88	708.19
70000	1102.76	1045.18	885.67	820.11	789.49	774.34	766.64	762.66
75000	1181.52	1119.84	948.94	878.69	845.88	829.65	821.40	817.14
80000	1260.29	1194.49	1012.20	937.27	902.27	884.96	876.16	871.62
85000	1339.06	1269.15	1075.46	995.84	958.67	940.27	930.92	926.09
90000	1417.83	1343.80	1138.72	1054.42	1015.06	995.58	985.68	980.57
95000	1496.60	1418.46	1201.99	1113.00	1071.45	1050.89	1040.44	1035.04
100000	1575.36	1493.11	1265.25	1171.58	1127.84	1106.20	1095.20	1089.52
105000	1654.13	1567.77	1328.51	1230.16	1184.23	1161.51	1149.96	1143.99
110000	1732.90	1642.42	1391.77	1288.74	1240.62	1216.82	1204.72	1198.47
115000	1811.67	1717.08	1455.03	1347.32	1297.02	1272.13	1259.48	1252.95
120000	1890.44	1791.73	1518.30	1405.90	1353.41	1327.44	1314.24	1307.42
125000	1969.20	1866.39	1581.56	1464.47	1409.80	1382.75	1369.00	1361.90
130000	2047.97	1941.04	1644.82	1523.05	1466.19	1438.06	1423.76	1416.37
135000	2126.74	2015.70	1708.08	1581.63	1522.58	1493.37	1478.52	1470.85
140000	2205.51	2090.36	1771.34	1640.21	1578.97	1548.68	1533.28	1525.32
145000	2284.28	2165.01	1834.61	1698.79	1635.37	1603.99	1588.04	1579.80
150000	2363.04	2239.67	1897.87	1757.37	1691.76	1659.30	1642.79	1634.28
155000	2441.81	2314.32	1961.13	1815.95	1748.15	1714.61	1697.55	1688.75
160000	2520.58	2388.98	2024.39	1874.53	1804.54	1769.92	1752.31	1743.23

39

13.250% MONTHLY AMORTIZING PAYMENTS

AMOUNT OF LOAN	NUMBER OF YEARS IN TERM							
	1	2	3	4	5	6	7	8
$ 50	4.48	2.39	1.70	1.35	1.15	1.02	.92	.85
100	8.95	4.77	3.39	2.70	2.29	2.03	1.84	1.70
200	17.89	9.54	6.77	5.40	4.58	4.05	3.67	3.39
300	26.84	14.30	10.15	8.09	6.87	6.07	5.50	5.09
400	35.78	19.07	13.53	10.79	9.16	8.09	7.34	6.78
500	44.72	23.83	16.91	13.48	11.45	10.11	9.17	8.48
600	53.67	28.60	20.29	16.18	13.73	12.13	11.00	10.17
700	62.61	33.37	23.68	18.87	16.02	14.15	12.83	11.87
800	71.55	38.13	27.06	21.57	18.31	16.17	14.67	13.56
900	80.50	42.90	30.44	24.26	20.60	18.19	16.50	15.26
1000	89.44	47.66	33.82	26.96	22.89	20.21	18.33	16.95
2000	178.87	95.32	67.63	53.91	45.77	40.42	36.66	33.90
3000	268.31	142.98	101.45	80.86	68.65	60.62	54.99	50.85
4000	357.74	190.64	135.26	107.81	91.53	80.83	73.32	67.79
5000	447.18	238.30	169.08	134.76	114.41	101.04	91.65	84.74
6000	536.61	285.96	202.89	161.72	137.29	121.24	109.97	101.69
7000	626.05	333.62	236.71	188.67	160.17	141.45	128.30	118.64
8000	715.48	381.28	270.52	215.62	183.06	161.66	146.63	135.58
9000	804.92	428.94	304.34	242.57	205.94	181.86	164.96	152.53
10000	894.35	476.60	338.15	269.52	228.82	202.07	183.29	169.48
11000	983.79	524.26	371.96	296.47	251.70	222.27	201.61	186.43
12000	1073.22	571.92	405.78	323.43	274.58	242.48	219.94	203.37
13000	1162.65	619.58	439.59	350.38	297.46	262.69	238.27	220.32
14000	1252.09	667.24	473.41	377.33	320.34	282.89	256.60	237.27
15000	1341.52	714.90	507.22	404.28	343.22	303.10	274.93	254.22
16000	1430.96	762.55	541.04	431.23	366.11	323.31	293.26	271.16
17000	1520.39	810.21	574.85	458.18	388.99	343.51	311.58	288.11
18000	1609.83	857.87	608.67	485.14	411.87	363.72	329.91	305.06
19000	1699.26	905.53	642.48	512.09	434.75	383.92	348.24	322.01
20000	1788.70	953.19	676.29	539.04	457.63	404.13	366.57	338.95
21000	1878.13	1000.85	710.11	565.99	480.51	424.34	384.90	355.90
22000	1967.57	1048.51	743.92	592.94	503.39	444.54	403.22	372.85
23000	2057.00	1096.17	777.74	619.90	526.27	464.75	421.55	389.80
24000	2146.44	1143.83	811.55	646.85	549.16	484.96	439.88	406.74
25000	2235.87	1191.49	845.37	673.80	572.04	505.16	458.21	423.69
26000	2325.30	1239.15	879.18	700.75	594.92	525.37	476.54	440.64
27000	2414.74	1286.81	913.00	727.70	617.80	545.57	494.87	457.58
28000	2504.17	1334.47	946.81	754.65	640.68	565.78	513.19	474.53
29000	2593.61	1382.13	980.63	781.61	663.56	585.99	531.52	491.48
30000	2683.04	1429.79	1014.44	808.56	686.44	606.19	549.85	508.43
31000	2772.48	1477.44	1048.26	835.51	709.32	626.40	568.18	525.37
32000	2861.91	1525.10	1082.07	862.46	732.21	646.61	586.51	542.32
33000	2951.35	1572.76	1115.88	889.41	755.09	666.81	604.83	559.27
34000	3040.78	1620.42	1149.70	916.36	777.97	687.02	623.16	576.22
35000	3130.22	1668.08	1183.51	943.32	800.85	707.23	641.49	593.16
40000	3577.39	1906.38	1352.58	1078.07	915.26	808.26	733.13	677.90
45000	4024.56	2144.68	1521.66	1212.83	1029.66	909.29	824.77	762.64
50000	4471.74	2382.97	1690.73	1347.59	1144.07	1010.32	916.41	847.38
55000	4918.91	2621.27	1859.80	1482.35	1258.47	1111.35	1008.05	932.11
60000	5366.08	2859.57	2028.87	1617.11	1372.88	1212.38	1099.69	1016.85
65000	5813.25	3097.86	2197.95	1751.87	1487.29	1313.41	1191.33	1101.59
70000	6260.43	3336.16	2367.02	1886.63	1601.69	1414.45	1282.98	1186.32
75000	6707.60	3574.46	2536.09	2021.39	1716.10	1515.48	1374.62	1271.06
80000	7154.77	3812.75	2705.16	2156.14	1830.51	1616.51	1466.26	1355.80
85000	7601.95	4051.05	2874.24	2290.90	1944.91	1717.54	1557.90	1440.53
90000	8049.12	4289.35	3043.31	2425.66	2059.32	1818.57	1649.54	1525.27
95000	8496.29	4527.64	3212.38	2560.42	2173.72	1919.60	1741.18	1610.01
100000	8943.47	4765.94	3381.45	2695.18	2288.13	2020.63	1832.82	1694.75
105000	9390.64	5004.24	3550.53	2829.94	2402.54	2121.67	1924.46	1779.48
110000	9837.81	5242.53	3719.60	2964.70	2516.94	2222.70	2016.10	1864.22
115000	10284.99	5480.83	3888.67	3099.46	2631.35	2323.73	2107.74	1948.96
120000	10732.16	5719.13	4057.74	3234.21	2745.76	2424.76	2199.38	2033.69
125000	11179.33	5957.42	4226.82	3368.97	2860.16	2525.79	2291.02	2118.43
130000	11626.50	6195.72	4395.89	3503.73	2974.57	2626.82	2382.66	2203.17
135000	12073.68	6434.02	4564.96	3638.49	3088.97	2727.85	2474.31	2287.90
140000	12520.85	6672.31	4734.03	3773.25	3203.38	2828.89	2565.95	2372.64
145000	12968.02	6910.61	4903.11	3908.01	3317.79	2929.92	2657.59	2457.38
150000	13415.20	7148.91	5072.18	4042.77	3432.19	3030.95	2749.23	2542.12
155000	13862.37	7387.20	5241.25	4177.53	3546.60	3131.98	2840.87	2626.85
160000	14309.54	7625.50	5410.32	4312.28	3661.01	3233.01	2932.51	2711.59

AMOUNT OF LOAN	NUMBER OF YEARS IN TERM							
	9	10	15	20	25	30	35	40
$ 50	.80	.76	.65	.60	.58	.57	.56	.56
100	1.59	1.51	1.29	1.19	1.15	1.13	1.12	1.11
200	3.18	3.02	2.57	2.38	2.30	2.26	2.24	2.22
300	4.77	4.53	3.85	3.57	3.45	3.38	3.35	3.33
400	6.36	6.04	5.13	4.76	4.59	4.51	4.47	4.44
500	7.95	7.54	6.41	5.95	5.74	5.63	5.58	5.55
600	9.54	9.05	7.70	7.14	6.89	6.76	6.70	6.66
700	11.13	10.56	8.98	8.33	8.03	7.89	7.81	7.77
800	12.72	12.07	10.26	9.52	9.18	9.01	8.93	8.88
900	14.31	13.58	11.54	10.71	10.33	10.14	10.04	9.99
1000	15.90	15.08	12.82	11.90	11.47	11.26	11.16	11.10
2000	31.80	30.16	25.64	23.79	22.94	22.52	22.31	22.20
3000	47.70	45.24	38.46	35.69	34.41	33.78	33.46	33.30
4000	63.60	60.32	51.27	47.58	45.87	45.04	44.61	44.40
5000	79.49	75.40	64.09	59.48	57.34	56.29	55.77	55.50
6000	95.39	90.48	76.91	71.37	68.81	67.55	66.92	66.60
7000	111.29	105.56	89.73	83.27	80.27	78.81	78.07	77.70
8000	127.19	120.64	102.54	95.16	91.74	90.07	89.22	88.79
9000	143.08	135.72	115.36	107.05	103.21	101.32	100.38	99.89
10000	158.98	150.79	128.18	118.95	114.68	112.58	111.53	110.99
11000	174.88	165.87	141.00	130.84	126.14	123.84	122.68	122.09
12000	190.78	180.95	153.81	142.74	137.61	135.10	133.83	133.19
13000	206.67	196.03	166.63	154.63	149.08	146.36	144.99	144.29
14000	222.57	211.11	179.45	166.53	160.54	157.61	156.14	155.39
15000	238.47	226.19	192.27	178.42	172.01	168.87	167.29	166.49
16000	254.37	241.27	205.08	190.31	183.48	180.13	178.44	177.58
17000	270.26	256.35	217.90	202.21	194.94	191.39	189.60	188.68
18000	286.16	271.43	230.72	214.10	206.41	202.64	200.75	199.78
19000	302.06	286.50	243.53	226.00	217.88	213.90	211.90	210.88
20000	317.96	301.58	256.35	237.89	229.35	225.16	223.05	221.98
21000	333.85	316.66	269.17	249.79	240.81	236.42	234.21	233.08
22000	349.75	331.74	281.99	261.68	252.28	247.68	245.36	244.18
23000	365.65	346.82	294.80	273.57	263.75	258.93	256.51	255.28
24000	381.55	361.90	307.62	285.47	275.21	270.19	267.66	266.37
25000	397.45	376.98	320.44	297.36	286.68	281.45	278.82	277.47
26000	413.34	392.06	333.26	309.26	298.15	292.71	289.97	288.57
27000	429.24	407.14	346.07	321.15	309.61	303.96	301.12	299.67
28000	445.14	422.21	358.89	333.05	321.08	315.22	312.27	310.77
29000	461.04	437.29	371.71	344.94	332.55	326.48	323.43	321.87
30000	476.93	452.37	384.53	356.83	344.02	337.74	334.58	332.97
31000	492.83	467.45	397.34	368.73	355.48	348.99	345.73	344.06
32000	508.73	482.53	410.16	380.62	366.95	360.25	356.88	355.16
33000	524.63	497.61	422.98	392.52	378.42	371.51	368.03	366.26
34000	540.52	512.69	435.80	404.41	389.88	382.77	379.19	377.36
35000	556.42	527.77	448.61	416.31	401.35	394.03	390.34	388.46
40000	635.91	603.16	512.70	475.78	458.69	450.31	446.10	443.95
45000	715.40	678.56	576.79	535.25	516.02	506.60	501.86	499.45
50000	794.89	753.95	640.87	594.72	573.36	562.89	557.63	554.94
55000	874.37	829.34	704.96	654.19	630.69	619.18	613.39	610.43
60000	953.86	904.74	769.05	713.66	688.03	675.47	669.15	665.93
65000	1033.35	980.13	833.13	773.13	745.36	731.76	724.91	721.42
70000	1112.84	1055.53	897.22	832.61	802.70	788.05	780.67	776.91
75000	1192.33	1130.92	961.31	892.08	860.03	844.34	836.44	832.41
80000	1271.81	1206.32	1025.39	951.55	917.37	900.62	892.20	887.90
85000	1351.30	1281.71	1089.48	1011.02	974.70	956.91	947.96	943.39
90000	1430.79	1357.11	1153.57	1070.49	1032.04	1013.20	1003.72	998.89
95000	1510.28	1432.50	1217.65	1129.96	1089.37	1069.49	1059.49	1054.38
100000	1589.77	1507.89	1281.74	1189.44	1146.71	1125.78	1115.25	1109.87
105000	1669.25	1583.29	1345.83	1248.91	1204.04	1182.07	1171.01	1165.37
110000	1748.74	1658.68	1409.92	1308.38	1261.38	1238.36	1226.77	1220.86
115000	1828.23	1734.08	1474.00	1367.85	1318.71	1294.64	1282.53	1276.36
120000	1907.72	1809.47	1538.09	1427.32	1376.05	1350.93	1338.30	1331.85
125000	1987.21	1884.87	1602.18	1486.79	1433.38	1407.22	1394.06	1387.34
130000	2066.70	1960.26	1666.26	1546.26	1490.72	1463.51	1449.82	1442.84
135000	2146.18	2035.66	1730.35	1605.74	1548.05	1519.80	1505.58	1498.33
140000	2225.67	2111.05	1794.44	1665.21	1605.39	1576.09	1561.34	1553.82
145000	2305.16	2186.44	1858.52	1724.68	1662.72	1632.38	1617.11	1609.32
150000	2384.65	2261.84	1922.61	1784.15	1720.06	1688.67	1672.87	1664.81
155000	2464.14	2337.23	1986.70	1843.62	1777.39	1744.95	1728.63	1720.30
160000	2543.62	2412.63	2050.78	1903.09	1834.73	1801.24	1784.39	1775.80

AMOUNT OF LOAN	NUMBER OF YEARS IN TERM							
	1	2	3	4	5	6	7	8
$ 50	4.48	2.39	1.70	1.36	1.16	1.02	.93	.86
100	8.96	4.78	3.40	2.71	2.31	2.04	1.85	1.71
200	17.92	9.56	6.79	5.42	4.61	4.07	3.70	3.42
300	26.87	14.34	10.19	8.13	6.91	6.11	5.54	5.13
400	35.83	19.12	13.58	10.84	9 21	8.14	7.39	6.84
500	44.78	23 89	16.97	13.54	11.51	10.17	9.24	8.55
600	53.74	28.67	20.37	16.25	13.81	12.21	11.08	10.26
700	62.69	33.45	23.76	18.96	16.11	14.24	12.93	11.97
800	71.65	38.23	27.15	21.67	18.41	16.28	14.78	13.68
900	80.60	43.00	30.55	24.37	20.71	18.31	16.62	15.38
1000	89.56	47.78	33.94	27.08	23.01	20.34	18 47	17.09
2000	179.11	95.56	67.88	54.16	46.02	40.68	36.93	34.18
3000	268.66	143.34	101.81	81.23	69.03	61.02	55.40	51.27
4000	358.21	191.11	135.75	108.31	92.04	81.36	73.86	68.36
5000	447.77	238.89	169.68	135.39	115.05	101.70	92.33	85.45
6000	537.32	286.67	203.62	162.46	138.06	122.04	110.79	102.53
7000	626.87	334.44	237.55	189.54	161.07	142.38	129.26	119.62
8000	716.42	382.22	271.49	216.62	184.08	162.72	147.72	136.71
9000	805.97	430.00	305.42	243.69	207.09	183.06	166.19	153.80
10000	895.53	477.78	339.36	270.77	230.10	203.39	184.65	170.89
11000	985.08	525.55	373.29	297.84	253.11	223.73	203.12	187.97
12000	1074.63	573.33	407.23	324.92	276.12	244.07	221.58	205.06
13000	1164.18	621.11	441.16	352.00	299.13	264.41	240.05	222.15
14000	1253.73	668.88	475.10	379.07	322.14	284.75	258.51	239.24
15000	1343.29	716.66	509.03	406.15	345.15	305.09	276.98	256.33
16000	1432.84	764.44	542.97	433.23	368.16	325.43	295.44	273.42
17000	1522.39	812.21	576.90	460.30	391.17	345.77	313.91	290.50
18000	1611.94	859.99	610.84	487.38	414.18	366.11	332.37	307.59
19000	1701.49	907.77	644.78	514.46	437.19	386.45	350.84	324.68
20000	1791.05	955.55	678.71	541.53	460.20	406.78	369.30	341.77
21000	1880.60	1003.32	712.65	568.61	483.21	427.12	387.77	358.86
22000	1970.15	1051.10	746.58	595.68	506.22	447.46	406.23	375.94
23000	2059.70	1098.88	780.52	622.76	529.23	467.80	424.70	393.03
24000	2149.25	1146.65	814.45	649.84	552.24	488.14	443.16	410.12
25000	2238.81	1194.43	848.39	676.91	575.25	508 48	461.63	427.21
26000	2328.36	1242.21	882.32	703.99	598.26	528.82	480.09	444.30
27000	2417.91	1289.98	916.26	731.07	621.27	549.16	498.56	461.39
28000	2507.46	1337.76	950.19	758.14	644.28	569.50	517.02	478.47
29000	2597.01	1385.54	984.13	785.22	667.29	589.83	535.49	495.56
30000	2686.57	1433.32	1018.06	812.29	690.30	610.17	553.95	512.65
31000	2776.12	1481.09	1052.00	839.37	713.31	630.51	572.42	529.74
32000	2865.67	1528.87	1085.93	866.45	736.32	650.85	590.88	546.83
33000	2955.22	1576.65	1119.87	893.52	759.33	671.19	609.35	563.91
34000	3044.77	1624.42	1153.80	920.60	782.34	691.53	627.81	581.00
35000	3134.33	1672.20	1187.74	947.68	805.35	711.87	646.28	598.09
40000	3582.09	1911.09	1357.42	1083.06	920.40	813.56	738.60	683.53
45000	4029.85	2149.97	1527.09	1218.44	1035.45	915.26	830.93	768.97
50000	4477.61	2388.86	1696.77	1353.82	1150.50	1016.95	923.25	854.41
55000	4925.37	2627.74	1866.45	1489.20	1265.55	1118.65	1015.57	939.85
60000	5373.13	2866.63	2036.12	1624.58	1380.60	1220.34	1107.90	1025.29
65000	5820.89	3105.51	2205.80	1759 97	1495.64	1322.04	1200.22	1110.74
70000	6268.65	3344.40	2375.48	1895.35	1610.69	1423.73	1292.55	1196.18
75000	6716.41	3583.28	2545.15	2030.73	1725.74	1525.43	1384.87	1281.62
80000	7164.17	3822.17	2714.83	2166.11	1840.79	1627.12	1477.20	1367.06
85000	7611.93	4061.05	2884.50	2301.49	1955.84	1728.82	1569.52	1452.50
90000	8059.69	4299.94	3054.18	2436.87	2070.89	1830.51	1661.85	1537.94
95000	8507.45	4538.82	3223.86	2572.26	2185.94	1932.21	1754.17	1623.38
100000	8955.22	4777.71	3393.53	2707.64	2300.99	2033.90	1846.49	1708.82
105000	9402.97	5016.59	3563.21	2843.02	2416.04	2135.60	1938.82	1794.26
110000	9850.73	5255.48	3732.89	2978.40	2531.09	2237.29	2031.14	1879.70
115000	10298.49	5494.36	3902.56	3113.78	2646.14	2338.99	2123.47	1965.14
120000	10746.25	5733.25	4072.24	3249.16	2761.19	2440.68	2215.79	2050.58
125000	11194.01	5972.13	4241.92	3384.55	2876.24	2542.38	2308.12	2136.02
130000	11641.77	6211.02	4411.59	3519.93	2991.28	2644.07	2400.44	2221.47
135000	12089.53	6449.90	4581.27	3655.31	3106.33	2745.76	2492.77	2306.91
140000	12537.29	6688.79	4750.95	3790.69	3221.38	2847.46	2585.09	2392.35
145000	12985.05	6927.67	4920.62	3926.07	3336.43	2949.15	2677.41	2477.79
150000	13432.81	7166.56	5090.30	4061.45	3451.48	3050.85	2769.74	2563.23
155000	13880.57	7405.44	5259.97	4196.84	3566.53	3152.54	2862.06	2648.67
160000	14328.33	7644.33	5429.65	4332.22	3681.58	3254.24	2954.39	2734.11

AMOUNT OF LOAN	NUMBER OF YEARS IN TERM							
	9	10	15	20	25	30	35	40
$ 50	.81	.77	.65	.61	.59	.58	.57	.57
100	1.61	1.53	1.30	1.21	1.17	1.15	1.14	1.14
200	3.21	3.05	2.60	2.42	2.34	2.30	2.28	2.27
300	4.82	4.57	3.90	3.63	3.50	3.44	3.41	3.40
400	6.42	6.10	5.20	4.83	4 67	4.59	4.55	4.53
500	8.03	7.62	6.50	6.04	5.83	5.73	5.68	5.66
600	9.63	9.14	7.79	7.25	7.00	6.88	6.82	6.79
700	11.23	10.66	9.09	8.46	8.16	8.02	7.95	7.92
800	12.84	12.19	10.39	9.66	9.33	9.17	9.09	9.05
900	14.44	13.71	11.69	10.87	10.50	10.31	10.22	10.18
1000	16.05	15.23	12.99	12.08	11.66	11.46	11.36	11.31
2000	32.09	30.46	25.97	24.15	23.32	22.91	22.71	22.61
3000	48.13	45.69	38.95	36.23	34.97	34.37	34.07	33.91
4000	64.17	60.91	51.94	48.30	46.63	45.82	45.42	45.22
5000	80.22	76.14	64.92	60.37	58.29	57.28	56.77	56.52
6000	96.26	91.37	77.90	72.45	69.94	68.73	68.13	67.82
7000	112.30	106.60	90.89	84.52	81.60	80.18	79.48	79.12
8000	128.34	121.82	103.87	96.59	93.26	91.64	90.83	90.43
9000	144.39	137.05	116.85	108.67	104.91	103.09	102 19	101.73
10000	160.43	152.28	129.84	120.74	116.57	114.55	113.54	113.03
11000	176.47	167.51	142.82	132.82	128.23	126.00	124.89	124.33
12000	192.51	182.73	155.80	144.89	139.88	137.45	136.25	135.64
13000	208.56	197.96	168.79	156.96	151.54	148.91	147.60	146.94
14000	224.60	213.19	181.77	169.04	163.20	160.36	158.95	158.24
15000	240.64	228.42	194.75	181.11	174.85	171.82	170.31	169.54
16000	256.68	243.64	207.74	193.18	186.51	183.27	181.66	180.85
17000	272.72	258.87	220.72	205.26	198.16	194.73	193.01	192.15
18000	288.77	274.10	233.70	217.33	209.82	206.18	204.37	203.45
19000	304.81	289.33	246.69	229.41	221.48	217.63	215.72	214.75
20000	320.85	304.55	259.67	241.48	233.13	229.09	227.07	226.06
21000	336.89	319.78	272.65	253.55	244.79	240.54	238.43	237.36
22000	352.94	335.01	285.64	265.63	256.45	252.00	249.78	248.66
23000	368.98	350.24	298.62	277.70	268.10	263.45	261.13	259.97
24000	385.02	365.46	311.60	289.77	279.76	274.90	272.49	271.27
25000	401.06	380.69	324.58	301.85	291.42	286.36	283.84	282.57
26000	417.11	395.92	337.57	313.92	303.07	297.81	295.19	293.87
27000	433.15	411.15	350.55	326.00	314.73	309.27	306.55	305.18
28000	449.19	426.37	363.53	338.07	326.39	320.72	317.90	316.48
29000	465.23	441.60	376.52	350.14	338.04	332.17	329.25	327.78
30000	481.27	456.83	389.50	362.22	349.70	343.63	340.61	339.08
31000	497.32	472.06	402.48	374.29	361.35	355.08	351.96	350.39
32000	513.36	487.28	415.47	386.36	373.01	366.54	363.31	361.69
33000	529.40	502.51	428.45	398.44	384.67	377.99	374.67	372.99
34000	545.44	517.74	441.43	410.51	396.32	389.45	386.02	384.29
35000	561.49	532.97	454.42	422.59	407.98	400.90	397.37	395.60
40000	641.70	609.10	519.33	482.95	466.26	458.17	454.14	452.11
45000	721.91	685.24	584.25	543.32	524.55	515.44	510.91	508.62
50000	802.12	761.38	649.16	603.69	582.83	572.71	567.68	565.14
55000	882.33	837.51	714.08	664.06	641.11	629.98	624.44	621.65
60000	962.54	913.65	779.00	724.43	699.39	687.25	681.21	678.16
65000	1042.76	989.79	843.91	784.80	757.67	744.52	737.98	734.67
70000	1122.97	1065.93	908.83	845.17	815.96	801.79	794.74	791.19
75000	1203.18	1142.06	973.74	905.54	874.24	859.06	851.51	847.70
80000	1283.39	1218.20	1038.66	965.90	932.52	916.33	908.28	904.21
85000	1363.60	1294.34	1103.58	1026.27	990.80	973.61	965.04	960.73
90000	1443.81	1370.47	1168.49	1086.64	1049.09	1030.88	1021.81	1017.24
95000	1524.02	1446.61	1233.41	1147.01	1107.37	1088.15	1078.58	1073.75
100000	1604.24	1522.75	1298.32	1207.38	1165.65	1145.42	1135.35	1130.27
105000	1684.45	1598.89	1363.24	1267.75	1223.93	1202.69	1192.11	1186.78
110000	1764.66	1675.02	1428.16	1328.12	1282.21	1259.96	1248.88	1243.29
115000	1844.87	1751.16	1493.07	1388.49	1340.50	1317.23	1305.65	1299.81
120000	1925.08	1827.30	1557.99	1448.85	1398.78	1374.50	1362.41	1356.32
125000	2005.29	1903.43	1622.90	1509.22	1457.06	1431.77	1419.18	1412.83
130000	2085.51	1979.57	1687.82	1569.59	1515.34	1489.04	1475.95	1469.34
135000	2165.72	2055.71	1752.74	1629.96	1573.63	1546.31	1532.71	1525.86
140000	2245.93	2131.85	1817.65	1690.33	1631.91	1603.58	1589.48	1582.37
145000	2326.14	2207.98	1882.57	1750.70	1690.19	1660.85	1646.25	1638.88
150000	2406.35	2284.12	1947.48	1811.07	1748.47	1718.12	1703.02	1695.40
155000	2486.56	2360.26	2012.40	1871.44	1806.75	1775.39	1759.78	1751.91
160000	2566.78	2436.39	2077.31	1931.80	1865.04	1832.66	1816.55	1808.42

13.750% MONTHLY AMORTIZING PAYMENTS

AMOUNT OF LOAN	NUMBER OF YEARS IN TERM							
	1	2	3	4	5	6	7	8
$ 50	4.49	2.40	1.71	1.37	1.16	1.03	.94	.87
100	8.97	4.79	3.41	2.73	2.32	2.05	1.87	1.73
200	17.94	9.58	6.82	5.45	4.63	4.10	3.73	3.45
300	26.91	14.37	10.22	8.17	6.95	6.15	5.59	5.17
400	35.87	19.16	13.63	10.89	9.26	8.19	7.45	6.90
500	44.84	23.95	17.03	13.61	11.57	10.24	9.31	8.62
600	53.81	28.74	20.44	16.33	13.89	12.29	11.17	10.34
700	62.77	33.53	23.84	19.05	16.20	14.34	13.03	12.07
800	71.74	38.32	27.25	21.77	18.52	16.38	14.89	13.79
900	80.71	43.11	30.66	24.49	20.83	18.43	16.75	15.51
1000	89.67	47.90	34.06	27.21	23.14	20.48	18.61	17.23
2000	179.34	95.79	68.12	54.41	46.28	40.95	37.21	34.46
3000	269.01	143.69	102.17	81.61	69.42	61.42	55.81	51.69
4000	358.68	191.58	136.23	108.81	92.56	81.89	74.41	68.92
5000	448.35	239.48	170.29	136.01	115.70	102.37	93.02	86.15
6000	538.02	287.37	204.34	163.21	138.84	122.84	111.62	103.38
7000	627.69	335.27	238.40	190.41	161.98	143.31	130.22	120.61
8000	717.36	383.16	272.46	217.61	185.12	163.78	148.82	137.84
9000	807.03	431.06	306.51	244.82	208.25	184.25	167.42	155.07
10000	896.70	478.95	340.57	272.02	231.39	204.73	186.03	172.30
11000	986.37	526.85	374.62	299.22	254.53	225.20	204.63	189.53
12000	1076.04	574.74	408.68	326.42	277.67	245.67	223.23	206.76
13000	1165.71	622.64	442.74	353.62	300.81	266.14	241.83	223.99
14000	1255.38	670.53	476.79	380.82	323.95	286.61	260.44	241.22
15000	1345.05	718.43	510.85	408.02	347.09	307.09	279.04	258.45
16000	1434.72	766.32	544.91	435.22	370.23	327.56	297.64	275.68
17000	1524.39	814.22	578.96	462.43	393.37	348.03	316.24	292.91
18000	1614.06	862.11	613.02	489.63	416.50	368.50	334.84	310.14
19000	1703.73	910.01	647.08	516.83	439.64	388.98	353.45	327.37
20000	1793.40	957.90	681.13	544.03	462.78	409.45	372.05	344.60
21000	1883.07	1005.80	715.19	571.23	485.92	429.92	390.65	361.83
22000	1972.73	1053.69	749.24	598.43	509.06	450.39	409.25	379.05
23000	2062.40	1101.59	783.30	625.63	532.20	470.86	427.86	396.28
24000	2152.07	1149.48	817.36	652.83	555.34	491.34	446.46	413.51
25000	2241.74	1197.38	851.41	680.04	578.48	511.81	465.06	430.74
26000	2331.41	1245.27	885.47	707.24	601.61	532.28	483.66	447.97
27000	2421.08	1293.17	919.53	734.44	624.75	552.75	502.26	465.20
28000	2510.75	1341.06	953.58	761.64	647.89	573.22	520.87	482.43
29000	2600.42	1388.96	987.64	788.84	671.03	593.70	539.47	499.66
30000	2690.09	1436.85	1021.69	816.04	694.17	614.17	558.07	516.89
31000	2779.76	1484.75	1055.75	843.24	717.31	634.64	576.67	534.12
32000	2869.43	1532.64	1089.81	870.44	740.45	655.11	595.27	551.35
33000	2959.10	1580.54	1123.86	897.65	763.59	675.58	613.88	568.58
34000	3048.77	1628.43	1157.92	924.85	786.73	696.06	632.48	585.81
35000	3138.44	1676.33	1191.98	952.05	809.86	716.53	651.08	603.04
40000	3586.79	1915.80	1362.26	1088.05	925.56	818.89	744.09	689.19
45000	4035.13	2155.27	1532.54	1224.06	1041.25	921.25	837.10	775.33
50000	4483.48	2394.75	1702.82	1360.07	1156.95	1023.61	930.11	861.48
55000	4931.83	2634.22	1873.10	1496.07	1272.64	1125.97	1023.12	947.63
60000	5380.18	2873.70	2043.38	1632.08	1388.34	1228.33	1116.14	1033.78
65000	5828.52	3113.17	2213.67	1768.09	1504.03	1330.69	1209.15	1119.92
70000	6276.87	3352.65	2383.95	1904.09	1619.72	1433.05	1302.16	1206.07
75000	6725.22	3592.12	2554.23	2040.10	1735.42	1535.41	1395.17	1292.22
80000	7173.57	3831.59	2724.51	2176.10	1851.11	1637.77	1488.18	1378.37
85000	7621.92	4071.07	2894.79	2312.11	1966.81	1740.13	1581.19	1464.51
90000	8070.26	4310.54	3065.07	2448.12	2082.50	1842.50	1674.20	1550.66
95000	8518.61	4550.02	3235.36	2584.12	2198.20	1944.86	1767.21	1636.81
100000	8966.96	4789.49	3405.64	2720.13	2313.89	2047.22	1860.22	1722.96
105000	9415.31	5028.97	3575.92	2856.13	2429.58	2149.58	1953.23	1809.11
110000	9863.65	5268.44	3746.20	2992.14	2545.28	2251.94	2046.24	1895.25
115000	10312.00	5507.91	3916.48	3128.15	2660.97	2354.30	2139.26	1981.40
120000	10760.35	5747.39	4086.76	3264.15	2776.67	2456.66	2232.27	2067.55
125000	11208.70	5986.86	4257.05	3400.16	2892.36	2559.02	2325.28	2153.70
130000	11657.04	6226.34	4427.33	3536.17	3008.05	2661.38	2418.29	2239.84
135000	12105.39	6465.81	4597.61	3672.17	3123.75	2763.74	2511.30	2325.99
140000	12553.74	6705.29	4767.89	3808.18	3239.44	2866.10	2604.31	2412.14
145000	13002.09	6944.76	4938.17	3944.18	3355.14	2968.46	2697.32	2498.29
150000	13450.43	7184.23	5108.45	4080.19	3470.83	3070.82	2790.33	2584.43
155000	13898.78	7423.71	5278.74	4216.20	3586.53	3173.18	2883.34	2670.58
160000	14347.13	7663.18	5449.02	4352.20	3702.22	3275.54	2976.35	2756.73

44

AMOUNT OF LOAN	NUMBER OF YEARS IN TERM							
	9	10	15	20	25	30	35	40
$ 50	.81	.77	.66	.62	.60	.59	.58	.58
100	1.62	1.54	1.32	1.23	1.19	1.17	1.16	1.16
200	3.24	3.08	2.63	2.46	2.37	2.34	2 32	2.31
300	4.86	4.62	3.95	3.68	3.56	3.50	3.47	3.46
400	6.48	6.16	5.26	4.91	4.74	4.67	4.63	4.61
500	8.10	7.69	6.58	6.13	5.93	5.83	5.78	5.76
600	9.72	9.23	7.89	7.36	7.11	7.00	6.94	6.91
700	11.34	10.77	9.21	8.58	8.30	8 16	8.09	8.06
800	12.96	12.31	10.52	9.81	9.48	9.33	9.25	9.21
900	14.57	13.84	11.84	11.03	10.67	10.49	10.40	10.36
1000	16.19	15.38	13.15	12.26	11.85	11.66	11.56	11.51
2000	32.38	30.76	26.30	24.51	23.70	23.31	23.11	23.02
3000	48.57	46.14	39.45	36.77	35.54	34.96	34.67	34.53
4000	64.76	61.51	52.60	49.02	47.39	46.61	46.22	46.03
5000	80.94	76.89	65.75	61.28	59.24	58.26	57.78	57.54
6000	97.13	92.27	78.90	73.53	71.08	69.91	69.33	69.05
7000	113.32	107.64	92.05	85.78	82.93	81.56	80.89	80.55
8000	129.51	123.02	105.20	98.04	94.78	93.21	92.44	92.06
9000	145.69	138.40	118.35	110.29	106.62	104.87	104.00	103.57
10000	161.88	153.77	131.50	122.55	118.47	116.52	115.55	115.07
11000	178.07	169.15	144.65	134.80	130.32	128.17	127.11	126.58
12000	194.26	184.53	157.80	147.05	142.16	139.82	138.66	138.09
13000	210.44	199.90	170.95	159.31	154.01	151.47	150.22	149.59
14000	226.63	215.28	184.10	171.56	165.86	163.12	161.77	161.10
15000	242.82	230.66	197.25	183.82	177.70	174.77	173.33	172.61
16000	259.01	246.03	210.40	196.07	189.55	186.42	184.88	184.11
17000	275.20	261.41	223.55	208.32	201.40	198.07	196.44	195.62
18000	291.38	276.79	236.70	220.58	213.24	209.73	207.99	207.13
19000	307.57	292.16	249.85	232.83	225.09	221.38	219.55	218.64
20000	323.76	307.54	263.00	245.09	236.94	233.03	231.10	230.14
21000	339.95	322.92	276.15	257.34	248.78	244.68	242.66	241.65
22000	356.13	338.29	289.30	269.59	260.63	256.33	254.21	253.16
23000	372.32	353.67	302.45	281.85	272.48	267.98	265.77	264.66
24000	388.51	369.05	315.60	294.10	284.32	279.63	277.32	276.17
25000	404.70	384.42	328.75	306.36	296.17	291.28	288.88	287.68
26000	420.88	399.80	341.90	318.61	308.02	302.93	300.43	299.18
27000	437.07	415.18	355.05	330.86	319.86	314.59	311.99	310.69
28000	453.26	430.55	368.20	343.12	331.71	326.24	323.54	322.20
29000	469.45	445.93	381.35	355.37	343.56	337.89	335.10	333.70
30000	485.64	461.31	394.50	367.63	355.40	349.54	346.65	345.21
31000	501.82	476.68	407.65	379.88	367.25	361.19	358.21	356.72
32000	518.01	492.06	420.80	392.13	379.10	372.84	369.76	368.22
33000	534.20	507.44	433.95	404.39	390.94	384.49	381.32	379.73
34000	550.39	522.81	447.10	416.64	402.79	396.14	392.87	391.24
35000	566.57	538.19	460.25	428.90	414.64	407.79	404.42	402.74
40000	647.51	615.07	526.00	490.17	473.87	466.05	462.20	460.28
45000	728.45	691.96	591.75	551.44	533.10	524.31	519.97	517.81
50000	809.39	768.84	657.50	612.71	592.34	582.56	577.75	575.35
55000	890.33	845.72	723.25	673.98	651.57	640.82	635.52	632.88
60000	971.27	922.61	789.00	735.25	710.80	699.07	693.30	690.42
65000	1052.20	999.49	854.75	796.52	770.04	757.33	751.07	747.95
70000	1133.14	1076.37	920.50	857.79	829.27	815.58	808.84	805.48
75000	1214.08	1153.26	986.25	919.06	888.50	873.84	866.62	863.02
80000	1295.02	1230.14	1051.99	980.33	947.74	932.10	924.39	920.55
85000	1375.96	1307.02	1117.74	1041.60	1006.97	990.35	982.17	978.09
90000	1456.90	1383.91	1183.49	1102.87	1066.20	1048.61	1039.94	1035.62
95000	1537.83	1460.79	1249.24	1164.14	1125.44	1106.86	1097.72	1093.16
100000	1618.77	1537.67	1314.99	1225.41	1184.67	1165.12	1155.49	1150.69
105000	1699.71	1614.56	1380.74	1286.68	1243.90	1223.37	1213.26	1208.22
110000	1780.65	1691.44	1446.49	1347.95	1303.14	1281.63	1271.04	1265.76
115000	1861.59	1768.32	1512.24	1409.22	1362.37	1339.88	1328.81	1323.29
120000	1942.53	1845.21	1577.99	1470.49	1421.60	1398.14	1386.59	1380.83
125000	2023.46	1922.09	1643.74	1531.76	1480.84	1456.40	1444.36	1438.36
130000	2104.40	1998.97	1709.49	1593.03	1540.07	1514.65	1502.14	1495.90
135000	2185.34	2075.86	1775.24	1654.30	1599.30	1572.91	1559.91	1553.43
140000	2266.28	2152.74	1840.99	1715.57	1658.54	1631.16	1617.68	1610.96
145000	2347.22	2229.62	1906.74	1776.84	1717.77	1689.42	1675.46	1668.50
150000	2428.16	2306.51	1972.49	1838.11	1777.00	1747.67	1733.23	1726.03
155000	2509.09	2383.39	2038.24	1899.38	1836.24	1805.93	1791.01	1783.57
160000	2590.03	2460.27	2103.98	1960.65	1895.47	1864.19	1848.78	1841.10

AMOUNT OF LOAN	NUMBER OF YEARS IN TERM							
	1	2	3	4	5	6	7	8
$ 50	4.49	2.41	1.71	1.37	1.17	1.04	.94	.87
100	8.98	4.81	3.42	2.74	2.33	2.07	1.88	1.74
200	17.96	9.61	6.84	5.47	4.66	4.13	3.75	3.48
300	26.94	14.41	10.26	8.20	6.99	6.19	5.63	5.22
400	35.92	19.21	13.68	10.94	9.31	8.25	7.50	6.95
500	44.90	24.01	17.09	13.67	11.64	10.31	9.38	8.69
600	53.88	28.81	20.51	16.40	13.97	12.37	11.25	10.43
700	62.86	33.61	23.93	19.13	16.29	14.43	13.12	12.17
800	71.83	38.42	27.35	21.87	18.62	16.49	15.00	13.90
900	80.81	43.22	30.76	24.60	20.95	18.55	16.87	15.64
1000	89.79	48.02	34.18	27.33	23.27	20.61	18.75	17.38
2000	179.58	96.03	68.36	54.66	46.54	41.22	37.49	34.75
3000	269.37	144.04	102.54	81.98	69.81	61.82	56.23	52.12
4000	359.15	192.06	136.72	109.31	93.08	82.43	74.97	69.49
5000	448.94	240.07	170.89	136.64	116.35	103.03	93.71	86.86
6000	538.73	288.08	205.07	163.96	139.61	123.64	112.45	104.23
7000	628.51	336.10	239.25	191.29	162.88	144.25	131.19	121.61
8000	718.30	384.11	273.43	218.62	186.15	164.85	149.93	138.98
9000	808.09	432.12	307.60	245.94	209.42	185.46	168.67	156.35
10000	897.88	480.13	341.78	273.27	232.69	206.06	187.41	173.72
11000	987.66	528.15	375.96	300.60	255.96	226.67	206.15	191.09
12000	1077.45	576.16	410.14	327.92	279.22	247.27	224.89	208.46
13000	1167.24	624.17	444.31	355.25	302.49	267.88	243.63	225.83
14000	1257.02	672.19	478.49	382.58	325.76	288.49	262.37	243.21
15000	1346.81	720.20	512.67	409.90	349.03	309.09	281.11	260.58
16000	1436.60	768.21	546.85	437.23	372.30	329.70	299.85	277.95
17000	1526.39	816.22	581.02	464.56	395.57	350.30	318.59	295.32
18000	1616.17	864.24	615.20	491.88	418.83	370.91	337.33	312.69
19000	1705.96	912.25	649.38	519.21	442.10	391.51	356.07	330.06
20000	1795.75	960.26	683.56	546.53	465.37	412.12	374.81	347.44
21000	1885.53	1008.28	717.74	573.86	488.64	432.73	393.55	364.81
22000	1975.32	1056.29	751.91	601.19	511.91	453.33	412.29	382.18
23000	2065.11	1104.30	786.09	628.51	535.17	473.94	431.03	399.55
24000	2154.90	1152.31	820.27	655.84	558.44	494.54	449.77	416.92
25000	2244.68	1200.33	854.45	683.17	581.71	515.15	468.51	434.29
26000	2334.47	1248.34	888.62	710.49	604.98	535.75	487.25	451.66
27000	2424.26	1296.35	922.80	737.82	628.25	556.36	505.99	469.04
28000	2514.04	1344.37	956.98	765.15	651.52	576.97	524.73	486.41
29000	2603.83	1392.38	991.16	792.47	674.78	597.57	543.47	503.78
30000	2693.62	1440.39	1025.33	819.80	698.05	618.18	562.21	521.15
31000	2783.41	1488.40	1059.51	847.13	721.32	638.78	580.95	538.52
32000	2873.19	1536.42	1093.69	874.45	744.59	659.39	599.69	555.89
33000	2962.98	1584.43	1127.87	901.78	767.86	679.99	618.43	573.26
34000	3052.77	1632.44	1162.04	929.11	791.13	700.60	637.17	590.64
35000	3142.55	1680.46	1196.22	956.43	814.39	721.21	655.91	608.01
40000	3591.49	1920.52	1367.11	1093.06	930.74	824.23	749.61	694.87
45000	4040.43	2160.58	1538.00	1229.70	1047.08	927.26	843.31	781.72
50000	4489.36	2400.65	1708.89	1366.33	1163.42	1030.29	937.0i	868.58
55000	4938.30	2640.71	1879.79	1502.96	1279.76	1133.32	1030.71	955.44
60000	5387.23	2880.78	2050.66	1639.59	1396.10	1236.35	1124.41	1042.30
65000	5836.17	3120.84	2221.55	1776.23	1512.44	1339.38	1218.11	1129.15
70000	6285.10	3360.91	2392.44	1912.86	1628.78	1442.41	1311.81	1216.01
75000	6734.04	3600.97	2563.33	2049.49	1745.12	1545.44	1405.51	1302.87
80000	7182.97	3841.04	2734.22	2186.12	1861.47	1648.46	1499.21	1389.73
85000	7631.91	4081.10	2905.10	2322.76	1977.81	1751.49	1592.91	1476.58
90000	8080.85	4321.16	3075.99	2459.39	2094.15	1854.52	1686.61	1563.44
95000	8529.78	4561.23	3246.88	2596.02	2210.49	1957.55	1780.31	1650.30
100000	8978.72	4801.29	3417.77	2732.65	2326.83	2060.58	1874.01	1737.16
105000	9427.65	5041.36	3588.66	2869.29	2443.17	2163.61	1967.71	1824.01
110000	9876.59	5281.42	3759.54	3005.92	2559.51	2266.64	2061.41	1910.87
115000	10325.52	5521.49	3930.43	3142.55	2675.85	2369.67	2155.11	1997.73
120000	10774.46	5761.55	4101.32	3279.18	2792.20	2472.69	2248.81	2084.59
125000	11223.40	6001.62	4272.21	3415.81	2908.54	2575.72	2342.51	2171.44
130000	11672.33	6241.68	4443.10	3552.45	3024.88	2678.75	2436.21	2258.30
135000	12121.27	6481.74	4613.98	3689.08	3141.22	2781.78	2529.91	2345.16
140000	12570.20	6721.81	4784.87	3825.71	3257.56	2884.81	2623.61	2432.02
145000	13019.14	6961.87	4955.76	3962.34	3373.90	2987.84	2717.31	2518.87
150000	13468.07	7201.94	5126.65	4098.98	3490.24	3090.87	2811.01	2605.73
155000	13917.01	7442.00	5297.54	4235.61	3606.58	3193.89	2904.71	2692.59
160000	14365.94	7682.07	5468.43	4372.24	3722.93	3296.92	2998.41	2779.45

MONTHLY AMORTIZING PAYMENTS 14.000%

AMOUNT OF LOAN	NUMBER OF YEARS IN TERM							
	9	10	15	20	25	30	35	40
$ 50	.82	.78	.67	.63	.61	.60	.59	.59
100	1.64	1.56	1.34	1.25	1.21	1.19	1.18	1.18
200	3.27	3.11	2.67	2.49	2.41	2.37	2.36	2.35
300	4.91	4.66	4.00	3.74	3.62	3.56	3.53	3.52
400	6.54	6.22	5.33	4.98	4.82	4.74	4.71	4.69
500	8.17	7.77	6.66	6.22	6.02	5.93	5.88	5.86
600	9.81	9.32	8.00	7.47	7.23	7.11	7.06	7.03
700	11.44	10.87	9.33	8.71	8.43	8.30	8.23	8.20
800	13.07	12.43	10.66	9.95	9.64	9.48	9.41	9.37
900	14.71	13.98	11.99	11.20	10.84	10.67	10.59	10.55
1000	16.34	15.53	13.32	12.44	12.04	11.85	11.76	11.72
2000	32.67	31.06	26.64	24.88	24.08	23.70	23.52	23.43
3000	49.01	46.58	39.96	37.31	36.12	35.55	35.28	35.14
4000	65.34	62.11	53.27	49.75	48.16	47.40	47.03	46.85
5000	81.67	77.64	66.59	62.18	60.19	59.25	58.79	58.56
6000	98.01	93.16	79.91	74.62	72.23	71.10	70.55	70.27
7000	114.34	108.69	93.23	87.05	84.27	82.95	82.30	81.98
8000	130.67	124.22	106.54	99.49	96.31	94.79	94.06	93.70
9000	147.01	139.74	119.86	111.92	108.34	106.64	105.82	105.41
10000	163.34	155.27	133.18	124.36	120.38	118.49	117.57	117.12
11000	179.68	170.80	146.50	136.79	132.42	130.34	129.33	128.83
12000	196.01	186.32	159.81	149.23	144.46	142.19	141.09	140.54
13000	212.34	201.85	173.13	161.66	156.49	154.04	152.84	152.25
14000	228.68	217.38	186.45	174.10	168.53	165.89	164.60	163.96
15000	245.01	232.90	199.77	186.53	180.57	177.74	176.36	175.68
16000	261.34	248.43	213.08	198.97	192.61	189.58	188.11	187.39
17000	277.68	263.96	226.40	211.40	204.64	201.43	199.87	199.10
18000	294.01	279.48	239.72	223.84	216.68	213.28	211.63	210.81
19000	310.35	295.01	253.04	236.27	228.72	225.13	223.38	222.52
20000	326.68	310.54	266.35	248.71	240.76	236.98	235.14	234.23
21000	343.01	326.06	279.67	261.14	252.79	248.83	246.90	245.94
22000	359.35	341.59	292.99	273.58	264.83	260.68	258.65	257.66
23000	375.68	357.12	306.31	286.01	276.87	272.53	270.41	269.37
24000	392.01	372.64	319.62	298.45	288.91	284.37	282.17	281.08
25000	408.35	388.17	332.94	310.89	300.95	296.22	293.92	292.79
26000	424.68	403.70	346.26	323.32	312.98	308.07	305.68	304.50
27000	441.01	419.22	359.58	335.76	325.02	319.92	317.44	316.21
28000	457.35	434.75	372.89	348.19	337.06	331.77	329.19	327.92
29000	473.68	450.28	386.21	360.63	349.10	343.62	340.95	339.64
30000	490.02	465.80	399.53	373.06	361.13	355.47	352.71	351.35
31000	506.35	481.33	412.84	385.50	373.17	367.32	364.46	363.06
32000	522.68	496.86	426.16	397.93	385.21	379.16	376.22	374.77
33000	539.02	512.38	439.48	410.37	397.25	391.01	387.98	386.48
34000	555.35	527.91	452.80	422.80	409.28	402.86	399.73	398.19
35000	571.68	543.44	466.11	435.24	421.32	414.71	411.49	409.90
40000	653.35	621.07	532.70	497.41	481.51	473.95	470.27	468.46
45000	735.02	698.70	599.29	559.59	541.70	533.20	529.06	527.02
50000	816.69	776.34	665.88	621.77	601.89	592.44	587.84	585.58
55000	898.36	853.97	732.46	683.94	662.07	651.68	646.63	644.13
60000	980.03	931.60	799.05	746.12	722.26	710.93	705.41	702.69
65000	1061.70	1009.24	865.64	808.29	782.45	770.17	764.19	761.25
70000	1143.36	1086.87	932.22	870.47	842.64	829.42	822.98	819.80
75000	1225.03	1164.50	998.81	932.65	902.83	888.66	881.76	878.36
80000	1306.70	1242.14	1065.40	994.82	963.01	947.90	940.54	936.92
85000	1388.37	1319.77	1131.99	1057.00	1023.20	1007.15	999.33	995.47
90000	1470.04	1397.40	1198.57	1119.17	1083.39	1066.39	1058.11	1054.03
95000	1551.71	1475.04	1265.16	1181.35	1143.58	1125.63	1116.89	1112.59
100000	1633.38	1552.67	1331.75	1243.53	1203.77	1184.88	1175.68	1171.15
105000	1715.04	1630.30	1398.33	1305.70	1263.95	1244.12	1234.46	1229.70
110000	1796.71	1707.94	1464.92	1367.88	1324.14	1303.36	1293.25	1288.26
115000	1878.38	1785.57	1531.51	1430.05	1384.33	1362.61	1352.03	1346.82
120000	1960.05	1863.20	1598.09	1492.23	1444.52	1421.85	1410.81	1405.37
125000	2041.72	1940.84	1664.68	1554.41	1504.71	1481.09	1469.60	1463.93
130000	2123.39	2018.47	1731.27	1616.58	1564.89	1540.34	1528.38	1522.49
135000	2205.05	2096.10	1797.86	1678.76	1625.08	1599.58	1587.16	1581.04
140000	2286.72	2173.74	1864.44	1740.93	1685.27	1658.83	1645.95	1639.60
145000	2368.39	2251.37	1931.03	1803.11	1745.46	1718.07	1704.73	1698.16
150000	2450.06	2329.00	1997.62	1865.29	1805.65	1777.31	1763.51	1756.72
155000	2531.73	2406.63	2064.20	1927.46	1865.83	1836.56	1822.30	1815.27
160000	2613.40	2484.27	2130.79	1989.64	1926.02	1895.80	1881.08	1873.83

14.250% MONTHLY AMORTIZING PAYMENTS

AMOUNT OF LOAN	NUMBER OF YEARS IN TERM							
	1	2	3	4	5	6	7	8
$ 50	4.50	2.41	1.72	1.38	1.17	1.04	.95	.88
100	9.00	4.82	3.43	2.75	2.34	2.08	1.89	1.76
200	17.99	9.63	6.86	5.50	4.68	4.15	3.78	3.51
300	26.98	14.44	10.29	8.24	7.02	6.23	5.67	5.26
400	35.97	19.26	13.72	10.99	9.36	8.30	7.56	7.01
500	44.96	24.07	17.15	13.73	11.70	10.37	9.44	8.76
600	53.95	28.88	20.58	16.48	14.04	12.45	11.33	10.51
700	62.94	33.70	24.01	19.22	16.38	14.52	13.22	12.26
800	71.93	38.51	27.44	21.97	18.72	16.60	15.11	14.02
900	80.92	43.32	30.87	24.71	21.06	18.67	17.00	15.77
1000	89.91	48.14	34.30	27.46	23.40	20.74	18.88	17.52
2000	179.81	96.27	68.60	54.91	46.80	41.48	37.76	35.03
3000	269.72	144.40	102.90	82.36	70.20	62.22	56.64	52.55
4000	359.62	192.53	137.20	109.81	93.60	82.96	75.52	70.06
5000	449.53	240.66	171.50	137.27	117.00	103.70	94.40	87.58
6000	539.43	288.79	205.80	164.72	140.39	124.44	113.28	105.09
7000	629.34	336.92	240.10	192.17	163.79	145.18	132.15	122.60
8000	719.24	385.05	274.40	219.62	187.19	165.92	151.03	140.12
9000	809.15	433.18	308.70	247.07	210.59	186.66	169.91	157.63
10000	899.05	481.32	343.00	274.53	233.99	207.40	188.79	175.15
11000	988.96	529.45	377.30	301.98	257.38	228.14	207.67	192.66
12000	1078.86	577.58	411.60	329.43	280.78	248.88	226.55	210.17
13000	1168.77	625.71	445.89	356.88	304.18	269.62	245.42	227.69
14000	1258.67	673.84	480.19	384.33	327.58	290.36	264.30	245.20
15000	1348.58	721.97	514.49	411.79	350.98	311.10	283.18	262.72
16000	1438.48	770.10	548.79	439.24	374.37	331.84	302.06	280.23
17000	1528.39	818.23	583.09	466.69	397.77	352.58	320.94	297.74
18000	1618.29	866.36	617.39	494.14	421.17	373.32	339.82	315.26
19000	1708.20	914.50	651.69	521.59	444.57	394.06	358.69	332.77
20000	1798.10	962.63	685.99	549.05	467.97	414.80	377.57	350.29
21000	1888.01	1010.76	720.29	576.50	491.36	435.54	396.45	367.80
22000	1977.91	1058.89	754.59	603.95	514.76	456.28	415.33	385.31
23000	2067.82	1107.02	788.89	631.40	538.16	477.02	434.21	402.83
24000	2157.72	1155.15	823.19	658.85	561.56	497.76	453.09	420.34
25000	2247.62	1203.28	857.48	686.31	584.96	518.50	471.96	437.86
26000	2337.53	1251.41	891.78	713.76	608.35	539.24	490.84	455.37
27000	2427.43	1299.54	926.08	741.21	631.75	559.98	509.72	472.89
28000	2517.34	1347.67	960.38	768.66	655.15	580.72	528.60	490.40
29000	2607.24	1395.81	994.68	796.11	678.55	601.46	547.48	507.91
30000	2697.15	1443.94	1028.98	823.57	701.95	622.20	566.36	525.43
31000	2787.05	1492.07	1063.28	851.02	725.34	642.94	585.24	542.94
32000	2876.96	1540.20	1097.58	878.47	748.74	663.68	604.11	560.46
33000	2966.86	1588.33	1131.88	905.92	772.14	684.42	622.99	577.97
34000	3056.77	1636.46	1166.18	933.37	795.54	705.16	641.87	595.48
35000	3146.67	1684.59	1200.48	960.83	818.94	725.90	660.75	613.00
40000	3596.20	1925.25	1371.97	1098.09	935.93	829.60	755.14	700.57
45000	4045.72	2165.90	1543.47	1235.35	1052.92	933.30	849.53	788.14
50000	4495.24	2406.56	1714.96	1372.61	1169.91	1037.00	943.92	875.71
55000	4944.77	2647.21	1886.46	1509.87	1286.90	1140.70	1038.32	963.28
60000	5394.29	2887.87	2057.96	1647.13	1403.89	1244.40	1132.71	1050.85
65000	5843.82	3128.52	2229.45	1784.39	1520.88	1348.09	1227.10	1138.42
70000	6293.34	3369.18	2400.95	1921.65	1637.87	1451.79	1321.49	1225.99
75000	6742.86	3609.84	2572.44	2058.91	1754.86	1555.49	1415.88	1313.56
80000	7192.39	3850.49	2743.94	2196.17	1871.85	1659.19	1510.28	1401.13
85000	7641.91	4091.15	2915.44	2333.43	1988.84	1762.89	1604.67	1488.70
90000	8091.44	4331.80	3086.93	2470.69	2105.83	1866.59	1699.06	1576.27
95000	8540.96	4572.46	3258.43	2607.95	2222.82	1970.29	1793.45	1663.84
100000	8990.48	4813.11	3429.92	2745.21	2339.81	2073.99	1887.84	1751.41
105000	9440.01	5053.77	3601.42	2882.47	2456.80	2177.69	1982.24	1838.98
110000	9889.53	5294.42	3772.91	3019.73	2573.79	2281.39	2076.63	1926.55
115000	10339.06	5535.08	3944.41	3156.99	2690.78	2385.09	2171.02	2014.12
120000	10788.58	5775.73	4115.91	3294.25	2807.77	2488.79	2265.41	2101.69
125000	11238.10	6016.39	4287.40	3431.51	2924.76	2592.49	2359.80	2189.26
130000	11687.63	6257.04	4458.90	3568.77	3041.75	2696.18	2454.20	2276.84
135000	12137.15	6497.70	4630.39	3706.03	3158.74	2799.88	2548.59	2364.41
140000	12586.68	6738.35	4801.89	3843.29	3275.73	2903.58	2642.98	2451.98
145000	13036.20	6979.01	4973.39	3980.55	3392.72	3007.28	2737.37	2539.55
150000	13485.72	7219.67	5144.88	4117.81	3509.71	3110.98	2831.76	2627.12
155000	13935.25	7460.32	5316.38	4255.07	3626.70	3214.68	2926.16	2714.69
160000	14384.77	7700.98	5487.87	4392.33	3743.70	3318.38	3020.55	2802.26

48

AMOUNT OF LOAN	NUMBER OF YEARS IN TERM							
	9	10	15	20	25	30	35	40
$ 50	.83	.79	.68	.64	.62	.61	.60	.60
100	1.65	1.57	1.35	1.27	1.23	1.21	1.20	1.20
200	3.30	3.14	2.70	2.53	2.45	2.41	2.40	2.39
300	4.95	4.71	4.05	3.79	3.67	3.62	3.59	3.58
400	6.60	6.28	5.40	5.05	4.90	4.82	4.79	4.77
500	8.25	7.84	6.75	6.31	6.12	6.03	5.98	5.96
600	9.89	9.41	8.10	7.58	7.34	7.23	7.18	7.15
700	11.54	10.98	9.45	8.84	8.57	8.44	8.38	8.35
800	13.19	12.55	10.79	10.10	9.79	9.64	9.57	9.54
900	14.84	14.11	12.14	11.36	11.01	10.85	10.77	10.73
1000	16.49	15.68	13.49	12.62	12.23	12.05	11.96	11.92
2000	32.97	31.36	26.98	25.24	24.46	24.10	23.92	23.84
3000	49.45	47.04	40.46	37.86	36.69	36.15	35.88	35.75
4000	65.93	62.71	53.95	50.47	48.92	48.19	47.84	47.67
5000	82.41	78.39	67.43	63.09	61.15	60.24	59.80	59.59
6000	98.89	94.07	80.92	75.71	73.38	72.29	71.76	71.50
7000	115.37	109.75	94.41	88.33	85.61	84.33	83.72	83.42
8000	131.85	125.42	107.89	100.94	97.84	96.38	95.68	95.33
9000	148.33	141.10	121.38	113.56	110.07	108.43	107.64	107.25
10000	164.81	156.78	134.86	126.18	122.30	120.47	119.60	119.17
11000	181.29	172.46	148.35	138.79	134.53	132.52	131.55	131.08
12000	197.77	188.13	161.83	151.41	146.76	144.57	143.51	143.00
13000	214.25	203.81	175.32	164.03	158.99	156.61	155.47	154.92
14000	230.73	219.49	188.81	176.65	171.21	168.66	167.43	166.83
15000	247.21	235.16	202.29	189.26	183.44	180.71	179.39	178.75
16000	263.69	250.84	215.78	201.88	195.67	192.75	191.35	190.66
17000	280.17	266.52	229.26	214.50	207.90	204.80	203.31	202.58
18000	296.65	282.20	242.75	227.11	220.13	216.85	215.27	214.50
19000	313.13	297.87	256.24	239.73	232.36	228.90	227.23	226.41
20000	329.61	313.55	269.72	252.35	244.59	240.94	239.19	238.33
21000	346.09	329.23	283.21	264.97	256.82	252.99	251.14	250.25
22000	362.57	344.91	296.69	277.58	269.05	265.04	263.10	262.16
23000	379.05	360.58	310.18	290.20	281.28	277.08	275.06	274.08
24000	395.53	376.26	323.66	302.82	293.51	289.13	287.02	285.99
25000	412.01	391.94	337.15	315.43	305.74	301.18	298.98	297.91
26000	428.49	407.62	350.64	328.05	317.97	313.22	310.94	309.83
27000	444.98	423.29	364.12	340.67	330.20	325.27	322.90	321.74
28000	461.46	438.97	377.61	353.29	342.42	337.32	334.86	333.66
29000	477.94	454.65	391.09	365.90	354.65	349.36	346.82	345.58
30000	494.42	470.32	404.58	378.52	366.88	361.41	358.78	357.49
31000	510.90	486.00	418.06	391.14	379.11	373.46	370.73	369.41
32000	527.38	501.68	431.55	403.76	391.34	385.50	382.69	381.32
33000	543.86	517.36	445.04	416.37	403.57	397.55	394.65	393.24
34000	560.34	533.03	458.52	428.99	415.80	409.60	406.61	405.16
35000	576.82	548.71	472.01	441.61	428.03	421.65	418.57	417.07
40000	659.22	627.10	539.44	504.69	489.18	481.88	478.37	476.65
45000	741.62	705.48	606.87	567.78	550.32	542.11	538.16	536.24
50000	824.02	783.87	674.29	630.86	611.47	602.35	597.96	595.82
55000	906.43	862.26	741.72	693.95	672.62	662.58	657.75	655.40
60000	988.83	940.64	809.15	757.04	733.76	722.82	717.55	714.98
65000	1071.23	1019.03	876.58	820.12	794.91	783.05	777.34	774.56
70000	1153.63	1097.42	944.01	883.21	856.05	843.29	837.14	834.14
75000	1236.03	1175.80	1011.44	946.29	917.20	903.52	896.93	893.72
80000	1318.44	1254.19	1078.87	1009.38	978.35	963.75	956.73	953.30
85000	1400.84	1332.58	1146.30	1072.47	1039.49	1023.99	1016.52	1012.88
90000	1483.24	1410.96	1213.73	1135.55	1100.64	1084.22	1076.32	1072.47
95000	1565.64	1489.35	1281.16	1198.64	1161.79	1144.46	1136.11	1132.05
100000	1648.04	1567.74	1348.58	1261.72	1222.93	1204.69	1195.91	1191.63
105000	1730.45	1646.12	1416.01	1324.81	1284.08	1264.93	1255.70	1251.21
110000	1812.85	1724.51	1483.44	1387.90	1345.23	1325.16	1315.50	1310.79
115000	1895.25	1802.90	1550.87	1450.98	1406.37	1385.40	1375.29	1370.37
120000	1977.65	1881.28	1618.30	1514.07	1467.52	1445.63	1435.09	1429.95
125000	2060.05	1959.67	1685.73	1577.15	1528.66	1505.86	1494.88	1489.53
130000	2142.45	2038.06	1753.16	1640.24	1589.81	1566.10	1554.68	1549.12
135000	2224.86	2116.44	1820.59	1703.33	1650.96	1626.33	1614.47	1608.70
140000	2307.26	2194.83	1888.02	1766.41	1712.10	1686.57	1674.27	1668.28
145000	2389.66	2273.22	1955.45	1829.50	1773.25	1746.80	1734.06	1727.86
150000	2472.06	2351.60	2022.87	1892.58	1834.40	1807.04	1793.86	1787.44
155000	2554.46	2429.99	2090.30	1955.67	1895.54	1867.27	1853.65	1847.02
160000	2636.87	2508.37	2157.73	2018.76	1956.69	1927.50	1913.45	1906.60

MONTHLY AMORTIZING PAYMENTS

AMOUNT OF LOAN	NUMBER OF YEARS IN TERM							
	1	2	3	4	5	6	7	8
$ 50	4.51	2.42	1.73	1.38	1.18	1.05	.96	.89
100	9.01	4.83	3.45	2.76	2.36	2.09	1.91	1.77
200	18.01	9.65	6.89	5.52	4.71	4.18	3.81	3.54
300	27.01	14.48	10.33	8.28	7.06	6.27	5.71	5.30
400	36.01	19.30	13.77	11.04	9.42	8.35	7.61	7.07
500	45.02	24.13	17.22	13.79	11.77	10.44	9.51	8.83
600	54.02	28.95	20.66	16.55	14.12	12.53	11.42	10.60
700	63.02	33.78	24.10	19.31	16.47	14.62	13.32	12.37
800	72.02	38.60	27.54	22.07	18.83	16.70	15.22	14.13
900	81.03	43.43	30.98	24.83	21.18	18.79	17.12	15.90
1000	90.03	48.25	34.43	27.58	23.53	20.88	19.02	17.66
2000	180.05	96.50	68.85	55.16	47.06	41.75	38.04	35.32
3000	270.07	144.75	103.27	82.74	70.59	62.63	57.06	52.98
4000	360.10	193.00	137.69	110.32	94.12	83.50	76.07	70.63
5000	450.12	241.25	172.11	137.89	117.65	104.38	95.09	88.29
6000	540.14	289.50	206.53	165.47	141.17	125.25	114.11	105.95
7000	630.16	337.75	240.95	193.05	164.70	146.13	133.13	123.61
8000	720.19	386.00	275.37	220.63	188.23	167.00	152.14	141.26
9000	810.21	434.25	309.79	248.21	211.76	187.87	171.16	158.92
10000	900.23	482.50	344.21	275.78	235.29	208.75	190.18	176.58
11000	990.25	530.75	378.64	303.36	258.82	229.62	209.20	194.23
12000	1080.28	579.00	413.06	330.94	282.34	250.50	228.21	211.89
13000	1170.30	627.25	447.48	358.52	305.87	271.37	247.23	229.55
14000	1260.32	675.50	481.90	386.10	329.40	292.25	266.25	247.21
15000	1350.34	723.75	516.32	413.67	352.93	313.12	285.26	264.86
16000	1440.37	772.00	550.74	441.25	376.46	334.00	304.28	282.52
17000	1530.39	820.25	585.16	468.83	399.99	354.87	323.30	300.18
18000	1620.41	868.49	619.58	496.41	423.51	375.74	342.32	317.84
19000	1710.43	916.74	654.00	523.99	447.04	396.62	361.33	335.49
20000	1800.46	964.99	688.42	551.56	470.57	417.49	380.35	353.15
21000	1890.48	1013.24	722.85	579.14	494.10	438.37	399.37	370.81
22000	1980.50	1061.49	757.27	606.72	517.63	459.24	418.39	388.46
23000	2070.52	1109.74	791.69	634.30	541.16	480.12	437.40	406.12
24000	2160.55	1157.99	826.11	661.88	564.68	500.99	456.42	423.78
25000	2250.57	1206.24	860.53	689.45	588.21	521.87	475.44	441.44
26000	2340.59	1254.49	894.95	717.03	611.74	542.74	494.45	459.09
27000	2430.61	1302.74	929.37	744.61	635.27	563.61	513.47	476.75
28000	2520.64	1350.99	963.79	772.19	658.80	584.49	532.49	494.41
29000	2610.66	1399.24	998.21	799.77	682.33	605.36	551.51	512.07
30000	2700.68	1447.49	1032.63	827.34	705.85	626.24	570.52	529.72
31000	2790.70	1495.74	1067.06	854.92	729.38	647.11	589.54	547.38
32000	2880.73	1543.99	1101.48	882.50	752.91	667.99	608.56	565.04
33000	2970.75	1592.24	1135.90	910.08	776.44	688.86	627.58	582.69
34000	3060.77	1640.49	1170.32	937.66	799.97	709.74	646.59	600.35
35000	3150.79	1688.73	1204.74	965.23	823.49	730.61	665.61	618.01
40000	3600.91	1929.98	1376.84	1103.12	941.14	834.98	760.70	706.30
45000	4051.02	2171.23	1548.95	1241.01	1058.78	939.35	855.78	794.58
50000	4501.13	2412.48	1721.05	1378.90	1176.42	1043.73	950.87	882.87
55000	4951.25	2653.72	1893.16	1516.79	1294.06	1148.10	1045.96	971.15
60000	5401.36	2894.97	2065.26	1654.68	1411.70	1252.47	1141.04	1059.44
65000	5851.47	3136.22	2237.37	1792.57	1529.34	1356.84	1236.13	1147.73
70000	6301.58	3377.46	2409.47	1930.46	1646.98	1461.21	1331.22	1236.01
75000	6751.70	3618.71	2581.58	2068.35	1764.63	1565.59	1426.30	1324.30
80000	7201.81	3859.96	2753.68	2206.24	1882.27	1669.96	1521.39	1412.59
85000	7651.92	4101.21	2925.79	2344.13	1999.91	1774.33	1616.48	1500.87
90000	8102.03	4342.45	3097.89	2482.02	2117.55	1878.70	1711.56	1589.16
95000	8552.15	4583.70	3270.00	2619.91	2235.19	1983.08	1806.65	1677.44
100000	9002.26	4824.95	3442.10	2757.80	2352.83	2087.45	1901.74	1765.73
105000	9452.37	5066.19	3614.21	2895.69	2470.47	2191.82	1996.82	1854.02
110000	9902.49	5307.44	3786.31	3033.58	2588.12	2296.19	2091.91	1942.30
115000	10352.60	5548.69	3958.42	3171.47	2705.76	2400.56	2186.99	2030.59
120000	10802.71	5789.94	4130.52	3309.36	2823.40	2504.94	2282.08	2118.88
125000	11252.82	6031.18	4302.63	3447.25	2941.04	2609.31	2377.17	2207.16
130000	11702.94	6272.43	4474.73	3585.14	3058.68	2713.68	2472.25	2295.45
135000	12153.05	6513.68	4646.84	3723.03	3176.32	2818.05	2567.34	2383.73
140000	12603.16	6754.92	4818.94	3860.92	3293.96	2922.42	2662.43	2472.02
145000	13053.27	6996.17	4991.05	3998.81	3411.61	3026.80	2757.51	2560.31
150000	13503.39	7237.42	5163.15	4136.70	3529.25	3131.17	2852.60	2648.59
155000	13953.50	7478.67	5335.26	4274.59	3646.89	3235.54	2947.69	2736.88
160000	14403.61	7719.91	5507.36	4412.48	3764.53	3339.91	3042.77	2825.17

AMOUNT OF LOAN	NUMBER OF YEARS IN TERM							
	9	10	15	20	25	30	35	40
$ 50	.84	.80	.69	.64	.63	.62	.61	.61
100	1.67	1.59	1.37	1.28	1.25	1.23	1.22	1.22
200	3.33	3.17	2.74	2.56	2.49	2.45	2.44	2.43
300	4.99	4.75	4.10	3.84	3.73	3.68	3.65	3.64
400	6.66	6.34	5.47	5.12	4.97	4.90	4.87	4.85
500	8.32	7.92	6.83	6.40	6.22	6.13	6.09	6.07
600	9.98	9.50	8.20	7.68	7.46	7.35	7.30	7.28
700	11.64	11.09	9.56	8.96	8.70	8.58	8.52	8.49
800	13.31	12.67	10.93	10.24	9.94	9.80	9.73	9.70
900	14.97	14.25	12.29	11.52	11.18	11.03	10.95	10.91
1000	16.63	15.83	13.66	12.80	12.43	12.25	12.17	12.13
2000	33.26	31.66	27.32	25.60	24.85	24.50	24.33	24.25
3000	49.89	47.49	40.97	38.40	37.27	36.74	36.49	36.37
4000	66.52	63.32	54.63	51.20	49.69	48.99	48.65	48.49
5000	83.14	79.15	68.28	64.00	62.11	61.23	60.81	60.61
6000	99.77	94.98	81.94	76.80	74.53	73.48	72.98	72.73
7000	116.40	110.81	95.59	89.60	86.96	85.72	85.14	84.85
8000	133.03	126.63	109.25	102.40	99.38	97.97	97.30	96.98
9000	149.65	142.46	122.90	115.20	111.80	122.46	109.46	109.10
10000	166.28	158.29	136.56	128.00	124.22	122.46	121.62	121.22
11000	182.91	174.12	150.21	140.80	136.64	134.71	133.78	133.34
12000	199.54	189.95	163.87	153.60	149.06	146.95	145.95	145.46
13000	216.17	205.78	177.52	166.40	161.49	159.20	158.11	157.58
14000	232.79	221.61	191.18	179.20	173.91	171.44	170.27	169.70
15000	249.42	237.44	204.83	192.00	186.33	183.69	182.43	181.82
16000	266.05	253.26	218.49	204.80	198.75	195.93	194.59	193.95
17000	282.68	269.09	232.14	217.60	211.17	208.18	206.75	206.07
18000	299.30	284.92	245.80	230.40	223.59	220.43	218.92	218.19
19000	315.93	300.75	259.45	243.20	236.02	232.67	231.08	230.31
20000	332.56	316.58	273.11	256.00	248.44	244.92	243.24	242.43
21000	349.19	332.41	286.76	268.80	260.86	257.16	255.40	254.55
22000	365.81	348.24	300.42	281.60	273.28	269.41	267.56	266.67
23000	382.44	364.06	314.07	294.40	285.70	281.65	279.72	278.80
24000	399.07	379.89	327.73	307.20	298.12	293.90	291.89	290.92
25000	415.70	395.72	341.38	320.00	310.55	306.14	304.05	303.04
26000	432.33	411.55	355.04	332.80	322.97	318.39	316.21	315.16
27000	448.95	427.38	368.69	345.60	335.39	330.64	328.37	327.28
28000	465.58	443.21	382.35	358.40	347.81	342.88	340.53	339.40
29000	482.21	459.04	396.00	371.20	360.23	355.13	352.69	351.52
30000	498.84	474.87	409.66	384.00	372.65	367.37	364.86	363.64
31000	515.46	490.69	423.31	396.80	385.08	379.62	377.02	375.77
32000	532.09	506.52	436.97	409.60	397.50	391.86	389.18	387.89
33000	548.72	522.35	450.62	422.40	409.92	404.11	401.34	400.01
34000	565.35	538.18	464.28	435.20	422.34	416.35	413.50	412.13
35000	581.98	554.01	477.93	448.00	434.76	428.60	425.66	424.25
40000	665.11	633.15	546.21	512.00	496.87	489.83	486.47	484.86
45000	748.25	712.30	614.48	576.00	558.98	551.06	547.28	545.46
50000	831.39	791.44	682.76	640.00	621.09	612.28	608.09	606.07
55000	914.53	870.58	751.03	704.00	683.19	673.51	668.90	666.68
60000	997.67	949.73	819.31	768.00	745.30	734.74	729.71	727.28
65000	1080.81	1028.87	887.58	832.00	807.41	795.97	790.52	787.89
70000	1163.95	1108.01	955.86	896.00	869.52	857.19	851.32	848.50
75000	1247.08	1187.16	1024.13	960.00	931.63	918.42	912.13	909.10
80000	1330.22	1266.30	1092.41	1024.00	993.74	979.65	972.94	969.71
85000	1413.36	1345.44	1160.68	1088.00	1055.84	1040.88	1033.75	1030.32
90000	1496.50	1424.59	1228.96	1152.00	1117.95	1102.11	1094.56	1090.92
95000	1579.64	1503.73	1297.23	1216.00	1180.06	1163.33	1155.37	1151.53
100000	1662.78	1582.87	1365.51	1280.00	1242.17	1224.56	1216.18	1212.14
105000	1745.92	1662.02	1433.78	1344.00	1304.28	1285.79	1276.98	1272.74
110000	1829.05	1741.16	1502.06	1408.00	1366.38	1347.02	1337.79	1333.35
115000	1912.19	1820.30	1570.33	1472.00	1428.49	1408.24	1398.60	1393.96
120000	1995.33	1899.45	1638.61	1536.00	1490.60	1469.47	1459.41	1454.56
125000	2078.47	1978.59	1706.88	1600.00	1552.71	1530.70	1520.22	1515.17
130000	2161.61	2057.73	1775.16	1664.00	1614.82	1591.93	1581.03	1575.78
135000	2244.75	2136.88	1843.43	1728.00	1676.92	1653.16	1641.84	1636.38
140000	2327.89	2216.02	1911.71	1792.00	1739.03	1714.38	1702.64	1696.99
145000	2411.02	2295.16	1979.98	1856.00	1801.14	1775.61	1763.45	1757.60
150000	2494.16	2374.31	2048.26	1920.00	1863.25	1836.84	1824.26	1818.20
155000	2577.30	2453.45	2116.53	1984.00	1925.36	1898.07	1885.07	1878.81
160000	2660.44	2532.59	2184.81	2048.00	1987.47	1959.29	1945.88	1939.42

14.750% MONTHLY AMORTIZING PAYMENTS

AMOUNT OF LOAN	NUMBER OF YEARS IN TERM							
	1	2	3	4	5	6	7	8
$ 50	4.51	2.42	1.73	1.39	1.19	1.06	.96	.90
100	9.02	4.84	3.46	2.78	2.37	2.11	1.92	1.79
200	18.03	9.68	6.91	5.55	4.74	4.21	3.84	3.57
300	27.05	14.52	10.37	8.32	7.10	6.31	5.75	5.35
400	36.06	19.35	13.82	11.09	9.47	8.41	7.67	7.13
500	45.08	24.19	17.28	13.86	11.83	10.51	9.58	8.91
600	54.09	29.03	20.73	16.63	14.20	12.61	11.50	10.69
700	63.10	33.86	24.19	19.40	16.57	14.71	13.41	12.47
800	72.12	38.70	27.64	22.17	18.93	16.81	15.33	14.25
900	81.13	43.54	31.09	24.94	21.30	18.91	17.25	16.03
1000	90.15	48.37	34.55	27.71	23.66	21.01	19.16	17.81
2000	180.29	96.74	69.09	55.41	47.32	42.02	38.32	35.61
3000	270.43	145.11	103.63	83.12	70.98	63.03	57.48	53.41
4000	360.57	193.48	138.18	110.82	94.64	84.04	76.63	71.21
5000	450.71	241.84	172.72	138.53	118.30	105.05	95.79	89.01
6000	540.85	290.21	207.26	166.23	141.96	126.06	114.95	106.81
7000	630.99	338.58	241.81	193.93	165.62	147.07	134.10	124.61
8000	721.13	386.95	276.35	221.64	189.28	168.08	153.26	142.41
9000	811.27	435.32	310.89	249.34	212.94	189.09	172.42	160.21
10000	901.41	483.68	345.44	277.05	236.59	210.10	191.57	178.02
11000	991.55	532.05	379.98	304.75	260.25	231.11	210.73	195.82
12000	1081.69	580.42	414.52	332.46	283.91	252.12	229.89	213.62
13000	1171.83	628.79	449.06	360.16	307.57	273.13	249.04	231.42
14000	1261.97	677.16	483.61	387.86	331.23	294.14	268.20	249.22
15000	1352.11	725.52	518.15	415.57	354.89	315.15	287.36	267.02
16000	1442.25	773.89	552.69	443.27	378.55	336.16	306.51	284.82
17000	1532.39	822.26	587.24	470.98	402.21	357.17	325.67	302.62
18000	1622.53	870.63	621.78	498.68	425.87	378.18	344.83	320.42
19000	1712.67	919.00	656.32	526.38	449.52	399.19	363.98	338.22
20000	1802.81	967.36	690.87	554.09	473.18	420.19	383.14	356.03
21000	1892.95	1015.73	725.41	581.79	496.84	441.20	402.30	373.83
22000	1983.09	1064.10	759.95	609.50	520.50	462.21	421.45	391.63
23000	2073.23	1112.47	794.49	637.20	544.16	483.22	440.61	409.43
24000	2163.37	1160.84	829.04	664.91	567.82	504.23	459.77	427.23
25000	2253.51	1209.20	863.58	692.61	591.48	525.24	478.92	445.03
26000	2343.66	1257.57	898.12	720.31	615.14	546.25	498.08	462.83
27000	2433.80	1305.94	932.67	748.02	638.80	567.26	517.24	480.63
28000	2523.94	1354.31	967.21	775.72	662.45	588.27	536.39	498.43
29000	2614.08	1402.68	1001.75	803.43	686.11	609.28	555.55	516.23
30000	2704.22	1451.04	1036.30	831.13	709.77	630.29	574.71	534.04
31000	2794.36	1499.41	1070.84	858.83	733.43	651.30	593.86	551.84
32000	2884.50	1547.78	1105.38	886.54	757.09	672.31	613.02	569.64
33000	2974.64	1596.15	1139.92	914.24	780.75	693.32	632.18	587.44
34000	3064.78	1644.52	1174.47	941.95	804.41	714.33	651.33	605.24
35000	3154.92	1692.88	1209.01	969.65	828.07	735.34	670.49	623.04
40000	3605.62	1934.72	1381.73	1108.17	946.36	840.38	766.28	712.05
45000	4056.32	2176.56	1554.44	1246.69	1064.66	945.43	862.06	801.05
50000	4507.02	2418.40	1727.16	1385.21	1182.95	1050.48	957.84	890.06
55000	4957.73	2660.24	1899.87	1523.74	1301.24	1155.53	1053.63	979.06
60000	5408.43	2902.08	2072.59	1662.26	1419.54	1260.57	1149.41	1068.07
65000	5859.13	3143.92	2245.30	1800.78	1537.83	1365.62	1245.19	1157.07
70000	6309.83	3385.76	2418.02	1939.30	1656.13	1470.67	1340.98	1246.08
75000	6760.53	3627.60	2590.73	2077.82	1774.42	1575.72	1436.76	1335.08
80000	7211.24	3869.44	2763.45	2216.34	1892.72	1680.76	1532.55	1424.09
85000	7661.94	4111.28	2936.16	2354.86	2011.01	1785.81	1628.33	1513.09
90000	8112.64	4353.12	3108.88	2493.38	2129.31	1890.86	1724.11	1602.10
95000	8563.34	4594.96	3281.59	2631.90	2247.60	1995.91	1819.90	1691.10
100000	9014.04	4836.80	3454.31	2770.42	2365.90	2100.95	1915.68	1780.11
105000	9464.75	5078.64	3627.02	2908.94	2484.19	2206.00	2011.46	1869.11
110000	9915.45	5320.48	3799.74	3047.47	2602.48	2311.05	2107.25	1958.12
115000	10366.15	5562.32	3972.45	3185.99	2720.78	2416.10	2203.03	2047.12
120000	10816.85	5804.16	4145.17	3324.51	2839.07	2521.14	2298.82	2136.13
125000	11267.55	6046.00	4317.88	3463.03	2957.37	2626.19	2394.60	2225.13
130000	11718.26	6287.84	4490.60	3601.55	3075.66	2731.24	2490.38	2314.14
135000	12168.96	6529.68	4663.31	3740.07	3193.96	2836.29	2586.17	2403.14
140000	12619.66	6771.52	4836.03	3878.59	3312.25	2941.33	2681.95	2492.15
145000	13070.36	7013.36	5008.74	4017.11	3430.55	3046.38	2777.74	2581.15
150000	13521.06	7255.20	5181.46	4155.63	3548.84	3151.43	2873.52	2670.16
155000	13971.76	7497.04	5354.17	4294.15	3667.14	3256.47	2969.30	2759.16
160000	14422.47	7738.88	5526.89	4432.67	3785.43	3361.52	3065.09	2848.17

52

AMOUNT OF LOAN	NUMBER OF YEARS IN TERM							
	9	10	15	20	25	30	35	40
$ 50	.84	.80	.70	.65	.64	.63	.62	.62
100	1.68	1.60	1.39	1.30	1.27	1.25	1.24	1.24
200	3.36	3.20	2.77	2.60	2.53	2.49	2.48	2.47
300	5.04	4.80	4.15	3.90	3.79	3.74	3.71	3.70
400	6.72	6.40	5.54	5.20	5.05	4.98	4.95	4.94
500	8.39	8.00	6.92	6.50	6.31	6.23	6.19	6.17
600	10.07	9.59	8.30	7.80	7.57	7.47	7.42	7.40
700	11.75	11.19	9.68	9.09	8.84	8.72	8.66	8.63
800	13.43	12.79	11.07	10.39	10.10	9.96	9.90	9.87
900	15.10	14.39	12.45	11.69	11.36	11.21	11.13	11.10
1000	16.78	15.99	13.83	12.99	12.62	12.45	12.37	12.33
2000	33.56	31.97	27.66	25.97	25.23	24.89	24.73	24.66
3000	50.33	47.95	41.48	38.96	37.85	37.34	37.10	36.99
4000	67.11	63.93	55.31	51.94	50.46	49.78	49.46	49.31
5000	83.88	79.91	69.13	64.92	63.08	62.23	61.83	61.64
6000	100.66	95.89	82.96	77.91	75.69	74.67	74.19	73.97
7000	117.43	111.87	96.78	90.89	88.31	87.12	86.56	86.29
8000	134.21	127.85	110.61	103.87	100.92	99.56	98.92	98.62
9000	150.99	143.83	124.43	116.86	113.54	112.01	111.29	110.95
10000	167.76	159.81	138.26	129.84	126.15	124.45	123.65	123.27
11000	184.54	175.79	152.08	142.82	138.77	136.90	136.02	135.60
12000	201.31	191.77	165.91	155.81	151.38	149.34	148.38	147.93
13000	218.09	207.75	179.73	168.79	164.00	161.79	160.75	160.25
14000	234.86	223.74	193.56	181.77	176.61	174.23	173.11	172.58
15000	251.64	239.72	207.38	194.76	189.22	186.68	185.48	184.91
16000	268.42	255.70	221.21	207.74	201.84	199.12	197.84	197.23
17000	285.19	271.68	235.03	220.73	214.45	211.57	210.21	209.56
18000	301.97	287.66	248.86	233.71	227.07	224.01	222.57	221.89
19000	318.74	303.64	262.68	246.69	239.68	236.46	234.94	234.21
20000	335.52	319.62	276.51	259.68	252.30	248.90	247.30	246.54
21000	352.29	335.60	290.33	272.66	264.91	261.34	259.66	258.87
22000	369.07	351.58	304.16	285.64	277.53	273.79	272.03	271.19
23000	385.85	367.56	317.98	298.63	290.14	286.23	284.39	283.52
24000	402.62	383.54	331.81	311.61	302.76	298.68	296.76	295.85
25000	419.40	399.52	345.63	324.59	315.37	311.12	309.12	308.17
26000	436.17	415.50	359.46	337.58	327.99	323.57	321.49	320.50
27000	452.95	431.49	373.28	350.56	340.60	336.01	333.85	332.83
28000	469.72	447.47	387.11	363.54	353.22	348.46	346.22	345.15
29000	486.50	463.45	400.93	376.53	365.83	360.90	358.58	357.48
30000	503.28	479.43	414.76	389.51	378.44	373.35	370.95	369.81
31000	520.05	495.41	428.58	402.50	391.06	385.79	383.31	382.13
32000	536.83	511.39	442.41	415.48	403.67	398.24	395.68	394.46
33000	553.60	527.37	456.23	428.46	416.29	410.68	408.04	406.79
34000	570.38	543.35	470.06	441.45	428.90	423.13	420.41	419.11
35000	587.15	559.33	483.88	454.43	441.52	435.57	432.77	431.44
40000	671.03	639.23	553.01	519.35	504.59	497.80	494.59	493.07
45000	754.91	719.14	622.13	584.26	567.66	560.02	556.42	554.71
50000	838.79	799.04	691.26	649.18	630.74	622.24	618.24	616.34
55000	922.67	878.95	760.38	714.10	693.81	684.47	680.07	677.97
60000	1006.55	958.85	829.51	779.02	756.88	746.69	741.89	739.61
65000	1090.43	1038.75	898.63	843.94	819.96	808.91	803.71	801.24
70000	1174.30	1118.66	967.76	908.85	883.03	871.14	865.54	862.87
75000	1258.18	1198.56	1036.88	973.77	946.10	933.36	927.36	924.51
80000	1342.06	1278.46	1106.01	1038.69	1009.18	995.59	989.18	986.14
85000	1425.94	1358.37	1175.13	1103.61	1072.25	1057.81	1051.01	1047.77
90000	1509.82	1438.27	1244.26	1168.52	1135.32	1120.03	1112.83	1109.41
95000	1593.70	1518.18	1313.38	1233.44	1198.40	1182.26	1174.66	1171.04
100000	1677.58	1598.08	1382.51	1298.36	1261.47	1244.48	1236.48	1232.67
105000	1761.45	1677.98	1451.63	1363.28	1324.54	1306.70	1298.30	1294.31
110000	1845.33	1757.89	1520.76	1428.20	1387.62	1368.93	1360.13	1355.94
115000	1929.21	1837.79	1589.88	1493.11	1450.69	1431.15	1421.95	1417.57
120000	2013.09	1917.69	1659.01	1558.03	1513.76	1493.38	1483.77	1479.21
125000	2096.97	1997.60	1728.13	1622.95	1576.84	1555.60	1545.60	1540.84
130000	2180.85	2077.50	1797.26	1687.87	1639.91	1617.82	1607.42	1602.47
135000	2264.73	2157.41	1866.39	1752.78	1702.98	1680.05	1669.25	1664.11
140000	2348.60	2237.31	1935.51	1817.70	1766.06	1742.27	1731.07	1725.74
145000	2432.48	2317.21	2004.64	1882.62	1829.13	1804.49	1792.89	1787.37
150000	2516.36	2397.12	2073.76	1947.54	1892.20	1866.72	1854.72	1849.01
155000	2600.24	2477.02	2142.89	2012.46	1955.28	1928.94	1916.54	1910.64
160000	2684.12	2556.92	2212.01	2077.37	2018.35	1991.16	1978.36	1972.27

MONTHLY AMORTIZING PAYMENTS

AMOUNT OF LOAN	NUMBER OF YEARS IN TERM							
	1	2	3	4	5	6	7	8
$ 50	4.52	2.43	1.74	1.40	1.19	1.06	.97	.90
100	9.03	4.85	3.47	2.79	2.38	2.12	1.93	1.80
200	18.06	9.70	6.94	5.57	4.76	4.23	3.86	3.59
300	27.08	14.55	10.40	8.35	7.14	6.35	5.79	5.39
400	36.11	19.40	13.87	11.14	9.52	8.46	7.72	7.18
500	45.13	24.25	17.34	13.92	11.90	10.58	9.65	8.98
600	54.16	29.10	20.80	16.70	14.28	12.69	11.58	10.77
700	63.19	33.95	24.27	19.49	16.66	14.81	13.51	12.57
800	72.21	38.79	27.74	22.27	19.04	16.92	15.44	14.36
900	81.24	43.64	31.20	25.05	21.42	19.04	17.37	16.16
1000	90.26	48.49	34.67	27.84	23.79	21.15	19.30	17.95
2000	180.52	96.98	69.34	55.67	47.58	42.30	38.60	35.90
3000	270.78	145.46	104.00	83.50	71.37	63.44	57.90	53.84
4000	361.04	193.95	138.67	111.33	95.16	84.59	77.19	71.79
5000	451.30	242.44	173.33	139.16	118.95	105.73	96.49	89.73
6000	541.55	290.92	208.00	166.99	142.74	126.88	115.79	107.68
7000	631.81	339.41	242.66	194.82	166.53	148.02	135.08	125.62
8000	722.07	387.90	277.33	222.65	190.32	169.17	154.38	143.57
9000	812.33	436.38	311.99	250.48	214.11	190.31	173.68	161.51
10000	902.59	484.87	346.66	278.31	237.90	211.46	192.97	179.46
11000	992.85	533.36	381.32	306.14	261.69	232.60	212.27	197.40
12000	1083.10	581.84	415.99	333.97	285.48	253.75	231.57	215.35
13000	1173.36	630.33	450.65	361.80	309.27	274.89	250.86	233.30
14000	1263.62	678.82	485.32	389.64	333.06	296.04	270.16	251.24
15000	1353.88	727.30	519.98	417.47	356.85	317.18	289.46	269.19
16000	1444.14	775.79	554.65	445.30	380.64	338.33	308.75	287.13
17000	1534.40	824.28	589.32	473.13	404.43	359.47	328.05	305.08
18000	1624.65	872.76	623.98	500.96	428.22	380.62	347.35	323.02
19000	1714.91	921.25	658.65	528.79	452.01	401.76	366.64	340.97
20000	1805.17	969.74	693.31	556.62	475.80	422.91	385.94	358.91
21000	1895.43	1018.22	727.98	584.45	499.59	444.05	405.24	376.86
22000	1985.69	1066.71	762.64	612.28	523.38	465.20	424.53	394.80
23000	2075.95	1115.20	797.31	640.11	547.17	486.34	443.83	412.75
24000	2166.20	1163.68	831.97	667.94	570.96	507.49	463.13	430.69
25000	2256.46	1212.17	866.64	695.77	594.75	528.63	482.42	448.64
26000	2346.72	1260.66	901.30	723.60	618.54	549.78	501.72	466.59
27000	2436.98	1309.14	935.97	751.44	642.33	570.92	521.02	484.53
28000	2527.24	1357.63	970.63	779.27	666.12	592.07	540.31	502.48
29000	2617.50	1406.12	1005.30	807.10	689.91	613.21	559.61	520.42
30000	2707.75	1454.60	1039.96	834.93	713.70	634.36	578.91	538.37
31000	2798.01	1503.09	1074.63	862.76	737.49	655.50	598.20	556.31
32000	2888.27	1551.58	1109.30	890.59	761.28	676.65	617.50	574.26
33000	2978.53	1600.06	1143.96	918.42	785.07	697.79	636.80	592.20
34000	3068.79	1648.55	1178.63	946.25	808.86	718.94	656.09	610.15
35000	3159.05	1697.04	1213.29	974.08	832.65	740.08	675.39	628.09
40000	3610.34	1939.47	1386.62	1113.23	951.60	845.81	771.88	717.82
45000	4061.63	2181.90	1559.94	1252.39	1070.55	951.53	868.36	807.55
50000	4512.92	2424.34	1733.27	1391.54	1189.50	1057.26	964.84	897.28
55000	4964.21	2666.77	1906.60	1530.70	1308.45	1162.98	1061.33	987.00
60000	5415.50	2909.20	2079.92	1669.85	1427.40	1268.71	1157.81	1076.73
65000	5866.80	3151.64	2253.25	1809.00	1546.35	1374.43	1254.29	1166.46
70000	6318.09	3394.07	2426.58	1948.16	1665.30	1480.16	1350.78	1256.18
75000	6769.38	3636.50	2599.90	2087.31	1784.25	1585.88	1447.26	1345.91
80000	7220.67	3878.94	2773.23	2226.46	1903.20	1691.61	1543.75	1435.64
85000	7671.96	4121.37	2946.56	2365.62	2022.15	1797.33	1640.23	1525.36
90000	8123.25	4363.80	3119.88	2504.77	2141.10	1903.06	1736.71	1615.09
95000	8574.54	4606.24	3293.21	2643.93	2260.05	2008.78	1833.20	1704.82
100000	9025.84	4848.67	3466.54	2783.08	2379.00	2114.51	1929.68	1794.55
105000	9477.13	5091.10	3639.86	2922.23	2497.95	2220.23	2026.16	1884.27
110000	9928.42	5333.54	3813.19	3061.39	2616.90	2325.96	2122.65	1974.00
115000	10379.71	5575.97	3986.52	3200.54	2735.85	2431.68	2219.13	2063.73
120000	10831.00	5818.40	4159.84	3339.69	2854.80	2537.41	2315.62	2153.45
125000	11282.29	6060.84	4333.17	3478.85	2973.75	2643.13	2412.10	2243.18
130000	11733.59	6303.27	4506.50	3618.00	3092.70	2748.86	2508.58	2332.91
135000	12184.88	6545.70	4679.82	3757.16	3211.65	2854.58	2605.07	2422.63
140000	12636.17	6788.14	4853.15	3896.31	3330.60	2960.31	2701.55	2512.36
145000	13087.46	7030.57	5026.48	4035.46	3449.54	3066.03	2798.03	2602.09
150000	13538.75	7273.00	5199.80	4174.62	3568.49	3171.76	2894.52	2691.82
155000	13990.04	7515.44	5373.13	4313.77	3687.44	3277.48	2991.00	2781.54
160000	14441.33	7757.87	5546.46	4452.92	3806.39	3383.21	3087.49	2871.27

AMOUNT OF LOAN	NUMBER OF YEARS IN TERM							
	9	10	15	20	25	30	35	40
$ 50	.85	.81	.70	.66	.65	.64	.63	.63
100	1.70	1.62	1.40	1.32	1.29	1.27	1.26	1.26
200	3.39	3.23	2.80	2.64	2.57	2.53	2.52	2.51
300	5.08	4.85	4.20	3.96	3.85	3.80	3.78	3.76
400	6.77	6.46	5.60	5.27	5.13	5.06	5.03	5.02
500	8.47	8.07	7.00	6.59	6.41	6.33	6.29	6.27
600	10.16	9.69	8.40	7.91	7.69	7.59	7.55	7.52
700	11.85	11.30	9.80	9.22	8.97	8.86	8.80	8.78
800	13.54	12.91	11.20	10.54	10.25	10.12	10.06	10.03
900	15.24	14.53	12.60	11.86	11.53	11.38	11.32	11.28
1000	16.93	16.14	14.00	13.17	12.81	12.65	12.57	12.54
2000	33.85	32.27	28.00	26.34	25.62	25.29	25.14	25.07
3000	50.78	48.41	41.99	39.51	38.43	37.94	37.71	37.60
4000	67.70	64.54	55.99	52.68	51.24	50.58	50.28	50.13
5000	84.63	80.67	69.98	65.84	64.05	63.23	62.85	62.67
6000	101.55	96.81	83.98	79.01	76.85	75.87	75.41	75.20
7000	118.48	112.94	97.98	92.18	89.66	88.52	87.98	87.73
8000	135.40	129.07	111.97	105.35	102.47	101.16	100.55	100.26
9000	152.32	145.21	125.97	118.52	115.28	113.80	113.12	112.80
10000	169.25	161.34	139.96	131.68	128.09	126.45	125.69	125.33
11000	186.17	177.47	153.96	144.85	140.90	139.09	138.25	137.86
12000	203.10	193.61	167.96	158.02	153.70	151.74	150.82	150.39
13000	220.02	209.74	181.95	171.19	166.51	164.38	163.39	162.92
14000	236.95	225.87	195.95	184.36	179.32	177.03	175.96	175.46
15000	253.87	242.01	209.94	197.52	192.13	189.67	188.53	187.99
16000	270.79	258.14	223.94	210.69	204.94	202.32	201.10	200.52
17000	287.72	274.27	237.93	223.86	217.75	214.96	213.66	213.05
18000	304.64	290.41	251.93	237.03	230.55	227.60	226.23	225.59
19000	321.57	306.54	265.93	250.20	243.36	240.25	238.80	238.12
20000	338.49	322.67	279.92	263.36	256.17	252.89	251.37	250.65
21000	355.42	338.81	293.92	276.53	268.98	265.54	263.94	263.18
22000	372.34	354.94	307.91	289.70	281.79	278.18	276.50	275.71
23000	389.26	371.08	321.91	302.87	294.60	290.83	289.07	288.25
24000	406.19	387.21	335.91	316.03	307.40	303.47	301.64	300.78
25000	423.11	403.34	349.90	329.20	320.21	316.12	314.21	313.31
26000	440.04	419.48	363.90	342.37	333.02	328.76	326.78	325.84
27000	456.96	435.61	377.89	355.54	345.83	341.40	339.34	338.38
28000	473.89	451.74	391.89	368.71	358.64	354.05	351.91	350.91
29000	490.81	467.88	405.89	381.87	371.45	366.69	364.48	363.44
30000	507.74	484.01	419.88	395.04	384.25	379.34	377.05	375.97
31000	524.66	500.14	433.88	408.21	397.06	391.98	389.62	388.50
32000	541.58	516.28	447.87	421.38	409.87	404.63	402.19	401.04
33000	558.51	532.41	461.87	434.55	422.68	417.27	414.75	413.57
34000	575.43	548.54	475.86	447.71	435.49	429.92	427.32	426.10
35000	592.36	564.68	489.86	460.88	448.30	442.56	439.89	438.63
40000	676.98	645.34	559.84	526.72	512.34	505.78	502.73	501.29
45000	761.60	726.01	629.82	592.56	576.38	569.00	565.57	563.96
50000	846.22	806.68	699.80	658.40	640.42	632.23	628.41	626.62
55000	930.84	887.35	769.78	724.24	704.46	695.45	691.25	689.28
60000	1015.47	968.01	839.76	790.08	768.50	758.67	754.09	751.94
65000	1100.09	1048.68	909.74	855.92	832.54	821.89	816.93	814.60
70000	1184.71	1129.35	979.72	921.76	896.59	885.12	879.77	877.26
75000	1269.33	1210.02	1049.70	987.60	960.63	948.34	942.61	939.92
80000	1353.95	1290.68	1119.67	1053.44	1024.67	1011.56	1005.46	1002.58
85000	1438.57	1371.35	1189.65	1119.28	1088.71	1074.78	1068.30	1065.25
90000	1523.20	1452.02	1259.63	1185.12	1152.75	1138.00	1131.14	1127.91
95000	1607.82	1532.69	1329.61	1250.96	1216.79	1201.23	1193.98	1190.57
100000	1692.44	1613.35	1399.59	1316.79	1280.84	1264.45	1256.82	1253.23
105000	1777.06	1694.02	1469.57	1382.63	1344.88	1327.67	1319.66	1315.89
110000	1861.68	1774.69	1539.55	1448.47	1408.92	1390.89	1382.50	1378.55
115000	1946.30	1855.36	1609.53	1514.31	1472.96	1454.12	1445.34	1441.21
120000	2030.93	1936.02	1679.51	1580.15	1537.00	1517.34	1508.18	1503.87
125000	2115.55	2016.69	1749.49	1645.99	1601.04	1580.56	1571.02	1566.54
130000	2200.17	2097.36	1819.47	1711.83	1665.08	1643.78	1633.86	1629.20
135000	2284.79	2178.03	1889.45	1777.67	1729.13	1707.00	1696.70	1691.86
140000	2369.41	2258.69	1959.43	1843.51	1793.17	1770.23	1759.54	1754.52
145000	2454.03	2339.36	2029.41	1909.35	1857.21	1833.45	1822.38	1817.18
150000	2538.66	2420.03	2099.39	1975.19	1921.25	1896.67	1885.22	1879.84
155000	2623.28	2500.70	2169.37	2041.03	1985.29	1959.89	1948.07	1942.50
160000	2707.90	2581.36	2239.34	2106.87	2049.33	2023.12	2010.91	2005.16

15.250% MONTHLY AMORTIZING PAYMENTS

AMOUNT OF LOAN	NUMBER OF YEARS IN TERM								
	1	2	3	4	5	6	7	8
$ 50	4.52	2.44	1.74	1.40	1.20	1.07	.98	.91
100	9.04	4.87	3.48	2.80	2.40	2.13	1.95	1.81
200	18.08	9.73	6.96	5.60	4.79	4.26	3.89	3.62
300	27.12	14.59	10.44	8.39	7.18	6.39	5.84	5.43
400	36.16	19.45	13.92	11.19	9.57	8.52	7.78	7.24
500	45.19	24.31	17.40	13.98	11.97	10.65	9.72	9.05
600	54.23	29.17	20.88	16.78	14.36	12.77	11.67	10.86
700	63.27	34.03	24.36	19.58	16.75	14.90	13.61	12.67
800	72.31	38.89	27.84	22.37	19.14	17.03	15.55	14.48
900	81.34	43.75	31.31	25.17	21.53	19.16	17.50	16.29
1000	90.38	48.61	34.79	27.96	23.93	21.29	19.44	18.10
2000	180.76	97.22	69.58	55.92	47.85	42.57	38.88	36.19
3000	271.13	145.82	104.37	83.88	71.77	63.85	58.32	54.28
4000	361.51	194.43	139.16	111.84	95.69	85.13	77.75	72.37
5000	451.89	243.03	173.94	139.79	119.61	106.41	97.19	90.46
6000	542.26	291.64	208.73	167.75	143.53	127.69	116.63	108.55
7000	632.64	340.24	243.52	195.71	167.45	148.97	136.07	126.64
8000	723.02	388.85	278.31	223.67	191.38	170.25	155.50	144.73
9000	813.39	437.45	313.10	251.62	215.30	191.53	174.94	162.82
10000	903.77	486.06	347.88	279.58	239.22	212.82	194.38	180.91
11000	994.14	534.67	382.67	307.54	263.14	234.10	213.82	199.00
12000	1084.52	583.27	417.46	335.50	287.06	255.38	233.25	217.09
13000	1174.90	631.88	452.25	363.45	310.98	276.66	252.69	235.18
14000	1265.27	680.48	487.04	391.41	334.90	297.94	272.13	253.27
15000	1355.65	729.09	521.82	419.37	358.83	319.22	291.56	271.36
16000	1446.03	777.69	556.61	447.33	382.75	340.50	311.00	289.45
17000	1536.40	826.30	591.40	475.28	406.67	361.78	330.44	307.54
18000	1626.78	874.90	626.19	503.24	430.59	383.06	349.88	325.63
19000	1717.16	923.51	660.97	531.20	454.51	404.34	369.31	343.72
20000	1807.53	972.12	695.76	559.16	478.43	425.63	388.75	361.81
21000	1897.91	1020.72	730.55	587.12	502.35	446.91	408.19	379.90
22000	1988.28	1069.33	765.34	615.07	526.27	468.19	427.63	397.99
23000	2078.66	1117.93	800.13	643.03	550.20	489.47	447.06	416.08
24000	2169.04	1166.54	834.91	670.99	574.12	510.75	466.50	434.17
25000	2259.41	1215.14	869.70	698.95	598.04	532.03	485.94	452.26
26000	2349.79	1263.75	904.49	726.90	621.96	553.31	505.37	470.35
27000	2440.17	1312.35	939.28	754.86	645.88	574.59	524.81	488.44
28000	2530.54	1360.96	974.07	782.82	669.80	595.87	544.25	506.54
29000	2620.92	1409.56	1008.85	810.78	693.72	617.15	563.69	524.63
30000	2711.29	1458.17	1043.64	838.73	717.65	638.44	583.12	542.72
31000	2801.67	1506.78	1078.43	866.69	741.57	659.72	602.56	560.81
32000	2892.05	1555.38	1113.22	894.65	765.49	681.00	622.00	578.90
33000	2982.42	1603.99	1148.01	922.61	789.41	702.28	641.44	596.99
34000	3072.80	1652.59	1182.79	950.56	813.33	723.56	660.87	615.08
35000	3163.18	1701.20	1217.58	978.52	837.25	744.84	680.31	633.17
40000	3615.06	1944.23	1391.52	1118.31	956.86	851.25	777.50	723.62
45000	4066.94	2187.25	1565.46	1258.10	1076.47	957.65	874.68	814.07
50000	4518.82	2430.28	1739.40	1397.89	1196.07	1064.06	971.87	904.52
55000	4970.70	2673.31	1913.34	1537.68	1315.68	1170.46	1069.06	994.98
60000	5422.58	2916.34	2087.28	1677.46	1435.29	1276.87	1166.24	1085.43
65000	5874.47	3159.36	2261.22	1817.25	1554.89	1383.27	1263.43	1175.88
70000	6326.35	3402.39	2435.16	1957.04	1674.50	1489.68	1360.61	1266.33
75000	6778.23	3645.42	2609.10	2096.83	1794.11	1596.08	1457.80	1356.78
80000	7230.11	3888.45	2783.04	2236.62	1913.71	1702.49	1554.99	1447.23
85000	7681.99	4131.47	2956.97	2376.40	2033.32	1808.89	1652.17	1537.69
90000	8133.87	4374.50	3130.91	2516.19	2152.93	1915.30	1749.36	1628.14
95000	8585.76	4617.53	3304.85	2655.98	2272.53	2021.70	1846.55	1718.59
100000	9037.64	4860.56	3478.79	2795.77	2392.14	2128.11	1943.73	1809.04
105000	9489.52	5103.58	3652.73	2935.56	2511.75	2234.51	2040.92	1899.49
110000	9941.40	5346.61	3826.67	3075.35	2631.35	2340.92	2138.11	1989.95
115000	10393.28	5589.64	4000.61	3215.13	2750.96	2447.32	2235.29	2080.40
120000	10845.16	5832.67	4174.55	3354.92	2870.57	2553.73	2332.48	2170.85
125000	11297.05	6075.69	4348.49	3494.71	2990.17	2660.13	2429.67	2261.30
130000	11748.93	6318.72	4522.43	3634.50	3109.78	2766.54	2526.85	2351.75
135000	12200.81	6561.75	4696.37	3774.29	3229.39	2872.94	2624.04	2442.20
140000	12652.69	6804.78	4870.31	3914.07	3349.00	2979.35	2721.22	2532.66
145000	13104.57	7047.80	5044.25	4053.86	3468.60	3085.75	2818.41	2623.11
150000	13556.45	7290.83	5218.19	4193.65	3588.21	3192.16	2915.60	2713.56
155000	14008.33	7533.86	5392.13	4333.44	3707.82	3298.56	3012.78	2804.01
160000	14460.22	7776.89	5566.07	4473.23	3827.42	3404.97	3109.97	2894.46

AMOUNT OF LOAN	NUMBER OF YEARS IN TERM							
	9	10	15	20	25	30	35	40
$ 50	.86	.82	.71	.67	.66	.65	.64	.64
100	1.71	1.63	1.42	1.34	1.31	1.29	1.28	1.28
200	3.42	3.26	2.84	2.68	2.61	2.57	2.56	2.55
300	5.13	4.89	4.26	4.01	3.91	3.86	3.84	3.83
400	6.83	6.52	5.67	5.35	5.21	5.14	5.11	5.10
500	8.54	8.15	7.09	6.68	6.51	6.43	6.39	6.37
600	10.25	9.78	8.51	8.02	7.81	7.71	7.67	7.65
700	11.96	11.41	9.92	9.35	9.11	9.00	8.95	8.92
800	13.66	13.03	11.34	10.69	10.41	10.28	10.22	10.20
900	15.37	14.66	12.76	12.02	11.71	11.57	11.50	11.47
1000	17.08	16.29	14.17	13.36	13.01	12.85	12.78	12.74
2000	34.15	32.58	28.34	26.71	26.01	25.69	25.55	25.48
3000	51.23	48.87	42.51	40.06	39.01	38.54	38.32	38.22
4000	68.30	65.15	56.67	53.42	52.02	51.38	51.09	50.96
5000	85.37	81.44	70.84	66.77	65.02	64.23	63.86	63.70
6000	102.45	97.73	85.01	80.12	78.02	77.07	76.64	76.43
7000	119.52	114.01	99.18	93.48	91.02	89.92	89.41	89.17
8000	136.59	130.30	113.34	106.83	104.03	102.76	102.18	101.91
9000	153.67	146.59	127.51	120.18	117.03	115.61	114.95	114.65
10000	170.74	162.87	141.68	133.53	130.03	128.45	127.72	127.39
11000	187.81	179.16	155.85	146.89	143.03	141.30	140.50	140.12
12000	204.89	195.45	170.01	160.24	156.04	154.14	153.27	152.86
13000	221.96	211.74	184.18	173.59	169.04	166.98	166.04	165.60
14000	239.04	228.02	198.35	186.95	182.04	179.83	178.81	178.34
15000	256.11	244.31	212.52	200.30	195.04	192.67	191.58	191.08
16000	273.18	260.60	226.68	213.65	208.05	205.52	204.35	203.81
17000	290.26	276.88	240.85	227.01	221.05	218.36	217.13	216.55
18000	307.33	293.17	255.02	240.36	234.05	231.21	229.90	229.29
19000	324.40	309.46	269.19	253.71	247.05	244.05	242.67	242.03
20000	341.48	325.74	283.35	267.06	260.06	256.90	255.44	254.77
21000	358.55	342.03	297.52	280.42	273.06	269.74	268.21	267.50
22000	375.62	358.32	311.69	293.77	286.06	282.59	280.99	280.24
23000	392.70	374.60	325.86	307.12	299.06	295.43	293.76	292.98
24000	409.77	390.89	340.02	320.48	312.07	308.28	306.53	305.72
25000	426.85	407.18	354.19	333.83	325.07	321.12	319.30	318.46
26000	443.92	423.47	368.36	347.18	338.07	333.96	332.07	331.19
27000	460.99	439.75	382.53	360.54	351.07	346.81	344.84	343.93
28000	478.07	456.04	396.69	373.89	364.08	359.65	357.62	356.67
29000	495.14	472.33	410.86	387.24	377.08	372.50	370.39	369.41
30000	512.21	488.61	425.03	400.59	390.08	385.34	383.16	382.15
31000	529.29	504.90	439.20	413.95	403.09	398.19	395.93	394.88
32000	546.36	521.19	453.36	427.30	416.09	411.03	408.70	407.62
33000	563.43	537.47	467.53	440.65	429.09	423.88	421.48	420.36
34000	580.51	553.76	481.70	454.01	442.09	436.72	434.25	433.10
35000	597.58	570.05	495.87	467.36	455.10	449.57	447.02	445.84
40000	682.95	651.48	566.70	534.12	520.11	513.79	510.88	509.53
45000	768.32	732.92	637.54	600.89	585.12	578.01	574.74	573.22
50000	853.69	814.35	708.38	667.65	650.13	642.23	638.60	636.91
55000	939.05	895.79	779.22	734.42	715.15	706.46	702.46	700.60
60000	1024.42	977.22	850.05	801.18	780.16	770.68	766.32	764.29
65000	1109.79	1058.66	920.89	867.95	845.17	834.90	830.17	827.98
70000	1195.16	1140.09	991.73	934.71	910.19	899.13	894.03	891.67
75000	1280.53	1221.53	1062.57	1001.48	975.20	963.35	957.89	955.36
80000	1365.89	1302.96	1133.40	1068.24	1040.21	1027.57	1021.75	1019.05
85000	1451.26	1384.39	1204.24	1135.01	1105.22	1091.79	1085.61	1082.74
90000	1536.63	1465.83	1275.08	1201.77	1170.24	1156.02	1149.47	1146.43
95000	1622.00	1547.26	1345.92	1268.54	1235.25	1220.24	1213.33	1210.12
100000	1707.37	1628.70	1416.75	1335.30	1300.26	1284.46	1277.19	1273.81
105000	1792.73	1710.13	1487.59	1402.07	1365.28	1348.69	1341.05	1337.50
110000	1878.10	1791.57	1558.43	1468.83	1430.29	1412.91	1404.91	1401.19
115000	1963.47	1873.00	1629.27	1535.60	1495.30	1477.13	1468.77	1464.88
120000	2048.84	1954.44	1700.10	1602.36	1560.31	1541.36	1532.63	1528.57
125000	2134.21	2035.87	1770.94	1669.13	1625.33	1605.58	1596.48	1592.26
130000	2219.57	2117.31	1841.78	1735.89	1690.34	1669.80	1660.34	1655.95
135000	2304.94	2198.74	1912.62	1802.66	1755.35	1734.02	1724.20	1719.64
140000	2390.31	2280.18	1983.45	1869.42	1820.37	1798.25	1788.06	1783.33
145000	2475.68	2361.61	2054.29	1936.19	1885.38	1862.47	1851.92	1847.02
150000	2561.05	2443.05	2125.13	2002.95	1950.39	1926.69	1915.78	1910.71
155000	2646.41	2524.48	2195.97	2069.72	2015.41	1990.92	1979.63	1974.40
160000	2731.78	2605.91	2266.80	2136.48	2080.42	2055.14	2043.50	2038.09

15.500% MONTHLY AMORTIZING PAYMENTS

AMOUNT OF LOAN	NUMBER OF YEARS IN TERM							
	1	2	3	4	5	6	7	8
$ 50	4.53	2.44	1.75	1.41	1.21	1.08	.98	.92
100	9.05	4.88	3.50	2.81	2.41	2.15	1.96	1.83
200	18.10	9.75	6.99	5.62	4.82	4.29	3.92	3.65
300	27.15	14.62	10.48	8.43	7.22	6.43	5.88	5.48
400	36.20	19.49	13.97	11.24	9.63	8.57	7.84	7.30
500	45.25	24.37	17.46	14.05	12.03	10.71	9.79	9.12
600	54.30	29.24	20.95	16.86	14.44	12.86	11.75	10.95
700	63.35	34.11	24.44	19.66	16.84	15.00	13.71	12.77
800	72.40	38.98	27.93	22.47	19.25	17.14	15.67	14.59
900	81.45	43.86	31.42	25.28	21.65	19.28	17.63	16.42
1000	90.50	48.73	34.92	28.09	24.06	21.42	19.58	18.24
2000	180.99	97.45	69.83	56.17	48.11	42.84	39.16	36.48
3000	271.49	146.18	104.74	84.26	72.16	64.26	58.74	54.71
4000	361.98	194.90	139.65	112.34	96.22	85.67	78.32	72.95
5000	452.48	243.63	174.56	140.43	120.27	107.09	97.90	91.18
6000	542.97	292.35	209.47	168.51	144.32	128.51	117.48	109.42
7000	633.47	341.08	244.38	196.60	168.38	149.93	137.05	127.66
8000	723.96	389.80	279.29	224.68	192.43	171.34	156.63	145.89
9000	814.45	438.53	314.20	252.77	216.48	192.76	176.21	164.13
10000	904.95	487.25	349.11	280.85	240.54	214.18	195.79	182.36
11000	995.44	535.97	384.02	308.94	264.59	235.60	215.37	200.60
12000	1085.94	584.70	418.93	337.02	288.64	257.01	234.95	218.84
13000	1176.43	633.42	453.84	365.11	312.70	278.43	254.52	237.07
14000	1266.93	682.15	488.75	393.19	336.75	299.85	274.10	255.31
15000	1357.42	730.87	523.67	421.28	360.80	321.27	293.68	273.54
16000	1447.92	779.60	558.58	449.36	384.86	342.68	313.26	291.78
17000	1538.41	828.32	593.49	477.45	408.91	364.10	332.84	310.02
18000	1628.90	877.05	628.40	505.53	432.96	385.52	352.42	328.25
19000	1719.40	925.77	663.31	533.62	457.02	406.94	371.99	346.49
20000	1809.89	974.50	698.22	561.70	481.07	428.35	391.57	364.72
21000	1900.39	1023.22	733.13	589.79	505.12	449.77	411.15	382.96
22000	1990.88	1071.94	768.04	617.87	529.18	471.19	430.73	401.20
23000	2081.38	1120.67	802.95	645.96	553.23	492.61	450.31	419.43
24000	2171.87	1169.39	837.86	674.04	577.28	514.02	469.89	437.67
25000	2262.37	1218.12	872.77	702.13	601.33	535.44	489.46	455.90
26000	2352.86	1266.84	907.68	730.21	625.39	556.86	509.04	474.14
27000	2443.35	1315.57	942.59	758.30	649.44	578.28	528.62	492.37
28000	2533.85	1364.29	977.50	786.38	673.49	599.69	548.20	510.61
29000	2624.34	1413.02	1012.41	814.47	697.55	621.11	567.78	528.85
30000	2714.84	1461.74	1047.33	842.55	721.60	642.53	587.36	547.08
31000	2805.33	1510.47	1082.24	870.64	745.65	663.95	606.93	565.32
32000	2895.83	1559.19	1117.15	898.72	769.71	685.36	626.51	583.55
33000	2986.32	1607.91	1152.06	926.81	793.76	706.78	646.09	601.79
34000	3076.82	1656.64	1186.97	954.89	817.81	728.20	665.67	620.03
35000	3167.31	1705.36	1221.88	982.98	841.87	749.62	685.25	638.26
40000	3619.78	1948.99	1396.43	1123.40	962.13	856.70	783.14	729.44
45000	4072.25	2192.61	1570.99	1263.82	1082.40	963.79	881.03	820.62
50000	4524.73	2436.23	1745.54	1404.25	1202.66	1070.88	978.92	911.80
55000	4977.20	2679.85	1920.09	1544.67	1322.93	1177.97	1076.81	1002.98
60000	5429.67	2923.48	2094.65	1685.10	1443.20	1285.05	1174.71	1094.16
65000	5882.14	3167.10	2269.20	1825.52	1563.46	1392.14	1272.60	1185.34
70000	6334.61	3410.72	2443.75	1965.95	1683.73	1499.23	1370.49	1276.52
75000	6787.09	3654.35	2618.31	2106.37	1803.99	1606.32	1468.38	1367.70
80000	7239.56	3897.97	2792.86	2246.79	1924.26	1713.40	1566.27	1458.88
85000	7692.03	4141.59	2967.41	2387.22	2044.53	1820.49	1664.16	1550.06
90000	8144.50	4385.21	3141.97	2527.64	2164.79	1927.58	1762.06	1641.24
95000	8596.97	4628.84	3316.52	2668.07	2285.06	2034.67	1859.95	1732.42
100000	9049.45	4872.46	3491.07	2808.49	2405.32	2141.75	1957.84	1823.60
105000	9501.92	5116.08	3665.63	2948.92	2525.59	2248.84	2055.73	1914.78
110000	9954.39	5359.70	3840.18	3089.34	2645.86	2355.93	2153.62	2005.96
115000	10406.86	5603.33	4014.73	3229.76	2766.12	2463.02	2251.51	2097.14
120000	10859.33	5846.95	4189.29	3370.19	2886.39	2570.10	2349.41	2188.32
125000	11311.81	6090.57	4363.84	3510.61	3006.65	2677.19	2447.30	2279.50
130000	11764.28	6334.20	4538.39	3651.04	3126.92	2784.28	2545.19	2370.67
135000	12216.75	6577.82	4712.95	3791.46	3247.19	2891.37	2643.08	2461.85
140000	12669.22	6821.44	4887.50	3931.89	3367.45	2998.45	2740.97	2553.03
145000	13121.70	7065.06	5062.05	4072.31	3487.72	3105.54	2838.87	2644.21
150000	13574.17	7308.69	5236.61	4212.73	3607.98	3212.63	2936.76	2735.39
155000	14026.64	7552.31	5411.16	4353.16	3728.25	3319.72	3034.65	2826.57
160000	14479.11	7795.93	5585.71	4493.58	3848.52	3426.80	3132.54	2917.75

58

AMOUNT OF LOAN	NUMBER OF YEARS IN TERM							
	9	10	15	20	25	30	35	40
$ 50	.87	.83	.72	.68	.66	.66	.65	.65
100	1.73	1.65	1.44	1.36	1.32	1.31	1.30	1.30
200	3.45	3.29	2.87	2.71	2.64	2.61	2.60	2.59
300	5.17	4.94	4.31	4.07	3.96	3.92	3.90	3.89
400	6.89	6.58	5.74	5.42	5.28	5.22	5.20	5.18
500	8.62	8.23	7.17	6.77	6.60	6.53	6.49	6.48
600	10.34	9.87	8.61	8.13	7.92	7.83	7.79	7.77
700	12.06	11.51	10.04	9.48	9.24	9.14	9.09	9.07
800	13.78	13.16	11.48	10.84	10.56	10.44	10.39	10.36
900	15.51	14.80	12.91	12.19	11.88	11.75	11.68	11.65
1000	17.23	16.45	14.34	13.54	13.20	13.05	12.98	12.95
2000	34.45	32.89	28.68	27.08	26.40	26.10	25.96	25.89
3000	51.68	49.33	43.02	40.62	39.60	39.14	38.93	38.84
4000	68.90	65.77	57.36	54.16	52.79	52.19	51.91	51.78
5000	86.12	82.21	71.70	67.70	65.99	65.23	64.88	64.72
6000	103.35	98.65	86.04	81.24	79.19	78.28	77.86	77.67
7000	120.57	115.09	100.38	94.78	92.39	91.32	90.84	90.61
8000	137.79	131.53	114.72	108.32	105.58	104.37	103.81	103.56
9000	155.02	147.97	129.06	121.85	118.78	117.41	116.79	116.50
10000	172.24	164.42	143.40	135.39	131.98	130.46	129.76	129.44
11000	189.46	180.86	157.74	148.93	145.18	143.50	142.74	142.39
12000	206.69	197.30	172.08	162.47	158.37	156.55	155.72	155.33
13000	223.91	213.74	186.42	176.01	171.57	169.59	168.69	168.28
14000	241.13	230.18	200.76	189.55	184.77	182.64	181.67	181.22
15000	258.36	246.62	215.10	203.09	197.97	195.68	194.64	194.16
16000	275.58	263.06	229.44	216.63	211.16	208.73	207.62	207.11
17000	292.80	279.50	243.78	230.16	224.36	221.77	220.59	220.05
18000	310.03	295.94	258.12	243.70	237.56	234.82	233.57	233.00
19000	327.25	312.39	272.46	257.24	250.76	247.86	246.55	245.94
20000	344.48	328.83	286.80	270.78	263.95	260.91	259.52	258.88
21000	361.70	345.27	301.14	284.32	277.15	273.95	272.50	271.83
22000	378.92	361.71	315.48	297.86	290.35	287.00	285.47	284.77
23000	396.15	378.15	329.82	311.40	303.55	300.04	298.45	297.72
24000	413.37	394.59	344.16	324.94	316.74	313.09	311.43	310.66
25000	430.59	411.03	358.50	338.48	329.94	326.13	324.40	323.60
26000	447.82	427.47	372.84	352.01	343.14	339.18	337.38	336.55
27000	465.04	443.91	387.18	365.55	356.34	352.22	350.35	349.49
28000	482.26	460.35	401.52	379.09	369.53	365.27	363.33	362.44
29000	499.49	476.80	415.86	392.63	382.73	378.31	376.30	375.38
30000	516.71	493.24	430.20	406.17	395.93	391.36	389.28	388.32
31000	533.93	509.68	444.54	419.71	409.13	404.41	402.26	401.27
32000	551.16	526.12	458.88	433.25	422.32	417.45	415.23	414.21
33000	568.38	542.56	473.22	446.79	435.52	430.50	428.21	427.16
34000	585.60	559.00	487.56	460.32	448.72	443.54	441.18	440.10
35000	602.83	575.44	501.90	473.86	461.92	456.59	454.16	453.04
40000	688.95	657.65	573.60	541.56	527.90	521.81	519.04	517.76
45000	775.06	739.85	645.30	609.25	593.89	587.04	583.92	582.48
50000	861.18	822.06	717.00	676.95	659.88	652.26	648.80	647.20
55000	947.30	904.26	788.70	744.64	725.86	717.49	713.68	711.92
60000	1033.42	986.47	860.40	812.33	791.85	782.72	778.56	776.64
65000	1119.53	1068.67	932.10	880.03	857.84	847.94	843.44	841.36
70000	1205.65	1150.88	1003.80	947.72	923.83	913.17	908.31	906.08
75000	1291.77	1233.08	1075.50	1015.42	989.81	978.39	973.19	970.80
80000	1377.89	1315.29	1147.20	1083.11	1055.80	1043.62	1038.07	1035.52
85000	1464.00	1397.49	1218.90	1150.80	1121.79	1108.84	1102.95	1100.24
90000	1550.12	1479.70	1290.60	1218.50	1187.78	1174.07	1167.83	1164.96
95000	1636.24	1561.91	1362.30	1286.19	1253.76	1239.30	1232.71	1229.68
100000	1722.36	1644.11	1434.00	1353.89	1319.75	1304.52	1297.59	1294.40
105000	1808.48	1726.32	1505.69	1421.58	1385.74	1369.75	1362.47	1359.12
110000	1894.59	1808.52	1577.39	1489.27	1451.72	1434.97	1427.35	1423.84
115000	1980.71	1890.73	1649.09	1556.97	1517.71	1500.20	1492.23	1488.56
120000	2066.83	1972.93	1720.79	1624.66	1583.70	1565.43	1557.11	1553.28
125000	2152.95	2055.14	1792.49	1692.36	1649.69	1630.65	1621.99	1618.00
130000	2239.06	2137.34	1864.19	1760.05	1715.67	1695.88	1686.87	1682.72
135000	2325.18	2219.55	1935.89	1827.74	1781.66	1761.10	1751.74	1747.44
140000	2411.30	2301.75	2007.59	1895.44	1847.65	1826.33	1816.62	1812.16
145000	2497.42	2383.96	2079.29	1963.13	1913.64	1891.55	1881.50	1876.88
150000	2583.53	2466.16	2150.99	2030.83	1979.62	1956.78	1946.38	1941.60
155000	2669.65	2548.37	2222.69	2098.52	2045.61	2022.01	2011.26	2006.32
160000	2755.77	2630.57	2294.39	2166.21	2111.60	2087.23	2076.14	2071.04

AMOUNT OF LOAN	NUMBER OF YEARS IN TERM							
	1	2	3	4	5	6	7	8
$ 50	4.54	2.45	1.76	1.42	1.21	1.08	.99	.92
100	9.07	4.89	3.51	2.83	2.42	2.16	1.98	1.84
200	18.13	9.77	7.01	5.65	4.84	4.32	3.95	3.68
300	27.19	14.66	10.52	8.47	7.26	6.47	5.92	5.52
400	36.25	19.54	14.02	11.29	9.68	8.63	7.89	7.36
500	45.31	24.43	17.52	14.11	12.10	10.78	9.86	9.20
600	54.37	29.31	21.03	16.93	14.52	12.94	11.84	11.03
700	63.43	34.20	24.53	19.75	16.93	15.09	13.81	12.87
800	72.50	39.08	28.03	22.57	19.35	17.25	15.78	14.71
900	81.56	43.96	31.54	25.40	21.77	19.40	17.75	16.55
1000	90.62	48.85	35.04	28.22	24.19	21.56	19.72	18.39
2000	181.23	97.69	70.07	56.43	48.38	43.11	39.44	36.77
3000	271.84	146.54	105.11	84.64	72.56	64.67	59.16	55.15
4000	362.46	195.38	140.14	112.85	96.75	86.22	78.88	73.53
5000	453.07	244.22	175.17	141.07	120.93	107.78	98.60	91.92
6000	543.68	293.07	210.21	169.28	145.12	129.33	118.32	110.30
7000	634.29	341.91	245.24	197.49	169.30	150.89	138.04	128.68
8000	724.91	390.75	280.27	225.70	193.49	172.44	157.76	147.06
9000	815.52	439.60	315.31	253.92	217.67	193.99	177.48	165.44
10000	906.13	488.44	350.34	282.13	241.86	215.55	197.20	183.83
11000	996.74	537.29	385.38	310.34	266.04	237.10	216.92	202.21
12000	1087.36	586.13	420.41	338.55	290.23	258.66	236.64	220.59
13000	1177.97	634.97	455.44	366.77	314.42	280.21	256.36	238.97
14000	1268.58	683.82	490.48	394.98	338.60	301.77	276.08	257.35
15000	1359.19	732.66	525.51	423.19	362.79	323.32	295.80	275.74
16000	1449.81	781.50	560.54	451.40	386.97	344.88	315.52	294.12
17000	1540.42	830.35	595.58	479.62	411.16	366.43	335.24	312.50
18000	1631.03	879.19	630.61	507.83	435.34	387.98	354.96	330.88
19000	1721.64	928.04	665.65	536.04	459.53	409.54	374.68	349.26
20000	1812.26	976.88	700.68	564.25	483.71	431.09	394.40	367.65
21000	1902.87	1025.72	735.71	592.47	507.90	452.65	414.12	386.03
22000	1993.48	1074.57	770.75	620.68	532.08	474.20	433.84	404.41
23000	2084.09	1123.41	805.78	648.89	556.27	495.76	453.56	422.79
24000	2174.71	1172.25	840.81	677.10	580.46	517.31	473.28	441.17
25000	2265.32	1221.10	875.85	705.32	604.64	538.87	493.00	459.56
26000	2355.93	1269.94	910.88	733.53	628.83	560.42	512.72	477.94
27000	2446.55	1318.79	945.92	761.74	653.01	581.97	532.44	496.32
28000	2537.16	1367.63	980.95	789.95	677.20	603.53	552.16	514.70
29000	2627.77	1416.47	1015.98	818.16	701.38	625.08	571.88	533.08
30000	2718.38	1465.32	1051.02	846.38	725.57	646.64	591.60	551.47
31000	2809.00	1514.16	1086.05	874.59	749.75	668.19	611.32	569.85
32000	2899.61	1563.00	1121.08	902.80	773.94	689.75	631.04	588.23
33000	2990.22	1611.85	1156.12	931.01	798.12	711.30	650.76	606.61
34000	3080.83	1660.69	1191.15	959.23	822.31	732.86	670.48	625.00
35000	3171.45	1709.54	1226.19	987.44	846.49	754.41	690.20	643.38
40000	3624.51	1953.75	1401.35	1128.50	967.42	862.18	788.80	735.29
45000	4077.57	2197.97	1576.52	1269.56	1088.35	969.95	887.40	827.20
50000	4530.63	2442.19	1751.69	1410.63	1209.28	1077.73	986.00	919.11
55000	4983.70	2686.41	1926.86	1551.69	1330.20	1185.50	1084.60	1011.02
60000	5436.76	2930.63	2102.03	1692.75	1451.13	1293.27	1183.20	1102.93
65000	5889.82	3174.85	2277.20	1833.81	1572.06	1401.04	1281.80	1194.84
70000	6342.89	3419.07	2452.37	1974.87	1692.98	1508.82	1380.40	1286.75
75000	6795.95	3663.29	2627.53	2115.94	1813.91	1616.59	1479.00	1378.66
80000	7249.01	3907.50	2802.70	2257.00	1934.84	1724.36	1577.60	1470.57
85000	7702.08	4151.72	2977.87	2398.06	2055.77	1832.13	1676.20	1562.48
90000	8155.14	4395.94	3153.04	2539.12	2176.69	1939.90	1774.80	1654.39
95000	8608.20	4640.16	3328.21	2680.18	2297.62	2047.68	1873.40	1746.30
100000	9061.26	4884.38	3503.38	2821.25	2418.55	2155.45	1972.00	1838.21
105000	9514.33	5128.60	3678.55	2962.31	2539.47	2263.22	2070.60	1930.12
110000	9967.39	5372.82	3853.72	3103.37	2660.40	2370.99	2169.20	2022.03
115000	10420.45	5617.04	4028.88	3244.43	2781.33	2478.76	2267.80	2113.94
120000	10873.52	5861.25	4204.05	3385.49	2902.26	2586.54	2366.40	2205.85
125000	11326.58	6105.47	4379.22	3526.56	3023.18	2694.31	2465.00	2297.76
130000	11779.64	6349.69	4554.39	3667.62	3144.11	2802.08	2563.60	2389.67
135000	12232.71	6593.91	4729.56	3808.68	3265.04	2909.85	2662.20	2481.58
140000	12685.77	6838.13	4904.73	3949.74	3385.96	3017.63	2760.80	2573.49
145000	13138.83	7082.35	5079.90	4090.80	3506.89	3125.40	2859.40	2665.40
150000	13591.89	7326.57	5255.06	4231.87	3627.82	3233.17	2958.00	2757.31
155000	14044.96	7570.79	5430.23	4372.93	3748.75	3340.94	3056.60	2849.22
160000	14498.02	7815.00	5605.40	4513.99	3869.67	3448.71	3155.20	2941.14

AMOUNT OF LOAN	NUMBER OF YEARS IN TERM							
	9	10	15	20	25	30	35	40
$ 50	.87	.83	.73	.69	.67	.67	.66	.66
100	1.74	1.66	1.46	1.38	1.34	1.33	1.32	1.32
200	3.48	3.32	2.91	2.75	2.68	2.65	2.64	2.64
300	5.22	4.98	4.36	4.12	4.02	3.98	3.96	3.95
400	6.95	6.64	5.81	5.50	5.36	5.30	5.28	5.27
500	8.69	8.30	7.26	6.87	6.70	6.63	6.60	6.58
600	10.43	9.96	8.71	8.24	8.04	7.95	7.91	7.90
700	12.17	11.62	10.16	9.61	9.38	9.28	9.23	9.21
800	13.90	13.28	11.62	10.99	10.72	10.60	10.55	10.53
900	15.64	14.94	13.07	12.36	12.06	11.93	11.87	11.84
1000	17.38	16.60	14.52	13.73	13.40	13.25	13.19	13.16
2000	34.75	33.20	29.03	27.46	26.79	26.50	26.37	26.31
3000	52.13	49.79	43.54	41.18	40.18	39.74	39.55	39.46
4000	69.50	66.39	58.06	54.91	53.58	52.99	52.73	52.61
5000	86.88	82.98	72.57	68.63	66.97	66.24	65.91	65.76
6000	104.25	99.58	87.08	82.36	80.36	79.48	79.09	78.91
7000	121.62	116.18	101.60	96.08	93.76	92.73	92.27	92.06
8000	139.00	132.77	116.11	109.81	107.15	105.97	105.45	105.21
9000	156.37	149.37	130.62	123.53	120.54	119.22	118.63	118.36
10000	173.75	165.96	145.14	137.26	133.93	132.47	131.81	131.51
11000	191.12	182.56	159.65	150.98	147.33	145.71	144.99	144.66
12000	208.49	199.16	174.16	164.71	160.72	158.96	158.17	157.81
13000	225.87	215.75	188.68	178.43	174.11	172.21	171.35	170.96
14000	243.24	232.35	203.19	192.16	187.51	185.45	184.53	184.11
15000	260.62	248.94	217.70	205.89	200.90	198.70	197.71	197.26
16000	277.99	265.54	232.21	219.61	214.29	211.94	210.89	210.41
17000	295.36	282.13	246.73	233.34	227.68	225.19	224.07	223.56
18000	312.74	298.73	261.24	247.06	241.08	238.44	237.25	236.71
19000	330.11	315.33	275.75	260.79	254.47	251.68	250.43	249.86
20000	347.49	331.92	290.27	274.51	267.86	264.93	263.61	263.01
21000	364.86	348.52	304.78	288.24	281.26	278.17	276.79	276.16
22000	382.23	365.11	319.29	301.96	294.65	291.42	289.97	289.31
23000	399.61	381.71	333.81	315.69	308.04	304.67	303.15	302.46
24000	416.98	398.31	348.32	329.41	321.43	317.91	316.33	315.61
25000	434.36	414.90	362.83	343.14	334.83	331.16	329.51	328.76
26000	451.73	431.50	377.35	356.86	348.22	344.41	342.69	341.91
27000	469.10	448.09	391.86	370.59	361.61	357.65	355.87	355.06
28000	486.48	464.69	406.37	384.31	375.01	370.90	369.05	368.21
29000	503.85	481.28	420.88	398.04	388.40	384.14	382.23	381.36
30000	521.23	497.88	435.40	411.77	401.79	397.39	395.41	394.51
31000	538.60	514.48	449.91	425.49	415.18	410.64	408.59	407.66
32000	555.98	531.07	464.42	439.22	428.58	423.88	421.77	420.81
33000	573.35	547.67	478.94	452.94	441.97	437.13	434.95	433.96
34000	590.72	564.26	493.45	466.67	455.36	450.37	448.13	447.11
35000	608.10	580.86	507.96	480.39	468.76	463.62	461.31	460.26
40000	694.97	663.84	580.53	549.02	535.72	529.85	527.21	526.01
45000	781.84	746.82	653.09	617.65	602.69	596.08	593.11	591.76
50000	868.71	829.80	725.66	686.27	669.65	662.31	659.01	657.51
55000	955.58	912.78	798.22	754.90	736.61	728.54	724.91	723.26
60000	1042.45	995.76	870.79	823.53	803.58	794.78	790.81	789.01
65000	1129.32	1078.74	943.36	892.15	870.54	861.01	856.71	854.77
70000	1216.19	1161.71	1015.90	960.78	937.51	927.24	922.61	920.52
75000	1303.06	1244.69	1088.49	1029.41	1004.47	993.47	988.52	986.27
80000	1389.93	1327.67	1161.05	1098.03	1071.44	1059.70	1054.42	1052.02
85000	1476.80	1410.65	1233.62	1166.66	1138.40	1125.93	1120.32	1117.77
90000	1563.67	1493.63	1306.18	1235.29	1205.37	1192.16	1186.22	1183.52
95000	1650.54	1576.61	1378.75	1303.91	1272.33	1258.39	1252.12	1249.27
100000	1737.41	1659.59	1451.31	1372.54	1339.29	1324.62	1318.02	1315.02
105000	1824.28	1742.57	1523.88	1441.17	1406.26	1390.85	1383.92	1380.77
110000	1911.15	1825.55	1596.44	1509.79	1473.22	1457.08	1449.82	1446.52
115000	1998.02	1908.53	1669.01	1578.42	1540.19	1523.31	1515.72	1512.27
120000	2084.89	1991.51	1741.57	1647.05	1607.15	1589.55	1581.62	1578.02
125000	2171.76	2074.49	1814.14	1715.67	1674.12	1655.78	1647.52	1643.77
130000	2258.63	2157.47	1886.71	1784.30	1741.08	1722.01	1713.42	1709.53
135000	2345.50	2240.44	1959.27	1852.93	1808.05	1788.24	1779.32	1775.28
140000	2432.38	2323.42	2031.84	1921.55	1875.01	1854.47	1845.22	1841.03
145000	2519.25	2406.40	2104.40	1990.18	1941.97	1920.70	1911.12	1906.78
150000	2606.12	2489.38	2176.97	2058.81	2008.94	1986.93	1977.03	1972.53
155000	2692.99	2572.36	2249.53	2127.43	2075.90	2053.16	2042.93	2038.28
160000	2779.86	2655.34	2322.10	2196.06	2142.87	2119.39	2108.83	2104.03

AMOUNT OF LOAN	NUMBER OF YEARS IN TERM							
	1	2	3	4	5	6	7	8
$ 50	4.54	2.45	1.76	1.42	1.22	1.09	1.00	.93
100	9.08	4.90	3.52	2.84	2.44	2.17	1.99	1.86
200	18.15	9.80	7.04	5.67	4.87	4.34	3.98	3.71
300	27.22	14.69	10.55	8.51	7.30	6.51	5.96	5.56
400	36.30	19.59	14.07	11.34	9.73	8.68	7.95	7.42
500	45.37	24.49	17.58	14.18	12.16	10.85	9.94	9.27
600	54.44	29.38	21.10	17.01	14.60	13.02	11.92	11.12
700	63.52	34.28	24.61	19.84	17.03	15.19	13.91	12.98
800	72.59	39.18	28.13	22.68	19.46	17.36	15.89	14.83
900	81.66	44.07	31.65	25.51	21.89	19.53	17.88	16.68
1000	90.74	48.97	35.16	28.35	24.32	21.70	19.87	18.53
2000	181.47	97.93	70.32	56.69	48.64	43.39	39.73	37.06
3000	272.20	146.89	105.48	85.03	72.96	65.08	59.59	55.59
4000	362.93	195.86	140.63	113.37	97.28	86.77	79.45	74.12
5000	453.66	244.82	175.79	141.71	121.60	108.46	99.32	92.65
6000	544.39	293.78	210.95	170.05	145.91	130.16	119.18	111.18
7000	635.12	342.75	246.10	198.39	170.23	151.85	139.04	129.71
8000	725.85	391.71	281.26	226.73	194.55	173.54	158.90	148.24
9000	816.58	440.67	316.42	255.07	218.87	195.23	178.76	166.76
10000	907.31	489.64	351.58	283.41	243.19	216.92	198.63	185.29
11000	998.04	538.60	386.73	311.75	267.50	238.62	218.49	203.82
12000	1088.78	587.56	421.89	340.09	291.82	260.31	238.35	222.35
13000	1179.51	636.53	457.05	368.43	316.14	282.00	258.21	240.88
14000	1270.24	685.49	492.20	396.77	340.46	303.69	278.07	259.41
15000	1360.97	734.45	527.36	425.11	364.78	325.38	297.94	277.94
16000	1451.70	783.41	562.52	453.45	389.09	347.07	317.80	296.47
17000	1542.43	832.38	597.67	481.79	413.41	368.77	337.66	314.99
18000	1633.16	881.34	632.83	510.13	437.73	390.46	357.52	333.52
19000	1723.89	930.30	667.99	538.47	462.05	412.15	377.38	352.05
20000	1814.62	979.27	703.15	566.81	486.37	433.84	397.25	370.58
21000	1905.35	1028.23	738.30	595.15	510.68	455.53	417.11	389.11
22000	1996.08	1077.19	773.46	623.49	535.00	477.23	436.97	407.64
23000	2086.81	1126.16	808.62	651.83	559.32	498.92	456.83	426.17
24000	2177.55	1175.12	843.77	680.17	583.64	520.61	476.69	444.70
25000	2268.28	1224.08	878.93	708.51	607.96	542.30	496.56	463.22
26000	2359.01	1273.05	914.09	736.85	632.27	563.99	516.42	481.75
27000	2449.74	1322.01	949.24	765.19	656.59	585.68	536.28	500.28
28000	2540.47	1370.97	984.40	793.53	680.91	607.38	556.14	518.81
29000	2631.20	1419.94	1019.56	821.87	705.23	629.07	576.00	537.34
30000	2721.93	1468.90	1054.72	850.21	729.55	650.76	595.87	555.87
31000	2812.66	1517.86	1089.87	878.55	753.86	672.45	615.73	574.40
32000	2903.39	1566.82	1125.03	906.89	778.18	694.14	635.59	592.93
33000	2994.12	1615.79	1160.19	935.23	802.50	715.84	655.45	611.46
34000	3084.85	1664.75	1195.34	963.57	826.82	737.53	675.32	629.98
35000	3175.59	1713.71	1230.50	991.91	851.14	759.22	695.18	648.51
40000	3629.24	1958.53	1406.29	1133.62	972.73	867.68	794.49	741.16
45000	4082.89	2203.34	1582.07	1275.32	1094.32	976.14	893.80	833.80
50000	4536.55	2448.16	1757.86	1417.02	1215.91	1084.60	993.11	926.44
55000	4990.20	2692.98	1933.64	1558.72	1337.50	1193.06	1092.42	1019.09
60000	5443.86	2937.79	2109.43	1700.42	1459.09	1301.52	1191.73	1111.73
65000	5897.51	3182.61	2285.21	1842.12	1580.68	1409.97	1291.04	1204.38
70000	6351.17	3427.42	2461.00	1983.82	1702.27	1518.43	1390.35	1297.02
75000	6804.82	3672.24	2636.78	2125.53	1823.86	1626.89	1489.66	1389.66
80000	7258.47	3917.05	2812.57	2267.23	1945.45	1735.35	1588.97	1482.31
85000	7712.13	4161.87	2988.35	2408.93	2067.04	1843.81	1688.28	1574.95
90000	8165.78	4406.68	3164.14	2550.63	2188.63	1952.27	1787.59	1667.60
95000	8619.44	4651.50	3339.92	2692.33	2310.22	2060.73	1886.90	1760.24
100000	9073.09	4896.32	3515.71	2834.03	2431.81	2169.19	1986.21	1852.88
105000	9526.75	5141.13	3691.49	2975.73	2553.40	2277.65	2085.52	1945.53
110000	9980.40	5385.95	3867.28	3117.44	2674.99	2386.11	2184.83	2038.17
115000	10434.05	5630.76	4043.06	3259.14	2796.58	2494.57	2284.14	2130.82
120000	10887.71	5875.58	4218.85	3400.84	2918.17	2603.03	2383.45	2223.46
125000	11341.36	6120.39	4394.63	3542.54	3039.76	2711.49	2482.76	2316.10
130000	11795.02	6365.21	4570.42	3684.24	3161.35	2819.94	2582.07	2408.75
135000	12248.67	6610.02	4746.20	3825.94	3282.94	2928.40	2681.38	2501.39
140000	12702.33	6854.84	4921.99	3967.64	3404.53	3036.86	2780.69	2594.04
145000	13155.98	7099.66	5097.77	4109.35	3526.12	3145.32	2880.00	2686.68
150000	13609.63	7344.47	5273.56	4251.05	3647.71	3253.78	2979.31	2779.32
155000	14063.29	7589.29	5449.35	4392.75	3769.30	3362.24	3078.62	2871.97
160000	14516.94	7834.10	5625.13	4534.45	3890.89	3470.70	3177.94	2964.61

AMOUNT OF LOAN	NUMBER OF YEARS IN TERM							
	9	10	15	20	25	30	35	40
$ 50	.88	.84	.74	.70	.68	.68	.67	.67
100	1.76	1.68	1.47	1.40	1.36	1.35	1.34	1.34
200	3.51	3.36	2.94	2.79	2.72	2.69	2.68	2.68
300	5.26	5.03	4.41	4.18	4.08	4.04	4.02	4.01
400	7.02	6.71	5.88	5.57	5.44	5.38	5.36	5.35
500	8.77	8.38	7.35	6.96	6.80	6.73	6.70	6.68
600	10.52	10.06	8.82	8.35	8.16	8.07	8.04	8.02
700	12.27	11.73	10.29	9.74	9.52	9.42	9.37	9.35
800	14.03	13.41	11.75	11.14	10.88	10.76	10.71	10.69
900	15.78	15.08	13.22	12.53	12.23	12.11	12.05	12.03
1000	17.53	16.76	14.69	13.92	13.59	13.45	13.39	13.36
2000	35.06	33.51	29.38	27.83	27.18	26.90	26.77	26.72
3000	52.58	50.26	44.07	41.74	40.77	40.35	40.16	40.07
4000	70.11	67.01	58.75	55.66	54.36	53.80	53.54	53.43
5000	87.63	83.76	73.44	69.57	67.95	67.24	66.93	66.79
6000	105.16	100.51	88.13	83.48	81.54	80.69	80.31	80.14
7000	122.68	117.26	102.81	97.39	95.13	94.14	93.70	93.50
8000	140.21	134.02	117.50	111.31	108.72	107.59	107.08	106.86
9000	157.73	150.77	132.19	125.22	122.30	121.03	120.47	120.21
10000	175.26	167.52	146.88	139.13	135.89	134.48	133.85	133.57
11000	192.78	184.27	161.56	153.04	149.48	147.93	147.24	146.93
12000	210.31	201.02	176.25	166.96	163.07	161.38	160.62	160.28
13000	227.83	217.77	190.94	180.87	176.66	174.82	174.01	173.64
14000	245.36	234.52	205.62	194.78	190.25	188.27	187.39	187.00
15000	262.88	251.27	220.31	208.69	203.84	201.72	200.78	200.35
16000	280.41	268.03	235.00	222.61	217.43	215.17	214.16	213.71
17000	297.93	284.78	249.68	236.52	231.02	228.61	227.54	227.07
18000	315.46	301.53	264.37	250.43	244.60	242.06	240.93	240.42
19000	332.98	318.28	279.06	264.34	258.19	255.51	254.31	253.78
20000	350.51	335.03	293.75	278.26	271.78	268.96	267.70	267.13
21000	368.04	351.78	308.43	292.17	285.37	282.40	281.08	280.49
22000	385.56	368.53	323.12	306.08	298.96	295.85	294.47	293.85
23000	403.09	385.29	337.81	319.99	312.55	309.30	307.85	307.20
24000	420.61	402.04	352.49	333.91	326.14	322.75	321.24	320.56
25000	438.14	418.79	367.18	347.82	339.73	336.19	334.62	333.92
26000	455.66	435.54	381.87	361.73	353.32	349.64	348.01	347.27
27000	473.19	452.29	396.55	375.64	366.90	363.09	361.39	360.63
28000	490.71	469.04	411.24	389.56	380.49	376.54	374.78	373.99
29000	508.24	485.79	425.93	403.47	394.08	389.98	388.16	387.34
30000	525.76	502.54	440.62	417.38	407.67	403.43	401.55	400.70
31000	543.29	519.30	455.30	431.29	421.26	416.88	414.93	414.06
32000	560.81	536.05	469.99	445.21	434.85	430.33	428.32	427.41
33000	578.34	552.80	484.68	459.12	448.44	443.77	441.70	440.77
34000	595.86	569.55	499.36	473.03	462.03	457.22	455.08	454.13
35000	613.39	586.30	514.05	486.94	475.62	470.67	468.47	467.48
40000	701.02	670.06	587.49	556.51	543.56	537.91	535.39	534.26
45000	788.64	753.81	660.92	626.07	611.50	605.15	602.32	601.05
50000	876.27	837.57	734.36	695.63	679.45	672.38	669.24	667.83
55000	963.89	921.33	807.79	765.20	747.39	739.62	736.16	734.61
60000	1051.52	1005.08	881.23	834.76	815.34	806.86	803.09	801.39
65000	1139.14	1088.84	954.66	904.32	883.28	874.10	870.01	868.18
70000	1226.77	1172.60	1028.10	973.88	951.23	941.33	936.93	934.96
75000	1314.40	1256.35	1101.53	1043.45	1019.17	1008.57	1003.86	1001.74
80000	1402.03	1340.11	1174.97	1113.01	1087.12	1075.81	1070.78	1068.52
85000	1489.65	1423.87	1248.46	1182.57	1155.06	1143.05	1137.70	1135.31
90000	1577.28	1507.62	1321.84	1252.14	1223.00	1210.29	1204.63	1202.09
95000	1664.90	1591.38	1395.27	1321.70	1290.95	1277.52	1271.55	1268.87
100000	1752.53	1675.14	1468.71	1391.26	1358.89	1344.76	1338.47	1335.65
105000	1840.16	1758.89	1542.14	1460.82	1426.84	1412.00	1405.40	1402.44
110000	1927.78	1842.65	1615.58	1530.39	1494.78	1479.24	1472.32	1469.22
115000	2015.41	1926.41	1689.01	1599.95	1562.73	1546.48	1539.24	1536.00
120000	2103.03	2010.16	1762.45	1669.51	1630.67	1613.71	1606.17	1602.78
125000	2190.66	2093.92	1835.88	1739.07	1698.62	1680.95	1673.09	1669.57
130000	2278.29	2177.68	1909.32	1808.64	1766.56	1748.19	1740.02	1736.35
135000	2365.91	2261.43	1982.75	1878.20	1834.50	1815.43	1806.94	1803.13
140000	2453.54	2345.19	2056.19	1947.76	1902.45	1882.66	1873.86	1869.91
145000	2541.17	2428.95	2129.62	2017.33	1970.39	1949.90	1940.79	1936.70
150000	2628.79	2512.70	2203.06	2086.89	2038.34	2017.14	2007.71	2003.48
155000	2716.42	2596.46	2276.49	2156.45	2106.28	2084.38	2074.63	2070.26
160000	2804.05	2680.21	2349.93	2226.01	2174.23	2151.62	2141.56	2137.04

16.250% MONTHLY AMORTIZING PAYMENTS

AMOUNT OF LOAN	NUMBER OF YEARS IN TERM							
	1	2	3	4	5	6	7	8
$ 50	4.55	2.46	1.77	1.43	1.23	1.10	1.01	.94
100	9.09	4.91	3.53	2.85	2.45	2.19	2.01	1.87
200	18.17	9.82	7.06	5.70	4.90	4.37	4.01	3.74
300	27.26	14.73	10.59	8.55	7.34	6.55	6.01	5.61
400	36.34	19.64	14.12	11.39	9.79	8.74	8.01	7.48
500	45.43	24.55	17.65	14.24	12.23	10.92	10.01	9.34
600	54.51	29.45	21.17	17.09	14.68	13.10	12.01	11.21
700	63.60	34.36	24.70	19.93	17.12	15.29	14.01	13.08
800	72.68	39.27	28.23	22.78	19.57	17.47	16.01	14.95
900	81.77	44.18	31.76	25.63	22.01	19.65	18.01	16.81
1000	90.85	49.09	35.29	28.47	24.46	21.83	20.01	18.68
2000	181.70	98.17	70.57	56.94	48.91	43.66	40.01	37.36
3000	272.55	147.25	105.85	85.41	73.36	65.49	60.02	56.03
4000	363.40	196.34	141.13	113.88	97.81	87.32	80.02	74.71
5000	454.25	245.42	176.41	142.35	122.26	109.15	100.03	93.39
6000	545.10	294.50	211.69	170.82	146.71	130.98	120.03	112.06
7000	635.95	343.58	246.97	199.28	171.16	152.81	140.04	130.74
8000	726.80	392.67	282.25	227.75	195.61	174.64	160.04	149.41
9000	817.65	441.75	317.53	256.22	220.06	196.47	180.05	168.09
10000	908.50	490.83	352.81	284.69	244.52	218.30	200.05	186.77
11000	999.35	539.91	388.09	313.16	268.97	240.13	220.06	205.44
12000	1090.20	589.00	423.37	341.63	293.42	261.96	240.06	224.12
13000	1181.04	638.08	458.65	370.10	317.87	283.79	260.07	242.79
14000	1271.89	687.16	493.93	398.56	342.32	305.62	280.07	261.47
15000	1362.74	736.24	529.21	427.03	366.77	327.45	300.08	280.15
16000	1453.59	785.33	564.49	455.50	391.22	349.28	320.08	298.82
17000	1544.44	834.41	599.77	483.97	415.67	371.11	340.09	317.50
18000	1635.29	883.49	635.06	512.44	440.12	392.94	360.09	336.17
19000	1726.14	932.58	670.34	540.91	464.58	414.77	380.09	354.85
20000	1816.99	981.66	705.62	569.37	489.03	436.60	400.10	373.53
21000	1907.84	1030.74	740.90	597.84	513.48	458.43	420.10	392.20
22000	1998.69	1079.82	776.18	626.31	537.93	480.26	440.11	410.88
23000	2089.54	1128.91	811.46	654.78	562.38	502.09	460.11	429.56
24000	2180.39	1177.99	846.74	683.25	586.83	523.92	480.12	448.23
25000	2271.24	1227.07	882.02	711.72	611.28	545.75	500.12	466.91
26000	2362.08	1276.15	917.30	740.19	635.73	567.58	520.13	485.58
27000	2452.93	1325.24	952.58	768.65	660.18	589.41	540.13	504.26
28000	2543.78	1374.32	987.86	797.12	684.64	611.24	560.14	522.94
29000	2634.63	1423.40	1023.14	825.59	709.09	633.07	580.14	541.61
30000	2725.48	1472.48	1058.42	854.06	733.54	654.90	600.15	560.29
31000	2816.33	1521.57	1093.70	882.53	757.99	676.73	620.15	578.96
32000	2907.18	1570.65	1128.98	911.00	782.44	698.56	640.16	597.64
33000	2998.03	1619.73	1164.26	939.46	806.89	720.39	660.16	616.32
34000	3088.88	1668.81	1199.54	967.93	831.34	742.22	680.17	634.99
35000	3179.73	1717.90	1234.83	996.40	855.79	764.05	700.17	653.67
40000	3633.97	1963.31	1411.23	1138.74	978.05	873.19	800.19	747.05
45000	4088.22	2208.72	1587.63	1281.09	1100.30	982.34	900.22	840.43
50000	4542.47	2454.14	1764.03	1423.43	1222.56	1091.49	1000.24	933.81
55000	4996.71	2699.55	1940.44	1565.77	1344.81	1200.64	1100.26	1027.19
60000	5450.96	2944.96	2116.84	1708.11	1467.07	1309.79	1200.29	1120.57
65000	5905.20	3190.38	2293.24	1850.46	1589.33	1418.94	1300.31	1213.95
70000	6359.45	3435.79	2469.65	1992.80	1711.58	1528.09	1400.33	1307.33
75000	6813.70	3681.20	2646.05	2135.14	1833.84	1637.23	1500.36	1400.71
80000	7267.94	3926.62	2822.45	2277.48	1956.09	1746.38	1600.38	1494.09
85000	7722.19	4172.03	2998.85	2419.83	2078.35	1855.53	1700.41	1587.47
90000	8176.43	4417.44	3175.26	2562.17	2200.60	1964.68	1800.43	1680.85
95000	8630.68	4662.86	3351.66	2704.51	2322.86	2073.83	1900.45	1774.23
100000	9084.93	4908.27	3528.06	2846.85	2445.11	2182.98	2000.48	1867.61
105000	9539.17	5153.68	3704.47	2989.20	2567.37	2292.13	2100.50	1960.99
110000	9993.42	5399.10	3880.87	3131.54	2689.62	2401.27	2200.52	2054.37
115000	10447.66	5644.51	4057.27	3273.88	2811.88	2510.42	2300.55	2147.76
120000	10901.91	5889.92	4233.67	3416.22	2934.14	2619.57	2400.57	2241.14
125000	11356.16	6135.34	4410.08	3558.57	3056.39	2728.72	2500.59	2334.52
130000	11810.40	6380.75	4586.48	3700.91	3178.65	2837.87	2600.62	2427.90
135000	12264.65	6626.16	4762.88	3843.25	3300.90	2947.02	2700.64	2521.28
140000	12718.89	6871.58	4939.29	3985.59	3423.16	3056.17	2800.66	2614.66
145000	13173.14	7116.99	5115.69	4127.93	3545.41	3165.31	2900.69	2708.04
150000	13627.39	7362.40	5292.09	4270.28	3667.67	3274.46	3000.71	2801.42
155000	14081.63	7607.82	5468.50	4412.62	3789.92	3383.61	3100.74	2894.80
160000	14535.88	7853.23	5644.90	4554.96	3912.18	3492.76	3200.76	2988.18

64

AMOUNT OF LOAN	NUMBER OF YEARS IN TERM							
	9	10	15	20	25	30	35	40
$ 50	.89	.85	.75	.71	.69	.69	.68	.68
100	1.77	1.70	1.49	1.42	1.38	1.37	1.36	1.36
200	3.54	3.39	2.98	2.83	2.76	2.73	2.72	2.72
300	5.31	5.08	4.46	4.24	4.14	4.10	4.08	4.07
400	7.08	6.77	5.95	5.65	5.52	5.46	5.44	5.43
500	8.84	8.46	7.44	7.06	6.90	6.83	6.80	6.79
600	10.61	10.15	8.92	8.47	8.28	8.19	8.16	8.14
700	12.38	11.84	10.41	9.88	9.65	9.56	9.52	9.50
800	14.15	13.53	11.89	11.29	11.03	10.92	10.88	10.86
900	15.91	15.22	13.38	12.70	12.41	12.29	12.24	12.21
1000	17.68	16.91	14.87	14.11	13.79	13.65	13.59	13.57
2000	35.36	33.82	29.73	28.21	27.58	27.30	27.18	27.13
3000	53.04	50.73	44.59	42.31	41.36	40.95	40.77	40.69
4000	70.71	67.63	59.45	56.41	55.15	54.60	54.36	54.26
5000	88.39	84.54	74.31	70.51	68.93	68.25	67.95	67.82
6000	106.07	101.45	89.18	84.61	82.72	81.90	81.54	81.38
7000	123.74	118.36	104.04	98.71	96.50	95.55	95.13	94.95
8000	141.42	135.26	118.90	112.81	110.29	109.20	108.72	108.51
9000	159.10	152.17	133.76	126.91	124.07	122.85	122.31	122.07
10000	176.78	169.08	148.62	141.01	137.86	136.50	135.90	135.63
11000	194.45	185.99	163.48	155.11	151.64	150.15	149.49	149.20
12000	212.13	202.89	178.35	169.21	165.43	163.80	163.08	162.76
13000	229.81	219.80	193.21	183.31	179.22	177.45	176.67	176.32
14000	247.48	236.71	208.07	197.41	193.00	191.10	190.26	189.89
15000	265.16	253.62	222.93	211.51	206.79	204.75	203.85	203.45
16000	282.84	270.52	237.79	225.61	220.57	218.39	217.44	217.01
17000	300.51	287.43	252.65	239.71	234.36	232.04	231.03	230.58
18000	318.19	304.34	267.52	253.81	248.14	245.69	244.62	244.14
19000	335.87	321.25	282.38	267.91	261.93	259.34	258.21	257.70
20000	353.55	338.15	297.24	282.01	275.71	272.99	271.79	271.26
21000	371.22	355.06	312.10	296.11	289.50	286.64	285.38	284.83
22000	388.90	371.97	326.96	310.22	303.28	300.29	298.97	298.39
23000	406.58	388.88	341.82	324.32	317.07	313.94	312.56	311.95
24000	424.25	405.78	356.69	338.42	330.85	327.59	326.15	325.52
25000	441.93	422.69	371.55	352.52	344.64	341.24	339.74	339.08
26000	459.61	439.60	386.41	366.62	358.43	354.89	353.33	352.64
27000	477.29	456.51	401.27	380.72	372.21	368.54	366.92	366.21
28000	494.96	473.41	416.13	394.82	386.00	382.19	380.51	379.77
29000	512.64	490.32	430.99	408.92	399.78	395.84	394.10	393.33
30000	530.32	507.23	445.86	423.02	413.57	409.49	407.69	406.89
31000	547.99	524.14	460.72	437.12	427.35	423.13	421.28	420.46
32000	565.67	541.04	475.58	451.22	441.14	436.78	434.87	434.02
33000	583.35	557.95	490.44	465.32	454.92	450.43	448.46	447.58
34000	601.02	574.86	505.30	479.42	468.71	464.08	462.05	461.15
35000	618.70	591.77	520.16	493.52	482.49	477.73	475.64	474.71
40000	707.09	676.30	594.47	564.02	551.42	545.98	543.58	542.52
45000	795.47	760.84	668.78	634.53	620.35	614.23	611.53	610.34
50000	883.86	845.38	743.09	705.03	689.28	682.47	679.48	678.15
55000	972.24	929.91	817.40	775.53	758.20	750.72	747.43	745.97
60000	1060.63	1014.45	891.71	846.03	827.13	818.97	815.37	813.78
65000	1149.01	1098.99	966.01	916.53	896.06	887.21	883.32	881.60
70000	1237.40	1183.53	1040.32	987.04	964.98	955.46	951.27	949.41
75000	1325.78	1268.06	1114.63	1057.54	1033.91	1023.71	1019.22	1017.23
80000	1414.17	1352.60	1188.94	1128.04	1102.84	1091.95	1087.16	1085.04
85000	1502.55	1437.14	1263.25	1198.54	1171.77	1160.20	1155.11	1152.86
90000	1590.94	1521.67	1337.56	1269.05	1240.69	1228.45	1223.06	1220.67
95000	1679.33	1606.21	1411.86	1339.55	1309.62	1296.69	1291.01	1288.49
100000	1767.71	1690.75	1486.17	1410.05	1378.55	1364.94	1358.95	1356.30
105000	1856.10	1775.29	1560.48	1480.55	1447.47	1433.19	1426.90	1424.12
110000	1944.48	1859.82	1634.79	1551.06	1516.40	1501.43	1494.85	1491.93
115000	2032.87	1944.36	1709.10	1621.56	1585.33	1569.68	1562.80	1559.75
120000	2121.25	2028.90	1783.41	1692.06	1654.25	1637.93	1630.74	1627.56
125000	2209.64	2113.44	1857.72	1762.56	1723.18	1706.17	1698.69	1695.38
130000	2298.02	2197.97	1932.02	1833.06	1792.11	1774.42	1766.64	1763.19
135000	2386.41	2282.51	2006.33	1903.57	1861.04	1842.67	1834.59	1831.01
140000	2474.79	2367.05	2080.64	1974.07	1929.96	1910.91	1902.53	1898.82
145000	2563.18	2451.58	2154.95	2044.57	1998.89	1979.16	1970.48	1966.64
150000	2651.56	2536.12	2229.26	2115.07	2067.82	2047.41	2038.43	2034.45
155000	2739.95	2620.66	2303.57	2185.58	2136.74	2115.65	2106.38	2102.26
160000	2828.33	2705.20	2377.87	2256.08	2205.67	2183.90	2174.32	2170.08

MONTHLY AMORTIZING PAYMENTS

AMOUNT OF LOAN	NUMBER OF YEARS IN TERM							
	1	2	3	4	5	6	7	8
$ 50	4.55	2.47	1.78	1.43	1.23	1.10	1.01	.95
100	9.10	4.93	3.55	2.86	2.46	2.20	2.02	1.89
200	18.20	9.85	7.09	5.72	4.92	4.40	4.03	3.77
300	27.30	14.77	10.63	8.58	7.38	6.60	6.05	5.65
400	36.39	19.69	14.17	11.44	9.84	8.79	8.06	7.53
500	45.49	24.61	17.71	14.30	12.30	10.99	10.08	9.42
600	54.59	29.53	21.25	17.16	14.76	13.19	12.09	11.30
700	63.68	34.45	24.79	20.02	17.21	15.38	14.11	13.18
800	72.78	39.37	28.33	22.88	19.67	17.58	16.12	15.06
900	81.88	44.29	31.87	25.74	22.13	19.78	18.14	16.95
1000	90.97	49.21	35.41	28.60	24.59	21.97	20.15	18.83
2000	181.94	98.41	70.81	57.20	49.17	43.94	40.30	37.65
3000	272.91	147.61	106.22	85.80	73.76	65.91	60.45	56.48
4000	363.88	196.81	141.62	114.39	98.34	87.88	80.60	75.30
5000	454.84	246.02	177.03	142.99	122.93	109.85	100.74	94.12
6000	545.81	295.22	212.43	171.59	147.51	131.81	120.89	112.95
7000	636.78	344.42	247.84	200.18	172.10	153.78	141.04	131.77
8000	727.75	393.62	283.24	228.78	196.68	175.75	161.19	150.60
9000	818.71	442.83	318.64	257.38	221.27	197.72	181.34	169.42
10000	909.68	492.03	354.05	285.98	245.85	219.69	201.48	188.24
11000	1000.65	541.23	389.45	314.57	270.43	241.65	221.63	207.07
12000	1091.62	590.43	424.86	343.17	295.02	263.62	241.78	225.89
13000	1182.58	639.64	460.26	371.77	319.60	285.59	261.93	244.72
14000	1273.55	688.84	495.67	400.36	344.19	307.56	282.08	263.54
15000	1364.52	738.04	531.07	428.96	368.77	329.53	302.22	282.36
16000	1455.49	787.24	566.48	457.56	393.36	351.49	322.37	301.19
17000	1546.45	836.44	601.88	486.15	417.94	373.46	342.52	320.01
18000	1637.42	885.65	637.28	514.75	442.53	395.43	362.67	338.84
19000	1728.39	934.85	672.69	543.35	467.11	417.40	382.81	357.66
20000	1819.36	984.05	708.09	571.95	491.70	439.37	402.96	376.48
21000	1910.33	1033.25	743.50	600.54	516.28	461.33	423.11	395.31
22000	2001.29	1082.46	778.90	629.14	540.86	483.30	443.26	414.13
23000	2092.26	1131.66	814.31	657.74	565.45	505.27	463.41	432.96
24000	2183.23	1180.86	849.71	686.33	590.03	527.24	483.55	451.78
25000	2274.20	1230.06	885.11	714.93	614.62	549.21	503.70	470.60
26000	2365.16	1279.27	920.52	743.53	639.20	571.17	523.85	489.43
27000	2456.13	1328.47	955.92	772.12	663.79	593.14	544.00	508.25
28000	2547.10	1377.67	991.33	800.72	688.37	615.11	564.15	527.08
29000	2638.07	1426.87	1026.73	829.32	712.96	637.08	584.29	545.90
30000	2729.03	1476.08	1062.14	857.92	737.54	659.05	604.44	564.72
31000	2820.00	1525.28	1097.54	886.51	762.13	681.01	624.59	583.55
32000	2910.97	1574.48	1132.95	915.11	786.71	702.98	644.74	602.37
33000	3001.94	1623.68	1168.35	943.71	811.29	724.95	664.89	621.20
34000	3092.90	1672.88	1203.75	972.30	835.88	746.92	685.03	640.02
35000	3183.87	1722.09	1239.16	1000.90	860.46	768.89	705.18	658.84
40000	3638.71	1968.10	1416.18	1143.89	983.39	878.73	805.92	752.96
45000	4093.55	2214.11	1593.20	1286.87	1106.31	988.57	906.66	847.08
50000	4548.39	2460.12	1770.22	1429.86	1229.23	1098.41	1007.40	941.20
55000	5003.23	2706.13	1947.25	1572.84	1352.15	1208.25	1108.14	1035.32
60000	5458.06	2952.15	2124.27	1715.83	1475.08	1318.09	1208.88	1129.44
65000	5912.90	3198.16	2301.29	1858.81	1598.00	1427.93	1309.62	1223.56
70000	6367.74	3444.17	2478.31	2001.80	1720.92	1537.77	1410.36	1317.68
75000	6822.58	3690.18	2655.33	2144.78	1843.84	1647.61	1511.10	1411.80
80000	7277.42	3936.19	2832.36	2287.77	1966.77	1757.45	1611.84	1505.92
85000	7732.25	4182.20	3009.38	2430.75	2089.69	1867.29	1712.58	1600.04
90000	8187.09	4428.22	3186.40	2573.74	2212.61	1977.13	1813.32	1694.16
95000	8641.93	4674.23	3363.42	2716.72	2335.53	2086.97	1914.05	1788.28
100000	9096.77	4920.24	3540.44	2859.71	2458.46	2196.81	2014.79	1882.40
105000	9551.61	5166.25	3717.47	3002.69	2581.38	2306.65	2115.53	1976.52
110000	10006.45	5412.26	3894.49	3145.68	2704.30	2416.49	2216.27	2070.64
115000	10461.28	5658.28	4071.51	3288.66	2827.22	2526.33	2317.01	2164.76
120000	10916.12	5904.29	4248.53	3431.65	2950.15	2636.17	2417.75	2258.88
125000	11370.96	6150.30	4425.55	3574.63	3073.07	2746.01	2518.49	2353.00
130000	11825.80	6396.31	4602.57	3717.62	3195.99	2855.85	2619.23	2447.12
135000	12280.64	6642.32	4779.60	3860.60	3318.92	2965.69	2719.97	2541.24
140000	12735.47	6888.33	4956.62	4003.59	3441.84	3075.53	2820.71	2635.36
145000	13190.31	7134.35	5133.64	4146.57	3564.76	3185.37	2921.45	2729.48
150000	13645.15	7380.36	5310.66	4289.56	3687.68	3295.21	3022.19	2823.60
155000	14099.99	7626.37	5487.68	4432.54	3810.61	3405.05	3122.93	2917.72
160000	14554.83	7872.38	5664.71	4575.53	3933.53	3514.89	3223.67	3011.84

AMOUNT OF LOAN	NUMBER OF YEARS IN TERM							
	9	10	15	20	25	30	35	40
$ 50	.90	.86	.76	.72	.70	.70	.69	.69
100	1.79	1.71	1.51	1.43	1.40	1.39	1.38	1.38
200	3.57	3.42	3.01	2.86	2.80	2.78	2.76	2.76
300	5.35	5.12	4.52	4.29	4.20	4.16	4.14	4.14
400	7.14	6.83	6.02	5.72	5.60	5.55	5.52	5.51
500	8.92	8.54	7.52	7.15	7.00	6.93	6.90	6.89
600	10.70	10.24	9.03	8.58	8.39	8.32	8.28	8.27
700	12.49	11.95	10.53	10.01	9.79	9.70	9.66	9.64
800	14.27	13.66	12.03	11.44	11.19	11.09	11.04	11.02
900	16.05	15.36	13.54	12.87	12.59	12.47	12.42	12.40
1000	17.83	17.07	15.04	14.29	13.99	13.86	13.80	13.77
2000	35.66	34.13	30.08	28.58	27.97	27.71	27.59	27.54
3000	53.49	51.20	45.12	42.87	41.95	41.56	41.39	41.31
4000	71.32	68.26	60.15	57.16	55.93	55.41	55.18	55.08
5000	89.15	85.33	75.19	71.45	69.92	69.26	68.98	68.85
6000	106.98	102.39	90.23	85.74	83.90	83.11	82.77	82.62
7000	124.81	119.45	105.26	100.03	97.88	96.97	96.57	96.39
8000	142.64	136.52	120.30	114.32	111.86	110.82	110.36	110.16
9000	160.47	153.58	135.34	128.61	125.85	124.67	124.16	123.93
10000	178.30	170.65	150.38	142.90	139.83	138.52	137.95	137.70
11000	196.13	187.71	165.41	157.18	153.81	152.37	151.74	151.47
12000	213.96	204.78	180.45	171.47	167.79	166.22	165.54	165.24
13000	231.79	221.84	195.49	185.76	181.78	180.07	179.33	179.01
14000	249.62	238.90	210.52	200.05	195.76	193.93	193.13	192.78
15000	267.45	255.97	225.56	214.34	209.74	207.78	206.92	206.55
16000	285.28	273.03	240.60	228.63	223.72	221.63	220.72	220.32
17000	303.11	290.10	255.64	242.92	237.71	235.48	234.51	234.09
18000	320.94	307.16	270.67	257.21	251.69	249.33	248.31	247.86
19000	338.77	324.23	285.71	271.50	265.67	263.18	262.10	261.63
20000	356.59	341.29	300.75	285.79	279.65	277.03	275.90	275.40
21000	374.42	358.35	315.78	300.07	293.64	290.89	289.69	289.17
22000	392.25	375.42	330.82	314.36	307.62	304.74	303.48	302.94
23000	410.08	392.48	345.86	328.65	321.60	318.59	317.28	316.71
24000	427.91	409.55	360.90	342.94	335.58	332.44	331.07	330.48
25000	445.74	426.61	375.93	357.23	349.57	346.29	344.87	344.24
26000	463.57	443.67	390.97	371.52	363.55	360.14	358.66	358.01
27000	481.40	460.74	406.01	385.81	377.53	373.99	372.46	371.78
28000	499.23	477.80	421.04	400.10	391.51	387.85	386.25	385.55
29000	517.06	494.87	436.08	414.39	405.50	401.70	400.05	399.32
30000	534.89	511.93	451.12	428.68	419.48	415.55	413.84	413.09
31000	552.72	529.00	466.15	442.96	433.46	429.40	427.64	426.86
32000	570.55	546.06	481.19	457.25	447.44	443.25	441.43	440.63
33000	588.38	563.12	496.23	471.54	461.43	457.10	455.22	454.40
34000	606.21	580.19	511.27	485.83	475.41	470.96	469.02	468.17
35000	624.04	597.25	526.30	500.12	489.39	484.81	482.81	481.94
40000	713.18	682.57	601.49	571.57	559.30	554.06	551.79	550.79
45000	802.33	767.90	676.67	643.01	629.22	623.32	620.76	619.64
50000	891.48	853.22	751.86	714.46	699.13	692.58	689.73	688.48
55000	980.63	938.54	827.04	785.90	769.04	761.84	758.70	757.33
60000	1069.77	1023.86	902.23	857.35	838.95	831.09	827.68	826.18
65000	1158.92	1109.18	977.42	928.79	908.86	900.35	896.65	895.03
70000	1248.07	1194.50	1052.60	1000.24	978.78	969.61	965.62	963.88
75000	1337.22	1279.82	1127.79	1071.68	1048.69	1038.87	1034.60	1032.72
80000	1426.36	1365.14	1202.97	1143.13	1118.60	1108.12	1103.57	1101.57
85000	1515.51	1450.46	1278.16	1214.57	1188.51	1177.38	1172.54	1170.42
90000	1604.66	1535.79	1353.34	1286.02	1258.43	1246.64	1241.51	1239.27
95000	1693.81	1621.11	1428.53	1357.46	1328.34	1315.90	1310.49	1308.12
100000	1782.95	1706.43	1503.71	1428.91	1398.25	1385.15	1379.46	1376.96
105000	1872.10	1791.75	1578.90	1500.35	1468.16	1454.41	1448.43	1445.81
110000	1961.25	1877.07	1654.08	1571.80	1538.07	1523.67	1517.40	1514.66
115000	2050.40	1962.39	1729.27	1643.24	1607.99	1592.93	1586.38	1583.51
120000	2139.54	2047.71	1804.46	1714.69	1677.90	1662.18	1655.35	1652.36
125000	2228.69	2133.03	1879.64	1786.13	1747.81	1731.44	1724.32	1721.20
130000	2317.84	2218.35	1954.83	1857.58	1817.72	1800.70	1793.30	1790.05
135000	2406.99	2303.68	2030.01	1929.02	1887.64	1869.95	1862.27	1858.90
140000	2496.13	2389.00	2105.20	2000.47	1957.55	1939.21	1931.24	1927.75
145000	2585.28	2474.32	2180.38	2071.91	2027.46	2008.47	2000.21	1996.60
150000	2674.43	2559.64	2255.57	2143.36	2097.37	2077.73	2069.19	2065.44
155000	2763.57	2644.96	2330.75	2214.80	2167.28	2146.98	2138.16	2134.29
160000	2852.72	2730.28	2405.94	2286.25	2237.20	2216.24	2207.13	2203.14

AMOUNT OF LOAN	NUMBER OF YEARS IN TERM							
	1	2	3	4	5	6	7	8
$ 50	4.56	2.47	1.78	1.44	1.24	1.11	1.02	.95
100	9.11	4.94	3.56	2.88	2.48	2.22	2.03	1.90
200	18.22	9.87	7.11	5.75	4.95	4.43	4.06	3.80
300	27.33	14.80	10.66	8.62	7.42	6.64	6.09	5.70
400	36.44	19.73	14.22	11.50	9.89	8.85	8.12	7.59
500	45.55	24.67	17.77	14.37	12.36	11.06	10.15	9.49
600	54.66	29.60	21.32	17.24	14.84	13.27	12.18	11.39
700	63.77	34.53	24.87	20.11	17.31	15.48	14.21	13.29
800	72.87	39.46	28.43	22.99	19.78	17.69	16.24	15.18
900	81.98	44.40	31.98	25.86	22.25	19.90	18.27	17.08
1000	91.09	49.33	35.53	28.73	24.72	22.11	20.30	18.98
2000	182.18	98.65	71.06	57.46	49.44	44.22	40.59	37.95
3000	273.26	147.97	106.59	86.18	74.16	66.33	60.88	56.92
4000	364.35	197.29	142.12	114.91	98.88	88.43	81.17	75.89
5000	455.44	246.62	177.65	143.63	123.60	110.54	101.46	94.87
6000	546.52	295.94	213.18	172.36	148.32	132.65	121.75	113.84
7000	637.61	345.26	248.70	201.09	173.03	154.75	142.05	132.81
8000	728.69	394.58	284.23	229.81	197.75	176.86	162.34	151.78
9000	819.78	443.91	319.76	258.54	222.47	198.97	182.63	170.76
10000	910.87	493.23	355.29	287.26	247.19	221.07	202.92	189.73
11000	1001.95	542.55	390.82	315.99	271.91	243.18	223.21	208.70
12000	1093.04	591.87	426.35	344.72	296.63	265.29	243.50	227.67
13000	1184.12	641.19	461.87	373.44	321.34	287.39	263.80	246.65
14000	1275.21	690.52	497.40	402.17	346.06	309.50	284.09	265.62
15000	1366.30	739.84	532.93	430.89	370.78	331.61	304.38	284.59
16000	1457.38	789.16	568.46	459.62	395.50	353.71	324.67	303.56
17000	1548.47	838.48	603.99	488.34	420.22	375.82	344.96	322.54
18000	1639.56	887.81	639.52	517.07	444.94	397.93	365.25	341.51
19000	1730.64	937.13	675.05	545.80	469.65	420.04	385.55	360.48
20000	1821.73	986.45	710.57	574.52	494.37	442.14	405.84	379.45
21000	1912.81	1035.77	746.10	603.25	519.09	464.25	426.13	398.43
22000	2003.90	1085.09	781.63	631.97	543.81	486.36	446.42	417.40
23000	2094.99	1134.42	817.16	660.70	568.53	508.46	466.71	436.37
24000	2186.07	1183.74	852.69	689.43	593.25	530.57	487.00	455.34
25000	2277.16	1233.06	888.22	718.15	617.96	552.68	507.29	474.32
26000	2368.24	1282.38	923.74	746.88	642.68	574.78	527.59	493.29
27000	2459.33	1331.71	959.27	775.60	667.40	596.89	547.88	512.26
28000	2550.42	1381.03	994.80	804.33	692.12	619.00	568.17	531.23
29000	2641.50	1430.35	1030.33	833.06	716.84	641.10	588.46	550.21
30000	2732.59	1479.67	1065.86	861.78	741.56	663.21	608.75	569.18
31000	2823.68	1528.99	1101.39	890.51	766.27	685.32	629.04	588.15
32000	2914.76	1578.32	1136.91	919.23	790.99	707.42	649.34	607.12
33000	3005.85	1627.64	1172.44	947.96	815.71	729.53	669.63	626.10
34000	3096.93	1676.96	1207.97	976.68	840.43	751.64	689.92	645.07
35000	3188.02	1726.28	1243.50	1005.41	865.15	773.75	710.21	664.04
40000	3643.45	1972.89	1421.14	1149.04	988.74	884.28	811.67	758.90
45000	4098.88	2219.51	1598.78	1292.67	1112.33	994.81	913.13	853.76
50000	4554.31	2466.12	1776.43	1436.30	1235.92	1105.35	1014.58	948.63
55000	5009.74	2712.73	1954.07	1579.93	1359.51	1215.88	1116.04	1043.49
60000	5465.17	2959.34	2131.71	1723.56	1483.11	1326.42	1217.50	1138.35
65000	5920.60	3205.95	2309.35	1867.19	1606.70	1436.95	1318.96	1233.21
70000	6376.04	3452.56	2487.00	2010.82	1730.29	1547.49	1420.42	1328.07
75000	6831.47	3699.17	2664.64	2154.44	1853.88	1658.02	1521.87	1422.94
80000	7286.90	3945.78	2842.28	2298.07	1977.47	1768.55	1623.33	1517.80
85000	7742.33	4192.39	3019.92	2441.70	2101.06	1879.09	1724.79	1612.66
90000	8197.76	4439.01	3197.56	2585.33	2224.66	1989.62	1826.25	1707.52
95000	8653.19	4685.62	3375.21	2728.96	2348.25	2100.16	1927.71	1802.39
100000	9108.62	4932.23	3552.85	2872.59	2471.84	2210.69	2029.16	1897.25
105000	9564.05	5178.84	3730.49	3016.22	2595.43	2321.23	2130.62	1992.11
110000	10019.48	5425.45	3908.13	3159.85	2719.02	2431.76	2232.08	2086.97
115000	10474.91	5672.06	4085.77	3303.48	2842.62	2542.29	2333.54	2181.83
120000	10930.34	5918.67	4263.42	3447.11	2966.21	2652.83	2435.00	2276.70
125000	11385.77	6165.28	4441.06	3590.74	3089.80	2763.36	2536.45	2371.56
130000	11841.20	6411.89	4618.70	3734.37	3213.39	2873.90	2637.91	2466.42
135000	12296.64	6658.51	4796.34	3878.00	3336.98	2984.43	2739.37	2561.28
140000	12752.07	6905.12	4973.99	4021.63	3460.57	3094.97	2840.83	2656.14
145000	13207.50	7151.73	5151.63	4165.26	3584.17	3205.50	2942.29	2751.01
150000	13662.93	7398.34	5329.27	4308.88	3707.76	3316.03	3043.74	2845.87
155000	14118.36	7644.95	5506.91	4452.51	3831.35	3426.57	3145.20	2940.73
160000	14573.79	7891.56	5684.55	4596.14	3954.94	3537.10	3246.66	3035.59

AMOUNT OF LOAN	NUMBER OF YEARS IN TERM							
	9	10	15	20	25	30	35	40
$ 50	.90	.87	.77	.73	.71	.71	.70	.70
100	1.80	1.73	1.53	1.45	1.42	1.41	1.40	1.40
200	3.60	3.45	3.05	2.90	2.84	2.82	2.80	2.80
300	5.40	5.17	4.57	4.35	4.26	4.22	4.20	4.20
400	7.20	6.89	6.09	5.80	5.68	5.63	5.60	5.60
500	9.00	8.62	7.61	7.24	7.09	7.03	7.00	6.99
600	10.79	10.34	9.13	8.69	8.51	8.44	8.40	8.39
700	12.59	12.06	10.65	10.14	9.93	9.84	9.80	9.79
800	14.39	13.78	12.18	11.59	11.35	11.25	11.20	11.19
900	16.19	15.50	13.70	13.04	12.77	12.65	12.60	12.58
1000	17.99	17.23	15.22	14.48	14.18	14.06	14.00	13.98
2000	35.97	34.45	30.43	28.96	28.36	28.11	28.00	27.96
3000	53.95	51.67	45.64	43.44	42.54	42.17	42.00	41.93
4000	71.94	68.89	60.86	57.92	56.72	56.22	56.00	55.91
5000	89.92	86.11	76.07	72.40	70.90	70.27	70.00	69.89
6000	107.90	103.34	91.28	86.87	85.08	84.33	84.00	83.86
7000	125.88	120.56	106.50	101.35	99.26	98.38	98.00	97.84
8000	143.87	137.78	121.71	115.83	113.44	112.44	112.00	111.82
9000	161.85	155.00	136.92	130.31	127.62	126.49	126.00	125.79
10000	179.83	172.22	152.14	144.79	141.80	140.54	140.00	139.77
11000	197.81	189.44	167.35	159.27	155.98	154.60	154.00	153.74
12000	215.80	206.67	182.56	173.74	170.16	168.65	168.00	167.72
13000	233.78	223.89	197.78	188.22	184.34	182.71	182.00	181.70
14000	251.76	241.11	212.99	202.70	198.52	196.76	196.00	195.67
15000	269.74	258.33	228.20	217.18	212.70	210.81	210.00	209.65
16000	287.73	275.55	243.42	231.66	226.88	224.87	224.00	223.63
17000	305.71	292.77	258.63	246.13	241.06	238.92	238.00	237.60
18000	323.69	310.00	273.84	260.61	255.24	252.98	252.00	251.58
19000	341.67	327.22	289.06	275.09	269.42	267.03	266.00	265.56
20000	359.66	344.44	304.27	289.57	283.60	281.08	280.00	279.53
21000	377.64	361.66	319.48	304.05	297.78	295.14	294.00	293.51
22000	395.62	378.88	334.70	318.53	311.95	309.19	308.00	307.48
23000	413.60	396.10	349.91	333.00	326.14	323.25	322.00	321.46
24000	431.59	413.33	365.12	347.48	340.32	337.30	336.00	335.44
25000	449.57	430.55	380.34	361.96	354.50	351.35	350.00	349.41
26000	467.55	447.77	395.55	376.44	368.68	365.41	364.00	363.39
27000	485.53	464.99	410.76	390.92	382.86	379.46	378.00	377.37
28000	503.52	482.21	425.97	405.39	397.04	393.52	392.00	391.34
29000	521.50	499.43	441.19	419.87	411.22	407.57	406.00	405.32
30000	539.48	516.66	456.40	434.35	425.40	421.62	420.00	419.30
31000	557.46	533.88	471.61	448.83	439.58	435.68	434.00	433.27
32000	575.45	551.10	486.83	463.31	453.76	449.73	448.00	447.25
33000	593.43	568.32	502.04	477.79	467.94	463.79	462.00	461.22
34000	611.41	585.54	517.25	492.26	482.12	477.84	476.00	475.20
35000	629.39	602.76	532.47	506.74	496.30	491.89	490.00	489.18
40000	719.31	688.87	608.53	579.13	567.20	562.16	560.00	559.06
45000	809.22	774.98	684.60	651.52	638.10	632.43	630.00	628.94
50000	899.13	861.09	760.67	723.91	709.00	702.70	699.99	698.82
55000	989.04	947.20	836.73	796.31	779.90	772.97	769.99	768.70
60000	1078.96	1033.31	912.80	868.70	850.80	843.24	839.99	838.59
65000	1168.87	1119.41	988.86	941.09	921.70	913.51	909.99	908.47
70000	1258.78	1205.52	1064.93	1013.48	992.60	983.78	979.99	978.35
75000	1348.69	1291.63	1141.00	1085.87	1063.50	1054.05	1049.99	1048.23
80000	1438.61	1377.74	1217.06	1158.26	1134.40	1124.32	1119.99	1118.11
85000	1528.52	1463.85	1293.13	1230.65	1205.30	1194.59	1189.99	1187.99
90000	1618.43	1549.96	1369.19	1303.04	1276.20	1264.86	1259.99	1257.88
95000	1708.35	1636.06	1445.26	1375.43	1347.10	1335.13	1329.99	1327.76
100000	1798.26	1722.17	1521.33	1447.82	1418.00	1405.40	1399.98	1397.64
105000	1888.17	1808.28	1597.39	1520.22	1488.90	1475.67	1469.98	1467.52
110000	1978.08	1894.39	1673.46	1592.61	1559.80	1545.94	1539.98	1537.40
115000	2068.00	1980.50	1749.52	1665.00	1630.70	1616.21	1609.98	1607.29
120000	2157.91	2066.61	1825.59	1737.39	1701.60	1686.48	1679.98	1677.17
125000	2247.82	2152.71	1901.66	1809.78	1772.50	1756.75	1749.98	1747.05
130000	2337.73	2238.82	1977.72	1882.17	1843.40	1827.02	1819.98	1816.93
135000	2427.65	2324.93	2053.79	1954.56	1914.30	1897.29	1889.98	1886.81
140000	2517.56	2411.04	2129.85	2026.95	1985.20	1967.56	1959.98	1956.69
145000	2607.47	2497.15	2205.92	2099.34	2056.10	2037.83	2029.98	2026.58
150000	2697.38	2583.26	2281.99	2171.73	2127.00	2108.10	2099.97	2096.46
155000	2787.30	2669.36	2358.05	2244.13	2197.90	2178.37	2169.97	2166.34
160000	2877.21	2755.47	2434.12	2316.52	2268.80	2248.64	2239.97	2236.22

MONTHLY AMORTIZING PAYMENTS

AMOUNT OF LOAN	NUMBER OF YEARS IN TERM							
	1	2	3	4	5	6	7	8
$ 50	4.57	2.48	1.79	1.45	1.25	1.12	1.03	.96
100	9.13	4.95	3.57	2.89	2.49	2.23	2.05	1.92
200	18.25	9.89	7.14	5.78	4.98	4.45	4.09	3.83
300	27.37	14.84	10.70	8.66	7.46	6.68	6.14	5.74
400	36.49	19.78	14.27	11.55	9.95	8.90	8.18	7.65
500	45.61	24.73	17.83	14.43	12.43	11.13	10.22	9.57
600	54.73	29.67	21.40	17.32	14.92	13.35	12.27	11.48
700	63.85	34.61	24.96	20.20	17.40	15.58	14.31	13.39
800	72.97	39.56	28.53	23.09	19.89	17.80	16.35	15.30
900	82.09	44.50	32.09	25.97	22.37	20.03	18.40	17.21
1000	91.21	49.45	35.66	28.86	24.86	22.25	20.44	19.13
2000	182.41	98.89	71.31	57.72	49.71	44.50	40.88	38.25
3000	273.62	148.33	106.96	86.57	74.56	66.74	61.31	57.37
4000	364.82	197.77	142.62	115.43	99.42	88.99	81.75	76.49
5000	456.03	247.22	178.27	144.28	124.27	111.24	102.18	95.61
6000	547.23	296.66	213.92	173.14	149.12	133.48	122.62	114.73
7000	638.44	346.10	249.57	201.99	173.97	155.73	143.06	133.86
8000	729.64	395.54	285.23	230.85	198.83	177.97	163.49	152.98
9000	820.85	444.99	320.88	259.70	223.68	200.22	183.93	172.10
10000	912.05	494.43	356.53	288.56	248.53	222.47	204.36	191.22
11000	1003.26	543.87	392.19	317.41	273.38	244.71	224.80	210.34
12000	1094.46	593.31	427.84	346.27	298.24	266.96	245.23	229.46
13000	1185.67	642.75	463.49	375.12	323.09	289.20	265.67	248.58
14000	1276.87	692.20	499.14	403.98	347.94	311.45	286.11	267.71
15000	1368.08	741.64	534.80	432.83	372.79	333.70	306.54	286.83
16000	1459.28	791.08	570.45	461.69	397.65	355.94	326.98	305.95
17000	1550.49	840.52	606.10	490.54	422.50	378.19	347.41	325.07
18000	1641.69	889.97	641.75	519.40	447.35	400.44	367.85	344.19
19000	1732.90	939.41	677.41	548.25	472.20	422.68	388.29	363.31
20000	1824.10	988.85	713.06	577.11	497.06	444.93	408.72	382.43
21000	1915.30	1038.29	748.71	605.96	521.91	467.17	429.16	401.56
22000	2006.51	1087.73	784.37	634.82	546.76	489.42	449.59	420.68
23000	2097.71	1137.18	820.02	663.67	571.61	511.67	470.03	439.80
24000	2188.92	1186.62	855.67	692.53	596.47	533.91	490.46	458.92
25000	2280.12	1236.06	891.32	721.38	621.32	556.16	510.90	478.04
26000	2371.33	1285.50	926.98	750.24	646.17	578.40	531.34	497.16
27000	2462.53	1334.95	962.63	779.09	671.02	600.65	551.77	516.28
28000	2553.74	1384.39	998.28	807.95	695.88	622.90	572.21	535.41
29000	2644.94	1433.83	1033.93	836.80	720.73	645.14	592.64	554.53
30000	2736.15	1483.27	1069.59	865.66	745.58	667.39	613.08	573.65
31000	2827.35	1532.72	1105.24	894.51	770.43	689.64	633.51	592.77
32000	2918.56	1582.16	1140.89	923.37	795.29	711.88	653.95	611.89
33000	3009.76	1631.60	1176.55	952.22	820.14	734.13	674.39	631.01
34000	3100.97	1681.04	1212.20	981.08	844.99	756.37	694.82	650.13
35000	3192.17	1730.48	1247.85	1009.93	869.85	778.62	715.26	669.26
40000	3648.20	1977.70	1426.11	1154.21	994.11	889.85	817.44	764.86
45000	4104.22	2224.91	1604.38	1298.48	1118.37	1001.08	919.62	860.47
50000	4560.24	2472.12	1782.64	1442.76	1242.63	1112.31	1021.80	956.08
55000	5016.27	2719.33	1960.91	1587.03	1366.90	1223.54	1123.97	1051.68
60000	5472.29	2966.54	2139.17	1731.31	1491.16	1334.77	1226.15	1147.29
65000	5928.31	3213.75	2317.43	1875.58	1615.42	1446.00	1328.33	1242.90
70000	6384.34	3460.96	2495.70	2019.86	1739.69	1557.23	1430.51	1338.51
75000	6840.36	3708.17	2673.96	2164.13	1863.95	1668.46	1532.69	1434.11
80000	7296.39	3955.39	2852.22	2308.41	1988.21	1779.70	1634.87	1529.72
85000	7752.41	4202.60	3030.49	2452.68	2112.47	1890.93	1737.05	1625.33
90000	8208.43	4449.81	3208.75	2596.96	2236.74	2002.16	1839.23	1720.94
95000	8664.46	4697.02	3387.01	2741.23	2361.00	2113.39	1941.41	1816.54
100000	9120.48	4944.23	3565.28	2885.51	2485.26	2224.62	2043.59	1912.15
105000	9576.50	5191.44	3743.54	3029.78	2609.53	2335.85	2145.76	2007.76
110000	10032.53	5438.65	3921.81	3174.06	2733.79	2447.08	2247.94	2103.36
115000	10488.55	5685.87	4100.07	3318.33	2858.05	2558.31	2350.12	2198.97
120000	10944.58	5933.08	4278.33	3462.61	2982.31	2669.54	2452.30	2294.58
125000	11400.60	6180.29	4456.60	3606.89	3106.58	2780.77	2554.48	2390.19
130000	11856.62	6427.50	4634.86	3751.16	3230.84	2892.00	2656.66	2485.79
135000	12312.65	6674.71	4813.12	3895.44	3355.10	3003.23	2758.84	2581.40
140000	12768.67	6921.92	4991.39	4039.71	3479.37	3114.46	2861.02	2677.01
145000	13224.69	7169.13	5169.65	4183.99	3603.63	3225.69	2963.20	2772.62
150000	13680.72	7416.34	5347.91	4328.26	3727.89	3336.92	3065.38	2868.22
155000	14136.74	7663.56	5526.18	4472.54	3852.15	3448.16	3167.55	2963.83
160000	14592.77	7910.77	5704.44	4616.81	3976.42	3559.39	3269.73	3059.44

AMOUNT OF LOAN	NUMBER OF YEARS IN TERM							
	9	10	15	20	25	30	35	40
$ 50	.91	.87	.77	.74	.72	.72	.72	.71
100	1.82	1.74	1.54	1.47	1.44	1.43	1.43	1.42
200	3.63	3.48	3.08	2.94	2.88	2.86	2.85	2.84
300	5.45	5.22	4.62	4.41	4.32	4.28	4.27	4.26
400	7.26	6.96	6.16	5.87	5.76	5.71	5.69	5.68
500	9.07	8.69	7.70	7.34	7.19	7.13	7.11	7.10
600	10.89	10.43	9.24	8.81	8.63	8.56	8.53	8.51
700	12.70	12.17	10.78	10.27	10.07	9.98	9.95	9.93
800	14.51	13.91	12.32	11.74	11.51	11.41	11.37	11.35
900	16.33	15.65	13.86	13.21	12.95	12.84	12.79	12.77
1000	18.14	17.38	15.40	14.67	14.38	14.26	14.21	14.19
2000	36.28	34.76	30.79	29.34	28.76	28.52	28.42	28.37
3000	54.41	52.14	46.18	44.01	43.14	42.78	42.62	42.55
4000	72.55	69.52	61.57	58.68	57.52	57.03	56.83	56.74
5000	90.69	86.90	76.96	73.35	71.89	71.29	71.03	70.92
6000	108.82	104.28	92.35	88.01	86.27	85.55	85.24	85.10
7000	126.96	121.66	107.74	102.68	100.65	99.80	99.44	99.29
8000	145.09	139.04	123.13	117.35	115.03	114.06	113.65	113.47
9000	163.23	156.42	138.52	132.02	129.41	128.32	127.85	127.65
10000	181.37	173.80	153.91	146.69	143.78	142.57	142.06	141.84
11000	199.50	191.18	169.30	161.35	158.16	156.83	156.26	156.02
12000	217.64	208.56	184.69	176.02	172.54	171.09	170.47	170.20
13000	235.78	225.94	200.08	190.69	186.92	185.34	184.67	184.39
14000	253.91	243.32	215.47	205.36	201.30	199.60	198.88	198.57
15000	272.05	260.70	230.86	220.03	215.67	213.86	213.08	212.75
16000	290.18	278.08	246.25	234.69	230.05	228.11	227.29	226.94
17000	308.32	295.46	261.64	249.36	244.43	242.37	241.49	241.12
18000	326.46	312.84	277.03	264.03	258.81	256.63	255.70	255.30
19000	344.59	330.22	292.42	278.70	273.19	270.88	269.90	269.49
20000	362.73	347.60	307.81	293.37	287.56	285.14	284.11	283.67
21000	380.86	364.98	323.20	308.03	301.94	299.40	298.32	297.85
22000	399.00	382.36	338.59	322.70	316.32	313.65	312.52	312.04
23000	417.14	399.74	353.98	337.37	330.70	327.91	326.73	326.22
24000	435.27	417.12	369.37	352.04	345.08	342.17	340.93	340.40
25000	453.41	434.50	384.76	366.71	359.45	356.42	355.14	354.59
26000	471.55	451.88	400.15	381.37	373.83	370.68	369.34	368.77
27000	489.68	469.26	415.54	396.04	388.21	384.94	383.55	382.95
28000	507.82	486.64	430.93	410.71	402.59	399.19	397.75	397.14
29000	525.95	504.02	446.32	425.38	416.97	413.45	411.96	411.32
30000	544.09	521.40	461.71	440.05	431.34	427.71	426.16	425.50
31000	562.23	538.78	477.10	454.71	445.72	441.96	440.37	439.69
32000	580.36	556.16	492.49	469.38	460.10	456.22	454.57	453.87
33000	598.50	573.54	507.88	484.05	474.48	470.48	468.78	468.05
34000	616.64	590.92	523.27	498.72	488.86	484.73	482.98	482.24
35000	634.77	608.30	538.66	513.39	503.23	498.99	497.19	496.42
40000	725.45	695.20	615.61	586.73	575.12	570.28	568.22	567.33
45000	816.13	782.09	692.56	660.07	647.01	641.56	639.24	638.25
50000	906.81	868.99	769.51	733.41	718.90	712.84	710.27	709.17
55000	997.50	955.89	846.46	806.75	790.79	784.13	781.29	780.08
60000	1088.18	1042.79	923.41	880.09	862.68	855.41	852.32	851.00
65000	1178.86	1129.69	1000.36	953.43	934.57	926.69	923.35	921.92
70000	1269.54	1216.59	1077.31	1026.77	1006.46	997.98	994.37	992.83
75000	1360.22	1303.49	1154.26	1100.11	1078.35	1069.26	1065.40	1063.75
80000	1450.90	1390.39	1231.21	1173.45	1150.24	1140.55	1136.43	1134.66
85000	1541.58	1477.29	1308.16	1246.79	1222.13	1211.83	1207.45	1205.58
90000	1632.26	1564.18	1385.11	1320.13	1294.02	1283.11	1278.48	1276.50
95000	1722.94	1651.08	1462.06	1393.47	1365.91	1354.40	1349.50	1347.41
100000	1813.62	1737.98	1539.01	1466.81	1437.80	1425.68	1420.53	1418.33
105000	1904.30	1824.88	1615.96	1540.15	1509.69	1496.96	1491.56	1489.24
110000	1994.99	1911.78	1692.91	1613.49	1581.58	1568.25	1562.58	1560.16
115000	2085.67	1998.68	1769.86	1686.83	1653.47	1639.53	1633.61	1631.08
120000	2176.35	2085.58	1846.81	1760.17	1725.36	1710.82	1704.64	1701.99
125000	2267.03	2172.48	1923.76	1833.51	1797.25	1782.10	1775.66	1772.91
130000	2357.71	2259.37	2000.71	1906.85	1869.14	1853.38	1846.69	1843.83
135000	2448.39	2346.27	2077.66	1980.19	1941.03	1924.67	1917.72	1914.74
140000	2539.07	2433.17	2154.61	2053.53	2012.92	1995.95	1988.74	1985.66
145000	2629.75	2520.07	2231.56	2126.87	2084.81	2067.23	2059.77	2056.57
150000	2720.43	2606.97	2308.51	2200.21	2156.70	2138.52	2130.79	2127.49
155000	2811.11	2693.87	2385.46	2273.55	2228.59	2209.80	2201.82	2198.41
160000	2901.80	2780.77	2462.41	2346.89	2300.48	2281.09	2272.85	2269.32

71

17.250% MONTHLY AMORTIZING PAYMENTS

AMOUNT OF LOAN	NUMBER OF YEARS IN TERM							
	1	2	3	4	5	6	7	8
$ 50	4.57	2.48	1.79	1.45	1.25	1.12	1.03	.97
100	9.14	4.96	3.58	2.90	2.50	2.24	2.06	1.93
200	18.27	9.92	7.16	5.80	5.00	4.48	4.12	3.86
300	27.40	14.87	10.74	8.70	7.50	6.72	6.18	5.79
400	36.53	19.83	14.32	11.60	10.00	8.96	8.24	7.71
500	45.67	24.79	17.89	14.50	12.50	11.20	10.30	9.64
600	54.80	29.74	21.47	17.40	15.00	13.44	12.35	11.57
700	63.93	34.70	25.05	20.29	17.50	15.68	14.41	13.49
800	73.06	39.65	28.63	23.19	19.99	17.91	16.47	15.42
900	82.20	44.61	32.20	26.09	22.49	20.15	18.53	17.35
1000	91.33	49.57	35.78	28.99	24.99	22.39	20.59	19.28
2000	182.65	99.13	71.56	57.97	49.98	44.78	41.17	38.55
3000	273.98	148.69	107.34	86.96	74.97	67.16	61.75	57.82
4000	365.30	198.25	143.11	115.94	99.95	89.55	82.33	77.09
5000	456.62	247.82	178.89	144.93	124.94	111.93	102.91	96.36
6000	547.95	297.38	214.67	173.91	149.93	134.32	123.49	115.63
7000	639.27	346.94	250.45	202.90	174.92	156.71	144.07	134.90
8000	730.59	396.50	286.22	231.88	199.90	179.09	164.65	154.17
9000	821.92	446.07	322.00	260.87	224.89	201.48	185.23	173.44
10000	913.24	495.63	357.78	289.85	249.88	223.86	205.81	192.72
11000	1004.56	545.19	393.55	318.84	274.86	246.25	226.39	211.99
12000	1095.89	594.75	429.33	347.82	299.85	268.64	246.97	231.26
13000	1187.21	644.32	465.11	376.80	324.84	291.02	267.55	250.53
14000	1278.53	693.88	500.89	405.79	349.83	313.41	288.13	269.80
15000	1369.86	743.44	536.66	434.77	374.81	335.79	308.71	289.07
16000	1461.18	793.00	572.44	463.76	399.80	358.18	329.29	308.34
17000	1552.50	842.57	608.22	492.74	424.79	380.56	349.87	327.61
18000	1643.83	892.13	644.00	521.73	449.77	402.95	370.45	346.88
19000	1735.15	941.69	679.77	550.71	474.76	425.34	391.04	366.15
20000	1826.47	991.25	715.55	579.70	499.75	447.72	411.62	385.43
21000	1917.80	1040.82	751.33	608.68	524.74	470.11	432.20	404.70
22000	2009.12	1090.38	787.10	637.67	549.72	492.49	452.78	423.97
23000	2100.44	1139.94	822.88	666.65	574.71	514.88	473.36	443.24
24000	2191.77	1189.50	858.66	695.63	599.70	537.27	493.94	462.51
25000	2283.09	1239.07	894.44	724.62	624.68	559.65	514.52	481.78
26000	2374.41	1288.63	930.21	753.60	649.67	582.04	535.10	501.05
27000	2465.74	1338.19	965.99	782.59	674.66	604.42	555.68	520.32
28000	2557.06	1387.75	1001.77	811.57	699.65	626.81	576.26	539.59
29000	2648.38	1437.32	1037.55	840.56	724.63	649.19	596.84	558.87
30000	2739.71	1486.88	1073.32	869.54	749.62	671.58	617.42	578.14
31000	2831.03	1536.44	1109.10	898.53	774.61	693.97	638.00	597.41
32000	2922.35	1586.00	1144.88	927.51	799.60	716.35	658.58	616.68
33000	3013.68	1635.57	1180.65	956.50	824.58	738.74	679.16	635.95
34000	3105.00	1685.13	1216.43	985.48	849.57	761.12	699.74	655.22
35000	3196.33	1734.69	1252.21	1014.46	874.56	783.51	720.32	674.49
40000	3652.94	1982.50	1431.10	1159.39	999.49	895.44	823.23	770.85
45000	4109.56	2230.32	1609.98	1304.31	1124.43	1007.37	926.13	867.20
50000	4566.18	2478.13	1788.87	1449.23	1249.36	1119.30	1029.03	963.56
55000	5022.79	2725.94	1967.75	1594.16	1374.30	1231.23	1131.93	1059.91
60000	5479.41	2973.75	2146.64	1739.08	1499.24	1343.16	1234.84	1156.27
65000	5936.03	3221.57	2325.53	1884.00	1624.17	1455.09	1337.74	1252.62
70000	6392.65	3469.38	2504.41	2028.92	1749.11	1567.02	1440.64	1348.98
75000	6849.26	3717.19	2683.30	2173.85	1874.04	1678.94	1543.55	1445.33
80000	7305.88	3965.00	2862.19	2318.77	1998.98	1790.87	1646.45	1541.69
85000	7762.50	4212.82	3041.07	2463.69	2123.92	1902.80	1749.35	1638.04
90000	8219.11	4460.63	3219.96	2608.61	2248.85	2014.73	1852.25	1734.40
95000	8675.73	4708.44	3398.85	2753.54	2373.79	2126.66	1955.16	1830.75
100000	9132.35	4956.25	3577.73	2898.46	2498.72	2238.59	2058.06	1927.11
105000	9588.97	5204.06	3756.62	3043.38	2623.66	2350.52	2160.96	2023.47
110000	10045.58	5451.88	3935.50	3188.31	2748.60	2462.45	2263.86	2119.82
115000	10502.20	5699.69	4114.39	3333.23	2873.53	2574.38	2366.77	2216.18
120000	10958.82	5947.50	4293.28	3478.15	2998.47	2686.31	2469.67	2312.53
125000	11415.45	6195.31	4472.16	3623.07	3123.40	2798.24	2572.57	2408.89
130000	11872.05	6443.13	4651.05	3768.00	3248.34	2910.17	2675.48	2505.24
135000	12328.67	6690.94	4829.94	3912.92	3373.28	3022.10	2778.38	2601.60
140000	12785.29	6938.75	5008.82	4057.84	3498.21	3134.03	2881.28	2697.95
145000	13241.90	7186.56	5187.71	4202.76	3623.15	3245.95	2984.18	2794.31
150000	13698.52	7434.38	5366.60	4347.69	3748.08	3357.88	3087.09	2890.66
155000	14155.14	7682.19	5545.48	4492.61	3873.02	3469.81	3189.99	2987.02
160000	14611.75	7930.00	5724.37	4637.53	3997.96	3581.74	3292.89	3083.37

72

MONTHLY AMORTIZING PAYMENTS 17.250%

AMOUNT OF LOAN	NUMBER OF YEARS IN TERM							
	9	10	15	20	25	30	35	40
$ 50	.92	.88	.78	.75	.73	.73	.73	.72
100	1.83	1.76	1.56	1.49	1.46	1.45	1.45	1.44
200	3.66	3.51	3.12	2.98	2.92	2.90	2.89	2.88
300	5.49	5.27	4.68	4.46	4.38	4.34	4.33	4.32
400	7.32	7.02	6.23	5.95	5.84	5.79	5.77	5.76
500	9.15	8.77	7.79	7.43	7.29	7.23	7.21	7.20
600	10.98	10.53	9.35	8.92	8.75	8.68	8.65	8.64
700	12.81	12.28	10.90	10.41	10.21	10.13	10.09	10.08
800	14.64	14.04	12.46	11.89	11.67	11.57	11.53	11.52
900	16.47	15.79	14.02	13.38	13.12	13.02	12.97	12.96
1000	18.30	17.54	15.57	14.86	14.58	14.46	14.42	14.40
2000	36.59	35.08	31.14	29.72	29.16	28.92	28.83	28.79
3000	54.88	52.62	46.71	44.58	43.73	43.38	43.24	43.18
4000	73.17	70.16	62.28	59.44	58.31	57.84	57.65	57.57
5000	91.46	87.70	77.84	74.30	72.89	72.30	72.06	71.96
6000	109.75	105.24	93.41	89.16	87.46	86.76	86.47	86.35
7000	128.04	122.77	108.98	104.01	102.04	101.22	100.88	100.74
8000	146.33	140.31	124.55	118.87	116.62	115.68	115.29	115.13
9000	164.62	157.85	140.11	133.73	131.19	130.14	129.70	129.52
10000	182.91	175.39	155.68	148.59	145.77	144.60	144.11	143.91
11000	201.20	192.93	171.25	163.45	160.35	159.06	158.53	158.30
12000	219.49	210.47	186.82	178.31	174.92	173.52	172.94	172.69
13000	237.78	228.01	202.38	193.16	189.50	187.98	187.35	187.08
14000	256.07	245.54	217.95	208.02	204.07	202.44	201.76	201.47
15000	274.36	263.08	233.52	222.88	218.65	216.90	216.17	215.86
16000	292.65	280.62	249.09	237.74	233.23	231.36	230.58	230.25
17000	310.94	298.16	264.65	252.60	247.80	245.82	244.99	244.64
18000	329.23	315.70	280.22	267.46	262.38	260.28	259.40	259.03
19000	347.52	333.24	295.79	282.31	276.96	274.74	273.81	273.42
20000	365.81	350.78	311.36	297.17	291.53	289.20	288.22	287.81
21000	384.10	368.31	326.92	312.03	306.11	303.66	302.63	302.20
22000	402.40	385.85	342.49	326.89	320.69	318.12	317.05	316.59
23000	420.69	403.39	358.06	341.75	335.26	332.58	331.46	330.98
24000	438.98	420.93	373.63	356.61	349.84	347.04	345.87	345.37
25000	457.27	438.47	389.19	371.47	364.42	361.50	360.28	359.76
26000	475.56	456.01	404.76	386.32	378.99	375.96	374.69	374.15
27000	493.85	473.54	420.33	401.18	393.57	390.42	389.10	388.54
28000	512.14	491.08	435.90	416.04	408.14	404.88	403.51	402.93
29000	530.43	508.62	451.46	430.90	422.72	419.34	417.92	417.32
30000	548.72	526.16	467.03	445.76	437.30	433.80	432.33	431.71
31000	567.01	543.70	482.60	460.62	451.87	448.26	446.74	446.10
32000	585.30	561.24	498.17	475.47	466.45	462.72	461.15	460.49
33000	603.59	578.78	513.73	490.33	481.03	477.18	475.57	474.88
34000	621.88	596.31	529.30	505.19	495.60	491.64	489.98	489.27
35000	640.17	613.85	544.87	520.05	510.18	506.10	504.39	503.66
40000	731.62	701.55	622.71	594.34	583.06	578.40	576.44	575.61
45000	823.08	789.24	700.55	668.63	655.94	650.70	648.50	647.57
50000	914.53	876.93	778.38	742.93	728.83	723.00	720.55	719.52
55000	1005.98	964.62	856.22	817.22	801.71	795.30	792.61	791.47
60000	1097.43	1052.32	934.06	891.51	874.59	867.60	864.66	863.42
65000	1188.88	1140.01	1011.90	965.80	947.47	939.90	936.71	935.37
70000	1280.34	1227.70	1089.73	1040.09	1020.35	1012.20	1008.77	1007.32
75000	1371.79	1315.39	1167.57	1114.39	1093.24	1084.49	1080.82	1079.27
80000	1463.24	1403.09	1245.41	1188.68	1166.12	1156.79	1152.88	1151.22
85000	1554.69	1490.78	1323.25	1262.97	1239.00	1229.09	1224.93	1223.17
90000	1646.15	1578.47	1401.09	1337.26	1311.88	1301.39	1296.99	1295.13
95000	1737.60	1666.16	1478.92	1411.55	1384.76	1373.69	1369.04	1367.08
100000	1829.05	1753.86	1556.76	1485.85	1457.65	1445.99	1441.10	1439.03
105000	1920.50	1841.55	1634.60	1560.14	1530.53	1518.29	1513.15	1510.98
110000	2011.96	1929.24	1712.44	1634.43	1603.41	1590.59	1585.21	1582.93
115000	2103.41	2016.93	1790.28	1708.72	1676.29	1662.89	1657.26	1654.88
120000	2194.86	2104.63	1868.11	1783.02	1749.17	1735.19	1729.32	1726.83
125000	2286.31	2192.32	1945.95	1857.31	1822.06	1807.49	1801.37	1798.78
130000	2377.76	2280.01	2023.79	1931.60	1894.94	1879.79	1873.42	1870.74
135000	2469.22	2367.70	2101.63	2005.89	1967.82	1952.09	1945.48	1942.69
140000	2560.67	2455.40	2179.46	2080.18	2040.70	2024.39	2017.53	2014.64
145000	2652.12	2543.09	2257.30	2154.48	2113.59	2096.68	2089.59	2086.59
150000	2743.57	2630.78	2335.14	2228.77	2186.47	2168.98	2161.64	2158.54
155000	2835.03	2718.47	2412.98	2303.06	2259.35	2241.28	2233.70	2230.49
160000	2926.48	2806.17	2490.82	2377.35	2332.23	2313.58	2305.75	2302.44

MONTHLY AMORTIZING PAYMENTS

AMOUNT OF LOAN	NUMBER OF YEARS IN TERM							
	1	2	3	4	5	6	7	8
$ 50	4.58	2.49	1.80	1.46	1.26	1.13	1.04	.98
100	9.15	4.97	3.60	2.92	2.52	2.26	2.08	1.95
200	18.29	9.94	7.19	5.83	5.03	4.51	4.15	3.89
300	27.44	14.91	10.78	8.74	7.54	6.76	6.22	5.83
400	36.58	19.88	14.37	11.65	10.05	9.02	8.30	7.77
500	45.73	24.85	17.96	14.56	12.57	11.27	10.37	9.72
600	54.87	29.81	21.55	17.47	15.08	13.52	12.44	11.66
700	64.01	34.78	25.14	20.39	17.59	15.77	14.51	13.60
800	73.16	39.75	28.73	23.30	20.10	18.03	16.59	15.54
900	82.30	44.72	32.32	26.21	22.61	20.28	18.66	17.48
1000	91.45	49.69	35.91	29.12	25.13	22.53	20.73	19.43
2000	182.89	99.37	71.81	58.23	50.25	45.06	41.46	38.85
3000	274.33	149.05	107.71	87.35	75.37	67.58	62.18	58.27
4000	365.77	198.74	143.61	116.46	100.49	90.11	82.91	77.69
5000	457.22	248.42	179.52	145.58	125.62	112.64	103.63	97.11
6000	548.66	298.10	215.42	174.69	150.74	135.16	124.36	116.53
7000	640.10	347.78	251.32	203.81	175.86	157.69	145.09	135.95
8000	731.54	397.47	287.22	232.92	200.98	180.21	165.81	155.37
9000	822.98	447.15	323.12	262.03	226.10	202.74	186.54	174.80
10000	914.43	496.83	359.03	291.15	251.23	225.27	207.26	194.22
11000	1005.87	546.52	394.93	320.26	276.35	247.79	227.99	213.64
12000	1097.31	596.20	430.83	349.38	301.47	270.32	248.71	233.06
13000	1188.75	645.88	466.73	378.49	326.59	292.84	269.44	252.48
14000	1280.20	695.56	502.63	407.61	351.72	315.37	290.17	271.90
15000	1371.64	745.25	538.54	436.72	376.84	337.90	310.89	291.32
16000	1463.08	794.93	574.44	465.83	401.96	360.42	331.62	310.74
17000	1554.52	844.61	610.34	494.95	427.08	382.95	352.34	330.17
18000	1645.96	894.30	646.24	524.06	452.20	405.47	373.07	349.59
19000	1737.41	943.98	682.14	553.18	477.33	428.00	393.80	369.01
20000	1828.85	993.66	718.05	582.29	502.45	450.53	414.52	388.43
21000	1920.29	1043.34	753.95	611.41	527.57	473.05	435.25	407.85
22000	2011.73	1093.03	789.85	640.52	552.69	495.58	455.97	427.27
23000	2103.18	1142.71	825.75	669.64	577.82	518.10	476.70	446.69
24000	2194.62	1192.39	861.65	698.75	602.94	540.63	497.42	466.11
25000	2286.06	1242.08	897.56	727.86	628.06	563.16	518.15	485.54
26000	2377.50	1291.76	933.46	756.98	653.18	585.68	538.88	504.96
27000	2468.94	1341.44	969.36	786.09	678.30	608.21	559.60	524.38
28000	2560.39	1391.12	1005.26	815.21	703.43	630.73	580.33	543.80
29000	2651.83	1440.81	1041.16	844.32	728.55	653.26	601.05	563.22
30000	2743.27	1490.49	1077.07	873.44	753.67	675.79	621.78	582.64
31000	2834.71	1540.17	1112.97	902.55	778.79	698.31	642.50	602.06
32000	2926.16	1589.86	1148.87	931.66	803.92	720.84	663.23	621.48
33000	3017.60	1639.54	1184.77	960.78	829.04	743.36	683.96	640.90
34000	3109.04	1689.22	1220.68	989.89	854.16	765.89	704.68	660.33
35000	3200.48	1738.90	1256.58	1019.01	879.28	788.42	725.41	679.75
40000	3657.69	1987.32	1436.09	1164.58	1004.89	901.05	829.04	776.85
45000	4114.90	2235.73	1615.60	1310.15	1130.51	1013.68	932.67	873.96
50000	4572.12	2484.15	1795.11	1455.72	1256.12	1126.31	1036.29	971.07
55000	5029.33	2732.56	1974.62	1601.30	1381.73	1238.94	1139.92	1068.17
60000	5486.54	2980.98	2154.13	1746.87	1507.34	1351.57	1243.55	1165.28
65000	5943.75	3229.39	2333.64	1892.44	1632.95	1464.20	1347.18	1262.38
70000	6400.96	3477.80	2513.15	2038.01	1758.56	1576.83	1450.81	1359.49
75000	6858.17	3726.22	2692.66	2183.58	1884.17	1689.46	1554.44	1456.60
80000	7315.38	3974.63	2872.17	2329.15	2009.78	1802.09	1658.07	1553.70
85000	7772.59	4223.05	3051.68	2474.73	2135.39	1914.72	1761.70	1650.81
90000	8229.80	4471.46	3231.19	2620.30	2261.00	2027.35	1865.33	1747.91
95000	8687.01	4719.88	3410.70	2765.87	2386.62	2139.98	1968.96	1845.02
100000	9144.23	4968.29	3590.21	2911.44	2512.23	2252.61	2072.58	1942.13
105000	9601.44	5216.70	3769.72	3057.01	2637.84	2365.24	2176.21	2039.23
110000	10058.65	5465.12	3949.23	3202.59	2763.45	2477.87	2279.84	2136.34
115000	10515.86	5713.53	4128.74	3348.16	2889.06	2590.50	2383.47	2233.44
120000	10973.07	5961.95	4308.25	3493.73	3014.67	2703.13	2487.10	2330.55
125000	11430.28	6210.36	4487.76	3639.30	3140.28	2815.76	2590.73	2427.66
130000	11887.49	6458.78	4667.27	3784.87	3265.89	2928.39	2694.36	2524.76
135000	12344.70	6707.19	4846.78	3930.45	3391.50	3041.02	2797.99	2621.87
140000	12801.91	6955.60	5026.29	4076.02	3517.11	3153.65	2901.62	2718.97
145000	13259.12	7204.02	5205.80	4221.59	3642.73	3266.28	3005.25	2816.08
150000	13716.34	7452.43	5385.31	4367.16	3768.34	3378.91	3108.87	2913.19
155000	14173.55	7700.85	5564.83	4512.73	3893.95	3491.54	3212.50	3010.29
160000	14630.76	7949.26	5744.34	4658.30	4019.56	3604.17	3316.13	3107.40

MONTHLY AMORTIZING PAYMENTS   17.500%

AMOUNT OF LOAN	NUMBER OF YEARS IN TERM							
	9	10	15	20	25	30	35	40
$ 50	.93	.89	.79	.76	.74	.74	.74	.73
100	1.85	1.77	1.58	1.51	1.48	1.47	1.47	1.46
200	3.69	3.54	3.15	3.01	2.96	2.94	2.93	2.92
300	5.54	5.31	4.73	4.52	4.44	4.40	4.39	4.38
400	7.38	7.08	6.30	6.02	5.92	5.87	5.85	5.84
500	9.23	8.85	7.88	7.53	7.39	7.34	7.31	7.30
600	11.07	10.62	9.45	9.03	8.87	8.80	8.78	8.76
700	12.92	12.39	11.03	10.54	10.35	10.27	10.24	10.22
800	14.76	14.16	12.60	12.04	11.83	11.74	11.70	11.68
900	16.61	15.93	14.18	13.55	13.30	13.20	13.16	13.14
1000	18.45	17.70	15.75	15.05	14.78	14.67	14.62	14.60
2000	36.90	35.40	31.50	30.10	29.56	29.33	29.24	29.20
3000	55.34	53.10	47.24	45.15	44.33	43.99	43.86	43.80
4000	73.79	70.80	62.99	60.20	59.11	58.66	58.47	58.39
5000	92.23	88.49	78.73	75.25	73.88	73.32	73.09	72.99
6000	110.68	106.19	94.48	90.30	88.66	87.98	87.71	87.59
7000	129.12	123.89	110.23	105.35	103.43	102.65	102.32	102.19
8000	147.57	141.59	125.97	120.40	118.21	117.31	116.94	116.78
9000	166.01	159.29	141.72	135.45	132.98	131.97	131.56	131.38
10000	184.46	176.98	157.46	150.50	147.76	146.64	146.17	145.98
11000	202.90	194.68	173.21	165.55	162.53	161.30	160.79	160.58
12000	221.35	212.38	188.95	180.60	177.31	175.96	175.41	175.17
13000	239.79	230.08	204.70	195.65	192.08	190.63	190.02	189.77
14000	258.24	247.78	220.45	210.70	206.86	205.29	204.64	204.37
15000	276.69	265.47	236.19	225.75	221.63	219.95	219.26	218.97
16000	295.13	283.17	251.94	240.80	236.41	234.62	233.87	233.56
17000	313.58	300.87	267.68	255.85	251.19	249.28	248.49	248.16
18000	332.02	318.57	283.43	270.89	265.96	263.94	263.11	262.76
19000	350.47	336.26	299.17	285.94	280.74	278.61	277.72	277.35
20000	368.91	353.96	314.92	300.99	295.51	293.27	292.34	291.95
21000	387.36	371.66	330.67	316.04	310.29	307.93	306.96	306.55
22000	405.80	389.36	346.41	331.09	325.06	322.60	321.57	321.15
23000	424.25	407.06	362.16	346.14	339.84	337.26	336.19	335.74
24000	442.69	424.75	377.90	361.19	354.61	351.92	350.81	350.34
25000	461.14	442.45	393.65	376.24	369.39	366.59	365.42	364.94
26000	479.58	460.15	409.40	391.28	384.16	381.25	380.04	379.54
27000	498.03	477.85	425.14	406.34	398.94	395.91	394.66	394.13
28000	516.47	495.55	440.89	421.39	413.71	410.58	409.27	408.73
29000	534.92	513.24	456.63	436.44	428.49	425.24	423.89	423.33
30000	553.37	530.94	472.38	451.49	443.26	439.90	438.51	437.93
31000	571.81	548.64	488.12	466.54	458.04	454.57	453.12	452.52
32000	590.26	566.34	503.87	481.59	472.81	469.23	467.74	467.12
33000	608.70	584.03	519.62	496.64	487.59	483.89	482.36	481.72
34000	627.15	601.73	535.36	511.69	502.37	498.56	496.97	496.31
35000	645.59	619.43	551.11	526.73	517.14	513.22	511.59	510.91
40000	737.82	707.92	629.84	601.98	591.02	586.54	584.68	583.90
45000	830.05	796.41	708.57	677.23	664.89	659.85	657.76	656.89
50000	922.27	884.90	787.29	752.48	738.77	733.17	730.84	729.87
55000	1014.50	973.39	866.02	827.72	812.65	806.48	803.93	802.86
60000	1106.73	1061.88	944.75	902.97	886.52	879.80	877.01	875.85
65000	1198.95	1150.37	1023.48	978.22	960.40	953.12	950.09	948.83
70000	1291.18	1238.86	1102.21	1053.46	1034.28	1026.43	1023.18	1021.82
75000	1383.41	1327.35	1180.94	1128.71	1108.15	1099.75	1096.26	1094.81
80000	1475.63	1415.84	1259.67	1203.96	1182.03	1173.07	1169.35	1167.79
85000	1567.86	1504.32	1338.40	1279.21	1255.91	1246.38	1242.43	1240.78
90000	1660.09	1592.81	1417.13	1354.45	1329.78	1319.70	1315.51	1313.77
95000	1752.31	1681.30	1495.85	1429.70	1403.66	1393.01	1388.60	1386.75
100000	1844.53	1769.79	1574.58	1504.95	1477.53	1466.33	1461.68	1459.74
105000	1936.77	1858.28	1653.31	1580.19	1551.41	1539.65	1534.76	1532.73
110000	2028.99	1946.77	1732.04	1655.44	1625.29	1612.96	1607.85	1605.71
115000	2121.22	2035.26	1810.77	1730.69	1699.16	1686.28	1680.93	1678.70
120000	2213.45	2123.75	1889.50	1805.94	1773.04	1759.60	1754.02	1751.69
125000	2305.67	2212.24	1968.23	1881.18	1846.92	1832.91	1827.10	1824.67
130000	2397.90	2300.73	2046.96	1956.43	1920.79	1906.23	1900.18	1897.66
135000	2490.13	2389.22	2125.69	2031.68	1994.67	1979.54	1973.27	1970.65
140000	2582.35	2477.71	2204.41	2106.92	2068.55	2052.86	2046.35	2043.63
145000	2674.58	2566.20	2283.14	2182.17	2142.42	2126.18	2119.43	2116.62
150000	2766.81	2654.69	2361.87	2257.42	2216.30	2199.49	2192.52	2189.61
155000	2859.03	2743.18	2440.60	2332.66	2290.18	2272.81	2265.60	2262.59
160000	2951.26	2831.67	2519.33	2407.91	2364.05	2346.13	2338.69	2335.58

MONTHLY AMORTIZING PAYMENTS

AMOUNT OF LOAN	NUMBER OF YEARS IN TERM							
	1	2	3	4	5	6	7	8
$ 50	4.58	2.50	1.81	1.47	1.27	1.14	1.05	.98
100	9.16	4.99	3.61	2.93	2.53	2.27	2.09	1.96
200	18.32	9.97	7.21	5.85	5.06	4.54	4.18	3.92
300	27.47	14.95	10.81	8.78	7.58	6.81	6.27	5.88
400	36.63	19.93	14.42	11.70	10.11	9.07	8.35	7.83
500	45.79	24.91	18.02	14.63	12.63	11.34	10.44	9.79
600	54.94	29.89	21.62	17.55	15.16	13.61	12.53	11.75
700	64.10	34.87	25.22	20.48	17.69	15.87	14.62	13.71
800	73.25	39.85	28.83	23.40	20.21	18.14	16.70	15.66
900	82.41	44.83	32.43	26.33	22.74	20.41	18.79	17.62
1000	91.57	49.81	36.03	29.25	25.26	22.67	20.88	19.58
2000	183.13	99.61	72.06	58.49	50.52	45.34	41.75	39.15
3000	274.69	149.42	108.09	87.74	75.78	68.01	62.62	58.72
4000	366.25	199.22	144.11	116.98	101.04	90.67	83.49	78.29
5000	457.81	249.02	180.14	146.23	126.29	113.34	104.36	97.86
6000	549.37	298.83	216.17	175.47	151.55	136.01	125.23	117.44
7000	640.93	348.63	252.19	204.72	176.81	158.67	146.11	137.01
8000	732.49	398.43	288.22	233.96	202.07	181.34	166.98	156.58
9000	824.05	448.24	324.25	263.21	227.32	204.01	187.85	176.15
10000	915.62	498.04	360.28	292.45	252.58	226.67	208.72	195.72
11000	1007.18	547.84	396.30	321.69	277.84	249.34	229.59	215.30
12000	1098.74	597.65	432.33	350.94	303.10	272.01	250.46	234.87
13000	1190.30	647.45	468.36	380.18	328.35	294.67	271.34	254.44
14000	1281.86	697.25	504.38	409.43	353.61	317.34	292.21	274.01
15000	1373.42	747.06	540.41	438.67	378.87	340.01	313.08	293.58
16000	1464.98	796.86	576.44	467.92	404.13	362.67	333.95	313.16
17000	1556.54	846.66	612.47	497.16	429.38	385.34	354.82	332.73
18000	1648.10	896.47	648.49	526.41	454.64	408.01	375.69	352.30
19000	1739.67	946.27	684.52	555.65	479.90	430.67	396.56	371.87
20000	1831.23	996.07	720.55	584.90	505.16	453.34	417.44	391.44
21000	1922.79	1045.88	756.57	614.14	530.42	476.01	438.31	411.02
22000	2014.35	1095.68	792.60	643.38	555.67	498.67	459.18	430.59
23000	2105.91	1145.48	828.63	672.63	580.93	521.34	480.05	450.16
24000	2197.47	1195.29	864.66	701.87	606.19	544.01	500.92	469.73
25000	2289.03	1245.09	900.68	731.12	631.45	566.67	521.79	489.30
26000	2380.59	1294.89	936.71	760.36	656.70	589.34	542.67	508.88
27000	2472.15	1344.70	972.74	789.61	681.96	612.01	563.54	528.45
28000	2563.71	1394.50	1008.76	818.85	707.22	634.67	584.41	548.02
29000	2655.28	1444.30	1044.79	848.10	732.48	657.34	605.28	567.59
30000	2746.84	1494.11	1080.82	877.34	757.73	680.01	626.15	587.16
31000	2838.40	1543.91	1116.85	906.59	782.99	702.67	647.02	606.73
32000	2929.96	1593.71	1152.87	935.83	808.25	725.34	667.89	626.31
33000	3021.52	1643.52	1188.90	965.07	833.51	748.01	688.77	645.88
34000	3113.08	1693.32	1224.93	994.32	858.76	770.67	709.64	665.45
35000	3204.64	1743.12	1260.95	1023.56	884.02	793.34	730.51	685.02
40000	3662.45	1992.14	1441.09	1169.79	1010.31	906.67	834.87	782.88
45000	4120.25	2241.16	1621.22	1316.01	1136.60	1020.01	939.23	880.74
50000	4578.06	2490.17	1801.36	1462.23	1262.89	1133.34	1043.58	978.60
55000	5035.86	2739.19	1981.50	1608.45	1389.17	1246.67	1147.94	1076.46
60000	5493.67	2988.21	2161.63	1754.68	1515.46	1360.01	1252.30	1174.32
65000	5951.47	3237.23	2341.77	1900.90	1641.75	1473.34	1356.66	1272.18
70000	6409.28	3486.24	2521.90	2047.12	1768.04	1586.68	1461.01	1370.04
75000	6867.08	3735.26	2702.04	2193.34	1894.33	1700.01	1565.37	1467.90
80000	7324.89	3984.28	2882.17	2339.57	2020.61	1813.34	1669.73	1565.76
85000	7782.69	4233.29	3062.31	2485.79	2146.90	1926.67	1774.09	1663.62
90000	8240.50	4482.31	3242.44	2632.01	2273.19	2040.01	1878.45	1761.48
95000	8698.31	4731.33	3422.58	2778.23	2399.48	2153.34	1982.80	1859.34
100000	9156.11	4980.34	3602.72	2924.46	2525.77	2266.67	2087.16	1957.20
105000	9613.92	5229.36	3782.85	3070.68	2652.06	2380.01	2191.52	2055.06
110000	10071.72	5478.38	3962.99	3216.90	2778.34	2493.34	2295.88	2152.92
115000	10529.53	5727.39	4143.12	3363.13	2904.63	2606.68	2400.23	2250.78
120000	10987.33	5976.41	4323.26	3509.35	3030.92	2720.01	2504.59	2348.64
125000	11445.14	6225.43	4503.39	3655.57	3157.21	2833.34	2608.95	2446.50
130000	11902.94	6474.45	4683.53	3801.79	3283.50	2946.67	2713.31	2544.36
135000	12360.75	6723.46	4863.66	3948.02	3409.78	3060.01	2817.67	2642.22
140000	12818.55	6972.48	5043.80	4094.24	3536.07	3173.34	2922.02	2740.08
145000	13276.36	7221.50	5223.94	4240.46	3662.36	3286.68	3026.38	2837.94
150000	13734.16	7470.51	5404.07	4386.68	3788.65	3400.01	3130.74	2935.79
155000	14191.97	7719.53	5584.21	4532.91	3914.94	3513.34	3235.10	3033.65
160000	14649.77	7968.55	5764.34	4679.13	4041.22	3626.68	3339.45	3131.51

AMOUNT OF LOAN	NUMBER OF YEARS IN TERM							
	9	10	15	20	25	30	35	40
$ 50	.94	.90	.80	.77	.75	.75	.75	.75
100	1.87	1.79	1.60	1.53	1.50	1.49	1.49	1.49
200	3.73	3.58	3.19	3.05	3.00	2.98	2.97	2.97
300	5.59	5.36	4.78	4.58	4.50	4.47	4.45	4.45
400	7.45	7.15	6.37	6.10	5.99	5.95	5.93	5.93
500	9.31	8.93	7.97	7.63	7.49	7.44	7.42	7.41
600	11.17	10.72	9.56	9.15	8.99	8.93	8.90	8.89
700	13.03	12.51	11.15	10.67	10.49	10.41	10.38	10.37
800	14.89	14.29	12.74	12.20	11.98	11.90	11.86	11.85
900	16.75	16.08	14.34	13.72	13.48	13.39	13.35	13.33
1000	18.61	17.86	15.93	15.25	14.98	14.87	14.83	14.81
2000	37.21	35.72	31.85	30.49	29.95	29.74	29.65	29.61
3000	55.81	53.58	47.78	45.73	44.93	44.61	44.47	44.42
4000	74.41	71.44	63.70	60.97	59.90	59.47	59.30	59.22
5000	93.01	89.29	79.63	76.21	74.88	74.34	74.12	74.03
6000	111.61	107.15	95.55	91.45	89.85	89.21	88.94	88.83
7000	130.21	125.01	111.48	106.69	104.83	104.07	103.76	103.64
8000	148.81	142.87	127.40	121.93	119.80	118.94	118.59	118.44
9000	167.41	160.73	143.33	137.17	134.78	133.81	133.41	133.25
10000	186.01	178.58	159.25	152.41	149.75	148.67	148.23	148.05
11000	204.61	196.44	175.18	167.66	164.73	163.54	163.06	162.85
12000	223.21	214.30	191.10	182.90	179.70	178.41	177.88	177.66
13000	241.82	232.16	207.03	198.14	194.67	193.27	192.70	192.46
14000	260.42	250.02	222.95	213.38	209.65	208.14	207.52	207.27
15000	279.02	267.87	238.87	228.62	224.62	223.01	222.35	222.07
16000	297.62	285.73	254.80	243.86	239.60	237.88	237.17	236.88
17000	316.22	303.59	270.72	259.10	254.57	252.74	251.99	251.68
18000	334.82	321.45	286.65	274.34	269.55	267.61	266.81	266.49
19000	353.42	339.30	302.57	289.58	284.52	282.48	281.64	281.29
20000	372.02	357.16	318.50	304.82	299.50	297.34	296.46	296.10
21000	390.62	375.02	334.42	320.07	314.47	312.21	311.28	310.90
22000	409.22	392.88	350.35	335.31	329.45	327.08	326.11	325.70
23000	427.82	410.74	366.27	350.55	344.42	341.94	340.93	340.51
24000	446.42	428.59	382.20	365.79	359.40	356.81	355.75	355.31
25000	465.03	446.45	398.12	381.03	374.37	371.68	370.57	370.12
26000	483.63	464.31	414.05	396.27	389.34	386.54	385.40	384.92
27000	502.23	482.17	429.97	411.51	404.32	401.41	400.22	399.73
28000	520.83	500.03	445.90	426.75	419.29	416.28	415.04	414.53
29000	539.43	517.88	461.82	441.99	434.27	431.15	429.86	429.34
30000	558.03	535.74	477.74	457.23	449.24	446.01	444.69	444.14
31000	576.63	553.60	493.67	472.48	464.22	460.88	459.51	458.95
32000	595.23	571.46	509.59	487.72	479.19	475.75	474.33	473.75
33000	613.83	589.32	525.52	502.96	494.17	490.61	489.16	488.55
34000	632.43	607.17	541.44	518.20	509.14	505.48	503.98	503.36
35000	651.03	625.03	557.37	533.44	524.12	520.35	518.80	518.16
40000	744.04	714.32	636.99	609.64	598.99	594.68	592.92	592.19
45000	837.04	803.61	716.61	685.85	673.86	669.02	667.03	666.21
50000	930.05	892.90	796.24	762.05	748.73	743.35	741.14	740.23
55000	1023.05	982.19	875.86	838.26	823.61	817.69	815.26	814.25
60000	1116.05	1071.48	955.48	914.46	898.48	892.02	889.37	888.28
65000	1209.06	1160.77	1035.11	990.67	973.35	966.35	963.48	962.30
70000	1302.06	1250.06	1114.73	1066.87	1048.23	1040.69	1037.60	1036.32
75000	1395.07	1339.35	1194.35	1143.08	1123.10	1115.02	1111.71	1110.35
80000	1488.07	1428.64	1273.98	1219.28	1197.97	1189.36	1185.83	1184.37
85000	1581.07	1517.93	1353.60	1295.49	1272.85	1263.69	1259.94	1258.39
90000	1674.08	1607.21	1433.22	1371.69	1347.72	1338.03	1334.05	1332.41
95000	1767.08	1696.50	1512.85	1447.90	1422.59	1412.36	1408.17	1406.44
100000	1860.09	1785.79	1592.47	1524.10	1497.46	1486.70	1482.28	1480.46
105000	1953.09	1875.08	1672.09	1600.31	1572.34	1561.03	1556.39	1554.48
110000	2046.09	1964.37	1751.72	1676.51	1647.21	1635.37	1630.51	1628.50
115000	2139.10	2053.66	1831.34	1752.72	1722.08	1709.70	1704.62	1702.53
120000	2232.10	2142.95	1910.96	1828.92	1796.96	1784.04	1778.74	1776.55
125000	2325.11	2232.24	1990.59	1905.13	1871.83	1858.37	1852.85	1850.57
130000	2418.11	2321.53	2070.21	1981.33	1946.70	1932.70	1926.96	1924.59
135000	2511.11	2410.82	2149.83	2057.54	2021.58	2007.04	2001.08	1998.62
140000	2604.12	2500.11	2229.46	2133.74	2096.45	2081.37	2075.19	2072.64
145000	2697.12	2589.40	2309.08	2209.95	2171.32	2155.71	2149.30	2146.66
150000	2790.13	2678.69	2388.70	2286.15	2246.19	2230.04	2223.42	2220.69
155000	2883.13	2767.98	2468.33	2362.36	2321.07	2304.38	2297.53	2294.71
160000	2976.13	2857.27	2547.95	2438.56	2395.94	2378.71	2371.65	2368.73

MONTHLY AMORTIZING PAYMENTS

AMOUNT OF LOAN	NUMBER OF YEARS IN TERM							
	1	2	3	4	5	6	7	8
$ 50	4.59	2.50	1.81	1.47	1.27	1.15	1.06	.99
100	9.17	5.00	3.62	2.94	2.54	2.29	2.11	1.98
200	18.34	9.99	7.24	5.88	5.08	4.57	4.21	3.95
300	27.51	14.98	10.85	8.82	7.62	6.85	6.31	5.92
400	36.68	19.97	14.47	11.75	10.16	9.13	8.41	7.89
500	45.84	24.97	18.08	14.69	12.70	11.41	10.51	9.87
600	55.01	29.96	21.70	17.63	15.24	13.69	12.62	11.84
700	64.18	34.95	25.31	20.57	17.78	15.97	14.72	13.81
800	73.35	39.94	28.93	23.50	20.32	18.25	16.82	15.78
900	82.52	44.94	32.54	26.44	22.86	20.53	18.92	17.76
1000	91.68	49.93	36.16	29.38	25.40	22.81	21.02	19.73
2000	183.36	99.85	72.31	58.75	50.79	45.62	42.04	39.45
3000	275.04	149.78	108.46	88.13	76.19	68.43	63.06	59.17
4000	366.72	199.70	144.61	117.50	101.58	91.24	84.08	78.90
5000	458.40	249.63	180.77	146.88	126.97	114.04	105.09	98.62
6000	550.08	299.55	216.92	176.25	152.37	136.85	126.11	118.34
7000	641.76	349.47	253.07	205.63	177.76	159.66	147.13	138.07
8000	733.44	399.40	289.22	235.00	203.15	182.47	168.15	157.79
9000	825.12	449.32	325.38	264.38	228.55	205.28	189.17	177.51
10000	916.80	499.25	361.53	293.75	253.94	228.08	210.18	197.24
11000	1008.48	549.17	397.68	323.13	279.33	250.89	231.20	216.96
12000	1100.16	599.09	433.83	352.50	304.73	273.70	252.22	236.68
13000	1191.84	649.02	469.99	381.88	330.12	296.51	273.24	256.41
14000	1283.52	698.94	506.14	411.25	355.51	319.31	294.25	276.13
15000	1375.20	748.87	542.29	440.63	380.91	342.12	315.27	295.85
16000	1466.88	798.79	578.44	470.00	406.30	364.93	336.29	315.58
17000	1558.56	848.71	614.60	499.38	431.69	387.74	357.31	335.30
18000	1650.24	898.64	650.75	528.75	457.09	410.55	378.33	355.02
19000	1741.92	948.56	686.90	558.13	482.48	433.35	399.34	374.75
20000	1833.60	998.49	723.05	587.50	507.87	456.16	420.36	394.47
21000	1925.28	1048.41	759.21	616.88	533.27	478.97	441.38	414.19
22000	2016.96	1098.34	795.36	646.25	558.66	501.78	462.40	433.92
23000	2108.64	1148.26	831.51	675.63	584.05	524.58	483.42	453.64
24000	2200.32	1198.18	867.66	705.00	609.45	547.39	504.43	473.36
25000	2292.00	1248.11	903.81	734.38	634.84	570.20	525.45	493.09
26000	2383.68	1298.03	939.97	763.75	660.23	593.01	546.47	512.81
27000	2475.36	1347.96	976.12	793.13	685.63	615.82	567.49	532.53
28000	2567.04	1397.88	1012.27	822.50	711.02	638.62	588.50	552.25
29000	2658.72	1447.80	1048.42	851.88	736.41	661.43	609.52	571.98
30000	2750.40	1497.73	1084.58	881.25	761.81	684.24	630.54	591.70
31000	2842.08	1547.65	1120.73	910.63	787.20	707.05	651.56	611.42
32000	2933.76	1597.58	1156.88	940.00	812.59	729.85	672.58	631.15
33000	3025.44	1647.50	1193.03	969.38	837.99	752.66	693.59	650.87
34000	3117.12	1697.42	1229.19	998.75	863.38	775.47	714.61	670.59
35000	3208.80	1747.35	1265.34	1028.13	888.77	798.28	735.63	690.32
40000	3667.20	1996.97	1446.10	1175.00	1015.74	912.32	840.72	788.93
45000	4125.60	2246.59	1626.86	1321.88	1142.71	1026.36	945.81	887.55
50000	4584.00	2496.21	1807.62	1468.75	1269.68	1140.39	1050.90	986.17
55000	5042.40	2745.83	1988.39	1615.63	1396.64	1254.43	1155.99	1084.78
60000	5500.80	2995.45	2169.15	1762.50	1523.61	1368.47	1261.08	1183.40
65000	5959.20	3245.07	2349.91	1909.38	1650.58	1482.51	1366.16	1282.01
70000	6417.60	3494.69	2530.67	2056.25	1777.54	1596.55	1471.25	1380.63
75000	6876.00	3744.31	2711.43	2203.13	1904.51	1710.59	1576.34	1479.25
80000	7334.40	3993.93	2892.20	2350.00	2031.48	1824.63	1681.43	1577.86
85000	7792.80	4243.55	3072.96	2496.88	2158.45	1938.67	1786.52	1676.48
90000	8251.20	4493.17	3253.72	2643.75	2285.41	2052.71	1891.61	1775.09
95000	8709.60	4742.79	3434.48	2790.63	2412.38	2166.75	1996.70	1873.71
100000	9168.00	4992.42	3615.24	2937.50	2539.35	2280.78	2101.79	1972.33
105000	9626.40	5242.04	3796.01	3084.38	2666.31	2394.82	2206.88	2070.94
110000	10084.80	5491.66	3976.77	3231.25	2793.28	2508.86	2311.97	2169.56
115000	10543.20	5741.28	4157.53	3378.13	2920.25	2622.90	2417.06	2268.17
120000	11001.60	5990.90	4338.29	3525.00	3047.22	2736.94	2522.15	2366.79
125000	11460.00	6240.52	4519.05	3671.88	3174.18	2850.98	2627.23	2465.41
130000	11918.40	6490.14	4699.82	3818.75	3301.15	2965.02	2732.32	2564.02
135000	12376.80	6739.76	4880.58	3965.63	3428.12	3079.06	2837.41	2662.64
140000	12835.20	6989.38	5061.34	4112.50	3555.08	3193.10	2942.50	2761.25
145000	13293.60	7239.00	5242.10	4259.38	3682.05	3307.13	3047.59	2859.87
150000	13752.00	7488.62	5422.86	4406.25	3809.02	3421.17	3152.68	2958.49
155000	14210.40	7738.24	5603.63	4553.13	3935.99	3535.21	3257.77	3057.10
160000	14668.80	7987.86	5784.39	4700.00	4062.95	3649.25	3362.86	3155.72

AMOUNT OF LOAN	NUMBER OF YEARS IN TERM							
	9	10	15	20	25	30	35	40
$ 50	.94	.91	.81	.78	.76	.76	.76	.76
100	1.88	1.81	1.62	1.55	1.52	1.51	1.51	1.51
200	3.76	3.61	3.23	3.09	3.04	3.02	3.01	3.01
300	5.63	5.41	4.84	4.63	4.56	4.53	4.51	4.51
400	7.51	7.21	6.45	6.18	6.07	6.03	6.02	6.01
500	9.38	9.01	8.06	7.72	7.59	7.54	7.52	7.51
600	11.26	10.82	9.67	9.26	9.11	9.05	9.02	9.01
700	13.13	12.62	11.28	10.81	10.63	10.55	10.53	10.51
800	15.01	14.42	12.89	12.35	12.14	12.06	12.03	12.01
900	16.89	16.22	14.50	13.89	13.66	13.57	13.53	13.52
1000	18.76	18.02	16.11	15.44	15.18	15.08	15.03	15.02
2000	37.52	36.04	32.21	30.87	30.35	30.15	30.06	30.03
3000	56.28	54.06	48.32	46.30	45.53	45.22	45.09	45.04
4000	75.03	72.08	64.42	61.74	60.70	60.29	60.12	60.05
5000	93.79	90.10	80.53	77.17	75.88	75.36	75.15	75.06
6000	112.55	108.12	96.63	92.60	91.05	90.43	90.18	90.08
7000	131.30	126.13	112.73	108.04	106.23	105.50	105.21	105.09
8000	150.06	144.15	128.84	123.47	121.40	120.57	120.24	120.10
9000	168.82	162.17	144.94	138.90	136.57	135.64	135.27	135.11
10000	187.57	180.19	161.05	154.34	151.75	150.71	150.29	150.12
11000	206.33	198.21	177.15	169.77	166.92	165.78	165.32	165.14
12000	225.09	216.23	193.26	185.20	182.10	180.86	180.35	180.15
13000	243.84	234.25	209.36	200.64	197.27	195.93	195.38	195.16
14000	262.60	252.26	225.46	216.07	212.45	211.00	210.41	210.17
15000	281.36	270.28	241.57	231.50	227.62	226.07	225.44	225.18
16000	300.12	288.30	257.67	246.93	242.79	241.14	240.47	240.19
17000	318.87	306.32	273.78	262.37	257.97	256.21	255.50	255.21
18000	337.63	324.34	289.88	277.80	273.14	271.28	270.53	270.22
19000	356.39	342.36	305.98	293.23	288.32	286.35	285.55	285.23
20000	375.14	360.38	322.09	308.67	303.49	301.42	300.58	300.24
21000	393.90	378.39	338.19	324.10	318.67	316.49	315.61	315.25
22000	412.66	396.41	354.30	339.53	333.84	331.56	330.64	330.27
23000	431.41	414.43	370.40	354.97	349.01	346.63	345.67	345.28
24000	450.17	432.45	386.51	370.40	364.19	361.71	360.70	360.29
25000	468.93	450.47	402.61	385.83	379.36	376.78	375.73	375.30
26000	487.68	468.49	418.71	401.27	394.54	391.85	390.76	390.31
27000	506.44	486.51	434.82	416.70	409.71	406.92	405.79	405.32
28000	525.20	504.52	450.92	432.13	424.89	421.99	420.81	420.34
29000	543.95	522.54	467.03	447.57	440.06	437.06	435.84	435.35
30000	562.71	540.56	483.13	463.00	455.23	452.13	450.87	450.36
31000	581.47	558.58	499.24	478.43	470.41	467.20	465.90	465.37
32000	600.23	576.60	515.34	493.86	485.58	482.27	480.93	480.38
33000	618.98	594.62	531.44	509.30	500.76	497.34	495.96	495.40
34000	637.74	612.63	547.55	524.73	515.93	512.41	510.99	510.41
35000	656.50	630.65	563.65	540.16	531.11	527.48	526.02	525.42
40000	750.28	720.75	644.17	617.33	606.98	602.84	601.16	600.48
45000	844.06	810.84	724.69	694.50	682.85	678.19	676.31	675.54
50000	937.85	900.93	805.22	771.66	758.72	753.55	751.45	750.60
55000	1031.63	991.02	885.74	848.83	834.59	828.90	826.60	825.66
60000	1125.42	1081.12	966.26	925.99	910.46	904.26	901.74	900.71
65000	1219.20	1171.21	1046.78	1003.16	986.33	979.61	976.88	975.77
70000	1312.99	1261.30	1127.30	1080.32	1062.21	1054.96	1052.03	1050.83
75000	1406.77	1351.39	1207.82	1157.49	1138.08	1130.32	1127.17	1125.89
80000	1500.56	1441.49	1288.34	1234.65	1213.95	1205.67	1202.32	1200.95
85000	1594.34	1531.58	1368.86	1311.82	1289.82	1281.03	1277.46	1276.01
90000	1688.12	1621.67	1449.38	1388.99	1365.69	1356.38	1352.61	1351.07
95000	1781.91	1711.76	1529.90	1466.15	1441.56	1431.74	1427.75	1426.13
100000	1875.69	1801.86	1610.43	1543.32	1517.43	1507.09	1502.90	1501.19
105000	1969.48	1891.95	1690.95	1620.48	1593.31	1582.44	1578.04	1576.25
110000	2063.26	1982.04	1771.47	1697.65	1669.18	1657.80	1653.19	1651.31
115000	2157.05	2072.13	1851.99	1774.81	1745.05	1733.15	1728.33	1726.36
120000	2250.83	2162.23	1932.51	1851.98	1820.92	1808.51	1803.48	1801.42
125000	2344.62	2252.32	2013.03	1929.14	1896.79	1883.86	1878.62	1876.48
130000	2438.40	2342.41	2093.55	2006.31	1972.66	1959.22	1953.76	1951.54
135000	2532.18	2432.51	2174.07	2083.48	2048.54	2034.57	2028.91	2026.60
140000	2625.97	2522.60	2254.59	2160.64	2124.41	2109.92	2104.05	2101.66
145000	2719.75	2612.69	2335.12	2237.81	2200.28	2185.28	2179.20	2176.72
150000	2813.54	2702.78	2415.64	2314.97	2276.15	2260.63	2254.34	2251.78
155000	2907.32	2792.88	2496.16	2392.14	2352.02	2335.99	2329.49	2326.84
160000	3001.11	2882.97	2576.68	2469.30	2427.89	2411.34	2404.63	2401.90

18.250% MONTHLY AMORTIZING PAYMENTS

AMOUNT OF LOAN	NUMBER OF YEARS IN TERM							
	1	2	3	4	5	6	7	8
$ 50	4.59	2.51	1.82	1.48	1.28	1.15	1.06	1.00
100	9.18	5.01	3.63	2.96	2.56	2.30	2.12	1.99
200	18.36	10.01	7.26	5.91	5.11	4.59	4.24	3.98
300	27.54	15.02	10.89	8.86	7.66	6.89	6.35	5.97
400	36.72	20.02	14.52	11.81	10.22	9.18	8.47	7.96
500	45.90	25.03	18.14	14.76	12.77	11.48	10.59	9.94
600	55.08	30.03	21.77	17.71	15.32	13.77	12.70	11.93
700	64.26	35.04	25.40	20.66	17.88	16.07	14.82	13.92
800	73.44	40.04	29.03	23.61	20.43	18.36	16.94	15.91
900	82.62	45.05	32.66	26.56	22.98	20.66	19.05	17.89
1000	91.80	50.05	36.28	29.51	25.53	22.95	21.17	19.88
2000	183.60	100.09	72.56	59.02	51.06	45.90	42.33	39.76
3000	275.40	150.14	108.84	88.52	76.59	68.85	63.50	59.63
4000	367.20	200.18	145.12	118.03	102.12	91.80	84.66	79.51
5000	459.00	250.23	181.39	147.53	127.65	114.75	105.83	99.38
6000	550.80	300.27	217.67	177.04	153.18	137.70	126.99	119.26
7000	642.60	350.32	253.95	206.55	178.71	160.65	148.16	139.13
8000	734.40	400.36	290.23	236.05	204.24	183.60	169.32	159.01
9000	826.20	450.41	326.51	265.56	229.77	206.55	190.49	178.88
10000	918.00	500.45	362.78	295.06	255.30	229.50	211.65	198.76
11000	1009.79	550.50	399.06	324.57	280.83	252.45	232.82	218.63
12000	1101.59	600.54	435.34	354.07	306.36	275.40	253.98	238.51
13000	1193.39	650.59	471.62	383.58	331.89	298.35	275.15	258.38
14000	1285.19	700.63	507.90	413.09	357.42	321.30	296.31	278.26
15000	1376.99	750.68	544.17	442.59	382.95	344.25	317.47	298.13
16000	1468.79	800.72	580.45	472.10	408.48	367.19	338.64	318.01
17000	1560.59	850.77	616.73	501.60	434.01	390.14	359.80	337.88
18000	1652.39	900.81	653.01	531.11	459.54	413.09	380.97	357.76
19000	1744.19	950.86	689.29	560.62	485.07	436.04	402.13	377.63
20000	1835.99	1000.90	725.56	590.12	510.60	458.99	423.30	397.51
21000	1927.78	1050.95	761.84	619.63	536.13	481.94	444.46	417.38
22000	2019.58	1100.99	798.12	649.13	561.66	504.89	465.63	437.26
23000	2111.38	1151.04	834.40	678.64	587.19	527.84	486.79	457.13
24000	2203.18	1201.08	870.68	708.14	612.72	550.79	507.96	477.01
25000	2294.98	1251.13	906.95	737.65	638.25	573.74	529.12	496.88
26000	2386.78	1301.17	943.23	767.16	663.78	596.69	550.29	516.76
27000	2478.58	1351.22	979.51	796.66	689.30	619.64	571.45	536.63
28000	2570.38	1401.26	1015.79	826.17	714.83	642.59	592.61	556.51
29000	2662.18	1451.31	1052.07	855.67	740.36	665.54	613.78	576.38
30000	2753.98	1501.35	1088.34	885.18	765.89	688.49	634.94	596.26
31000	2845.77	1551.40	1124.62	914.68	791.42	711.43	656.11	616.13
32000	2937.57	1601.44	1160.90	944.19	816.95	734.38	677.27	636.01
33000	3029.37	1651.49	1197.18	973.70	842.48	757.33	698.44	655.88
34000	3121.17	1701.53	1233.45	1003.20	868.01	780.28	719.60	675.76
35000	3212.97	1751.58	1269.73	1032.71	893.54	803.23	740.77	695.63
40000	3671.97	2001.80	1451.12	1180.24	1021.19	917.98	846.59	795.01
45000	4130.96	2252.03	1632.51	1327.77	1148.84	1032.73	952.41	894.38
50000	4589.96	2502.25	1813.90	1475.29	1276.49	1147.47	1058.24	993.76
55000	5048.95	2752.48	1995.29	1622.82	1404.13	1262.22	1164.06	1093.13
60000	5507.95	3002.70	2176.68	1770.35	1531.78	1376.97	1269.88	1192.51
65000	5966.94	3252.93	2358.07	1917.88	1659.43	1491.71	1375.71	1291.88
70000	6425.94	3503.15	2539.46	2065.41	1787.08	1606.46	1481.53	1391.26
75000	6884.93	3753.38	2720.85	2212.94	1914.73	1721.21	1587.35	1490.63
80000	7343.93	4003.60	2902.24	2360.47	2042.37	1835.95	1693.18	1590.01
85000	7802.92	4253.83	3083.63	2508.00	2170.02	1950.70	1799.00	1689.38
90000	8261.92	4504.05	3265.02	2655.53	2297.67	2065.45	1904.82	1788.76
95000	8720.91	4754.28	3446.41	2803.06	2425.32	2180.19	2010.64	1888.13
100000	9179.91	5004.50	3627.80	2950.58	2552.97	2294.94	2116.47	1987.51
105000	9638.90	5254.73	3809.19	3098.11	2680.62	2409.69	2222.29	2086.89
110000	10097.90	5504.95	3990.58	3245.64	2808.26	2524.43	2328.11	2186.26
115000	10556.89	5755.18	4171.97	3393.17	2935.91	2639.18	2433.94	2285.64
120000	11015.89	6005.40	4353.36	3540.70	3063.56	2753.93	2539.76	2385.01
125000	11474.88	6255.63	4534.75	3688.23	3191.21	2868.67	2645.58	2484.39
130000	11933.88	6505.85	4716.14	3835.76	3318.86	2983.42	2751.41	2583.76
135000	12392.87	6756.08	4897.53	3983.29	3446.50	3098.17	2857.23	2683.14
140000	12851.87	7006.30	5078.92	4130.82	3574.15	3212.91	2963.05	2782.51
145000	13310.86	7256.53	5260.31	4278.35	3701.80	3327.66	3068.88	2881.89
150000	13769.86	7506.75	5441.69	4425.87	3829.45	3442.41	3174.70	2981.26
155000	14228.85	7756.98	5623.08	4573.40	3957.10	3557.15	3280.52	3080.64
160000	14687.85	8007.20	5804.47	4720.93	4084.74	3671.90	3386.35	3180.01

80

MONTHLY AMORTIZING PAYMENTS 18.250%

AMOUNT OF LOAN	NUMBER OF YEARS IN TERM							
	9	10	15	20	25	30	35	40
$ 50	.95	.91	.82	.79	.77	.77	.77	.77
100	1.90	1.82	1.63	1.57	1.54	1.53	1.53	1.53
200	3.79	3.64	3.26	3.13	3.08	3.06	3.05	3.05
300	5.68	5.46	4.89	4.69	4.62	4.59	4.58	4.57
400	7.57	7.28	6.52	6.26	6.15	6.12	6.10	6.09
500	9.46	9.09	8.15	7.82	7.69	7.64	7.62	7.61
600	11.35	10.91	9.78	9.38	9.23	9.17	9.15	9.14
700	13.24	12.73	11.40	10.94	10.77	10.70	10.67	10.66
800	15.14	14.55	13.03	12.51	12.30	12.23	12.19	12.18
900	17.03	16.37	14.66	14.07	13.84	13.75	13.72	13.70
1000	18.92	18.18	16.29	15.63	15.38	15.28	15.24	15.22
2000	37.83	36.36	32.57	31.26	30.75	30.56	30.48	30.44
3000	56.75	54.54	48.86	46.88	46.13	45.83	45.71	45.66
4000	75.66	72.72	65.14	62.51	61.50	61.11	60.95	60.88
5000	94.57	90.90	81.43	78.13	76.88	76.38	76.18	76.10
6000	113.49	109.08	97.71	93.76	92.25	91.66	91.42	91.32
7000	132.40	127.26	114.00	109.39	107.63	106.93	106.65	106.54
8000	151.31	145.44	130.28	125.01	123.00	122.21	121.89	121.76
9000	170.23	163.62	146.56	140.64	138.37	137.48	137.12	136.98
10000	189.14	181.80	162.85	156.26	153.75	152.76	152.36	152.20
11000	208.05	199.98	179.13	171.89	169.12	168.03	167.59	167.42
12000	226.97	218.16	195.42	187.51	184.50	183.31	182.83	182.64
13000	245.88	236.34	211.70	203.14	199.87	198.58	198.06	197.85
14000	264.79	254.52	227.99	218.77	215.25	213.86	213.30	213.07
15000	283.71	272.70	244.27	234.39	230.62	229.13	228.53	228.29
16000	302.62	290.88	260.56	250.02	246.00	244.41	243.77	243.51
17000	321.54	309.06	276.84	265.64	261.37	259.68	259.00	258.73
18000	340.45	327.24	293.12	281.27	276.74	274.96	274.24	273.95
19000	359.36	345.42	309.41	296.89	292.12	290.23	289.47	289.17
20000	378.28	363.60	325.69	312.52	307.49	305.51	304.71	304.39
21000	397.19	381.78	341.98	328.15	322.87	320.78	319.94	319.61
22000	416.10	399.96	358.26	343.77	338.24	336.06	335.18	334.83
23000	435.02	418.14	374.55	359.40	353.62	351.33	350.42	350.05
24000	453.93	436.32	390.83	375.02	368.99	366.61	365.65	365.27
25000	472.84	454.50	407.12	390.65	384.36	381.88	380.89	380.48
26000	491.76	472.68	423.40	406.28	399.74	397.16	396.12	395.70
27000	510.67	490.86	439.68	421.90	415.11	412.43	411.36	410.92
28000	529.58	509.04	455.97	437.53	430.49	427.71	426.59	426.14
29000	548.50	527.22	472.25	453.15	445.86	442.98	441.83	441.36
30000	567.41	545.40	488.54	468.78	461.24	458.26	457.06	456.58
31000	586.33	563.58	504.82	484.40	476.61	473.53	472.30	471.80
32000	605.24	581.76	521.11	500.03	491.99	488.81	487.53	487.02
33000	624.15	599.94	537.39	515.66	507.36	504.08	502.77	502.24
34000	643.07	618.12	553.67	531.28	522.73	519.36	518.00	517.46
35000	661.98	636.30	569.96	546.91	538.11	534.63	533.24	532.68
40000	756.55	727.20	651.38	625.04	614.98	611.01	609.41	608.77
45000	851.12	818.10	732.80	703.17	691.85	687.38	685.59	684.87
50000	945.68	908.99	814.23	781.29	768.72	763.76	761.77	760.96
55000	1040.25	999.89	895.65	859.42	845.60	840.13	837.94	837.06
60000	1134.82	1090.79	977.07	937.55	922.47	916.51	914.12	913.16
65000	1229.39	1181.69	1058.49	1015.68	999.34	992.88	990.29	989.25
70000	1323.95	1272.59	1139.91	1093.81	1076.21	1069.26	1066.47	1065.35
75000	1418.52	1363.49	1221.34	1171.94	1153.08	1145.63	1142.65	1141.44
80000	1513.09	1454.39	1302.76	1250.07	1229.96	1222.01	1218.82	1217.54
85000	1607.66	1545.29	1384.18	1328.20	1306.83	1298.38	1295.00	1293.64
90000	1702.23	1636.19	1465.60	1406.33	1383.70	1374.76	1371.18	1369.73
95000	1796.79	1727.08	1547.02	1484.45	1460.57	1451.13	1447.35	1445.83
100000	1891.36	1817.98	1628.45	1562.58	1537.44	1527.51	1523.53	1521.92
105000	1985.93	1908.88	1709.87	1640.71	1614.32	1603.88	1599.70	1598.02
110000	2080.50	1999.78	1791.29	1718.84	1691.19	1680.26	1675.88	1674.12
115000	2175.06	2090.68	1872.71	1796.97	1768.06	1756.63	1752.06	1750.21
120000	2269.63	2181.58	1954.13	1875.10	1844.93	1833.01	1828.23	1826.31
125000	2364.20	2272.48	2035.56	1953.23	1921.80	1909.38	1904.41	1902.40
130000	2458.77	2363.38	2116.98	2031.36	1998.68	1985.76	1980.58	1978.50
135000	2553.34	2454.28	2198.40	2109.49	2075.55	2062.13	2056.76	2054.60
140000	2647.90	2545.17	2279.82	2187.61	2152.42	2138.51	2132.94	2130.69
145000	2742.47	2636.07	2361.24	2265.74	2229.29	2214.88	2209.11	2206.79
150000	2837.04	2726.97	2442.67	2343.87	2306.16	2291.26	2285.29	2282.88
155000	2931.61	2817.87	2524.09	2422.00	2383.03	2367.64	2361.47	2358.98
160000	3026.17	2908.77	2605.51	2500.13	2459.91	2444.01	2437.64	2435.08

81

MONTHLY AMORTIZING PAYMENTS

AMOUNT OF LOAN	NUMBER OF YEARS IN TERM							
	1	2	3	4	5	6	7	8
$ 50	4.60	2.51	1.83	1.49	1.29	1.16	1.07	1.01
100	9.20	5.02	3.65	2.97	2.57	2.31	2.14	2.01
200	18.39	10.04	7.29	5.93	5.14	4.62	4.27	4.01
300	27.58	15.05	10.93	8.90	7.70	6.93	6.40	6.01
400	36.77	20.07	14.57	11.86	10.27	9.24	8.53	8.02
500	45.96	25.09	18.21	14.82	12.84	11.55	10.66	10.02
600	55.16	30.10	21.85	17.79	15.40	13.86	12.79	12.02
700	64.35	35.12	25.49	20.75	17.97	16.17	14.92	14.02
800	73.54	40.14	29.13	23.71	20.54	18.48	17.05	16.03
900	82.73	45.15	32.77	26.68	23.10	20.79	19.19	18.03
1000	91.92	50.17	36.41	29.64	25.67	23.10	21.32	20.03
2000	183.84	100.34	72.81	59.28	51.34	46.19	42.63	40.06
3000	275.76	150.50	109.22	88.92	77.00	69.28	63.94	60.09
4000	367.68	200.67	145.62	118.55	102.67	92.37	85.25	80.11
5000	459.60	250.84	182.02	148.19	128.34	115.46	106.56	100.14
6000	551.51	301.00	218.43	177.83	154.00	138.55	127.88	120.17
7000	643.43	351.17	254.83	207.46	179.67	161.64	149.19	140.20
8000	735.35	401.33	291.23	237.10	205.33	184.74	170.50	160.22
9000	827.27	451.50	327.64	266.74	231.00	207.83	191.81	180.25
10000	919.19	501.67	364.04	296.37	256.67	230.92	213.12	200.28
11000	1011.10	551.83	400.45	326.01	282.33	254.01	234.44	220.31
12000	1103.02	602.00	436.85	355.65	308.00	277.10	255.75	240.33
13000	1194.94	652.16	473.25	385.28	333.67	300.19	277.06	260.36
14000	1286.86	702.33	509.66	414.92	359.33	323.28	298.37	280.39
15000	1378.78	752.50	546.06	444.56	385.00	346.38	319.68	300.42
16000	1470.69	802.66	582.46	474.20	410.66	369.47	341.00	320.44
17000	1562.61	852.83	618.87	503.83	436.33	392.56	362.31	340.47
18000	1654.53	902.99	655.27	533.47	462.00	415.65	383.62	360.50
19000	1746.45	953.16	691.68	563.11	487.66	438.74	404.93	380.53
20000	1838.37	1003.33	728.08	592.74	513.33	461.83	426.24	400.55
21000	1930.29	1053.49	764.48	622.38	539.00	484.92	447.56	420.58
22000	2022.20	1103.66	800.89	652.02	564.66	508.01	468.87	440.61
23000	2114.12	1153.82	837.29	681.65	590.33	531.11	490.18	460.64
24000	2206.04	1203.99	873.69	711.29	615.99	554.20	511.49	480.66
25000	2297.96	1254.16	910.10	740.93	641.66	577.29	532.80	500.69
26000	2389.88	1304.32	946.50	770.56	667.33	600.38	554.11	520.72
27000	2481.79	1354.49	982.91	800.20	692.99	623.47	575.43	540.75
28000	2573.71	1404.65	1019.31	829.84	718.66	646.56	596.74	560.77
29000	2665.63	1454.82	1055.71	859.48	744.33	669.65	618.05	580.80
30000	2757.55	1504.99	1092.12	889.11	769.99	692.75	639.36	600.83
31000	2849.47	1555.15	1128.52	918.75	795.66	715.84	660.67	620.86
32000	2941.38	1605.32	1164.92	948.39	821.32	738.93	681.99	640.88
33000	3033.30	1655.48	1201.33	978.02	846.99	762.02	703.30	660.91
34000	3125.22	1705.65	1237.73	1007.66	872.66	785.11	724.61	680.94
35000	3217.14	1755.82	1274.13	1037.30	898.32	808.20	745.92	700.97
40000	3676.73	2006.65	1456.15	1185.48	1026.65	923.66	852.48	801.10
45000	4136.32	2257.48	1638.17	1333.67	1154.98	1039.12	959.04	901.24
50000	4595.91	2508.31	1820.19	1481.85	1283.32	1154.57	1065.60	1001.38
55000	5055.50	2759.14	2002.21	1630.04	1411.65	1270.03	1172.16	1101.51
60000	5515.09	3009.97	2184.23	1778.22	1539.98	1385.49	1278.72	1201.65
65000	5974.68	3260.80	2366.25	1926.40	1668.31	1500.94	1385.28	1301.79
70000	6434.27	3511.63	2548.27	2074.59	1796.64	1616.40	1491.84	1401.93
75000	6893.86	3762.46	2730.28	2222.77	1924.97	1731.86	1598.40	1502.06
80000	7353.45	4013.29	2912.30	2370.96	2053.30	1847.31	1704.96	1602.20
85000	7813.04	4264.12	3094.32	2519.14	2181.63	1962.77	1811.52	1702.34
90000	8272.64	4514.95	3276.34	2667.33	2309.96	2078.23	1918.08	1802.47
95000	8732.23	4765.78	3458.36	2815.51	2438.29	2193.68	2024.64	1902.61
100000	9191.82	5016.61	3640.38	2963.70	2566.63	2309.14	2131.20	2002.75
105000	9651.41	5267.44	3822.40	3111.88	2694.96	2424.60	2237.76	2102.89
110000	10111.00	5518.27	4004.41	3260.07	2823.29	2540.05	2344.32	2203.02
115000	10570.59	5769.10	4186.43	3408.25	2951.62	2655.51	2450.88	2303.16
120000	11030.18	6019.93	4368.45	3556.43	3079.95	2770.97	2557.44	2403.30
125000	11489.77	6270.76	4550.47	3704.62	3208.28	2886.42	2663.99	2503.44
130000	11949.36	6521.59	4732.49	3852.80	3336.61	3001.88	2770.55	2603.57
135000	12408.95	6772.42	4914.51	4000.99	3464.94	3117.34	2877.11	2703.71
140000	12868.54	7023.25	5096.53	4149.17	3593.27	3232.79	2983.67	2803.85
145000	13328.13	7274.08	5278.54	4297.36	3721.61	3348.25	3090.23	2903.98
150000	13787.72	7524.91	5460.56	4445.54	3849.94	3463.71	3196.79	3004.12
155000	14247.31	7775.74	5642.58	4593.73	3978.27	3579.16	3303.35	3104.26
160000	14706.90	8026.57	5824.60	4741.91	4106.60	3694.62	3409.91	3204.40

AMOUNT OF LOAN	NUMBER OF YEARS IN TERM							
	9	10	15	20	25	30	35	40
$ 50	.96	.92	.83	.80	.78	.78	.78	.78
100	1.91	1.84	1.65	1.59	1.56	1.55	1.55	1.55
200	3.82	3.67	3.30	3.17	3.12	3.10	3.09	3.09
300	5.73	5.51	4.94	4.75	4.68	4.65	4.64	4.63
400	7.63	7.34	6.59	6.33	6.23	6.20	6.18	6.18
500	9.54	9.18	8.24	7.91	7.79	7.74	7.73	7.72
600	11.45	11.01	9.88	9.50	9.35	9.29	9.27	9.26
700	13.35	12.84	11.53	11.08	10.91	10.84	10.81	10.80
800	15.26	14.68	13.18	12.66	12.46	12.39	12.36	12.35
900	17.17	16.51	14.82	14.24	14.02	13.94	13.90	13.89
1000	19.08	18.35	16.47	15.82	15.58	15.48	15.45	15.43
2000	38.15	36.69	32.94	31.64	31.15	30.96	30.89	30.86
3000	57.22	55.03	49.40	47.46	46.73	46.44	46.33	46.28
4000	76.29	73.37	65.87	63.28	62.30	61.92	61.77	61.71
5000	95.36	91.71	82.33	79.10	77.88	77.40	77.21	77.14
6000	114.43	110.05	98.80	94.92	93.45	92.88	92.66	92.56
7000	133.50	128.40	115.26	110.74	109.03	108.36	108.10	107.99
8000	152.57	146.74	131.73	126.56	124.60	123.84	123.54	123.42
9000	171.64	165.08	148.19	142.38	140.18	139.32	138.98	138.84
10000	190.71	183.42	164.66	158.19	155.75	154.80	154.42	154.27
11000	209.78	201.76	181.12	174.01	171.33	170.28	169.86	169.70
12000	228.85	220.10	197.59	189.83	186.90	185.76	185.31	185.12
13000	247.93	238.45	214.05	205.65	202.48	201.24	200.75	200.55
14000	267.00	256.79	230.52	221.47	218.05	216.72	216.19	215.98
15000	286.07	275.13	246.98	237.29	233.63	232.20	231.63	231.40
16000	305.14	293.47	263.45	253.11	249.20	247.68	247.07	246.83
17000	324.21	311.81	279.91	268.93	264.78	263.16	262.51	262.26
18000	343.28	330.15	296.38	284.75	280.35	278.64	277.96	277.68
19000	362.35	348.50	312.84	300.57	295.93	294.11	293.40	293.11
20000	381.42	366.84	329.31	316.38	311.50	309.59	308.84	308.54
21000	400.49	385.18	345.77	332.20	327.08	325.07	324.28	323.96
22000	419.56	403.52	362.24	348.02	342.65	340.55	339.72	339.39
23000	438.63	421.86	378.71	363.84	358.23	356.03	355.16	354.82
24000	457.70	440.20	395.17	379.66	373.80	371.51	370.61	370.24
25000	476.78	458.55	411.64	395.48	389.38	386.99	386.05	385.67
26000	495.85	476.89	428.10	411.30	404.95	402.47	401.49	401.10
27000	514.92	495.23	444.57	427.12	420.53	417.95	416.93	416.52
28000	533.99	513.57	461.03	442.94	436.10	433.43	432.37	431.95
29000	553.06	531.91	477.50	458.76	451.68	448.91	447.81	447.38
30000	572.13	550.25	493.96	474.57	467.25	464.39	463.26	462.80
31000	591.20	568.60	510.43	490.39	482.83	479.87	478.70	478.23
32000	610.27	586.94	526.89	506.21	498.40	495.35	494.14	493.66
33000	629.34	605.28	543.36	522.03	513.97	510.83	509.58	509.08
34000	648.41	623.62	559.82	537.85	529.55	526.31	525.02	524.51
35000	667.48	641.96	576.29	553.67	545.12	541.79	540.46	539.94
40000	762.84	733.67	658.61	632.76	623.00	619.18	617.67	617.07
45000	858.19	825.38	740.94	711.86	700.87	696.58	694.88	694.20
50000	953.55	917.09	823.27	790.95	778.75	773.98	772.09	771.34
55000	1048.90	1008.80	905.59	870.05	856.62	851.37	849.30	848.47
60000	1144.25	1100.50	987.92	949.14	934.50	928.77	926.51	925.60
65000	1239.61	1192.21	1070.25	1028.24	1012.37	1006.17	1003.71	1002.74
70000	1334.96	1283.92	1152.57	1107.33	1090.24	1083.57	1080.92	1079.87
75000	1430.32	1375.63	1234.90	1186.43	1168.12	1160.96	1158.13	1157.00
80000	1525.67	1467.34	1317.22	1265.52	1245.99	1238.36	1235.34	1234.14
85000	1621.02	1559.05	1399.55	1344.62	1323.87	1315.76	1312.55	1311.27
90000	1716.38	1650.75	1481.88	1423.71	1401.74	1393.16	1389.76	1388.40
95000	1811.73	1742.46	1564.20	1502.81	1479.61	1470.55	1466.96	1465.54
100000	1907.09	1834.17	1646.53	1581.90	1557.49	1547.95	1544.17	1542.67
105000	2002.44	1925.88	1728.85	1661.00	1635.36	1625.35	1621.38	1619.80
110000	2097.79	2017.59	1811.18	1740.09	1713.24	1702.74	1698.59	1696.94
115000	2193.15	2109.30	1893.51	1819.19	1791.11	1780.14	1775.80	1774.07
120000	2288.50	2201.00	1975.83	1898.28	1868.99	1857.54	1853.01	1851.20
125000	2383.86	2292.71	2058.16	1977.38	1946.86	1934.94	1930.21	1928.34
130000	2479.21	2384.42	2140.49	2056.47	2024.73	2012.33	2007.42	2005.47
135000	2574.57	2476.13	2222.81	2135.57	2102.61	2089.73	2084.63	2082.60
140000	2669.92	2567.84	2305.14	2214.66	2180.48	2167.13	2161.84	2159.74
145000	2765.27	2659.54	2387.46	2293.76	2258.36	2244.52	2239.05	2236.87
150000	2860.63	2751.25	2469.79	2372.85	2336.23	2321.92	2316.26	2314.00
155000	2955.98	2842.96	2552.12	2451.94	2414.11	2399.32	2393.46	2391.13
160000	3051.34	2934.67	2634.44	2531.04	2491.98	2476.72	2470.67	2468.27

83

18.750% MONTHLY AMORTIZING PAYMENTS

AMOUNT OF LOAN	NUMBER OF YEARS IN TERM							
	1	2	3	4	5	6	7	8
$ 50	4.61	2.52	1.83	1.49	1.30	1.17	1.08	1.01
100	9.21	5.03	3.66	2.98	2.59	2.33	2.15	2.02
200	18.41	10.06	7.31	5.96	5.17	4.65	4.30	4.04
300	27.62	15.09	10.96	8.94	7.75	6.98	6.44	6.06
400	36.82	20.12	14.62	11.91	10.33	9.30	8.59	8.08
500	46.02	25.15	18.27	14.89	12.91	11.62	10.73	10.10
600	55.23	30.18	21.92	17.87	15.49	13.95	12.88	12.11
700	64.43	35.21	25.58	20.84	18.07	16.27	15.03	14.13
800	73.63	40.23	29.23	23.82	20.65	18.59	17.17	16.15
900	82.84	45.26	32.88	26.80	23.23	20.92	19.32	18.17
1000	92.04	50.29	36.53	29.77	25.81	23.24	21.46	20.19
2000	184.08	100.58	73.06	59.54	51.61	46.47	42.92	40.37
3000	276.12	150.87	109.59	89.31	77.41	69.71	64.38	60.55
4000	368.15	201.15	146.12	119.08	103.22	92.94	85.84	80.73
5000	460.19	251.44	182.65	148.85	129.02	116.17	107.30	100.91
6000	552.23	301.73	219.18	178.62	154.82	139.41	128.76	121.09
7000	644.27	352.02	255.71	208.38	180.63	162.64	150.22	141.27
8000	736.30	402.30	292.24	238.15	206.43	185.88	171.68	161.45
9000	828.34	452.59	328.77	267.92	232.23	209.11	193.14	181.63
10000	920.38	502.88	365.30	297.69	258.04	232.34	214.60	201.81
11000	1012.42	553.16	401.83	327.46	283.84	255.58	236.06	221.99
12000	1104.45	603.45	438.36	357.23	309.64	278.81	257.52	242.17
13000	1196.49	653.74	474.89	386.99	335.45	302.04	278.98	262.35
14000	1288.53	704.03	511.42	416.76	361.25	325.28	300.44	282.53
15000	1380.56	754.31	547.95	446.53	387.05	348.51	321.90	302.71
16000	1472.60	804.60	584.48	476.30	412.86	371.75	343.36	322.89
17000	1564.64	854.89	621.01	506.07	438.66	394.98	364.82	343.07
18000	1656.68	905.18	657.54	535.84	464.46	418.21	386.28	363.25
19000	1748.71	955.46	694.07	565.60	490.27	441.45	407.74	383.43
20000	1840.75	1005.75	730.60	595.37	516.07	464.68	429.20	403.61
21000	1932.79	1056.04	767.13	625.14	541.87	487.92	450.66	423.79
22000	2024.83	1106.32	803.66	654.91	567.68	511.15	472.12	443.97
23000	2116.86	1156.61	840.19	684.68	593.48	534.38	493.58	464.15
24000	2208.90	1206.90	876.72	714.45	619.28	557.62	515.04	484.33
25000	2300.94	1257.19	913.25	744.21	645.08	580.85	536.50	504.51
26000	2392.97	1307.47	949.78	773.98	670.89	604.08	557.96	524.69
27000	2485.01	1357.76	986.31	803.75	696.69	627.32	579.42	544.88
28000	2577.05	1408.05	1022.84	833.52	722.49	650.55	600.88	565.06
29000	2669.09	1458.33	1059.37	863.29	748.30	673.79	622.34	585.24
30000	2761.12	1508.62	1095.90	893.06	774.10	697.02	643.80	605.42
31000	2853.16	1558.91	1132.43	922.82	799.90	720.25	665.26	625.60
32000	2945.20	1609.20	1168.96	952.59	825.71	743.49	686.72	645.78
33000	3037.24	1659.48	1205.49	982.36	851.51	766.72	708.18	665.96
34000	3129.27	1709.77	1242.02	1012.13	877.31	789.95	729.64	686.14
35000	3221.31	1760.06	1278.55	1041.90	903.12	813.19	751.10	706.32
40000	3681.50	2011.49	1461.19	1190.74	1032.13	929.36	858.39	807.22
45000	4141.68	2262.93	1643.84	1339.58	1161.15	1045.53	965.69	908.12
50000	4601.87	2514.37	1826.49	1488.42	1290.16	1161.70	1072.99	1009.02
55000	5062.06	2765.80	2009.14	1637.26	1419.18	1277.86	1180.29	1109.93
60000	5522.24	3017.24	2191.79	1786.11	1548.20	1394.03	1287.59	1210.83
65000	5982.43	3268.68	2374.44	1934.95	1677.21	1510.20	1394.89	1311.73
70000	6442.62	3520.11	2557.09	2083.79	1806.23	1626.37	1502.19	1412.63
75000	6902.80	3771.55	2739.74	2232.63	1935.24	1742.54	1609.48	1513.53
80000	7362.99	4022.98	2922.38	2381.47	2064.26	1858.71	1716.78	1614.44
85000	7823.18	4274.42	3105.03	2530.32	2193.28	1974.88	1824.08	1715.34
90000	8283.36	4525.86	3287.68	2679.16	2322.29	2091.05	1931.38	1816.24
95000	8743.55	4777.29	3470.33	2828.00	2451.31	2207.22	2038.68	1917.14
100000	9203.74	5028.73	3652.98	2976.84	2580.32	2323.39	2145.98	2018.04
105000	9663.92	5280.16	3835.63	3125.68	2709.34	2439.56	2253.28	2118.94
110000	10124.11	5531.60	4018.28	3274.52	2838.36	2555.72	2360.57	2219.85
115000	10584.30	5783.04	4200.93	3423.37	2967.37	2671.89	2467.87	2320.75
120000	11044.48	6034.47	4383.57	3572.21	3096.39	2788.06	2575.17	2421.65
125000	11504.67	6285.91	4566.22	3721.05	3225.40	2904.23	2682.47	2522.55
130000	11964.85	6537.35	4748.87	3869.89	3354.42	3020.40	2789.77	2623.45
135000	12425.04	6788.78	4931.52	4018.73	3483.44	3136.57	2897.07	2724.36
140000	12885.23	7040.22	5114.17	4167.57	3612.45	3252.74	3004.37	2825.26
145000	13345.41	7291.65	5296.82	4316.42	3741.47	3368.91	3111.66	2926.16
150000	13805.60	7543.09	5479.47	4465.26	3870.48	3485.08	3218.96	3027.06
155000	14265.79	7794.53	5662.12	4614.10	3999.50	3601.25	3326.26	3127.96
160000	14725.97	8045.96	5844.76	4762.94	4128.51	3717.42	3433.56	3228.87

84

AMOUNT OF LOAN	NUMBER OF YEARS IN TERM							
	9	10	15	20	25	30	35	40
$ 50	.97	.93	.84	.81	.79	.79	.79	.79
100	1.93	1.86	1.67	1.61	1.58	1.57	1.57	1.57
200	3.85	3.71	3.33	3.21	3.16	3.14	3.13	3.13
300	5.77	5.56	5.00	4.81	4.74	4.71	4.70	4.70
400	7.70	7.41	6.66	6.41	6.32	6.28	6.26	6.26
500	9.62	9.26	8.33	8.01	7.89	7.85	7.83	7.82
600	11.54	11.11	9.99	9.61	9.47	9.42	9.39	9.39
700	13.47	12.96	11.66	11.21	11.05	10.98	10.96	10.95
800	15.39	14.81	13.32	12.82	12.63	12.55	12.52	12.51
900	17.31	16.66	14.99	14.42	14.20	14.12	14.09	14.08
1000	19.23	18.51	16.65	16.02	15.78	15.69	15.65	15.64
2000	38.46	37.01	33.30	32.03	31.56	31.37	31.30	31.27
3000	57.69	55.52	49.95	48.04	47.33	47.06	46.95	46.91
4000	76.92	74.02	66.59	64.06	63.11	62.74	62.60	62.54
5000	96.15	92.53	83.24	80.07	78.88	78.43	78.25	78.18
6000	115.38	111.03	99.89	96.08	94.66	94.11	93.89	93.81
7000	134.61	129.53	116.53	112.09	110.43	109.79	109.54	109.44
8000	153.83	148.04	133.18	128.11	126.21	125.48	125.19	125.08
9000	173.06	166.54	149.83	144.12	141.99	141.16	140.84	140.71
10000	192.29	185.05	166.47	160.13	157.76	156.85	156.49	156.35
11000	211.52	203.55	183.12	176.14	173.54	172.53	172.14	171.98
12000	230.75	222.05	199.77	192.16	189.31	188.21	187.78	187.61
13000	249.98	240.56	216.41	208.17	205.09	203.90	203.43	203.25
14000	269.21	259.06	233.06	224.18	220.86	219.58	219.08	218.88
15000	288.43	277.57	249.71	240.19	236.64	235.27	234.73	234.52
16000	307.66	296.07	266.35	256.21	252.42	250.95	250.38	250.15
17000	326.89	314.58	283.00	272.22	268.19	266.64	266.03	265.79
18000	346.12	333.08	299.65	288.23	283.97	282.32	281.67	281.42
19000	365.35	351.58	316.29	304.25	299.74	298.00	297.32	297.05
20000	384.58	370.09	332.94	320.26	315.52	313.69	312.97	312.69
21000	403.81	388.59	349.59	336.27	331.29	329.37	328.62	328.32
22000	423.04	407.10	366.23	352.28	347.07	345.05	344.27	343.96
23000	442.26	425.60	382.88	368.30	362.84	360.74	359.91	359.59
24000	461.49	444.10	399.53	384.31	378.62	376.42	375.56	375.22
25000	480.72	462.61	416.17	400.32	394.40	392.11	391.21	390.86
26000	499.95	481.11	432.82	416.33	410.17	407.79	406.86	406.49
27000	519.18	499.62	449.47	432.35	425.95	423.48	422.51	422.13
28000	538.41	518.12	466.11	448.36	441.72	439.16	438.16	437.76
29000	557.64	536.63	482.76	464.37	457.50	454.84	453.80	453.40
30000	576.86	555.13	499.41	480.38	473.27	470.53	469.45	469.03
31000	596.09	573.63	516.05	496.40	489.05	486.21	485.10	484.66
32000	615.32	592.14	532.70	512.41	504.83	501.90	500.75	500.30
33000	634.55	610.64	549.35	528.42	520.60	517.58	516.40	515.93
34000	653.78	629.15	565.99	544.44	536.38	533.26	532.05	531.57
35000	673.01	647.65	582.64	560.45	552.15	548.95	547.69	547.20
40000	769.15	740.17	665.87	640.51	631.03	627.37	625.94	625.37
45000	865.29	832.69	749.11	720.57	709.91	705.79	704.18	703.54
50000	961.44	925.21	832.34	800.64	788.79	784.21	782.42	781.71
55000	1057.58	1017.73	915.57	880.70	867.67	862.63	860.66	859.88
60000	1153.72	1110.25	998.81	960.76	946.54	941.05	938.90	938.05
65000	1249.86	1202.77	1082.04	1040.83	1025.42	1019.47	1017.14	1016.23
70000	1346.01	1295.29	1165.27	1120.89	1104.30	1097.89	1095.38	1094.40
75000	1442.15	1387.82	1248.51	1200.95	1183.18	1176.31	1173.62	1172.57
80000	1538.30	1480.34	1331.74	1281.02	1262.06	1254.73	1251.87	1250.74
85000	1634.44	1572.86	1414.97	1361.08	1340.94	1333.15	1330.11	1328.91
90000	1730.58	1665.38	1498.21	1441.14	1419.81	1411.57	1408.35	1407.08
95000	1826.73	1757.90	1581.44	1521.21	1498.69	1489.99	1486.59	1485.25
100000	1922.87	1850.42	1664.67	1601.27	1577.57	1568.41	1564.83	1563.42
105000	2019.01	1942.94	1747.91	1681.33	1656.45	1646.83	1643.07	1641.59
110000	2115.16	2035.46	1831.14	1761.40	1735.33	1725.25	1721.31	1719.76
115000	2211.30	2127.98	1914.37	1841.46	1814.20	1803.67	1799.55	1797.93
120000	2307.44	2220.50	1997.61	1921.52	1893.08	1882.09	1877.80	1876.10
125000	2403.59	2313.02	2080.84	2001.59	1971.96	1960.52	1956.04	1954.28
130000	2499.73	2405.54	2164.07	2081.65	2050.84	2038.94	2034.28	2032.45
135000	2595.87	2498.06	2247.31	2161.71	2129.72	2117.36	2112.52	2110.62
140000	2692.02	2590.58	2330.54	2241.78	2208.60	2195.78	2190.76	2188.79
145000	2788.16	2683.11	2413.78	2321.84	2287.47	2274.20	2269.00	2266.96
150000	2884.30	2775.63	2497.01	2401.90	2366.35	2352.62	2347.24	2345.13
155000	2980.45	2868.15	2580.24	2481.97	2445.23	2431.04	2425.48	2423.30
160000	3076.59	2960.67	2663.48	2562.03	2524.11	2509.46	2503.73	2501.47

MONTHLY AMORTIZING PAYMENTS

AMOUNT OF LOAN	NUMBER OF YEARS IN TERM							
	1	2	3	4	5	6	7	8
$ 50	4.61	2.53	1.84	1.50	1.30	1.17	1.09	1.02
100	9.22	5.05	3.67	3.00	2.60	2.34	2.17	2.04
200	18.44	10.09	7.34	5.99	5.19	4.68	4.33	4.07
300	27.65	15.13	11.00	8.98	7.79	7.02	6.49	6.11
400	36.87	20.17	14.67	11.97	10.38	9.36	8.65	8.14
500	46.08	25.21	18.33	14.96	12.98	11.69	10.81	10.17
600	55.30	30.25	22.00	17.95	15.57	14.03	12.97	12.21
700	64.51	35.29	25.66	20.94	18.16	16.37	15.13	14.24
800	73.73	40.33	29.33	23.93	20.76	18.71	17.29	16.27
900	82.95	45.37	33.00	26.92	23.35	21.04	19.45	18.31
1000	92.16	50.41	36.66	29.91	25.95	23.38	21.61	20.34
2000	184.32	100.82	73.32	59.81	51.89	46.76	43.22	40.67
3000	276.47	151.23	109.97	89.71	77.83	70.14	64.83	61.01
4000	368.63	201.64	146.63	119.61	103.77	93.51	86.44	81.34
5000	460.79	252.05	183.29	149.51	129.71	116.89	108.05	101.67
6000	552.94	302.46	219.94	179.41	155.65	140.27	129.65	122.01
7000	645.10	352.87	256.60	209.31	181.59	163.64	151.26	142.34
8000	737.26	403.27	293.25	239.21	207.53	187.02	172.87	162.68
9000	829.41	453.68	329.91	269.11	233.47	210.40	194.48	183.01
10000	921.57	504.09	366.57	299.01	259.41	233.77	216.09	203.34
11000	1013.73	554.50	403.22	328.91	285.35	257.15	237.69	223.68
12000	1105.88	604.91	439.88	358.81	311.29	280.53	259.30	244.01
13000	1198.04	655.32	476.53	388.71	337.23	303.90	280.91	264.35
14000	1290.20	705.73	513.19	418.61	363.17	327.28	302.52	284.68
15000	1382.35	756.13	549.85	448.51	389.11	350.66	324.13	305.01
16000	1474.51	806.54	586.50	478.41	415.05	374.03	345.73	325.35
17000	1566.67	856.95	623.16	508.31	440.99	397.41	367.34	345.68
18000	1658.82	907.36	659.81	538.21	466.93	420.79	388.95	366.01
19000	1750.98	957.77	696.47	568.11	492.88	444.16	410.56	386.35
20000	1843.14	1008.18	733.13	598.01	518.82	467.54	432.17	406.68
21000	1935.29	1058.59	769.78	627.91	544.76	490.92	453.77	427.02
22000	2027.45	1108.99	806.44	657.81	570.70	514.29	475.38	447.35
23000	2119.61	1159.40	843.09	687.71	596.64	537.67	496.99	467.68
24000	2211.76	1209.81	879.75	717.61	622.58	561.05	518.60	488.02
25000	2303.92	1260.22	916.41	747.51	648.52	584.42	540.21	508.35
26000	2396.08	1310.63	953.06	777.41	674.46	607.80	561.81	528.69
27000	2488.23	1361.04	989.72	807.31	700.40	631.18	583.42	549.02
28000	2580.39	1411.45	1026.37	837.21	726.34	654.55	605.03	569.35
29000	2672.55	1461.85	1063.03	867.11	752.28	677.93	626.64	589.69
30000	2764.70	1512.26	1099.69	897.01	778.22	701.31	648.25	610.02
31000	2856.86	1562.67	1136.34	926.91	804.16	724.68	669.85	630.35
32000	2949.02	1613.08	1173.00	956.81	830.10	748.06	691.46	650.69
33000	3041.17	1663.49	1209.65	986.71	856.04	771.44	713.07	671.02
34000	3133.33	1713.90	1246.31	1016.61	881.98	794.81	734.68	691.36
35000	3225.49	1764.31	1282.97	1046.51	907.92	818.19	756.29	711.69
40000	3686.27	2016.35	1466.25	1196.01	1037.63	935.07	864.33	813.36
45000	4147.05	2268.39	1649.53	1345.51	1167.33	1051.96	972.37	915.03
50000	4607.83	2520.44	1832.81	1495.01	1297.03	1168.84	1080.41	1016.70
55000	5068.62	2772.48	2016.09	1644.51	1426.74	1285.72	1188.45	1118.37
60000	5529.40	3024.52	2199.37	1794.01	1556.44	1402.61	1296.49	1220.04
65000	5990.18	3276.57	2382.65	1943.51	1686.14	1519.49	1404.53	1321.71
70000	6450.97	3528.61	2565.93	2093.01	1815.84	1636.38	1512.57	1423.38
75000	6911.75	3780.65	2749.21	2242.51	1945.55	1753.26	1620.61	1525.04
80000	7372.53	4032.69	2932.49	2392.01	2075.25	1870.14	1728.65	1626.71
85000	7833.31	4284.74	3115.77	2541.52	2204.95	1987.03	1836.69	1728.38
90000	8294.10	4536.78	3299.05	2691.02	2334.65	2103.91	1944.73	1830.05
95000	8754.88	4788.82	3482.33	2840.52	2464.36	2220.79	2052.77	1931.72
100000	9215.66	5040.87	3665.61	2990.02	2594.06	2337.68	2160.81	2033.39
105000	9676.45	5292.91	3848.89	3139.52	2723.76	2454.56	2268.85	2135.06
110000	10137.23	5544.95	4032.17	3289.02	2853.47	2571.44	2376.89	2236.73
115000	10598.01	5797.00	4215.45	3438.52	2983.17	2688.33	2484.93	2338.40
120000	11058.79	6049.04	4398.73	3588.02	3112.87	2805.21	2592.97	2440.07
125000	11519.58	6301.08	4582.01	3737.52	3242.57	2922.10	2701.01	2541.74
130000	11980.36	6553.13	4765.29	3887.02	3372.28	3038.98	2809.05	2643.41
135000	12441.14	6805.17	4948.57	4036.52	3501.98	3155.86	2917.09	2745.08
140000	12901.93	7057.21	5131.85	4186.02	3631.68	3272.75	3025.13	2846.75
145000	13362.71	7309.25	5315.13	4335.52	3761.38	3389.63	3133.17	2948.42
150000	13823.49	7561.30	5498.41	4485.02	3891.09	3506.51	3241.21	3050.08
155000	14284.27	7813.34	5681.69	4634.52	4020.79	3623.40	3349.25	3151.75
160000	14745.06	8065.38	5864.97	4784.02	4150.49	3740.28	3457.29	3253.42

MONTHLY AMORTIZING PAYMENTS 19.000%

AMOUNT OF LOAN	NUMBER OF YEARS IN TERM							
	9	10	15	20	25	30	35	40
$ 50	.97	.94	.85	.82	.80	.80	.80	.80
100	1.94	1.87	1.69	1.63	1.60	1.59	1.59	1.59
200	3.88	3.74	3.37	3.25	3.20	3.18	3.18	3.17
300	5.82	5.61	5.05	4.87	4.80	4.77	4.76	4.76
400	7.76	7.47	6.74	6.49	6.40	6.36	6.35	6.34
500	9.70	9.34	8.42	8.11	7.99	7.95	7.93	7.93
600	11.64	11.21	10.10	9.73	9.59	9.54	9.52	9.51
700	13.58	13.07	11.79	11.35	11.19	11.13	11.10	11.09
800	15.51	14.94	13.47	12.97	12.79	12.72	12.69	12.68
900	17.45	16.81	15.15	14.59	14.38	14.31	14.27	14.26
1000	19.39	18.67	16.83	16.21	15.98	15.89	15.86	15.85
2000	38.78	37.34	33.66	32.42	31.96	31.78	31.71	31.69
3000	58.17	56.01	50.49	48.63	47.94	47.67	47.57	47.53
4000	77.55	74.67	67.32	64.83	63.91	63.56	63.42	63.37
5000	96.94	93.34	84.15	81.04	79.89	79.45	79.28	79.21
6000	116.33	112.01	100.98	97.25	95.87	95.34	95.13	95.06
7000	135.71	130.68	117.81	113.45	111.84	111.23	110.99	110.90
8000	155.10	149.34	134.64	129.66	127.82	127.12	126.84	126.74
9000	174.49	168.01	151.46	145.87	143.80	143.01	142.70	142.58
10000	193.88	186.68	168.29	162.07	159.77	158.89	158.55	158.42
11000	213.26	205.34	185.12	178.28	175.75	174.78	174.41	174.26
12000	232.65	224.01	201.95	194.49	191.73	190.67	190.26	190.11
13000	252.04	242.68	218.78	210.69	207.70	206.56	206.12	205.95
14000	271.42	261.35	235.61	226.90	223.68	222.45	221.97	221.79
15000	290.81	280.01	252.44	243.11	239.66	238.34	237.83	237.63
16000	310.20	298.68	269.27	259.31	255.63	254.23	253.68	253.47
17000	329.59	317.35	286.09	275.52	271.61	270.12	269.54	269.31
18000	348.97	336.02	302.92	291.73	287.59	286.01	285.39	285.16
19000	368.36	354.68	319.75	307.94	303.56	301.89	301.25	301.00
20000	387.75	373.35	336.58	324.14	319.54	317.78	317.10	316.84
21000	407.13	392.02	353.41	340.35	335.52	333.67	332.96	332.68
22000	426.52	410.68	370.24	356.56	351.49	349.56	348.81	348.52
23000	445.91	429.35	387.07	372.76	367.47	365.45	364.67	364.37
24000	465.29	448.02	403.90	388.97	383.45	381.34	380.52	380.21
25000	484.68	466.69	420.72	405.18	399.43	397.23	396.38	396.05
26000	504.07	485.35	437.55	421.38	415.40	413.12	412.23	411.89
27000	523.46	504.02	454.38	437.59	431.38	429.01	428.09	427.73
28000	542.84	522.69	471.21	453.80	447.36	444.89	443.94	443.57
29000	562.23	541.35	488.04	470.00	463.33	460.78	459.80	459.42
30000	581.62	560.02	504.87	486.21	479.31	476.67	475.65	475.26
31000	601.00	578.69	521.70	502.42	495.29	492.56	491.51	491.10
32000	620.39	597.36	538.53	518.62	511.26	508.45	507.36	506.94
33000	639.78	616.02	555.35	534.83	527.24	524.34	523.22	522.78
34000	659.17	634.69	572.18	551.04	543.22	540.23	539.07	538.62
35000	678.55	653.36	589.01	567.24	559.19	556.12	554.93	554.47
40000	775.49	746.69	673.16	648.28	639.08	635.56	634.20	633.67
45000	872.42	840.03	757.30	729.31	718.96	715.01	713.48	712.88
50000	969.36	933.37	841.44	810.35	798.85	794.45	792.75	792.09
55000	1066.29	1026.70	925.59	891.38	878.73	873.90	872.03	871.30
60000	1163.23	1120.04	1009.73	972.42	958.61	953.34	951.30	950.51
65000	1260.17	1213.38	1093.87	1053.45	1038.50	1032.79	1030.58	1029.72
70000	1357.10	1306.71	1178.02	1134.48	1118.38	1112.23	1109.85	1108.93
75000	1454.04	1400.05	1262.16	1215.52	1198.27	1191.67	1189.13	1188.14
80000	1550.97	1493.38	1346.31	1296.55	1278.15	1271.12	1268.40	1267.34
85000	1647.91	1586.72	1430.45	1377.59	1358.03	1350.56	1347.68	1346.55
90000	1744.84	1680.06	1514.59	1458.62	1437.92	1430.01	1426.95	1425.76
95000	1841.78	1773.39	1598.74	1539.66	1517.80	1509.45	1506.22	1504.97
100000	1938.71	1866.73	1682.88	1620.69	1597.69	1588.90	1585.50	1584.18
105000	2035.65	1960.06	1767.02	1701.72	1677.57	1668.34	1664.77	1663.39
110000	2132.58	2053.40	1851.17	1782.76	1757.45	1747.79	1744.05	1742.60
115000	2229.52	2146.74	1935.31	1863.79	1837.34	1827.23	1823.32	1821.81
120000	2326.45	2240.07	2019.46	1944.83	1917.22	1906.68	1902.60	1901.01
125000	2423.39	2333.41	2103.60	2025.86	1997.11	1986.12	1981.87	1980.22
130000	2520.33	2426.75	2187.74	2106.90	2076.99	2065.57	2061.15	2059.43
135000	2617.26	2520.08	2271.89	2187.93	2156.87	2145.01	2140.42	2138.64
140000	2714.20	2613.42	2356.03	2268.96	2236.76	2224.45	2219.70	2217.85
145000	2811.13	2706.75	2440.18	2350.00	2316.64	2303.90	2298.97	2297.06
150000	2908.07	2800.09	2524.32	2431.03	2396.53	2383.34	2378.25	2376.27
155000	3005.00	2893.43	2608.46	2512.07	2476.41	2462.79	2457.52	2455.48
160000	3101.94	2986.76	2692.61	2593.10	2556.29	2542.23	2536.80	2534.68

19.250%   MONTHLY AMORTIZING PAYMENTS

AMOUNT OF LOAN	NUMBER OF YEARS IN TERM							
	1	2	3	4	5	6	7	8
$ 50	4.62	2.53	1.84	1.51	1.31	1.18	1.09	1.03
100	9.23	5.06	3.68	3.01	2.61	2.36	2.18	2.05
200	18.46	10.11	7.36	6.01	5.22	4.71	4.36	4.10
300	27.69	15.16	11.04	9.01	7.83	7.06	6.53	6.15
400	36.92	20.22	14.72	12.02	10.44	9.41	8.71	8.20
500	46.14	25.27	18.40	15.02	13.04	11.77	10.88	10.25
600	55.37	30.32	22.07	18.02	15.65	14.12	13.06	12.30
700	64.60	35.38	25.75	21.03	18.26	16.47	15.23	14.35
800	73.83	40.43	29.43	24.03	20.87	18.82	17.41	16.40
900	83.05	45.48	33.11	27.03	23.48	21.17	19.59	18.44
1000	92.28	50.54	36.79	30.04	26.08	23.53	21.76	20.49
2000	184.56	101.07	73.57	60.07	52.16	47.05	43.52	40.98
3000	276.83	151.60	110.35	90.10	78.24	70.57	65.28	61.47
4000	369.11	202.13	147.14	120.13	104.32	94.09	87.03	81.96
5000	461.38	252.66	183.92	150.17	130.40	117.61	108.79	102.44
6000	553.66	303.19	220.70	180.20	156.47	141.13	130.55	122.93
7000	645.94	353.72	257.48	210.23	182.55	164.65	152.30	143.42
8000	738.21	404.25	294.27	240.26	208.63	188.17	174.06	163.91
9000	830.49	454.78	331.05	270.29	234.71	211.69	195.82	184.40
10000	922.76	505.31	367.83	300.33	260.79	235.21	217.57	204.88
11000	1015.04	555.84	404.61	330.36	286.87	258.73	239.33	225.37
12000	1107.32	606.37	441.40	360.39	312.94	282.25	261.09	245.86
13000	1199.59	656.90	478.18	390.42	339.02	305.77	282.84	266.35
14000	1291.87	707.43	514.96	420.46	365.10	329.29	304.60	286.84
15000	1384.14	757.96	551.74	450.49	391.18	352.81	326.36	307.32
16000	1476.42	808.49	588.53	480.52	417.26	376.33	348.11	327.81
17000	1568.70	859.02	625.31	510.55	443.34	399.85	369.87	348.30
18000	1660.97	909.55	662.09	540.58	469.41	423.37	391.63	368.79
19000	1753.25	960.08	698.87	570.62	495.49	446.89	413.38	389.27
20000	1845.52	1010.61	735.66	600.65	521.57	470.41	435.14	409.76
21000	1937.80	1061.14	772.44	630.68	547.65	493.93	456.90	430.25
22000	2030.08	1111.67	809.22	660.71	573.73	517.45	478.66	450.74
23000	2122.35	1162.20	846.00	690.75	599.81	540.97	500.41	471.23
24000	2214.63	1212.73	882.79	720.78	625.88	564.49	522.17	491.71
25000	2306.90	1263.26	919.57	750.81	651.96	588.01	543.93	512.20
26000	2399.18	1313.79	956.35	780.84	678.04	611.53	565.68	532.69
27000	2491.46	1364.32	993.13	810.87	704.12	635.05	587.44	553.18
28000	2583.73	1414.85	1029.92	840.91	730.20	658.57	609.20	573.67
29000	2676.01	1465.38	1066.70	870.94	756.28	682.09	630.95	594.15
30000	2768.28	1515.91	1103.48	900.97	782.35	705.61	652.71	614.64
31000	2860.56	1566.44	1140.26	931.00	808.43	729.13	674.47	635.13
32000	2952.83	1616.97	1177.05	961.04	834.51	752.65	696.22	655.62
33000	3045.11	1667.50	1213.83	991.07	860.59	776.17	717.98	676.11
34000	3137.39	1718.03	1250.61	1021.10	886.67	799.69	739.74	696.59
35000	3229.66	1768.56	1287.39	1051.13	912.75	823.21	761.49	717.08
40000	3691.04	2021.21	1471.31	1201.29	1043.14	940.81	870.28	819.52
45000	4152.42	2273.86	1655.22	1351.45	1173.53	1058.41	979.06	921.96
50000	4613.80	2526.51	1839.13	1501.62	1303.92	1176.01	1087.85	1024.40
55000	5075.18	2779.16	2023.04	1651.78	1434.31	1293.61	1196.63	1126.84
60000	5536.56	3031.81	2206.96	1801.94	1564.70	1411.21	1305.41	1229.28
65000	5997.94	3284.47	2390.87	1952.10	1695.09	1528.81	1414.20	1331.72
70000	6459.32	3537.12	2574.78	2102.26	1825.49	1646.41	1522.98	1434.16
75000	6920.70	3789.77	2758.70	2252.42	1955.88	1764.01	1631.77	1536.60
80000	7382.08	4042.42	2942.61	2402.58	2086.27	1881.61	1740.55	1639.04
85000	7843.46	4295.07	3126.52	2552.74	2216.66	1999.21	1849.33	1741.48
90000	8304.84	4547.72	3310.43	2702.90	2347.05	2116.81	1958.12	1843.92
95000	8766.22	4800.37	3494.35	2853.06	2477.44	2234.41	2066.90	1946.35
100000	9227.60	5053.02	3678.26	3003.23	2607.84	2352.01	2175.69	2048.79
105000	9688.98	5305.67	3862.17	3153.39	2738.23	2469.61	2284.47	2151.23
110000	10150.36	5558.32	4046.08	3303.55	2868.62	2587.21	2393.26	2253.67
115000	10611.74	5810.97	4230.00	3453.71	2999.01	2704.81	2502.04	2356.11
120000	11073.12	6063.62	4413.91	3603.87	3129.40	2822.41	2610.82	2458.55
125000	11534.50	6316.28	4597.82	3754.03	3259.79	2940.02	2719.61	2560.99
130000	11995.88	6568.93	4781.74	3904.19	3390.18	3057.62	2828.39	2663.43
135000	12457.26	6821.58	4965.65	4054.35	3520.58	3175.22	2937.18	2765.87
140000	12918.64	7074.23	5149.56	4204.51	3650.97	3292.82	3045.96	2868.31
145000	13380.02	7326.88	5333.47	4354.67	3781.36	3410.42	3154.74	2970.75
150000	13841.40	7579.53	5517.39	4504.84	3911.75	3528.02	3263.53	3073.19
155000	14302.77	7832.18	5701.30	4655.00	4042.14	3645.62	3372.31	3175.63
160000	14764.15	8084.83	5885.21	4805.16	4172.53	3763.22	3481.10	3278.07

AMOUNT OF LOAN	NUMBER OF YEARS IN TERM							
	9	10	15	20	25	30	35	40
$ 50	.98	.95	.86	.83	.81	.81	.81	.81
100	1.96	1.89	1.71	1.65	1.62	1.61	1.61	1.61
200	3.91	3.77	3.41	3.29	3.24	3.22	3.22	3.21
300	5.87	5.65	5.11	4.93	4.86	4.83	4.82	4.82
400	7.82	7.54	6.81	6.57	6.48	6.44	6.43	6.42
500	9.78	9.42	8.51	8.21	8.09	8.05	8.04	8.03
600	11.73	11.30	10.21	9.85	9.71	9.66	9.64	9.63
700	13.69	13.19	11.91	11.49	11.33	11.27	11.25	11.24
800	15.64	15.07	13.61	13.13	12.95	12.88	12.85	12.84
900	17.60	16.95	15.32	14.77	14.57	14.49	14.46	14.45
1000	19.55	18.84	17.02	16.41	16.18	16.10	16.07	16.05
2000	39.10	37.67	34.03	32.81	32.36	32.19	32.13	32.10
3000	58.64	56.50	51.04	49.21	48.54	48.29	48.19	48.15
4000	78.19	75.33	68.05	65.61	64.72	64.38	64.25	64.20
5000	97.74	94.16	85.06	82.01	80.90	80.47	80.31	80.25
6000	117.28	112.99	102.07	98.41	97.07	96.57	96.38	96.30
7000	136.83	131.82	119.09	114.82	113.25	112.66	112.44	112.35
8000	156.37	150.65	136.10	131.22	129.43	128.76	128.50	128.40
9000	175.92	169.48	153.11	147.62	145.61	144.85	144.56	144.45
10000	195.47	188.31	170.12	164.02	161.79	160.94	160.62	160.50
11000	215.01	207.15	187.13	180.42	177.97	177.04	176.68	176.55
12000	234.56	225.98	204.14	196.82	194.14	193.13	192.75	192.60
13000	254.10	244.81	221.15	213.22	210.32	209.23	208.81	208.65
14000	273.65	263.64	238.17	229.63	226.50	225.32	224.87	224.70
15000	293.20	282.47	255.18	246.03	242.68	241.41	240.93	240.75
16000	312.74	301.30	272.19	262.43	258.86	257.51	256.99	256.80
17000	332.29	320.13	289.20	278.83	275.04	273.60	273.05	272.84
18000	351.83	338.96	306.21	295.23	291.21	289.70	289.12	288.89
19000	371.38	357.79	323.22	311.63	307.39	305.79	305.18	304.94
20000	390.93	376.62	340.23	328.04	323.57	321.88	321.24	320.99
21000	410.47	395.45	357.25	344.44	339.75	337.98	337.30	337.04
22000	430.02	414.29	374.26	360.84	355.93	354.07	353.36	353.09
23000	449.56	433.12	391.27	377.24	372.11	370.17	369.43	369.14
24000	469.11	451.95	408.28	393.64	388.28	386.26	385.49	385.19
25000	488.66	470.78	425.29	410.04	404.46	402.35	401.55	401.24
26000	508.20	489.61	442.30	426.44	420.64	418.45	417.61	417.29
27000	527.75	508.44	459.31	442.85	436.82	434.54	433.67	433.34
28000	547.30	527.27	476.33	459.25	453.00	450.64	449.73	449.39
29000	566.84	546.10	493.34	475.65	469.17	466.73	465.80	465.44
30000	586.39	564.93	510.35	492.05	485.35	482.82	481.86	481.49
31000	605.93	583.76	527.36	508.45	501.53	498.92	497.92	497.54
32000	625.48	602.59	544.37	524.85	517.71	515.01	513.98	513.59
33000	645.03	621.43	561.38	541.25	533.89	531.11	530.04	529.63
34000	664.57	640.26	578.39	557.66	550.07	547.20	546.10	545.68
35000	684.12	659.09	595.41	574.06	566.24	563.29	562.17	561.73
40000	781.85	753.24	680.46	656.07	647.14	643.76	642.48	641.98
45000	879.58	847.40	765.52	738.07	728.03	724.23	722.78	722.23
50000	977.31	941.55	850.58	820.08	808.92	804.70	803.09	802.47
55000	1075.04	1035.71	935.63	902.09	889.81	885.17	883.40	882.72
60000	1172.77	1129.86	1020.69	984.10	970.70	965.64	963.71	962.97
65000	1270.50	1224.02	1105.75	1066.10	1051.59	1046.11	1044.02	1043.22
70000	1368.23	1318.17	1190.81	1148.11	1132.48	1126.58	1124.33	1123.46
75000	1465.96	1412.32	1275.86	1230.12	1213.38	1207.05	1204.64	1203.71
80000	1563.69	1506.48	1360.92	1312.13	1294.27	1287.52	1284.95	1283.96
85000	1661.42	1600.63	1445.98	1394.13	1375.16	1367.99	1365.25	1364.20
90000	1759.15	1694.79	1531.03	1476.14	1456.05	1448.46	1445.56	1444.45
95000	1856.88	1788.94	1616.09	1558.15	1536.94	1528.93	1525.87	1524.70
100000	1954.61	1883.10	1701.15	1640.16	1617.83	1609.40	1606.18	1604.94
105000	2052.34	1977.25	1786.21	1722.16	1698.72	1689.87	1686.49	1685.19
110000	2150.07	2071.41	1871.26	1804.17	1779.62	1770.34	1766.80	1765.44
115000	2247.80	2165.56	1956.32	1886.18	1860.51	1850.81	1847.11	1845.69
120000	2345.54	2259.72	2041.38	1968.19	1941.40	1931.28	1927.42	1925.93
125000	2443.27	2353.87	2126.43	2050.19	2022.29	2011.75	2007.72	2006.18
130000	2541.00	2448.03	2211.49	2132.20	2103.18	2092.22	2088.03	2086.43
135000	2638.73	2542.18	2296.55	2214.21	2184.07	2172.69	2168.34	2166.67
140000	2736.46	2636.34	2381.61	2296.22	2264.96	2253.16	2248.65	2246.92
145000	2834.19	2730.49	2466.66	2378.22	2345.85	2333.63	2328.96	2327.17
150000	2931.92	2824.64	2551.72	2460.23	2426.75	2414.10	2409.27	2407.41
155000	3029.65	2918.80	2636.78	2542.24	2507.64	2494.57	2489.58	2487.66
160000	3127.38	3012.95	2721.83	2624.25	2588.53	2575.04	2569.89	2567.91

19.500%   MONTHLY AMORTIZING PAYMENTS

AMOUNT OF LOAN	NUMBER OF YEARS IN TERM							
	1	2	3	4	5	6	7	8
$ 50	4.62	2.54	1.85	1.51	1.32	1.19	1.10	1.04
100	9.24	5.07	3.70	3.02	2.63	2.37	2.20	2.07
200	18.48	10.14	7.39	6.04	5.25	4.74	4.39	4.13
300	27.72	15.20	11.08	9.05	7.87	7.10	6.58	6.20
400	36.96	20.27	14.77	12.07	10.49	9.47	8.77	8.26
500	46.20	25.33	18.46	15.09	13.11	11.84	10.96	10.33
600	55.44	30.40	22.15	18.10	15.73	14.20	13.15	12.39
700	64.68	35.46	25.84	21.12	18.36	16.57	15.34	14.45
800	73.92	40.53	29.53	24.14	20.98	18.94	17.53	16.52
900	83.16	45.59	33.22	27.15	23.60	21.30	19.72	18.58
1000	92.40	50.66	36.91	30.17	26.22	23.67	21.91	20.65
2000	184.80	101.31	73.82	60.33	52.44	47.33	43.82	41.29
3000	277.19	151.96	110.73	90.50	78.65	71.00	65.72	61.93
4000	369.59	202.61	147.64	120.66	104.87	94.66	87.63	82.57
5000	461.98	253.26	184.55	150.83	131.09	118.32	109.54	103.22
6000	554.38	303.92	221.46	180.99	157.30	141.99	131.44	123.86
7000	646.77	354.57	258.37	211.16	183.52	165.65	153.35	144.50
8000	739.17	405.22	295.28	241.32	209.74	189.32	175.25	165.14
9000	831.56	455.87	332.19	271.49	235.95	212.98	197.16	185.79
10000	923.96	506.52	369.10	301.65	262.17	236.64	219.07	206.43
11000	1016.35	557.18	406.01	331.82	288.39	260.31	240.97	227.07
12000	1108.75	607.83	442.92	361.98	314.60	283.97	262.88	247.71
13000	1201.14	658.48	479.83	392.14	340.82	307.64	284.78	268.36
14000	1293.54	709.13	516.74	422.31	367.04	331.30	306.69	289.00
15000	1385.94	759.78	553.64	452.47	393.25	354.96	328.60	309.64
16000	1478.33	810.44	590.55	482.64	419.47	378.63	350.50	330.28
17000	1570.73	861.09	627.46	512.80	445.68	402.29	372.41	350.93
18000	1663.12	911.74	664.37	542.97	471.90	425.95	394.32	371.57
19000	1755.52	962.39	701.28	573.13	498.12	449.62	416.22	392.21
20000	1847.91	1013.04	738.19	603.30	524.33	473.28	438.13	412.85
21000	1940.31	1063.69	775.10	633.46	550.55	496.95	460.03	433.50
22000	2032.70	1114.35	812.01	663.63	576.77	520.61	481.94	454.14
23000	2125.10	1165.00	848.92	693.79	602.98	544.27	503.85	474.78
24000	2217.49	1215.65	885.83	723.96	629.20	567.94	525.75	495.42
25000	2309.89	1266.30	922.74	754.12	655.42	591.60	547.66	516.07
26000	2402.28	1316.95	959.65	784.28	681.63	615.27	569.56	536.71
27000	2494.68	1367.61	996.56	814.45	707.85	638.93	591.47	557.35
28000	2587.08	1418.26	1033.47	844.61	734.07	662.59	613.38	577.99
29000	2679.47	1468.91	1070.38	874.78	760.28	686.26	635.28	598.64
30000	2771.87	1519.56	1107.28	904.94	786.50	709.92	657.19	619.28
31000	2864.26	1570.21	1144.19	935.11	812.71	733.59	679.09	639.92
32000	2956.66	1620.87	1181.10	965.27	838.93	757.25	701.00	660.56
33000	3049.05	1671.52	1218.01	995.44	865.15	780.91	722.91	681.21
34000	3141.45	1722.17	1254.92	1025.60	891.36	804.58	744.81	701.85
35000	3233.84	1772.82	1291.83	1055.77	917.58	828.24	766.72	722.49
40000	3695.82	2026.08	1476.38	1206.59	1048.66	946.56	876.25	825.70
45000	4157.80	2279.34	1660.92	1357.41	1179.75	1064.88	985.78	928.92
50000	4619.77	2532.60	1845.47	1508.24	1310.83	1183.20	1095.31	1032.13
55000	5081.75	2785.86	2030.02	1659.06	1441.91	1301.52	1204.84	1135.34
60000	5543.73	3039.12	2214.56	1809.88	1572.99	1419.84	1314.37	1238.55
65000	6005.70	3292.38	2399.11	1960.70	1704.07	1538.16	1423.90	1341.76
70000	6467.68	3545.64	2583.66	2111.53	1835.16	1656.48	1533.43	1444.98
75000	6929.66	3798.90	2768.20	2262.35	1966.24	1774.80	1642.96	1548.19
80000	7391.63	4052.16	2952.75	2413.17	2097.32	1893.12	1752.49	1651.40
85000	7853.61	4305.41	3137.30	2564.00	2228.40	2011.44	1862.03	1754.61
90000	8315.59	4558.67	3321.84	2714.82	2359.49	2129.75	1971.56	1857.83
95000	8777.57	4811.93	3506.39	2865.64	2490.57	2248.07	2081.09	1961.04
100000	9239.54	5065.19	3690.94	3016.47	2621.65	2366.39	2190.62	2064.25
105000	9701.52	5318.45	3875.48	3167.29	2752.73	2484.71	2300.15	2167.46
110000	10163.50	5571.71	4060.03	3318.11	2883.81	2603.03	2409.68	2270.68
115000	10625.47	5824.97	4244.58	3468.93	3014.90	2721.35	2519.21	2373.89
120000	11087.45	6078.23	4429.12	3619.76	3145.98	2839.67	2628.74	2477.10
125000	11549.43	6331.49	4613.67	3770.58	3277.06	2957.99	2738.27	2580.31
130000	12011.40	6584.75	4798.22	3921.40	3408.14	3076.31	2847.80	2683.52
135000	12473.38	6838.01	4982.76	4072.23	3539.23	3194.63	2957.33	2786.74
140000	12935.36	7091.27	5167.31	4223.05	3670.31	3312.95	3066.86	2889.95
145000	13397.33	7344.53	5351.86	4373.87	3801.39	3431.27	3176.39	2993.16
150000	13859.31	7597.79	5536.40	4524.70	3932.47	3549.59	3285.92	3096.37
155000	14321.29	7851.05	5720.95	4675.52	4063.55	3667.91	3395.45	3199.59
160000	14783.26	8104.31	5905.49	4826.34	4194.64	3786.23	3504.98	3302.80

AMOUNT OF LOAN	NUMBER OF YEARS IN TERM							
	9	10	15	20	25	30	35	40
$ 50	.99	.95	.86	.83	.82	.82	.82	.82
100	1.98	1.90	1.72	1.66	1.64	1.63	1.63	1.63
200	3.95	3.80	3.44	3.32	3.28	3.26	3.26	3.26
300	5.92	5.70	5.16	4.98	4.92	4.89	4.89	4.88
400	7.89	7.60	6.88	6.64	6.56	6.52	6.51	6.51
500	9.86	9.50	8.60	8.30	8.20	8.15	8.14	8.13
600	11.83	11.40	10.32	9.96	9.83	9.78	9.77	9.76
700	13.80	13.30	12.04	11.62	11.47	11.41	11.39	11.38
800	15.77	15.20	13.76	13.28	13.11	13.04	13.02	13.01
900	17.74	17.10	15.48	14.94	14.75	14.67	14.65	14.64
1000	19.71	19.00	17.20	16.60	16.39	16.30	16.27	16.26
2000	39.42	38.00	34.39	33.20	32.77	32.60	32.54	32.52
3000	59.12	56.99	51.59	49.79	49.15	48.90	48.81	48.78
4000	78.83	75.99	68.78	66.39	65.53	65.20	65.08	65.03
5000	98.53	94.98	85.98	82.99	81.91	81.50	81.35	81.29
6000	118.24	113.98	103.17	99.58	98.29	97.80	97.62	97.55
7000	137.94	132.97	120.37	116.18	114.67	114.10	113.89	113.80
8000	157.65	151.97	137.56	132.78	131.05	130.40	130.15	130.06
9000	177.36	170.96	154.76	149.37	147.43	146.70	146.42	146.32
10000	197.06	189.96	171.95	165.97	163.81	163.00	162.69	162.58
11000	216.77	208.95	189.15	182.57	180.19	179.30	178.96	178.83
12000	236.47	227.95	206.34	199.16	196.57	195.60	195.23	195.09
13000	256.18	246.94	223.54	215.76	212.95	211.89	211.50	211.35
14000	275.88	265.94	240.73	232.36	229.33	228.19	227.77	227.60
15000	295.59	284.93	257.93	248.95	245.71	244.49	244.04	243.86
16000	315.30	303.93	275.12	265.55	262.09	260.79	260.30	260.12
17000	335.00	322.92	292.31	282.15	278.47	277.09	276.57	276.38
18000	354.71	341.92	309.51	298.74	294.85	293.39	292.84	292.63
19000	374.41	360.91	326.70	315.34	311.23	309.69	309.11	308.89
20000	394.12	379.91	343.90	331.94	327.61	325.99	325.38	325.15
21000	413.82	398.90	361.09	348.53	343.99	342.29	341.65	341.40
22000	433.53	417.90	378.29	365.13	360.37	358.59	357.92	357.66
23000	453.24	436.89	395.48	381.73	376.75	374.89	374.18	373.92
24000	472.94	455.89	412.68	398.32	393.13	391.19	390.45	390.18
25000	492.65	474.89	429.87	414.92	409.51	407.48	406.72	406.43
26000	512.35	493.88	447.07	431.52	425.89	423.78	422.99	422.69
27000	532.06	512.88	464.26	448.11	442.27	440.08	439.26	438.95
28000	551.76	531.87	481.46	464.71	458.65	456.38	455.53	455.20
29000	571.47	550.87	498.65	481.31	475.03	472.68	471.80	471.46
30000	591.17	569.86	515.85	497.90	491.41	488.98	488.07	487.72
31000	610.88	588.86	533.04	514.50	507.79	505.28	504.33	503.97
32000	630.59	607.85	550.24	531.10	524.17	521.58	520.60	520.23
33000	650.29	626.85	567.43	547.69	540.55	537.88	536.87	536.49
34000	670.00	645.84	584.62	564.29	556.93	554.18	553.14	552.75
35000	689.70	664.84	601.82	580.89	573.31	570.48	569.41	569.00
40000	788.23	759.81	687.79	663.87	655.21	651.97	650.75	650.29
45000	886.76	854.79	773.77	746.85	737.11	733.47	732.10	731.57
50000	985.29	949.77	859.74	829.84	819.01	814.96	813.44	812.86
55000	1083.82	1044.74	945.71	912.82	900.91	896.46	894.78	894.15
60000	1182.34	1139.72	1031.69	995.80	982.81	977.96	976.13	975.43
65000	1280.87	1234.69	1117.66	1078.79	1064.71	1059.45	1057.47	1056.72
70000	1379.40	1329.67	1203.63	1161.77	1146.61	1140.95	1138.81	1138.00
75000	1477.93	1424.65	1289.61	1244.75	1228.51	1222.44	1220.16	1219.29
80000	1576.46	1519.62	1375.58	1327.74	1310.41	1303.94	1301.50	1300.57
85000	1674.99	1614.60	1461.55	1410.72	1392.31	1385.44	1382.84	1381.86
90000	1773.51	1709.57	1547.53	1493.70	1474.21	1466.93	1464.19	1463.14
95000	1872.04	1804.55	1633.50	1576.69	1556.11	1548.43	1545.53	1544.43
100000	1970.57	1899.53	1719.48	1659.67	1638.01	1629.93	1626.87	1625.71
105000	2069.10	1994.50	1805.45	1742.65	1719.91	1711.42	1708.22	1707.00
110000	2167.63	2089.48	1891.42	1825.64	1801.81	1792.92	1789.56	1788.29
115000	2266.16	2184.46	1977.40	1908.62	1883.71	1874.41	1870.90	1869.57
120000	2364.68	2279.43	2063.37	1991.60	1965.61	1955.91	1952.25	1950.86
125000	2463.21	2374.41	2149.34	2074.59	2047.51	2037.41	2033.59	2032.14
130000	2561.74	2469.38	2235.32	2157.57	2129.41	2118.90	2114.93	2113.43
135000	2660.27	2564.36	2321.29	2240.55	2211.31	2200.40	2196.28	2194.71
140000	2758.80	2659.34	2407.26	2323.54	2293.21	2281.89	2277.62	2276.00
145000	2857.33	2754.31	2493.24	2406.52	2375.11	2363.39	2358.96	2357.28
150000	2955.85	2849.29	2579.21	2489.50	2457.01	2444.89	2440.31	2438.57
155000	3054.38	2944.26	2665.18	2572.49	2538.91	2526.38	2521.65	2519.85
160000	3152.91	3039.24	2751.16	2655.47	2620.81	2607.88	2602.99	2601.14

19.750% MONTHLY AMORTIZING PAYMENTS

AMOUNT OF LOAN	NUMBER OF YEARS IN TERM							
	1	2	3	4	5	6	7	8
$ 50	4.63	2.54	1.86	1.52	1.32	1.20	1.11	1.04
100	9.26	5.08	3.71	3.03	2.64	2.39	2.21	2.08
200	18.51	10.16	7.41	6.06	5.28	4.77	4.42	4.16
300	27.76	15.24	11.12	9.09	7.91	7.15	6.62	6.24
400	37.01	20.31	14.82	12.12	10.55	9.53	8.83	8.32
500	46.26	25.39	18.52	15.15	13.18	11.91	11.03	10.40
600	55.51	30.47	22.23	18.18	15.82	14.29	13.24	12.48
700	64.77	35.55	25.93	21.21	18.45	16.67	15.44	14.56
800	74.02	40.62	29.63	24.24	21.09	19.05	17.65	16.64
900	83.27	45.70	33.34	27.27	23.72	21.43	19.86	18.72
1000	92.52	50.78	37.04	30.30	26.36	23.81	22.06	20.80
2000	185.03	101.55	74.08	60.60	52.71	47.62	44.12	41.60
3000	277.55	152.33	111.11	90.90	79.07	71.43	66.17	62.40
4000	370.06	203.10	148.15	121.19	105.42	95.24	88.23	83.20
5000	462.58	253.87	185.19	151.49	131.78	119.05	110.28	103.99
6000	555.09	304.65	222.22	181.79	158.13	142.85	132.34	124.79
7000	647.61	355.42	259.26	212.09	184.49	166.66	154.40	145.59
8000	740.12	406.20	296.30	242.38	210.84	190.47	176.45	166.39
9000	832.64	456.97	333.33	272.68	237.20	214.28	198.51	187.18
10000	925.15	507.74	370.37	302.98	263.55	238.09	220.56	207.98
11000	1017.67	558.52	407.40	333.28	289.91	261.89	242.62	228.78
12000	1110.18	609.29	444.44	363.57	316.26	285.70	264.68	249.58
13000	1202.70	660.06	481.48	393.87	342.62	309.51	286.73	270.37
14000	1295.21	710.84	518.51	424.17	368.97	333.32	308.79	291.17
15000	1387.73	761.61	555.55	454.46	395.33	357.13	330.84	311.97
16000	1480.24	812.39	592.59	484.76	421.68	380.94	352.90	332.77
17000	1572.76	863.16	629.62	515.06	448.04	404.74	374.96	353.56
18000	1665.27	913.93	666.66	545.36	474.39	428.55	397.01	374.36
19000	1757.79	964.71	703.70	575.65	500.75	452.36	419.07	395.16
20000	1850.30	1015.48	740.73	605.95	527.10	476.17	441.12	415.96
21000	1942.82	1066.25	777.77	636.25	553.46	499.98	463.18	436.75
22000	2035.33	1117.03	814.80	666.55	579.81	523.78	485.24	457.55
23000	2127.85	1167.80	851.84	696.84	606.17	547.59	507.29	478.35
24000	2220.36	1218.58	888.88	727.14	632.52	571.40	529.35	499.15
25000	2312.88	1269.35	925.91	757.44	658.88	595.21	551.40	519.94
26000	2405.39	1320.12	962.95	787.74	685.23	619.02	573.46	540.74
27000	2497.91	1370.90	999.99	818.03	711.59	642.82	595.51	561.54
28000	2590.42	1421.67	1037.02	848.33	737.94	666.63	617.57	582.34
29000	2682.94	1472.44	1074.06	878.63	764.30	690.44	639.63	603.13
30000	2775.45	1523.22	1111.09	908.92	790.65	714.25	661.68	623.93
31000	2867.97	1573.99	1148.13	939.22	817.01	738.06	683.74	644.73
32000	2960.48	1624.77	1185.17	969.52	843.36	761.87	705.79	665.53
33000	3053.00	1675.54	1222.20	999.82	869.72	785.67	727.85	686.32
34000	3145.51	1726.31	1259.24	1030.11	896.07	809.48	749.91	707.12
35000	3238.03	1777.09	1296.28	1060.41	922.43	833.29	771.96	727.92
40000	3700.60	2030.96	1481.46	1211.90	1054.20	952.33	882.24	831.91
45000	4163.18	2284.82	1666.64	1363.38	1185.98	1071.37	992.52	935.90
50000	4625.75	2538.69	1851.82	1514.87	1317.75	1190.41	1102.80	1039.88
55000	5088.32	2792.56	2037.00	1666.36	1449.53	1309.45	1213.08	1143.87
60000	5550.90	3046.43	2222.18	1817.84	1581.30	1428.49	1323.36	1247.86
65000	6013.47	3300.30	2407.37	1969.33	1713.08	1547.53	1433.64	1351.85
70000	6476.05	3554.17	2592.55	2120.82	1844.85	1666.57	1543.92	1455.83
75000	6938.62	3808.04	2777.73	2272.30	1976.63	1785.62	1654.20	1559.82
80000	7401.20	4061.91	2962.91	2423.79	2108.40	1904.66	1764.48	1663.81
85000	7863.77	4315.77	3148.09	2575.28	2240.18	2023.70	1874.76	1767.80
90000	8326.35	4569.64	3333.27	2726.76	2371.95	2142.74	1985.04	1871.79
95000	8788.92	4823.51	3518.46	2878.25	2503.73	2261.78	2095.32	1975.77
100000	9251.49	5077.38	3703.64	3029.74	2635.50	2380.82	2205.60	2079.76
105000	9714.07	5331.25	3888.82	3181.22	2767.28	2499.86	2315.88	2183.75
110000	10176.64	5585.12	4074.00	3332.71	2899.05	2618.90	2426.16	2287.74
115000	10639.22	5838.99	4259.18	3484.20	3030.83	2737.94	2536.43	2391.72
120000	11101.79	6092.86	4444.36	3635.68	3162.60	2856.98	2646.71	2495.71
125000	11564.37	6346.72	4629.55	3787.17	3294.38	2976.02	2756.99	2599.70
130000	12026.94	6600.59	4814.73	3938.66	3426.15	3095.06	2867.27	2703.69
135000	12489.52	6854.46	4999.91	4090.14	3557.93	3214.10	2977.55	2807.68
140000	12952.09	7108.33	5185.09	4241.63	3689.70	3333.14	3087.83	2911.66
145000	13414.67	7362.20	5370.27	4393.12	3821.48	3452.18	3198.11	3015.65
150000	13877.24	7616.07	5555.45	4544.60	3953.25	3571.23	3308.39	3119.64
155000	14339.81	7869.94	5740.64	4696.09	4085.03	3690.27	3418.67	3223.63
160000	14802.39	8123.81	5925.82	4847.58	4216.80	3809.31	3528.95	3327.62

92

AMOUNT OF LOAN	NUMBER OF YEARS IN TERM							
	9	10	15	20	25	30	35	40
$ 50	1.00	.96	.87	.84	.83	.83	.83	.83
100	1.99	1.92	1.74	1.68	1.66	1.66	1.65	1.65
200	3.98	3.84	3.48	3.36	3.32	3.31	3.30	3.30
300	5.96	5.75	5.22	5.04	4.98	4.96	4.95	4.94
400	7.95	7.67	6.96	6.72	6.64	6.61	6.60	6.59
500	9.94	9.59	8.69	8.40	8.30	8.26	8.24	8.24
600	11.92	11.50	10.43	10.08	9.95	9.91	9.89	9.88
700	13.91	13.42	12.17	11.76	11.61	11.56	11.54	11.53
800	15.90	15.33	13.91	13.44	13.27	13.21	13.19	13.18
900	17.88	17.25	15.65	15.12	14.93	14.86	14.83	14.82
1000	19.87	19.17	17.38	16.80	16.59	16.51	16.48	16.47
2000	39.74	38.33	34.76	33.59	33.17	33.01	32.96	32.93
3000	59.60	57.49	52.14	50.38	49.75	49.52	49.43	49.40
4000	79.47	76.65	69.52	67.17	66.33	66.02	65.91	65.86
5000	99.33	95.81	86.90	83.97	82.92	82.53	82.38	82.33
6000	119.20	114.97	104.28	100.76	99.50	99.03	98.86	98.79
7000	139.07	134.13	121.65	117.55	116.08	115.54	115.33	115.26
8000	158.93	153.29	139.03	134.34	132.66	132.04	131.81	131.72
9000	178.80	172.45	156.41	151.14	149.24	148.55	148.29	148.19
10000	198.66	191.61	173.79	167.93	165.83	165.05	164.76	164.65
11000	218.53	210.77	191.17	184.72	182.41	181.56	181.24	181.12
12000	238.39	229.93	208.55	201.51	198.99	198.06	197.71	197.58
13000	258.26	249.09	225.93	218.30	215.57	214.56	214.19	214.05
14000	278.13	268.25	243.30	235.10	232.16	231.07	230.66	230.51
15000	297.99	287.41	260.68	251.89	248.74	247.57	247.14	246.98
16000	317.86	306.57	278.06	268.68	265.32	264.08	263.62	263.44
17000	337.72	325.73	295.44	285.47	281.90	280.58	280.09	279.91
18000	357.59	344.89	312.82	302.27	298.48	297.09	296.57	296.37
19000	377.46	364.05	330.20	319.06	315.07	313.59	313.04	312.84
20000	397.32	383.21	347.58	335.85	331.65	330.10	329.52	329.30
21000	417.19	402.37	364.95	352.64	348.23	346.60	345.99	345.77
22000	437.05	421.53	382.33	369.43	364.81	363.11	362.47	362.23
23000	456.92	440.69	399.71	386.23	381.39	379.61	378.95	378.70
24000	476.78	459.85	417.09	403.02	397.98	396.12	395.42	395.16
25000	496.65	479.01	434.47	419.81	414.56	412.62	411.90	411.63
26000	516.52	498.17	451.85	436.60	431.14	429.12	428.37	428.09
27000	536.38	517.33	469.23	453.40	447.72	445.63	444.85	444.56
28000	556.25	536.49	486.60	470.19	464.31	462.13	461.32	461.02
29000	576.11	555.65	503.98	486.98	480.89	478.64	477.80	477.49
30000	595.98	574.81	521.36	503.77	497.47	495.14	494.28	493.95
31000	615.84	593.97	538.74	520.56	514.05	511.65	510.75	510.42
32000	635.71	613.13	556.12	537.36	530.63	528.15	527.23	526.88
33000	655.58	632.29	573.50	554.15	547.22	544.66	543.70	543.34
34000	675.44	651.45	590.88	570.94	563.80	561.16	560.18	559.81
35000	695.31	670.61	608.25	587.73	580.38	577.67	576.65	576.27
40000	794.64	766.41	695.15	671.69	663.29	660.19	659.03	658.60
45000	893.97	862.21	782.04	755.66	746.20	742.71	741.41	740.92
50000	993.29	958.01	868.93	839.62	829.11	825.24	823.79	823.25
55000	1092.62	1053.81	955.83	923.58	912.02	907.76	906.17	905.57
60000	1191.95	1149.61	1042.72	1007.54	994.93	990.28	988.55	987.90
65000	1291.28	1245.41	1129.61	1091.50	1077.84	1072.80	1070.92	1070.22
70000	1390.61	1341.21	1216.50	1175.46	1160.76	1155.33	1153.30	1152.54
75000	1489.94	1437.01	1303.40	1259.42	1243.67	1237.85	1235.68	1234.87
80000	1589.27	1532.81	1390.29	1343.38	1326.58	1320.37	1318.06	1317.19
85000	1688.60	1628.61	1477.18	1427.34	1409.49	1402.90	1400.44	1399.52
90000	1787.93	1724.41	1564.07	1511.31	1492.40	1485.42	1482.82	1481.84
95000	1887.26	1820.21	1650.97	1595.27	1575.31	1567.94	1565.19	1564.17
100000	1986.58	1916.02	1737.86	1679.23	1658.22	1650.47	1647.57	1646.49
105000	2085.91	2011.82	1824.75	1763.19	1741.13	1732.99	1729.95	1728.81
110000	2185.24	2107.62	1911.65	1847.15	1824.04	1815.51	1812.33	1811.14
115000	2284.57	2203.42	1998.54	1931.11	1906.95	1898.04	1894.71	1893.46
120000	2383.90	2299.22	2085.43	2015.07	1989.86	1980.56	1977.09	1975.79
125000	2483.23	2395.02	2172.32	2099.03	2072.77	2063.08	2059.47	2058.11
130000	2582.56	2490.82	2259.22	2182.99	2155.68	2145.60	2141.84	2140.43
135000	2681.89	2586.62	2346.11	2266.96	2238.59	2228.13	2224.22	2222.76
140000	2781.22	2682.42	2433.00	2350.92	2321.51	2310.65	2306.60	2305.08
145000	2880.55	2778.22	2519.89	2434.88	2404.42	2393.17	2388.98	2387.41
150000	2979.87	2874.02	2606.79	2518.84	2487.33	2475.70	2471.36	2469.73
155000	3079.20	2969.82	2693.68	2602.80	2570.24	2558.22	2553.74	2552.06
160000	3178.53	3065.62	2780.57	2686.76	2653.15	2640.74	2636.11	2634.38

AMOUNT OF LOAN	NUMBER OF YEARS IN TERM							
	1	2	3	4	5	6	7	8
$ 50	4.64	2.55	1.86	1.53	1.33	1.20	1.12	1.05
100	9.27	5.09	3.72	3.05	2.65	2.40	2.23	2.10
200	18.53	10.18	7.44	6.09	5.30	4.80	4.45	4.20
300	27.80	15.27	11.15	9.13	7.95	7.19	6.67	6.29
400	37.06	20.36	14.87	12.18	10.60	9.59	8.89	8.39
500	46.32	25.45	18.59	15.22	13.25	11.98	11.11	10.48
600	55.59	30.54	22.30	18.26	15.90	14.38	13.33	12.58
700	64.85	35.63	26.02	21.31	18.55	16.77	15.55	14.67
800	74.11	40.72	29.74	24.35	21.20	19.17	17.77	16.77
900	83.38	45.81	33.45	27.39	23.85	21.56	19.99	18.86
1000	92.64	50.90	37.17	30.44	26.50	23.96	22.21	20.96
2000	185.27	101.80	74.33	60.87	52.99	47.91	44.42	41.91
3000	277.91	152.69	111.50	91.30	79.49	71.86	66.62	62.86
4000	370.54	203.59	148.66	121.73	105.98	95.82	88.83	83.82
5000	463.18	254.48	185.82	152.16	132.47	119.77	111.04	104.77
6000	555.81	305.38	222.99	182.59	158.97	143.72	133.24	125.72
7000	648.45	356.28	260.15	213.02	185.46	167.67	155.45	146.68
8000	741.08	407.17	297.31	243.45	211.96	191.63	177.65	167.63
9000	833.72	458.07	334.48	273.88	238.45	215.58	199.86	188.58
10000	926.35	508.96	371.64	304.31	264.94	239.53	222.07	209.54
11000	1018.98	559.86	408.80	334.74	291.44	263.49	244.27	230.49
12000	1111.62	610.75	445.97	365.17	317.93	287.44	266.48	251.44
13000	1204.25	661.65	483.13	395.60	344.43	311.39	288.69	272.40
14000	1296.89	712.55	520.30	426.03	370.92	335.34	310.89	293.35
15000	1389.52	763.44	557.46	456.46	397.41	359.30	333.10	314.30
16000	1482.16	814.34	594.62	486.89	423.91	383.25	355.30	335.26
17000	1574.79	865.23	631.79	517.32	450.40	407.20	377.51	356.21
18000	1667.43	916.13	668.95	547.75	476.89	431.16	399.72	377.16
19000	1760.06	967.03	706.11	578.18	503.39	455.11	421.92	398.12
20000	1852.70	1017.92	743.28	608.61	529.88	479.06	444.13	419.07
21000	1945.33	1068.82	780.44	639.04	556.38	503.01	466.34	440.02
22000	2037.96	1119.71	817.60	669.47	582.87	526.97	488.54	460.98
23000	2130.60	1170.61	854.77	699.90	609.36	550.92	510.75	481.93
24000	2223.23	1221.50	891.93	730.33	635.86	574.87	532.95	502.88
25000	2315.87	1272.40	929.09	760.76	662.35	598.83	555.16	523.84
26000	2408.50	1323.30	966.26	791.19	688.85	622.78	577.37	544.79
27000	2501.14	1374.19	1003.42	821.62	715.34	646.73	599.57	565.74
28000	2593.77	1425.09	1040.59	852.06	741.83	670.68	621.78	586.69
29000	2686.41	1475.98	1077.75	882.49	768.33	694.64	643.98	607.65
30000	2779.04	1526.88	1114.91	912.92	794.82	718.59	666.19	628.60
31000	2871.67	1577.77	1152.08	943.35	821.32	742.54	688.40	649.55
32000	2964.31	1628.67	1189.24	973.78	847.81	766.50	710.60	670.51
33000	3056.94	1679.57	1226.40	1004.21	874.30	790.45	732.81	691.46
34000	3149.58	1730.46	1263.57	1034.64	900.80	814.40	755.02	712.41
35000	3242.21	1781.36	1300.73	1065.07	927.29	838.35	777.22	733.37
40000	3705.39	2035.84	1486.55	1217.22	1059.76	958.12	888.25	838.13
45000	4168.56	2290.32	1672.37	1369.37	1192.23	1077.88	999.28	942.90
50000	4631.73	2544.80	1858.18	1521.52	1324.70	1197.65	1110.31	1047.67
55000	5094.90	2799.27	2044.00	1673.67	1457.17	1317.41	1221.35	1152.43
60000	5558.08	3053.75	2229.82	1825.83	1589.64	1437.17	1332.38	1257.20
65000	6021.25	3308.23	2415.64	1977.98	1722.11	1556.94	1443.41	1361.96
70000	6484.42	3562.71	2601.46	2130.13	1854.58	1676.70	1554.44	1466.73
75000	6947.59	3817.19	2787.27	2282.28	1987.05	1796.47	1665.47	1571.50
80000	7410.77	4071.67	2973.09	2434.43	2119.52	1916.23	1776.50	1676.26
85000	7873.94	4326.15	3158.91	2586.59	2251.99	2036.00	1887.53	1781.03
90000	8337.11	4580.63	3344.73	2738.74	2384.45	2155.76	1998.56	1885.79
95000	8800.28	4835.11	3530.55	2890.89	2516.92	2275.52	2109.59	1990.56
100000	9263.46	5089.59	3716.36	3043.04	2649.39	2395.29	2220.62	2095.33
105000	9726.63	5344.06	3902.18	3195.19	2781.86	2515.05	2331.66	2200.09
110000	10189.80	5598.54	4088.00	3347.34	2914.33	2634.82	2442.69	2304.86
115000	10652.97	5853.02	4273.82	3499.50	3046.80	2754.58	2553.72	2409.62
120000	11116.15	6107.50	4459.64	3651.65	3179.27	2874.34	2664.75	2514.39
125000	11579.32	6361.98	4645.45	3803.80	3311.74	2994.11	2775.78	2619.16
130000	12042.49	6616.46	4831.27	3955.95	3444.21	3113.87	2886.81	2723.92
135000	12505.66	6870.94	5017.09	4108.10	3576.68	3233.64	2997.84	2828.69
140000	12968.84	7125.42	5202.91	4260.26	3709.15	3353.40	3108.87	2933.45
145000	13432.01	7379.90	5388.72	4412.41	3841.62	3473.16	3219.90	3038.22
150000	13895.18	7634.38	5574.54	4564.56	3974.09	3592.93	3330.93	3142.99
155000	14358.35	7888.85	5760.36	4716.71	4106.56	3712.69	3441.97	3247.75
160000	14821.53	8143.33	5946.18	4868.86	4239.03	3832.46	3553.00	3352.52

MONTHLY AMORTIZING PAYMENTS 20.000%

AMOUNT OF LOAN	NUMBER OF YEARS IN TERM							
	9	10	15	20	25	30	35	40
$ 50	1.01	.97	.88	.85	.84	.84	.84	.84
100	2.01	1.94	1.76	1.70	1.68	1.68	1.67	1.67
200	4.01	3.87	3.52	3.40	3.36	3.35	3.34	3.34
300	6.01	5.80	5.27	5.10	5.04	5.02	5.01	5.01
400	8.02	7.74	7.03	6.80	6.72	6.69	6.68	6.67
500	10.02	9.67	8.79	8.50	8.40	8.36	8.35	8.34
600	12.02	11.60	10.54	10.20	10.08	10.03	10.01	10.01
700	14.02	13.53	12.30	11.90	11.75	11.70	11.68	11.68
800	16.03	15.47	14.06	13.60	13.43	13.37	13.35	13.34
900	18.03	17.40	15.81	15.29	15.11	15.04	15.02	15.01
1000	20.03	19.33	17.57	16.99	16.79	16.72	16.69	16.68
2000	40.06	38.66	35.13	33.98	33.57	33.43	33.37	33.35
3000	60.08	57.98	52.69	50.97	50.36	50.14	50.05	50.02
4000	80.11	77.31	70.26	67.96	67.14	66.85	66.74	66.70
5000	100.14	96.63	87.82	84.95	83.93	83.56	83.42	83.37
6000	120.16	115.96	105.38	101.93	100.71	100.27	100.10	100.04
7000	140.19	135.28	122.95	118.92	117.50	116.98	116.78	116.71
8000	160.22	154.61	140.51	135.91	134.28	133.69	133.47	133.39
9000	180.24	173.94	158.07	152.90	151.07	150.40	150.15	150.06
10000	200.27	193.26	175.63	169.89	167.85	167.11	166.83	166.73
11000	220.30	212.59	193.20	186.88	184.63	183.82	183.52	183.40
12000	240.32	231.91	210.76	203.86	201.42	200.53	200.20	200.08
13000	260.35	251.24	228.32	220.85	218.20	217.24	216.88	216.75
14000	280.38	270.56	245.89	237.84	234.99	233.95	233.56	233.42
15000	300.40	289.89	263.45	254.83	251.77	250.66	250.25	250.09
16000	320.43	309.21	281.01	271.82	268.56	267.37	266.93	266.77
17000	340.46	328.54	298.58	288.81	285.34	284.08	283.61	283.44
18000	360.48	347.87	316.14	305.79	302.13	300.79	300.30	300.11
19000	380.51	367.19	333.70	322.78	318.91	317.50	316.98	316.79
20000	400.54	386.52	351.26	339.77	335.70	334.21	333.66	333.46
21000	420.56	405.84	368.83	356.76	352.48	350.92	350.34	350.13
22000	440.59	425.17	386.39	373.75	369.26	367.63	367.03	366.80
23000	460.61	444.49	403.95	390.73	386.05	384.34	383.71	383.48
24000	480.64	463.82	421.52	407.72	402.83	401.05	400.39	400.15
25000	500.67	483.14	439.08	424.71	419.62	417.76	417.07	416.82
26000	520.69	502.47	456.64	441.70	436.40	434.47	433.76	433.49
27000	540.72	521.80	474.21	458.69	453.19	451.18	450.44	450.17
28000	560.75	541.12	491.77	475.68	469.97	467.89	467.12	466.84
29000	580.77	560.45	509.33	492.66	486.76	484.60	483.81	483.51
30000	600.80	579.77	526.89	509.65	503.54	501.31	500.49	500.18
31000	620.83	599.10	544.46	526.64	520.33	518.02	517.17	516.86
32000	640.85	618.42	562.02	543.63	537.11	534.73	533.85	533.53
33000	660.88	637.75	579.58	560.62	553.89	551.44	550.54	550.20
34000	680.91	657.07	597.15	577.61	570.68	568.15	567.22	566.87
35000	700.93	676.40	614.71	594.59	587.46	584.86	583.90	583.55
40000	801.07	773.03	702.52	679.53	671.39	668.41	667.32	666.91
45000	901.20	869.66	790.34	764.48	755.31	751.96	750.73	750.27
50000	1001.33	966.28	878.15	849.42	839.23	835.51	834.14	833.64
55000	1101.46	1062.91	965.97	934.36	923.15	919.07	917.56	917.00
60000	1201.60	1159.54	1053.78	1019.30	1007.08	1002.62	1000.97	1000.36
65000	1301.73	1256.17	1141.60	1104.24	1091.00	1086.17	1084.39	1083.73
70000	1401.86	1352.79	1229.41	1189.18	1174.92	1169.72	1167.80	1167.09
75000	1501.99	1449.42	1317.23	1274.12	1258.84	1253.27	1251.21	1250.45
80000	1602.13	1546.05	1405.04	1359.06	1342.77	1336.82	1334.63	1333.82
85000	1702.26	1642.68	1492.86	1444.01	1426.69	1420.37	1418.04	1417.18
90000	1802.39	1739.31	1580.67	1528.95	1510.61	1503.92	1501.46	1500.54
95000	1902.52	1835.93	1668.49	1613.89	1594.53	1587.47	1584.87	1583.91
100000	2002.66	1932.56	1756.30	1698.83	1678.46	1671.02	1668.28	1667.27
105000	2102.79	2029.19	1844.12	1783.77	1762.38	1754.57	1751.70	1750.63
110000	2202.92	2125.82	1931.93	1868.71	1846.30	1838.13	1835.11	1834.00
115000	2303.05	2222.45	2019.75	1953.65	1930.22	1921.68	1918.53	1917.36
120000	2403.19	2319.07	2107.56	2038.59	2014.15	2005.23	2001.94	2000.72
125000	2503.32	2415.70	2195.38	2123.54	2098.07	2088.78	2085.35	2084.09
130000	2603.45	2512.33	2283.19	2208.48	2181.99	2172.33	2168.77	2167.45
135000	2703.58	2608.96	2371.01	2293.42	2265.91	2255.88	2252.18	2250.81
140000	2803.72	2705.58	2458.82	2378.36	2349.84	2339.43	2335.59	2334.17
145000	2903.85	2802.21	2546.63	2463.30	2433.76	2422.98	2419.01	2417.54
150000	3003.98	2898.84	2634.45	2548.24	2517.68	2506.53	2502.42	2500.90
155000	3104.11	2995.47	2722.26	2633.18	2601.61	2590.08	2585.84	2584.26
160000	3204.25	3092.10	2810.08	2718.12	2685.53	2673.65	2669.25	2667.63

AMOUNT OF LOAN	NUMBER OF YEARS IN TERM							
	1	2	3	4	5	6	7	8
$ 50	4.64	2.56	1.87	1.53	1.34	1.21	1.12	1.06
100	9.28	5.11	3.73	3.06	2.67	2.41	2.24	2.12
200	18.56	10.21	7.46	6.12	5.33	4.82	4.48	4.23
300	27.83	15.31	11.19	9.17	7.99	7.23	6.71	6.34
400	37.11	20.41	14.92	12.23	10.66	9.64	8.95	8.45
500	46.38	25.51	18.65	15.29	13.32	12.05	11.18	10.56
600	55.66	30.62	22.38	18.34	15.98	14.46	13.42	12.67
700	64.93	35.72	26.11	21.40	18.65	16.87	15.65	14.78
800	74.21	40.82	29.84	24.46	21.31	19.28	17.89	16.89
900	83.48	45.92	33.57	27.51	23.97	21.69	20.13	19.00
1000	92.76	51.02	37.30	30.57	26.64	24.10	22.36	21.11
2000	185.51	102.04	74.59	61.13	53.27	48.20	44.72	42.22
3000	278.27	153.06	111.88	91.70	79.90	72.30	67.08	63.33
4000	371.02	204.08	149.17	122.26	106.54	96.40	89.43	84.44
5000	463.78	255.10	186.46	152.82	133.17	120.49	111.79	105.55
6000	556.53	306.11	223.75	183.39	159.80	144.59	134.15	126.66
7000	649.28	357.13	261.04	213.95	186.44	168.69	156.50	147.77
8000	742.04	408.15	298.33	244.51	213.07	192.79	178.86	168.88
9000	834.79	459.17	335.62	275.08	239.70	216.89	201.22	189.99
10000	927.55	510.19	372.92	305.64	266.34	240.98	223.57	211.10
11000	1020.30	561.20	410.21	336.21	292.97	265.08	245.93	232.21
12000	1113.06	612.22	447.50	366.77	319.60	289.18	268.29	253.32
13000	1205.81	663.24	484.79	397.33	346.24	313.28	290.65	274.43
14000	1298.56	714.26	522.08	427.90	372.87	337.38	313.00	295.54
15000	1391.32	765.28	559.37	458.46	399.50	361.47	335.36	316.65
16000	1484.07	816.29	596.66	489.02	426.14	385.57	357.72	337.75
17000	1576.83	867.31	633.95	519.59	452.77	409.67	380.07	358.86
18000	1669.58	918.33	671.24	550.15	479.40	433.77	402.43	379.97
19000	1762.33	969.35	708.54	580.72	506.04	457.87	424.79	401.08
20000	1855.09	1020.37	745.83	611.28	532.67	481.96	447.14	422.19
21000	1947.84	1071.38	783.12	641.84	559.30	506.06	469.50	443.30
22000	2040.60	1122.40	820.41	672.41	585.93	530.16	491.86	464.41
23000	2133.35	1173.42	857.70	702.97	612.57	554.26	514.22	485.52
24000	2226.11	1224.44	894.99	733.53	639.20	578.36	536.57	506.63
25000	2318.86	1275.46	932.28	764.10	665.83	602.45	558.93	527.74
26000	2411.61	1326.47	969.57	794.66	692.47	626.55	581.29	548.85
27000	2504.37	1377.49	1006.86	825.23	719.10	650.65	603.64	569.96
28000	2597.12	1428.51	1044.16	855.79	745.73	674.75	626.00	591.07
29000	2689.88	1479.53	1081.45	886.35	772.37	698.85	648.36	612.18
30000	2782.63	1530.55	1118.74	916.92	799.00	722.94	670.71	633.29
31000	2875.39	1581.56	1156.03	947.48	825.63	747.04	693.07	654.40
32000	2968.14	1632.58	1193.32	978.04	852.27	771.14	715.43	675.50
33000	3060.89	1683.60	1230.61	1008.61	878.90	795.24	737.79	696.61
34000	3153.65	1734.62	1267.90	1039.17	905.53	819.34	760.14	717.72
35000	3246.40	1785.64	1305.19	1069.74	932.17	843.43	782.50	738.83
40000	3710.17	2040.73	1491.65	1222.55	1065.33	963.92	894.28	844.38
45000	4173.94	2295.82	1678.10	1375.37	1198.50	1084.41	1006.07	949.93
50000	4637.71	2550.91	1864.56	1528.19	1331.66	1204.90	1117.85	1055.47
55000	5101.49	2806.00	2051.01	1681.01	1464.83	1325.39	1229.64	1161.02
60000	5565.26	3061.09	2237.47	1833.83	1598.00	1445.88	1341.42	1266.57
65000	6029.03	3316.18	2423.93	1986.65	1731.16	1566.37	1453.21	1372.11
70000	6492.80	3571.27	2610.38	2139.47	1864.33	1686.86	1564.99	1477.66
75000	6956.57	3826.36	2796.84	2292.28	1997.49	1807.35	1676.78	1583.21
80000	7420.34	4081.45	2983.29	2445.10	2130.66	1927.84	1788.56	1688.75
85000	7884.11	4336.54	3169.75	2597.92	2263.83	2048.33	1900.35	1794.30
90000	8347.88	4591.63	3356.20	2750.74	2396.99	2168.82	2012.13	1899.85
95000	8811.65	4846.72	3542.66	2903.56	2530.16	2289.31	2123.92	2005.39
100000	9275.42	5101.81	3729.11	3056.38	2663.32	2409.80	2235.70	2110.94
105000	9739.20	5356.90	3915.57	3209.20	2796.49	2530.29	2347.49	2216.49
110000	10202.97	5611.99	4102.02	3362.01	2929.65	2650.78	2459.27	2322.04
115000	10666.74	5867.08	4288.48	3514.83	3062.82	2771.27	2571.06	2427.58
120000	11130.51	6122.17	4474.94	3667.65	3195.99	2891.76	2682.84	2533.13
125000	11594.28	6377.26	4661.39	3820.47	3329.15	3012.25	2794.63	2638.68
130000	12058.05	6632.35	4847.85	3973.29	3462.32	3132.74	2906.41	2744.22
135000	12521.82	6887.44	5034.30	4126.11	3595.48	3253.23	3018.20	2849.77
140000	12985.59	7142.53	5220.76	4278.93	3728.65	3373.72	3129.98	2955.32
145000	13449.36	7397.62	5407.21	4431.74	3861.82	3494.21	3241.77	3060.86
150000	13913.13	7652.71	5593.67	4584.56	3994.98	3614.70	3353.55	3166.41
155000	14376.91	7907.80	5780.12	4737.38	4128.15	3735.19	3465.34	3271.96
160000	14840.68	8162.89	5966.58	4890.20	4261.31	3855.68	3577.12	3377.50

AMOUNT OF LOAN	NUMBER OF YEARS IN TERM							
	9	10	15	20	25	30	35	40
$ 50	1.01	.98	.89	.86	.85	.85	.85	.85
100	2.02	1.95	1.78	1.72	1.70	1.70	1.69	1.69
200	4.04	3.90	3.55	3.44	3.40	3.39	3.38	3.38
300	6.06	5.85	5.33	5.16	5.10	5.08	5.07	5.07
400	8.08	7.80	7.10	6.88	6.80	6.77	6.76	6.76
500	10.10	9.75	8.88	8.60	8.50	8.46	8.45	8.45
600	12.12	11.70	10.65	10.32	10.20	10.15	10.14	10.13
700	14.14	13.65	12.43	12.03	11.90	11.85	11.83	11.82
800	16.16	15.60	14.20	13.75	13.59	13.54	13.52	13.51
900	18.17	17.55	15.98	15.47	15.29	15.23	15.21	15.20
1000	20.19	19.50	17.75	17.19	16.99	16.92	16.89	16.89
2000	40.38	38.99	35.50	34.37	33.98	33.84	33.78	33.77
3000	60.57	58.48	53.25	51.56	50.97	50.75	50.67	50.65
4000	80.76	77.97	71.00	68.74	67.95	67.67	67.56	67.53
5000	100.94	97.46	88.74	85.93	84.94	84.58	84.45	84.41
6000	121.13	116.95	106.49	103.11	101.93	101.50	101.34	101.29
7000	141.32	136.45	124.24	120.30	118.92	118.42	118.23	118.17
8000	161.51	155.94	141.99	137.48	135.90	135.33	135.12	135.05
9000	181.69	175.43	159.74	154.67	152.89	152.25	152.01	151.93
10000	201.88	194.92	177.48	171.85	169.88	169.16	168.90	168.81
11000	222.07	214.41	195.23	189.04	186.86	186.08	185.79	185.69
12000	242.26	233.90	212.98	206.22	203.85	203.00	202.68	202.57
13000	262.45	253.40	230.73	223.41	220.84	219.91	219.57	219.45
14000	282.63	272.89	248.48	240.59	237.83	236.83	236.46	236.33
15000	302.82	292.38	266.22	257.78	254.81	253.74	253.35	253.21
16000	323.01	311.87	283.97	274.96	271.80	270.66	270.24	270.09
17000	343.20	331.36	301.72	292.14	288.79	287.58	287.13	286.97
18000	363.38	350.85	319.47	309.33	305.77	304.49	304.02	303.85
19000	383.57	370.35	337.22	326.51	322.76	321.41	320.91	320.73
20000	403.76	389.84	354.96	343.70	339.75	338.32	337.80	337.61
21000	423.95	409.33	372.71	360.88	356.74	355.24	354.69	354.50
22000	444.14	428.82	390.46	378.07	373.72	372.16	371.58	371.38
23000	464.32	448.31	408.21	395.25	390.71	389.07	388.47	388.26
24000	484.51	467.80	425.96	412.44	407.70	405.99	405.36	405.14
25000	504.70	487.30	443.70	429.62	424.68	422.90	422.25	422.02
26000	524.89	506.79	461.45	446.81	441.67	439.82	439.14	438.90
27000	545.07	526.28	479.20	463.99	458.66	456.73	456.03	455.78
28000	565.26	545.77	496.95	481.18	475.65	473.65	472.92	472.66
29000	585.45	565.26	514.70	498.36	492.63	490.57	489.81	489.54
30000	605.64	584.75	532.44	515.55	509.62	507.48	506.70	506.42
31000	625.83	604.24	550.19	532.73	526.61	524.40	523.59	523.30
32000	646.01	623.74	567.94	549.92	543.59	541.31	540.48	540.18
33000	666.20	643.23	585.69	567.10	560.58	558.23	557.37	557.06
34000	686.39	662.72	603.44	584.28	577.57	575.15	574.26	573.94
35000	706.58	682.21	621.18	601.47	594.56	592.06	591.15	590.82
40000	807.52	779.67	709.92	687.39	679.49	676.64	675.60	675.22
45000	908.45	877.13	798.66	773.32	764.43	761.22	760.05	759.63
50000	1009.39	974.59	887.40	859.24	849.36	845.80	844.50	844.03
55000	1110.33	1072.04	976.14	945.16	934.30	930.38	928.95	928.43
60000	1211.27	1169.50	1064.88	1031.09	1019.23	1014.96	1013.40	1012.83
65000	1312.21	1266.96	1153.62	1117.01	1104.17	1099.54	1097.85	1097.24
70000	1413.15	1364.42	1242.36	1202.93	1189.11	1184.12	1182.30	1181.64
75000	1514.09	1461.88	1331.10	1288.86	1274.04	1268.70	1266.75	1266.04
80000	1615.03	1559.33	1419.84	1374.78	1358.98	1353.28	1351.20	1350.44
85000	1715.97	1656.79	1508.58	1460.70	1443.91	1437.86	1435.65	1434.85
90000	1816.90	1754.25	1597.32	1546.63	1528.85	1522.44	1520.10	1519.25
95000	1917.84	1851.71	1686.06	1632.55	1613.79	1607.02	1604.55	1603.65
100000	2018.78	1949.17	1774.80	1718.47	1698.72	1691.60	1689.00	1688.05
105000	2119.72	2046.62	1863.54	1804.40	1783.66	1776.18	1773.45	1772.46
110000	2220.66	2144.08	1952.28	1890.32	1868.59	1860.76	1857.90	1856.86
115000	2321.60	2241.54	2041.02	1976.24	1953.53	1945.34	1942.35	1941.26
120000	2422.54	2339.00	2129.76	2062.17	2038.46	2029.92	2026.80	2025.66
125000	2523.48	2436.46	2218.50	2148.09	2123.40	2114.50	2111.25	2110.07
130000	2624.41	2533.91	2307.24	2234.01	2208.34	2199.08	2195.70	2194.47
135000	2725.35	2631.37	2395.98	2319.94	2293.27	2283.65	2280.15	2278.87
140000	2826.29	2728.83	2484.72	2405.86	2378.21	2368.23	2364.60	2363.27
145000	2927.23	2826.29	2573.46	2491.78	2463.14	2452.81	2449.05	2447.67
150000	3028.17	2923.75	2662.20	2577.71	2548.08	2537.39	2533.50	2532.08
155000	3129.11	3021.20	2750.94	2663.63	2633.02	2621.97	2617.95	2616.48
160000	3230.05	3118.66	2839.68	2749.56	2717.95	2706.55	2702.40	2700.88

20.500% MONTHLY AMORTIZING PAYMENTS

AMOUNT OF LOAN	\multicolumn{8}{c}{NUMBER OF YEARS IN TERM}
	1	**2**	**3**	**4**	**5**	**6**	**7**	**8**
$ 50	4.65	2.56	1.88	1.54	1.34	1.22	1.13	1.07
100	9.29	5.12	3.75	3.07	2.68	2.43	2.26	2.13
200	18.58	10.23	7.49	6.14	5.36	4.85	4.51	4.26
300	27.87	15.35	11.23	9.21	8.04	7.28	6.76	6.38
400	37.15	20.46	14.97	12.28	10.71	9.70	9.01	8.51
500	46.44	25.58	18.71	15.35	13.39	12.13	11.26	10.64
600	55.73	30.69	22.46	18.42	16.07	14.55	13.51	12.76
700	65.02	35.80	26.20	21.49	18.75	16.98	15.76	14.89
800	74.30	40.92	29.94	24.56	21.42	19.40	18.01	17.02
900	83.59	46.03	33.68	27.63	24.10	21.82	20.26	19.14
1000	92.88	51.15	37.42	30.70	26.78	24.25	22.51	21.27
2000	185.75	102.29	74.84	61.40	53.55	48.49	45.02	42.54
3000	278.63	153.43	112.26	92.10	80.32	72.74	67.53	63.80
4000	371.50	204.57	149.68	122.79	107.10	96.98	90.04	85.07
5000	464.37	255.71	187.10	153.49	133.87	121.22	112.55	106.34
6000	557.25	306.85	224.52	184.19	160.64	145.47	135.05	127.60
7000	650.12	357.99	261.94	214.89	187.42	169.71	157.56	148.87
8000	743.00	409.13	299.36	245.58	214.19	193.95	180.07	170.13
9000	835.87	460.27	336.77	276.28	240.96	218.20	202.58	191.40
10000	928.74	511.41	374.19	306.98	267.73	242.44	225.09	212.67
11000	1021.62	562.55	411.61	337.68	294.51	266.68	247.60	233.93
12000	1114.49	613.69	449.03	368.37	321.28	290.93	270.10	255.20
13000	1207.37	664.83	486.45	399.07	348.05	315.17	292.61	276.46
14000	1300.24	715.97	523.87	429.77	374.83	339.41	315.12	297.73
15000	1393.11	767.11	561.29	460.47	401.60	363.66	337.63	319.00
16000	1485.99	818.25	598.71	491.16	428.37	387.90	360.14	340.26
17000	1578.86	869.39	636.13	521.86	455.14	412.15	382.65	361.53
18000	1671.74	920.53	673.54	552.56	481.92	436.39	405.15	382.79
19000	1764.61	971.67	710.96	583.26	508.69	460.63	427.66	404.06
20000	1857.48	1022.81	748.38	613.95	535.46	484.88	450.17	425.33
21000	1950.36	1073.95	785.80	644.65	562.24	509.12	472.68	446.59
22000	2043.23	1125.09	823.22	675.35	589.01	533.36	495.19	467.86
23000	2136.11	1176.23	860.64	706.05	615.78	557.61	517.69	489.12
24000	2228.98	1227.37	898.06	736.74	642.55	581.85	540.20	510.39
25000	2321.85	1278.51	935.48	767.44	669.33	606.09	562.71	531.66
26000	2414.73	1329.66	972.89	798.14	696.10	630.34	585.22	552.92
27000	2507.60	1380.80	1010.31	828.83	722.87	654.58	607.73	574.19
28000	2600.48	1431.94	1047.73	859.53	749.65	678.82	630.24	595.45
29000	2693.35	1483.08	1085.15	890.23	776.42	703.07	652.74	616.72
30000	2786.22	1534.22	1122.57	920.93	803.19	727.31	675.25	637.99
31000	2879.10	1585.36	1159.99	951.62	829.96	751.55	697.76	659.25
32000	2971.97	1636.50	1197.41	982.32	856.74	775.80	720.27	680.52
33000	3064.85	1687.64	1234.83	1013.02	883.51	800.04	742.78	701.78
34000	3157.72	1738.78	1272.25	1043.72	910.28	824.29	765.29	723.05
35000	3250.59	1789.92	1309.66	1074.41	937.06	848.53	787.79	744.32
40000	3714.96	2045.62	1496.76	1227.90	1070.92	969.75	900.33	850.65
45000	4179.33	2301.32	1683.85	1381.39	1204.78	1090.96	1012.88	956.98
50000	4643.70	2557.02	1870.95	1534.87	1338.65	1212.18	1125.42	1063.31
55000	5108.07	2812.73	2058.04	1688.36	1472.51	1333.40	1237.96	1169.64
60000	5572.44	3068.43	2245.14	1841.85	1606.38	1454.62	1350.50	1275.97
65000	6036.81	3324.13	2432.23	1995.34	1740.24	1575.83	1463.04	1382.30
70000	6501.18	3579.83	2619.32	2148.82	1874.11	1697.05	1575.58	1488.63
75000	6965.55	3835.53	2806.42	2302.31	2007.97	1818.27	1688.12	1594.96
80000	7429.92	4091.24	2993.51	2455.80	2141.83	1939.49	1800.66	1701.29
85000	7894.29	4346.94	3180.61	2609.28	2275.70	2060.71	1913.21	1807.62
90000	8358.66	4602.64	3367.70	2762.77	2409.56	2181.92	2025.75	1913.95
95000	8823.03	4858.34	3554.79	2916.26	2543.43	2303.14	2138.29	2020.28
100000	9287.40	5114.04	3741.89	3069.74	2677.29	2424.36	2250.83	2126.61
105000	9751.77	5369.75	3928.98	3223.23	2811.16	2545.58	2363.37	2232.94
110000	10216.14	5625.45	4116.08	3376.72	2945.02	2666.79	2475.91	2339.27
115000	10680.51	5881.15	4303.17	3530.21	3078.88	2788.01	2588.45	2445.60
120000	11144.88	6136.85	4490.27	3683.69	3212.75	2909.23	2700.99	2551.93
125000	11609.25	6392.55	4677.36	3837.18	3346.61	3030.45	2813.54	2658.26
130000	12073.62	6648.26	4864.45	3990.67	3480.48	3151.66	2926.08	2764.59
135000	12537.99	6903.96	5051.55	4144.15	3614.34	3272.88	3038.62	2870.92
140000	13002.36	7159.66	5238.64	4297.64	3748.21	3394.10	3151.16	2977.25
145000	13466.73	7415.36	5425.74	4451.13	3882.07	3515.32	3263.70	3083.58
150000	13931.10	7671.06	5612.83	4604.61	4015.93	3636.54	3376.24	3189.91
155000	14395.47	7926.77	5799.92	4758.10	4149.80	3757.75	3488.78	3296.24
160000	14859.84	8182.47	5987.02	4911.59	4283.66	3878.97	3601.32	3402.57

98

AMOUNT OF LOAN	NUMBER OF YEARS IN TERM							
	9	10	15	20	25	30	35	40
$ 50	1.02	.99	.90	.87	.86	.86	.86	.86
100	2.04	1.97	1.80	1.74	1.72	1.72	1.71	1.71
200	4.07	3.94	3.59	3.48	3.44	3.43	3.42	3.42
300	6.11	5.90	5.39	5.22	5.16	5.14	5.13	5.13
400	8.14	7.87	7.18	6.96	6.88	6.85	6.84	6.84
500	10.18	9.83	8.97	8.70	8.60	8.57	8.55	8.55
600	12.21	11.80	10.77	10.43	10.32	10.28	10.26	10.26
700	14.25	13.77	12.56	12.17	12.04	11.99	11.97	11.97
800	16.28	15.73	14.35	13.91	13.76	13.70	13.68	13.68
900	18.32	17.70	16.15	15.65	15.48	15.41	15.39	15.38
1000	20.35	19.66	17.94	17.39	17.20	17.13	17.10	17.09
2000	40.70	39.32	35.87	34.77	34.39	34.25	34.20	34.18
3000	61.05	58.98	53.81	52.15	51.58	51.37	51.30	51.27
4000	81.40	78.64	71.74	69.53	68.77	68.49	68.39	68.36
5000	101.75	98.30	89.67	86.91	85.96	85.61	85.49	85.45
6000	122.10	117.95	107.61	104.29	103.15	102.74	102.59	102.54
7000	142.45	137.61	125.54	121.68	120.34	119.86	119.69	119.62
8000	162.80	157.27	143.47	139.06	137.53	136.98	136.78	136.71
9000	183.15	176.93	161.41	156.44	154.72	154.10	153.88	153.80
10000	203.50	196.59	179.34	173.82	171.91	171.22	170.98	170.89
11000	223.85	216.25	197.27	191.20	189.10	188.34	188.07	187.98
12000	244.20	235.90	215.21	208.58	206.29	205.47	205.17	205.07
13000	264.55	255.56	233.14	225.97	223.48	222.59	222.27	222.15
14000	284.90	275.22	251.07	243.35	240.67	239.71	239.37	239.24
15000	305.25	294.88	269.01	260.73	257.86	256.83	256.46	256.33
16000	325.60	314.54	286.94	278.11	275.05	273.95	273.56	273.42
17000	345.95	334.19	304.87	295.49	292.24	291.08	290.66	290.51
18000	366.30	353.85	322.81	312.87	309.43	308.20	307.76	307.60
19000	386.65	373.51	340.74	330.25	326.62	325.32	324.85	324.68
20000	407.00	393.17	358.67	347.64	343.81	342.44	341.95	341.77
21000	427.35	412.83	376.61	365.02	361.00	359.56	359.05	358.86
22000	447.70	432.49	394.54	382.40	378.19	376.68	376.14	375.95
23000	468.05	452.14	412.47	399.78	395.38	393.81	393.24	393.04
24000	488.40	471.80	430.41	417.16	412.57	410.93	410.34	410.13
25000	508.74	491.46	448.34	434.54	429.76	428.05	427.44	427.21
26000	529.09	511.12	466.28	451.93	446.95	445.17	444.53	444.30
27000	549.44	530.78	484.21	469.31	464.14	462.29	461.63	461.39
28000	569.79	550.44	502.14	486.69	481.33	479.42	478.73	478.48
29000	590.14	570.09	520.08	504.07	498.52	496.54	495.82	495.57
30000	610.49	589.75	538.01	521.45	515.71	513.66	512.92	512.66
31000	630.84	609.41	555.94	538.83	532.90	530.78	530.02	529.74
32000	651.19	629.07	573.88	556.21	550.09	547.90	547.12	546.83
33000	671.54	648.73	591.81	573.60	567.28	565.02	564.21	563.92
34000	691.89	668.38	609.74	590.98	584.47	582.15	581.31	581.01
35000	712.24	688.04	627.68	608.36	601.66	599.27	598.41	598.10
40000	813.99	786.33	717.34	695.27	687.61	684.88	683.89	683.54
45000	915.74	884.63	807.01	782.17	773.56	770.49	769.38	768.98
50000	1017.48	982.92	896.68	869.08	859.51	856.10	854.87	854.42
55000	1119.23	1081.21	986.35	955.99	945.46	941.70	940.35	939.86
60000	1220.98	1179.50	1076.01	1042.90	1031.41	1027.31	1025.84	1025.31
65000	1322.73	1277.79	1165.68	1129.81	1117.36	1112.92	1111.33	1110.75
70000	1424.48	1376.08	1255.35	1216.71	1203.31	1198.53	1196.81	1196.19
75000	1526.22	1474.37	1345.02	1303.62	1289.26	1284.14	1282.30	1281.63
80000	1627.97	1572.66	1434.68	1390.53	1375.21	1369.75	1367.78	1367.07
85000	1729.72	1670.95	1524.35	1477.44	1461.16	1455.36	1453.27	1452.52
90000	1831.47	1769.25	1614.02	1564.34	1547.11	1540.97	1538.76	1537.96
95000	1933.22	1867.54	1703.68	1651.25	1633.06	1626.58	1624.24	1623.40
100000	2034.96	1965.83	1793.35	1738.16	1719.01	1712.19	1709.73	1708.84
105000	2136.71	2064.12	1883.02	1825.07	1804.96	1797.80	1795.22	1794.28
110000	2238.46	2162.41	1972.69	1911.97	1890.91	1883.40	1880.70	1879.72
115000	2340.21	2260.70	2062.35	1998.88	1976.86	1969.01	1966.19	1965.17
120000	2441.96	2358.99	2152.02	2085.79	2062.81	2054.62	2051.67	2050.61
125000	2543.70	2457.28	2241.69	2172.70	2148.76	2140.23	2137.16	2136.05
130000	2645.45	2555.57	2331.36	2259.61	2234.71	2225.84	2222.65	2221.49
135000	2747.20	2653.87	2421.02	2346.51	2320.66	2311.45	2308.13	2306.93
140000	2848.95	2752.16	2510.69	2433.42	2406.61	2397.06	2393.62	2392.38
145000	2950.69	2850.45	2600.36	2520.33	2492.57	2482.67	2479.10	2477.82
150000	3052.44	2948.74	2690.03	2607.24	2578.52	2568.28	2564.59	2563.26
155000	3154.19	3047.03	2779.69	2694.14	2664.47	2653.89	2650.08	2648.70
160000	3255.94	3145.32	2869.36	2781.05	2750.42	2739.49	2735.56	2734.14

AMOUNT OF LOAN	NUMBER OF YEARS IN TERM							
	1	2	3	4	5	6	7	8
$ 50	4.65	2.57	1.88	1.55	1.35	1.22	1.14	1.08
100	9.30	5.13	3.76	3.09	2.70	2.44	2.27	2.15
200	18.60	10.26	7.51	6.17	5.39	4.88	4.54	4.29
300	27.90	15.38	11.27	9.25	8.08	7.32	6.80	6.43
400	37.20	20.51	15.02	12.34	10.77	9.76	9.07	8.57
500	46.50	25.64	18.78	15.42	13.46	12.20	11.33	10.72
600	55.80	30.76	22.53	18.50	16.15	14.64	13.60	12.86
700	65.10	35.89	26.29	21.59	18.84	17.08	15.87	15.00
800	74.40	41.02	30.04	24.67	21.54	19.52	18.13	17.14
900	83.70	46.14	33.80	27.75	24.23	21.96	20.40	19.29
1000	93.00	51.27	37.55	30.84	26.92	24.39	22.66	21.43
2000	185.99	102.53	75.10	61.67	53.83	48.78	45.32	42.85
3000	278.99	153.79	112.65	92.50	80.74	73.17	67.98	64.27
4000	371.98	205.06	150.19	123.33	107.66	97.56	90.64	85.70
5000	464.97	256.32	187.74	154.16	134.57	121.95	113.30	107.12
6000	557.97	307.58	225.29	184.99	161.48	146.34	135.96	128.54
7000	650.96	358.85	262.83	215.82	188.40	170.73	158.62	149.97
8000	743.96	410.11	300.38	246.66	215.31	195.12	181.28	171.39
9000	836.95	461.37	337.93	277.49	242.22	219.51	203.94	192.81
10000	929.94	512.63	375.47	308.32	269.13	243.90	226.60	214.24
11000	1022.94	563.90	413.02	339.15	296.05	268.29	249.26	235.66
12000	1115.93	615.16	450.57	369.98	322.96	292.68	271.92	257.08
13000	1208.92	666.42	488.11	400.81	349.87	317.07	294.58	278.51
14000	1301.92	717.69	525.66	431.64	376.79	341.46	317.24	299.93
15000	1394.91	768.95	563.21	462.48	403.70	365.85	339.90	321.35
16000	1487.91	820.21	600.75	493.31	430.61	390.24	362.56	342.78
17000	1580.90	871.47	638.30	524.14	457.52	414.63	385.22	364.20
18000	1673.89	922.74	675.85	554.97	484.44	439.02	407.88	385.62
19000	1766.89	974.00	713.39	585.80	511.35	463.41	430.54	407.05
20000	1859.88	1025.26	750.94	616.63	538.26	487.80	453.20	428.47
21000	1952.88	1076.53	788.49	647.46	565.18	512.19	475.86	449.89
22000	2045.87	1127.79	826.04	678.30	592.09	536.58	498.52	471.32
23000	2138.86	1179.05	863.58	709.13	619.00	560.96	521.18	492.74
24000	2231.86	1230.32	901.13	739.96	645.92	585.35	543.84	514.16
25000	2324.85	1281.58	938.68	770.79	672.83	609.74	566.50	535.59
26000	2417.84	1332.84	976.22	801.62	699.74	634.13	589.16	557.01
27000	2510.84	1384.10	1013.77	832.45	726.65	658.52	611.82	578.43
28000	2603.83	1435.37	1051.32	863.28	753.57	682.91	634.48	599.86
29000	2696.83	1486.63	1088.86	894.12	780.48	707.30	657.14	621.28
30000	2789.82	1537.89	1126.41	924.95	807.39	731.69	679.80	642.70
31000	2882.81	1589.16	1163.96	955.78	834.31	756.08	702.46	664.13
32000	2975.81	1640.42	1201.50	986.61	861.22	780.47	725.12	685.55
33000	3068.80	1691.68	1239.05	1017.44	888.13	804.86	747.78	706.97
34000	3161.80	1742.94	1276.60	1048.27	915.04	829.25	770.44	728.40
35000	3254.79	1794.21	1314.14	1079.10	941.96	853.64	793.10	749.82
40000	3719.76	2050.52	1501.88	1233.26	1076.52	975.59	906.40	856.94
45000	4184.73	2306.84	1689.61	1387.42	1211.09	1097.53	1019.70	964.05
50000	4649.70	2563.15	1877.35	1541.57	1345.65	1219.48	1133.00	1071.17
55000	5114.67	2819.47	2065.08	1695.73	1480.22	1341.43	1246.30	1178.29
60000	5579.63	3075.78	2252.81	1849.89	1614.78	1463.38	1359.60	1285.40
65000	6044.60	3332.10	2440.55	2004.05	1749.34	1585.33	1472.90	1392.52
70000	6509.57	3588.41	2628.28	2158.20	1883.91	1707.27	1586.20	1499.63
75000	6974.54	3844.73	2816.02	2312.36	2018.47	1829.22	1699.50	1606.75
80000	7439.51	4101.04	3003.75	2466.52	2153.04	1951.17	1812.80	1713.87
85000	7904.48	4357.35	3191.49	2620.67	2287.60	2073.12	1926.10	1820.98
90000	8369.45	4613.67	3379.22	2774.83	2422.17	2195.06	2039.40	1928.10
95000	8834.42	4869.98	3566.95	2928.99	2556.73	2317.01	2152.70	2035.22
100000	9299.39	5126.30	3754.69	3083.14	2691.30	2438.96	2266.00	2142.33
105000	9764.36	5382.61	3942.42	3237.30	2825.86	2560.91	2379.30	2249.45
110000	10229.33	5638.93	4130.16	3391.46	2960.43	2682.86	2492.60	2356.57
115000	10694.30	5895.24	4317.89	3545.61	3094.99	2804.80	2605.90	2463.68
120000	11159.26	6151.56	4505.62	3699.77	3229.56	2926.75	2719.20	2570.80
125000	11624.23	6407.87	4693.36	3853.93	3364.12	3048.70	2832.50	2677.91
130000	12089.20	6664.19	4881.09	4008.09	3498.68	3170.65	2945.80	2785.03
135000	12554.17	6920.50	5068.83	4162.24	3633.25	3292.59	3059.10	2892.15
140000	13019.14	7176.82	5256.56	4316.40	3767.81	3414.54	3172.40	2999.26
145000	13484.11	7433.13	5444.30	4470.56	3902.38	3536.49	3285.70	3106.38
150000	13949.08	7689.45	5632.03	4624.71	4036.94	3658.44	3399.00	3213.50
155000	14414.05	7945.76	5819.76	4778.87	4171.51	3780.38	3512.30	3320.61
160000	14879.02	8202.08	6007.50	4933.03	4306.07	3902.33	3625.60	3427.73

AMOUNT OF LOAN	NUMBER OF YEARS IN TERM							
	9	10	15	20	25	30	35	40
$ 50	1.03	1.00	.91	.88	.87	.87	.87	.87
100	2.06	1.99	1.82	1.76	1.74	1.74	1.74	1.73
200	4.11	3.97	3.63	3.52	3.48	3.47	3.47	3.46
300	6.16	5.95	5.44	5.28	5.22	5.20	5.20	5.19
400	8.21	7.94	7.25	7.04	6.96	6.94	6.93	6.92
500	10.26	9.92	9.06	8.79	8.70	8.67	8.66	8.65
600	12.31	11.90	10.88	10.55	10.44	10.40	10.39	10.38
700	14.36	13.88	12.69	12.31	12.18	12.13	12.12	12.11
800	16.41	15.87	14.50	14.07	13.92	13.87	13.85	13.84
900	18.47	17.85	16.31	15.83	15.66	15.60	15.58	15.57
1000	20.52	19.83	18.12	17.58	17.40	17.33	17.31	17.30
2000	41.03	39.66	36.24	35.16	34.79	34.66	34.61	34.60
3000	61.54	59.48	54.36	52.74	52.18	51.99	51.92	51.89
4000	82.05	79.31	72.48	70.32	69.58	69.32	69.22	69.19
5000	102.56	99.13	90.60	87.90	86.97	86.64	86.53	86.49
6000	123.08	118.96	108.72	105.48	104.36	103.97	103.83	103.78
7000	143.59	138.78	126.84	123.06	121.76	121.30	121.14	121.08
8000	164.10	158.61	144.96	140.64	139.15	138.63	138.44	138.38
9000	184.61	178.43	163.08	158.21	156.54	155.96	155.75	155.67
10000	205.12	198.26	181.20	175.79	173.94	173.28	173.05	172.97
11000	225.64	218.08	199.32	193.37	191.33	190.61	190.36	190.26
12000	246.15	237.91	217.44	210.95	208.72	207.94	207.66	207.56
13000	266.66	257.74	235.56	228.53	226.12	225.27	224.96	224.86
14000	287.17	277.56	253.68	246.11	243.51	242.59	242.27	242.15
15000	307.68	297.39	271.80	263.69	260.90	259.92	259.57	259.45
16000	328.20	317.21	289.92	281.27	278.30	277.25	276.88	276.75
17000	348.71	337.04	308.04	298.84	295.69	294.58	294.18	294.04
18000	369.22	356.86	326.16	316.42	313.08	311.91	311.49	311.34
19000	389.73	376.69	344.28	334.00	330.48	329.23	328.79	328.63
20000	410.24	396.51	362.40	351.58	347.87	346.56	346.10	345.93
21000	430.76	416.34	380.52	369.16	365.26	363.89	363.40	363.23
22000	451.27	436.16	398.63	386.74	382.66	381.22	380.71	380.52
23000	471.78	455.99	416.75	404.32	400.05	398.55	398.01	397.82
24000	492.29	475.82	434.87	421.90	417.44	415.87	415.31	415.12
25000	512.80	495.64	452.99	439.47	434.84	433.20	432.62	432.41
26000	533.32	515.47	471.11	457.05	452.23	450.53	449.92	449.71
27000	553.83	535.29	489.23	474.63	469.62	467.86	467.23	467.00
28000	574.34	555.12	507.35	492.21	487.02	485.18	484.53	484.30
29000	594.85	574.94	525.47	509.79	504.41	502.51	501.84	501.60
30000	615.36	594.77	543.59	527.37	521.80	519.84	519.14	518.89
31000	635.88	614.59	561.71	544.95	539.20	537.17	536.45	536.19
32000	656.39	634.42	579.83	562.53	556.59	554.50	553.75	553.49
33000	676.90	654.24	597.95	580.11	573.98	571.82	571.06	570.78
34000	697.41	674.07	616.07	597.68	591.37	589.15	588.36	588.08
35000	717.92	693.89	634.19	615.26	608.77	606.48	605.67	605.37
40000	820.48	793.02	724.79	703.16	695.73	693.12	692.19	691.86
45000	923.04	892.15	815.38	791.05	782.70	779.76	778.71	778.34
50000	1025.60	991.28	905.98	878.94	869.67	866.40	865.23	864.82
55000	1128.16	1090.40	996.58	966.84	956.63	953.04	951.76	951.30
60000	1230.72	1189.53	1087.18	1054.73	1043.60	1039.68	1038.28	1037.78
65000	1333.28	1288.66	1177.77	1142.63	1130.56	1126.31	1124.80	1124.26
70000	1435.84	1387.78	1268.37	1230.52	1217.53	1212.95	1211.33	1210.74
75000	1538.40	1486.91	1358.97	1318.41	1304.50	1299.59	1297.85	1297.23
80000	1640.96	1586.04	1449.57	1406.31	1391.46	1386.23	1384.37	1383.71
85000	1743.52	1685.17	1540.17	1494.20	1478.43	1472.87	1470.89	1470.19
90000	1846.08	1784.29	1630.76	1582.10	1565.40	1559.51	1557.42	1556.67
95000	1948.64	1883.42	1721.36	1669.99	1652.36	1646.15	1643.94	1643.15
100000	2051.20	1982.55	1811.96	1757.88	1739.33	1732.79	1730.46	1729.63
105000	2153.76	2081.67	1902.56	1845.78	1826.29	1819.43	1816.99	1816.11
110000	2256.32	2180.80	1993.15	1933.67	1913.26	1906.07	1903.51	1902.60
115000	2358.88	2279.93	2083.75	2021.57	2000.23	1992.71	1990.03	1989.08
120000	2461.44	2379.06	2174.35	2109.46	2087.19	2079.35	2076.55	2075.56
125000	2564.00	2478.18	2264.95	2197.35	2174.16	2165.98	2163.08	2162.04
130000	2666.56	2577.31	2355.54	2285.25	2261.12	2252.62	2249.60	2248.52
135000	2769.12	2676.44	2446.14	2373.14	2348.09	2339.26	2336.12	2335.00
140000	2871.68	2775.56	2536.74	2461.04	2435.06	2425.90	2422.65	2421.48
145000	2974.24	2874.69	2627.34	2548.93	2522.02	2512.54	2509.17	2507.97
150000	3076.80	2973.82	2717.93	2636.82	2608.99	2599.18	2595.69	2594.45
155000	3179.36	3072.94	2808.53	2724.72	2695.96	2685.82	2682.21	2680.93
160000	3281.92	3172.07	2899.13	2812.61	2782.92	2772.46	2768.74	2767.41

MONTHLY AMORTIZING PAYMENTS

AMOUNT OF LOAN	NUMBER OF YEARS IN TERM							
	1	2	3	4	5	6	7	8
$ 50	4.66	2.57	1.89	1.55	1.36	1.23	1.15	1.08
100	9.32	5.14	3.77	3.10	2.71	2.46	2.29	2.16
200	18.63	10.28	7.54	6.20	5.42	4.91	4.57	4.32
300	27.94	15.42	11.31	9.29	8.12	7.37	6.85	6.48
400	37.25	20.56	15.08	12.39	10.83	9.82	9.13	8.64
500	46.56	25.70	18.84	15.49	13.53	12.27	11.41	10.80
600	55.87	30.84	22.61	18.58	16.24	14.73	13.69	12.95
700	65.18	35.97	26.38	21.68	18.94	17.18	15.97	15.11
800	74.50	41.11	30.15	24.78	21.65	19.63	18.25	17.27
900	83.81	46.25	33.91	27.87	24.35	22.09	20.54	19.43
1000	93.12	51.39	37.68	30.97	27.06	24.54	22.82	21.59
2000	186.23	102.78	75.36	61.94	54.11	49.08	45.63	43.17
3000	279.35	154.16	113.03	92.90	81.17	73.61	68.44	64.75
4000	372.46	205.55	150.71	123.87	108.22	98.15	91.25	86.33
5000	465.57	256.93	188.38	154.83	135.27	122.68	114.07	107.91
6000	558.69	308.32	226.06	185.80	162.33	147.22	136.88	129.49
7000	651.80	359.70	263.73	216.76	189.38	171.76	159.69	151.07
8000	744.92	411.09	301.41	247.73	216.43	196.29	182.50	172.65
9000	838.03	462.48	339.08	278.70	243.49	220.83	205.32	194.23
10000	931.14	513.86	376.76	309.66	270.54	245.36	228.13	215.82
11000	1024.26	565.25	414.43	340.63	297.59	269.90	250.94	237.40
12000	1117.37	616.63	452.11	371.59	324.65	294.44	273.75	258.98
13000	1210.48	668.02	489.78	402.56	351.70	318.97	296.56	280.56
14000	1303.60	719.40	527.46	433.52	378.75	343.51	319.38	302.14
15000	1396.71	770.79	565.13	464.49	405.81	368.04	342.19	323.72
16000	1489.83	822.18	602.81	495.46	432.86	392.58	365.00	345.30
17000	1582.94	873.56	640.48	526.42	459.91	417.12	387.81	366.88
18000	1676.05	924.95	678.16	557.39	486.97	441.65	410.63	388.46
19000	1769.17	976.33	715.83	588.35	514.02	466.19	433.44	410.04
20000	1862.28	1027.72	753.51	619.32	541.07	490.72	456.25	431.63
21000	1955.39	1079.10	791.18	650.28	568.13	515.26	479.06	453.21
22000	2048.51	1130.49	828.86	681.25	595.18	539.80	501.87	474.79
23000	2141.62	1181.87	866.53	712.22	622.23	564.33	524.69	496.37
24000	2234.74	1233.26	904.21	743.18	649.29	588.87	547.50	517.95
25000	2327.85	1284.65	941.88	774.15	676.34	613.40	570.31	539.53
26000	2420.96	1336.03	979.56	805.11	703.39	637.94	593.12	561.11
27000	2514.08	1387.42	1017.23	836.08	730.45	662.48	615.94	582.69
28000	2607.19	1438.80	1054.91	867.04	757.50	687.01	638.75	604.27
29000	2700.30	1490.19	1092.58	898.01	784.55	711.55	661.56	625.85
30000	2793.42	1541.57	1130.26	928.98	811.61	736.08	684.37	647.44
31000	2886.53	1592.96	1167.93	959.94	838.66	760.62	707.18	669.02
32000	2979.65	1644.35	1205.61	990.91	865.71	785.16	730.00	690.60
33000	3072.76	1695.73	1243.28	1021.87	892.77	809.69	752.81	712.18
34000	3165.87	1747.12	1280.96	1052.84	919.82	834.23	775.62	733.76
35000	3258.99	1798.50	1318.63	1083.80	946.87	858.76	798.43	755.34
40000	3724.56	2055.43	1507.01	1238.63	1082.14	981.44	912.49	863.25
45000	4190.12	2312.36	1695.38	1393.46	1217.41	1104.12	1026.56	971.15
50000	4655.69	2569.29	1883.76	1548.29	1352.67	1226.80	1140.62	1079.06
55000	5121.26	2826.22	2072.13	1703.12	1487.94	1349.48	1254.68	1186.96
60000	5586.83	3083.14	2260.51	1857.95	1623.21	1472.16	1368.74	1294.87
65000	6052.40	3340.07	2448.88	2012.78	1758.47	1594.84	1482.80	1402.77
70000	6517.97	3597.00	2637.26	2167.60	1893.74	1717.52	1596.86	1510.68
75000	6983.54	3853.93	2825.64	2322.43	2029.01	1840.20	1710.92	1618.58
80000	7449.11	4110.86	3014.01	2477.26	2164.27	1962.88	1824.98	1726.49
85000	7914.68	4367.79	3202.39	2632.09	2299.54	2085.56	1939.04	1834.39
90000	8380.24	4624.71	3390.76	2786.92	2434.81	2208.24	2053.11	1942.30
95000	8845.81	4881.64	3579.14	2941.75	2570.07	2330.92	2167.17	2050.20
100000	9311.38	5138.57	3767.51	3096.57	2705.34	2453.60	2281.23	2158.11
105000	9776.95	5395.50	3955.89	3251.40	2840.61	2576.28	2395.29	2266.01
110000	10242.52	5652.43	4144.26	3406.23	2975.87	2698.96	2509.35	2373.92
115000	10708.09	5909.35	4332.64	3561.06	3111.14	2821.64	2623.41	2481.82
120000	11173.66	6166.28	4521.01	3715.89	3246.41	2944.32	2737.47	2589.73
125000	11639.23	6423.21	4709.39	3870.72	3381.67	3067.00	2851.53	2697.63
130000	12104.80	6680.14	4897.76	4025.55	3516.94	3189.68	2965.59	2805.54
135000	12570.36	6937.07	5086.14	4180.37	3652.21	3312.36	3079.66	2913.44
140000	13035.93	7194.00	5274.51	4335.20	3787.48	3435.04	3193.72	3021.35
145000	13501.50	7450.92	5462.89	4490.03	3922.74	3557.72	3307.78	3129.25
150000	13967.07	7707.85	5651.27	4644.86	4058.01	3680.40	3421.84	3237.16
155000	14432.64	7964.78	5839.64	4799.69	4193.28	3803.08	3535.90	3345.06
160000	14898.21	8221.71	6028.02	4954.52	4328.54	3925.76	3649.96	3452.97

AMOUNT OF LOAN	NUMBER OF YEARS IN TERM							
	9	10	15	20	25	30	35	40
$ 50	1.04	1.00	.92	.89	.88	.88	.88	.88
100	2.07	2.00	1.84	1.78	1.76	1.76	1.76	1.76
200	4.14	4.00	3.67	3.56	3.52	3.51	3.51	3.51
300	6.21	6.00	5.50	5.34	5.28	5.27	5.26	5.26
400	8.27	8.00	7.33	7.12	7.04	7.02	7.01	7.01
500	10.34	10.00	9.16	8.89	8.80	8.77	8.76	8.76
600	12.41	12.00	10.99	10.67	10.56	10.53	10.51	10.51
700	14.48	14.00	12.82	12.45	12.32	12.28	12.26	12.26
800	16.54	16.00	14.65	14.23	14.08	14.03	14.01	14.01
900	18.61	18.00	16.48	16.00	15.84	15.79	15.77	15.76
1000	20.68	20.00	18.31	17.78	17.60	17.54	17.52	17.51
2000	41.35	39.99	36.62	35.56	35.20	35.07	35.03	35.01
3000	62.03	59.98	54.92	53.33	52.79	52.61	52.54	52.52
4000	82.70	79.98	73.23	71.11	70.39	70.14	70.05	70.02
5000	103.38	99.97	91.54	88.89	87.99	87.68	87.56	87.53
6000	124.05	119.96	109.84	106.66	105.58	105.21	105.08	105.03
7000	144.73	139.96	128.15	124.44	123.18	122.74	122.59	122.53
8000	165.40	159.95	146.45	142.22	140.78	140.28	140.10	140.04
9000	186.08	179.94	164.76	159.99	158.37	157.81	157.61	157.54
10000	206.75	199.94	183.07	177.77	175.97	175.35	175.12	175.05
11000	227.43	219.93	201.37	195.55	193.57	192.88	192.64	192.55
12000	248.10	239.92	219.68	213.32	211.16	210.41	210.15	210.06
13000	268.78	259.92	237.98	231.10	228.76	227.95	227.66	227.56
14000	289.45	279.91	256.29	248.88	246.36	245.48	245.17	245.06
15000	310.13	299.90	274.60	266.65	263.95	263.02	262.68	262.57
16000	330.80	319.90	292.90	284.43	281.55	280.55	280.20	280.07
17000	351.48	339.89	311.21	302.20	299.15	298.08	297.71	297.58
18000	372.15	359.88	329.52	319.98	316.74	315.62	315.22	315.08
19000	392.83	379.88	347.82	337.76	334.34	333.15	332.73	332.59
20000	413.50	399.87	366.13	355.53	351.94	350.69	350.24	350.09
21000	434.18	419.86	384.43	373.31	369.53	368.22	367.76	367.59
22000	454.85	439.85	402.74	391.09	387.13	385.75	385.27	385.10
23000	475.53	459.85	421.05	408.86	404.73	403.29	402.78	402.60
24000	496.20	479.84	439.35	426.64	422.32	420.82	420.29	420.11
25000	516.88	499.83	457.66	444.42	439.92	438.36	437.80	437.61
26000	537.55	519.83	475.96	462.19	457.52	455.89	455.32	455.12
27000	558.23	539.82	494.27	479.97	475.11	473.42	472.83	472.62
28000	578.90	559.81	512.58	497.75	492.71	490.96	490.34	490.12
29000	599.58	579.81	530.88	515.52	510.31	508.49	507.85	507.63
30000	620.25	599.80	549.19	533.30	527.90	526.03	525.36	525.13
31000	640.93	619.79	567.49	551.07	545.50	543.56	542.88	542.64
32000	661.60	639.79	585.80	568.85	563.10	561.09	560.39	560.14
33000	682.28	659.78	604.11	586.63	580.69	578.63	577.90	577.64
34000	702.95	679.77	622.41	604.40	598.29	596.16	595.41	595.15
35000	723.63	699.77	640.72	622.18	615.89	613.70	612.92	612.65
40000	827.00	799.73	732.25	711.06	703.87	701.37	700.48	700.17
45000	930.37	899.70	823.78	799.94	791.85	789.04	788.04	787.70
50000	1033.75	999.66	915.31	888.83	879.84	876.71	875.60	875.22
55000	1137.12	1099.63	1006.84	977.71	967.82	964.38	963.16	962.74
60000	1240.50	1199.60	1098.37	1066.59	1055.80	1052.05	1050.72	1050.26
65000	1343.87	1299.56	1189.90	1155.47	1143.79	1139.72	1138.28	1137.78
70000	1447.25	1399.53	1281.43	1244.36	1231.77	1227.39	1225.84	1225.30
75000	1550.62	1499.49	1372.96	1333.24	1319.75	1315.06	1313.40	1312.82
80000	1653.99	1599.46	1464.49	1422.12	1407.74	1402.73	1400.96	1400.34
85000	1757.37	1699.42	1556.03	1511.00	1495.72	1490.40	1488.52	1487.86
90000	1860.74	1799.39	1647.56	1599.88	1583.70	1578.07	1576.08	1575.39
95000	1964.12	1899.36	1739.09	1688.77	1671.68	1665.74	1663.64	1662.91
100000	2067.49	1999.32	1830.62	1777.65	1759.67	1753.41	1751.20	1750.43
105000	2170.87	2099.29	1922.15	1866.53	1847.65	1841.08	1838.76	1837.95
110000	2274.24	2199.25	2013.68	1955.41	1935.63	1928.75	1926.32	1925.47
115000	2377.61	2299.22	2105.21	2044.29	2023.62	2016.42	2013.88	2012.99
120000	2480.99	2399.19	2196.74	2133.18	2111.60	2104.09	2101.44	2100.51
125000	2584.36	2499.15	2288.27	2222.06	2199.58	2191.76	2189.00	2188.03
130000	2687.74	2599.12	2379.80	2310.94	2287.57	2279.43	2276.56	2275.56
135000	2791.11	2699.08	2471.33	2399.82	2375.55	2367.10	2364.12	2363.08
140000	2894.49	2799.05	2562.86	2488.71	2463.53	2454.77	2451.68	2450.60
145000	2997.86	2899.01	2654.39	2577.59	2551.52	2542.44	2539.24	2538.12
150000	3101.24	2998.98	2745.92	2666.47	2639.50	2630.11	2626.80	2625.64
155000	3204.61	3098.95	2837.45	2755.35	2727.48	2717.78	2714.36	2713.16
160000	3307.98	3198.91	2928.98	2844.23	2815.47	2805.45	2801.92	2800.68

21.250%   MONTHLY AMORTIZING PAYMENTS

AMOUNT OF LOAN	NUMBER OF YEARS IN TERM							
	1	2	3	4	5	6	7	8
$ 50	4.67	2.58	1.90	1.56	1.36	1.24	1.15	1.09
100	9.33	5.16	3.79	3.12	2.72	2.47	2.30	2.18
200	18.65	10.31	7.57	6.23	5.44	4.94	4.60	4.35
300	27.98	15.46	11.35	9.34	8.16	7.41	6.89	6.53
400	37.30	20.61	15.13	12.45	10.88	9.88	9.19	8.70
500	46.62	25.76	18.91	15.56	13.60	12.35	11.49	10.87
600	55.95	30.91	22.69	18.67	16.32	14.81	13.78	13.05
700	65.27	36.06	26.47	21.78	19.04	17.28	16.08	15.22
800	74.59	41.21	30.25	24.89	21.76	19.75	18.38	17.40
900	83.92	46.36	34.03	28.00	24.48	22.22	20.67	19.57
1000	93.24	51.51	37.81	31.11	27.20	24.69	22.97	21.74
2000	186.47	103.02	75.61	62.21	54.39	49.37	45.93	43.48
3000	279.71	154.53	113.42	93.31	81.59	74.05	68.90	65.22
4000	372.94	206.04	151.22	124.41	108.78	98.74	91.86	86.96
5000	466.17	257.55	189.02	155.51	135.98	123.42	114.83	108.70
6000	559.41	309.06	226.83	186.61	163.17	148.10	137.79	130.44
7000	652.64	360.56	264.63	217.71	190.36	172.79	160.76	152.18
8000	745.88	412.07	302.43	248.81	217.56	197.47	183.72	173.92
9000	839.11	463.58	340.24	279.91	244.75	222.15	206.69	195.66
10000	932.34	515.09	378.04	311.01	271.95	246.83	229.65	217.40
11000	1025.58	566.60	415.84	342.11	299.14	271.52	252.62	239.14
12000	1118.81	618.11	453.65	373.21	326.34	296.20	275.58	260.88
13000	1212.04	669.62	491.45	404.31	353.53	320.88	298.55	282.62
14000	1305.28	721.12	529.25	435.41	380.72	345.57	321.51	304.35
15000	1398.51	772.63	567.06	466.51	407.92	370.25	344.48	326.09
16000	1491.75	824.14	604.86	497.61	435.11	394.93	367.44	347.83
17000	1584.98	875.65	642.67	528.71	462.31	419.61	390.41	369.57
18000	1678.21	927.16	680.47	559.81	489.50	444.30	413.37	391.31
19000	1771.45	978.67	718.27	590.91	516.69	468.98	436.34	413.05
20000	1864.68	1030.18	756.08	622.01	543.89	493.66	459.30	434.79
21000	1957.91	1081.68	793.88	653.11	571.08	518.35	482.27	456.53
22000	2051.15	1133.19	831.68	684.21	598.28	543.03	505.23	478.27
23000	2144.38	1184.70	869.49	715.31	625.47	567.71	528.20	500.01
24000	2237.62	1236.21	907.29	746.41	652.67	592.39	551.16	521.75
25000	2330.85	1287.72	945.09	777.51	679.86	617.08	574.13	543.49
26000	2424.08	1339.23	982.90	808.61	707.05	641.76	597.09	565.23
27000	2517.32	1390.74	1020.70	839.71	734.25	666.44	620.06	586.97
28000	2610.55	1442.24	1058.50	870.81	761.44	691.13	643.02	608.70
29000	2703.79	1493.75	1096.31	901.91	788.64	715.81	665.99	630.44
30000	2797.02	1545.26	1134.11	933.01	815.83	740.49	688.95	652.18
31000	2890.25	1596.77	1171.92	964.11	843.02	765.17	711.92	673.92
32000	2983.49	1648.28	1209.72	995.22	870.22	789.86	734.88	695.66
33000	3076.72	1699.79	1247.52	1026.32	897.41	814.54	757.85	717.40
34000	3169.95	1751.29	1285.33	1057.42	924.61	839.22	780.81	739.14
35000	3263.19	1802.80	1323.13	1088.52	951.80	863.91	803.78	760.88
40000	3729.36	2060.35	1512.15	1244.02	1087.77	987.32	918.60	869.58
45000	4195.53	2317.89	1701.16	1399.52	1223.74	1110.73	1033.43	978.27
50000	4661.69	2575.43	1890.18	1555.02	1359.71	1234.15	1148.25	1086.97
55000	5127.86	2832.97	2079.20	1710.52	1495.68	1357.56	1263.08	1195.66
60000	5594.03	3090.52	2268.22	1866.02	1631.66	1480.98	1377.90	1304.36
65000	6060.20	3348.06	2457.24	2021.53	1767.63	1604.39	1492.73	1413.06
70000	6526.37	3605.60	2646.25	2177.03	1903.60	1727.81	1607.55	1521.75
75000	6992.54	3863.14	2835.27	2332.53	2039.57	1851.22	1722.38	1630.45
80000	7458.71	4120.69	3024.29	2488.03	2175.54	1974.64	1837.20	1739.15
85000	7924.88	4378.23	3213.31	2643.53	2311.51	2098.05	1952.02	1847.84
90000	8391.05	4635.77	3402.32	2799.03	2447.48	2221.46	2066.85	1956.54
95000	8857.22	4893.32	3591.34	2954.54	2583.45	2344.88	2181.67	2065.23
100000	9323.38	5150.86	3780.36	3110.04	2719.42	2468.29	2296.50	2173.93
105000	9789.55	5408.40	3969.38	3265.54	2855.39	2591.71	2411.32	2282.63
110000	10255.72	5665.94	4158.40	3421.04	2991.36	2715.12	2526.15	2391.32
115000	10721.89	5923.49	4347.41	3576.54	3127.34	2838.54	2640.97	2500.02
120000	11188.06	6181.03	4536.43	3732.04	3263.31	2961.95	2755.80	2608.72
125000	11654.23	6438.57	4725.45	3887.54	3399.28	3085.37	2870.62	2717.41
130000	12120.40	6696.11	4914.47	4043.05	3535.25	3208.78	2985.45	2826.11
135000	12586.57	6953.66	5103.48	4198.55	3671.22	3332.19	3100.27	2934.81
140000	13052.74	7211.20	5292.50	4354.05	3807.19	3455.61	3215.10	3043.50
145000	13518.91	7468.74	5481.52	4509.55	3943.16	3579.02	3329.92	3152.20
150000	13985.07	7726.28	5670.54	4665.05	4079.13	3702.44	3444.75	3260.89
155000	14451.24	7983.83	5859.56	4820.55	4215.10	3825.85	3559.57	3369.59
160000	14917.41	8241.37	6048.56	4976.06	4351.07	3949.27	3674.40	3478.29

104

AMOUNT OF LOAN	NUMBER OF YEARS IN TERM							
	9	10	15	20	25	30	35	40
$ 50	1.05	1.01	.93	.90	.90	.89	.89	.89
100	2.09	2.02	1.85	1.80	1.79	1.78	1.78	1.78
200	4.17	4.04	3.70	3.60	3.57	3.55	3.55	3.55
300	6.26	6.05	5.55	5.40	5.35	5.33	5.32	5.32
400	8.34	8.07	7.40	7.19	7.13	7.10	7.09	7.09
500	10.42	10.09	9.25	8.99	8.91	8.88	8.86	8.86
600	12.51	12.10	11.10	10.79	10.69	10.65	10.64	10.63
700	14.59	14.12	12.95	12.59	12.47	12.42	12.41	12.40
800	16.68	16.13	14.80	14.38	14.25	14.20	14.18	14.17
900	18.76	18.15	16.65	16.18	16.03	15.97	15.95	15.95
1000	20.84	20.17	18.50	17.98	17.81	17.75	17.72	17.72
2000	41.68	40.33	36.99	35.95	35.61	35.49	35.44	35.43
3000	62.52	60.49	55.48	53.93	53.41	53.23	53.16	53.14
4000	83.36	80.65	73.98	71.90	71.21	70.97	70.88	70.85
5000	104.20	100.81	92.47	89.88	89.01	88.71	88.60	88.57
6000	125.03	120.97	110.96	107.85	106.81	106.45	106.32	106.28
7000	145.87	141.14	129.46	125.83	124.61	124.19	124.04	123.99
8000	166.71	161.30	147.95	143.80	142.41	141.93	141.76	141.70
9000	187.55	181.46	166.44	161.77	160.21	159.67	159.48	159.41
10000	208.39	201.62	184.94	179.75	178.01	177.41	177.20	177.13
11000	229.23	221.78	203.43	197.72	195.81	195.15	194.92	194.84
12000	250.06	241.94	221.92	215.70	213.61	212.89	212.64	212.55
13000	270.90	262.10	240.42	233.67	231.41	230.63	230.36	230.26
14000	291.74	282.27	258.91	251.65	249.21	248.37	248.08	247.98
15000	312.58	302.43	277.40	269.62	267.01	266.11	265.80	265.69
16000	333.42	322.59	295.90	287.60	284.81	283.85	283.52	283.40
17000	354.26	342.75	314.39	305.57	302.61	301.59	301.24	301.11
18000	375.09	362.91	332.88	323.54	320.41	319.33	318.96	318.82
19000	395.93	383.07	351.38	341.52	338.21	337.07	336.67	336.54
20000	416.77	403.23	369.87	359.49	356.01	354.81	354.39	354.25
21000	437.61	423.40	388.36	377.47	373.81	372.55	372.11	371.96
22000	458.45	443.56	406.86	395.44	391.61	390.29	389.83	389.67
23000	479.29	463.72	425.35	413.42	409.41	408.03	407.55	407.39
24000	500.12	483.88	443.84	431.39	427.21	425.77	425.27	425.10
25000	520.96	504.04	462.34	449.37	445.01	443.51	442.99	442.81
26000	541.80	524.20	480.83	467.34	462.81	461.25	460.71	460.52
27000	562.64	544.36	499.32	485.31	480.61	478.99	478.43	478.23
28000	583.48	564.53	517.82	503.29	498.41	496.73	496.15	495.95
29000	604.32	584.69	536.31	521.26	516.21	514.47	513.87	513.66
30000	625.15	604.85	554.80	539.24	534.01	532.21	531.59	531.37
31000	645.99	625.01	573.30	557.21	551.81	549.95	549.31	549.08
32000	666.83	645.17	591.79	575.19	569.61	567.69	567.03	566.80
33000	687.67	665.33	610.28	593.16	587.41	585.43	584.75	584.51
34000	708.51	685.50	628.77	611.14	605.21	603.17	602.47	602.22
35000	729.35	705.66	647.27	629.11	623.01	620.92	620.19	619.93
40000	833.54	806.46	739.73	718.98	712.02	709.62	708.78	708.49
45000	937.73	907.27	832.20	808.85	801.02	798.32	797.38	797.05
50000	1041.92	1008.08	924.67	898.73	890.02	887.02	885.98	885.62
55000	1146.11	1108.89	1017.13	988.60	979.02	975.72	974.58	974.18
60000	1250.30	1209.69	1109.60	1078.47	1068.02	1064.42	1063.17	1062.74
65000	1354.50	1310.50	1202.07	1168.34	1157.02	1153.12	1151.77	1151.30
70000	1458.69	1411.31	1294.53	1258.22	1246.02	1241.83	1240.37	1239.86
75000	1562.88	1512.12	1387.00	1348.09	1335.02	1330.53	1328.97	1328.42
80000	1667.07	1612.92	1479.46	1437.96	1424.03	1419.23	1417.56	1416.98
85000	1771.26	1713.73	1571.93	1527.83	1513.03	1507.93	1506.16	1505.54
90000	1875.45	1814.54	1664.40	1617.70	1602.03	1596.63	1594.76	1594.10
95000	1979.65	1915.35	1756.86	1707.58	1691.03	1685.33	1683.35	1682.67
100000	2083.84	2016.15	1849.33	1797.45	1780.03	1774.03	1771.95	1771.23
105000	2188.03	2116.96	1941.79	1887.32	1869.03	1862.74	1860.55	1859.79
110000	2292.22	2217.77	2034.26	1977.19	1958.03	1951.44	1949.15	1948.35
115000	2396.41	2318.57	2126.73	2067.07	2047.03	2040.14	2037.74	2036.91
120000	2500.60	2419.38	2219.19	2156.94	2136.04	2128.84	2126.34	2125.47
125000	2604.80	2520.19	2311.66	2246.81	2225.04	2217.54	2214.94	2214.03
130000	2708.99	2621.00	2404.13	2336.68	2314.04	2306.24	2303.54	2302.59
135000	2813.18	2721.80	2496.59	2426.55	2403.04	2394.94	2392.13	2391.15
140000	2917.37	2822.61	2589.06	2516.43	2492.04	2483.65	2480.73	2479.72
145000	3021.56	2923.42	2681.52	2606.30	2581.04	2572.35	2569.33	2568.28
150000	3125.75	3024.23	2773.99	2696.17	2670.04	2661.05	2657.93	2656.84
155000	3229.95	3125.03	2866.46	2786.04	2759.04	2749.75	2746.52	2745.40
160000	3334.14	3225.84	2958.92	2875.92	2848.05	2838.45	2835.12	2833.96

AMOUNT OF LOAN	NUMBER OF YEARS IN TERM							
	1	2	3	4	5	6	7	8
$ 50	4.67	2.59	1.90	1.57	1.37	1.25	1.16	1.10
100	9.34	5.17	3.80	3.13	2.74	2.49	2.32	2.19
200	18.68	10.33	7.59	6.25	5.47	4.97	4.63	4.38
300	28.01	15.49	11.38	9.38	8.21	7.45	6.94	6.57
400	37.35	20.66	15.18	12.50	10.94	9.94	9.25	8.76
500	46.68	25.82	18.97	15.62	13.67	12.42	11.56	10.95
600	56.02	30.98	22.76	18.75	16.41	14.90	13.88	13.14
700	65.35	36.15	26.56	21.87	19.14	17.39	16.19	15.33
800	74.69	41.31	30.35	24.99	21.87	19.87	18.50	17.52
900	84.02	46.47	34.14	28.12	24.61	22.35	20.81	19.71
1000	93.36	51.64	37.94	31.24	27.34	24.84	23.12	21.90
2000	186.71	103.27	75.87	62.48	54.68	49.67	46.24	43.80
3000	280.07	154.90	113.80	93.71	82.01	74.50	69.36	65.70
4000	373.42	206.53	151.73	124.95	109.35	99.33	92.48	87.60
5000	466.77	258.16	189.67	156.18	136.68	124.16	115.60	109.50
6000	560.13	309.79	227.60	187.42	164.02	148.99	138.71	131.39
7000	653.48	361.43	265.53	218.65	191.35	173.82	161.83	153.29
8000	746.84	413.06	303.46	249.89	218.69	198.65	184.95	175.19
9000	840.19	464.69	341.40	281.12	246.02	223.48	208.07	197.09
10000	933.54	516.32	379.33	312.36	273.36	248.31	231.19	218.99
11000	1026.90	567.95	417.26	343.59	300.69	273.14	254.30	240.88
12000	1120.25	619.58	455.19	374.83	328.03	297.97	277.42	262.78
13000	1213.61	671.22	493.12	406.06	355.36	322.80	300.54	284.68
14000	1306.96	722.85	531.06	437.30	382.70	347.63	323.66	306.58
15000	1400.31	774.48	568.99	468.53	410.04	372.46	346.78	328.48
16000	1493.67	826.11	606.92	499.77	437.37	397.29	369.90	350.37
17000	1587.02	877.74	644.85	531.00	464.71	422.12	393.01	372.27
18000	1680.38	929.37	682.79	562.24	492.04	446.95	416.13	394.17
19000	1773.73	981.00	720.72	593.47	519.38	471.78	439.25	416.07
20000	1867.08	1032.64	758.65	624.71	546.71	496.61	462.37	437.97
21000	1960.44	1084.27	796.58	655.95	574.05	521.44	485.49	459.86
22000	2053.79	1135.90	834.52	687.18	601.38	546.27	508.60	481.76
23000	2147.14	1187.53	872.45	718.42	628.72	571.10	531.72	503.66
24000	2240.50	1239.16	910.38	749.65	656.05	595.93	554.84	525.56
25000	2333.85	1290.79	948.31	780.89	683.39	620.76	577.96	547.46
26000	2427.21	1342.43	986.24	812.12	710.72	645.59	601.08	569.35
27000	2520.56	1394.06	1024.18	843.36	738.06	670.42	624.19	591.25
28000	2613.91	1445.69	1062.11	874.59	765.40	695.25	647.31	613.15
29000	2707.27	1497.32	1100.04	905.83	792.73	720.08	670.43	635.05
30000	2800.62	1548.95	1137.97	937.06	820.07	744.91	693.55	656.95
31000	2893.98	1600.58	1175.91	968.30	847.40	769.74	716.67	678.84
32000	2987.33	1652.22	1213.84	999.53	874.74	794.57	739.79	700.74
33000	3080.68	1703.85	1251.77	1030.77	902.07	819.40	762.90	722.64
34000	3174.04	1755.48	1289.70	1062.00	929.41	844.23	786.02	744.54
35000	3267.39	1807.11	1327.63	1093.24	956.74	869.06	809.14	766.44
40000	3734.16	2065.27	1517.30	1249.42	1093.42	993.21	924.73	875.93
45000	4200.93	2323.43	1706.96	1405.59	1230.10	1117.36	1040.32	985.42
50000	4667.70	2581.58	1896.62	1561.77	1366.77	1241.51	1155.91	1094.91
55000	5134.47	2839.74	2086.28	1717.94	1503.45	1365.67	1271.50	1204.40
60000	5601.24	3097.90	2275.94	1874.12	1640.13	1489.82	1387.09	1313.89
65000	6068.01	3356.06	2465.60	2030.30	1776.80	1613.97	1502.68	1423.38
70000	6534.78	3614.21	2655.26	2186.47	1913.48	1738.12	1618.27	1532.87
75000	7001.55	3872.37	2844.93	2342.65	2050.16	1862.27	1733.87	1642.36
80000	7468.32	4130.53	3034.59	2498.83	2186.84	1986.42	1849.46	1751.85
85000	7935.09	4388.69	3224.25	2655.00	2323.51	2110.57	1965.05	1861.34
90000	8401.86	4646.85	3413.91	2811.18	2460.19	2234.72	2080.64	1970.83
95000	8868.63	4905.00	3603.57	2967.35	2596.87	2358.87	2196.23	2080.32
100000	9335.40	5163.16	3793.23	3123.53	2733.54	2483.02	2311.82	2189.81
105000	9802.17	5421.32	3982.89	3279.71	2870.22	2607.18	2427.41	2299.30
110000	10268.94	5679.48	4172.56	3435.88	3006.90	2731.33	2543.00	2408.79
115000	10735.70	5937.64	4362.22	3592.06	3143.57	2855.48	2658.59	2518.28
120000	11202.47	6195.79	4551.88	3748.24	3280.25	2979.63	2774.18	2627.77
125000	11669.24	6453.95	4741.54	3904.41	3416.93	3103.78	2889.77	2737.26
130000	12136.01	6712.11	4931.20	4060.59	3553.60	3227.93	3005.36	2846.75
135000	12602.78	6970.27	5120.86	4216.76	3690.28	3352.08	3120.95	2956.24
140000	13069.55	7228.42	5310.52	4372.94	3826.96	3476.23	3236.54	3065.73
145000	13536.32	7486.58	5500.18	4529.12	3963.64	3600.38	3352.13	3175.22
150000	14003.09	7744.74	5689.85	4685.29	4100.31	3724.53	3467.73	3284.71
155000	14469.86	8002.90	5879.51	4841.47	4236.99	3848.69	3583.32	3394.20
160000	14936.63	8261.06	6069.17	4997.65	4373.67	3972.84	3698.91	3503.69

AMOUNT OF LOAN	NUMBER OF YEARS IN TERM							
	9	10	15	20	25	30	35	40
$ 50	1.06	1.02	.94	.91	.91	.90	.90	.90
100	2.11	2.04	1.87	1.82	1.81	1.80	1.80	1.80
200	4.21	4.07	3.74	3.64	3.61	3.59	3.59	3.59
300	6.31	6.10	5.61	5.46	5.41	5.39	5.38	5.38
400	8.41	8.14	7.48	7.27	7.21	7.18	7.18	7.17
500	10.51	10.17	9.35	9.09	9.01	8.98	8.97	8.97
600	12.61	12.20	11.21	10.91	10.81	10.77	10.76	10.76
700	14.71	14.24	13.08	12.73	12.61	12.57	12.55	12.55
800	16.81	16.27	14.95	14.54	14.41	14.36	14.35	14.34
900	18.91	18.30	16.82	16.36	16.21	16.16	16.14	16.13
1000	21.01	20.34	18.69	18.18	18.01	17.95	17.93	17.93
2000	42.01	40.67	37.37	36.35	36.01	35.90	35.86	35.85
3000	63.01	61.00	56.05	54.52	54.02	53.85	53.79	53.77
4000	84.01	81.33	74.73	72.70	72.02	71.79	71.71	71.69
5000	105.02	101.66	93.41	90.87	90.03	89.74	89.64	89.61
6000	126.02	121.99	112.09	109.04	108.03	107.69	107.57	107.53
7000	147.02	142.32	130.77	127.21	126.03	125.63	125.49	125.45
8000	168.02	162.65	149.45	145.39	144.04	143.58	143.42	143.37
9000	189.03	182.98	168.13	163.56	162.04	161.53	161.35	161.29
10000	210.03	203.31	186.81	181.73	180.05	179.47	179.28	179.21
11000	231.03	223.64	205.49	199.91	198.05	197.42	197.20	197.13
12000	252.03	243.97	224.18	218.08	216.05	215.37	215.13	215.05
13000	273.04	264.30	242.86	236.25	234.06	233.31	233.06	232.97
14000	294.04	284.63	261.54	254.42	252.06	251.26	250.98	250.89
15000	315.04	304.96	280.22	272.60	270.07	269.21	268.91	268.81
16000	336.04	325.29	298.90	290.77	288.07	287.15	286.84	286.73
17000	357.04	345.62	317.58	308.94	306.07	305.10	304.76	304.65
18000	378.05	365.95	336.26	327.12	324.08	323.05	322.69	322.57
19000	399.05	386.28	354.94	345.29	342.08	340.99	340.62	340.49
20000	420.05	406.61	373.62	363.46	360.09	358.94	358.55	358.41
21000	441.05	426.94	392.30	381.63	378.09	376.89	376.47	376.33
22000	462.06	447.27	410.98	399.81	396.10	394.83	394.40	394.25
23000	483.06	467.60	429.66	417.98	414.10	412.78	412.33	412.17
24000	504.06	487.93	448.35	436.15	432.10	430.73	430.25	430.09
25000	525.06	508.26	467.03	454.33	450.11	448.67	448.18	448.01
26000	546.07	528.59	485.71	472.50	468.11	466.62	466.11	465.93
27000	567.07	548.92	504.39	490.67	486.12	484.57	484.03	483.85
28000	588.07	569.25	523.07	508.84	504.12	502.51	501.96	501.77
29000	609.07	589.58	541.75	527.02	522.12	520.46	519.89	519.69
30000	630.07	609.92	560.43	545.19	540.13	538.41	537.82	537.61
31000	651.08	630.25	579.11	563.36	558.13	556.35	555.74	555.53
32000	672.08	650.58	597.79	581.54	576.14	574.30	573.67	573.45
33000	693.08	670.91	616.47	599.71	594.14	592.25	591.60	591.37
34000	714.08	691.24	635.15	617.88	612.14	610.19	609.52	609.29
35000	735.09	711.57	653.83	636.05	630.15	628.14	627.45	627.21
40000	840.10	813.22	747.24	726.92	720.17	717.87	717.09	716.81
45000	945.11	914.87	840.64	817.78	810.19	807.61	806.72	806.42
50000	1050.12	1016.52	934.05	908.65	900.21	897.34	896.36	896.02
55000	1155.13	1118.17	1027.45	999.51	990.23	987.07	985.99	985.62
60000	1260.14	1219.83	1120.86	1090.37	1080.25	1076.81	1075.63	1075.22
65000	1365.16	1321.48	1214.26	1181.24	1170.27	1166.54	1165.26	1164.82
70000	1470.17	1423.13	1307.66	1272.10	1260.29	1256.27	1254.90	1254.42
75000	1575.18	1524.78	1401.07	1362.97	1350.31	1346.01	1344.53	1344.02
80000	1680.19	1626.43	1494.47	1453.83	1440.33	1435.74	1434.17	1433.62
85000	1785.20	1728.08	1587.88	1544.69	1530.35	1525.47	1523.80	1523.22
90000	1890.21	1829.74	1681.28	1635.56	1620.37	1615.21	1613.44	1612.83
95000	1995.23	1931.39	1774.69	1726.42	1710.40	1704.94	1703.07	1702.43
100000	2100.24	2033.04	1868.09	1817.29	1800.42	1794.67	1792.71	1792.03
105000	2205.25	2134.69	1961.49	1908.15	1890.44	1884.41	1882.34	1881.63
110000	2310.26	2236.34	2054.90	1999.01	1980.46	1974.14	1971.98	1971.23
115000	2415.27	2337.99	2148.30	2089.88	2070.48	2063.88	2061.61	2060.83
120000	2520.28	2439.65	2241.71	2180.74	2160.50	2153.61	2151.25	2150.43
125000	2625.29	2541.30	2335.11	2271.61	2250.52	2243.34	2240.88	2240.03
130000	2730.31	2642.95	2428.52	2362.47	2340.54	2333.08	2330.52	2329.63
135000	2835.32	2744.60	2521.92	2453.33	2430.56	2422.81	2420.15	2419.24
140000	2940.33	2846.25	2615.32	2544.20	2520.58	2512.54	2509.79	2508.84
145000	3045.34	2947.90	2708.73	2635.06	2610.60	2602.28	2599.42	2598.44
150000	3150.35	3049.56	2802.13	2725.93	2700.62	2692.01	2689.06	2688.04
155000	3255.36	3151.21	2895.54	2816.79	2790.64	2781.74	2778.69	2777.64
160000	3360.38	3252.86	2988.94	2907.66	2880.66	2871.48	2868.33	2867.24

21.750%   MONTHLY AMORTIZING PAYMENTS

AMOUNT OF LOAN	NUMBER OF YEARS IN TERM							
	1	2	3	4	5	6	7	8
$ 50	4.68	2.59	1.91	1.57	1.38	1.25	1.17	1.11
100	9.35	5.18	3.81	3.14	2.75	2.50	2.33	2.21
200	18.70	10.36	7.62	6.28	5.50	5.00	4.66	4.42
300	28.05	15.53	11.42	9.42	8.25	7.50	6.99	6.62
400	37.39	20.71	15.23	12.55	11.00	10.00	9.31	8.83
500	46.74	25.88	19.04	15.69	13.74	12.49	11.64	11.03
600	56.09	31.06	22.84	18.83	16.49	14.99	13.97	13.24
700	65.44	36.23	26.65	21.96	19.24	17.49	16.30	15.45
800	74.78	41.41	30.45	25.10	21.99	19.99	18.62	17.65
900	84.13	46.58	34.26	28.24	24.73	22.49	20.95	19.86
1000	93.48	51.76	38.07	31.38	27.48	24.98	23.28	22.06
2000	186.95	103.51	76.13	62.75	54.96	49.96	46.55	44.12
3000	280.43	155.27	114.19	94.12	82.44	74.94	69.82	66.18
4000	373.90	207.02	152.25	125.49	109.91	99.92	93.09	88.23
5000	467.38	258.78	190.31	156.86	137.39	124.89	116.36	110.29
6000	560.85	310.53	228.37	188.23	164.87	149.87	139.64	132.35
7000	654.32	362.29	266.43	219.60	192.34	174.85	162.91	154.41
8000	747.80	414.04	304.49	250.97	219.82	199.83	186.18	176.46
9000	841.27	465.80	342.56	282.34	247.30	224.81	209.45	198.52
10000	934.75	517.55	380.62	313.71	274.77	249.78	232.72	220.58
11000	1028.22	569.31	418.68	345.08	302.25	274.76	255.99	242.64
12000	1121.69	621.06	456.74	376.45	329.73	299.74	279.27	264.69
13000	1215.17	672.82	494.80	407.82	357.21	324.72	302.54	286.75
14000	1308.64	724.57	532.86	439.19	384.68	349.70	325.81	308.81
15000	1402.12	776.33	570.92	470.56	412.16	374.67	349.08	330.86
16000	1495.59	828.08	608.98	501.93	439.64	399.65	372.35	352.92
17000	1589.06	879.84	647.05	533.30	467.11	424.63	395.63	374.98
18000	1682.54	931.59	685.11	564.67	494.59	449.61	418.90	397.04
19000	1776.01	983.35	723.17	596.04	522.07	474.59	442.17	419.09
20000	1869.49	1035.10	761.23	627.42	549.54	499.56	465.44	441.15
21000	1962.96	1086.86	799.29	658.79	577.02	524.54	488.71	463.21
22000	2056.44	1138.61	837.35	690.16	604.50	549.52	511.98	485.27
23000	2149.91	1190.36	875.41	721.53	631.98	574.50	535.26	507.32
24000	2243.38	1242.12	913.47	752.90	659.45	599.48	558.53	529.38
25000	2336.86	1293.87	951.54	784.27	686.93	624.45	581.80	551.44
26000	2430.33	1345.63	989.60	815.64	714.41	649.43	605.07	573.49
27000	2523.81	1397.38	1027.66	847.01	741.88	674.41	628.34	595.55
28000	2617.28	1449.14	1065.72	878.38	769.36	699.39	651.62	617.61
29000	2710.75	1500.89	1103.78	909.75	796.84	724.37	674.89	639.67
30000	2804.23	1552.65	1141.84	941.12	824.31	749.34	698.16	661.72
31000	2897.70	1604.40	1179.90	972.49	851.79	774.32	721.43	683.78
32000	2991.18	1656.16	1217.96	1003.86	879.27	799.30	744.70	705.84
33000	3084.65	1707.91	1256.03	1035.23	906.74	824.28	767.97	727.90
34000	3178.12	1759.67	1294.09	1066.60	934.22	849.26	791.25	749.95
35000	3271.60	1811.42	1332.15	1097.97	961.70	874.23	814.52	772.01
40000	3738.97	2070.20	1522.45	1254.83	1099.08	999.12	930.88	882.30
45000	4206.34	2328.97	1712.76	1411.68	1236.47	1124.01	1047.24	992.58
50000	4673.71	2587.74	1903.07	1568.53	1373.85	1248.90	1163.60	1102.87
55000	5141.08	2846.52	2093.37	1725.38	1511.24	1373.79	1279.95	1213.16
60000	5608.45	3105.29	2283.68	1882.24	1648.62	1498.68	1396.31	1323.44
65000	6075.82	3364.07	2473.99	2039.09	1786.01	1623.57	1512.67	1433.73
70000	6543.19	3622.84	2664.29	2195.94	1923.39	1748.46	1629.03	1544.02
75000	7010.56	3881.61	2854.60	2352.79	2060.78	1873.35	1745.39	1654.30
80000	7477.93	4140.39	3044.90	2509.65	2198.16	1998.24	1861.75	1764.59
85000	7945.30	4399.16	3235.21	2666.50	2335.55	2123.13	1978.11	1874.88
90000	8412.67	4657.94	3425.52	2823.35	2472.93	2248.02	2094.47	1985.16
95000	8880.04	4916.71	3615.82	2980.20	2610.32	2372.91	2210.83	2095.45
100000	9347.42	5175.48	3806.13	3137.06	2747.70	2497.80	2327.19	2205.73
105000	9814.79	5434.26	3996.44	3293.91	2885.09	2622.69	2443.54	2316.02
110000	10282.16	5693.03	4186.74	3450.76	3022.47	2747.58	2559.90	2426.31
115000	10749.53	5951.80	4377.05	3607.61	3159.86	2872.47	2676.26	2536.59
120000	11216.90	6210.58	4567.35	3764.47	3297.24	2997.36	2792.62	2646.88
125000	11684.27	6469.35	4757.66	3921.32	3434.62	3122.25	2908.98	2757.17
130000	12151.64	6728.13	4947.97	4078.17	3572.01	3247.14	3025.34	2867.45
135000	12619.01	6986.90	5138.27	4235.02	3709.39	3372.03	3141.70	2977.74
140000	13086.38	7245.67	5328.58	4391.88	3846.78	3496.92	3258.06	3088.03
145000	13553.75	7504.45	5518.89	4548.73	3984.16	3621.81	3374.42	3198.31
150000	14021.12	7763.22	5709.19	4705.58	4121.55	3746.70	3490.78	3308.60
155000	14488.49	8022.00	5899.50	4862.43	4258.93	3871.59	3607.13	3418.89
160000	14955.86	8280.77	6089.80	5019.29	4396.32	3996.48	3723.49	3529.17

108

AMOUNT OF LOAN	NUMBER OF YEARS IN TERM							
	9	10	15	20	25	30	35	40
$ 50	1.06	1.03	.95	.92	.92	.91	.91	.91
100	2.12	2.05	1.89	1.84	1.83	1.82	1.82	1.82
200	4.24	4.10	3.78	3.68	3.65	3.64	3.63	3.63
300	6.36	6.15	5.67	5.52	5.47	5.45	5.45	5.44
400	8.47	8.20	7.55	7.35	7.29	7.27	7.26	7.26
500	10.59	10.25	9.44	9.19	9.11	9.08	9.07	9.07
600	12.71	12.30	11.33	11.03	10.93	10.90	10.89	10.88
700	14.82	14.35	13.21	12.87	12.75	12.71	12.70	12.69
800	16.94	16.40	15.10	14.70	14.57	14.53	14.51	14.51
900	19.06	18.45	16.99	16.54	16.39	16.34	16.33	16.32
1000	21.17	20.50	18.87	18.38	18.21	18.16	18.14	18.13
2000	42.34	41.00	37.74	36.75	36.42	36.31	36.27	36.26
3000	63.51	61.50	56.61	55.12	54.63	54.46	54.41	54.39
4000	84.67	82.00	75.48	73.49	72.84	72.62	72.54	72.52
5000	105.84	102.50	94.35	91.86	91.05	90.77	90.68	90.65
6000	127.01	123.00	113.22	110.23	109.25	108.92	108.81	108.77
7000	148.17	143.50	132.09	128.61	127.46	127.08	126.95	126.90
8000	169.34	164.00	150.96	146.98	145.67	145.23	145.08	145.03
9000	190.51	184.50	169.83	165.35	163.88	163.38	163.22	163.16
10000	211.67	205.00	188.69	183.72	182.09	181.54	181.35	181.29
11000	232.84	225.50	207.56	202.09	200.29	199.69	199.49	199.42
12000	254.01	246.00	226.43	220.46	218.50	217.84	217.62	217.54
13000	275.17	266.50	245.30	238.83	236.71	236.00	235.75	235.67
14000	296.34	287.00	264.17	257.21	254.92	254.15	253.89	253.80
15000	317.51	307.50	283.04	275.58	273.13	272.30	272.02	271.93
16000	338.67	328.00	301.91	293.95	291.34	290.46	290.16	290.06
17000	359.84	348.50	320.78	312.32	309.54	308.61	308.29	308.19
18000	381.01	369.00	339.65	330.69	327.75	326.76	326.43	326.31
19000	402.18	389.50	358.52	349.06	345.96	344.92	344.56	344.44
20000	423.34	410.00	377.38	367.44	364.17	363.07	362.70	362.57
21000	444.51	430.50	396.25	385.81	382.38	381.22	380.83	380.70
22000	465.68	451.00	415.12	404.18	400.58	399.38	398.97	398.83
23000	486.84	471.50	433.99	422.55	418.79	417.53	417.10	416.96
24000	508.01	492.00	452.86	440.92	437.00	435.68	435.24	435.08
25000	529.18	512.50	471.73	459.29	455.21	453.84	453.37	453.21
26000	550.34	533.00	490.60	477.66	473.42	471.99	471.50	471.34
27000	571.51	553.50	509.47	496.04	491.63	490.14	489.64	489.47
28000	592.68	574.00	528.34	514.41	509.83	508.30	507.77	507.60
29000	613.84	594.50	547.20	532.78	528.04	526.45	525.91	525.72
30000	635.01	615.00	566.07	551.15	546.25	544.60	544.04	543.85
31000	656.18	635.50	584.94	569.52	564.46	562.75	562.18	561.98
32000	677.34	656.00	603.81	587.89	582.67	580.91	580.31	580.11
33000	698.51	676.50	622.68	606.27	600.87	599.06	598.45	598.24
34000	719.68	697.00	641.55	624.64	619.08	617.21	616.58	616.37
35000	740.84	717.50	660.42	643.01	637.29	635.37	634.72	634.49
40000	846.68	819.99	754.76	734.87	728.33	726.13	725.39	725.14
45000	952.51	922.49	849.11	826.72	819.37	816.90	816.06	815.78
50000	1058.35	1024.99	943.45	918.58	910.41	907.67	906.73	906.42
55000	1164.18	1127.49	1037.80	1010.44	1001.45	998.43	997.41	997.06
60000	1270.02	1229.99	1132.14	1102.30	1092.49	1089.20	1088.08	1087.70
65000	1375.85	1332.49	1226.49	1194.15	1183.54	1179.96	1178.75	1178.34
70000	1481.68	1434.99	1320.83	1286.01	1274.58	1270.73	1269.43	1268.98
75000	1587.52	1537.49	1415.18	1377.87	1365.62	1361.50	1360.10	1359.62
80000	1693.35	1639.98	1509.52	1469.73	1456.66	1452.26	1450.77	1450.27
85000	1799.19	1742.48	1603.87	1561.59	1547.70	1543.03	1541.45	1540.91
90000	1905.02	1844.98	1698.21	1653.44	1638.74	1633.79	1632.12	1631.55
95000	2010.86	1947.48	1792.56	1745.30	1729.78	1724.56	1722.79	1722.19
100000	2116.69	2049.98	1886.90	1837.16	1820.82	1815.33	1813.46	1812.83
105000	2222.52	2152.48	1981.25	1929.02	1911.86	1906.09	1904.14	1903.47
110000	2328.36	2254.98	2075.59	2020.87	2002.90	1996.86	1994.81	1994.11
115000	2434.19	2357.48	2169.94	2112.73	2093.94	2087.63	2085.48	2084.76
120000	2540.03	2459.97	2264.28	2204.59	2184.98	2178.39	2176.16	2175.40
125000	2645.86	2562.47	2358.63	2296.45	2276.03	2269.16	2266.83	2266.04
130000	2751.69	2664.97	2452.97	2388.30	2367.07	2359.92	2357.50	2356.68
135000	2857.53	2767.47	2547.31	2480.16	2458.11	2450.69	2448.18	2447.32
140000	2963.36	2869.97	2641.66	2572.02	2549.15	2541.46	2538.85	2537.96
145000	3069.20	2972.47	2736.00	2663.88	2640.19	2632.22	2629.52	2628.60
150000	3175.03	3074.97	2830.35	2755.74	2731.23	2722.99	2720.19	2719.24
155000	3280.87	3177.46	2924.69	2847.59	2822.27	2813.75	2810.87	2809.89
160000	3386.70	3279.96	3019.04	2939.45	2913.31	2904.52	2901.54	2900.53

22.000% MONTHLY AMORTIZING PAYMENTS

AMOUNT OF LOAN	NUMBER OF YEARS IN TERM							
	1	2	3	4	5	6	7	8
$ 50	4.68	2.60	1.91	1.58	1.39	1.26	1.18	1.12
100	9.36	5.19	3.82	3.16	2.77	2.52	2.35	2.23
200	18.72	10.38	7.64	6.31	5.53	5.03	4.69	4.45
300	28.08	15.57	11.46	9.46	8.29	7.54	7.03	6.67
400	37.44	20.76	15.28	12.61	11.05	10.06	9.38	8.89
500	46.80	25.94	19.10	15.76	13.81	12.57	11.72	11.11
600	56.16	31.13	22.92	18.91	16.58	15.08	14.06	13.34
700	65.52	36.32	26.74	22.06	19.34	17.59	16.40	15.56
800	74.88	41.51	30.56	25.21	22.10	20.11	18.75	17.78
900	84.24	46.70	34.38	28.36	24.86	22.62	21.09	20.00
1000	93.60	51.88	38.20	31.51	27.62	25.13	23.43	22.22
2000	187.19	103.76	76.39	63.02	55.24	50.26	46.86	44.44
3000	280.79	155.64	114.58	94.52	82.86	75.38	70.28	66.66
4000	374.38	207.52	152.77	126.03	110.48	100.51	93.71	88.87
5000	467.98	259.40	190.96	157.54	138.10	125.64	117.13	111.09
6000	561.57	311.27	229.15	189.04	165.72	150.76	140.56	133.31
7000	655.17	363.15	267.34	220.55	193.34	175.89	163.99	155.52
8000	748.76	415.03	305.53	252.05	220.96	201.01	187.41	177.74
9000	842.35	466.91	343.72	283.56	248.58	226.14	210.84	199.96
10000	935.95	518.79	381.91	315.07	276.19	251.27	234.26	222.18
11000	1029.54	570.66	420.10	346.57	303.81	276.39	257.69	244.39
12000	1123.14	622.54	458.29	378.08	331.43	301.52	281.12	266.61
13000	1216.73	674.42	496.48	409.58	359.05	326.64	304.54	288.83
14000	1310.33	726.30	534.67	441.09	386.67	351.77	327.97	311.04
15000	1403.92	778.18	572.86	472.60	414.29	376.90	351.39	333.26
16000	1497.52	830.06	611.05	504.10	441.91	402.02	374.82	355.48
17000	1591.11	881.93	649.24	535.61	469.53	427.15	398.25	377.70
18000	1684.70	933.81	687.43	567.11	497.15	452.28	421.67	399.91
19000	1778.30	985.69	725.62	598.62	524.76	477.40	445.10	422.13
20000	1871.89	1037.57	763.81	630.13	552.38	502.53	468.52	444.35
21000	1965.49	1089.45	802.00	661.63	580.00	527.65	491.95	466.56
22000	2059.08	1141.32	840.19	693.14	607.62	552.78	515.38	488.78
23000	2152.68	1193.20	878.39	724.64	635.24	577.91	538.80	511.00
24000	2246.27	1245.08	916.58	756.15	662.86	603.03	562.23	533.21
25000	2339.86	1296.96	954.77	787.66	690.48	628.16	585.65	555.43
26000	2433.46	1348.84	992.96	819.16	718.10	653.28	609.08	577.65
27000	2527.05	1400.72	1031.15	850.67	745.72	678.41	632.51	599.87
28000	2620.65	1452.59	1069.34	882.18	773.33	703.54	655.93	622.08
29000	2714.24	1504.47	1107.53	913.68	800.95	728.66	679.36	644.30
30000	2807.84	1556.35	1145.72	945.19	828.57	753.79	702.78	666.52
31000	2901.43	1608.23	1183.91	976.69	856.19	778.91	726.21	688.73
32000	2995.03	1660.11	1222.10	1008.20	883.81	804.04	749.64	710.95
33000	3088.62	1711.98	1260.29	1039.71	911.43	829.17	773.06	733.17
34000	3182.21	1763.86	1298.48	1071.21	939.05	854.29	796.49	755.39
35000	3275.31	1815.74	1336.67	1102.72	966.67	879.42	819.91	777.60
40000	3743.78	2075.13	1527.62	1260.25	1104.76	1005.05	937.04	888.69
45000	4211.75	2334.52	1718.58	1417.78	1242.86	1130.68	1054.17	999.77
50000	4679.72	2593.91	1909.53	1575.31	1380.95	1256.31	1171.30	1110.86
55000	5147.70	2853.30	2100.48	1732.84	1519.05	1381.94	1288.43	1221.94
60000	5615.67	3112.69	2291.43	1890.37	1657.14	1507.57	1405.56	1333.03
65000	6083.64	3372.09	2482.38	2047.90	1795.23	1633.20	1522.69	1444.12
70000	6551.61	3631.48	2673.34	2205.43	1933.33	1758.83	1639.82	1555.20
75000	7019.58	3890.87	2864.29	2362.96	2071.42	1884.46	1756.95	1666.29
80000	7487.56	4150.26	3055.24	2520.49	2209.52	2010.10	1874.08	1777.37
85000	7955.53	4409.65	3246.19	2678.02	2347.61	2135.73	1991.21	1888.46
90000	8423.50	4669.04	3437.15	2835.55	2485.71	2261.36	2108.34	1999.54
95000	8891.47	4928.43	3628.10	2993.08	2623.80	2386.99	2225.47	2110.63
100000	9359.44	5187.82	3819.05	3150.61	2761.90	2512.62	2342.60	2221.71
105000	9827.41	5447.21	4010.00	3308.14	2899.99	2638.25	2459.73	2332.80
110000	10295.39	5706.60	4200.95	3465.67	3038.09	2763.88	2576.86	2443.88
115000	10763.36	5965.99	4391.91	3623.20	3176.18	2889.51	2693.99	2554.97
120000	11231.33	6225.38	4582.86	3780.73	3314.27	3015.14	2811.12	2666.05
125000	11699.30	6484.77	4773.81	3938.26	3452.37	3140.77	2928.25	2777.14
130000	12167.27	6744.17	4964.76	4095.80	3590.46	3266.40	3045.38	2888.23
135000	12635.25	7003.56	5155.72	4253.33	3728.56	3392.03	3162.51	2999.31
140000	13103.22	7262.95	5346.67	4410.86	3866.65	3517.66	3279.64	3110.40
145000	13571.19	7522.34	5537.62	4568.39	4004.75	3643.29	3396.77	3221.48
150000	14039.16	7781.73	5728.57	4725.92	4142.84	3768.92	3513.90	3332.57
155000	14507.13	8041.12	5919.53	4883.45	4280.94	3894.55	3631.03	3443.65
160000	14975.11	8300.51	6110.48	5040.98	4419.03	4020.19	3748.16	3554.74

110

AMOUNT OF LOAN	NUMBER OF YEARS IN TERM							
	9	10	15	20	25	30	35	40
$ 50	1.07	1.04	.96	.93	.93	.92	.92	.92
100	2.14	2.07	1.91	1.86	1.86	1.85	1.84	1.84
200	4.27	4.14	3.82	3.72	3.69	3.68	3.67	3.67
300	6.40	6.21	5.72	5.58	5.53	5.51	5.51	5.51
400	8.54	8.27	7.63	7.43	7.37	7.35	7.34	7.34
500	10.67	10.34	9.53	9.29	9.21	9.18	9.18	9.17
600	12.80	12.41	11.44	11.15	11.05	11.02	11.01	11.01
700	14.94	14.47	13.35	13.00	12.89	12.86	12.84	12.84
800	17.07	16.54	15.25	14.86	14.73	14.69	14.68	14.67
900	19.20	18.61	17.16	16.72	16.58	16.53	16.51	16.51
1000	21.34	20.67	19.06	18.58	18.42	18.36	18.35	18.34
2000	42.67	41.34	38.12	37.15	36.83	36.72	36.69	36.68
3000	64.00	62.01	57.18	55.72	55.24	55.08	55.03	55.01
4000	85.33	82.68	76.24	74.29	73.65	73.44	73.37	73.35
5000	106.66	103.35	95.29	92.86	92.07	91.80	91.72	91.69
6000	128.00	124.02	114.35	111.43	110.48	110.16	110.06	110.02
7000	149.33	144.69	133.41	130.00	128.89	128.52	128.40	128.36
8000	170.66	165.36	152.47	148.57	147.30	146.88	146.74	146.70
9000	191.99	186.03	171.52	167.14	165.72	165.24	165.09	165.03
10000	213.32	206.70	190.58	185.71	184.13	183.60	183.43	183.37
11000	234.66	227.37	209.64	204.28	202.54	201.96	201.77	201.70
12000	255.99	248.04	228.70	222.85	220.95	220.32	220.11	220.04
13000	277.32	268.71	247.75	241.42	239.37	238.68	238.45	238.38
14000	298.65	289.38	266.81	259.99	257.78	257.04	256.80	256.71
15000	319.98	310.05	285.87	278.56	276.19	275.40	275.14	275.05
16000	341.32	330.72	304.93	297.13	294.60	293.76	293.48	293.39
17000	362.65	351.39	323.98	315.71	313.02	312.12	311.82	311.72
18000	383.98	372.06	343.04	334.28	331.43	330.48	330.17	330.06
19000	405.31	392.73	362.10	352.85	349.84	348.84	348.51	348.40
20000	426.64	413.40	381.16	371.42	368.25	367.20	366.85	366.73
21000	447.97	434.07	400.21	389.99	386.67	385.56	385.19	385.07
22000	469.31	454.74	419.27	408.56	405.08	403.92	403.53	403.40
23000	490.64	475.41	438.33	427.13	423.49	422.28	421.88	421.74
24000	511.97	496.08	457.39	445.70	441.90	440.64	440.22	440.08
25000	533.30	516.75	476.44	464.27	460.32	459.00	458.56	458.41
26000	554.63	537.42	495.50	482.84	478.73	477.36	476.90	476.75
27000	575.97	558.09	514.56	501.41	497.14	495.72	495.25	495.09
28000	597.30	578.76	533.62	519.98	515.55	514.08	513.59	513.42
29000	618.63	599.43	552.67	538.55	533.97	532.44	531.93	531.76
30000	639.96	620.10	571.73	557.12	552.38	550.80	550.27	550.09
31000	661.29	640.77	590.79	575.69	570.79	569.16	568.61	568.43
32000	682.63	661.44	609.85	594.26	589.20	587.52	586.96	586.77
33000	703.96	682.10	628.90	612.83	607.61	605.88	605.30	605.10
34000	725.29	702.77	647.96	631.41	626.03	624.24	623.64	623.44
35000	746.62	723.44	667.02	649.98	644.44	642.60	641.98	641.78
40000	853.28	826.79	762.31	742.83	736.50	734.40	733.69	733.46
45000	959.94	930.14	857.60	835.68	828.56	826.20	825.41	825.14
50000	1066.60	1033.49	952.88	928.53	920.63	918.00	917.12	916.82
55000	1173.26	1136.84	1048.17	1021.39	1012.69	1009.80	1008.83	1008.50
60000	1279.92	1240.19	1143.46	1114.24	1104.75	1100.54	1100.54	1100.18
65000	1386.58	1343.53	1238.75	1207.09	1196.81	1193.40	1192.25	1191.87
70000	1493.24	1446.88	1334.03	1299.95	1288.87	1285.19	1283.96	1283.55
75000	1599.90	1550.23	1429.32	1392.80	1380.94	1376.99	1375.67	1375.23
80000	1706.56	1653.58	1524.61	1485.65	1473.00	1468.79	1467.38	1466.91
85000	1813.22	1756.93	1619.90	1578.51	1565.06	1560.59	1559.10	1558.59
90000	1919.88	1860.28	1715.19	1671.36	1657.12	1652.39	1650.81	1650.27
95000	2026.54	1963.63	1810.47	1764.21	1749.19	1744.19	1742.52	1741.96
100000	2133.20	2066.97	1905.76	1857.06	1841.25	1835.99	1834.23	1833.64
105000	2239.85	2170.32	2001.05	1949.92	1933.31	1927.79	1925.94	1925.32
110000	2346.51	2273.67	2096.34	2042.77	2025.37	2019.59	2017.65	2017.00
115000	2453.17	2377.02	2191.62	2135.62	2117.43	2111.39	2109.36	2108.68
120000	2559.83	2480.37	2286.91	2228.48	2209.50	2203.19	2201.07	2200.36
125000	2666.49	2583.72	2382.20	2321.33	2301.56	2294.99	2292.78	2292.05
130000	2773.15	2687.06	2477.49	2414.18	2393.62	2386.79	2384.50	2383.73
135000	2879.81	2790.41	2572.78	2507.04	2485.68	2478.58	2476.21	2475.41
140000	2986.47	2893.76	2668.06	2599.89	2577.74	2570.38	2567.92	2567.09
145000	3093.13	2997.11	2763.35	2692.74	2669.81	2662.18	2659.63	2658.77
150000	3199.79	3100.46	2858.64	2785.59	2761.87	2753.98	2751.34	2750.45
155000	3306.45	3203.81	2953.93	2878.45	2853.93	2845.78	2843.05	2842.14
160000	3413.11	3307.16	3049.21	2971.30	2945.99	2937.58	2934.76	2933.82

22.250% MONTHLY AMORTIZING PAYMENTS

AMOUNT OF LOAN	NUMBER OF YEARS IN TERM							
	1	2	3	4	5	6	7	8
$ 50	4.69	2.61	1.92	1.59	1.39	1.27	1.18	1.12
100	9.38	5.21	3.84	3.17	2.78	2.53	2.36	2.24
200	18.75	10.41	7.67	6.33	5.56	5.06	4.72	4.48
300	28.12	15.61	11.50	9.50	8.33	7.59	7.08	6.72
400	37.49	20.81	15.33	12.66	11.11	10.11	9.44	8.96
500	46.86	26.01	19.16	15.83	13.89	12.64	11.80	11.19
600	56.23	31.21	23.00	18.99	16.66	15.17	14.15	13.43
700	65.61	36.41	26.83	22.15	19.44	17.70	16.51	15.67
800	74.98	41.61	30.66	25.32	22.21	20.22	18.87	17.91
900	84.35	46.81	34.49	28.48	24.99	22.75	21.23	20.14
1000	93.72	52.01	38.32	31.65	27.77	25.28	23.59	22.38
2000	187.43	104.01	76.64	63.29	55.53	50.55	47.17	44.76
3000	281.15	156.01	114.96	94.93	83.29	75.83	70.75	67.14
4000	374.86	208.01	153.28	126.57	111.05	101.10	94.33	89.51
5000	468.58	260.01	191.60	158.21	138.81	126.38	117.91	111.89
6000	562.29	312.01	229.92	189.86	166.57	151.65	141.49	134.27
7000	656.01	364.02	268.24	221.50	194.33	176.93	165.07	156.65
8000	749.72	416.02	306.56	253.14	222.09	202.20	188.65	179.02
9000	843.44	468.02	344.88	284.78	249.86	227.48	212.23	201.40
10000	937.15	520.02	383.20	316.42	277.62	252.75	235.81	223.78
11000	1030.87	572.02	421.52	348.07	305.38	278.03	259.39	246.16
12000	1124.58	624.03	459.84	379.71	333.14	303.30	282.97	268.53
13000	1218.30	676.03	498.16	411.35	360.90	328.58	306.55	290.91
14000	1312.01	728.03	536.48	442.99	388.66	353.85	330.13	313.29
15000	1405.73	780.03	574.80	474.63	416.42	379.13	353.71	335.67
16000	1499.44	832.03	613.12	506.28	444.18	404.40	377.29	358.04
17000	1593.16	884.03	651.44	537.92	471.95	429.68	400.87	380.42
18000	1686.87	936.04	689.76	569.56	499.71	454.95	424.46	402.80
19000	1780.59	988.04	728.08	601.20	527.47	480.22	448.04	425.17
20000	1874.30	1040.04	766.40	632.84	555.23	505.50	471.62	447.55
21000	1968.01	1092.04	804.72	664.49	582.99	530.77	495.20	469.93
22000	2061.73	1144.04	843.04	696.13	610.75	556.05	518.78	492.31
23000	2155.44	1196.04	881.36	727.77	638.51	581.32	542.36	514.68
24000	2249.16	1248.05	919.68	759.41	666.27	606.60	565.94	537.06
25000	2342.87	1300.05	958.00	791.05	694.04	631.87	589.52	559.44
26000	2436.59	1352.05	996.32	822.70	721.80	657.15	613.10	581.82
27000	2530.30	1404.05	1034.64	854.34	749.56	682.42	636.68	604.19
28000	2624.02	1456.05	1072.96	885.98	777.32	707.70	660.26	626.57
29000	2717.73	1508.05	1111.28	917.62	805.08	732.97	683.84	648.95
30000	2811.45	1560.06	1149.60	949.26	832.84	758.25	707.42	671.33
31000	2905.16	1612.06	1187.92	980.91	860.60	783.52	731.00	693.70
32000	2998.88	1664.06	1226.24	1012.55	888.36	808.80	754.58	716.08
33000	3092.59	1716.06	1264.56	1044.19	916.13	834.07	778.16	738.46
34000	3186.31	1768.06	1302.88	1075.83	943.89	859.35	801.74	760.84
35000	3280.02	1820.06	1341.20	1107.47	971.65	884.62	825.32	783.21
40000	3748.59	2080.07	1532.80	1265.68	1110.45	1010.99	943.23	895.10
45000	4217.17	2340.08	1724.40	1423.89	1249.26	1137.37	1061.13	1006.99
50000	4685.74	2600.09	1916.00	1582.10	1388.07	1263.74	1179.03	1118.87
55000	5154.32	2860.10	2107.60	1740.31	1526.87	1390.12	1296.94	1230.76
60000	5622.89	3120.11	2299.20	1898.52	1665.68	1516.49	1414.84	1342.65
65000	6091.46	3380.12	2490.80	2056.73	1804.49	1642.86	1532.74	1454.53
70000	6560.04	3640.12	2682.40	2214.94	1943.29	1769.24	1650.64	1566.42
75000	7028.61	3900.13	2874.00	2373.15	2082.10	1895.61	1768.55	1678.31
80000	7497.18	4160.14	3065.60	2531.36	2220.90	2021.98	1886.45	1790.19
85000	7965.76	4420.15	3257.20	2689.57	2359.71	2148.36	2004.35	1902.08
90000	8434.33	4680.16	3448.80	2847.78	2498.52	2274.73	2122.26	2013.97
95000	8902.91	4940.17	3640.40	3005.99	2637.32	2401.10	2240.16	2125.85
100000	9371.48	5200.17	3832.00	3164.20	2776.13	2527.48	2358.06	2237.74
105000	9840.05	5460.18	4023.60	3322.41	2914.94	2653.85	2475.96	2349.63
110000	10308.63	5720.19	4215.19	3480.62	3053.74	2780.23	2593.87	2461.51
115000	10777.20	5980.20	4406.79	3638.83	3192.55	2906.60	2711.77	2573.40
120000	11245.77	6240.21	4598.39	3797.04	3331.35	3032.97	2829.67	2685.29
125000	11714.35	6500.22	4789.99	3955.25	3470.16	3159.35	2947.57	2797.18
130000	12182.92	6760.23	4981.59	4113.46	3608.97	3285.72	3065.48	2909.06
135000	12651.49	7020.23	5173.19	4271.67	3747.77	3412.09	3183.38	3020.95
140000	13120.07	7280.24	5364.79	4429.88	3886.58	3538.47	3301.28	3132.84
145000	13588.64	7540.25	5556.39	4588.09	4025.39	3664.84	3419.19	3244.72
150000	14057.22	7800.26	5747.99	4746.30	4164.19	3791.22	3537.09	3356.61
155000	14525.79	8060.27	5939.59	4904.51	4303.00	3917.59	3654.99	3468.50
160000	14994.36	8320.28	6131.19	5062.72	4441.80	4043.96	3772.89	3580.38

MONTHLY AMORTIZING PAYMENTS 22.250%

AMOUNT OF LOAN	NUMBER OF YEARS IN TERM							
	9	10	15	20	25	30	35	40
$ 50	1.08	1.05	.97	.94	.94	.93	.93	.93
100	2.15	2.09	1.93	1.88	1.87	1.86	1.86	1.86
200	4.30	4.17	3.85	3.76	3.73	3.72	3.71	3.71
300	6.45	6.26	5.78	5.64	5.59	5.57	5.57	5.57
400	8.60	8.34	7.70	7.51	7.45	7.43	7.42	7.42
500	10.75	10.43	9.63	9.39	9.31	9.29	9.28	9.28
600	12.90	12.51	11.55	11.27	11.18	11.14	11.13	11.13
700	15.05	14.59	13.48	13.14	13.04	13.00	12.99	12.99
800	17.20	16.68	15.40	15.02	14.90	14.86	14.84	14.84
900	19.35	18.76	17.33	16.90	16.76	16.71	16.70	16.69
1000	21.50	20.85	19.25	18.77	18.62	18.57	18.55	18.55
2000	43.00	41.69	38.50	37.54	37.24	37.14	37.10	37.09
3000	64.50	62.53	57.74	56.31	55.86	55.70	55.65	55.64
4000	85.99	83.37	76.99	75.08	74.47	74.27	74.20	74.18
5000	107.49	104.21	96.24	93.85	93.09	92.84	92.75	92.73
6000	128.99	125.05	115.48	112.62	111.71	111.40	111.30	111.27
7000	150.49	145.89	134.73	131.39	130.32	129.97	129.85	129.82
8000	171.98	166.73	153.98	150.16	148.94	148.54	148.40	148.36
9000	193.48	187.57	173.22	168.93	167.56	167.10	166.95	166.90
10000	214.98	208.41	192.47	187.70	186.17	185.67	185.50	185.45
11000	236.48	229.25	211.72	206.47	204.79	204.24	204.05	203.99
12000	257.97	250.09	230.96	225.24	223.41	222.80	222.60	222.54
13000	279.47	270.93	250.21	244.01	242.02	241.37	241.15	241.08
14000	300.97	291.77	269.46	262.78	260.64	259.94	259.70	259.63
15000	322.47	312.61	288.70	281.55	279.26	278.50	278.25	278.17
16000	343.96	333.45	307.95	300.32	297.88	297.07	296.80	296.72
17000	365.46	354.29	327.20	319.09	316.49	315.64	315.35	315.26
18000	386.96	375.13	346.44	337.86	335.11	334.20	333.90	333.80
19000	408.46	395.97	365.69	356.63	353.73	352.77	352.45	352.35
20000	429.95	416.81	384.94	375.40	372.34	371.34	371.00	370.89
21000	451.45	437.65	404.18	394.17	390.96	389.90	389.55	389.44
22000	472.95	458.49	423.43	412.94	409.58	408.47	408.10	407.98
23000	494.45	479.33	442.68	431.71	428.19	427.04	426.65	426.53
24000	515.94	500.17	461.92	450.48	446.81	445.60	445.20	445.07
25000	537.44	521.01	481.17	469.25	465.43	464.17	463.75	463.62
26000	558.94	541.85	500.42	488.02	484.04	482.74	482.30	482.16
27000	580.44	562.69	519.66	506.79	502.66	501.30	500.85	500.70
28000	601.93	583.53	538.91	525.56	521.28	519.87	519.40	519.25
29000	623.43	604.37	558.16	544.33	539.89	538.44	537.95	537.79
30000	644.93	625.21	577.40	563.10	558.51	557.00	556.50	556.34
31000	666.43	646.05	596.65	581.87	577.13	575.57	575.05	574.88
32000	687.92	666.89	615.90	600.64	595.75	594.14	593.60	593.43
33000	709.42	687.73	635.14	619.41	614.36	612.70	612.15	611.97
34000	730.92	708.57	654.39	638.18	632.98	631.27	630.70	630.51
35000	752.42	729.41	673.64	656.95	651.60	649.84	649.25	649.06
40000	859.90	833.61	769.87	750.80	744.68	742.67	742.00	741.78
45000	967.39	937.81	866.10	844.65	837.76	835.50	834.75	834.50
50000	1074.88	1042.01	962.34	938.50	930.85	928.33	927.50	927.23
55000	1182.37	1146.21	1058.57	1032.35	1023.93	1021.17	1020.25	1019.95
60000	1289.85	1250.42	1154.80	1126.20	1117.02	1114.00	1113.00	1112.67
65000	1397.34	1354.62	1251.04	1220.05	1210.10	1206.83	1205.75	1205.39
70000	1504.83	1458.82	1347.27	1313.90	1303.19	1299.67	1298.50	1298.11
75000	1612.32	1563.02	1443.50	1407.75	1396.27	1392.50	1391.25	1390.84
80000	1719.80	1667.22	1539.74	1501.60	1489.36	1485.33	1484.00	1483.56
85000	1827.29	1771.42	1635.97	1595.45	1582.44	1578.16	1576.75	1576.28
90000	1934.78	1875.62	1732.20	1689.30	1675.52	1671.00	1669.50	1669.00
95000	2042.27	1979.82	1828.44	1783.15	1768.61	1763.83	1762.25	1761.72
100000	2149.75	2084.02	1924.67	1877.00	1861.69	1856.66	1855.00	1854.45
105000	2257.24	2188.22	2020.90	1970.85	1954.78	1949.50	1947.75	1947.17
110000	2364.73	2292.42	2117.14	2064.70	2047.86	2042.33	2040.50	2039.89
115000	2472.22	2396.62	2213.37	2158.55	2140.95	2135.16	2133.25	2132.61
120000	2579.70	2500.83	2309.60	2252.40	2234.03	2227.99	2226.00	2225.33
125000	2687.19	2605.03	2405.83	2346.25	2327.11	2320.83	2318.75	2318.06
130000	2794.68	2709.23	2502.07	2440.10	2420.20	2413.66	2411.50	2410.78
135000	2902.16	2813.43	2598.30	2533.95	2513.28	2506.49	2504.25	2503.50
140000	3009.65	2917.63	2694.53	2627.80	2606.37	2599.33	2597.00	2596.22
145000	3117.14	3021.83	2790.77	2721.65	2699.45	2692.16	2689.75	2688.94
150000	3224.63	3126.03	2887.00	2815.50	2792.54	2784.99	2782.49	2781.67
155000	3332.11	3230.23	2983.23	2909.35	2885.62	2877.82	2875.24	2874.39
160000	3439.60	3334.43	3079.47	3003.20	2978.71	2970.66	2967.99	2967.11

113

AMOUNT OF LOAN	NUMBER OF YEARS IN TERM							
	1	2	3	4	5	6	7	8
$ 50	4.70	2.61	1.93	1.59	1.40	1.28	1.19	1.13
100	9.39	5.22	3.85	3.18	2.80	2.55	2.38	2.26
200	18.77	10.43	7.69	6.36	5.59	5.09	4.75	4.51
300	28.16	15.64	11.54	9.54	8.38	7.63	7.13	6.77
400	37.54	20.86	15.38	12.72	11.17	10.17	9.50	9.02
500	46.92	26.07	19.23	15.89	13.96	12.72	11.87	11.27
600	56.31	31.28	23.07	19.07	16.75	15.26	14.25	13.53
700	65.69	36.49	26.92	22.25	19.54	17.80	16.62	15.78
800	75.07	41.71	30.76	25.43	22.33	20.34	18.99	18.04
900	84.46	46.92	34.61	28.61	25.12	22.89	21.37	20.29
1000	93.84	52.13	38.45	31.78	27.91	25.43	23.74	22.54
2000	187.68	104.26	76.90	63.56	55.81	50.85	47.48	45.08
3000	281.51	156.38	115.35	95.34	83.72	76.28	71.21	67.62
4000	375.35	208.51	153.80	127.12	111.62	101.70	94.95	90.16
5000	469.18	260.63	192.25	158.90	139.52	127.12	118.68	112.70
6000	563.02	312.76	230.70	190.67	167.43	152.55	142.42	135.23
7000	656.85	364.88	269.15	222.45	195.33	177.97	166.15	157.77
8000	750.69	417.01	307.60	254.23	223.24	203.40	189.89	180.31
9000	844.52	469.13	346.05	286.01	251.14	228.82	213.63	202.85
10000	938.36	521.26	384.50	317.79	279.04	254.24	237.36	225.39
11000	1032.19	573.38	422.95	349.56	306.95	279.67	261.10	247.92
12000	1126.03	625.51	461.40	381.34	334.85	305.09	284.83	270.46
13000	1219.86	677.64	499.85	413.12	362.76	330.51	308.57	293.00
14000	1313.70	729.76	538.30	444.90	390.66	355.94	332.30	315.54
15000	1407.53	781.89	576.75	476.68	418.56	381.36	356.04	338.08
16000	1501.37	834.01	615.20	508.46	446.47	406.79	379.78	360.62
17000	1595.20	886.14	653.65	540.23	474.37	432.21	403.51	383.15
18000	1689.04	938.26	692.10	572.01	502.28	457.63	427.25	405.69
19000	1782.87	990.39	730.55	603.79	530.18	483.06	450.98	428.23
20000	1876.71	1042.51	769.00	635.57	558.08	508.48	474.72	450.77
21000	1970.54	1094.64	807.45	667.35	585.99	533.90	498.45	473.31
22000	2064.38	1146.76	845.90	699.12	613.89	559.33	522.19	495.84
23000	2158.21	1198.89	884.35	730.90	641.80	584.75	545.92	518.38
24000	2252.05	1251.01	922.80	762.68	669.70	610.18	569.66	540.92
25000	2345.88	1303.14	961.25	794.46	697.60	635.60	593.40	563.46
26000	2439.72	1355.27	999.69	826.24	725.51	661.02	617.13	586.00
27000	2533.55	1407.39	1038.14	858.02	753.41	686.45	640.87	608.53
28000	2627.39	1459.52	1076.59	889.79	781.32	711.87	664.60	631.07
29000	2721.23	1511.64	1115.04	921.57	809.22	737.29	688.34	653.61
30000	2815.06	1563.77	1153.49	953.35	837.12	762.72	712.07	676.15
31000	2908.90	1615.89	1191.94	985.13	865.03	788.14	735.81	698.69
32000	3002.73	1668.02	1230.39	1016.91	892.93	813.57	759.55	721.23
33000	3096.57	1720.14	1268.84	1048.68	920.84	838.99	783.28	743.76
34000	3190.40	1772.27	1307.29	1080.46	948.74	864.41	807.02	766.30
35000	3284.24	1824.39	1345.74	1112.24	976.64	889.84	830.75	788.84
40000	3753.41	2085.02	1537.99	1271.13	1116.16	1016.96	949.43	901.53
45000	4222.59	2345.65	1730.24	1430.02	1255.68	1144.07	1068.11	1014.22
50000	4691.76	2606.27	1922.49	1588.91	1395.20	1271.19	1186.79	1126.91
55000	5160.94	2866.90	2114.73	1747.80	1534.72	1398.31	1305.47	1239.60
60000	5630.12	3127.53	2306.98	1906.69	1674.24	1525.43	1424.14	1352.29
65000	6099.29	3388.16	2499.23	2065.58	1813.76	1652.55	1542.82	1464.98
70000	6568.47	3648.78	2691.48	2224.48	1953.28	1779.67	1661.50	1577.68
75000	7037.64	3909.41	2883.73	2383.37	2092.80	1906.79	1780.18	1690.37
80000	7506.82	4170.04	3075.97	2542.26	2232.32	2033.91	1898.86	1803.06
85000	7976.00	4430.66	3268.22	2701.15	2371.84	2161.03	2017.53	1915.75
90000	8445.17	4691.29	3460.47	2860.04	2511.36	2288.14	2136.21	2028.44
95000	8914.35	4951.92	3652.72	3018.93	2650.88	2415.26	2254.89	2141.13
100000	9383.52	5212.54	3844.97	3177.82	2790.40	2542.38	2373.57	2253.82
105000	9852.70	5473.17	4037.21	3336.71	2929.92	2669.50	2492.25	2366.51
110000	10321.88	5733.80	4229.46	3495.60	3069.44	2796.62	2610.93	2479.20
115000	10791.05	5994.43	4421.71	3654.49	3208.96	2923.74	2729.60	2591.89
120000	11260.23	6255.05	4613.96	3813.38	3348.48	3050.86	2848.28	2704.58
125000	11729.40	6515.68	4806.21	3972.27	3488.00	3177.98	2966.96	2817.27
130000	12198.58	6776.31	4998.45	4131.16	3627.52	3305.09	3085.64	2929.96
135000	12667.75	7036.93	5190.70	4290.06	3767.04	3432.21	3204.32	3042.65
140000	13136.93	7297.56	5382.95	4448.95	3906.56	3559.33	3322.99	3155.35
145000	13606.11	7558.19	5575.20	4607.84	4046.08	3686.45	3441.67	3268.04
150000	14075.28	7818.81	5767.45	4766.73	4185.60	3813.57	3560.35	3380.73
155000	14544.46	8079.44	5959.69	4925.62	4325.12	3940.69	3679.03	3493.42
160000	15013.63	8340.07	6151.94	5084.51	4464.64	4067.81	3797.71	3606.11

AMOUNT OF LOAN	NUMBER OF YEARS IN TERM							
	9	10	15	20	25	30	35	40
$ 50	1.09	1.06	.98	.95	.95	.94	.94	.94
100	2.17	2.11	1.95	1.90	1.89	1.88	1.88	1.88
200	4.34	4.21	3.89	3.80	3.77	3.76	3.76	3.76
300	6.50	6.31	5.84	5.70	5.65	5.64	5.63	5.63
400	8.67	8.41	7.78	7.59	7.53	7.51	7.51	7.51
500	10.84	10.51	9.72	9.49	9.42	9.39	9.38	9.38
600	13.00	12.61	11.67	11.39	11.30	11.27	11.26	11.26
700	15.17	14.71	13.61	13.28	13.18	13.15	13.14	13.13
800	17.34	16.81	15.55	15.18	15.06	15.02	15.01	15.01
900	19.50	18.92	17.50	17.08	16.94	16.90	16.89	16.88
1000	21.67	21.02	19.44	18.97	18.83	18.78	18.76	18.76
2000	43.33	42.03	38.88	37.94	37.65	37.55	37.52	37.51
3000	65.00	63.04	58.31	56.91	56.47	56.33	56.28	56.26
4000	86.66	84.05	77.75	75.88	75.29	75.10	75.04	75.02
5000	108.32	105.06	97.19	94.85	94.11	93.87	93.79	93.77
6000	129.99	126.07	116.62	113.82	112.93	112.65	112.55	112.52
7000	151.65	147.08	136.06	132.79	131.76	131.42	131.31	131.27
8000	173.31	168.09	155.49	151.76	150.58	150.19	150.07	150.03
9000	194.98	189.11	174.93	170.73	169.40	168.97	168.82	168.78
10000	216.64	210.12	194.37	189.70	188.22	187.74	187.58	187.53
11000	238.30	231.13	213.80	208.67	207.04	206.51	206.34	206.28
12000	259.97	252.14	233.24	227.64	225.86	225.29	225.10	225.04
13000	281.63	273.15	252.68	246.61	244.68	244.06	243.85	243.79
14000	303.30	294.16	272.11	265.58	263.51	262.83	262.61	262.54
15000	324.96	315.17	291.55	284.55	282.33	281.61	281.37	281.29
16000	346.62	336.18	310.98	303.52	301.15	300.38	300.13	300.05
17000	368.29	357.20	330.42	322.49	319.97	319.15	318.89	318.80
18000	389.95	378.21	349.86	341.46	338.79	337.93	337.64	337.55
19000	411.61	399.22	369.29	360.43	357.61	356.70	356.40	356.30
20000	433.28	420.23	388.73	379.40	376.44	375.47	375.16	375.06
21000	454.94	441.24	408.16	398.37	395.26	394.25	393.92	393.81
22000	476.60	462.25	427.60	417.34	414.08	413.02	412.67	412.56
23000	498.27	483.26	447.04	436.31	432.90	431.79	431.43	431.31
24000	519.93	504.27	466.47	455.28	451.72	450.57	450.19	450.07
25000	541.59	525.28	485.91	474.25	470.54	469.34	468.95	468.82
26000	563.26	546.30	505.35	493.22	489.36	488.11	487.70	487.57
27000	584.92	567.31	524.78	512.19	508.19	506.89	506.46	506.32
28000	606.59	588.32	544.22	531.16	527.01	525.66	525.22	525.08
29000	628.25	609.33	563.65	550.13	545.83	544.43	543.98	543.83
30000	649.91	630.34	583.09	569.10	564.65	563.21	562.74	562.58
31000	671.58	651.35	602.53	588.07	583.47	581.98	581.49	581.33
32000	693.24	672.36	621.96	607.04	602.29	600.75	600.25	600.09
33000	714.90	693.37	641.40	626.01	621.11	619.53	619.01	618.84
34000	736.57	714.39	660.84	644.97	639.94	638.30	637.77	637.59
35000	758.23	735.40	680.27	663.94	658.76	657.07	656.52	656.34
40000	866.55	840.45	777.45	758.79	752.87	750.94	750.31	750.11
45000	974.87	945.51	874.63	853.64	846.97	844.81	844.10	843.87
50000	1083.18	1050.56	971.81	948.49	941.08	938.67	937.89	937.63
55000	1191.50	1155.62	1068.99	1043.34	1035.19	1032.54	1031.68	1031.39
60000	1299.82	1260.68	1166.18	1138.19	1129.30	1126.41	1125.47	1125.16
65000	1408.14	1365.73	1263.36	1233.04	1223.40	1220.28	1219.25	1218.92
70000	1516.46	1470.79	1360.54	1327.88	1317.51	1314.14	1313.04	1312.68
75000	1624.77	1575.84	1457.72	1422.73	1411.62	1408.01	1406.83	1406.44
80000	1733.09	1680.90	1554.90	1517.58	1505.73	1501.88	1500.62	1500.21
85000	1841.41	1785.96	1652.08	1612.43	1599.83	1595.74	1594.41	1593.97
90000	1949.73	1891.01	1749.26	1707.28	1693.94	1689.61	1688.20	1687.73
95000	2058.05	1996.07	1846.44	1802.13	1788.05	1783.48	1781.98	1781.49
100000	2166.36	2101.12	1943.62	1896.98	1882.16	1877.34	1875.77	1875.26
105000	2274.68	2206.18	2040.80	1991.82	1976.26	1971.21	1969.56	1969.02
110000	2383.00	2311.24	2137.98	2086.67	2070.37	2065.08	2063.35	2062.78
115000	2491.32	2416.29	2235.17	2181.52	2164.48	2158.95	2157.14	2156.54
120000	2599.63	2521.35	2332.35	2276.37	2258.59	2252.81	2250.93	2250.31
125000	2707.95	2626.40	2429.53	2371.22	2352.69	2346.68	2344.71	2344.07
130000	2816.27	2731.46	2526.71	2466.07	2446.80	2440.55	2438.50	2437.83
135000	2924.59	2836.51	2623.89	2560.91	2540.91	2534.41	2532.29	2531.59
140000	3032.91	2941.57	2721.07	2655.76	2635.02	2628.28	2626.08	2625.36
145000	3141.22	3046.63	2818.25	2750.61	2729.12	2722.15	2719.87	2719.12
150000	3249.54	3151.68	2915.43	2845.46	2823.23	2816.01	2813.66	2812.88
155000	3357.86	3256.74	3012.61	2940.31	2917.34	2909.88	2907.44	2906.64
160000	3466.18	3361.79	3109.79	3035.16	3011.45	3003.75	3001.23	3000.41

22.750% MONTHLY AMORTIZING PAYMENTS

AMOUNT OF LOAN	NUMBER OF YEARS IN TERM							
	1	2	3	4	5	6	7	8
$ 50	4.70	2.62	1.93	1.60	1.41	1.28	1.20	1.14
100	9.40	5.23	3.86	3.20	2.81	2.56	2.39	2.27
200	18.80	10.45	7.72	6.39	5.61	5.12	4.78	4.54
300	28.19	15.68	11.58	9.58	8.42	7.68	7.17	6.81
400	37.59	20.90	15.44	12.77	11.22	10.23	9.56	9.08
500	46.98	26.13	19.29	15.96	14.03	12.79	11.95	11.35
600	56.38	31.35	23.15	19.15	16.83	15.35	14.34	13.62
700	65.77	36.58	27.01	22.35	19.64	17.91	16.73	15.89
800	75.17	41.80	30.87	25.54	22.44	20.46	19.12	18.16
900	84.57	47.03	34.73	28.73	25.25	23.02	21.51	20.43
1000	93.96	52.25	38.58	31.92	28.05	25.58	23.90	22.70
2000	187.92	104.50	77.16	63.83	56.10	51.15	47.79	45.40
3000	281.87	156.75	115.74	95.75	84.15	76.72	71.68	68.10
4000	375.83	209.00	154.32	127.66	112.19	102.30	95.57	90.80
5000	469.78	261.25	192.90	159.58	140.24	127.87	119.46	113.50
6000	563.74	313.50	231.48	191.49	168.29	153.44	143.35	136.20
7000	657.69	365.75	270.06	223.41	196.33	179.02	167.24	158.90
8000	751.65	418.00	308.64	255.32	224.38	204.59	191.13	181.60
9000	845.61	470.25	347.22	287.24	252.43	230.16	215.03	204.30
10000	939.56	522.50	385.80	319.15	280.48	255.74	238.92	227.00
11000	1033.52	574.75	424.38	351.07	308.52	281.31	262.81	249.70
12000	1127.47	627.00	462.96	382.98	336.57	306.88	286.70	272.40
13000	1221.43	679.25	501.54	414.90	364.62	332.46	310.59	295.10
14000	1315.38	731.49	540.12	446.81	392.66	358.03	334.48	317.80
15000	1409.34	783.74	578.70	478.72	420.71	383.60	358.37	340.50
16000	1503.30	835.99	617.28	510.64	448.76	409.18	382.26	363.20
17000	1597.25	888.24	655.86	542.55	476.80	434.75	406.16	385.90
18000	1691.21	940.49	694.44	574.47	504.85	460.32	430.05	408.59
19000	1785.16	992.74	733.02	606.38	532.90	485.90	453.94	431.29
20000	1879.12	1044.99	771.60	638.30	560.95	511.47	477.83	453.99
21000	1973.07	1097.24	810.18	670.21	588.99	537.04	501.72	476.69
22000	2067.03	1149.49	848.75	702.13	617.04	562.62	525.61	499.39
23000	2160.99	1201.74	887.33	734.04	645.09	588.19	549.50	522.09
24000	2254.94	1253.99	925.91	765.96	673.13	613.76	573.39	544.79
25000	2348.90	1306.24	964.49	797.87	701.18	639.34	597.28	567.49
26000	2442.85	1358.49	1003.07	829.79	729.23	664.91	621.18	590.19
27000	2536.81	1410.74	1041.65	861.70	757.27	690.48	645.07	612.89
28000	2630.76	1462.98	1080.23	893.62	785.32	716.06	668.96	635.59
29000	2724.72	1515.23	1118.81	925.53	813.37	741.63	692.85	658.29
30000	2818.68	1567.48	1157.39	957.44	841.42	767.20	716.74	680.99
31000	2912.63	1619.73	1195.97	989.36	869.46	792.78	740.63	703.69
32000	3006.59	1671.98	1234.55	1021.27	897.51	818.35	764.52	726.39
33000	3100.54	1724.23	1273.13	1053.19	925.56	843.92	788.41	749.09
34000	3194.50	1776.48	1311.71	1085.10	953.60	869.49	812.31	771.79
35000	3288.45	1828.73	1350.29	1117.02	981.65	895.07	836.20	794.48
40000	3758.23	2089.98	1543.19	1276.59	1121.89	1022.93	955.65	907.98
45000	4228.01	2351.22	1736.08	1436.16	1262.12	1150.80	1075.11	1021.48
50000	4697.79	2612.47	1928.98	1595.74	1402.36	1278.67	1194.56	1134.98
55000	5167.57	2873.71	2121.88	1755.31	1542.59	1406.53	1314.02	1248.47
60000	5637.35	3134.96	2314.78	1914.88	1682.83	1534.40	1433.48	1361.97
65000	6107.13	3396.21	2507.68	2074.46	1823.06	1662.26	1552.93	1475.47
70000	6576.90	3657.45	2700.57	2234.03	1963.30	1790.13	1672.39	1588.96
75000	7046.68	3918.70	2893.47	2393.60	2103.53	1918.00	1791.84	1702.46
80000	7516.46	4179.95	3086.37	2553.18	2243.77	2045.86	1911.30	1815.96
85000	7986.24	4441.19	3279.27	2712.75	2384.00	2173.73	2030.76	1929.46
90000	8456.02	4702.44	3472.16	2872.32	2524.24	2301.60	2150.21	2042.95
95000	8925.80	4963.69	3665.06	3031.90	2664.47	2429.46	2269.67	2156.45
100000	9395.58	5224.93	3857.96	3191.47	2804.71	2557.33	2389.12	2269.95
105000	9865.35	5486.18	4050.86	3351.04	2944.94	2685.19	2508.58	2383.44
110000	10335.13	5747.42	4243.75	3510.62	3085.18	2813.06	2628.04	2496.94
115000	10804.91	6008.67	4436.65	3670.19	3225.41	2940.93	2747.49	2610.44
120000	11274.69	6269.92	4629.55	3829.76	3365.65	3068.79	2866.95	2723.94
125000	11744.47	6531.16	4822.45	3989.34	3505.88	3196.66	2986.40	2837.43
130000	12214.25	6792.41	5015.35	4148.91	3646.12	3324.52	3105.86	2950.93
135000	12684.03	7053.66	5208.24	4308.48	3786.35	3452.39	3225.31	3064.43
140000	13153.80	7314.90	5401.14	4468.06	3926.59	3580.26	3344.77	3177.92
145000	13623.58	7576.15	5594.04	4627.63	4066.82	3708.12	3464.23	3291.42
150000	14093.36	7837.40	5786.94	4787.20	4207.06	3835.99	3583.68	3404.92
155000	14563.14	8098.64	5979.83	4946.78	4347.29	3963.86	3703.14	3518.42
160000	15032.92	8359.89	6172.73	5106.35	4487.53	4091.72	3822.59	3631.91

AMOUNT OF LOAN	NUMBER OF YEARS IN TERM							
	9	10	15	20	25	30	35	40
$ 50	1.10	1.06	.99	.96	.96	.95	.95	.95
100	2.19	2.12	1.97	1.92	1.91	1.90	1.90	1.90
200	4.37	4.24	3.93	3.84	3.81	3.80	3.80	3.80
300	6.55	6.36	5.89	5.76	5.71	5.70	5.69	5.69
400	8.74	8.48	7.86	7.67	7.62	7.60	7.59	7.59
500	10.92	10.60	9.82	9.59	9.52	9.50	9.49	9.49
600	13.10	12.71	11.78	11.51	11.42	11.39	11.38	11.38
700	15.29	14.83	13.74	13.42	13.32	13.29	13.28	13.28
800	17.47	16.95	15.71	15.34	15.23	15.19	15.18	15.17
900	19.65	19.07	17.67	17.26	17.13	17.09	17.07	17.07
1000	21.84	21.19	19.63	19.17	19.03	18.99	18.97	18.97
2000	43.67	42.37	39.26	38.34	38.06	37.97	37.94	37.93
3000	65.50	63.55	58.88	57.51	57.08	56.95	56.90	56.89
4000	87.33	84.74	78.51	76.68	76.11	75.93	75.87	75.85
5000	109.16	105.92	98.14	95.85	95.14	94.91	94.83	94.81
6000	130.99	127.10	117.76	115.02	114.16	113.89	113.80	113.77
7000	152.82	148.28	137.39	134.19	133.19	132.87	132.76	132.73
8000	174.65	169.47	157.01	153.36	152.22	151.85	151.73	151.69
9000	196.48	190.65	176.64	172.53	171.24	170.83	170.69	170.65
10000	218.31	211.83	196.27	191.70	190.27	189.81	189.66	189.61
11000	240.14	233.01	215.89	210.87	209.29	208.79	208.62	208.57
12000	261.97	254.20	235.52	230.04	228.32	227.77	227.59	227.53
13000	283.80	275.38	255.15	249.21	247.35	246.75	246.56	246.49
14000	305.63	296.56	274.77	268.38	266.37	265.73	265.52	265.45
15000	327.46	317.75	294.40	287.55	285.40	284.71	284.49	284.41
16000	349.29	338.93	314.02	306.72	304.43	303.69	303.45	303.38
17000	371.12	360.11	333.65	325.89	323.45	322.67	322.42	322.34
18000	392.95	381.29	353.28	345.06	342.48	341.65	341.38	341.30
19000	414.78	402.48	372.90	364.23	361.51	360.63	360.35	360.26
20000	436.61	423.66	392.53	383.40	380.53	379.61	379.31	379.22
21000	458.44	444.84	412.15	402.57	399.56	398.59	398.28	398.18
22000	480.27	466.02	431.78	421.74	418.58	417.57	417.24	417.14
23000	502.10	487.21	451.41	440.91	437.61	436.55	436.21	436.10
24000	523.93	508.39	471.03	460.08	456.64	455.53	455.18	455.06
25000	545.76	529.57	490.66	479.25	475.66	474.51	474.14	474.02
26000	567.59	550.76	510.29	498.42	494.69	493.49	493.11	492.98
27000	589.42	571.94	529.91	517.59	513.72	512.47	512.07	511.94
28000	611.25	593.12	549.54	536.76	532.74	531.45	531.04	530.90
29000	633.08	614.30	569.16	555.93	551.77	550.43	550.00	549.86
30000	654.91	635.49	588.79	575.10	570.79	569.41	568.97	568.82
31000	676.74	656.67	608.42	594.27	589.82	588.39	587.93	587.78
32000	698.57	677.85	628.04	613.44	608.85	607.37	606.90	606.75
33000	720.40	699.03	647.67	632.61	627.87	626.36	625.86	625.71
34000	742.23	720.22	667.30	651.78	646.90	645.34	644.83	644.67
35000	764.06	741.40	686.92	670.95	665.93	664.32	663.80	663.63
40000	873.21	847.31	785.05	766.79	761.06	759.22	758.62	758.43
45000	982.36	953.23	883.18	862.64	856.19	854.12	853.45	853.23
50000	1091.51	1059.14	981.31	958.49	951.32	949.02	948.28	948.04
55000	1200.67	1165.05	1079.45	1054.34	1046.45	1043.92	1043.10	1042.84
60000	1309.82	1270.97	1177.58	1150.19	1141.58	1138.82	1137.93	1137.64
65000	1418.97	1376.88	1275.71	1246.04	1236.72	1233.73	1232.76	1232.45
70000	1528.12	1482.80	1373.84	1341.89	1331.85	1328.63	1327.59	1327.25
75000	1637.27	1588.71	1471.97	1437.73	1426.98	1423.53	1422.41	1422.05
80000	1746.42	1694.62	1570.10	1533.58	1522.11	1518.43	1517.24	1516.86
85000	1855.57	1800.54	1668.23	1629.43	1617.24	1613.33	1612.07	1611.66
90000	1964.72	1906.45	1766.36	1725.28	1712.37	1708.23	1706.90	1706.46
95000	2073.87	2012.36	1864.49	1821.13	1807.51	1803.13	1801.72	1801.27
100000	2183.02	2118.28	1962.62	1916.98	1902.64	1898.04	1896.55	1896.07
105000	2292.18	2224.19	2060.75	2012.83	1997.77	1992.94	1991.38	1990.87
110000	2401.33	2330.10	2158.89	2108.67	2092.90	2087.84	2086.20	2085.68
115000	2510.48	2436.02	2257.02	2204.52	2188.03	2182.74	2181.03	2180.48
120000	2619.63	2541.93	2355.15	2300.37	2283.16	2277.64	2275.86	2275.28
125000	2728.78	2647.85	2453.28	2396.22	2378.30	2372.54	2370.69	2370.08
130000	2837.93	2753.76	2551.41	2492.07	2473.43	2467.45	2465.51	2464.89
135000	2947.08	2859.67	2649.54	2587.92	2568.56	2562.35	2560.34	2559.69
140000	3056.23	2965.59	2747.67	2683.77	2663.69	2657.25	2655.17	2654.49
145000	3165.38	3071.50	2845.80	2779.61	2758.82	2752.15	2750.00	2749.30
150000	3274.53	3177.41	2943.93	2875.46	2853.95	2847.05	2844.82	2844.10
155000	3383.69	3283.33	3042.06	2971.31	2949.08	2941.95	2939.65	2938.90
160000	3492.84	3389.24	3140.19	3067.16	3044.22	3036.85	3034.48	3033.71

23.000% MONTHLY AMORTIZING PAYMENTS

AMOUNT OF LOAN	NUMBER OF YEARS IN TERM							
	1	2	3	4	5	6	7	8
$ 50	4.71	2.62	1.94	1.61	1.41	1.29	1.21	1.15
100	9.41	5.24	3.88	3.21	2.82	2.58	2.41	2.29
200	18.82	10.48	7.75	6.42	5.64	5.15	4.81	4.58
300	28.23	15.72	11.62	9.62	8.46	7.72	7.22	6.86
400	37.64	20.95	15.49	12.83	11.28	10.29	9.62	9.15
500	47.04	26.19	19.36	16.03	14.10	12.87	12.03	11.44
600	56.45	31.43	23.23	19.24	16.92	15.44	14.43	13.72
700	65.86	36.67	27.10	22.44	19.74	18.01	16.84	16.01
800	75.27	41.90	30.97	25.65	22.56	20.58	19.24	18.29
900	84.67	47.14	34.84	28.85	25.38	23.16	21.65	20.58
1000	94.08	52.38	38.71	32.06	28.20	25.73	24.05	22.87
2000	188.16	104.75	77.42	64.11	56.39	51.45	48.10	45.73
3000	282.23	157.12	116.13	96.16	84.58	77.17	72.15	68.59
4000	376.31	209.50	154.84	128.21	112.77	102.90	96.19	91.45
5000	470.39	261.87	193.55	160.26	140.96	128.62	120.24	114.31
6000	564.46	314.24	232.26	192.31	169.15	154.34	144.29	137.17
7000	658.54	366.62	270.97	224.37	197.34	180.07	168.34	160.03
8000	752.62	418.99	309.68	256.42	225.53	205.79	192.38	182.89
9000	846.69	471.36	348.39	288.47	253.72	231.51	216.43	205.76
10000	940.77	523.74	387.10	320.52	281.91	257.24	240.48	228.62
11000	1034.84	576.11	425.81	352.57	310.10	282.96	264.52	251.48
12000	1128.92	628.48	464.52	384.62	338.29	308.68	288.57	274.34
13000	1223.00	680.86	503.23	416.67	366.48	334.41	312.62	297.20
14000	1317.07	733.23	541.94	448.73	394.67	360.13	336.67	320.06
15000	1411.15	785.60	580.65	480.78	422.86	385.85	360.71	342.92
16000	1505.23	837.98	619.36	512.83	451.05	411.57	384.76	365.78
17000	1599.30	890.35	658.07	544.88	479.24	437.30	408.81	388.65
18000	1693.38	942.72	696.78	576.93	507.43	463.02	432.85	411.51
19000	1787.46	995.10	735.49	608.98	535.62	488.74	456.90	434.37
20000	1881.53	1047.47	774.20	641.03	563.81	514.47	480.95	457.23
21000	1975.61	1099.84	812.91	673.09	592.00	540.19	505.00	480.09
22000	2069.68	1152.22	851.62	705.14	620.20	565.91	529.04	502.95
23000	2163.76	1204.59	890.33	737.19	648.39	591.64	553.09	525.81
24000	2257.84	1256.96	929.04	769.24	676.58	617.36	577.14	548.67
25000	2351.91	1309.34	967.75	801.29	704.77	643.08	601.18	571.53
26000	2445.99	1361.71	1006.46	833.34	732.96	668.81	625.23	594.40
27000	2540.07	1414.08	1045.17	865.39	761.15	694.53	649.28	617.26
28000	2634.14	1466.46	1083.88	897.45	789.34	720.25	673.33	640.12
29000	2728.22	1518.83	1122.59	929.50	817.53	745.98	697.37	662.98
30000	2822.29	1571.20	1161.30	961.55	845.72	771.70	721.42	685.84
31000	2916.37	1623.58	1200.01	993.60	873.91	797.42	745.47	708.70
32000	3010.45	1675.95	1238.72	1025.65	902.10	823.14	769.52	731.56
33000	3104.52	1728.32	1277.43	1057.70	930.29	848.87	793.56	754.42
34000	3198.60	1780.70	1316.14	1089.76	958.48	874.59	817.61	777.29
35000	3292.68	1833.07	1354.85	1121.81	986.67	900.31	841.66	800.15
40000	3763.06	2094.94	1548.39	1282.06	1127.62	1028.93	961.89	914.45
45000	4233.44	2356.80	1741.94	1442.32	1268.58	1157.54	1082.13	1028.76
50000	4703.82	2618.67	1935.49	1602.58	1409.53	1286.16	1202.36	1143.06
55000	5174.20	2880.54	2129.04	1762.84	1550.48	1414.78	1322.60	1257.37
60000	5644.58	3142.40	2322.59	1923.09	1691.43	1543.39	1442.84	1371.68
65000	6114.97	3404.27	2516.14	2083.35	1832.39	1672.01	1563.07	1485.98
70000	6585.35	3666.14	2709.69	2243.61	1973.34	1800.62	1683.31	1600.29
75000	7055.73	3928.00	2903.23	2403.87	2114.29	1929.24	1803.54	1714.59
80000	7526.11	4189.87	3096.78	2564.12	2255.24	2057.85	1923.78	1828.90
85000	7996.49	4451.74	3290.33	2724.38	2396.20	2186.47	2044.02	1943.21
90000	8466.87	4713.60	3483.88	2884.64	2537.15	2315.08	2164.25	2057.51
95000	8937.26	4975.47	3677.43	3044.89	2678.10	2443.70	2284.49	2171.82
100000	9407.64	5237.34	3870.98	3205.15	2819.05	2572.32	2404.72	2286.12
105000	9878.02	5499.20	4064.53	3365.41	2960.00	2700.93	2524.96	2400.43
110000	10348.40	5761.07	4258.07	3525.67	3100.96	2829.55	2645.20	2514.74
115000	10818.78	6022.94	4451.62	3685.92	3241.91	2958.16	2765.43	2629.04
120000	11289.16	6284.80	4645.17	3846.18	3382.86	3086.78	2885.67	2743.35
125000	11759.55	6546.67	4838.72	4006.44	3523.81	3215.39	3005.90	2857.65
130000	12229.93	6808.53	5032.27	4166.70	3664.77	3344.01	3126.14	2971.96
135000	12700.31	7070.40	5225.82	4326.95	3805.72	3472.62	3246.38	3086.27
140000	13170.69	7332.27	5419.37	4487.21	3946.67	3601.24	3366.61	3200.57
145000	13641.07	7594.13	5612.91	4647.47	4087.62	3729.86	3486.85	3314.88
150000	14111.45	7856.00	5806.46	4807.73	4228.58	3858.47	3607.08	3429.18
155000	14581.83	8117.87	6000.01	4967.98	4369.53	3987.09	3727.32	3543.49
160000	15052.22	8379.73	6193.56	5128.24	4510.48	4115.70	3847.56	3657.80

AMOUNT OF LOAN	NUMBER OF YEARS IN TERM							
	9	10	15	20	25	30	35	40
$ 50	1.10	1.07	1.00	.97	.97	.96	.96	.96
100	2.20	2.14	1.99	1.94	1.93	1.92	1.92	1.92
200	4.40	4.28	3.97	3.88	3.85	3.84	3.84	3.84
300	6.60	6.41	5.95	5.82	5.77	5.76	5.76	5.76
400	8.80	8.55	7.93	7.75	7.70	7.68	7.67	7.67
500	11.00	10.68	9.91	9.69	9.62	9.60	9.59	9.59
600	13.20	12.82	11.89	11.63	11.54	11.52	11.51	11.51
700	15.40	14.95	13.88	13.56	13.47	13.44	13.43	13.42
800	17.60	17.09	15.86	15.50	15.39	15.35	15.34	15.34
900	19.80	19.22	17.84	17.44	17.31	17.27	17.26	17.26
1000	22.00	21.36	19.82	19.38	19.24	19.19	19.18	19.17
2000	44.00	42.71	39.64	38.75	38.47	38.38	38.35	38.34
3000	66.00	64.07	59.45	58.12	57.70	57.57	57.52	57.51
4000	87.99	85.42	79.27	77.49	76.93	76.75	76.70	76.68
5000	109.99	106.78	99.09	96.86	96.16	95.94	95.87	95.85
6000	131.99	128.13	118.90	116.23	115.39	115.13	115.04	115.02
7000	153.99	149.49	138.72	135.60	134.62	134.32	134.22	134.19
8000	175.98	170.84	158.54	154.97	153.86	153.50	153.39	153.36
9000	197.98	192.20	178.35	174.34	173.09	172.69	172.56	172.52
10000	219.98	213.55	198.17	193.71	192.32	191.88	191.74	191.69
11000	241.98	234.91	217.99	213.08	211.55	211.07	210.91	210.86
12000	263.97	256.26	237.80	232.45	230.78	230.25	230.08	230.03
13000	285.97	277.62	257.62	251.82	250.01	249.44	249.26	249.20
14000	307.97	298.97	277.44	271.19	269.24	268.63	268.43	268.37
15000	329.96	320.33	297.25	290.56	288.47	287.81	287.60	287.54
16000	351.96	341.68	317.07	309.93	307.71	307.00	306.78	306.71
17000	373.96	363.04	336.89	329.30	326.94	326.19	325.95	325.87
18000	395.96	384.39	356.70	348.67	346.17	345.38	345.12	345.04
19000	417.95	405.75	376.52	368.04	365.40	364.56	364.30	364.21
20000	439.95	427.10	396.34	387.41	384.63	383.75	383.47	383.38
21000	461.95	448.46	416.15	406.78	403.86	402.94	402.64	402.55
22000	483.95	469.81	435.97	426.15	423.09	422.13	421.82	421.72
23000	505.94	491.16	455.79	445.52	442.32	441.31	440.99	440.89
24000	527.94	512.52	475.60	464.89	461.56	460.50	460.16	460.06
25000	549.94	533.87	495.42	484.26	480.79	479.69	479.34	479.22
26000	571.94	555.23	515.24	503.63	500.02	498.88	498.51	498.39
27000	593.93	576.58	535.05	523.00	519.25	518.06	517.68	517.56
28000	615.93	597.94	554.87	542.37	538.48	537.25	536.86	536.73
29000	637.93	619.29	574.69	561.74	557.71	556.44	556.03	555.90
30000	659.92	640.65	594.50	581.11	576.94	575.62	575.20	575.07
31000	681.92	662.00	614.32	600.48	596.18	594.81	594.38	594.24
32000	703.92	683.36	634.14	619.85	615.41	614.00	613.55	613.41
33000	725.92	704.71	653.95	639.22	634.64	633.19	632.72	632.57
34000	747.91	726.07	673.77	658.59	653.87	652.37	651.90	651.74
35000	769.91	747.42	693.59	677.96	673.10	671.56	671.07	670.91
40000	879.90	854.20	792.67	774.81	769.26	767.50	766.94	766.76
45000	989.88	960.97	891.75	871.66	865.41	863.43	862.80	862.60
50000	1099.87	1067.74	990.84	968.51	961.57	959.37	958.67	958.44
55000	1209.86	1174.52	1089.92	1065.36	1057.73	1055.31	1054.53	1054.29
60000	1319.84	1281.29	1189.00	1162.21	1153.88	1151.24	1150.40	1150.13
65000	1429.83	1388.07	1288.09	1259.06	1250.04	1247.18	1246.27	1245.98
70000	1539.82	1494.84	1387.17	1355.91	1346.20	1343.12	1342.13	1341.82
75000	1649.80	1601.61	1486.25	1452.76	1442.35	1439.05	1438.00	1437.66
80000	1759.79	1708.39	1585.34	1549.61	1538.51	1534.99	1533.87	1533.51
85000	1869.78	1815.16	1684.42	1646.46	1634.67	1630.93	1629.73	1629.35
90000	1979.76	1921.94	1783.50	1743.31	1730.82	1726.86	1725.60	1725.20
95000	2089.75	2028.71	1882.59	1840.16	1826.98	1822.80	1821.47	1821.04
100000	2199.74	2135.48	1981.67	1937.01	1923.13	1918.74	1917.33	1916.88
105000	2309.72	2242.26	2080.75	2033.86	2019.29	2014.67	2013.20	2012.73
110000	2419.71	2349.03	2179.83	2130.71	2115.45	2110.61	2109.06	2108.57
115000	2529.70	2455.80	2278.92	2227.56	2211.60	2206.55	2204.93	2204.41
120000	2639.68	2562.58	2378.00	2324.41	2307.76	2302.48	2300.80	2300.26
125000	2749.67	2669.35	2477.08	2421.26	2403.92	2398.42	2396.66	2396.10
130000	2859.66	2776.13	2576.17	2518.11	2500.07	2494.36	2492.53	2491.95
135000	2969.64	2882.90	2675.25	2614.96	2596.23	2590.29	2588.40	2587.79
140000	3079.63	2989.67	2774.33	2711.81	2692.39	2686.23	2684.26	2683.63
145000	3189.62	3096.45	2873.42	2808.66	2788.54	2782.16	2780.13	2779.48
150000	3299.60	3203.22	2972.50	2905.51	2884.70	2878.10	2876.00	2875.32
155000	3409.59	3310.00	3071.58	3002.36	2980.86	2974.04	2971.86	2971.17
160000	3519.58	3416.77	3170.67	3099.21	3077.01	3069.97	3067.73	3067.01

AMOUNT OF LOAN	NUMBER OF YEARS IN TERM							
	1	2	3	4	5	6	7	8
$ 50	4.71	2.63	1.95	1.61	1.42	1.30	1.22	1.16
100	9.42	5.25	3.89	3.22	2.84	2.59	2.43	2.31
200	18.84	10.50	7.77	6.44	5.67	5.18	4.85	4.61
300	28.26	15.75	11.66	9.66	8.51	7.77	7.27	6.91
400	37.68	21.00	15.54	12.88	11.34	10.35	9.69	9.21
500	47.10	26.25	19.43	16.10	14.17	12.94	12.11	11.52
600	56.52	31.50	23.31	19.32	17.01	15.53	14.53	13.82
700	65.94	36.75	27.19	22.54	19.84	18.12	16.95	16.12
800	75.36	42.00	31.08	25.76	22.67	20.70	19.37	18.42
900	84.78	47.25	34.96	28.97	25.51	23.29	21.79	20.73
1000	94.20	52.50	38.85	32.19	28.34	25.88	24.21	23.03
2000	188.40	105.00	77.69	64.38	56.67	51.75	48.41	46.05
3000	282.60	157.50	116.53	96.57	85.01	77.63	72.62	69.08
4000	376.79	210.00	155.37	128.76	113.34	103.50	96.82	92.10
5000	470.99	262.49	194.21	160.95	141.68	129.37	121.02	115.12
6000	565.19	314.99	233.05	193.14	170.01	155.25	145.23	138.15
7000	659.38	367.49	271.89	225.33	198.35	181.12	169.43	161.17
8000	753.58	419.99	310.73	257.51	226.68	206.99	193.63	184.19
9000	847.78	472.48	349.57	289.70	255.01	232.87	217.84	207.22
10000	941.98	524.98	388.41	321.89	283.35	258.74	242.04	230.24
11000	1036.17	577.48	427.25	354.08	311.68	284.61	266.25	253.26
12000	1130.37	629.98	466.09	386.27	340.02	310.49	290.45	276.29
13000	1224.57	682.47	504.93	418.46	368.35	336.36	314.65	299.31
14000	1318.76	734.97	543.77	450.65	396.69	362.23	338.86	322.33
15000	1412.96	787.47	582.61	482.83	425.02	388.11	363.06	345.36
16000	1507.16	839.97	621.45	515.02	453.35	413.98	387.26	368.38
17000	1601.35	892.46	660.29	547.21	481.69	439.85	411.47	391.40
18000	1695.55	944.96	699.13	579.40	510.02	465.73	435.67	414.43
19000	1789.75	997.46	737.97	611.59	538.36	491.60	459.87	437.45
20000	1883.95	1049.96	776.81	643.78	566.69	517.47	484.08	460.47
21000	1978.14	1102.45	815.65	675.97	595.03	543.35	508.28	483.50
22000	2072.34	1154.95	854.49	708.15	623.36	569.22	532.49	506.52
23000	2166.53	1207.45	893.33	740.34	651.69	595.09	556.69	529.54
24000	2260.73	1259.95	932.17	772.53	680.03	620.97	580.89	552.57
25000	2354.93	1312.44	971.01	804.72	708.36	646.84	605.10	575.59
26000	2449.13	1364.94	1009.85	836.91	736.70	672.71	629.30	598.61
27000	2543.32	1417.44	1048.69	869.10	765.03	698.59	653.50	621.64
28000	2637.52	1469.94	1087.53	901.29	793.37	724.46	677.71	644.66
29000	2731.72	1522.43	1126.37	933.47	821.70	750.33	701.91	667.69
30000	2825.92	1574.93	1165.21	965.66	850.03	776.21	726.11	690.71
31000	2920.11	1627.43	1204.05	997.85	878.37	802.08	750.32	713.73
32000	3014.31	1679.93	1242.89	1030.04	906.70	827.95	774.52	736.76
33000	3108.51	1732.42	1281.73	1062.23	935.04	853.83	798.73	759.78
34000	3202.70	1784.92	1320.57	1094.42	963.37	879.70	822.93	782.80
35000	3296.90	1837.42	1359.41	1126.61	991.71	905.57	847.13	805.83
40000	3767.89	2099.91	1553.61	1287.55	1133.38	1034.94	968.15	920.94
45000	4238.87	2362.39	1747.81	1448.49	1275.05	1164.31	1089.17	1036.06
50000	4709.86	2624.88	1942.01	1609.43	1416.72	1293.68	1210.19	1151.18
55000	5180.84	2887.37	2136.21	1770.38	1558.39	1423.04	1331.21	1266.29
60000	5651.83	3149.86	2330.41	1931.32	1700.06	1552.41	1452.22	1381.41
65000	6122.81	3412.34	2524.61	2092.26	1841.73	1681.78	1573.24	1496.53
70000	6593.80	3674.83	2718.82	2253.21	1983.41	1811.14	1694.26	1611.65
75000	7064.78	3937.32	2913.02	2414.15	2125.08	1940.51	1815.28	1726.76
80000	7535.77	4199.81	3107.22	2575.09	2266.75	2069.88	1936.30	1841.88
85000	8006.75	4462.29	3301.42	2736.04	2408.42	2199.25	2057.32	1957.00
90000	8477.74	4724.78	3495.62	2896.98	2550.09	2328.61	2178.33	2072.12
95000	8948.72	4987.27	3689.82	3057.92	2691.76	2457.98	2299.35	2187.23
100000	9419.71	5249.76	3884.02	3218.86	2833.43	2587.35	2420.37	2302.35
105000	9890.69	5512.24	4078.22	3379.81	2975.11	2716.71	2541.39	2417.47
110000	10361.68	5774.73	4272.42	3540.75	3116.78	2846.08	2662.41	2532.58
115000	10832.66	6037.22	4466.62	3701.69	3258.45	2975.45	2783.43	2647.70
120000	11303.65	6299.71	4660.82	3862.64	3400.12	3104.81	2904.44	2762.82
125000	11774.63	6562.19	4855.02	4023.58	3541.79	3234.18	3025.46	2877.94
130000	12245.62	6824.68	5049.22	4184.52	3683.46	3363.55	3146.48	2993.05
135000	12716.60	7087.17	5243.42	4345.47	3825.13	3492.92	3267.50	3108.17
140000	13187.59	7349.66	5437.63	4506.41	3966.81	3622.28	3388.52	3223.29
145000	13658.57	7612.14	5631.83	4667.35	4108.48	3751.65	3509.54	3338.41
150000	14129.56	7874.63	5826.03	4828.29	4250.15	3881.02	3630.55	3453.52
155000	14600.54	8137.12	6020.23	4989.24	4391.82	4010.38	3751.57	3568.64
160000	15071.53	8399.61	6214.43	5150.18	4533.49	4139.75	3872.59	3683.76

AMOUNT OF LOAN	NUMBER OF YEARS IN TERM							
	9	10	15	20	25	30	35	40
$ 50	1.11	1.08	1.01	.98	.98	.97	.97	.97
100	2.22	2.16	2.01	1.96	1.95	1.94	1.94	1.94
200	4.44	4.31	4.01	3.92	3.89	3.88	3.88	3.88
300	6.65	6.46	6.01	5.88	5.84	5.82	5.82	5.82
400	8.87	8.62	8.01	7.83	7.78	7.76	7.76	7.76
500	11.09	10.77	10.01	9.79	9.72	9.70	9.70	9.69
600	13.30	12.92	12.01	11.75	11.67	11.64	11.63	11.63
700	15.52	15.07	14.01	13.70	13.61	13.58	13.57	13.57
800	17.74	17.23	16.01	15.66	15.55	15.52	15.51	15.51
900	19.95	19.38	18.01	17.62	17.50	17.46	17.45	17.44
1000	22.17	21.53	20.01	19.58	19.44	19.40	19.39	19.38
2000	44.33	43.06	40.02	39.15	38.88	38.79	38.77	38.76
3000	66.50	64.59	60.03	58.72	58.31	58.19	58.15	58.14
4000	88.66	86.11	80.04	78.29	77.75	77.58	77.53	77.51
5000	110.83	107.64	100.04	97.86	97.19	96.98	96.91	96.89
6000	132.99	129.17	120.05	117.43	116.62	116.37	116.29	116.27
7000	155.16	150.70	140.06	137.00	136.06	135.77	135.67	135.64
8000	177.32	172.22	160.07	156.57	155.50	155.16	155.05	155.02
9000	199.49	193.75	180.08	176.14	174.93	174.55	174.44	174.40
10000	221.65	215.28	200.08	195.71	194.37	193.95	193.82	193.77
11000	243.82	236.81	220.09	215.28	213.81	213.34	213.20	213.15
12000	265.98	258.33	240.10	234.85	233.24	232.74	232.58	232.53
13000	288.15	279.86	260.10	254.42	252.68	252.13	251.96	251.91
14000	310.31	301.39	280.11	273.99	272.12	271.53	271.34	271.28
15000	332.48	322.92	300.12	293.56	291.55	290.92	290.72	290.66
16000	354.64	344.44	320.13	313.14	310.99	310.32	310.10	310.04
17000	376.81	365.97	340.13	332.71	330.42	329.71	329.48	329.41
18000	398.97	387.50	360.14	352.28	349.86	349.10	348.87	348.79
19000	421.14	409.02	380.15	371.85	369.30	368.50	368.25	368.17
20000	443.30	430.55	400.16	391.42	388.73	387.89	387.63	387.54
21000	465.47	452.08	420.16	410.99	408.17	407.29	407.01	406.92
22000	487.63	473.61	440.17	430.56	427.61	426.68	426.39	426.30
23000	509.80	495.13	460.18	450.13	447.04	446.08	445.77	445.67
24000	531.96	516.66	480.19	469.70	466.48	465.47	465.15	465.05
25000	554.13	538.19	500.19	489.27	485.92	484.86	484.53	484.43
26000	576.29	559.72	520.20	508.84	505.35	504.26	503.91	503.81
27000	598.46	581.24	540.21	528.41	524.79	523.65	523.30	523.18
28000	620.62	602.77	560.22	547.98	544.23	543.05	542.68	542.56
29000	642.79	624.30	580.22	567.55	563.66	562.44	562.06	561.94
30000	664.95	645.83	600.23	587.12	583.10	581.84	581.44	581.31
31000	687.12	667.35	620.24	606.69	602.53	601.23	600.82	600.69
32000	709.28	688.88	640.25	626.27	621.97	620.63	620.20	620.07
33000	731.45	710.41	660.25	645.84	641.41	640.02	639.58	639.44
34000	753.61	731.93	680.26	665.41	660.84	659.41	658.96	658.82
35000	775.78	753.46	700.27	684.98	680.28	678.81	678.34	678.20
40000	886.60	861.10	800.31	782.83	777.46	775.78	775.25	775.08
45000	997.43	968.74	900.34	880.68	874.64	872.75	872.16	871.97
50000	1108.25	1076.37	1000.38	978.54	971.83	969.72	969.06	968.85
55000	1219.08	1184.01	1100.42	1076.39	1069.01	1066.70	1065.97	1065.74
60000	1329.90	1291.65	1200.46	1174.24	1166.19	1163.67	1162.87	1162.62
65000	1440.73	1399.28	1300.49	1272.10	1263.37	1260.64	1259.78	1259.51
70000	1551.55	1506.92	1400.53	1369.95	1360.56	1357.61	1356.68	1356.39
75000	1662.38	1614.56	1500.57	1467.80	1457.74	1454.58	1453.59	1453.28
80000	1773.20	1722.19	1600.61	1565.66	1554.92	1551.56	1550.50	1550.16
85000	1884.03	1829.83	1700.64	1663.51	1652.10	1648.53	1647.40	1647.04
90000	1994.85	1937.47	1800.68	1761.36	1749.28	1745.50	1744.31	1743.93
95000	2105.68	2045.10	1900.72	1859.22	1846.47	1842.47	1841.21	1840.81
100000	2216.50	2152.74	2000.76	1957.07	1943.65	1939.44	1938.12	1937.70
105000	2327.33	2260.38	2100.80	2054.92	2040.83	2036.42	2035.02	2034.58
110000	2438.15	2368.01	2200.83	2152.78	2138.01	2133.39	2131.93	2131.47
115000	2548.97	2475.65	2300.87	2250.63	2235.20	2230.36	2228.83	2228.35
120000	2659.80	2583.29	2400.91	2348.48	2332.38	2327.33	2325.74	2325.24
125000	2770.62	2690.92	2500.95	2446.33	2429.56	2424.30	2422.65	2422.12
130000	2881.45	2798.56	2600.98	2544.19	2526.74	2521.27	2519.55	2519.01
135000	2992.27	2906.20	2701.02	2642.04	2623.92	2618.25	2616.46	2615.89
140000	3103.10	3013.83	2801.06	2739.89	2721.11	2715.22	2713.36	2712.78
145000	3213.92	3121.47	2901.10	2837.75	2818.29	2812.19	2810.27	2809.66
150000	3324.75	3229.11	3001.13	2935.60	2915.47	2909.16	2907.17	2906.55
155000	3435.57	3336.74	3101.17	3033.45	3012.65	3006.13	3004.08	3003.43
160000	3546.40	3444.38	3201.21	3131.31	3109.83	3103.11	3100.99	3100.31

23.500% MONTHLY AMORTIZING PAYMENTS

AMOUNT OF LOAN	NUMBER OF YEARS IN TERM							
	1	2	3	4	5	6	7	8
$ 50	4.72	2.64	1.95	1.62	1.43	1.31	1.22	1.16
100	9.44	5.27	3.90	3.24	2.85	2.61	2.44	2.32
200	18.87	10.53	7.80	6.47	5.70	5.21	4.88	4.64
300	28.30	15.79	11.70	9.70	8.55	7.81	7.31	6.96
400	37.73	21.05	15.59	12.93	11.40	10.41	9.75	9.28
500	47.16	26.32	19.49	16.17	14.24	13.02	12.19	11.60
600	56.60	31.58	23.39	19.40	17.09	15.62	14.62	13.92
700	66.03	36.84	27.28	22.63	19.94	18.22	17.06	16.24
800	75.46	42.10	31.18	25.87	22.79	20.82	19.49	18.55
900	84.89	47.36	35.08	29.10	25.64	23.43	21.93	20.87
1000	94.32	52.63	38.98	32.33	28.48	26.03	24.37	23.19
2000	188.64	105.25	77.95	64.66	56.96	52.05	48.73	46.38
3000	282.96	157.87	116.92	96.98	85.44	78.08	73.09	69.56
4000	377.28	210.49	155.89	129.31	113.92	104.10	97.45	92.75
5000	471.59	263.11	194.86	161.64	142.40	130.13	121.81	115.94
6000	565.91	315.74	233.83	193.96	170.88	156.15	146.17	139.12
7000	660.23	368.36	272.80	226.29	199.35	182.17	170.53	162.31
8000	754.55	420.98	311.77	258.61	227.83	208.20	194.89	185.49
9000	848.87	473.60	350.74	290.94	256.31	234.22	219.25	208.68
10000	943.18	526.22	389.71	323.27	284.79	260.25	243.61	231.87
11000	1037.50	578.85	428.68	355.59	313.27	286.27	267.97	255.05
12000	1131.82	631.47	467.65	387.92	341.75	312.29	292.33	278.24
13000	1226.14	684.09	506.63	420.24	370.23	338.32	316.69	301.43
14000	1320.45	736.71	545.60	452.57	398.70	364.34	341.05	324.61
15000	1414.77	789.33	584.57	484.90	427.18	390.37	365.41	347.80
16000	1509.09	841.95	623.54	517.22	455.66	416.39	389.77	370.98
17000	1603.41	894.58	662.51	549.55	484.14	442.42	414.14	394.17
18000	1697.73	947.20	701.48	581.87	512.62	468.44	438.50	417.36
19000	1792.04	999.82	740.45	614.20	541.10	494.46	462.86	440.54
20000	1886.36	1052.44	779.42	646.53	569.57	520.49	487.22	463.73
21000	1980.68	1105.06	818.39	678.85	598.05	546.51	511.58	486.92
22000	2075.00	1157.69	857.36	711.18	626.53	572.54	535.94	510.10
23000	2169.31	1210.31	896.33	743.50	655.01	598.56	560.30	533.29
24000	2263.63	1262.93	935.30	775.83	683.49	624.58	584.66	556.47
25000	2357.95	1315.55	974.28	808.16	711.97	650.61	609.02	579.66
26000	2452.27	1368.17	1013.25	840.48	740.45	676.63	633.38	602.85
27000	2546.59	1420.80	1052.22	872.81	768.92	702.66	657.74	626.03
28000	2640.90	1473.42	1091.19	905.13	797.40	728.68	682.10	649.22
29000	2735.22	1526.04	1130.16	937.46	825.88	754.70	706.46	672.40
30000	2829.54	1578.66	1169.13	969.79	854.36	780.73	730.82	695.59
31000	2923.86	1631.28	1208.10	1002.11	882.84	806.75	755.18	718.78
32000	3018.17	1683.90	1247.07	1034.44	911.32	832.78	779.54	741.96
33000	3112.49	1736.53	1286.04	1066.76	939.79	858.80	803.90	765.15
34000	3206.81	1789.15	1325.01	1099.09	968.27	884.83	828.27	788.34
35000	3301.13	1841.77	1363.98	1131.42	996.75	910.85	852.63	811.52
40000	3772.72	2104.88	1558.84	1293.05	1139.14	1040.97	974.43	927.45
45000	4244.31	2367.99	1753.69	1454.68	1281.54	1171.09	1096.23	1043.38
50000	4715.89	2631.10	1948.55	1616.31	1423.93	1301.21	1218.03	1159.31
55000	5187.48	2894.21	2143.40	1777.94	1566.32	1431.33	1339.84	1275.25
60000	5659.07	3157.32	2338.25	1939.57	1708.71	1561.45	1461.64	1391.18
65000	6130.66	3420.43	2533.11	2101.20	1851.11	1691.57	1583.44	1507.11
70000	6602.25	3683.54	2727.96	2262.83	1993.50	1821.69	1705.25	1623.04
75000	7073.84	3946.65	2922.82	2424.46	2135.89	1951.82	1827.05	1738.97
80000	7545.43	4209.76	3117.67	2586.09	2278.28	2081.94	1948.85	1854.90
85000	8017.02	4472.86	3312.52	2747.72	2420.68	2212.06	2070.66	1970.83
90000	8488.61	4735.97	3507.38	2909.35	2563.07	2342.18	2192.46	2086.76
95000	8960.20	4999.08	3702.23	3070.98	2705.46	2472.30	2314.26	2202.69
100000	9431.78	5262.19	3897.09	3232.61	2847.85	2602.42	2436.06	2318.62
105000	9903.37	5525.30	4091.94	3394.24	2990.25	2732.54	2557.87	2434.56
110000	10374.96	5788.41	4286.79	3555.87	3132.64	2862.66	2679.67	2550.49
115000	10846.55	6051.52	4481.65	3717.50	3275.03	2992.78	2801.47	2666.42
120000	11318.14	6314.63	4676.50	3879.13	3417.42	3122.90	2923.28	2782.35
125000	11789.73	6577.74	4871.36	4040.76	3559.82	3253.02	3045.08	2898.28
130000	12261.32	6840.85	5066.21	4202.39	3702.21	3383.14	3166.88	3014.21
135000	12732.91	7103.96	5261.06	4364.02	3844.60	3513.26	3288.68	3130.14
140000	13204.50	7367.07	5455.92	4525.65	3986.99	3643.38	3410.49	3246.07
145000	13676.08	7630.18	5650.77	4687.28	4129.38	3773.50	3532.29	3362.00
150000	14147.67	7893.29	5845.63	4848.91	4271.78	3903.63	3654.09	3477.93
155000	14619.26	8156.40	6040.48	5010.54	4414.17	4033.75	3775.90	3593.87
160000	15090.85	8419.50	6235.33	5172.17	4556.56	4163.87	3897.70	3709.80

MONTHLY AMORTIZING PAYMENTS 23.500%

AMOUNT OF LOAN	NUMBER OF YEARS IN TERM							
	9	10	15	20	25	30	35	40
$ 50	1.12	1.09	1.01	.99	.99	.99	.98	.98
100	2.24	2.18	2.02	1.98	1.97	1.97	1.96	1.96
200	4.47	4.35	4.04	3.96	3.93	3.93	3.92	3.92
300	6.70	6.52	6.06	5.94	5.90	5.89	5.88	5.88
400	8.94	8.69	8.08	7.91	7.86	7.85	7.84	7.84
500	11.17	10.86	10.10	9.89	9.83	9.81	9.80	9.80
600	13.40	13.03	12.12	11.87	11.79	11.77	11.76	11.76
700	15.64	15.20	14.14	13.85	13.75	13.73	13.72	13.71
800	17.87	17.37	16.16	15.82	15.72	15.69	15.68	15.67
900	20.10	19.54	18.18	17.80	17.68	17.65	17.64	17.63
1000	22.34	21.71	20.20	19.78	19.65	19.61	19.59	19.59
2000	44.67	43.41	40.40	39.55	39.29	39.21	39.18	39.18
3000	67.00	65.11	60.60	59.32	58.93	58.81	58.77	58.76
4000	89.34	86.81	80.80	79.09	78.57	78.41	78.36	78.35
5000	111.67	108.51	101.00	98.86	98.21	98.01	97.95	97.93
6000	134.00	130.21	121.20	118.63	117.86	117.61	117.54	117.52
7000	156.34	151.91	141.40	138.41	137.50	137.22	137.13	137.10
8000	178.67	173.61	161.60	158.18	157.14	156.82	156.72	156.69
9000	201.00	195.31	181.79	177.95	176.78	176.42	176.31	176.27
10000	223.34	217.01	201.99	197.72	196.42	196.02	195.90	195.86
11000	245.67	238.71	222.19	217.49	216.06	215.62	215.48	215.44
12000	268.00	260.41	242.39	237.26	235.71	235.22	235.07	235.03
13000	290.34	282.11	262.59	257.03	255.35	254.82	254.66	254.61
14000	312.67	303.81	282.79	276.81	274.99	274.43	274.25	274.20
15000	335.00	325.51	302.99	296.58	294.63	294.03	293.84	293.78
16000	357.33	347.21	323.19	316.35	314.27	313.63	313.43	313.37
17000	379.67	368.91	343.39	336.12	333.91	333.23	333.02	332.95
18000	402.00	390.61	363.58	355.89	353.56	352.83	352.61	352.54
19000	424.33	412.31	383.78	375.66	373.20	372.43	372.20	372.12
20000	446.67	434.01	403.98	395.44	392.84	392.04	391.79	391.71
21000	469.00	455.71	424.18	415.21	412.48	411.64	411.37	411.29
22000	491.33	477.41	444.38	434.98	432.12	431.24	430.96	430.88
23000	513.67	499.11	464.58	454.75	451.76	450.84	450.55	450.46
24000	536.00	520.82	484.78	474.52	471.41	470.44	470.14	470.05
25000	558.33	542.52	504.98	494.29	491.05	490.04	489.73	489.63
26000	580.67	564.22	525.17	514.06	510.69	509.64	509.32	509.22
27000	603.00	585.92	545.37	533.84	530.33	529.25	528.91	528.80
28000	625.33	607.62	565.57	553.61	549.97	548.85	548.50	548.39
29000	647.66	629.32	585.77	573.38	569.62	568.45	568.09	567.97
30000	670.00	651.02	605.97	593.15	589.26	588.05	587.68	587.56
31000	692.33	672.72	626.17	612.92	608.90	607.65	607.26	607.14
32000	714.66	694.42	646.37	632.69	628.54	627.25	626.85	626.73
33000	737.00	716.12	666.57	652.47	648.18	646.86	646.44	646.31
34000	759.33	737.82	686.77	672.24	667.82	666.46	666.03	665.90
35000	781.66	759.52	706.96	692.01	687.47	686.06	685.62	685.48
40000	893.33	868.02	807.96	790.87	785.67	784.07	783.57	783.41
45000	1004.99	976.52	908.95	889.72	883.88	882.07	881.51	881.33
50000	1116.65	1085.03	1009.95	988.58	982.09	980.08	979.46	979.26
55000	1228.32	1193.53	1110.94	1087.44	1080.30	1078.09	1077.40	1077.19
60000	1339.99	1302.03	1211.94	1186.30	1178.51	1176.10	1175.35	1175.11
65000	1451.66	1410.53	1312.93	1285.15	1276.72	1274.10	1273.29	1273.04
70000	1563.32	1519.04	1413.92	1384.01	1374.93	1372.11	1371.24	1370.96
75000	1674.99	1627.54	1514.92	1482.87	1473.13	1470.12	1469.18	1468.89
80000	1786.65	1736.04	1615.91	1581.73	1571.34	1568.13	1567.13	1566.81
85000	1898.32	1844.54	1716.91	1680.58	1669.55	1666.14	1665.07	1664.74
90000	2009.98	1953.04	1817.90	1779.44	1767.76	1764.14	1763.02	1762.66
95000	2121.65	2061.55	1918.90	1878.30	1865.97	1862.15	1860.96	1860.59
100000	2233.31	2170.05	2019.89	1977.16	1964.18	1960.16	1958.91	1958.52
105000	2344.98	2278.55	2120.88	2076.01	2062.39	2058.17	2056.85	2056.44
110000	2456.64	2387.05	2221.88	2174.87	2160.59	2156.17	2154.80	2154.37
115000	2568.31	2495.55	2322.87	2273.73	2258.80	2254.18	2252.74	2252.29
120000	2679.98	2604.06	2423.87	2372.59	2357.01	2352.19	2350.69	2350.22
125000	2791.64	2712.56	2524.86	2471.44	2455.22	2450.20	2448.63	2448.14
130000	2903.31	2821.06	2625.85	2570.30	2553.43	2548.20	2546.58	2546.07
135000	3014.97	2929.56	2726.85	2669.16	2651.64	2646.21	2644.52	2643.99
140000	3126.64	3038.07	2827.84	2768.02	2749.85	2744.22	2742.47	2741.92
145000	3238.30	3146.57	2928.84	2866.88	2848.06	2842.23	2840.41	2839.85
150000	3349.97	3255.07	3029.83	2965.73	2946.26	2940.24	2938.36	2937.77
155000	3461.63	3363.57	3130.83	3064.59	3044.47	3038.24	3036.30	3035.70
160000	3573.30	3472.07	3231.82	3163.45	3142.68	3136.25	3134.25	3133.62

23.750% MONTHLY AMORTIZING PAYMENTS

AMOUNT OF LOAN	NUMBER OF YEARS IN TERM							
	1	2	3	4	5	6	7	8
$ 50	4.73	2.64	1.96	1.63	1.44	1.31	1.23	1.17
100	9.45	5.28	3.92	3.25	2.87	2.62	2.46	2.34
200	18.89	10.55	7.83	6.50	5.73	5.24	4.91	4.67
300	28.34	15.83	11.74	9.74	8.59	7.86	7.36	7.01
400	37.78	21.10	15.65	12.99	11.45	10.48	9.81	9.34
500	47.22	26.38	19.56	16.24	14.32	13.09	12.26	11.68
600	56.67	31.65	23.47	19.48	17.18	15.71	14.72	14.01
700	66.11	36.93	27.38	22.73	20.04	18.33	17.17	16.35
800	75.56	42.20	31.29	25.98	22.90	20.95	19.62	18.68
900	85.00	47.48	35.20	29.22	25.77	23.56	22.07	21.02
1000	94.44	52.75	39.11	32.47	28.63	26.18	24.52	23.35
2000	188.88	105.50	78.21	64.93	57.25	52.36	49.04	46.70
3000	283.32	158.24	117.31	97.40	85.87	78.53	73.56	70.05
4000	377.76	210.99	156.41	129.86	114.50	104.71	98.08	93.40
5000	472.20	263.74	195.51	162.32	143.12	130.88	122.59	116.75
6000	566.64	316.48	234.62	194.79	171.74	157.06	147.11	140.10
7000	661.08	369.23	273.72	227.25	200.37	183.23	171.63	163.45
8000	755.51	421.98	312.82	259.72	228.99	209.41	196.15	186.80
9000	849.95	474.72	351.92	292.18	257.61	235.58	220.67	210.15
10000	944.39	527.47	391.02	324.64	286.24	261.76	245.18	233.50
11000	1038.83	580.22	430.12	357.11	314.86	287.93	269.70	256.85
12000	1133.27	632.96	469.23	389.57	343.48	314.11	294.22	280.20
13000	1227.71	685.71	508.33	422.03	372.10	340.28	318.74	303.55
14000	1322.15	738.45	547.43	454.50	400.73	366.46	343.26	326.90
15000	1416.58	791.20	586.53	486.96	429.35	392.63	367.77	350.25
16000	1511.02	843.95	625.63	519.43	457.97	418.81	392.29	373.60
17000	1605.46	896.69	664.73	551.89	486.60	444.98	416.81	396.95
18000	1699.90	949.44	703.84	584.35	515.22	471.16	441.33	420.29
19000	1794.34	1002.19	742.94	616.82	543.84	497.34	465.85	443.64
20000	1888.78	1054.93	782.04	649.28	572.47	523.51	490.36	466.99
21000	1983.22	1107.68	821.14	681.74	601.09	549.69	514.88	490.34
22000	2077.66	1160.43	860.24	714.21	629.71	575.86	539.40	513.69
23000	2172.09	1213.17	899.34	746.67	658.33	602.04	563.92	537.04
24000	2266.53	1265.92	938.45	779.14	686.96	628.21	588.44	560.39
25000	2360.97	1318.67	977.55	811.60	715.58	654.39	612.95	583.74
26000	2455.41	1371.41	1016.65	844.06	744.20	680.56	637.47	607.09
27000	2549.85	1424.16	1055.75	876.53	772.83	706.74	661.99	630.44
28000	2644.29	1476.90	1094.85	908.99	801.45	732.91	686.51	653.79
29000	2738.73	1529.65	1133.95	941.45	830.07	759.09	711.03	677.14
30000	2833.16	1582.40	1173.06	973.92	858.70	785.26	735.54	700.49
31000	2927.60	1635.14	1212.16	1006.38	887.32	811.44	760.06	723.84
32000	3022.04	1687.89	1251.26	1038.85	915.94	837.61	784.58	747.19
33000	3116.48	1740.64	1290.36	1071.31	944.57	863.79	809.10	770.54
34000	3210.92	1793.38	1329.46	1103.77	973.19	889.96	833.62	793.89
35000	3305.36	1846.13	1368.56	1136.24	1001.81	916.14	858.13	817.23
40000	3777.55	2109.86	1564.07	1298.56	1144.93	1047.02	980.72	933.98
45000	4249.74	2373.59	1759.58	1460.88	1288.04	1177.89	1103.31	1050.73
50000	4721.94	2637.33	1955.09	1623.19	1431.16	1308.77	1225.90	1167.48
55000	5194.13	2901.06	2150.60	1785.51	1574.27	1439.65	1348.49	1284.23
60000	5666.32	3164.79	2346.11	1947.83	1717.39	1570.52	1471.08	1400.97
65000	6138.52	3428.52	2541.62	2110.15	1860.50	1701.40	1593.67	1517.72
70000	6610.71	3692.25	2737.12	2272.47	2003.62	1832.27	1716.26	1634.46
75000	7082.90	3955.99	2932.63	2434.79	2146.73	1963.15	1838.85	1751.21
80000	7555.10	4219.72	3128.14	2597.11	2289.85	2094.03	1961.44	1867.96
85000	8027.29	4483.45	3323.65	2759.43	2432.96	2224.90	2084.03	1984.71
90000	8499.48	4747.18	3519.16	2921.75	2576.08	2355.78	2206.62	2101.45
95000	8971.68	5010.91	3714.67	3084.06	2719.19	2486.66	2329.21	2218.20
100000	9443.87	5274.65	3910.18	3246.38	2862.31	2617.53	2451.80	2334.95
105000	9916.06	5538.38	4105.68	3408.70	3005.42	2748.41	2574.39	2451.69
110000	10388.26	5802.11	4301.19	3571.02	3148.54	2879.29	2696.98	2568.44
115000	10860.45	6065.84	4496.70	3733.34	3291.65	3010.16	2819.57	2685.19
120000	11332.64	6329.57	4692.21	3895.66	3434.77	3141.04	2942.16	2801.94
125000	11804.83	6593.31	4887.72	4057.98	3577.88	3271.91	3064.75	2918.68
130000	12277.03	6857.04	5083.23	4220.30	3721.00	3402.79	3187.34	3035.43
135000	12749.22	7120.77	5278.74	4382.62	3864.12	3533.67	3309.93	3152.18
140000	13221.42	7384.50	5474.24	4544.93	4007.23	3664.54	3432.52	3268.92
145000	13693.61	7648.23	5669.75	4707.25	4150.35	3795.42	3555.11	3385.67
150000	14165.80	7911.97	5865.26	4869.57	4293.46	3926.30	3677.70	3502.42
155000	14638.00	8175.70	6060.77	5031.89	4436.58	4057.17	3800.29	3619.17
160000	15110.19	8439.43	6256.28	5194.21	4579.69	4188.05	3922.88	3735.91

124

MONTHLY AMORTIZING PAYMENTS 23.750%

AMOUNT OF LOAN	NUMBER OF YEARS IN TERM							
	9	10	15	20	25	30	35	40
$ 50	1.13	1.10	1.02	1.00	1.00	1.00	.99	.99
100	2.26	2.19	2.04	2.00	1.99	1.99	1.98	1.98
200	4.51	4.38	4.08	4.00	3.97	3.97	3.96	3.96
300	6.76	6.57	6.12	6.00	5.96	5.95	5.94	5.94
400	9.01	8.75	8.16	7.99	7.94	7.93	7.92	7.92
500	11.26	10.94	10.20	9.99	9.93	9.91	9.90	9.90
600	13.51	13.13	12.24	11.99	11.91	11.89	11.88	11.88
700	15.76	15.32	14.28	13.99	13.90	13.87	13.86	13.86
800	18.01	17.50	16.32	15.98	15.88	15.85	15.84	15.84
900	20.26	19.69	18.36	17.98	17.87	17.83	17.82	17.82
1000	22.51	21.88	20.40	19.98	19.85	19.81	19.80	19.80
2000	45.01	43.75	40.79	39.95	39.70	39.62	39.60	39.59
3000	67.51	65.63	61.18	59.92	59.55	59.43	59.40	59.38
4000	90.01	87.50	81.57	79.90	79.39	79.24	79.19	79.18
5000	112.51	109.38	101.96	99.87	99.24	99.05	98.99	98.97
6000	135.02	131.25	122.35	119.84	119.09	118.86	118.79	118.76
7000	157.52	153.12	142.74	139.81	138.94	138.67	138.58	138.56
8000	180.02	175.00	163.13	159.79	158.78	158.48	158.38	158.35
9000	202.52	196.87	183.52	179.76	178.63	178.28	178.18	178.14
10000	225.02	218.75	203.91	199.73	198.48	198.09	197.97	197.94
11000	247.52	240.62	224.30	219.70	218.32	217.90	217.77	217.73
12000	270.03	262.49	244.69	239.68	238.17	237.71	237.57	237.52
13000	292.53	284.37	265.08	259.65	258.02	257.52	257.37	257.32
14000	315.03	306.24	285.47	279.62	277.86	277.32	277.17	277.11
15000	337.53	328.12	305.86	299.60	297.71	297.14	296.96	296.90
16000	360.03	349.99	326.25	319.57	317.56	316.95	316.76	316.70
17000	382.53	371.86	346.64	339.54	337.41	336.75	336.55	336.49
18000	405.04	393.74	367.04	359.51	357.25	356.56	356.35	356.28
19000	427.54	415.61	387.43	379.49	377.10	376.37	376.15	376.08
20000	450.04	437.49	407.82	399.46	396.95	396.18	395.94	395.87
21000	472.54	459.36	428.21	419.43	416.80	415.99	415.74	415.66
22000	495.04	481.23	448.60	439.40	436.64	435.80	435.54	435.46
23000	517.54	503.11	468.99	459.38	456.49	455.61	455.33	455.25
24000	540.05	524.98	489.38	479.35	476.34	475.42	475.13	475.04
25000	562.55	546.86	509.77	499.32	496.18	495.22	494.93	494.84
26000	585.05	568.73	530.16	519.29	516.03	515.03	514.73	514.63
27000	607.55	590.60	550.55	539.27	535.88	534.84	534.52	534.42
28000	630.05	612.48	570.94	559.24	555.73	554.65	554.32	554.22
29000	652.55	634.35	591.33	579.21	575.57	574.46	574.12	574.01
30000	675.06	656.23	611.72	599.19	595.42	594.27	593.91	593.80
31000	697.56	678.10	632.11	619.16	615.27	614.08	613.71	613.60
32000	720.06	699.97	652.50	639.13	635.11	633.89	633.51	633.39
33000	742.56	721.85	672.89	659.10	654.96	653.69	653.30	653.18
34000	765.06	743.72	693.28	679.08	674.81	673.50	673.10	672.98
35000	787.57	765.60	713.68	699.05	694.66	693.31	692.90	692.77
40000	900.07	874.97	815.63	798.91	793.89	792.36	791.88	791.74
45000	1012.58	984.34	917.58	898.78	893.13	891.40	890.87	890.70
50000	1125.09	1093.71	1019.53	998.64	992.36	990.44	989.85	989.67
55000	1237.60	1203.08	1121.49	1098.50	1091.60	1089.49	1088.84	1088.64
60000	1350.11	1312.45	1223.44	1198.37	1190.83	1188.53	1187.82	1187.60
65000	1462.62	1421.82	1325.39	1298.23	1290.07	1287.57	1286.81	1286.57
70000	1575.13	1531.19	1427.35	1398.09	1389.31	1386.62	1385.79	1385.54
75000	1687.63	1640.56	1529.30	1497.96	1488.54	1485.66	1484.78	1484.50
80000	1800.14	1749.93	1631.25	1597.82	1587.78	1584.71	1583.76	1583.47
85000	1912.65	1859.30	1733.20	1697.68	1687.01	1683.75	1682.74	1682.43
90000	2025.16	1968.67	1835.16	1797.55	1786.25	1782.79	1781.73	1781.40
95000	2137.67	2078.04	1937.11	1897.41	1885.49	1881.84	1880.71	1880.37
100000	2250.18	2187.41	2039.06	1997.27	1984.72	1980.88	1979.70	1979.33
105000	2362.69	2296.78	2141.02	2097.14	2083.96	2079.92	2078.68	2078.30
110000	2475.19	2406.15	2242.97	2197.00	2183.19	2178.97	2177.67	2177.27
115000	2587.70	2515.52	2344.92	2296.86	2282.43	2278.01	2276.65	2276.23
120000	2700.21	2624.89	2446.88	2396.73	2381.66	2377.06	2375.64	2375.20
125000	2812.72	2734.26	2548.83	2496.59	2480.90	2476.10	2474.62	2474.17
130000	2925.23	2843.63	2650.78	2596.45	2580.14	2575.14	2573.61	2573.13
135000	3037.74	2953.00	2752.73	2696.32	2679.37	2674.19	2672.59	2672.10
140000	3150.25	3062.37	2854.69	2796.18	2778.61	2773.23	2771.58	2771.07
145000	3262.75	3171.74	2956.64	2896.04	2877.84	2872.27	2870.56	2870.03
150000	3375.26	3281.11	3058.59	2995.91	2977.08	2971.32	2969.55	2969.00
155000	3487.77	3390.48	3160.55	3095.77	3076.32	3070.36	3068.53	3067.97
160000	3600.28	3499.85	3262.50	3195.63	3175.55	3169.41	3167.51	3166.93

125

24.000% MONTHLY AMORTIZING PAYMENTS

AMOUNT OF LOAN	NUMBER OF YEARS IN TERM							
	1	2	3	4	5	6	7	8
$ 50	4.73	2.65	1.97	1.64	1.44	1.32	1.24	1.18
100	9.46	5.29	3.93	3.27	2.88	2.64	2.47	2.36
200	18.92	10.58	7.85	6.53	5.76	5.27	4.94	4.71
300	28.37	15.87	11.77	9.79	8.64	7.90	7.41	7.06
400	37.83	21.15	15.70	13.05	11.51	10.54	9.88	9.41
500	47.28	26.44	19.62	16.31	14.39	13.17	12.34	11.76
600	56.74	31.73	23.54	19.57	17.27	15.80	14.81	14.11
700	66.20	37.01	27.47	22.83	20.14	18.43	17.28	16.46
800	75.65	42.30	31.39	26.09	23.02	21.07	19.75	18.82
900	85.11	47.59	35.31	29.35	25.90	23.70	22.21	21.17
1000	94.56	52.88	39.24	32.61	28.77	26.33	24.68	23.52
2000	189.12	105.75	78.47	65.21	57.54	52.66	49.36	47.03
3000	283.68	158.62	117.70	97.81	86.31	78.99	74.03	70.54
4000	378.24	211.49	156.94	130.41	115.08	105.31	98.71	94.06
5000	472.80	264.36	196.17	163.01	143.84	131.64	123.38	117.57
6000	567.36	317.23	235.40	195.62	172.61	157.97	148.06	141.08
7000	661.92	370.10	274.63	228.22	201.38	184.29	172.74	164.60
8000	756.48	422.97	313.87	260.82	230.15	210.62	197.41	188.11
9000	851.04	475.84	353.10	293.42	258.92	236.95	222.09	211.62
10000	945.60	528.72	392.33	326.02	287.68	263.27	246.76	235.14
11000	1040.16	581.59	431.57	358.63	316.45	289.60	271.44	258.65
12000	1134.72	634.46	470.80	391.23	345.22	315.93	296.11	282.16
13000	1229.28	687.33	510.03	423.83	373.99	342.25	320.79	305.68
14000	1323.84	740.20	549.26	456.43	402.76	368.58	345.47	329.19
15000	1418.40	793.07	588.50	489.03	431.52	394.91	370.14	352.70
16000	1512.96	845.94	627.73	521.63	460.29	421.23	394.82	376.22
17000	1607.52	898.81	666.96	554.24	489.06	447.56	419.49	399.73
18000	1702.08	951.68	706.20	586.84	517.83	473.89	444.17	423.24
19000	1796.64	1004.56	745.43	619.44	546.60	500.21	468.85	446.75
20000	1891.20	1057.43	784.66	652.04	575.36	526.54	493.52	470.27
21000	1985.76	1110.30	823.89	684.64	604.13	552.87	518.20	493.78
22000	2080.32	1163.17	863.13	717.25	632.90	579.20	542.87	517.29
23000	2174.88	1216.04	902.36	749.85	661.67	605.52	567.55	540.81
24000	2269.44	1268.91	941.59	782.45	690.44	631.85	592.22	564.32
25000	2363.99	1321.78	980.83	815.05	719.20	658.18	616.90	587.83
26000	2458.55	1374.65	1020.06	847.65	747.97	684.50	641.58	611.35
27000	2553.11	1427.52	1059.29	880.25	776.74	710.83	666.25	634.86
28000	2647.67	1480.40	1098.52	912.86	805.51	737.16	690.93	658.37
29000	2742.23	1533.27	1137.76	945.46	834.28	763.48	715.60	681.89
30000	2836.79	1586.14	1176.99	978.06	863.04	789.81	740.28	705.40
31000	2931.35	1639.01	1216.22	1010.66	891.81	816.14	764.96	728.91
32000	3025.91	1691.88	1255.46	1043.26	920.58	842.46	789.63	752.43
33000	3120.47	1744.75	1294.69	1075.87	949.35	868.79	814.31	775.94
34000	3215.03	1797.62	1333.92	1108.47	978.12	895.12	838.98	799.45
35000	3309.59	1850.49	1373.15	1141.07	1006.88	921.44	863.66	822.96
40000	3782.39	2114.85	1569.32	1304.08	1150.72	1053.08	987.04	940.53
45000	4255.19	2379.20	1765.48	1467.09	1294.56	1184.71	1110.42	1058.10
50000	4727.98	2643.56	1961.65	1630.10	1438.40	1316.35	1233.80	1175.66
55000	5200.78	2907.92	2157.81	1793.11	1582.24	1447.98	1357.17	1293.23
60000	5673.58	3172.27	2353.98	1956.12	1726.08	1579.61	1480.55	1410.79
65000	6146.38	3436.63	2550.14	2119.12	1869.92	1711.25	1603.93	1528.36
70000	6619.18	3700.98	2746.30	2282.13	2013.76	1842.88	1727.31	1645.92
75000	7091.97	3965.34	2942.47	2445.14	2157.60	1974.52	1850.69	1763.49
80000	7564.77	4229.69	3138.63	2608.15	2301.44	2106.15	1974.07	1881.06
85000	8037.57	4494.05	3334.80	2771.16	2445.28	2237.79	2097.45	1998.62
90000	8510.37	4758.40	3530.96	2934.17	2589.12	2369.42	2220.83	2116.19
95000	8983.17	5022.76	3727.13	3097.18	2732.96	2501.05	2344.21	2233.75
100000	9455.96	5287.11	3923.29	3260.19	2876.80	2632.69	2467.59	2351.32
105000	9928.76	5551.47	4119.45	3423.20	3020.64	2764.32	2590.97	2468.88
110000	10401.56	5815.83	4315.62	3586.21	3164.48	2895.96	2714.36	2586.45
115000	10874.36	6080.18	4511.78	3749.22	3308.32	3027.59	2837.72	2704.01
120000	11347.16	6344.54	4707.95	3912.23	3452.16	3159.22	2961.10	2821.58
125000	11819.95	6608.89	4904.11	4075.23	3596.00	3290.86	3084.48	2939.15
130000	12292.75	6873.25	5100.28	4238.24	3739.84	3422.49	3207.86	3056.71
135000	12765.55	7137.60	5296.44	4401.25	3883.68	3554.13	3331.24	3174.28
140000	13238.35	7401.96	5492.60	4564.26	4027.52	3685.76	3454.62	3291.84
145000	13711.15	7666.31	5688.77	4727.27	4171.36	3817.40	3578.00	3409.41
150000	14183.94	7930.67	5884.93	4890.28	4315.20	3949.03	3701.38	3526.97
155000	14656.74	8195.03	6081.10	5053.29	4459.04	4080.66	3824.76	3644.54
160000	15129.54	8459.38	6277.26	5216.30	4602.88	4212.30	3948.13	3762.11

126

AMOUNT OF LOAN	NUMBER OF YEARS IN TERM							
	9	10	15	20	25	30	35	40
$ 50	1.14	1.11	1.03	1.01	1.01	1.01	1.01	1.01
100	2.27	2.21	2.06	2.02	2.01	2.01	2.01	2.01
200	4.54	4.41	4.12	4.04	4.02	4.01	4.01	4.01
300	6.81	6.62	6.18	6.06	6.02	6.01	6.01	6.01
400	9.07	8.82	8.24	8.07	8.03	8.01	8.01	8.01
500	11.34	11.03	10.30	10.09	10.03	10.01	10.01	10.01
600	13.61	13.23	12.35	12.11	12.04	12.01	12.01	12.01
700	15.87	15.44	14.41	14.13	14.04	14.02	14.01	14.01
800	18.14	17.64	16.47	16.14	16.05	16.02	16.01	16.01
900	20.41	19.85	18.53	18.16	18.05	18.02	18.01	18.01
1000	22.68	22.05	20.59	20.18	20.06	20.02	20.01	20.01
2000	45.35	44.10	41.17	40.35	40.11	40.04	40.01	40.01
3000	68.02	66.15	61.75	60.53	60.16	60.05	60.02	60.01
4000	90.69	88.20	82.34	80.70	80.22	80.07	80.02	80.01
5000	113.36	110.25	102.92	100.88	100.27	100.09	100.03	100.01
6000	136.03	132.29	123.50	121.05	120.32	120.10	120.03	120.01
7000	158.70	154.34	144.08	141.22	140.37	140.12	140.04	140.02
8000	181.37	176.39	164.67	161.40	160.43	160.13	160.04	160.02
9000	204.04	198.44	185.25	181.57	180.48	180.15	180.05	180.02
10000	226.71	220.49	205.83	201.75	200.53	200.17	200.05	200.02
11000	249.38	242.53	226.42	221.92	220.59	220.18	220.06	220.02
12000	272.06	264.58	247.00	242.09	240.64	240.20	240.06	240.02
13000	294.73	286.63	267.58	262.27	260.69	260.21	260.07	260.02
14000	317.40	308.68	288.16	282.44	280.74	280.23	280.07	280.03
15000	340.07	330.73	308.75	302.62	300.80	300.25	300.08	300.03
16000	362.74	352.77	329.33	322.79	320.85	320.26	320.08	320.03
17000	385.41	374.82	349.91	342.96	340.90	340.28	340.09	340.03
18000	408.08	396.87	370.49	363.14	360.95	360.29	360.09	360.03
19000	430.75	418.92	391.08	383.31	381.01	380.31	380.10	380.03
20000	453.42	440.97	411.66	403.49	401.06	400.33	400.10	400.03
21000	476.09	463.02	432.24	423.66	421.11	420.34	420.11	420.04
22000	498.76	485.06	452.83	443.83	441.17	440.36	440.11	440.04
23000	521.43	507.11	473.41	464.01	461.22	460.37	460.12	460.04
24000	544.11	529.16	493.99	484.18	481.27	480.39	480.12	480.04
25000	566.78	551.21	514.57	504.36	501.32	500.41	500.13	500.04
26000	589.45	573.26	535.16	524.53	521.38	520.42	520.13	520.04
27000	612.12	595.30	555.74	544.71	541.43	540.44	540.14	540.05
28000	634.79	617.35	576.32	564.88	561.48	560.45	560.14	560.05
29000	657.46	639.40	596.90	585.05	581.53	580.47	580.15	580.05
30000	680.13	661.45	617.49	605.23	601.59	600.49	600.15	600.05
31000	702.80	683.50	638.07	625.40	621.64	620.50	620.16	620.05
32000	725.47	705.54	658.65	645.58	641.69	640.52	640.16	640.05
33000	748.14	727.59	679.24	665.75	661.75	660.53	660.17	660.05
34000	770.81	749.64	699.82	685.92	681.80	680.55	680.17	680.06
35000	793.48	771.69	720.40	706.10	701.85	700.57	700.18	700.06
40000	906.84	881.93	823.31	806.97	802.11	800.65	800.20	800.06
45000	1020.19	992.17	926.23	907.84	902.38	900.73	900.22	900.07
50000	1133.55	1102.41	1029.14	1008.71	1002.64	1000.81	1000.25	1000.08
55000	1246.90	1212.65	1132.06	1109.58	1102.91	1100.89	1100.27	1100.09
60000	1360.26	1322.89	1234.97	1210.45	1203.17	1200.97	1200.30	1200.09
65000	1473.61	1433.13	1337.88	1311.32	1303.43	1301.05	1300.32	1300.10
70000	1586.96	1543.37	1440.80	1412.19	1403.70	1401.13	1400.35	1400.11
75000	1700.32	1653.61	1543.71	1513.06	1503.96	1501.21	1500.37	1500.12
80000	1813.67	1763.85	1646.62	1613.93	1604.22	1601.29	1600.40	1600.12
85000	1927.03	1874.09	1749.54	1714.80	1704.49	1701.37	1700.42	1700.13
90000	2040.38	1984.33	1852.45	1815.67	1804.75	1801.45	1800.44	1800.14
95000	2153.74	2094.57	1955.36	1916.54	1905.02	1901.53	1900.47	1900.15
100000	2267.09	2204.81	2058.28	2017.41	2005.28	2001.61	2000.49	2000.15
105000	2380.44	2315.06	2161.19	2118.28	2105.54	2101.69	2100.52	2100.16
110000	2493.80	2425.30	2264.11	2219.15	2205.81	2201.77	2200.54	2200.17
115000	2607.15	2535.54	2367.02	2320.02	2306.07	2301.85	2300.57	2300.18
120000	2720.51	2645.78	2469.93	2420.89	2406.33	2401.93	2400.59	2400.18
125000	2833.86	2756.02	2572.85	2521.77	2506.60	2502.01	2500.62	2500.19
130000	2947.22	2866.26	2675.76	2622.64	2606.86	2602.09	2600.64	2600.20
135000	3060.57	2976.50	2778.68	2723.51	2707.12	2702.17	2700.66	2700.21
140000	3173.92	3086.74	2881.59	2824.38	2807.39	2802.25	2800.69	2800.21
145000	3287.28	3196.98	2984.50	2925.25	2907.65	2902.33	2900.71	2900.22
150000	3400.63	3307.22	3087.42	3026.12	3007.92	3002.41	3000.74	3000.23
155000	3513.99	3417.46	3190.33	3126.99	3108.18	3102.49	3100.76	3100.24
160000	3627.34	3527.70	3293.24	3227.86	3208.44	3202.57	3200.79	3200.24

AMOUNT OF LOAN	NUMBER OF YEARS IN TERM							
	1	2	3	4	5	6	7	8
$ 50	4.74	2.65	1.97	1.64	1.45	1.33	1.25	1.19
100	9.47	5.30	3.94	3.28	2.90	2.65	2.49	2.37
200	18.94	10.60	7.88	6.55	5.79	5.30	4.97	4.74
300	28.41	15.90	11.81	9.83	8.68	7.95	7.46	7.11
400	37.88	21.20	15.75	13.10	11.57	10.60	9.94	9.48
500	47.35	26.50	19.69	16.38	14.46	13.24	12.42	11.84
600	56.81	31.80	23.62	19.65	17.35	15.89	14.91	14.21
700	66.28	37.10	27.56	22.92	20.24	18.54	17.39	16.58
800	75.75	42.40	31.50	26.20	23.14	21.19	19.87	18.95
900	85.22	47.70	35.43	29.47	26.03	23.84	22.36	21.31
1000	94.69	53.00	39.37	32.75	28.92	26.48	24.84	23.68
2000	189.37	106.00	78.73	65.49	57.83	52.96	49.67	47.36
3000	284.05	158.99	118.10	98.23	86.74	79.44	74.51	71.04
4000	378.73	211.99	157.46	130.97	115.66	105.92	99.34	94.71
5000	473.41	264.98	196.83	163.71	144.57	132.40	124.18	118.39
6000	568.09	317.98	236.19	196.45	173.48	158.88	149.01	142.07
7000	662.77	370.98	275.55	229.19	202.40	185.36	173.84	165.75
8000	757.45	423.97	314.92	261.93	231.31	211.84	198.68	189.42
9000	852.13	476.97	354.28	294.67	260.22	238.31	223.51	213.10
10000	946.81	529.96	393.65	327.41	289.14	264.79	248.35	236.78
11000	1041.49	582.96	433.01	360.15	318.05	291.27	273.18	260.46
12000	1136.17	635.96	472.38	392.89	346.96	317.75	298.01	284.13
13000	1230.85	688.95	511.74	425.63	375.88	344.23	322.85	307.81
14000	1325.53	741.95	551.10	458.37	404.79	370.71	347.68	331.49
15000	1420.21	794.94	590.47	491.11	433.70	397.19	372.52	355.16
16000	1514.89	847.94	629.83	523.85	462.62	423.67	397.35	378.84
17000	1609.58	900.94	669.20	556.59	491.53	450.14	422.18	402.52
18000	1704.26	953.93	708.56	589.33	520.44	476.62	447.02	426.20
19000	1798.94	1006.93	747.93	622.07	549.36	503.10	471.85	449.87
20000	1893.62	1059.92	787.29	654.81	578.27	529.58	496.69	473.55
21000	1988.30	1112.92	826.65	687.55	607.18	556.06	521.52	497.23
22000	2082.98	1165.92	866.02	720.29	636.10	582.54	546.36	520.91
23000	2177.66	1218.91	905.38	753.03	665.01	609.02	571.19	544.58
24000	2272.34	1271.91	944.75	785.77	693.92	635.50	596.02	568.26
25000	2367.02	1324.90	984.11	818.51	722.84	661.98	620.86	591.94
26000	2461.70	1377.90	1023.48	851.25	751.75	688.45	645.69	615.62
27000	2556.38	1430.90	1052.84	883.99	780.66	714.93	670.53	639.29
28000	2651.06	1483.89	1102.20	916.73	809.58	741.41	695.36	662.97
29000	2745.74	1536.89	1141.57	949.47	838.49	767.89	720.19	686.65
30000	2840.42	1589.88	1180.93	982.21	867.40	794.37	745.03	710.32
31000	2935.10	1642.88	1220.30	1014.95	896.32	820.85	769.86	734.00
32000	3029.78	1695.88	1259.66	1047.69	925.23	847.33	794.70	757.68
33000	3124.47	1748.87	1299.02	1080.43	954.14	873.81	819.53	781.36
34000	3219.15	1801.87	1338.39	1113.17	983.06	900.28	844.36	805.03
35000	3313.83	1854.86	1377.75	1145.91	1011.97	926.76	869.20	828.71
40000	3787.23	2119.84	1574.57	1309.61	1156.54	1059.16	993.37	947.10
45000	4260.63	2384.82	1771.40	1473.31	1301.10	1191.55	1117.54	1065.48
50000	4734.04	2649.80	1968.22	1637.01	1445.67	1323.95	1241.71	1183.87
55000	5207.44	2914.78	2165.04	1800.72	1590.23	1456.34	1365.88	1302.26
60000	5680.84	3179.76	2361.86	1964.42	1734.80	1588.73	1490.05	1420.64
65000	6154.25	3444.74	2558.68	2128.12	1879.37	1721.13	1614.22	1539.03
70000	6627.65	3709.72	2755.50	2291.82	2023.93	1853.52	1738.39	1657.42
75000	7101.05	3974.70	2952.32	2455.52	2168.50	1985.92	1862.56	1775.80
80000	7574.45	4239.68	3149.14	2619.22	2313.07	2118.31	1986.73	1894.19
85000	8047.86	4504.66	3345.97	2782.92	2457.63	2250.70	2110.90	2012.58
90000	8521.26	4769.64	3542.79	2946.62	2602.20	2383.10	2235.07	2130.96
95000	8994.66	5034.62	3739.61	3110.32	2746.76	2515.49	2359.24	2249.35
100000	9468.07	5299.60	3936.43	3274.02	2891.33	2647.89	2483.41	2367.74
105000	9941.47	5564.58	4133.25	3437.73	3035.90	2780.28	2607.59	2486.12
110000	10414.87	5829.56	4330.07	3601.43	3180.46	2912.67	2731.76	2604.51
115000	10888.28	6094.54	4526.89	3765.13	3325.03	3045.07	2855.93	2722.90
120000	11361.68	6359.52	4723.71	3928.83	3469.60	3177.46	2980.10	2841.28
125000	11835.08	6624.50	4920.53	4092.53	3614.16	3309.86	3104.27	2959.67
130000	12308.49	6889.48	5117.36	4256.23	3758.73	3442.25	3228.44	3078.06
135000	12781.89	7154.46	5314.18	4419.93	3903.29	3574.64	3352.61	3196.44
140000	13255.29	7419.44	5511.00	4583.63	4047.86	3707.04	3476.78	3314.83
145000	13728.70	7684.42	5707.82	4747.33	4192.43	3839.43	3600.95	3433.21
150000	14202.10	7949.40	5904.64	4911.03	4336.99	3971.83	3725.12	3551.60
155000	14675.50	8214.38	6101.46	5074.74	4481.56	4104.22	3849.29	3669.99
160000	15148.90	8479.36	6298.28	5238.44	4626.13	4236.61	3973.46	3788.37

AMOUNT OF LOAN	NUMBER OF YEARS IN TERM							
	9	10	15	20	25	30	35	40
$ 50	1.15	1.12	1.04	1.02	1.02	1.02	1.02	1.02
100	2.29	2.23	2.08	2.04	2.03	2.03	2.03	2.03
200	4.57	4.45	4.16	4.08	4.06	4.05	4.05	4.05
300	6.86	6.67	6.24	6.12	6.08	6.07	6.07	6.07
400	9.14	8.89	8.32	8.16	8.11	8.09	8.09	8.09
500	11.43	11.12	10.39	10.19	10.13	10.12	10.11	10.11
600	13.71	13.34	12.47	12.23	12.16	12.14	12.13	12.13
700	15.99	15.56	14.55	14.27	14.19	14.16	14.15	14.15
800	18.28	17.78	16.63	16.31	16.21	16.18	16.18	16.17
900	20.56	20.01	18.70	18.34	18.24	18.21	18.20	18.19
1000	22.85	22.23	20.78	20.38	20.26	20.23	20.22	20.21
2000	45.69	44.45	41.56	40.76	40.52	40.45	40.43	40.42
3000	68.53	66.67	62.33	61.13	60.78	60.68	60.64	60.63
4000	91.37	88.90	83.11	81.51	81.04	80.90	80.86	80.84
5000	114.21	111.12	103.88	101.88	101.30	101.13	101.07	101.05
6000	137.05	133.34	124.66	122.26	121.56	121.35	121.28	121.26
7000	159.89	155.56	145.43	142.64	141.81	141.57	141.50	141.47
8000	182.73	177.79	166.21	163.01	162.07	161.79	161.71	161.68
9000	205.57	200.01	186.98	183.39	182.33	182.02	181.92	181.89
10000	228.41	222.23	207.76	203.76	202.59	202.24	202.13	202.10
11000	251.25	244.45	228.53	224.14	222.85	222.46	222.35	222.31
12000	274.09	266.68	249.31	244.51	243.11	242.69	242.56	242.52
13000	296.93	288.90	270.08	264.89	263.36	262.91	262.77	262.73
14000	319.77	311.12	290.86	285.27	283.62	283.13	282.99	282.94
15000	342.61	333.35	311.63	305.64	303.88	303.36	303.20	303.15
16000	365.45	355.57	332.41	326.02	324.14	323.58	323.41	323.36
17000	388.29	377.79	353.18	346.39	344.40	343.80	343.62	343.57
18000	411.13	400.01	373.96	366.77	364.66	364.03	363.84	363.78
19000	433.97	422.24	394.74	387.14	384.92	384.25	384.05	383.99
20000	456.81	444.46	415.51	407.52	405.17	404.47	404.26	404.20
21000	479.65	466.68	436.29	427.90	425.43	424.70	424.48	424.41
22000	502.50	488.90	457.06	448.27	445.69	444.92	444.69	444.62
23000	525.34	511.13	477.84	468.65	465.95	465.14	464.90	464.83
24000	548.18	533.35	498.61	489.02	486.21	485.37	485.11	485.04
25000	571.02	555.57	519.39	509.40	506.47	505.59	505.33	505.25
26000	593.86	577.79	540.16	529.77	526.72	525.81	525.54	525.46
27000	616.70	600.02	560.94	550.15	546.98	546.04	545.75	545.67
28000	639.54	622.24	581.71	570.53	567.24	566.26	565.97	565.88
29000	662.38	644.46	602.49	590.90	587.50	586.48	586.18	586.09
30000	685.22	666.69	623.26	611.28	607.76	606.71	606.39	606.30
31000	708.06	688.91	644.04	631.65	628.02	626.93	626.60	626.51
32000	730.90	711.13	664.81	652.03	648.28	647.15	646.82	646.72
33000	753.74	733.35	685.59	672.40	668.53	667.38	667.03	666.93
34000	776.58	755.58	706.36	692.78	688.79	687.60	687.24	687.13
35000	799.42	777.80	727.14	713.16	709.05	707.82	707.46	707.34
40000	913.62	888.91	831.02	815.03	810.34	808.94	808.52	808.39
45000	1027.83	1000.03	934.89	916.91	911.64	910.06	909.58	909.44
50000	1142.03	1111.14	1038.77	1018.79	1012.93	1011.17	1010.65	1010.49
55000	1256.23	1222.25	1142.65	1120.67	1114.22	1112.29	1111.71	1111.54
60000	1370.43	1333.37	1246.52	1222.55	1215.51	1213.41	1212.78	1212.59
65000	1484.64	1444.48	1350.40	1324.43	1316.80	1314.53	1313.84	1313.64
70000	1598.84	1555.59	1454.28	1426.31	1418.10	1415.64	1414.91	1414.68
75000	1713.04	1666.71	1558.15	1528.19	1519.39	1516.76	1515.97	1515.73
80000	1827.24	1777.82	1662.03	1630.06	1620.68	1617.88	1617.03	1616.78
85000	1941.44	1888.93	1765.90	1731.94	1721.97	1718.99	1718.10	1717.83
90000	2055.65	2000.05	1869.78	1833.82	1823.27	1820.11	1819.16	1818.88
95000	2169.85	2111.16	1973.66	1935.70	1924.56	1921.23	1920.23	1919.93
100000	2284.05	2222.27	2077.53	2037.58	2025.85	2022.34	2021.29	2020.97
105000	2398.25	2333.39	2181.41	2139.46	2127.14	2123.46	2122.36	2122.02
110000	2512.46	2444.50	2285.29	2241.34	2228.43	2224.58	2223.42	2223.07
115000	2626.66	2555.61	2389.16	2343.22	2329.73	2325.70	2324.48	2324.12
120000	2740.86	2666.73	2493.04	2445.09	2431.02	2426.81	2425.55	2425.17
125000	2855.06	2777.84	2596.92	2546.97	2532.31	2527.93	2526.61	2526.22
130000	2969.27	2888.95	2700.79	2648.85	2633.60	2629.05	2627.68	2627.27
135000	3083.47	3000.07	2804.67	2750.73	2734.90	2730.16	2728.74	2728.31
140000	3197.67	3111.18	2908.55	2852.61	2836.19	2831.28	2829.81	2829.36
145000	3311.87	3222.29	3012.42	2954.49	2937.48	2932.40	2930.87	2930.41
150000	3426.07	3333.41	3116.30	3056.37	3038.77	3033.51	3031.93	3031.46
155000	3540.28	3444.52	3220.18	3158.25	3140.06	3134.63	3133.00	3132.51
160000	3654.48	3555.63	3324.05	3260.12	3241.36	3235.75	3234.06	3233.56

MONTHLY AMORTIZING PAYMENTS

AMOUNT OF LOAN	NUMBER OF YEARS IN TERM							
	1	2	3	4	5	6	7	8
$ 50	4.75	2.66	1.98	1.65	1.46	1.34	1.25	1.20
100	9.49	5.32	3.95	3.29	2.91	2.67	2.50	2.39
200	18.97	10.63	7.90	6.58	5.82	5.33	5.00	4.77
300	28.45	15.94	11.85	9.87	8.72	7.99	7.50	7.16
400	37.93	21.25	15.80	13.16	11.63	10.66	10.00	9.54
500	47.41	26.57	19.75	16.44	14.53	13.32	12.50	11.93
600	56.89	31.88	23.70	19.73	17.44	15.98	15.00	14.31
700	66.37	37.19	27.65	23.02	20.35	18.65	17.50	16.69
800	75.85	42.50	31.60	26.31	23.25	21.31	20.00	19.08
900	85.33	47.81	35.55	29.60	26.16	23.97	22.50	21.46
1000	94.81	53.13	39.50	32.88	29.06	26.64	25.00	23.85
2000	189.61	106.25	79.00	65.76	58.12	53.27	49.99	47.69
3000	284.41	159.37	118.49	98.64	87.18	79.90	74.98	71.53
4000	379.21	212.49	157.99	131.52	116.24	106.53	99.98	95.37
5000	474.01	265.61	197.48	164.40	145.30	133.16	124.97	119.21
6000	568.82	318.73	236.98	197.28	174.36	159.79	149.96	143.06
7000	663.62	371.85	276.48	230.16	203.42	186.43	174.95	166.90
8000	758.42	424.97	315.97	263.04	232.48	213.05	199.95	190.74
9000	853.22	478.09	355.47	295.91	261.54	239.69	224.94	214.58
10000	948.02	531.21	394.96	328.79	290.59	266.32	249.93	238.42
11000	1042.82	584.34	434.46	361.67	319.65	292.95	274.93	262.27
12000	1137.63	637.46	473.96	394.55	348.71	319.58	299.92	286.11
13000	1232.43	690.58	513.45	427.43	377.77	346.21	324.91	309.95
14000	1327.23	743.70	552.95	460.31	406.83	372.84	349.90	333.79
15000	1422.03	796.82	592.44	493.19	435.89	399.47	374.90	357.63
16000	1516.83	849.94	631.94	526.07	464.95	426.10	399.89	381.48
17000	1611.63	903.06	671.43	558.95	494.01	452.74	424.88	405.32
18000	1706.44	956.18	710.93	591.82	523.07	479.37	449.88	429.16
19000	1801.24	1009.30	750.43	624.70	552.12	506.00	474.87	453.00
20000	1896.04	1062.42	789.92	657.58	581.18	532.63	499.86	476.84
21000	1990.84	1115.55	829.42	690.46	610.24	559.26	524.85	500.69
22000	2085.64	1168.67	868.91	723.34	639.30	585.89	549.85	524.53
23000	2180.44	1221.79	908.41	756.22	668.36	612.52	574.84	548.37
24000	2275.25	1274.91	947.91	789.10	697.42	639.15	599.83	572.21
25000	2370.05	1328.03	987.40	821.98	726.48	665.78	624.83	596.05
26000	2464.85	1381.15	1026.90	854.86	755.54	692.42	649.82	619.90
27000	2559.65	1434.27	1066.39	887.73	784.60	719.05	674.81	643.74
28000	2654.45	1487.39	1105.89	920.61	813.65	745.68	699.80	667.58
29000	2749.26	1540.51	1145.38	953.49	842.71	772.31	724.80	691.42
30000	2844.06	1593.63	1184.88	986.37	871.77	798.94	749.79	715.26
31000	2938.86	1646.76	1224.38	1019.25	900.83	825.57	774.78	739.11
32000	3033.66	1699.88	1263.87	1052.13	929.89	852.20	799.78	762.95
33000	3128.46	1753.00	1303.37	1085.01	958.95	878.83	824.77	786.79
34000	3223.26	1806.12	1342.86	1117.89	988.01	905.47	849.76	810.63
35000	3318.07	1859.24	1382.36	1150.77	1017.07	932.10	874.75	834.47
40000	3792.07	2124.84	1579.84	1315.16	1162.36	1065.25	999.72	953.68
45000	4266.08	2390.45	1777.32	1479.55	1307.66	1198.41	1124.68	1072.89
50000	4740.09	2656.05	1974.80	1643.95	1452.95	1331.56	1249.65	1192.10
55000	5214.10	2921.66	2172.28	1808.34	1598.25	1464.72	1374.61	1311.31
60000	5688.11	3187.26	2369.76	1972.74	1743.54	1597.88	1499.58	1430.52
65000	6162.12	3452.87	2567.24	2137.13	1888.83	1731.03	1624.54	1549.73
70000	6636.13	3718.47	2764.72	2301.53	2034.13	1864.19	1749.50	1668.94
75000	7110.14	3984.08	2962.19	2465.92	2179.42	1997.34	1874.47	1788.15
80000	7584.14	4249.68	3159.67	2630.31	2324.72	2130.50	1999.43	1907.36
85000	8058.15	4515.29	3357.15	2794.71	2470.01	2263.66	2124.40	2026.57
90000	8532.16	4780.89	3554.63	2959.10	2615.31	2396.81	2249.36	2145.78
95000	9006.17	5046.50	3752.11	3123.50	2760.60	2529.97	2374.32	2264.99
100000	9480.18	5312.10	3949.59	3287.89	2905.90	2663.12	2499.29	2384.20
105000	9954.19	5577.71	4147.07	3452.29	3051.19	2796.28	2624.25	2503.41
110000	10428.20	5843.31	4344.55	3616.68	3196.49	2929.44	2749.22	2622.62
115000	10902.20	6108.92	4542.03	3781.07	3341.78	3062.59	2874.18	2741.83
120000	11376.21	6374.52	4739.51	3945.47	3487.07	3195.75	2999.15	2861.04
125000	11850.22	6640.13	4936.99	4109.86	3632.37	3328.90	3124.11	2980.25
130000	12324.23	6905.73	5134.47	4274.26	3777.66	3462.06	3249.07	3099.46
135000	12798.24	7171.34	5331.95	4438.65	3922.96	3595.21	3374.04	3218.67
140000	13272.25	7436.94	5529.43	4603.05	4068.25	3728.37	3499.00	3337.88
145000	13746.26	7702.55	5726.90	4767.44	4213.55	3861.53	3623.97	3457.09
150000	14220.27	7968.15	5924.38	4931.84	4358.84	3994.68	3748.93	3576.30
155000	14694.27	8233.76	6121.86	5096.23	4504.14	4127.84	3873.89	3695.51
160000	15168.28	8499.36	6319.34	5260.62	4649.43	4260.99	3998.86	3814.72

AMOUNT OF LOAN	NUMBER OF YEARS IN TERM							
	9	10	15	20	25	30	35	40
$ 50	1.16	1.12	1.05	1.03	1.03	1.03	1.03	1.03
100	2.31	2.24	2.10	2.06	2.05	2.05	2.05	2.05
200	4.61	4.48	4.20	4.12	4.10	4.09	4.09	4.09
300	6.91	6.72	6.30	6.18	6.14	6.13	6.13	6.13
400	9.21	8.96	8.39	8.24	8.19	8.18	8.17	8.17
500	11.51	11.20	10.49	10.29	10.24	10.22	10.22	10.21
600	13.81	13.44	12.59	12.35	12.28	12.26	12.26	12.26
700	16.11	15.68	14.68	14.41	14.33	14.31	14.30	14.30
800	18.41	17.92	16.78	16.47	16.38	16.35	16.34	16.34
900	20.71	20.16	18.88	18.52	18.42	18.39	18.38	18.38
1000	23.02	22.40	20.97	20.58	20.47	20.44	20.43	20.42
2000	46.03	44.80	41.94	41.16	40.93	40.87	40.85	40.84
3000	69.04	67.20	62.91	61.74	61.40	61.30	61.27	61.26
4000	92.05	89.60	83.88	82.32	81.86	81.73	81.69	81.68
5000	115.06	111.99	104.85	102.89	102.33	102.16	102.11	102.09
6000	138.07	134.39	125.81	123.47	122.79	122.59	122.53	122.51
7000	161.08	156.79	146.78	144.05	143.25	143.02	142.95	142.93
8000	184.09	179.19	167.75	164.63	163.72	163.45	163.37	163.35
9000	207.10	201.58	188.72	185.20	184.18	183.88	183.79	183.77
10000	230.11	223.98	209.69	205.78	204.65	204.31	204.21	204.18
11000	253.12	246.38	230.66	226.36	225.11	224.74	224.63	224.60
12000	276.13	268.78	251.62	246.94	245.58	245.17	245.06	245.02
13000	299.14	291.18	272.59	267.51	266.04	265.61	265.48	265.44
14000	322.15	313.57	293.56	288.09	286.50	286.04	285.90	285.86
15000	345.16	335.97	314.53	308.67	306.97	306.47	306.32	306.27
16000	368.17	358.37	335.50	329.25	327.43	326.90	326.74	326.69
17000	391.18	380.77	356.47	349.83	347.90	347.33	347.16	347.11
18000	414.20	403.17	377.43	370.40	368.36	367.76	367.58	367.53
19000	437.21	425.56	398.40	390.98	388.83	388.19	388.00	387.95
20000	460.22	447.96	419.37	411.56	409.29	408.62	408.42	408.36
21000	483.23	470.36	440.34	432.14	429.75	429.05	428.84	428.78
22000	506.24	492.76	461.31	452.71	450.22	449.48	449.26	449.20
23000	529.25	515.15	482.27	473.29	470.68	469.91	469.68	469.62
24000	552.26	537.55	503.24	493.87	491.15	490.34	490.11	490.03
25000	575.27	559.95	524.21	514.45	511.61	510.78	510.53	510.45
26000	598.28	582.35	545.18	535.02	532.08	531.21	530.95	530.87
27000	621.29	604.74	566.15	555.60	552.54	551.64	551.37	551.29
28000	644.30	627.14	587.12	576.18	573.00	572.07	571.79	571.71
29000	667.31	649.54	608.08	596.76	593.47	592.50	592.21	592.12
30000	690.32	671.94	629.05	617.33	613.93	612.93	612.63	612.54
31000	713.33	694.33	650.02	637.91	634.40	633.36	633.05	632.96
32000	736.34	716.73	670.99	658.49	654.86	653.79	653.47	653.38
33000	759.35	739.13	691.96	679.07	675.33	674.22	673.89	673.80
34000	782.36	761.53	712.93	699.65	695.79	694.65	694.31	694.21
35000	805.37	783.93	733.89	720.22	716.25	715.08	714.74	714.63
40000	920.43	895.91	838.73	823.11	818.58	817.24	816.84	816.72
45000	1035.48	1007.90	943.58	926.00	920.90	919.39	918.94	918.81
50000	1150.53	1119.89	1048.42	1028.89	1023.22	1021.55	1021.05	1020.90
55000	1265.59	1231.88	1153.26	1131.78	1125.54	1123.70	1123.15	1122.99
60000	1380.64	1343.87	1258.10	1234.66	1227.86	1225.85	1225.26	1225.08
65000	1495.69	1455.86	1362.94	1337.55	1330.18	1328.01	1327.36	1327.17
70000	1610.74	1567.85	1467.78	1440.44	1432.50	1430.16	1429.47	1429.26
75000	1725.80	1679.83	1572.62	1543.33	1534.83	1532.32	1531.57	1531.35
80000	1840.85	1791.82	1677.46	1646.22	1637.15	1634.47	1633.67	1633.44
85000	1955.90	1903.81	1782.31	1749.11	1739.47	1736.62	1735.78	1735.53
90000	2070.96	2015.80	1887.15	1851.99	1841.79	1838.78	1837.88	1837.62
95000	2186.01	2127.79	1991.99	1954.88	1944.11	1940.93	1939.99	1939.71
100000	2301.06	2239.78	2096.83	2057.77	2046.43	2043.09	2042.09	2041.80
105000	2416.11	2351.77	2201.67	2160.66	2148.75	2145.24	2144.20	2143.89
110000	2531.17	2463.76	2306.51	2263.55	2251.08	2247.39	2246.30	2245.98
115000	2646.22	2575.74	2411.35	2366.43	2353.40	2349.55	2348.40	2348.07
120000	2761.27	2687.73	2516.19	2469.32	2455.72	2451.70	2450.51	2450.15
125000	2876.33	2799.72	2621.04	2572.21	2558.04	2553.86	2552.61	2552.24
130000	2991.38	2911.71	2725.88	2675.10	2660.36	2656.01	2654.72	2654.33
135000	3106.43	3023.70	2830.72	2777.99	2762.68	2758.16	2756.82	2756.42
140000	3221.48	3135.69	2935.56	2880.88	2865.00	2860.32	2858.93	2858.51
145000	3336.54	3247.68	3040.40	2983.76	2967.33	2962.47	2961.03	2960.60
150000	3451.59	3359.66	3145.24	3086.65	3069.65	3064.63	3063.14	3062.69
155000	3566.64	3471.65	3250.08	3189.54	3171.97	3166.78	3165.24	3164.78
160000	3681.70	3583.64	3354.92	3292.43	3274.29	3268.93	3267.34	3266.87

AMOUNT OF LOAN	NUMBER OF YEARS IN TERM							
	1	2	3	4	5	6	7	8
$ 50	4.75	2.67	1.99	1.66	1.47	1.34	1.26	1.21
100	9.50	5.33	3.97	3.31	2.93	2.68	2.52	2.41
200	18.99	10.65	7.93	6.61	5.85	5.36	5.04	4.81
300	28.48	15.98	11.89	9.91	8.77	8.04	7.55	7.21
400	37.97	21.30	15.86	13.21	11.69	10.72	10.07	9.61
500	47.47	26.63	19.82	16.51	14.61	13.40	12.58	12.01
600	56.96	31.95	23.78	19.82	17.53	16.08	15.10	14.41
700	66.45	37.28	27.74	23.12	20.45	18.75	17.61	16.81
800	75.94	42.60	31.71	26.42	23.37	21.43	20.13	19.21
900	85.44	47.93	35.67	29.72	26.29	24.11	22.64	21.61
1000	94.93	53.25	39.63	33.02	29.21	26.79	25.16	24.01
2000	189.85	106.50	79.26	66.04	58.41	53.57	50.31	48.02
3000	284.77	159.74	118.89	99.06	87.62	80.36	75.46	72.03
4000	379.70	212.99	158.52	132.08	116.82	107.14	100.61	96.03
5000	474.62	266.24	198.14	165.09	146.03	133.92	125.77	120.04
6000	569.54	319.48	237.77	198.11	175.23	160.71	150.92	144.05
7000	664.47	372.73	277.40	231.13	204.44	187.49	176.07	168.05
8000	759.39	425.97	317.03	264.15	233.64	214.28	201.22	192.06
9000	854.31	479.22	356.65	297.17	262.85	241.06	226.37	216.07
10000	949.23	532.47	396.28	330.18	292.05	267.84	251.53	240.08
11000	1044.16	585.71	435.91	363.20	321.26	294.63	276.68	264.08
12000	1139.08	638.96	475.54	396.22	350.46	321.41	301.83	288.09
13000	1234.00	692.21	515.17	429.24	379.67	348.20	326.98	312.10
14000	1328.93	745.45	554.79	462.25	408.87	374.98	352.13	336.10
15000	1423.85	798.70	594.42	495.27	438.08	401.76	377.29	360.11
16000	1518.77	851.94	634.05	528.29	467.28	428.55	402.44	384.12
17000	1613.69	905.19	673.68	561.31	496.49	455.33	427.59	408.13
18000	1708.62	958.44	713.30	594.33	525.69	482.12	452.74	432.13
19000	1803.54	1011.68	752.93	627.34	554.90	508.90	477.89	456.14
20000	1898.46	1064.93	792.56	660.36	584.10	535.68	503.05	480.15
21000	1993.39	1118.17	832.19	693.38	613.31	562.47	528.20	504.15
22000	2088.31	1171.42	871.81	726.40	642.51	589.25	553.35	528.16
23000	2183.23	1224.67	911.44	759.42	671.72	616.04	578.50	552.17
24000	2278.16	1277.91	951.07	792.43	700.92	642.82	603.65	576.17
25000	2373.08	1331.16	990.70	825.45	730.13	669.60	628.81	600.18
26000	2468.00	1384.41	1030.33	858.47	759.33	696.39	653.96	624.19
27000	2562.92	1437.65	1069.95	891.49	788.54	723.17	679.11	648.20
28000	2657.85	1490.90	1109.58	924.50	817.74	749.96	704.26	672.20
29000	2752.77	1544.14	1149.21	957.52	846.95	776.74	729.41	696.21
30000	2847.69	1597.39	1188.84	990.54	876.15	803.52	754.57	720.22
31000	2942.62	1650.64	1228.46	1023.56	905.36	830.31	779.72	744.22
32000	3037.54	1703.88	1268.09	1056.58	934.56	857.09	804.87	768.23
33000	3132.46	1757.13	1307.72	1089.59	963.77	883.88	830.02	792.24
34000	3227.38	1810.37	1347.35	1122.61	992.97	910.66	855.17	816.25
35000	3322.31	1863.62	1386.98	1155.63	1022.18	937.44	880.33	840.25
40000	3796.92	2129.85	1585.11	1320.72	1168.20	1071.36	1006.09	960.29
45000	4271.54	2396.08	1783.25	1485.81	1314.23	1205.28	1131.85	1080.32
50000	4746.15	2662.31	1981.39	1650.90	1460.25	1339.20	1257.61	1200.36
55000	5220.77	2928.54	2179.53	1815.99	1606.28	1473.12	1383.37	1320.39
60000	5695.38	3194.78	2377.67	1981.08	1752.30	1607.04	1509.13	1440.43
65000	6170.00	3461.01	2575.81	2146.16	1898.33	1740.96	1634.89	1560.47
70000	6644.61	3727.24	2773.95	2311.25	2044.35	1874.88	1760.65	1680.50
75000	7119.22	3993.47	2972.08	2476.34	2190.38	2008.80	1886.41	1800.54
80000	7593.84	4259.70	3170.22	2641.43	2336.40	2142.72	2012.17	1920.57
85000	8068.45	4525.93	3368.36	2806.52	2482.42	2276.64	2137.93	2040.61
90000	8543.07	4792.16	3566.50	2971.61	2628.45	2410.56	2263.69	2160.64
95000	9017.68	5058.39	3764.64	3136.70	2774.47	2544.48	2389.45	2280.68
100000	9492.30	5324.62	3962.78	3301.79	2920.50	2678.40	2515.21	2400.71
105000	9966.91	5590.85	4160.92	3466.88	3066.52	2812.32	2640.97	2520.75
110000	10441.53	5857.08	4359.05	3631.97	3212.55	2946.24	2766.73	2640.78
115000	10916.14	6123.31	4557.19	3797.06	3358.57	3080.16	2892.49	2760.82
120000	11390.76	6389.55	4755.33	3962.15	3504.60	3214.08	3018.25	2880.85
125000	11865.37	6655.78	4953.47	4127.24	3650.62	3348.00	3144.01	3000.89
130000	12339.99	6922.01	5151.61	4292.32	3796.65	3481.92	3269.77	3120.93
135000	12814.60	7188.24	5349.75	4457.41	3942.67	3615.84	3395.53	3240.96
140000	13289.21	7454.47	5547.89	4622.50	4088.70	3749.76	3521.29	3361.00
145000	13763.83	7720.70	5746.02	4787.59	4234.72	3883.68	3647.05	3481.03
150000	14238.44	7986.93	5944.16	4952.68	4380.75	4017.60	3772.81	3601.07
155000	14713.06	8253.16	6142.30	5117.77	4526.77	4151.52	3898.57	3721.10
160000	15187.67	8519.39	6340.44	5282.86	4672.80	4285.44	4024.33	3841.14

AMOUNT OF LOAN	NUMBER OF YEARS IN TERM							
	9	10	15	20	25	30	35	40
$ 50	1.16	1.13	1.06	1.04	1.04	1.04	1.04	1.04
100	2.32	2.26	2.12	2.08	2.07	2.07	2.07	2.07
200	4.64	4.52	4.24	4.16	4.14	4.13	4.13	4.13
300	6.96	6.78	6.35	6.24	6.21	6.20	6.19	6.19
400	9.28	9.03	8.47	8.32	8.27	8.26	8.26	8.26
500	11.60	11.29	10.59	10.39	10.34	10.32	10.32	10.32
600	13.91	13.55	12.70	12.47	12.41	12.39	12.38	12.38
700	16.23	15.81	14.82	14.55	14.47	14.45	14.45	14.44
800	18.55	18.06	16.93	16.63	16.54	16.52	16.51	16.51
900	20.87	20.32	19.05	18.71	18.61	18.58	18.57	18.57
1000	23.19	22.58	21.17	20.78	20.68	20.64	20.63	20.63
2000	46.37	45.15	42.33	41.56	41.35	41.28	41.26	41.26
3000	69.55	67.72	63.49	62.34	62.02	61.92	61.89	61.88
4000	92.73	90.30	84.65	83.12	82.69	82.56	82.52	82.51
5000	115.91	112.87	105.81	103.90	103.36	103.20	103.15	103.14
6000	139.09	135.44	126.97	124.68	124.03	123.83	123.78	123.76
7000	162.27	158.02	148.14	145.46	144.70	144.47	144.41	144.39
8000	185.45	180.59	169.30	166.24	165.37	165.11	165.04	165.01
9000	208.64	203.16	190.46	187.02	186.04	185.75	185.67	185.64
10000	231.82	225.74	211.62	207.80	206.71	206.39	206.29	206.27
11000	255.00	248.31	232.78	228.58	227.38	227.03	226.92	226.89
12000	278.18	270.88	253.94	249.36	248.05	247.66	247.55	247.52
13000	301.36	293.46	275.11	270.14	268.72	268.30	268.18	268.14
14000	324.54	316.03	296.27	290.92	289.39	288.94	288.81	288.77
15000	347.72	338.60	317.43	311.70	310.06	309.58	309.44	309.40
16000	370.90	361.18	338.59	332.48	330.73	330.22	330.07	330.02
17000	394.08	383.75	359.75	353.26	351.40	350.86	350.70	350.65
18000	417.27	406.32	380.91	374.04	372.07	371.49	371.33	371.28
19000	440.45	428.90	402.07	394.82	392.74	392.13	391.95	391.90
20000	463.63	451.47	423.24	415.60	413.41	412.77	412.58	412.53
21000	486.81	474.04	444.40	436.38	434.08	433.41	433.21	433.15
22000	509.99	496.62	465.56	457.16	454.75	454.05	453.84	453.78
23000	533.17	519.19	486.72	477.94	475.42	474.69	474.47	474.41
24000	556.35	541.76	507.88	498.72	496.09	495.32	495.10	495.03
25000	579.53	564.34	529.04	519.50	516.76	515.96	515.73	515.66
26000	602.71	586.91	550.21	540.28	537.43	536.60	536.36	536.28
27000	625.90	609.48	571.37	561.06	558.10	557.24	556.99	556.91
28000	649.08	632.06	592.53	581.84	578.77	577.88	577.61	577.54
29000	672.26	654.63	613.69	602.62	599.44	598.51	598.24	598.16
30000	695.44	677.20	634.85	623.40	620.11	619.15	618.87	618.79
31000	718.62	699.78	656.01	644.18	640.78	639.79	639.50	639.42
32000	741.80	722.35	677.18	664.96	661.45	660.43	660.13	660.04
33000	764.98	744.92	698.34	685.74	682.12	681.07	680.76	680.67
34000	788.16	767.50	719.50	706.52	702.79	701.71	701.39	701.29
35000	811.34	790.07	740.66	727.30	723.46	722.34	722.02	721.92
40000	927.25	902.94	846.47	831.20	826.81	825.54	825.16	825.05
45000	1043.16	1015.80	952.28	935.10	930.17	928.73	928.31	928.18
50000	1159.06	1128.67	1058.08	1038.99	1033.52	1031.92	1031.45	1031.31
55000	1274.97	1241.54	1163.89	1142.89	1136.87	1135.11	1134.59	1134.44
60000	1390.87	1354.40	1269.70	1246.79	1240.22	1238.30	1237.74	1237.57
65000	1506.78	1467.27	1375.51	1350.69	1343.57	1341.49	1340.88	1340.70
70000	1622.68	1580.13	1481.32	1454.59	1446.92	1444.68	1444.03	1443.84
75000	1738.59	1693.00	1587.12	1558.49	1550.27	1547.88	1547.17	1546.97
80000	1854.50	1805.87	1692.93	1662.39	1653.62	1651.07	1650.32	1650.10
85000	1970.40	1918.73	1798.74	1766.29	1756.98	1754.26	1753.46	1753.23
90000	2086.31	2031.60	1904.55	1870.19	1860.33	1857.45	1856.61	1856.36
95000	2202.21	2144.47	2010.35	1974.09	1963.68	1960.64	1959.75	1959.49
100000	2318.12	2257.33	2116.16	2077.98	2067.03	2063.83	2062.89	2062.62
105000	2434.02	2370.20	2221.97	2181.88	2170.38	2167.02	2166.04	2165.75
110000	2549.93	2483.07	2327.78	2285.78	2273.73	2270.21	2269.18	2268.88
115000	2665.84	2595.93	2433.59	2389.68	2377.08	2373.41	2372.33	2372.01
120000	2781.74	2708.80	2539.39	2493.58	2480.43	2476.60	2475.47	2475.14
125000	2897.65	2821.66	2645.20	2597.48	2583.78	2579.79	2578.62	2578.27
130000	3013.55	2934.53	2751.01	2701.38	2687.14	2682.98	2681.76	2681.40
135000	3129.46	3047.40	2856.82	2805.28	2790.49	2786.17	2784.91	2784.53
140000	3245.36	3160.26	2962.63	2909.18	2893.84	2889.36	2888.05	2887.67
145000	3361.27	3273.13	3068.43	3013.08	2997.19	2992.55	2991.19	2990.80
150000	3477.18	3386.00	3174.24	3116.97	3100.54	3095.75	3094.34	3093.93
155000	3593.08	3498.86	3280.05	3220.87	3203.89	3198.94	3197.48	3197.06
160000	3708.99	3611.73	3385.86	3324.77	3307.24	3302.13	3300.63	3300.19

MONTHLY AMORTIZING PAYMENTS

AMOUNT OF LOAN	NUMBER OF YEARS IN TERM							
	1	2	3	4	5	6	7	8
$ 50	4.76	2.67	1.99	1.66	1.47	1.35	1.27	1.21
100	9.51	5.34	3.98	3.32	2.94	2.70	2.54	2.42
200	19.01	10.68	7.96	6.64	5.88	5.39	5.07	4.84
300	28.52	16.02	11.93	9.95	8.81	8.09	7.60	7.26
400	38.02	21.35	15.91	13.27	11.75	10.78	10.13	9.67
500	47.53	26.69	19.88	16.58	14.68	13.47	12.66	12.09
600	57.03	32.03	23.86	19.90	17.62	16.17	15.19	14.51
700	66.54	37.37	27.84	23.21	20.55	18.86	17.72	16.93
800	76.04	42.70	31.81	26.53	23.49	21.55	20.25	19.34
900	85.54	48.04	35.79	29.85	26.42	24.25	22.79	21.76
1000	95.05	53.38	39.76	33.16	29.36	26.94	25.32	24.18
2000	190.09	106.75	79.52	66.32	58.71	53.88	50.63	48.35
3000	285.14	160.12	119.28	99.48	88.06	80.82	75.94	72.52
4000	380.18	213.49	159.04	132.63	117.41	107.75	101.25	96.70
5000	475.23	266.86	198.80	165.79	146.76	134.69	126.56	120.87
6000	570.27	320.23	238.56	198.95	176.11	161.63	151.87	145.04
7000	665.31	373.61	278.32	232.10	205.46	188.57	177.19	169.21
8000	760.36	426.98	318.08	265.26	234.82	215.50	202.50	193.39
9000	855.40	480.35	357.84	298.42	264.17	242.44	227.81	217.56
10000	950.45	533.72	397.60	331.58	293.52	269.38	253.12	241.73
11000	1045.49	587.09	437.36	364.73	322.87	296.31	278.43	265.90
12000	1140.54	640.46	477.12	397.89	352.22	323.25	303.74	290.08
13000	1235.58	693.83	516.88	431.05	381.57	350.19	329.06	314.25
14000	1330.62	747.21	556.64	464.20	410.92	377.13	354.37	338.42
15000	1425.67	800.58	596.40	497.36	440.27	404.06	379.68	362.59
16000	1520.71	853.95	636.16	530.52	469.63	431.00	404.99	386.77
17000	1615.76	907.32	675.92	563.68	498.98	457.94	430.30	410.94
18000	1710.80	960.69	715.68	596.83	528.33	484.87	455.61	435.11
19000	1805.84	1014.06	755.44	629.99	557.68	511.81	480.93	459.29
20000	1900.89	1067.44	795.20	663.15	587.03	538.75	506.24	483.46
21000	1995.93	1120.81	834.96	696.30	616.38	565.69	531.55	507.63
22000	2090.98	1174.18	874.72	729.46	645.73	592.62	556.86	531.80
23000	2186.02	1227.55	914.48	762.62	675.09	619.56	582.17	555.98
24000	2281.07	1280.92	954.24	795.78	704.44	646.50	607.48	580.15
25000	2376.11	1334.29	994.00	828.93	733.79	673.43	632.80	604.32
26000	2471.15	1387.66	1033.76	862.09	763.14	700.37	658.11	628.49
27000	2566.20	1441.04	1073.52	895.25	792.49	727.31	683.42	652.67
28000	2661.24	1494.41	1113.28	928.40	821.84	754.25	708.73	676.84
29000	2756.29	1547.78	1153.04	961.56	851.19	781.18	734.04	701.01
30000	2851.33	1601.15	1192.80	994.72	880.54	808.12	759.35	725.18
31000	2946.38	1654.52	1232.56	1027.88	909.90	835.06	784.67	749.36
32000	3041.42	1707.89	1272.32	1061.03	939.25	861.99	809.98	773.53
33000	3136.46	1761.27	1312.08	1094.19	968.60	888.93	835.29	797.70
34000	3231.51	1814.64	1351.84	1127.35	997.95	915.87	860.60	821.88
35000	3326.55	1868.01	1391.60	1160.50	1027.30	942.81	885.91	846.05
40000	3801.77	2134.87	1590.40	1326.29	1174.06	1077.49	1012.47	966.91
45000	4276.99	2401.72	1789.20	1492.08	1320.81	1212.18	1139.03	1087.77
50000	4752.22	2668.58	1988.00	1657.86	1467.57	1346.86	1265.59	1208.64
55000	5227.44	2935.44	2186.80	1823.65	1614.33	1481.55	1392.14	1329.50
60000	5702.66	3202.30	2385.59	1989.43	1761.08	1616.24	1518.70	1450.36
65000	6177.88	3469.15	2584.39	2155.22	1907.84	1750.92	1645.26	1571.23
70000	6653.10	3736.01	2783.19	2321.00	2054.60	1885.61	1771.82	1692.09
75000	7128.32	4002.87	2981.99	2486.79	2201.35	2020.29	1898.38	1812.95
80000	7603.54	4269.73	3180.79	2652.58	2348.11	2154.98	2024.94	1933.82
85000	8078.76	4536.58	3379.59	2818.36	2494.87	2289.67	2151.49	2054.68
90000	8553.98	4803.44	3578.39	2984.15	2641.62	2424.35	2278.05	2175.54
95000	9029.20	5070.30	3777.19	3149.93	2788.38	2559.04	2404.61	2296.41
100000	9504.43	5337.16	3975.99	3315.72	2935.14	2693.72	2531.17	2417.27
105000	9979.65	5604.01	4174.79	3481.50	3081.89	2828.41	2657.73	2538.13
110000	10454.87	5870.87	4373.59	3647.29	3228.65	2963.09	2784.28	2659.00
115000	10930.09	6137.73	4572.38	3813.07	3375.41	3097.78	2910.84	2779.86
120000	11405.31	6404.59	4771.18	3978.86	3522.16	3232.47	3037.40	2900.72
125000	11880.53	6671.45	4969.98	4144.65	3668.92	3367.15	3163.96	3021.59
130000	12355.75	6938.30	5168.78	4310.43	3815.68	3501.84	3290.52	3142.45
135000	12830.97	7205.16	5367.58	4476.22	3962.43	3636.52	3417.08	3263.31
140000	13306.19	7472.02	5566.38	4642.00	4109.19	3771.21	3543.63	3384.18
145000	13781.41	7738.88	5765.18	4807.79	4255.95	3905.90	3670.19	3505.04
150000	14256.64	8005.73	5963.98	4973.57	4402.70	4040.58	3796.75	3625.90
155000	14731.86	8272.59	6162.78	5139.36	4549.46	4175.27	3923.31	3746.77
160000	15207.08	8539.45	6361.58	5305.15	4696.22	4309.95	4049.87	3867.63

AMOUNT OF LOAN	NUMBER OF YEARS IN TERM							
	9	10	15	20	25	30	35	40
$ 50	1.17	1.14	1.07	1.05	1.05	1.05	1.05	1.05
100	2.34	2.28	2.14	2.10	2.09	2.09	2.09	2.09
200	4.68	4.55	4.28	4.20	4.18	4.17	4.17	4.17
300	7.01	6.83	6.41	6.30	6.27	6.26	6.26	6.26
400	9.35	9.10	8.55	8.40	8.36	8.34	8.34	8.34
500	11.68	11.38	10.68	10.50	10.44	10.43	10.42	10.42
600	14.02	13.65	12.82	12.59	12.53	12.51	12.51	12.51
700	16.35	15.93	14.95	14.69	14.62	14.60	14.59	14.59
800	18.69	18.20	17.09	16.79	16.71	16.68	16.67	16.67
900	21.02	20.48	19.22	18.89	18.79	18.77	18.76	18.76
1000	23.36	22.75	21.36	20.99	20.88	20.85	20.84	20.84
2000	46.71	45.50	42.72	41.97	41.76	41.70	41.68	41.67
3000	70.06	68.25	64.07	62.96	62.63	62.54	62.52	62.51
4000	93.41	91.00	85.43	83.93	83.51	83.39	83.35	83.34
5000	116.77	113.75	106.78	104.92	104.39	104.23	104.19	104.18
6000	140.12	136.50	128.14	125.90	125.26	125.08	125.03	125.01
7000	163.47	159.25	149.49	146.88	146.14	145.93	145.86	145.85
8000	186.82	182.00	170.85	167.86	167.02	166.77	166.70	166.68
9000	210.17	204.75	192.20	188.84	187.89	187.62	187.54	187.51
10000	233.53	227.50	213.56	209.83	208.77	208.46	208.37	208.35
11000	256.88	250.25	234.91	230.81	229.64	229.31	229.21	229.18
12000	280.23	273.00	256.27	251.79	250.52	250.15	250.05	250.02
13000	303.58	295.75	277.62	272.77	271.40	271.00	270.89	270.85
14000	326.94	318.50	298.98	293.76	292.27	291.85	291.72	291.69
15000	350.29	341.24	320.33	314.74	313.15	312.69	312.56	312.52
16000	373.64	363.99	341.69	335.72	334.03	333.54	333.40	333.36
17000	396.99	386.74	363.04	356.70	354.90	354.38	354.23	354.19
18000	420.34	409.49	384.40	377.68	375.78	375.23	375.07	375.02
19000	443.70	432.24	405.76	398.67	396.65	396.07	395.91	395.86
20000	467.05	454.99	427.11	419.65	417.53	416.92	416.74	416.69
21000	490.40	477.74	448.47	440.63	438.41	437.77	437.58	437.53
22000	513.75	500.49	469.82	461.61	459.28	458.61	458.42	458.36
23000	537.11	523.24	491.18	482.59	480.16	479.46	479.25	479.20
24000	560.46	545.99	512.53	503.58	501.04	500.30	500.09	500.03
25000	583.81	568.74	533.89	524.56	521.91	521.15	520.93	520.86
26000	607.16	591.49	555.24	545.54	542.79	542.00	541.77	541.70
27000	630.51	614.24	576.60	566.52	563.67	562.84	562.60	562.53
28000	653.87	636.99	597.95	587.51	584.54	583.69	583.44	583.37
29000	677.22	659.73	619.31	608.49	605.42	604.53	604.28	604.20
30000	700.57	682.48	640.66	629.47	626.29	625.38	625.11	625.04
31000	723.92	705.23	662.02	650.45	647.17	646.22	645.95	645.87
32000	747.28	727.98	683.37	671.43	668.05	667.07	666.79	666.71
33000	770.63	750.73	704.73	692.42	688.92	687.92	687.62	687.54
34000	793.98	773.48	726.08	713.40	709.80	708.76	708.46	708.37
35000	817.33	796.23	747.44	734.38	730.68	729.61	729.30	729.21
40000	934.09	909.98	854.22	839.29	835.06	833.84	833.48	833.38
45000	1050.85	1023.72	960.99	944.20	939.44	938.07	937.67	937.55
50000	1167.61	1137.47	1067.77	1049.11	1043.82	1042.29	1041.85	1041.72
55000	1284.38	1251.22	1174.55	1154.02	1148.20	1146.52	1146.04	1145.90
60000	1401.14	1364.96	1281.32	1258.93	1252.58	1250.75	1250.22	1250.07
65000	1517.90	1478.71	1388.10	1363.85	1356.96	1354.98	1354.41	1354.24
70000	1634.66	1592.46	1494.88	1468.76	1461.35	1459.21	1458.59	1458.41
75000	1751.42	1706.20	1601.65	1573.67	1565.73	1563.44	1562.78	1562.58
80000	1868.18	1819.95	1708.43	1678.58	1670.11	1667.67	1666.96	1666.76
85000	1984.94	1933.70	1815.20	1783.49	1774.49	1771.90	1771.15	1770.93
90000	2101.70	2047.44	1921.98	1888.40	1878.87	1876.13	1875.33	1875.10
95000	2218.46	2161.19	2028.76	1993.31	1983.25	1980.35	1979.51	1979.27
100000	2335.22	2274.93	2135.53	2098.22	2087.64	2084.58	2083.70	2083.44
105000	2451.99	2388.68	2242.31	2203.13	2192.02	2188.81	2187.88	2187.62
110000	2568.75	2502.43	2349.09	2308.04	2296.40	2293.04	2292.07	2291.79
115000	2685.51	2616.17	2455.86	2412.95	2400.78	2397.27	2396.25	2395.96
120000	2802.27	2729.92	2562.64	2517.86	2505.16	2501.50	2500.44	2500.13
125000	2919.03	2843.67	2669.42	2622.78	2609.54	2605.73	2604.62	2604.30
130000	3035.79	2957.41	2776.19	2727.69	2713.92	2709.96	2708.81	2708.47
135000	3152.55	3071.16	2882.97	2832.60	2818.31	2814.19	2812.99	2812.65
140000	3269.31	3184.91	2989.75	2937.51	2922.69	2918.42	2917.18	2916.82
145000	3386.07	3298.65	3096.52	3042.42	3027.07	3022.64	3021.36	3020.99
150000	3502.83	3412.40	3203.30	3147.33	3131.45	3126.87	3125.55	3125.16
155000	3619.60	3526.15	3310.07	3252.24	3235.83	3231.10	3229.73	3229.33
160000	3736.36	3639.89	3416.85	3357.15	3340.21	3335.33	3333.92	3333.51

AMOUNT OF LOAN	NUMBER OF YEARS IN TERM							
	1	2	3	4	5	6	7	8
$ 50	4.76	2.68	2.00	1.67	1.48	1.36	1.28	1.22
100	9.52	5.35	3.99	3.33	2.95	2.71	2.55	2.44
200	19.04	10.70	7.98	6.66	5.90	5.42	5.10	4.87
300	28.55	16.05	11.97	9.99	8.85	8.13	7.65	7.31
400	38.07	21.40	15.96	13.32	11.80	10.84	10.19	9.74
500	47.59	26.75	19.95	16.65	14.75	13.55	12.74	12.17
600	57.10	32.10	23.94	19.98	17.70	16.26	15.29	14.61
700	66.62	37.45	27.93	23.31	20.65	18.97	17.84	17.04
800	76.14	42.80	31.92	26.64	23.60	21.68	20.38	19.48
900	85.65	48.15	35.91	29.97	26.55	24.39	22.93	21.91
1000	95.17	53.50	39.90	33.30	29.50	27.10	25.48	24.34
2000	190.34	107.00	79.79	66.60	59.00	54.19	50.95	48.68
3000	285.50	160.50	119.68	99.90	88.50	81.28	76.42	73.02
4000	380.67	213.99	159.57	133.19	118.00	108.37	101.89	97.36
5000	475.83	267.49	199.47	166.49	147.50	135.46	127.36	121.70
6000	571.00	320.99	239.36	199.79	176.99	162.55	152.84	146.04
7000	666.16	374.48	279.25	233.08	206.49	189.64	178.31	170.38
8000	761.33	427.98	319.14	266.38	235.99	216.73	203.78	194.71
9000	856.50	481.48	359.03	299.68	265.49	243.82	229.25	219.05
10000	951.66	534.98	398.93	332.97	294.99	270.91	254.72	243.39
11000	1046.83	588.47	438.82	366.27	324.48	298.00	280.19	267.73
12000	1141.99	641.97	478.71	399.57	353.98	325.09	305.67	292.07
13000	1237.16	695.47	518.60	432.86	383.48	352.19	331.14	316.41
14000	1332.32	748.96	558.50	466.16	412.98	379.28	356.61	340.75
15000	1427.49	802.46	598.39	499.46	442.48	406.37	382.08	365.09
16000	1522.65	855.96	638.28	532.75	471.97	433.46	407.55	389.42
17000	1617.82	909.45	678.17	566.05	501.47	460.55	433.02	413.76
18000	1712.99	962.95	718.06	599.35	530.97	487.64	458.50	438.10
19000	1808.15	1016.45	757.96	632.64	560.47	514.73	483.97	462.44
20000	1903.32	1069.95	797.85	665.94	589.97	541.82	509.44	486.78
21000	1998.48	1123.44	837.74	699.24	619.46	568.91	534.91	511.12
22000	2093.65	1176.94	877.63	732.53	648.96	596.00	560.38	535.46
23000	2188.81	1230.44	917.52	765.83	678.46	623.09	585.85	559.80
24000	2283.98	1283.93	957.42	799.13	707.96	650.18	611.33	584.13
25000	2379.14	1337.43	997.31	832.42	737.46	677.27	636.80	608.47
26000	2474.31	1390.93	1037.20	865.72	766.95	704.37	662.27	632.81
27000	2569.48	1444.42	1077.09	899.02	796.45	731.46	687.74	657.15
28000	2664.64	1497.92	1116.99	932.31	825.95	758.55	713.21	681.49
29000	2759.81	1551.42	1156.88	965.61	855.45	785.64	738.68	705.83
30000	2854.97	1604.92	1196.77	998.91	884.95	812.73	764.16	730.17
31000	2950.14	1658.41	1236.66	1032.20	914.45	839.82	789.63	754.51
32000	3045.30	1711.91	1276.55	1065.50	943.94	866.91	815.10	778.84
33000	3140.47	1765.41	1316.45	1098.80	973.44	894.00	840.57	803.18
34000	3235.63	1818.90	1356.34	1132.09	1002.94	921.09	866.04	827.52
35000	3330.80	1872.40	1396.23	1165.39	1032.44	948.18	891.51	851.86
40000	3806.63	2139.89	1595.69	1331.87	1179.93	1083.64	1018.87	973.55
45000	4282.46	2407.37	1795.15	1498.36	1327.42	1219.09	1146.23	1095.25
50000	4758.28	2674.86	1994.61	1664.84	1474.91	1354.54	1273.59	1216.94
55000	5234.11	2942.34	2194.07	1831.32	1622.40	1490.00	1400.95	1338.63
60000	5709.94	3209.83	2393.54	1997.81	1769.89	1625.45	1528.31	1460.33
65000	6185.77	3477.31	2593.00	2164.29	1917.38	1760.91	1655.67	1582.02
70000	6661.59	3744.80	2792.46	2330.78	2064.87	1896.36	1783.02	1703.71
75000	7137.42	4012.28	2991.92	2497.26	2212.36	2031.81	1910.38	1825.41
80000	7613.25	4279.77	3191.38	2663.74	2359.85	2167.27	2037.74	1947.10
85000	8089.08	4547.25	3390.84	2830.23	2507.34	2302.72	2165.10	2068.80
90000	8564.91	4814.74	3590.30	2996.71	2654.83	2438.18	2292.46	2190.49
95000	9040.73	5082.22	3789.76	3163.19	2802.32	2573.63	2419.82	2312.18
100000	9516.56	5349.71	3989.22	3329.68	2949.81	2709.08	2547.17	2433.88
105000	9992.39	5617.19	4188.68	3496.16	3097.30	2844.54	2674.53	2555.57
110000	10468.22	5884.68	4388.14	3662.64	3244.79	2979.99	2801.89	2677.26
115000	10944.04	6152.16	4587.60	3829.13	3392.28	3115.45	2929.25	2798.96
120000	11419.87	6419.65	4787.07	3995.61	3539.77	3250.90	3056.61	2920.65
125000	11895.70	6687.13	4986.53	4162.09	3687.26	3386.35	3183.97	3042.34
130000	12371.53	6954.62	5185.99	4328.58	3834.75	3521.81	3311.33	3164.04
135000	12847.36	7222.10	5385.45	4495.06	3982.24	3657.26	3438.68	3285.73
140000	13323.18	7489.59	5584.91	4661.55	4129.73	3792.71	3566.04	3407.42
145000	13799.01	7757.08	5784.37	4828.03	4277.23	3928.17	3693.40	3529.12
150000	14274.84	8024.56	5983.83	4994.51	4424.72	4063.62	3820.76	3650.81
155000	14750.67	8292.05	6183.29	5161.00	4572.21	4199.08	3948.12	3772.51
160000	15226.50	8559.53	6382.75	5327.48	4719.70	4334.53	4075.48	3894.20

MONTHLY AMORTIZING PAYMENTS   25.250%

AMOUNT OF LOAN	NUMBER OF YEARS IN TERM							
	9	10	15	20	25	30	35	40
$ 50	1.18	1.15	1.08	1.06	1.06	1.06	1.06	1.06
100	2.36	2.30	2.16	2.12	2.11	2.11	2.11	2.11
200	4.71	4.59	4.31	4.24	4.22	4.22	4.21	4.21
300	7.06	6.88	6.47	6.36	6.33	6.32	6.32	6.32
400	9.41	9.18	8.62	8.48	8.44	8.43	8.42	8.42
500	11.77	11.47	10.78	10.60	10.55	10.53	10.53	10.53
600	14.12	13.76	12.93	12.72	12.65	12.64	12.63	12.63
700	16.47	16.05	15.09	14.83	14.76	14.74	14.74	14.73
800	18.82	18.35	17.24	16.95	16.87	16.85	16.84	16.84
900	21.18	20.64	19.40	19.07	18.98	18.95	18.95	18.94
1000	23.53	22.93	21.55	21.19	21.09	21.06	21.05	21.05
2000	47.05	45.86	43.10	42.37	42.17	42.11	42.10	42.09
3000	70.58	68.78	64.65	63.56	63.25	63.17	63.14	63.13
4000	94.10	91.71	86.20	84.74	84.33	84.22	84.19	84.18
5000	117.62	114.63	107.75	105.93	105.42	105.27	105.23	105.22
6000	141.15	137.56	129.30	127.11	126.50	126.33	126.28	126.26
7000	164.67	160.49	150.85	148.30	147.58	147.38	147.32	147.30
8000	188.19	183.41	172.40	169.48	168.66	168.43	168.37	168.35
9000	211.72	206.34	193.95	190.67	189.75	189.49	189.41	189.39
10000	235.24	229.26	215.50	211.85	210.83	210.54	210.46	210.43
11000	258.77	252.19	237.05	233.04	231.91	231.59	231.50	231.47
12000	282.29	275.11	258.60	254.22	252.99	252.65	252.55	252.52
13000	305.81	298.04	280.15	275.41	274.08	273.70	273.59	273.56
14000	329.34	320.97	301.70	296.59	295.16	294.75	294.64	294.60
15000	352.86	343.89	323.25	317.78	316.24	315.81	315.68	315.64
16000	376.38	366.82	344.79	338.96	337.32	336.86	336.73	336.69
17000	399.91	389.74	366.34	360.15	358.41	357.91	357.77	357.73
18000	423.43	412.67	387.89	381.33	379.49	378.97	378.82	378.77
19000	446.96	435.59	409.44	402.52	400.57	400.02	399.86	399.81
20000	470.48	458.52	430.99	423.70	421.65	421.07	420.91	420.86
21000	494.00	481.45	452.54	444.88	442.74	442.13	441.95	441.90
22000	517.53	504.37	474.09	466.07	463.82	463.18	463.00	462.94
23000	541.05	527.30	495.64	487.25	484.90	484.23	484.04	483.99
24000	564.57	550.22	517.19	508.44	505.98	505.29	505.09	505.03
25000	588.10	573.15	538.74	529.62	527.07	526.34	526.13	526.07
26000	611.62	596.08	560.29	550.81	548.15	547.39	547.18	547.11
27000	635.15	619.00	581.84	571.99	569.23	568.45	568.22	568.16
28000	658.67	641.93	603.39	593.18	590.31	589.50	589.27	589.20
29000	682.19	664.85	624.94	614.36	611.40	610.55	610.31	610.24
30000	705.72	687.78	646.49	635.55	632.48	631.61	631.36	631.28
31000	729.24	710.70	668.04	656.73	653.56	652.66	652.40	652.33
32000	752.76	733.63	689.58	677.92	674.64	673.71	673.45	673.37
33000	776.29	756.56	711.13	699.10	695.73	694.77	694.49	694.41
34000	799.81	779.48	732.68	720.29	716.81	715.82	715.54	715.45
35000	823.34	802.41	754.23	741.47	737.89	736.87	736.58	736.50
40000	940.95	917.04	861.98	847.40	843.30	842.14	841.81	841.71
45000	1058.57	1031.67	969.73	953.32	948.72	947.41	947.03	946.92
50000	1176.19	1146.29	1077.47	1059.24	1054.13	1052.67	1052.26	1052.14
55000	1293.81	1260.92	1185.22	1165.17	1159.54	1157.94	1157.48	1157.35
60000	1411.43	1375.55	1292.97	1271.09	1264.95	1263.21	1262.71	1262.56
65000	1529.05	1490.18	1400.71	1377.01	1370.37	1368.47	1367.93	1367.78
70000	1646.67	1604.81	1508.46	1482.94	1475.78	1473.74	1473.16	1472.99
75000	1764.28	1719.44	1616.21	1588.86	1581.19	1579.01	1578.38	1578.20
80000	1881.90	1834.07	1723.95	1694.79	1686.60	1684.27	1683.61	1683.42
85000	1999.52	1948.70	1831.70	1800.71	1792.02	1789.54	1788.83	1788.63
90000	2117.14	2063.33	1939.45	1906.63	1897.43	1894.81	1894.06	1893.84
95000	2234.76	2177.95	2047.20	2012.56	2002.84	2000.07	1999.28	1999.05
100000	2352.38	2292.58	2154.94	2118.48	2108.25	2105.34	2104.51	2104.27
105000	2470.00	2407.21	2262.69	2224.40	2213.67	2210.61	2209.73	2209.48
110000	2587.61	2521.84	2370.44	2330.33	2319.08	2315.87	2314.96	2314.69
115000	2705.23	2636.47	2478.18	2436.25	2424.49	2421.14	2420.18	2419.91
120000	2822.85	2751.10	2585.93	2542.18	2529.90	2526.41	2525.41	2525.12
125000	2940.47	2865.73	2693.68	2648.10	2635.32	2631.67	2630.63	2630.33
130000	3058.09	2980.36	2801.42	2754.02	2740.73	2736.94	2735.86	2735.55
135000	3175.71	3094.99	2909.17	2859.95	2846.14	2842.21	2841.08	2840.76
140000	3293.33	3209.62	3016.92	2965.87	2951.55	2947.47	2946.31	2945.97
145000	3410.95	3324.24	3124.66	3071.79	3056.97	3052.74	3051.53	3051.19
150000	3528.56	3438.87	3232.41	3177.72	3162.38	3158.01	3156.76	3156.40
155000	3646.18	3553.50	3340.16	3283.64	3267.79	3263.27	3261.98	3261.61
160000	3763.80	3668.13	3447.90	3389.57	3373.20	3368.54	3367.21	3366.83

25.500%   MONTHLY AMORTIZING PAYMENTS

AMOUNT OF LOAN	\multicolumn{8}{c}{NUMBER OF YEARS IN TERM}
	1	**2**	**3**	**4**	**5**	**6**	**7**	**8**
$ 50	4.77	2.69	2.01	1.68	1.49	1.37	1.29	1.23
100	9.53	5.37	4.01	3.35	2.97	2.73	2.57	2.46
200	19.06	10.73	8.01	6.69	5.93	5.45	5.13	4.91
300	28.59	16.09	12.01	10.04	8.90	8.18	7.69	7.36
400	38.12	21.45	16.01	13.38	11.86	10.90	10.26	9.81
500	47.65	26.82	20.02	16.72	14.83	13.63	12.82	12.26
600	57.18	32.18	24.02	20.07	17.79	16.35	15.38	14.71
700	66.71	37.54	28.02	23.41	20.76	19.08	17.95	17.16
800	76.23	42.90	32.02	26.75	23.72	21.80	20.51	19.61
900	85.76	48.27	36.03	30.10	26.69	24.53	23.07	22.06
1000	95.29	53.63	40.03	33.44	29.65	27.25	25.64	24.51
2000	190.58	107.25	80.05	66.88	59.30	54.49	51.27	49.02
3000	285.87	160.87	120.08	100.31	88.94	81.74	76.90	73.52
4000	381.15	214.50	160.10	133.75	118.59	108.98	102.53	98.03
5000	476.44	268.12	200.13	167.19	148.23	136.23	128.17	122.53
6000	571.73	321.74	240.15	200.62	177.88	163.47	153.80	147.04
7000	667.01	375.36	280.18	234.06	207.52	190.72	179.43	171.54
8000	762.30	428.99	320.20	267.50	237.17	217.96	205.06	196.05
9000	857.59	482.61	360.23	300.93	266.81	245.21	230.69	220.55
10000	952.88	536.23	400.25	334.37	296.46	272.45	256.33	245.06
11000	1048.16	589.85	440.28	367.81	326.10	299.70	281.96	269.56
12000	1143.45	643.48	480.30	401.24	355.75	326.94	307.59	294.07
13000	1238.74	697.10	520.33	434.68	385.39	354.19	333.22	318.57
14000	1334.02	750.72	560.35	468.12	415.04	381.43	358.86	343.08
15000	1429.31	804.35	600.38	501.55	444.68	408.68	384.49	367.58
16000	1524.60	857.97	640.40	534.99	474.33	435.92	410.12	392.09
17000	1619.88	911.59	680.43	568.43	503.97	463.17	435.75	416.59
18000	1715.17	965.21	720.45	601.86	533.62	490.41	461.38	441.10
19000	1810.46	1018.84	760.48	635.30	563.26	517.66	487.02	465.60
20000	1905.75	1072.46	800.50	668.74	592.91	544.90	512.65	490.11
21000	2001.03	1126.08	840.52	702.17	622.55	572.15	538.28	514.61
22000	2096.32	1179.70	880.55	735.61	652.20	599.39	563.91	539.12
23000	2191.61	1233.33	920.57	769.05	681.84	626.64	589.55	563.62
24000	2286.89	1286.95	960.60	802.48	711.49	653.88	615.18	588.13
25000	2382.18	1340.57	1000.62	835.92	741.13	681.12	640.81	612.64
26000	2477.47	1394.20	1040.65	869.36	770.78	708.37	666.44	637.14
27000	2572.75	1447.82	1080.67	902.79	800.42	735.61	692.07	661.65
28000	2668.04	1501.44	1120.70	936.23	830.07	762.86	717.71	686.15
29000	2763.33	1555.06	1160.72	969.67	859.72	790.10	743.34	710.66
30000	2858.62	1608.69	1200.75	1003.10	889.36	817.35	768.97	735.16
31000	2953.90	1662.31	1240.77	1036.54	919.01	844.59	794.60	759.67
32000	3049.19	1715.93	1280.80	1069.98	948.65	871.84	820.24	784.17
33000	3144.48	1769.55	1320.82	1103.41	978.30	899.08	845.87	808.68
34000	3239.76	1823.18	1360.85	1136.85	1007.94	926.33	871.50	833.18
35000	3335.05	1876.80	1400.87	1170.29	1037.59	953.57	897.13	857.69
40000	3811.49	2144.91	1600.99	1337.47	1185.81	1089.80	1025.29	980.21
45000	4287.92	2413.03	1801.12	1504.65	1334.04	1226.02	1153.45	1102.74
50000	4764.36	2681.14	2001.24	1671.84	1482.26	1362.24	1281.61	1225.27
55000	5240.79	2949.25	2201.37	1839.02	1630.49	1498.47	1409.78	1347.79
60000	5717.23	3217.37	2401.49	2006.20	1778.72	1634.69	1537.94	1470.32
65000	6193.66	3485.48	2601.61	2173.38	1926.94	1770.92	1666.10	1592.84
70000	6670.10	3753.60	2801.74	2340.57	2075.17	1907.14	1794.26	1715.37
75000	7146.53	4021.71	3001.86	2507.75	2223.39	2043.36	1922.42	1837.90
80000	7622.97	4289.82	3201.98	2674.93	2371.62	2179.59	2050.58	1960.42
85000	8099.40	4557.94	3402.11	2842.12	2519.85	2315.81	2178.74	2082.95
90000	8575.84	4826.05	3602.23	3009.30	2668.07	2452.04	2306.90	2205.47
95000	9052.27	5094.16	3802.36	3176.48	2816.30	2588.26	2435.06	2328.00
100000	9528.71	5362.28	4002.48	3343.67	2964.52	2724.48	2563.22	2450.53
105000	10005.14	5630.39	4202.60	3510.85	3112.75	2860.71	2691.39	2573.05
110000	10481.58	5898.50	4402.73	3678.03	3260.97	2996.93	2819.55	2695.58
115000	10958.01	6166.62	4602.85	3845.22	3409.20	3133.16	2947.71	2818.10
120000	11434.45	6434.73	4802.97	4012.40	3557.43	3269.38	3075.87	2940.63
125000	11910.88	6702.84	5003.10	4179.58	3705.65	3405.60	3204.03	3063.16
130000	12387.32	6970.96	5203.22	4346.76	3853.88	3541.83	3332.19	3185.68
135000	12863.75	7239.07	5403.35	4513.95	4002.10	3678.05	3460.35	3308.21
140000	13340.19	7507.19	5603.47	4681.13	4150.33	3814.28	3588.51	3430.74
145000	13816.62	7775.30	5803.59	4848.31	4298.56	3950.50	3716.67	3553.26
150000	14293.06	8043.41	6003.72	5015.50	4446.78	4086.72	3844.83	3675.79
155000	14769.49	8311.53	6203.84	5182.68	4595.01	4222.95	3973.00	3798.31
160000	15245.93	8579.64	6403.96	5349.86	4743.23	4359.17	4101.16	3920.84

138

AMOUNT OF LOAN	NUMBER OF YEARS IN TERM							
	9	10	15	20	25	30	35	40
$ 50	1.19	1.16	1.09	1.07	1.07	1.07	1.07	1.07
100	2.37	2.32	2.18	2.14	2.13	2.13	2.13	2.13
200	4.74	4.63	4.35	4.28	4.26	4.26	4.26	4.26
300	7.11	6.94	6.53	6.42	6.39	6.38	6.38	6.38
400	9.48	9.25	8.70	8.56	8.52	8.51	8.51	8.51
500	11.85	11.56	10.88	10.70	10.65	10.64	10.63	10.63
600	14.22	13.87	13.05	12.84	12.78	12.76	12.76	12.76
700	16.59	16.18	15.23	14.98	14.91	14.89	14.88	14.88
800	18.96	18.49	17.40	17.12	17.04	17.01	17.01	17.01
900	21.33	20.80	19 57	19.25	19.16	19.14	19.13	19.13
1000	23.70	23.11	21.75	21.39	21.29	21.27	21.26	21.26
2000	47.40	46.21	43.49	42.78	42.58	42.53	42.51	42.51
3000	71.09	69.31	65.24	64.17	63.87	63.79	63.76	63.76
4000	94.79	92.42	86.98	85.56	85.16	85.05	85.02	85.01
5000	118.48	115.52	108.72	106.94	106.44	106.31	106.27	106.26
6000	142.18	138.62	130.47	128.33	127.74	127.57	127.52	127.51
7000	165.88	161.72	152.21	149.72	149.03	148.83	148.78	148.76
8000	189.57	184.83	173.96	171.11	170.32	170.09	170.03	170.01
9000	213.27	207.93	195.70	192.49	191.60	191.35	191.28	191.26
10000	236.96	231.03	217.44	213.88	212.89	212.61	212.54	212.51
11000	260.66	254.14	239.19	235.27	234.18	233.88	233.79	233.76
12000	284.35	277.24	260.93	256.66	255.47	255.14	255.05	255.02
13000	308.05	300.34	282.67	278.04	276.76	276.40	276.30	276.27
14000	331.75	323.44	304.42	299.43	298.05	297.66	297.55	297.52
15000	355.44	346.55	326.16	320.82	319.34	318.92	318.80	318.77
16000	379.14	369.65	347.91	342.21	340.63	340.18	340.05	340.02
17000	402.83	392.75	369.65	363.59	361.91	361.44	361.31	361.27
18000	426.53	415.85	391.39	384.98	383.20	382.70	382.56	382.52
19000	450.22	438.96	413.14	406.37	404.49	403.96	403.81	403.77
20000	473.92	462.06	434.88	427.76	425.78	425.22	425.07	425.02
21000	497.62	485.16	456.63	449.14	447.07	446.49	446.32	446.27
22000	521.31	508.27	478.37	470.53	468.36	467.75	467.57	467.52
23000	545.01	531.37	500.11	491.92	489.65	489.01	488.83	488.78
24000	568.70	554.47	521.86	513.31	510.94	510.27	510.08	510.03
25000	592.40	577.57	543.60	534.69	532.22	531.53	531.33	531.28
26000	616.09	600.68	565.34	556.08	553.51	552.79	552.59	552.53
27000	639.79	623.78	587.09	577.47	574.80	574.05	573.84	573.78
28000	663.49	646.88	608.83	598.86	596.09	595.31	595.09	595.03
29000	687.18	669.98	630.58	620.24	617.38	616.57	616.35	616.28
30000	710.88	693.09	652.32	641.63	638.67	637.83	637.60	637.53
31000	734.57	716.19	674.06	663.02	659.96	659.09	658.85	658.78
32000	758.27	739.29	695.81	684.41	681.25	680.36	680.10	680.03
33000	781.96	762.40	717.55	705.79	702.53	701.62	701.36	701.28
34000	805.66	785.50	739.29	727.18	723.82	722.88	722.61	722.53
35000	829.36	808.60	761.04	748.57	745.11	744.14	743.86	743.79
40000	947.83	924.11	869.76	855.51	851.56	850.44	850.13	850.04
45000	1066.45	1039.63	978.48	962.44	958.00	956.75	956.39	956.29
50000	1184.79	1155.14	1087.20	1069.38	1064.44	1063.05	1062.66	1062.55
55000	1303.27	1270.66	1195.91	1176.32	1170.89	1169.36	1168.93	1168.80
60000	1421.75	1386.17	1304.63	1283.26	1277.33	1275.66	1275.19	1275.06
65000	1540.23	1501.68	1413.35	1390.20	1383.78	1381.97	1381.46	1381.31
70000	1658.71	1617.20	1522.07	1497.13	1490.22	1488.27	1487.72	1487.57
75000	1777.18	1732.71	1630.79	1604.07	1596.66	1594.58	1593.99	1593.82
80000	1895.66	1848.22	1739.51	1711.01	1703.11	1700.88	1700.25	1700.08
85000	2014.14	1963.74	1848.23	1817.95	1809.55	1807.19	1806.52	1806.33
90000	2132.62	2079.25	1956.95	1924.88	1915.99	1913.49	1912.78	1912.58
95000	2251.10	2194.77	2065.67	2031.82	2022.44	2019.80	2019.05	2018.84
100000	2369.58	2310.28	2174.39	2138.76	2128.88	2126.10	2125.32	2125.09
105000	2488.06	2425.79	2283.11	2245.70	2235.33	2232.41	2231.58	2231.35
110000	2606.53	2541.31	2391.82	2352.64	2341.77	2338.71	2337.85	2337.60
115000	2725.01	2656.82	2500.54	2459.57	2448.21	2445.02	2444.11	2443.86
120000	2843.49	2772.33	2609.26	2566.51	2554.66	2551.32	2550.38	2550.11
125000	2961.97	2887.85	2717.98	2673.45	2661.10	2657.63	2656.64	2656.36
130000	3080.45	3003.36	2826.70	2780.39	2767.55	2763.93	2762.91	2762.62
135000	3198.93	3118.88	2935.42	2887.32	2873.99	2870.24	2869.17	2868.87
140000	3317.41	3234.39	3044.14	2994.26	2980.43	2976.54	2975.44	2975.13
145000	3435.88	3349.90	3152.86	3101.20	3086.88	3082.85	3081.71	3081.38
150000	3554.36	3465.42	3261.58	3208.14	3193.32	3189.15	3187.97	3187.64
155000	3672.84	3580.93	3370.30	3315.08	3299.76	3295.45	3294.24	3293.89
160000	3791.32	3696.44	3479.02	3422.01	3406.21	3401.76	3400.50	3400.15

AMOUNT OF LOAN	NUMBER OF YEARS IN TERM							
	1	2	3	4	5	6	7	8
$ 50	4.78	2.69	2.01	1.68	1.49	1.37	1.29	1.24
100	9.55	5.38	4.02	3.36	2.98	2.74	2.58	2.47
200	19.09	10.75	8.04	6.72	5.96	5.48	5.16	4.94
300	28.63	16.13	12.05	10.08	8.94	8.22	7.74	7.41
400	38.17	21.50	16.07	13.44	11.92	10.96	10.32	9.87
500	47.71	26.88	20.08	16.79	14.90	13.70	12.90	12.34
600	57.25	32.25	24.10	20.15	17.88	16.44	15.48	14.81
700	66.79	37.63	28.12	23.51	20.86	19.18	18.06	17.28
800	76.33	43.00	32.13	26.87	23.84	21.92	20.64	19.74
900	85.87	48.38	36.15	30.22	26.82	24.66	23.22	22.21
1000	95.41	53.75	40.16	33.58	29.80	27.40	25.80	24.68
2000	190.82	107.50	80.32	67.16	59.59	54.80	51.59	49.35
3000	286.23	161.25	120.48	100.74	89.38	82.20	77.38	74.02
4000	381.64	215.00	160.64	134.31	119.18	109.60	103.18	98.69
5000	477.05	268.75	200.79	167.89	148.97	137.00	128.97	123.37
6000	572.46	322.50	240.95	201.47	178.76	164.40	154.76	148.04
7000	667.86	376.24	281.11	235.04	208.55	191.80	180.56	172.71
8000	763.27	429.99	321.27	268.62	238.35	219.20	206.35	197.38
9000	858.68	483.74	361.42	302.20	268.14	246.60	232.14	222.05
10000	954.09	537.49	401.58	335.77	297.93	274.00	257.94	246.73
11000	1049.50	591.24	441.74	369.35	327.72	301.40	283.73	271.40
12000	1144.91	644.99	481.90	402.93	357.52	328.80	309.52	296.07
13000	1240.32	698.74	522.05	436.50	387.31	356.19	335.32	320.74
14000	1335.72	752.48	562.21	470.08	417.10	383.59	361.11	345.42
15000	1431.13	806.23	602.37	503.66	446.89	410.99	386.90	370.09
16000	1526.54	859.98	642.53	537.23	476.69	438.39	412.70	394.76
17000	1621.95	913.73	682.68	570.81	506.48	465.79	438.49	419.43
18000	1717.36	967.48	722.84	604.39	536.27	493.19	464.28	444.10
19000	1812.77	1021.23	763.00	637.96	566.07	520.59	490.07	468.78
20000	1908.18	1074.98	803.16	671.54	595.86	547.99	515.87	493.45
21000	2003.58	1128.72	843.31	705.12	625.65	575.39	541.66	518.12
22000	2098.99	1182.47	883.47	738.69	655.44	602.79	567.45	542.79
23000	2194.40	1236.22	923.63	772.27	685.24	630.19	593.25	567.47
24000	2289.81	1289.97	963.79	805.85	715.03	657.59	619.04	592.14
25000	2385.22	1343.72	1003.94	839.43	744.82	684.99	644.83	616.81
26000	2480.63	1397.47	1044.10	873.00	774.61	712.38	670.63	641.48
27000	2576.04	1451.22	1084.26	906.58	804.41	739.78	696.42	666.15
28000	2671.44	1504.96	1124.42	940.16	834.20	767.18	722.21	690.83
29000	2766.85	1558.71	1164.57	973.73	863.99	794.58	748.01	715.50
30000	2862.26	1612.46	1204.73	1007.31	893.78	821.98	773.80	740.17
31000	2957.67	1666.21	1244.89	1040.89	923.58	849.38	799.59	764.84
32000	3053.08	1719.96	1285.05	1074.46	953.37	876.78	825.39	789.51
33000	3148.49	1773.71	1325.20	1108.04	983.16	904.18	851.18	814.19
34000	3243.90	1827.46	1365.36	1141.62	1012.95	931.58	876.97	838.86
35000	3339.30	1881.20	1405.52	1175.19	1042.75	958.98	902.76	863.53
40000	3816.35	2149.95	1606.31	1343.08	1191.71	1095.97	1031.73	986.89
45000	4293.39	2418.69	1807.10	1510.96	1340.67	1232.97	1160.70	1110.25
50000	4770.43	2687.43	2007.88	1678.85	1489.64	1369.97	1289.66	1233.61
55000	5247.47	2956.18	2208.67	1846.73	1638.60	1506.96	1418.63	1356.97
60000	5724.52	3224.92	2409.46	2014.61	1787.56	1643.96	1547.59	1480.34
65000	6201.56	3493.66	2610.25	2182.50	1936.53	1780.95	1676.56	1603.70
70000	6678.60	3762.40	2811.03	2350.38	2085.49	1917.95	1805.52	1727.06
75000	7155.64	4031.15	3011.82	2518.27	2234.45	2054.95	1934.49	1850.42
80000	7632.69	4299.89	3212.61	2686.15	2383.42	2191.94	2063.46	1973.78
85000	8109.73	4568.63	3413.40	2854.03	2532.38	2328.94	2192.42	2097.14
90000	8586.77	4837.38	3614.19	3021.92	2681.34	2465.93	2321.39	2220.50
95000	9063.82	5106.12	3814.97	3189.80	2830.31	2602.93	2450.35	2343.86
100000	9540.86	5374.86	4015.76	3357.69	2979.27	2739.93	2579.32	2467.22
105000	10017.90	5643.60	4216.55	3525.57	3128.23	2876.92	2708.28	2590.58
110000	10494.94	5912.35	4417.34	3693.45	3277.20	3013.92	2837.25	2713.94
115000	10971.99	6181.09	4618.12	3861.34	3426.16	3150.91	2966.22	2837.31
120000	11449.03	6449.83	4818.91	4029.22	3575.12	3287.91	3095.18	2960.67
125000	11926.07	6718.57	5019.70	4197.11	3724.09	3424.91	3224.15	3084.03
130000	12403.11	6987.32	5220.49	4364.99	3873.05	3561.90	3353.11	3207.39
135000	12880.16	7256.06	5421.28	4532.87	4022.01	3698.90	3482.08	3330.75
140000	13357.20	7524.80	5622.06	4700.76	4170.98	3835.90	3611.04	3454.11
145000	13834.24	7793.55	5822.85	4868.64	4319.94	3972.89	3740.01	3577.47
150000	14311.28	8062.29	6023.64	5036.53	4468.90	4109.89	3868.97	3700.83
155000	14788.33	8331.03	6224.43	5204.41	4617.86	4246.88	3997.94	3824.19
160000	15265.37	8599.77	6425.22	5372.29	4766.83	4383.88	4126.91	3947.55

AMOUNT OF LOAN	NUMBER OF YEARS IN TERM							
	9	10	15	20	25	30	35	40
$ 50	1.20	1.17	1.10	1.08	1.08	1.08	1.08	1.08
100	2.39	2.33	2.20	2.16	2.15	2.15	2.15	2.15
200	4.78	4.66	4.39	4.32	4.30	4.30	4.30	4.30
300	7.17	6.99	6.59	6.48	6.45	6.45	6.44	6.44
400	9.55	9.32	8.78	8.64	8.60	8.59	8.59	8.59
500	11.94	11.65	10.97	10.80	10.75	10.74	10.74	10.73
600	14.33	13.97	13.17	12.96	12.90	12.89	12.88	12.88
700	16.71	16.30	15.36	15.12	15.05	15.03	15.03	15.03
800	19.10	18.63	17.56	17.28	17.20	17.18	17.17	17.17
900	21.49	20.96	19.75	19.44	19.35	19.33	19.32	19.32
1000	23.87	23.29	21.94	21.60	21.50	21.47	21.47	21.46
2000	47.74	46.57	43.88	43.19	43.00	42.94	42.93	42.92
3000	71.61	69.85	65.82	64.78	64.49	64.41	64.39	64.38
4000	95.48	93.13	87.76	86.37	85.99	85.88	85.85	85.84
5000	119.35	116.41	109.70	107.96	107.48	107.35	107.31	107.30
6000	143.21	139.69	131.64	129.55	128.98	128.82	128.77	128.76
7000	167.08	162.97	153.58	151.14	150.47	150.29	150.23	150.22
8000	190.95	186.25	175.51	172.73	171.97	171.75	171.69	171.68
9000	214.82	209.53	197.45	194.32	193.46	193.22	193.16	193.14
10000	238.69	232.81	219.39	215.91	214.96	214.69	214.62	214.60
11000	262.55	256.09	241.33	237.50	236.45	236.16	236.08	236.06
12000	286.42	279.37	263.27	259.09	257.95	257.63	257.54	257.51
13000	310.29	302.65	285.21	280.68	279.44	279.10	279.00	278.97
14000	334.16	325.93	307.15	302.27	300.94	300.57	300.46	300.43
15000	358.03	349.21	329.08	323.86	322.43	322.03	321.92	321.89
16000	381.90	372.49	351.02	345.45	343.93	343.50	343.38	343.35
17000	405.76	395.77	372.96	367.04	365.42	364.97	364.85	364.81
18000	429.63	419.05	394.90	388.64	386.92	386.44	386.31	386.27
19000	453.50	442.33	416.84	410.23	408.41	407.91	407.77	407.73
20000	477.37	465.61	438.78	431.82	429.91	429.38	429.23	429.19
21000	501.24	488.89	460.72	453.41	451.40	450.85	450.69	450.65
22000	525.10	512.17	482.65	475.00	472.90	472.31	472.15	472.11
23000	548.97	535.45	504.59	496.59	494.39	493.78	493.61	493.57
24000	572.84	558.73	526.53	518.18	515.89	515.25	515.07	515.02
25000	596.71	582.01	548.47	539.77	537.38	536.72	536.54	536.48
26000	620.58	605.29	570.41	561.36	558.88	558.19	558.00	557.94
27000	644.45	628.57	592.35	582.95	580.37	579.66	579.46	579.40
28000	668.31	651.85	614.29	604.54	601.87	601.13	600.92	600.86
29000	692.18	675.13	636.22	626.13	623.36	622.60	622.38	622.32
30000	716.05	698.41	658.16	647.72	644.86	644.06	643.84	643.78
31000	739.92	721.69	680.10	669.31	666.35	665.53	665.30	665.24
32000	763.79	744.97	702.04	690.90	687.85	687.00	686.76	686.70
33000	787.65	768.25	723.98	712.49	709.35	708.47	708.22	708.16
34000	811.52	791.53	745.92	734.08	730.84	729.94	729.69	729.62
35000	835.39	814.81	767.86	755.67	752.34	751.41	751.15	751.07
40000	954.73	931.21	877.55	863.63	859.81	858.75	858.45	858.37
45000	1074.07	1047.61	987.24	971.58	967.29	966.09	965.76	965.67
50000	1193.41	1164.01	1096.94	1079.53	1074.76	1073.44	1073.07	1072.96
55000	1312.75	1280.41	1206.63	1187.49	1182.24	1180.78	1180.37	1180.26
60000	1432.10	1396.81	1316.32	1295.44	1289.71	1288.12	1287.68	1287.55
65000	1551.44	1513.22	1426.01	1403.39	1397.19	1395.47	1394.98	1394.85
70000	1670.78	1629.62	1535.71	1511.34	1504.67	1502.81	1502.29	1502.14
75000	1790.12	1746.02	1645.40	1619.30	1612.14	1610.15	1609.59	1609.44
80000	1909.46	1862.42	1755.09	1727.25	1719.62	1717.49	1716.90	1716.74
85000	2028.80	1978.82	1864.79	1835.20	1827.09	1824.84	1824.21	1824.03
90000	2148.14	2095.22	1974.48	1943.16	1934.57	1932.18	1931.51	1931.33
95000	2267.48	2211.62	2084.17	2051.11	2042.05	2039.52	2038.82	2038.62
100000	2386.82	2328.02	2193.87	2159.06	2149.52	2146.87	2146.13	2145.92
105000	2506.16	2444.42	2303.56	2267.01	2257.00	2254.21	2253.43	2253.21
110000	2625.50	2560.82	2413.25	2374.97	2364.47	2361.55	2360.74	2360.51
115000	2744.85	2677.22	2522.95	2482.92	2471.95	2468.90	2468.04	2467.81
120000	2864.19	2793.62	2632.64	2590.87	2579.42	2576.24	2575.35	2575.10
125000	2983.53	2910.03	2742.33	2698.82	2686.90	2683.58	2682.66	2682.40
130000	3102.87	3026.43	2852.02	2806.78	2794.38	2790.93	2789.96	2789.69
135000	3222.21	3142.83	2961.72	2914.73	2901.85	2898.27	2897.27	2896.99
140000	3341.55	3259.23	3071.41	3022.68	3009.33	3005.61	3004.57	3004.28
145000	3460.89	3375.63	3181.10	3130.64	3116.80	3112.96	3111.88	3111.58
150000	3580.23	3492.03	3290.80	3238.59	3224.28	3220.30	3219.19	3218.88
155000	3699.57	3608.43	3400.49	3346.54	3331.75	3327.64	3326.49	3326.17
160000	3818.91	3724.83	3510.18	3454.49	3439.23	3434.98	3433.80	3433.47

AMOUNT OF LOAN	NUMBER OF YEARS IN TERM							
	1	2	3	4	5	6	7	8
$ 50	4.78	2.70	2.02	1.69	1.50	1.38	1 30	1.25
100	9.56	5.39	4.03	3.38	3.00	2.76	2.60	2.49
200	19.11	10.78	8.06	6.75	5.99	5.52	5.20	4.97
300	28.66	16.17	12.09	10.12	8.99	8.27	7.79	7.46
400	38.22	21.55	16.12	13.49	11.98	11.03	10.39	9.94
500	47.77	26.94	20.15	16.86	14.98	13.78	12.98	12.42
600	57.32	32.33	24.18	20.24	17.97	16.54	15.58	14.91
700	66.88	37.72	28.21	23.61	20.96	19.29	18.17	17.39
800	76.43	43.10	32.24	26.98	23.96	22.05	20.77	19.88
900	85.98	48.49	36.27	30.35	26.95	24.80	23.36	22.36
1000	95.54	53.88	40.30	33.72	29.95	27.56	25.96	24.84
2000	191.07	107.75	80.59	67.44	59.89	55.11	51.91	49.68
3000	286.60	161.63	120.88	101.16	89.83	82.67	77.87	74.52
4000	382.13	215.50	161.17	134.87	119.77	110.22	103.82	99.36
5000	477.66	269.38	201.46	168.59	149.71	137.78	129.78	124.20
6000	573.19	323.25	241.75	202.31	179.65	165.33	155.73	149.04
7000	668.72	377.13	282.04	236.03	209.59	192.88	181.69	173.88
8000	764.25	431.00	322.33	269.74	239.53	220.44	207.64	198.72
9000	859.78	484.88	362.62	303.46	269.47	247.99	233.60	223.56
10000	955.31	538.75	402.91	337.18	299.41	275.55	259.55	248.40
11000	1050.84	592.63	443.20	370.90	329.35	303.10	285.50	273.24
12000	1146.37	646.50	483.49	404.61	359.29	330.65	311.46	298.08
13000	1241.90	700.37	523.78	438.33	389.23	358.21	337.41	322.92
14000	1337.43	754.25	564.07	472.05	419.17	385.76	363.37	347.76
15000	1432.96	808.12	604.36	505.76	449.11	413.32	389.32	372.60
16000	1528.49	862.00	644.65	539.48	479.05	440.87	415.28	397.44
17000	1624.02	915.87	684.95	573.20	508.99	468.42	441.23	422.28
18000	1719.55	969.75	725.24	606.92	538.93	495.98	467.19	447.12
19000	1815.08	1023.62	765.53	640.63	568.87	523.53	493.14	471.96
20000	1910.61	1077.50	805.82	674.35	598.81	551.09	519.09	496.80
21000	2006.14	1131.37	846.11	708.07	628.75	578.64	545.05	521.64
22000	2101.67	1185.25	886.40	741.79	658.70	606.19	571.00	546.48
23000	2197.20	1239.12	926.69	775.50	688.64	633.75	596.96	571.32
24000	2292.73	1292.99	966.98	809.22	718.58	661.30	622.91	596.16
25000	2388.26	1346.87	1007.27	842.94	748.52	688.86	648.87	620.99
26000	2483.79	1400.74	1047.56	876.65	778.46	716.41	674.82	645.83
27000	2579.32	1454.62	1087.85	910.37	808.40	743.96	700.78	670.67
28000	2674.85	1508.49	1128.14	944.09	838.34	771.52	726.73	695.51
29000	2770.38	1562.37	1168.43	977.81	868.28	799.07	752.69	720.35
30000	2865.91	1616.24	1208.72	1011.52	898.22	826.63	778.64	745.19
31000	2961.44	1670.12	1249.01	1045.24	928.16	854.18	804.59	770.03
32000	3056.97	1723.99	1289.30	1078.96	958.10	881.73	830.55	794.87
33000	3152.50	1777.87	1329.60	1112.68	988.04	909.29	856.50	819.71
34000	3248.03	1831.74	1369.89	1146.39	1017.98	936.84	882.46	844.55
35000	3343.56	1885.61	1410.18	1180.11	1047.92	964.40	908.41	869.39
40000	3821.21	2154.99	1611.63	1348.70	1197.62	1102.17	1038.18	993.59
45000	4298.86	2424.36	1813.08	1517.28	1347.33	1239.94	1167.96	1117.79
50000	4776.51	2693.73	2014.54	1685.87	1497.03	1377.71	1297.73	1241.98
55000	5254.16	2963.11	2215.99	1854.46	1646.73	1515.48	1427.50	1366.18
60000	5731.81	3232.48	2417.44	2023.04	1796.43	1653.25	1557.27	1490.38
65000	6209.46	3501.85	2618.90	2191.63	1946.14	1791.02	1687.05	1614.58
70000	6687.11	3771.22	2820.35	2360.22	2095.84	1928.79	1816.82	1738.78
75000	7164.77	4040.60	3021.80	2528.80	2245.54	2066.56	1946.59	1862.97
80000	7642.42	4309.97	3223.25	2697.39	2395.24	2204.33	2076.36	1987.17
85000	8120.07	4579.34	3424.71	2865.98	2544.94	2342.10	2206.14	2111.37
90000	8597.72	4848.72	3626.16	3034.56	2694.65	2479.87	2335.91	2235.57
95000	9075.37	5118.09	3827.61	3203.15	2844.35	2617.64	2465.68	2359.77
100000	9553.02	5387.46	4029.07	3371.74	2994.05	2755.41	2595.45	2483.96
105000	10030.67	5656.83	4230.52	3540.32	3143.75	2893.18	2725.23	2608.16
110000	10508.32	5926.21	4431.97	3708.91	3293.46	3030.95	2855.00	2732.36
115000	10985.97	6195.58	4633.43	3877.50	3443.16	3168.72	2984.77	2856.56
120000	11463.62	6464.95	4834.88	4046.08	3592.86	3306.49	3114.54	2980.76
125000	11941.27	6734.33	5036.33	4214.67	3742.56	3444.26	3244.32	3104.95
130000	12418.92	7003.70	5237.79	4383.25	3892.27	3582.03	3374.09	3229.15
135000	12896.57	7273.07	5439.24	4551.84	4041.97	3719.80	3503.86	3353.35
140000	13374.22	7542.44	5640.69	4720.43	4191.67	3857.57	3633.63	3477.55
145000	13851.88	7811.82	5842.14	4889.01	4341.37	3995.34	3763.41	3601.74
150000	14329.53	8081.19	6043.60	5057.60	4491.08	4133.11	3893.18	3725.94
155000	14807.18	8350.56	6245.05	5226.19	4640.78	4270.88	4022.95	3850.14
160000	15284.83	8619.94	6446.50	5394.77	4790.48	4408.65	4152.72	3974.34

AMOUNT OF LOAN	NUMBER OF YEARS IN TERM							
	9	10	15	20	25	30	35	40
$ 50	1.21	1.18	1.11	1.09	1.09	1.09	1.09	1.09
100	2.41	2.35	2.22	2.18	2.18	2.17	2.17	2.17
200	4.81	4.70	4.43	4.36	4.35	4.34	4.34	4.34
300	7.22	7.04	6.65	6.54	6.52	6.51	6.51	6.51
400	9.62	9.39	8.86	8.72	8.69	8.68	8.67	8.67
500	12.03	11.73	11.07	10.90	10.86	10.84	10.84	10.84
600	14.43	14.08	13.29	13.08	13.03	13.01	13.01	13.01
700	16.83	16.43	15.50	15.26	15.20	15.18	15.17	15.17
800	19.24	18.77	17.71	17.44	17.37	17.35	17.34	17.34
900	21.64	21.12	19.93	19.62	19.54	19.51	19.51	19.51
1000	24.05	23.46	22.14	21.80	21.71	21.68	21.67	21.67
2000	48.09	46.92	44.27	43.59	43.41	43.36	43.34	43.34
3000	72.13	70.38	66.41	65.39	65.11	65.03	65.01	65.01
4000	96.17	93.84	88.54	87.18	86.81	86.71	86.68	86.67
5000	120.21	117.30	110.67	108.97	108.51	108.39	108.35	108.34
6000	144.25	140.75	132.81	130.77	130.21	130.06	130.02	130.01
7000	168.29	164.21	154.94	152.56	151.92	151.74	151.69	151.68
8000	192.33	187.67	177.08	174.36	173.62	173.42	173.36	173.34
9000	216.37	211.13	199.21	196.15	195.32	195.09	195.03	195.01
10000	240.42	234.59	221.34	217.94	217.02	216.77	216.70	216.68
11000	264.46	258.04	243.48	239.74	238.72	238.44	238.37	238.35
12000	288.50	281.50	265.61	261.53	260.42	260.12	260.04	260.01
13000	312.54	304.96	287.74	283.32	282.13	281.80	281.71	281.68
14000	336.58	328.42	309.88	305.12	303.83	303.47	303.38	303.35
15000	360.62	351.88	332.01	326.91	325.53	325.15	325.04	325.02
16000	384.66	375.33	354.15	348.71	347.23	346.83	346.71	346.68
17000	408.70	398.79	376.28	370.50	368.93	368.50	368.38	368.35
18000	432.74	422.25	398.41	392.29	390.63	390.18	390.05	390.02
19000	456.79	445.71	420.55	414.09	412.34	411.86	411.72	411.69
20000	480.83	469.17	442.68	435.88	434.04	433.53	433.39	433.35
21000	504.87	492.62	464.81	457.67	455.74	455.21	455.06	455.02
22000	528.91	516.08	486.95	479.47	477.44	476.88	476.73	476.69
23000	552.95	539.54	509.08	501.26	499.14	498.56	498.40	498.36
24000	576.99	563.00	531.22	523.06	520.84	520.24	520.07	520.02
25000	601.03	586.46	553.35	544.85	542.55	541.91	541.74	541.69
26000	625.07	609.91	575.48	566.64	564.25	563.59	563.41	563.36
27000	649.11	633.37	597.62	588.44	585.95	585.27	585.08	585.02
28000	673.16	656.83	619.75	610.23	607.65	606.94	606.75	606.69
29000	697.20	680.29	641.88	632.02	629.35	628.62	628.42	628.36
30000	721.24	703.75	664.02	653.82	651.05	650.29	650.08	650.03
31000	745.28	727.20	686.15	675.61	672.76	671.97	671.75	671.69
32000	769.32	750.66	708.29	697.41	694.46	693.65	693.42	693.36
33000	793.36	774.12	730.42	719.20	716.16	715.32	715.09	715.03
34000	817.40	797.58	752.55	740.99	737.86	737.00	736.76	736.70
35000	841.44	821.04	774.69	762.79	759.56	758.68	758.43	758.36
40000	961.65	938.33	885.36	871.76	868.07	867.06	866.78	866.70
45000	1081.85	1055.62	996.02	980.72	976.58	975.44	975.12	975.04
50000	1202.06	1172.91	1106.69	1089.69	1085.09	1083.82	1083.47	1083.38
55000	1322.26	1290.20	1217.36	1198.66	1193.60	1192.20	1191.82	1191.71
60000	1442.47	1407.49	1328.03	1307.63	1302.10	1300.58	1300.16	1300.05
65000	1562.68	1524.78	1438.70	1416.60	1410.61	1408.97	1408.51	1408.39
70000	1682.88	1642.07	1549.37	1525.57	1519.12	1517.35	1516.86	1516.72
75000	1803.09	1759.36	1660.04	1634.54	1627.63	1625.73	1625.21	1625.06
80000	1923.29	1876.65	1770.71	1743.51	1736.14	1734.11	1733.55	1733.40
85000	2043.50	1993.94	1881.37	1852.47	1844.64	1842.49	1841.90	1841.73
90000	2163.70	2111.23	1992.04	1961.44	1953.15	1950.87	1950.25	1950.07
95000	2283.91	2228.52	2102.71	2070.41	2061.66	2059.26	2058.59	2058.41
100000	2404.11	2345.81	2213.38	2179.38	2170.17	2167.64	2166.94	2166.75
105000	2524.32	2463.10	2324.05	2288.35	2278.68	2276.02	2275.29	2275.08
110000	2644.52	2580.39	2434.72	2397.32	2387.19	2384.40	2383.63	2383.42
115000	2764.73	2697.68	2545.39	2506.29	2495.69	2492.78	2491.98	2491.76
120000	2884.94	2814.97	2656.06	2615.26	2604.20	2601.16	2600.33	2600.09
125000	3005.14	2932.26	2766.72	2724.22	2712.71	2709.54	2708.67	2708.43
130000	3125.35	3049.55	2877.39	2833.19	2821.22	2817.93	2817.02	2816.77
135000	3245.55	3166.84	2988.06	2942.16	2929.73	2926.31	2925.37	2925.10
140000	3365.76	3284.13	3098.73	3051.13	3038.23	3034.69	3033.71	3033.44
145000	3485.96	3401.42	3209.40	3160.10	3146.74	3143.07	3142.06	3141.78
150000	3606.17	3518.71	3320.07	3269.07	3255.25	3251.45	3250.41	3250.12
155000	3726.37	3636.00	3430.74	3378.04	3363.76	3359.83	3358.75	3358.45
160000	3846.58	3753.29	3541.41	3487.01	3472.27	3468.22	3467.10	3466.79

NOTES